THE CATHERINE CORE READER

St. Catherine University

Printed in the United States of America

ISBN 13: 978-1-58390-136-6

Cover art courtesy of Elizabeth Erickson. *Hildegard's House of Light*. Mixed media, 2011, 22 x 18 inches

This painting depicts a version of a visionary moment as experienced by Hildegard of Bingen. Hildegard was a twelfth century mystic, as well as a writer, composer and a Benedictine abbess in what is now Germany. She founded monasteries, corresponded with popes and emperors, wrote theological and medicinal texts and liturgical songs, and oversaw the creation of illuminations based on her visions. An accomplished and renowned woman in a time and place that restricted women's social participation, Hildegard described her visions as "the living light of God." Hildegard died in 1179.

St. Catherine University Web site: www.stkate.edu

XanEdu
Change the course.

530 Great Road
Acton, MA 01720
800-562-2147

Editors

Cecilia Konchar Farr
Sr. Mona Riley Endowed Chair in the Humanities
Professor, English & Women's Studies

Martha M. Phillips
Director of Core Curriculum & Professor, Biology

Nancy A. Heitzeg
Professor, Sociology & Critical Studies of Race & Ethnicity

Acknowledgements

The editors would like to thank the *TRW* Reader Revision Committee for their thorough and inspired reworking of the Reflective Woman section of this book: Shanan Custer, Nicole Montana, Jenny McDougal, Katharine Glassman, Cynthia Olson, Pamela Fletcher and Kristin Chalberg.

Thanks are also due to the *Global Search for Justice* Reader Revision Committee: Deep Shikha, Nasrin Jewell, Helen Howell, Catherine Spaeth and Pamela Fletcher.

And special thanks to Professor Patricia Olson, for her cover design and help in gathering the art works that appear here.

The Catherine Core Curriculum marks its twentieth year this year, 1995–2015. The constant attention to assessment and revision, particularly of the two "bookend courses"—TRW and GSJ—could not have happened without the collaborative work of many colleagues—faculty, staff, students and administrators—over many years, through seven editions of *The Reflective Woman* Reader and four editions of *The Global Search for Justice* Reader. This new gathering of texts for what we have called "the whole core" is inspired by their work. The editors (and former core directors) would particularly like to thank each previous Core Director—Brian Fogarty, Cecilia Konchar Farr, Suzanne Hendricks, Marla Martin Hanley, and Sharon Doherty—for their leadership.

Thanks, finally, to all who developed and sustain this mission-driven baccalaureate liberal arts core curriculum. May it continue to invite all of our students to lead, influence, seek justice, and "claim an education."

Contents

Introduction

What does it mean to be educated? Does it mean possessing a wealth of factual knowledge, being a walking Wikipedia? Does it mean applying a wide range of theories or principles to a question or engaging professional skills or practices? Does it mean having a good memory, talking a good line, shifting quickly from idea to idea?

A St. Kate's education, in the liberal arts tradition, requires reflective judgment—the ability not only to access information and talk about it, but also to incorporate knowledge with experience. Reflective judgment includes understanding, reflection, and, perhaps most importantly, the application of knowledge to the real decisions of life.

In St. Catherine University's baccalaureate women's college we have a long tradition of "educating women to lead and influence." Our model of education is active. Together we read, study, research, connect, assess, write, discuss, and reflect—in the liberal arts core and across our majors. We take one another seriously, doing collaborative research, engaging in lively discussions. And we take that active education into the world, making changes that matter.

In the earliest days of St. Kate's, our founding Sisters of St. Joseph determined that theirs would be a liberal arts college, one that encouraged students to be thinkers and scholars as well as teachers, health care workers, lawyers and judges, scientists, artists, social workers, and professional women of every sort. And so it has been.

Our Core Curriculum is twenty years old in 2015, and this *Catherine Core Reader* gets to the heart of the core, with readings for The Reflective Woman, the liberal arts core courses and Global Search for Justice. Our hope is that this book will go with you through your years at St. Kate's and beyond, posing interesting questions, reminding you of striking insights, and cementing your social justice commitments. Here you can "claim an education," practice "lace-making" with the CSJs, "walk away from Omelas," pay attention to trifles, see mathematics in poetry (and poetry in math), find "truth without certainty" and "optimism in uncertainty," link justice to action, and be a "citizen of the universe."

What you learn in school should help you make life choices that matter. Being an educated woman means making creative connections and living with conviction and purpose. We hope this book will guide you through that lifelong process.

Welcome to the Catherine Core Curriculum.

Martha M. Phillips
Nancy A. Heitzeg
Cecilia Konchar Farr

The Reflective Woman

Oppositional Gaze
Anna Garski
charcoal on paper
2011, 22 x 30-inches

Introduction:
The Reflective Woman

Welcome to St. Catherine University and the unique liberal arts education it offers you. We believe real education begins, as Adrienne Rich writes, by "refusing to let others do your thinking, talking, and naming for you; it means learning to respect and use your own brains and instinct." This is the work of a lifetime. You began this learning before you came here, of course, and none of us can know where it will ultimately take you. At St. Kate's, both in and out of the classroom, you will have opportunities to affirm what you know, to test it, to deepen it, to revise it. Through courses, campus organizations and activities, groups of friends and teams of co-workers, internships or activism in the wider community, study or travel abroad, a St. Catherine education supports you and challenges you to move beyond what is known and familiar. You are invited to explore further a vast universe of knowledge, values, and skills: where they come from, how well they work, how to create them, how they fit together, and how to use them.

Our vision for a St. Catherine education has been developing since the Sisters of St. Joseph of Carondelet founded the College of St. Catherine in 1905 and St. Mary's School of Nursing in 1887, through braiding together three interlocking threads: Catholic, liberal arts, and women. Just as the sisters in France taught lace making to help women support themselves, St. Kate's helps you weave an education by drawing together Catholic intellectual traditions and social teachings with the liberating disciplines of the humanities, arts, and sciences in a learning environment uniquely suited to women. To prepare women to lead and influence, we have developed a set of Goals of a Liberal Arts Education at SCU to guide both curriculum (courses) and co-curriculum (programs available outside the classroom). The strategies to help you achieve the knowledge, skills, and values articulated in these goals are woven throughout the liberal arts core and the major requirements. In addition, St. Catherine University offers a rich variety of opportunities outside the classroom to develop your interests and skills, which we encourage you to explore with your advisor throughout your years here and by using the St. Catherine Experience pamphlet focused on your major.

Many students enter college with the main goal of completing a major, and studying deeply in one field is certainly important. Regardless of the discipline of your major—whether a professional major, such as business, or a liberal arts major, such as biology—the whole of your education, grounded in the liberal arts and sciences through the liberal arts core requirements, prepares you for much more than a job. It prepares you to navigate a complex and constantly changing world, to understand issues no one is yet discussing, to make decisions none of us can predict, to take on work that has not even been invented, and to enrich your life with meaning, purpose, and satisfaction. Learning requires rigorous study in a variety of subjects, taking risks to try new and challenging experiences, and a commitment to excellence—expecting the very best of yourself. In this kind of education, you invest your time and energy in learning that will be valuable no matter what life brings you.

In St. Catherine University's College for Women, you start your educational journey in **The Reflective Woman** (TRW). This unique course is an essential part of an education that prepares women to lead and influence. As a gateway common experience, it will introduce you to and connect you with the mission and vision of St. Catherine's. At the same time, this discussion-based and writing intensive course will further develop your academic skills, using various frameworks from liberal arts traditions and emphasizing critical thinking, effective communication and cultural analysis.

Every section of TRW course is built around three themes (Composing a Life, Searching for Truths, and Working Towards Community and Justice) with a focus on connections to art and aesthetics throughout. The themes names are intentionally active, recognizing that you and your education are a work in progress.

Composing a Life: This theme explores identity—what are the choices we make in order to compose a life that expresses who we want to become? What role do ethnicity, race and gender play in how we conceive of ourselves or how others conceive of us?

St. Catherine University itself has an identity, composed around its mission and the mission the Sisters of Carondelet who founded it. The first few readings in this reader introduce you to St. Kate's. By describing the work of the Sisters of St. Joseph and the early days of the College of St. Catherine, these readings reveal how history has shaped us and how stories continue to have a powerful influence on who we think we are.

The selections relating to this theme include a variety of stories to give you the opportunity to reflect further on your own identity and the many creative processes—including our educations—that combine throughout a lifetime to form us. Personal narratives allow us to hear diverse voices, as authors describe who they are and what forces have contributed to and hindered their developing, understanding, and expressing who they are. Gender, class, race/ethnicity, sexual orientation, and language are just some of the differences these writers explore. The processes of composing a life and expressing who we are transpire both within us as individuals and within our social contexts. The interplay of the individual and her social and physical environment is a central theme throughout literature and the arts, and a key question that theories in science and the social sciences explore as well. Why is it that some individuals feel invisible and others empowered? Why are some oppressed and others privileged? How are different groups represented in our culture, and how do we respond to these representations? How do we develop our distinctive identities? How do we safeguard others' rights to discover and express themselves authentically? What importance does knowing oneself have for claiming an education?

Searching for Truths: How do we know what we know? Under this second theme of TRW the goals are to improve your skills as a critical reader and thinker, to develop your awareness of the variety of disciplinary approaches for exploring truths, and to hone your skills in evaluating the assertions of those around us. We will ask, "What is truth? How do we recognize it?" And we will ask those questions from different angles—philosophical, aesthetic, theological, and scientific. We will also consider the differences between opinion and evidence and how we construct a reasoned argument. How should we make a claim and support it with logic and evidence?

TRW students begin in different places; regardless of your skill set as you start this course, expect to further develop skills in how to: read academic essays; learn collaboratively; communicate orally and visually; structure an argument; question objectively; sift through perceived truths; develop an opinion from knowledge, not just habit; agree to disagree; recognize stakeholders and claims to power in arguments; and argue not to "win" but to listen, learn, and understand. We will also approach the question of how to know truth in a practical way in the context of library research. In other words, how do you find different types of information and distinguish between reliable and not-so-reliable sources?

By way of a "Structured Controversy" project or research paper, you will have a chance to increase your capacity for reflective judgment on matters of fact and conflicting ideas, and to connect that capacity to your education, aesthetic, and spiritual experiences. You will also experience the process of writing as you revise, rework, and re-examine your writing and thinking in small groups and with your instructor. In the end, this theme is about helping you clarify the relationship between self-knowledge and academic learning.

Working Toward Community and Justice: The readings related to this final theme are a combination of the theoretical and the personal, but each asks a central question: if, as Martin Luther King, Jr. proposes, we are all "caught in an inescapable network," how do we work to heal, mend, strengthen, and enrich that interdependent, interlaced web? Each author advocates principles to guide us in understanding justice and taking action for the common good.

Early work in The Reflective Woman is designed to assist you in approaching this final theme with these insights and questions: Who is my neighbor? What vision of our common life is compelling and just? What principles help me determine whether a particular action or decision would help bring that vision into reality? What forces or conditions prevent or delay our communities in achieving that vision?

More importantly, however, the St. Catherine University is founded on the conviction that educated women have a right and a responsibility to lead and influence for a more just society. As you explore the principles, positions, and strategies of these authors, we invite you to reflect on what you believe the purpose of your life is, how the work you choose to do can best offer your own skills, interests, and understandings, and how you connect with and engage ever-wider circles of community. A liberal arts education is a life-long pursuit to liberate ourselves to know who we are, not just who we are told we are; to seek truths, not passively accept what others would lead us to believe; and to claim our own visions and voices for creating the world we live in and leave for others. This theme connects the concepts of identity and searching for truths with your life's work. As the poet Mary Oliver asks, "What is it you plan to do with your one wild and precious life?"

TRW lays the foundation for your learning at SCU and introduces you to the structure of liberal arts core requirements every student, regardless of her major, will complete. These requirements are built on the principle that an individual best prepared to deal with a complex, diverse and changing world has broad knowledge of human cultures and the physical and natural world, as well as in-depth knowledge of a specific field. Our goal is to provide a curriculum that helps you achieve an understanding of the breadth of human scientific, artistic and intellectual achievement throughout history and across cultures and that develops your understanding of distinct methods for exploring truths across the disciplines in natural and social sciences, arts and humanities. The set of readings in the middle of this reader are aimed at connecting you with these various disciplinary ways of thinking.

The final course in The Catherine Core is the capstone senior-level course, **The Global Search for Justice**. GSJ challenges you to apply the lessons of your education to issues of justice throughout the world. In this course you will analyze a justice issue in depth, such as environmental racism, homelessness, or health disparities, and explore the responsibility of global citizens to work for change.

We have designed a liberal arts education with *you* at its heart, respecting your own uniqueness, appreciating the perspectives you bring, and trusting in your capacity to claim this education for your own.

Martha M. Phillips, PhD
Director of the Core Curriculum
March 2014

Sr. Joan Mitchell, CSJ, is a St. Kate's alumna and a member of the Board of Trustees of the university. A founding editor of Good Ground Press, Sr. Joan now blogs and edits Sunday by Sunday *and* Spirit for Teens, *weekly faith sharing magazines.*

All Women Can Be: The Spirit of the Sisters of St. Joseph

Joan Mitchell, CSJ

I feel a personal passion for St. Catherine's because I found my life here in my undergraduate years 1958–1962. My four years were a journey of empowerment. I came undereducated and afraid; I left able to write, think, and perform. I also found a community of women, the Sisters of St. Joseph of Carondelet, with whom to invest my life in service.

Empowering is what Sisters of St. Joseph have been about from their beginning in 1650. Pre-revolutionary France had terrible social and economic inequalities. With wealth concentrated in the church and nobility the country suffered much the same chronic problems as Third World countries today. The desperate needs of the people at the bottom gave birth to *apostolic* orders, whose cloisters became the streets, whose prayer became the works of mercy.

Among their ministries the first sisters helped young women forced to support themselves through prostitution to learn lacemaking and become self-supporting. Many marriageable young men had gone to the New World, leaving many young women without the possibility of marriage. The sisters gave these women at the bottom of society a stepping stone to their own place in its economic life beyond the social norm of their day.

The College of St. Catherine has educated and empowered most of the present members of the Sisters of St. Joseph of the St. Paul Province. Most sisters attended St. Catherine as beleaguered teachers coming on Saturday mornings or during the hot days of summer sessions, to finish degrees on the twenty-year plan. Many attended in the days before the Second Vatican Council, when we were forbidden to talk to the other students and cut off from the community life of the college. Many sisters have returned to St. Catherine's to do graduate work, for example, in the Master of Arts in Organizational Leadership, theology, and spirituality, and their work has nurtured the community.

However, norms for women also affected us. Our community educated many women to the doctoral level but never in medicine, nor did we train our own women in advanced theology degrees until after Vatican II. Sister Rosalie Ryan led that small revolution toward the college theology department of today. In her research and writing she is one of the pioneering women bible scholars who have recovered the importance of women among Jesus's disciples, those women who follow and serve him and are with him from the beginning in Galilee but whose presence was lost to us in the scant two and three verses the gospel gives to their presence.

The Sisters of St. Joseph College Consortium, which has twelve member colleges, funded a study of their mission and image, surveying 480 people, twenty-five on this campus, four of them sisters. Sister Karen Kennelly, formerly academic dean on the St. Paul Campus and now president of Mount St. Mary's in Los Angeles, chairs this consortium. Their study reports five distinctive characteristics of these colleges, which include St. Catherine:

1) Hospitality and caring community
2) Concern for all without distinction
3) Addressing the needs of the time
4) Striving for excellence in all endeavors
5) Making a difference in local and world community

These same characteristics reach back to our beginnings as a community. Our houses were to be hubs of hospitality, caring, and outreach to our neighbors. The first foundation of the Sisters of St. Joseph was a secret society. It lasted only two years. This was a small group of pious women who wanted to help others. The Jesuit Father Medaille, who articulated the spirituality of these women, describes the community as a "little design," called by the name of St. Joseph, a model of hidden service, like the self-emptying humility of Jesus hidden in the tabernacle among the people. What lasted of this first foundation is its identity with Joseph, of whom little is known but his care for Mary and Jesus. From this name we take an ethic of *charity to the dear neighbor without distinction.*

To address the needs of the time was why the community of St. Joseph began anew in 1650 in LePuy, France, with the support of Bishop de Maupas, in a hospital. The first sisters formed a hub from which the spokes of the wheel of ministry went out. Our first constitutions directed the sisters to "divide the city into various sections, and either by visiting the sick personally or through the lay associates of the congregation . . . make every effort to learn what disorders prevail in each quarter so that they may remedy them either by their own efforts or by the intermediary of those who have some power over the person engaged in these disorders."

Striving for excellence is an ethic at the heart of St. Catherine. Seventeenth-century piety used the word *zeal* and the concept of *the more* to express this value that we know so well from the history of the St. Paul campus where Mother Antonia sent six young sisters to study in European universities. They became the living endowment of the college's early years. We know this quality well, too, from the history of the Minneapolis campus where the faculty practically had to teach in the stairwells as second and third year nursing students contended for space with the first class of the junior college Sister Ann Joachim founded.

The *more* is an ethic of liberation that envisioned the sisters being all women could be and envisioned people at the bottom of society empowered to be all they could be. At our general chapter as a congregation in 1993 we asked ourselves again, "What more is being asked of us now in our commitment to justice?" You see the clear common roots of the two campuses in these characteristics:

- Hospitality and caring
- Concern for the dear neighbor without distinction
- Addressing the needs of the time
- Striving for excellence

They add up to making a difference.

Sometimes when I hear people talk about *the sisters*, I sense they are not talking about me or sisters today but about women farther back, perhaps those who founded St. Catherine's or those who formed the academic community in the past. I share reverence for these sisters, but I suspect they seem wise and foresighted rather than dangerous and single-minded because they are safely dead. We laud Mother Antonia today but would we have sided with her when she put up Mendel Hall to stop Prior from going through the St. Paul Campus? Where beyond the status quo would her passion for excellence and education for women lead her today? Perhaps where it has led our 1989 general chapter, which declared, "We support the exercise of the gifts of all the baptized for ministry." And what more? Conflict, conversation, argument—these are creative processes.

George Arbunckle, a cultural anthropologist, Marist priest, and New Zealander, says the Catholic Church missed the modern era. At the Council of Trent, which met twenty-five times between 1546 and 1563, the Church responded to the Protestant Reformation by effectively freezing itself in a medieval time warp that lasted until the Second Vatican Council 402 years later.

In the Church's fixed self-understanding prior to Vatican II, sisters' permanent vowed commitment gave them a special, privileged place in the structure of the Church, lower than the clergy but higher than the faithful laity. The Second Vatican Council radically flattened these hierarchical gradations by stressing the common call to holiness all Christians share, none more than others, by reason of the baptism.

Thirty years ago we sisters lived our higher spiritual vocation by being set apart from lay people. Today we are part of the ordinary life of the human community rather than apart from it. We understand ourselves not only as a community of vowed members but a vast inclusive network of relationships with colleagues in ministry, former members, families, and friends. We share life, prayer, ministry, and companionship with consociates who link themselves with us through interest and shared charism rather than vows.

There are positives in missing the modern era. Catholic consciousness remains very shaped by the communal experience that antedates the Enlightenment focus on individual subjectivity. Books such as *Habits of the Heart* call for churches to become the glue of fragmented postmodern society. Catholic tradition and sisters' experience in creating community together have something to offer the civic community toward this need, not in going backward to a community that buries the individual but forward to communities of mutuality and interdependence. In fact, in Latin America a base-community movement has arisen reinventing Christian community at the grassroots level. This movement is spreading here in the U.S., too.

The Second Vatican Council called Christians to serve the poor and make a difference in this world. "The joys and the hopes, the griefs and the anxieties of the people of this age, especially those who are poor or are in any way afflicted, those too are the joys and hopes, the griefs and anxieties of the followers of Christ," it said (*Pastoral Constitution on the Church in the Modern World, #1*). Our ministries as a community have radically broadened in response to this call. Our history in this century had been one of participating in the building of the Catholic school system in this country and the Catholic health care system. Things were gained in this national endeavor—immigrant Catholics were educated and assimilated into the American culture. This era also made us semi-cloistered in our convents and limited to staffing schools and hospitals. Since Vatican II we have rediscovered we are an order founded to serve on the streets and form partnerships with lay people. We were founded to "divide the city in various sections."

At first, this emphasis strained relations between people who moved out of their classroom to give direct service to the poor and those who stayed in institutions such as the college. Now, thirty years later, we see very clearly the importance of higher education in people's journey out of poverty, welfare, and hunger. I'll bet anyone who heard the student from the Minneapolis campus with the six children and the disabled husband who spoke one year at our Student/Board of Trustees Dialog still remembers her and the difference her education was making for all of them. I remember Anita Pampusch remarking at the tenth anniversary of Weekend College that those who established educational policies in large corporations probably did not have in mind educating the numbers of women in secretarial work who took advantage of these programs to earn bachelors' degrees.

The Sisters of St. Joseph have profoundly changed in the last thirty years and we want you to know who we are today. We continue to have sisters on the college faculty and staff, but fewer than in the past. In the past thirty years sisters have developed new ministries that offer sites for volunteer work, internships, and mentoring programs. Sisters are actively involved with Peace House, where Rose Tillemans welcomes and shares lunch and prayer with street people in a community of respect right next to the Dairy Queen near Franklin and Portland. Down Portland is St. Joseph House, which Char Madigan helped start and so many keep going as a place that welcomes battered women and nurtures clients as staff members. HOPE, Homes on Portland Enterprises, has refurbished former crack houses on the same block. At Incarnation House sisters helped found and staff this place for women with young children; at Ascension Place, women are struggling out of addictions. Sisters are teaching in literacy programs in the Frogtown area and at the Administration Center and Carondelet Center next door. In these new ministries as in our earliest ministries we partner with lay people.

Few people in the Church have changed more than sisters as a group. We were readied to respond to the needs of the time by good educations. We have roared through modern consciousness into the postmodern. Today we pursue our own talents and gifts in ministry rather than getting educated to fill a waiting position. Today we are working out new forms of governance that build vision from the bottom up by hearing into words all our voices.

The Second Vatican Council was part of the social change and challenge of the 1960's that also revived the women's movement. This movement began in the last century among Quaker and Unitarian women who joined the cause for abolition and moved on to women's suffrage. In the last twenty years Catholic women have taken their place in the movement, especially in the theological fields.

Elisabeth Schussler Fiorenza has put feminist methodologies to work retrieving the importance of women in the bible, theorizing that the first Christian communities formed a discipleship of equals and aiming to make the scriptures no longer tablets of stone but bread to nourish women and men today.

Rosemary Radford Ruether, pioneer Catholic woman historian, godmothers younger feminists. She insists women rape victims in her classes can relate to Jesus because of his experience of violence. He is Christ and Christa. Mary Daly's prodigious research chronicles violence to women in many cultures and creates new language for women's experience. Elizabeth Johnson is a Sister of St. Joseph of Brentwood and professor at Fordham who suggests, in her book *She Who Is* that we no longer neglect the feminine imagery of God as Spirit and recognize the imminent presence of God as Spirit cogiven with all life. Hispanic sisters have formed Las Hermanas to further the struggle for liberation among Hispanic women. The Black Sisters Conference has contributed its own voices—Toinette Eugene, Jamie Phelps, Thea Bowman.

Catholic women and men stand at a threshold today. People ask sisters, "How can you stay in the Catholic Church? It's so patriarchal. How can you let the pope tell you what to do?" How can one care about educating men and women for interdependency and community and stay in the church? I should point out that these are not only women's questions. St. Catherine honored Bishop Raymond Lucker for his support of women during the debates about the women's pastoral.

At the last board retreat I attended we had to draw an image of St. Catherine. I found myself drawing the stacks of books in the library and beside them the big doors of the chapel. I drew the shelves open but put a lock on the chapel. How does a Catholic college educate women to be all they can be when the church does not welcome their gifts for ministry?

Withdrawing from the church is the easiest answer. It's the answer of preference among Catholics in their twenties. It's not mine. It's not a lot of people's. As a Sister of St. Joseph I am a publicly committed woman of the church. I say, "We are the Church. This is our home. We won't be put out." More than that, women have always belonged here. Scripture gives us evidence of women disciples, apostles, deacons, prophets. Church history tells us Hilda of Whitby and Brigid of Ireland were abbesses of double monasteries of men and women. Shawn Madigan's research identifies women mystics in every age.

What do the Sisters of St. Joseph ask and offer this college toward the future? We are here today asking for dialog. We have to offer our struggle to change since Vatican II and a long history as an alternative Christian community within the Church. Feminist and other liberation theologies locate authority in the voices of the oppressed struggling for justice. These liberation theologies call us to speak the truth of our experience and to make room for others through listening them into speech.

A cultural anthropologist looks at the current movement to restore the pre-Vatican II Catholic Church and says that it's surprising the backlash isn't worse because the social upheaval and chaos have been so profound. This is the restoration church. On the other side, another kind of church is taking form in small Christian communities of lay men and women who break open the word together, do justice together, seek equality together. This is the emergent church.

The restoration church says the conversation is over. The emergent church says we must begin a conversation that includes everyone and invites all to speak for themselves as their most fundamental act of being human. We are asking for dialog and engagement in improvising a useful future.

Pope John Paul II's statement on Catholic education, *Ex Corde Ecclesiae,* has renewed conversation about what Catholic means in the missions of institutions of higher learning. In *America,* for May 28, 1994, Father Joseph Feeney of St. Joseph University in Philadelphia asks familiar questions: "While Jesuit colleges do and should welcome students of all faiths and no faith, has a diverse student body clouded institutional vision? How is Jesuit education defined? As liberal-arts based? Humanistic? Christian humanistic? Faith and justice based? How to link campus ministry and classroom? How to cherish diversity and build community?"

The Sisters of St. Joseph who came to the United States in 1836 from France to New Orleans, up the Mississippi to St. Louis, to the town of Carondelet just south of St. Louis, came to do what had to be done in the New World. In 1851 sisters came upstream to St. Paul to teach Indians, but they wound up founding the first hospital in the state, St. Joseph's, because a cholera epidemic demanded their school become a hospital. They improvised a useful future.

Sister Rita Steinhagen is a legend among the sisters for all she has initiated as a result of Father Harry Bury taking her to the streets of Cedar Riverside, where she began hearing people's needs and started a Free Store, the West Bank Clinic, the Bridge for runaway kids, and with Char Madigan St. Joseph House for Battered Women. Rita and Char taught us to listen to the needs of the dear neighbor without distinction as the confraternities of mercy had done in France in the beginning.

At our last all-community gathering Sister Marian Louwaige brought to the eucharistic table a piece of Belgian lace. She saw in its airy pattern a symbol of room for all in the design of the community and its future. Sister Sharon Howell brought to the altar a piece of kinte cloth, a tightly woven African cloth. She saw in the weave a symbol of the solidarity in which we must stand together. What we really ask of you is to continue the lacemaking with us, to weave a future that continues to reintegrate those who have least with those who have most, that makes of the threads of our lives a pattern of grace that is both open to all and tight enough not to come undone, or fray, but last as an intricacy where sisters cared and joined hands with lasting friends in entwining circles of learning and care, love and service.

Jane Carroll is a Phi Beta Kappa graduate of St. Kate's (1980), where, as a senior, she earned the prestigious Mother Antonia McHugh Award for a student who "could go on to be a professor that Mother Antonia would be proud to have on the faculty." True to the prediction, she earned a PhD in history at the University of Minnesota and is now Professor of History at St. Kate's. The essay included here is about the extraordinary influence Mother Antonia exerted on the conception and development of our college for women. Professor Carroll's essay demonstrates why Mother Antonia stories are still so prevalent in our community. How did Mother Antonia demonstrate "extravagantly visionary leadership"? In what ways does her vision play out in the university you are attending today?

Extravagantly Visionary Leadership

The Irelands and Sister Antonia McHugh

Jane Lamm Carroll

> It is the aim of those in charge to make this college the best and highest of its kind in the Northwest.[1]

> When I think of Mother Antonia, I think of strength and firmness, and the authority of her presence. I think she invented vigor. She held up to us an example of invincibility—that is if you really made up your mind to do it, you could conquer—you could win.[2]

> The College is unwilling to grant her degrees to mere bridge—players or mere bookworms—both of whom may be spendthrifts of their inheritance; she would keep her reward for what she aims to ensure, the development of the happy, energetic, richly educated and therefore resourceful girls—ready, capable, glad to serve, with the strength and beauty of Catholic womanhood.[3]

Many Catholic women religious in the United States have long histories of educating girls and young women, and their experience in running female academies for generations in the nineteenth century laid the intellectual and practical foundations for the later successful conduct of their women's colleges.[4] According to Karen Kennelly:

> Virtually every congregation that established colleges during the pioneer period from 1890 to 1920 had by that time one—and often two or three—generations of members who had taught in academies. The academy curricula offered by sister-faculty had expanded during the late nineteenth-century as sisters recognized changing expectations for women and adapted classical structures many had brought with them from European convent schools. Such experience was antecedent to the scholarly seriousness necessary for the development of a collegiate atmosphere.[5]

The Sisters of St. Joseph (CSJ) illustrate this pattern in the history of Catholic women's colleges. They founded St. Joseph's Academy, the first female academy in St. Paul, almost immediately upon their arrival in 1851. One of the first graduates of St. Joseph's Academy to enter the Sisters of St. Joseph, Ellen Ireland (Sister Seraphine), would later found the College of St. Catherine. [6] Just a few years prior to the 1905 opening of the College of St. Catherine, the first graduates of St. Mary's School of Nursing received diplomas. The Sisters of St. Joseph had been operating St. Mary's Hospital in Minneapolis since 1887. As the hospital expanded and nursing became increasingly technical and professional, the Sisters themselves could not meet St. Mary's demand for nurses. Hence, they established a school of nursing at the hospital in the early 1900s. After a decade of collaborating with St. Mary's in developing nursing education, the College of St. Catherine established a full nursing degree program on its campus in the early 1940s, leaving St. Mary's providing only the clinical aspects of nursing education for students. In 1958 the two institutions separated again, and in 1963 the Sisters replaced the Nursing School with St. Mary's Junior College. St. Catherine's and St. Mary's eventually merged in 1986.

Sisters: Educators and Leaders

Women's colleges created spaces that allowed their students and faculty to develop their own intellectual and social identities as women, becoming islands of liberty in which women were, first and foremost, human beings.[7] However, when the first women's colleges were founded in the late nineteenth and early twentieth centuries, they were faced with multiple missions and placed in a rather defensive position *vis-á-vis* social expectations and fears about female education. Not only did women's colleges have to prove to society that women were capable of undertaking a rigorously intellectual education, but they also had to show that such an education did not impair women's health, make them less feminine, encourage sexual impropriety, or discourage women from becoming wives and mothers.[8]

The women religious who founded and operated Catholic women's colleges have historically offered a "counter social model" of life for young women in a way that non-Catholic women's colleges could not. Catholic women's colleges, earlier than their secular counterparts, recognized that women could have vocations in life other than marriage and motherhood and that many women needed an education in order to become self-supporting. Moreover, unlike some prominent non-Catholic women's colleges, in Catholic institutions, the presidents, administrators, and faculty were almost entirely, if not exclusively, women.[9]

Earlier in the twentieth century, the Sisters in particular were exemplars of women living lives that were alternatives to the social roles of marriage and motherhood and that challenged the social assumption that women were or should be dependent upon men.[10] To establish, expand, fund and maintain their institutions, the Sisters operated successfully in a male-dominated world. Indeed, their religious sisterhood empowered them to act in ways that were highly unusual for laywomen of their own times. Thus the Sisters were inspiring examples of what women could be and do.

At Catholic women's colleges, to an even greater extent than at secular women's colleges, women's leadership in all aspects of institutional life was particularly evident. At Catholic women's colleges, Sisters established, operated, and staffed the institutions, subsidizing them with their own intellectual and physical labor.[11] In her analysis of religious sisterhoods and Catholic higher education, Mary Oates claims that, "in deliberately choosing to live in large female communities, nuns were radically challenging the social prescription that women belonged in the home."[12]

At the College of St. Catherine, St. Mary's Hospital, and St. Mary's School of Nursing, the Sisters of St. Joseph who served as administrators, faculty, and staff were influential role models for their students. They functioned in positions of power over men or in collaboration with them, including professionals (doctors, interns, and chaplains) and staff (orderlies, maintenance men), positions rare for women during the first half and even later decades, of the twentieth century. Hospital and Nursing School administrators, like Presidents of the College, also had to be skilled at raising funds in the wider community, which meant seeking financial support from male business owners and philanthropists.[13]

Roots and Founders: The Sisters of St. Joseph and the Irelands

The Sisters of St. Joseph began their charitable and educational work in 1650 in LePuy, France. Dedicating themselves to combating poverty and ignorance, they established orphanages, hospitals, free and tuition schools and hospices for the aged. By the time of the French Revolution, the Sisters had developed over 150 communities across France. The Revolution (1789–1794) brought the virtual dissolution of the congregation, as the zeal of the revolutionaries to create a completely secular state led to the widespread oppression of the clergy and Catholic religious communities. During the Revolution, the Sisters were scattered and persecuted. French authorities imprisoned many and executed five of the Sisters. One Sister who narrowly escaped the guillotine, Mother St. John Fontbonne, lived to rebuild the congregation based in Lyons. By the time of her death in 1843 the Sisters of St. Joseph had 244 houses and 3,000 members.[14]

In 1836, under Mother St. John Fontbonne's leadership, the congregation's first mission outside France was sent to North America, to a French settlement, Carondelet, on the Mississippi River near St. Louis. In 1851,

Bishop Joseph Cretin of Minnesota Territory invited the Sisters of St. Joseph to journey up the Mississippi to teach immigrant and American Indian children in St. Paul. Four Sisters arrived that same year and settled in a small shanty on the riverbank. In a nearby log cabin that was the frontier town's first and only Catholic church, the Sisters immediately established St. Joseph's Academy for girls, the first female academy in the region. The log cabin church also served as a hospital where the Sisters treated victims of the 1853 cholera epidemic.[15]

By 1901, when the Sisters of St. Joseph of Carondelet celebrated their 50th Jubilee, they had founded and were operating two hospitals, two nursing schools, two girls' academies, a conservatory for art and music, several orphanages, and numerous parish schools in the Twin Cities of Minneapolis and St. Paul as well as in rural areas of Minnesota and the Dakotas.[16] The first graduates of St. Mary's School of Nursing in Minneapolis matriculated in 1903.[17] Archbishop John Ireland and his sister, Sister Seraphine Ireland, the Provincial Superior of the Sisters of St. Joseph since 1884, worked closely together on all of the Sisters' endeavors.[18]

John Ireland was one of the influential leaders of a movement among American Catholics in the late nineteenth century seeking to "Americanize" the Church in order to remove the stigma attached to Catholics as immigrants and second-class citizens in a predominantly Protestant nation. One important aspect of the Americanization movement was the effort to make all levels of the Catholic educational system the equal of secular and Protestant institutions.[19]

Archbishop Ireland was particularly anxious that Catholic women have access to the higher education they needed to answer the new demands of American womanhood that were apparent by 1900. He saw his own sister, Mother Seraphine, and her Sisters of St. Joseph of St. Paul as the valuable vanguard who would realize his goals for the higher education of Catholic women in the Northwest.[20] In his 1901 address to the Sisters of St. Joseph on the occasion of their 50th Jubilee, Ireland expressed his desire to see Catholic women educated to become effective and capable American citizens:

> Your special province is the training of womanhood. In this new world of ours, there is in a true and honorable sense of the word, the new woman. Beyond a doubt, the sphere of woman's activities has widened; women's influence reaches much farther than ever before: and for such new conditions she must be prepared by an intellectual training higher and more thorough than has heretofore been necessary. . . . I am a firm believer in the higher education of women: I covet for the daughters of the people, . . . the opportunities of receiving under the protecting hand of religion the fullest intellectual equipment of which woman is capable.[21]

The Sisters of St. Joseph had planned to open their college in the 1890s, but the severe financial panic of 1893 and the subsequent recession created financial difficulties that delayed their plans. Eventually the economic situation improved, and in 1900 the Archbishop spurred a renewal of the effort by giving the Sisters the royalties from his newest book, which they peddled on the streets to raise $60,000. In addition, Archbishop Ireland persuaded a local Catholic farmer, Hugh Derham, to donate $25,000 to the Sisters' college fund. In 1903 the Sisters broke ground for the College of St. Catherine's first building, Derham Hall. The first students came in January 1905, just weeks after the first Sisters arrived in a snowstorm to prepare the new building for occupants.[22]

The Irelands were extravagantly visionary in establishing the College of St. Catherine in 1905, for at the time none of the Sisters of St. Joseph had a bachelor of arts degree.[23] Among the 27 Sisters who transferred from St. Joseph's Academy to Derham Hall, however, there was a cadre of exceptional and experienced teachers who would form the nucleus of the College's first faculty.[24] Although they lacked the requisite credentials for college teaching, according to Sister Teresa Toomey, "they were well equipped in learning, in appreciation of art and music, in enthusiasm for literature, classical and modern, and in an understanding of the demands of scholarship."[25]

Moreover, the Sisters acted quickly to educate themselves further and to earn their degrees. The College developed and prospered in direct proportion to the cultivation of the Sisters of St. Joseph who served as its faculty. In the year before the College opened, Mother Seraphine sent Sister Hyacinth Werden, a German teacher and the first superior of the College, and Sister Bridget Bohan, the music teacher, on a wide-ranging tour of Europe to study its systems of higher education and to visit its great cultural and historic sites.[26] Most of the Sisters took correspondence courses and attended summer school courses to work toward degrees. In the summer of 1905 the Sisters who taught history, English, math, and science left to obtain bachelor's degrees, two at Harvard University and two at the University of Chicago. Sister Antonia McHugh, the history teacher, was allowed several leaves of absence from teaching to complete two bachelor's degrees by 1908 in education and philosophy, and by 1909 a master's degree in philosophy. By 1913, two Sisters teaching at the College had bachelor's degrees and three had master's degrees.[28] After 1913, the challenge of continuing to build a qualified faculty from the ranks of the Sisters would fall to Sister Antonia as Dean, and later President, of the College. In later years, Sister Antonia would argue successfully, as she sought accreditation and a chapter of Phi Beta Kappa for St. Catherine's, that her faculty of Sisters was the College's endowment.[29]

The Sisters operated a preparatory program and the early college program side-by-side in Derham Hall. In 1905–1906, its first year, the College of St. Catherine had seven students and attracted between five and nine students each year between 1906 and 1910. Until 1911, the Sisters offered no courses for juniors and seniors, so students who wanted to finish their degrees went on to the University of Minnesota. In 1909, the first student enrolled who would complete all four years of the bachelor's degree at St. Catherine's. The College found it very difficult to retain students in the years before 1911; in its first six years, only seven of 43 students stayed to begin their sophomore year and none of those seven returned as juniors.[30] The tide turned in 1911–1912, when an unprecedented 19 students enrolled, starting a dramatic upward trend that was not reversed. By 1914–1915, the College had 51 students, by 1916–1917 it had 116, and by 1919–1920 there were 238 enrolled. A decade later, 404 women attended the College and throughout the 1930s, despite the Depression, enrollment continued to rise; by 1934–1935 there were 573 students.[31]

The Irelands, Mother Seraphine and Archbishop John, were 62 and 66 years of age, respectively, when the College of St. Catherine opened its doors. They were the founders of an institution that they saw as the crowning and appropriate achievement of over a half-century of work by the Sisters of St. Joseph of St. Paul. However, it would be the next generation of Sisters, under the remarkable acumen and leadership of Sister Antonia McHugh, who would actually create the College that the Irelands had first envisioned in the 1880s. Indeed, perhaps the Archbishop's greatest legacy to the College, having provided it with the necessary financial foundation, was to single out Sister Antonia McHugh as especially talented and to recommend her to Mother Seraphine as the Sister he thought most capable of leading St. Catherine's into the new century.

Sister Antonia: Converting Vision into Reality

It may be impossible to overstate the significance of Sister Antonia McHugh's vision, leadership, and influence upon the development of the College of St. Catherine. Among the Sisters of St. Joseph, it was Sister Antonia who determined what the College should be and how to make that vision a reality. It was Sister Antonia, in turn, who chose and cultivated other Sisters who shared her vision and subscribed to the College ethos she created, and who in subsequent generations would carry the work forward. Many Sisters made essential and lasting contributions to the College of St. Catherine in the first decades of its existence. However, it was Sister Antonia McHugh, more than any other person, who was responsible for establishing a sound financial base for the College, building its community of scholars, refining and expanding its curriculum, and constructing most of its buildings, all of which were essential to the creation of a nationally recognized liberal arts institution. In 1937, her remarkable achievements culminated in the endowment for the College of a chapter of the nation's oldest and most prestigious honor society, Phi Beta Kappa.[32] Notably, the College of St. Catherine was the first Catholic college in the United States deemed worthy of this honor by the Phi Beta Kappa Society. Key to gaining the Gamma Chapter of Phi Beta Kappa was the Society's assessment of the College's faculty, which it described as:

> Young, capable and well qualified. It is the committee's strong conviction that the College of St. Catherine has an alert, well trained, scholarly, interested and deeply intellectual group of administrators and teachers.[33]

It should not be forgotten, however, that Sister Antonia's leadership and vision, to the extent that they changed the lives of her sister religious, also created tensions within the Sisters of St. Joseph community. Committed to building a faculty and college on the model of the University of Chicago, Sister Antonia sent Sisters off to earn degrees at prestigious secular and even Protestant universities all over the world. She also required Sisters to travel to Europe and New York City as part of their educations.[34] When Sister Antonia became Dean of the College in 1914, only three of the Sisters teaching at the College had master's degrees. Under her leadership as dean, and later president, the Sisters obtained master's and doctorate degrees at a breakneck pace: by 1936, an additional 25 advanced degrees had been earned. In addition, at least 13 Sisters had had the opportunity to travel abroad.[35]

Education and cultural activities beyond the convent walls, especially travel and study far from St. Paul, did not sit well with all the Sisters, especially those of the older generation. As Sister Helen Angela Hurley explained in her history of the Sisters of St. Joseph of St. Paul:

> Going outside the convent for higher education was a distinct departure from custom. Yet each of the sisters thus developed a stronger individuality and assurance about the proper way to conduct activities in her field. Sister Antonia was regarded as aggressive and domineering, but she differed from her companions in degree rather than kind. None of them contemplated any departure from either the letter or spirit of their religious profession. They felt that they were merely carrying out the prescriptions of the Third Plenary council of ·Baltimore, which insisted that Catholic schools should be at least as good as public schools of a similar grade. The pronouncements and the ideas of Pope Leo XIll on the subject they had heard many times from Archbishop Ireland.[36]

Sister Teresa Toomey, a historian who began teaching at St. Catherine's in 1918, says Sister Antonia's superiors in the community often got in her way as she acted to implement her vision as Dean of the College. Significantly, Sister Antonia would not be named President of the College until1929 and never held any office in the Sisters of St. Joseph community higher than superior to the Sisters of the College (1931 to 1937).[37] Thus, during most of the years she labored to build the College, Sister Antonia contended with authority figures in the community who were not always supportive of her plans. In 1958, Toomey, in reflecting upon the College's early years, provided the following assessment of the situation:

> Sister Antonia's labors were made the heavier, but unintentionally so, by some who were above her office in the community, and who withheld from her that degree of authority within her assigned area of action which she deemed indispensable for success. In her mind, since she had been given a work to do for God, it could not have been intended that she fail therein, and fail she certainly would not. She took a broad interpretation of the powers inherent in the mandate given her to run the college, and with unflinching courage returned again and again to the charge in behalf of all the demands she kept making for the progress of St. Catherine's. Often it seemed that it was easier for her to go to New York and secure a substantial grant of money for the college than to win a point concerning the study or travel of the sisters.[38]

Even Mother Seraphine, Provincial Superior until 1921 and founder of the College, was at times taken aback by the changes in the lives of the Sisters wrought by Sister Antonia's leadership. According to Hurley, "Mother Seraphine gasped at some of the developments under Sister Antonia, not in disapproval, but as a sort of reminder to the community that all of them were not acts of God and the letter of the law was still in force."[39] Sister Antonia was apparently too progressive and liberal for some in the community; it was she whom Sisters sought out for support in undertaking unusual opportunities that required waivers from "religious restrictions."[40] Always convinced that her way was the best way, and apparently frequently dismissive of those who dared to disagree, she made "more than a few enemies" during her years as dean and president.[41] According to Hurley, if a Sister questioned Sister Antonia's plan to send her to a secular institution to earn an advanced degree, "she was apt to have a new address by the fall. "[42] Those who challenged her ideas or did not meet with her approval in some way were dismissed as "jackasses" or "babies," and told their claims were "nonsense. "[43]

In her unwavering determination and effort to build a community of scholars of the highest caliber, Sister Antonia McHugh was seen by some as ruthless and insensitive to the personal needs of some Sisters. Driven by a desire for excellence as well as a virtual obsession with achieving the best possible credentials for the College, and disappointed that she herself had been unable to earn a doctorate degree, Sister Antonia drove her Sisters to quickly obtain advanced degrees with little reference to individual needs or wishes. [44] Sacrificed for the greater good of the College, some bore scars.

What enabled Sister Antonia to be as successful as she was, despite obstacles within the CSJ community, was the support of Archbishop Ireland. Sister Antonia was his protégé. It was he who had singled her out as one of a small group of young teachers who should be sent to Harvard and the

University of Chicago for bachelor's degrees. It was the Archbishop who had "insisted" to his sister, Mother Seraphine, that Sister Antonia be named Dean of the College. Sister Antonia's intelligence, frankness, and self-confidence had brought her to the Archbishop's attention. Later in her life, Sister Antonia would recall: "The Archbishop liked me. I would talk to him. He knew I wasn't afraid of him."[45] Until his death in 1918, the Archbishop, a frequent visitor to the College, offered unflagging support for Sister Antonia's efforts on behalf of the College. According to Sister Helen Angela Hurley, "publicly and privately he encouraged Sister Antonia, and he kept his eyes open to see that she was not being hampered in her plans."[46] Thus, the Archbishop exercised his considerable influence with Mother Seraphine and the Sisters of St. Joseph on her behalf.[47]

Anna McHugh first encountered the Sisters of St. Joseph in 1885 at the age of 12, when she traveled from her home in North Dakota to attend St. Joseph's Academy for girls in St. Paul. Anna spent only a year in St. Paul and then, because it was closer to her home, transferred to St. Mary's Academy in Winnipeg, Canada, run by the Sisters of the Holy Name, also known as the Gray Nuns. Unexpectedly and to the particular dismay of her father, Anna decided after her academy education that she wanted to become a Gray Nun herself. Her father insisted she delay entering the convent for a year, during which time he presumably hoped Anna would reconsider. However, Anna remained determined. Upon learning that the Gray Nuns required a steep dowry to enter their order, she entered the Sisters of St. Joseph novitiate instead in 1890, at 17 years of age. Anna was better educated than most of the other young women who entered the novitiate in St. Paul that year, and was quickly put to work teaching both the other novices and the St. Joseph academy students. She took the name Antonia and made her permanent vows in 1898.[48]

In addition to her convent education, Anna's parents and her experiences growing up on the North Dakota frontier were significant in forming her character and vision. Her father, Patrick McHugh, was a prominent businessman and politician who took Anna with him to political conventions and on business trips in between her terms at boarding school. In the year before Anna entered the novitiate, Patrick and Anna traveled through Yellowstone Park and attended the North Dakota constitutional convention. As Karen Kennelly explains:

> Childhood experiences in the Dakotas, in the 1870s and 1880s taught Anna to confront all manner of people and situations with curiosity rather than fear and to associate the idea of education with people, travel, and events, as much as with book learning and schools. She came also to conceive of women's work in an expansive way, not just in the religious precepts taught by her grandmother and mother but in their personal examples of courage and generosity.[49]

In 1904 Sister Antonia McHugh was among the first group of Sisters who left St. Joseph's Academy and moved to Derham Hall, the nucleus of the College of St. Catherine. There she met a demanding routine of teaching, cleaning, housekeeping, supervising resident students, and attending daily prayers. As a teacher of history, Sister Antonia was both loved and feared, but always respected. An alumna from the earliest years at the College remembered that Sister Antonia

> knew everything about us, every thought, every idle dream, every latent possibility. . . . It was plain that she would tolerate no indirectness, superficiality, bad manners, slovenly thinking, sham or nonsense in any shape or form. . . . She respected us too much to accept from us a standard lower than the highest.[50]

Sister Helen Angela Hurley describes Sister Antonia's significant impact on her students as a teacher in the years before she became Dean of the College in 1914:

> She was just a teacher, not an official for the first ten years after Derham Hall opened, but no girl ever took her lightly. "Energize yourself," she would pronounce and they moved. There was an endless calendar of her oft-repeated dicta. . . . "It's terrible to have a stagnant mind," "self-pity is a destructive force," "fill your minds with great things and there will be no trivialities," and "she who would be a woman must avoid mediocrity." . . . Room 12 was Sister Antonia's classroom and the place whence apples and advice were dealt out with an impartial hand to the starved and the maladjusted. . . . It was always the hub of the universe to the students, even though not officially so designated.[51]

As dean, Sister Antonia commanded even more respect from students and novices. Sister Marie Philip Haley recalled that when she first arrived at the College in 1917, Sister Antonia loomed very large:

> I knew from the minute I set my foot here that she was the most important one on campus. She was the one I loved most, feared most, respected most, and she certainly was running things. There was no doubt about who was running the students. [52]

Just as Sister Antonia took her students seriously as scholars, she devoted her free time to furthering her own scholarship, attending summer school and taking correspondence courses during the school year from the University of Chicago. Finally allowed a leave of absence to attend the University during regular sessions, she completed a bachelor's degree in philosophy and education by 1908 and a master's degree in history by 1909.[53]

The University of Chicago provided Sister Antonia not only with an education, but also with important friends and mentors from among its faculty and administrators. One of these, Dr. George Edgar Vincent, the Dean of the Faculty, would prove to be a useful and influential ally as she struggled to build St. Catherine's. Vincent became president of the University of Minnesota in 1911 and was close enough for the next five years to act as a frequent consultant.[54] Sister Antonia later recalled:

> During his administration, from 1911 to 1916, St. Catherine's was in the hazardous days of its beginnings, and it was Dr. Vincent, more than anyone else, who helped make it secure. With his characteristic generosity and splendid spirit of service, he made clear to me what to do, how to organize, and how to bring about the improvements that made the accrediting of the college possible.[55]

Dr. Vincent left the University of Minnesota in 1917 and, serendipitously for Sister Antonia, became the head of the Rockefeller Foundation's General Education Fund. She applied to the Foundation in 1918 for funds and largely credited Vincent for the $100,000 grant she obtained for the College.[56]

At Chicago, Sister Antonia also developed close ties with Dr. James Angell, her professor of psychology, and Dr. William Rainey Harper, the president of the University. Attending Harper's convocations at Chicago, Sister Antonia said, gave her a "burning desire to have some part, however small, in the work in education in the Northwest."[57] Sister Antonia adopted Harper's idea that a university should be a community of scholars and, after becoming dean in 1914, she was determined to implement his model at St. Catherine's. Angell would prove an essential ally; when he later served as a board member of both the Carnegie and Rockefeller Foundations, Sister Antonia applied to both for funding for the College. In 1926, under Angell's auspices, the Carnegie Foundation gave the College a five-year grant totaling $40,000. In the late 1920s, the Rockefeller Foundation granted St. Catherine's an additional $400,000 to build a science building and health center (Mendel and Fontbonne Halls).[58] Another former teacher and friend from the University of Chicago, Professor Charles Judd, helped Sister Antonia present a successful case for accreditation of the College. At the meeting of the North Central Association of Colleges and Universities in 1916, their novel argument was that the Sisters, as faculty, constituted the equivalent of a cash endowment.[59]

Sister Antonia concerned herself with all facets of the College's development; in addition to ordering the curriculum and raising funds, she oversaw construction of six buildings, the landscaping of the campus, the recruiting of students, advertising, and obtaining accreditation. Most importantly, she knew that the development of her faculty was key to creating the fine liberal arts college she envisioned. Consequently, Sister Antonia set her sights on building a community of scholars on the Chicago model and achieving accreditation for the College as quickly as possible. These dual goals meant the continued, swift cultivation of her faculty of Sisters. St. Catherine's was not unusual in its drive to rapidly develop its faculty; this was the norm for all Catholic women's colleges in the first half of the twentieth century. According to Karen Kennelly, because congregations wanted to teach students themselves rather than hire lay faculty, women religious "were soon greatly exceeding the rate of earning of advanced degrees by lay women in the United States and Europe."[60]

Sister Agnes Rita Lingl, who earned a doctorate in German from the University of Munich in 1933, remembered that Sister Antonia's insistence that the Sisters obtain degrees from the most prominent universities was controversial among Catholics:

> To the horror of some people, sometimes bishops, she sent the sisters out to many non-Catholic or rather secular universities. . . . She saw to it that the sisters got to Chicago, Columbia, to other secular institutions. . . . When we went to the secular institutions at that time, the sisters from other communities were all being sent to the Catholic University or Notre Dame.[61]

Despite Sister Rita's recollection, other Catholic women's colleges in the United States did send their sisters for graduate educations at non-Catholic universities, mainly because few Catholic universities offered advanced degrees in the fields needed by the women religious running colleges.[62] Moreover, Sister Antonia shared Archbishop Ireland's insistence that the credentials of faculty teaching at all levels of Catholic education be comparable to that of faculty at secular and Protestant institutions.[63]

Sister Antonia's grueling program of faculty development required that Sisters obtain doctorates before the age of 35. Sisters teaching in the preparatory program who did not have bachelor's degrees were required to take college courses on Saturdays and during the summer. These younger sisters were sent on trips to learn how to travel and attended local cultural events and institutions as part of their educations as well. Once a Sister obtained her bachelor's degree, she was immediately sent off to earn a master's degree or doctorate at a prestigious institution in the United States or Europe.[64] Sister Helen Angela Hurley described the swift pace of faculty development under Sister Antonia's leadership:

> With factory-like speed Sisters were hurried through college and shipped away for graduate work. College and high school graduates began entering the novitiate. The instant they were released from the religious training required of them by Canon Law, Sister Antonia insisted on taking them over. . . . The young sisters grasped the intellectual challenge and pleasure which foot-loose travel and study, the necessary concomitants of Sister Antonia's ideas in education, brought them. Not a few scars must be attributed to the reckless distribution of opportunities.[65]

Sister Antonia's plans for faculty improvement suffered a temporary setback in 1920–1921, when five of the Sisters who had earned advanced degrees, apparently rankled by her leadership, requested and obtained assignments at other institutions. Sister Maris Stella Smith, who was a student at the time, recalled her impression of why the five Sisters left the College:

> I was here for a year with Sister Clara as principal of Derham Hall High School. Sister Clara wasn't here when I was a Senior. I think she went to St. Margaret's or some place; I suppose she got a mission. I think perhaps there was an element of Sister Clara and Sister Antonia not seeing eye-to-eye. . . . Sister Clara was more conventional. Sister Mary John and Sister Eva were also more of the conventional school, and they dropped out somewhere when I was in the novitiate. They were, I think you might call them casualties.[66]

Sister Antonia's response to the loss was to immediately enact an even more ambitious plan to prepare faculty for the College. She quickly selected the most promising young Sisters from the novitiate, including Sisters Maris Stella Smith, Teresa Joseph Griswold, Helen Margaret Peck, Antonius Kennelly, Agnes Rita Lingl, Jeanne D'Arc Hurley, and Cecilia Manion, to pursue advanced studies. Sister Antonia also acted to free some of the College's faculty for a term, summer, or year to pursue further graduate studies. She made it possible for several of the Sisters to travel and study abroad over the next 10 years. Finally, to ensure the College would not lose ground, she employed highly competent instructors from nearby institutions, including the University of Minnesota, as substitutes for these Sisters. [67]

Under Sister Antonia's program of faculty development, the Sisters of St. Joseph at the College of St. Catherine rapidly accumulated advanced degrees at prestigious institutions, including the University of Munich, Columbia University, and the University of Louvain in Belgium, as well as the universities of Chicago, Minnesota, Michigan, and Catholic University. Two other Sisters received master's degrees from Oxford University.[68] Other Sisters spent several years traveling and studying in Europe. In the early 1920s, Sister Anna Goulet and Sister Cecilia Manion went to Paris to study music under the composer Marcel Dupre. Sister Eleanor Michel studied art history at the University of Madrid for a year and continued her studies in Florence, Paris, and Havana, Cuba.[69] By 1933, the College's faculty included 47 Sisters of St. Joseph and 19 laywomen. About two-thirds of the Sisters held advanced degrees from a variety of American and European universities. In contrast, most of the lay female faculty held degrees from regional institutions.[70]

In addition to cultivating the faculty, Sister Antonia's objectives for the College included building a financial endowment, raising the funds necessary to erect new buildings, maintaining an adequate library, and achieving national recognition for the scholastic achievements of the College.[71] During her tenure as dean, and then president, she successfully solicited funds from both the Carnegie and Rockefeller Foundations that totaled $540,000. In addition, the Archdiocese of St. Paul gave the College a grant of $200,000 out of the Archbishop Ireland Educational Fund in 1921; it was the last time in the College's history that the Archdiocese would provide St. Catherine's with financial support. In response to a stipulation of the Rockefeller grant, Sister Antonia also organized the College's first Board of Trustees in 1920.[72]

Successful fundraising allowed Sister Antonia to pursue an ambitious plan for constructing new buildings and landscaping the College campus. As the newly appointed dean in 1914, she oversaw the construction already under way of Whitby Hall. Between 1921 and 1932 she built Caecilian, Mendel, and Fontbonne Halls and Our Lady of Victory Chapel. Funding from the Carnegie Foundation allowed Sister Antonia to expand the libarary's holdings from 12,000 books in 1916 to 50,000 volumes by 1937.[73] National recognition of the College of St. Catherine resulted from Sister Antonia's leadership and the scholarly achievements of her faculty Sisters. Having achieved regional accreditation in 1916, Sister Antonia immediately turned to the National Association of American Universities, receiving its stamp of approval in 1917. By 1924, she had successfully won for the College membership in the Association of American University Women.[74] Sister Antonia herself served as president of the Minnesota Association of Colleges and as chair of the National Catholic Educational Association Conference of Colleges for Women; she also held executive positions in the American Association of Colleges and participated in a White House conference on Child Health and Protection in 1930. Sister Antonia received papal honors in 1931, an honorary degree from the University of Minnesota in 1936, and a Distinguished Alumni award from the University of Chicago in 1937.[75] However, her greatest triumph and the crowning achievement of her administrative career was securing a chapter of the nation's oldest and most prestigious academic honor society, Phi Beta Kappa, for the College.

Sister Antonia had been dogged in her pursuit of Phi Beta Kappa membership. She first applied for a chapter of the Society in 1921, but was forced to abandon the effort due to a lack of support from administrators of liberal arts institutions that were already members of Phi Beta Kappa.[76] According to Sister Rosalie Ryan, there were subsequent unsuccessful attempts to secure a chapter as well. At one point, Sister Antonia was told that the College's library holdings were insufficient and the French Department was too weak. Sister Antonia's response to such rejections was to right whatever the review committee found wrong with the College and to try again.[77] Despite persistent obstacles, Sister Antonia was resolute in her determination to gain Phi Beta Kappa's imprimatur for the College. As Charles Buzicky explains, "The achievement of a Phi Beta Kappa chapter became an obsession with her; it was the measuring stick of her success as an educator."[78]

The final application to the Society began in 1933, when Sister Antonia asked Sister Jeanne Marie Bonnett, who had earned a doctorate in psychology from the University of Louvain, to steer the College through the review process. Sister Jeanne Marie wrote a 138-page report highlighting the College's qualifications as a liberal arts institution with a highly accomplished, committed faculty. To ensure that St. Catherine's would receive a site visit, Sister Jeanne Marie traveled to New York to meet with the Society's president, "to refute rumors that Catholic colleges curtailed academic freedom or suffered from 'in-breeding' of faculty." The Society conducted a site visit of St. Catherine's in December 1936. Early in 1937, the Society voted to grant the College membership.[79] For many years, St. Catherine's would remain the only Catholic college in the nation with a Phi Beta Kappa chapter, a stunning achievement for a young, small, Catholic women's college in the Upper Midwest.

It is difficult to exaggerate the import of Sister Antonia McHugh's influence and leadership in the history of the College of St. Catherine. Sister Antonia's expansive vision, heroic efforts, remarkable achievements, and devotion to mission constitute her continuing legacy to the College. Indeed, she is still with us at the College in many symbolic ways, such as the Antonian Scholars Program and the Mother Antonia McHugh Award. Moreover, Antonia lore (some of which, as with all legends, is not accurate) still abounds. Certainly the essential matter of her legacy remains: the conviction that the liberal arts and sciences should be the core, if not the entire substance, of a woman's college education. But she was not a saint, nor was her leadership always easy for others to bear: "her yoke was not always sweet or her burden light. "[80] Sister Antonia's relentless pursuit of excellence brought change, brought "gasps" from her superiors, and flung some of her Sisters aside, yet it also created a Catholic college for women of the highest caliber, one on par with the best secular institutions of its time. The genius beind her leadership was her ability to envision the future and to act as if it were already accomplished, which somehow, in the end, made it so. Like the Irelands before her, she too was extravagantly visionary. In 1936, the College's student fine arts publication, Ariston, explained Sister Antonia's talent for effecting change:

> But always to her St. Catherine's had been a great college, even when it was only a dream. Never just a building on a hill, it was a growing family of buildings: Caeciliaan, Mendel, the Health Center, the Chapel. All these she planned, built and peopled in her mind long before the architects were ever summoned. The pews of Our Lady of Victory Chapel were filled with girls in caps and gowns when the old chapel on Fourth Derham was still adequate to the College needs. It is that vision for the future, that aspiration for excellence and the creative power to convert vision into reality that has distinguished Mother Antonia's work in the entire field of education.[81]

Notes

1. 1904 Announcement of Opening of the College of St. Catherine, St. Paul, Minnesota, College of St. Catherine (CSC) Archives.

2. Helena Caven Murray, CSC Alumna, Class of 1937, Alumnae Reminiscences of Mother Antonia McHugh, 1973, McHugh Papers, CSC Archives, Box 8.

3. Mother Antonia McHugh, "Address to the National Catholic Council of Women," undated, McHugh Papers, CSC Archives, Box 8.

4. Karen Kennelly, "Faculties and What They Taught," in Tracy Schler and Cynthia Russett, *Catholic Women's Colleges in America* (Baltimore: Johns Hopkins University Press, 2002), pp. 98–121.

5. *Ibid*, p. 98.

6. Sister Helen Angela Hurley, *On Good Ground: The Sisters of St. Joseph of Carondelet* (Minneapolis: University of Minnesota Press, 1957), p. 86.

7. Nancy Woloch, *Women and the American Experience* (Boston: McGraw Hill, 2000), 3rd edition, chapters 4, 6, 8, 10, 12; M. Elizabeth Tidball, Daryl Smith, Charles Tidball, and Lisa Wolf-Wendel, *Taking Women Seriously* (Phoenix: American Council on Education, 1999), pp. 69–70.

8. Woloch, pp. 281–292.

9. Jill Ker Conway, "Faith, Knowledge and Gender," in *Catholic Women's Colleges in America*, pp. 11–16, at pp. 13–15; Kennelly, pp. 99–100; Woloch, p. 284. Wellesley was the only prominent non-Catholic women's college with the tradition of a female president and all-female faculty in the late nineteenth century.

10. Woloch, chapters 14, 16, 18, 20.

11. Mary Oates, "Sisterhoods and Catholic Higher Education," in Catholic Women's Colleges in America, p. 164.

12. Ibid., p. 171.

13. Sister Anne Thomasine Sampson, *Care With a Prayer* (Minneapolis: St. Mary's Hospital, 1987); Sister Rosalie Ryan and Sr. John Christine Wolkerstorfer, *More Than A Dream* (St. Paul: College of St. Catherine, 1992); Charles Buzicky, "Mother Antonia's Impossible Dream: The College of St. Catherine," Scan (Fall 1973), pp. 5–12; Woloch, *Women and the American Experience*, chapters 10, 12, 14, 18.

14. Hurley, pp. 1–8.

15. Hurley, pp. 5–20.

16. Hurley, pp. 113–193.

17. Sampson, p. 11.

18. Hurley, pp. 164, 197–227. The Archbishop's cousin, Sister Celestine Howard, and another of his sisters, Sister St. John Ireland, were also prominent leaders in the order.

19. Hurley, pp. 200–210; William Watts Folwell, *A History of Minnesota* (St. Paul: Minnesota Historical Society, 1926), Volume IV, pp. 180–182; Reverend John Ireland, *The Church and Modern Society* (St. Paul: Pioneer Press, 1904).

[20] Hurley, p. 225; Karen Kennelly, "The Dynamic Sister Antonia and the College of St. Catherine," *Ramsey County History* (Fall/Winter 1978), pp. 3–18 at p. 7.

[21] As quoted in Buzicky, p. 7; Ireland, *The Church and Modern Society*, pp. 300–301.

[22] Hurley, pp. 228–229; Kennelly, 'The Dynamic Sister Antonia," p. 7. Derham donated $20,000 for the building and $5,000 for a scholarship fund.

[23] Sister Teresa Toomey, "The Best and Highest of Its Kind," Scan (Spring 1958), p. 10.

[24] Toomey, p. 11.

[25] Toomey, p. 10.

[26] Toomey, p. 11; Sister Helen Margaret Peck, "An Academic History of the College of St. Catherine," (unpublished manuscript, 1982), Volume II, College of St. Catherine Archives, p. 29.

[27] Peck, pp. 28–29. They were Sister Antonia, Sister De Sales Kilty, Sister Mary Joseph Kelly, and Sister Clara Graham.

[28] Toomey, p. 12.

[29] Kennelly, "The Dynamic Sister Antonia," p. 13.

[30] Peck, "Academic History," pp. 1–2.

[31] Sister Helen Margaret Peck. "The Growth and Expansion of the College of St. Catherine to the End of the Presidency of Sister Antonia McHugh," (unpublished manuscript, 1982), CSC Archives, pp. 3–4.

[32] Buzicky, pp. 11–13; Kennelly, "The Dynamic Sister Antonia," pp. 11–12.

[33] "PBK Investigative Report," 1937, as quoted in Buzicky, p. 12.

[34] Toomey, pp. 13–14; Kennelly, "The Dynamic Sister Antonia," pp. 13–14.

[35] Kennelly, "The Dynamic Sister Antonia," p. 13; Toomey, p. 14.

[36] Hurley, pp. 236–237.

[37] Hurley, p. 254, p. 264.

[38] Toomey, p. 13.

[39] Hurley, p. 229.

[40] Hurley, p. 254.

[41] Kennelly, "The Dynamic Sister Antonia," p. 16; Hurley, p. 245.

[42] Hurley, p. 245.

[43] Hurley, p. 245; Kennelly, "The Dynamic Sister Antonia," p. 16.

[44] Buzicky, p. 12.

[45] Kennelly, "The Dynamic Sister Antonia," p. 11; Hurley, p. 236.

[46] Hurley, p. 248.

[47] Hurley, p. 247.

[48] Kennelly, "The Dynamic Sister Antonia," pp. 8–9; Ryan and Wolkerstorfer, p. 8.

[49] Kennelly, "The Dynamic Sister Antonia," p. 8.

[50] As quoted in Buzicky, p. 9.

[51] Hurley, pp. 240–241.

[52] Sister Marie Philip Haley, Oral History Interview, June 16, 1975, as quoted in Ryan manuscript for *More Than A Dream*, CSC Archives, p. 12a.

[53] Sister Rosalie Ryan, Manuscript for *More Than a Dream*, CSC Archives, pp. 9–10.

[54] Buzicky, p. 8.

[55] Sister Antonia McHugh, "Recollections," Box 9, CSC Archives, as quoted in Ryan manuscript, p. 10.

[56] Ryan manuscript, p. 10; Hurley, p. 248.

[57] Sister Antonia, as quoted in Ryan manuscript, p. 10; Hurley, p. 23S; Buzicky, pp. 8–10.

[58] Hurley, p. 249.

[59] Kennelly, "The Dynamic Sister Antonia," p. 13; Toomey, p. 20; Hurley, p. 244.

[60] Kennelly, "Faculties and What They Taught," p. 105.

[61] Sister Agnes Rita Lingl, Oral History, p. 13, as quoted in Ryan manuscript, p. 22a.

[62] Kennelly, "Faculties and What They Taught," pp. 105–108.

[63] Hurley, p. 245.

[64] Toomey, p. 14.

[65] Hurley, p. 245.

[66] Sister Maris Stella Smith Oral Interview, January 14, 1975, CSC Archives, as quoted in Ryan manuscript, CSC Archives.

[67] Peck, "Growth and Expansion," p. 47.

[68] Kennelly, "The Dynamic Sister Antonia," p. 13.

[69] Ryan manuscript, pp. 23, 25b.

[70] Kennelly, "Faculties and What They Taught," p. 105.

[71] Toomey, Material Collected on Sister Antonia McHugh, Box 8, CSC Archives, as quoted in Ryan manuscript, p. 19.

[72] Toomey, p. 20.

[73] Ibid.

[74] Ibid.

[75] Kennelly, "The Dynamic Sister Antonia," p. 16.

[76] Kennelly, "The Dynamic Sister Antonia," p. 15.

[77] Ryan and Wolkerstorfer, *More than a Dream*, pp. 31–32.

[78] Buzicky, p. 12.

[79] Buzicky, p. 12.

[80] Buzicky, p. 12.

[81] Ariston, 1936, as quoted in Peck, "Growth and Expansion," p. 118.

Rosalie Ryan (1925–2013) was a 1936 graduate of St. Kate's who returned as an English professor in 1958. She later served as admissions director and academic dean and retired in 1985 from the theology department. John Christine Wolkerstorfer, CSJ, is also a St. Kate's graduate. She was professor of American history at CSC, with special interests in oral history and in the U.S. Civil War. She retired in 1997. The following excerpt is taken from their work, More than a Dream: Eighty-five Years at the College of St. Catherine, *published in 1992. They present a detailed history of the College calling attention to a number of key figures who played essential roles in making the college what it is today. What do you find noteworthy in this history? How does this history affect your thinking about your education here?*

from More than a Dream
Eighty-five Years at the College of St. Catherine

Rosalie Ryan, CSJ, and John Christine Wolkerstorfer, CSJ

Chapter One: A Vision of Excellence

Early in 1905, a bulletin announced that a new Catholic college for women would introduce "the third epoch in the development of the educational work of the Sisters of St. Joseph in the Northwest. In 1851 they opened the first Catholic elementary school . . . some years later they built St. Joseph's Academy, the first preparatory school; and finally they founded St. Catherine's . . . the purpose of those in charge is to make this college the best and highest school of its kind in the Northwest." Twenty-seven sisters had already begun to fulfill this vision in a single building on isolated farmland west of St. Paul.

The College of St. Catherine opened to students in January 1905, but the project had been long in the making. Archbishop John Ireland had begun to plan for the college in the early 1890s, helping his sister Ellen—Mother Seraphine Ireland—acquire 110 acres of land at the comer of Randolph and Cleveland avenues. A financial panic in 1893 postponed the project, and ten years passed before the work continued. Not everyone greeted plans for the new college with enthusiasm. Institutions for the higher education of women had not found favor in the United States in the late 1800s. Women's education was carried on chiefly by "female seminaries," which gave courses in "domestic training": needlework, manners, and a host of other topics intended to prepare a woman for her place in the home. Toward the end of the century, individual women began asking for more, and the heads of some colleges moved towards providing education in literature and the sciences to prepare women for teaching and other professions. George Schmidt wrote of what this entailed in *The Liberal Arts College: A Chapter in American Cultural History*: "To reach the college level . . . it would be necessary to slough off the many fashionable and vocational scraps of knowledge and concentrate on the solid subjects which sharpened the understanding and disciplined the mind. This meant the higher reaches of Latin, Greek, mathematics, mental and moral philosophy." Efforts to create greater intellectual challenge for women often met with shock, alarm, or derision. "Such an experience," said one critic, "can only be hardening and deforming." Another said, "This borders on the vulgar."

Historian Thomas Woody wrote that the Reverend John Todd, a Protestant minister, absolutely denounced the idea: "As for training young ladies through a long intellectual course, as we do young men, it can never be done. They will die in the process . . . The poor thing has her brain crowded with history, grammar, arithmetic, geography, natural history, chemistry . . . metaphysics, French, often German, Latin, perhaps Greek. . . . She must be on the strain all the school hours, study in the evening till her eyes ache, her brain whirls, her spine yields and gives way, and she comes through the process of education enervated, feeble, without courage or vigor, elasticity or strength."

The naysayers deterred neither the sisters nor Archbishop Ireland, who had already given material as well as moral support. In 1900 he had signed over to the sisters the rights to his book, *The Church and Modern Society*, which they peddled from door to door, selling 20,000 copies and raising $60,000 for the college building fund. In 1902, Hugh Derham, a wealthy farmer from Rosemount, asked the archbishop to name a special charity. Ireland suggested he support the effort toward a new Catholic liberal arts college for women. Derham donated $20,000 toward the erection of the first building and $5,000 for a scholarship. Later, Mother Seraphine said of the gift: "It may not seem very large . . . but it gave us courage to go on. He well deserved to have Derham Hall named for him."

Because of problems with construction, the school, scheduled to open in September 1904, was not ready for occupancy until the end of that year. On December 26, 1904, twenty-seven sisters walked a mile in a snowstorm from St. Joseph's Academy in downtown St. Paul to board the Grand Avenue streetcar at Seven Corners. They got off the bus at Cleveland Avenue, then walked another mile south to Randolph Avenue. The elements did not discourage their excitement over the new building. Sister Bridget Bohan later reminisced that on December 27 Archbishop Ireland came out with a team of horses. With him were Mother Seraphine and Sister Celestine Howard. Promptly at 7:00 A.M., the archbishop offered the first Mass. Then he blessed the rooms of Derham. Hall: "They had lanterns to light their way around the house . . . a cat followed . . . Sister Jarlath [Noonan] said that Sister Eulalia [Dress] brought the cat from the academy in a bag . . . The cat went into all the rooms as they were being blessed. Whenever the archbishop shook the holy water, the cat went up to receive . . . Finally he said, 'What's that doing here?'" Because of the continuing snow, the three guests left after breakfast. A few days later the boarding students from St. Joseph's Academy arrived to become students of Derham Hall.

The sisters had started from scratch in furnishing the new school, and they sometimes came up short. According to Sister Bridget: "We had about ninety boarders, and when their trunks came out with everything, we had sheets enough for about forty-eight or fifty beds . . . And this was the Christmas holidays. Sister Hyacinth [Werden] said, 'I don't know what to do.' 'Well,' I said, 'give us some money, and we'll do the buying.' Sister Edith [Hogan] and I went over to Minneapolis, and you couldn't get sheets ready-made. You had to buy the bolt of unbleached muslin . . . We rented [sewing] machines and Sister Antonia [McHugh] and I sat at those machines from dawn to dark, and Sister Monica [Berghs] made up the sheets. And the boarders took them without being laundered. They made nothing of it . . . Unbleached, oh, it was unspeakable!" Nevertheless, the school shortly offered an "academic" (college preparatory) course, music, art, and domestic arts. In September 1905, college courses formally began, with seven students registered as freshmen.

The challenge of building enrollment engaged the sisters from the start. Brochures extolled the beauty of the campus, and, later, paid advertisements in the *Catholic Bulletin* lured prospective students. The first printed materials read: "On this spot Nature has poured her beauty with a prodigal hand. To the west of the college is the Mississippi, just recovering from its dash over the Falls [of St. Anthony]; further still to the west, the laughing waters of Minnehaha make constant melody, and on all sides alternating stretches of unkempt forest and billowy greensward complete the beauty of the scene."

Later notices stressed the healthfulness of the site. In 1906: "No school in the United States for the education of young ladies is more favorably situated . . . in regard to the healthfulness and sanitation . . . The drainage and plumbing are as nearly perfect as can be found anywhere." Another ad read: "In the construction of the college building the comfort and safety of its inmates were taken into consideration . . . The wide corridors which extend through the whole length of the building afford space for recreation and exercise in inclement weather." And in 1907, signed by Charles Meade, physician for the college: "The site is exceptionally healthful, and the extensive grounds afford ample opportunity for free outdoor life and exercise in the bracing Minnesota air." Would such claims refute accusations of the likes of the Reverend Todd?

The earliest catalog stated plainly the college's objectives:

- to give the students a liberal education to train and develop all their powers simultaneously
- to train Catholic "girls" to be solidly virtuous and religious—to teach all, irrespective of their denominational differences, to respect, appreciate, and encourage religion and Christian morality.

Despite the publicity, enrollment grew slowly, and for the first six years the College of St. Catherine was really a small high school with just a handful of "specials" doing postsecondary work. Most students wishing to continue beyond the sophomore year transferred to the University of Minnesota. Finally in 1911, two students who had completed the sophomore year, Gertrude Malloy and Marguerite McCusker (Testor), returned as juniors. They remained to graduate in 1913. . . . That year Sisters Frances Clare Bardon, Margaret Kerby, and Antonia McHugh filed a certificate of incorporation for the College of St. Catherine to promote letters, sciences, and the arts through the care, protection, housing, and instruction of students in subjects including the practice of religion.

The next year, at the insistence of Archbishop Ireland, Sister Antonia McHugh was appointed the first dean (chief administrative officer). Building a great college for women was the object of her unceasing labor for the next twenty-four years.

Fit for Pioneer Work

Sister Antonia's background fitted her for pioneering work. She was born Anna McHugh in Omaha in 1873 of an itinerant frontier family. Her father, Patrick McHugh, after several moves in the Dakotas, settled in Langdon, North Dakota, to serve as mayor, postmaster, and bank director. He was elected a commissioner of Cavalier County, then to the territorial legislature for three terms and to the North Dakota legislature for four. Patrick McHugh often took young Anna with him on his business and political travels in the territory.

When she was twelve years old, Anna's father took her to St. Joseph's Academy in St. Paul to study and prepare for her first Holy Communion. During the next three years, she attended St. Mary's Academy in Winnipeg, which was closer to home. Sister Mary Joseph Calasenz, SNJM, remembered Anna McHugh from her days in high school: "She was remarkable in her practical piety, application to study, and generosity. Her outspokenness was proverbial among her companions; her frankness was of a nature to abash those who were not lovers of the truth." Said Sister Teresa Toomey: "During the whole of her life as an educator, Sister Antonia showed herself to be a true daughter of pioneers, alert, eager, undaunted by difficulties, and bold in her dreams of what Catholic schools in the Northwest could mean for both the Church and the nation she loved."

In 1890 Anna entered the novitiate of the Sisters of St. Joseph in St. Paul, then began teaching third and fourth grades at St. Joseph's Academy. She was among the first group of sisters at the new college. There she threw herself into a routine of cleaning and housekeeping, teaching, supervising resident students, and attending daily prayers. She continued her education with classes at the University of Chicago in summer and correspondence courses during the school year. . . Sister Antonia attended four successive seminars beginning in 1905, with a full year of study arranged for 1908. By December of that year, she had a bachelor's degree in philosophy and education. In 1909 she received a master's degree in history. . . .

Sister Antonia had returned from studies in Chicago to teach at the College of St. Catherine with characteristic enthusiasm. Her classes in history were filled with love of the classical age of Greece and Rome. For study of the Middle Ages she had collected hundreds of pictures of cathedrals and castles. She had spent much time in the study of geology and geography, so the map of Europe became familiar to her students. Her knowledge of music and art was extensive.

Sister Antonia sprinkled her teaching with dozens of maxims and phrases. When she said, "energize yourself," the student moved. She considered some responses "clear as mud" or "windy." Outside of class she might comment that "things for sale are in windows" or "only horses hang their heads" or "she who would be a woman must avoid mediocrity." From Room 12, she impartially handed out apples and advice. Her classroom was a place where young women found out what was the matter with them even when they didn't want to know. But there was also talk about books and stars and music and pictures. The seriousness of a particular conference with a student could be gauged by whether the door to Room 12 was open or closed.

In these ways Sister Antonia impressed students deeply: "I certainly knew, from the minute I set my foot here, that she was the most important one on the campus. She was the one I loved most, respected most, feared most, and she certainly was running things," said Sister Marie Philip Haley '21.

Spreading the News

When Sister Antonia became dean in 1914, eighteen students were enrolled in the college, but the sisters were determined to attract more. News items, articles, and full-page advertisements in the *Catholic Bulletin* helped make the public aware of the college's facilities: "Come to the College of St. Catherine. Don't put it off. Decide now. If you need financial help, write to us. We will do all we can. Many students earn their way through college. A college education is worth a big sacrifice. Come." On June 3, 1916, pictures first graced an ad. Around the same time, the college began placing ads in the St. Paul *Pioneer Press* and St. Paul *Dispatch* and publishing more and better brochures. The start of a regular run of the no-fare "dinky" from Snelling to Cleveland on Randolph in 1916 supported recruitment for day students, too. Earlier, the nearest streetcar lines were a mile east and north, on Snelling and Grand Avenues. . . .

Students in area elementary and secondary schools were advised by their teachers of opportunities at the college. Family members, friends, and acquaintances of students spoke highly of it. Sometimes a parish priest recommended a student, and alumnae visitors also spread the news. In response to laws passed in Minnesota and North Dakota requiring all teachers in elementary and high schools to meet requirements for state certification, Sister Antonia assisted the sisters in her congregation as well as those of others. She received letters from sisters in all parts of the country, asking for help in evaluating credits and meeting the new requirements, usually including a bachelor's degree. She gave advice and education, tuition-free at the college, in the hope that the recipients would send future students to their alma mater. In 1921–22, for example, five Sisters of the Holy Names from Vancouver, two Missionary Sisters of the Most Holy Trinity from Alabama, and two Sisters of St. Joseph from Crookston, Minnesota, registered at the college.

These strategies all helped toward increasing enrollment from 30 students in 1914 to 218 in 1920. But the most direct recruiting method—the personal visit—met with the most success. Genevieve Lamb (Oberly) recalled that every year the sisters stayed at her grandmother's home while visiting her hometown of Michigan, North Dakota. A teenager of fourteen or fifteen, she was called upon to drive a surrey carrying the sisters and their lunches to neighboring towns such as Crary. Obtaining the names of Catholic girls from the parish priest, the sisters then visited them in their homes. With no Catholic college in the state, North Dakota was a rich field for recruitment, and enrollment from the area increased from one in 1911 to thirty-one in 1919.

The sisters traveled to Minnesota towns, branching out to Wisconsin and Montana. They went to and from the coast on the Northern Pacific and Great Northern railways on passes granted by the railroads on the assumption that students would come back as paying fares. Each pair of sisters carried fifty dollars in cash to cover six weeks' travel expenses. They stopped in every fair-sized town along the way, staying without cost in convents or hospitals and in the homes of students or alumnae. They visited the homes of those who had inquired about the college or who were known as prospective recruits by students or alumnae from the town. Difficulties were compensated for by their success at bringing in registrants and the chance to see the West—including Yellowstone and Glacier parks, as arranged by alumnae or parents of students.

The college took a step forward in recruiting techniques in 1924–25 with the production of a movie on campus life called *A Day at St. Catherine's*. Its plot centered on the adventures of a new student. Athletic events (including a field day and a tennis tournament), music classes, the dedication of the chapel, and a commencement procession were shown. Two years later, the college announced the availability of honor tuition scholarships in Catholic high schools throughout Minnesota and surrounding states. This strategy, coupled with a student service program initiated in 1922, helped to increase enrollment even during the economic depression of the 1930s.

Sister Antonia clearly was not interested in enrollment for enrollment's sake, however, and she carefully planned for every facet of college development. Sister Teresa remembered that she labored, usually in several areas at once, to carry through this fourfold program:

1. to obtain national and international recognition for the scholastic work
2. to offer to the sisters of the college the opportunity for a wide cultural background and for professional education at outstanding American and European centers of learning
3. to work out a schedule of study and activity ensuring education at once religious, humanistic, and professional
4. to secure funding for the erection of new buildings, the maintenance of an adequate library, and the establishment of an endowment fund.

Official Recognition

Between 1916 and 1920, the college was accredited by the North Central Association of Colleges, the National Educational Association, the National Catholic Educational Association, and the Association of American Colleges. . . . Accreditation by the North Central Association of Colleges had been particularly complicated, since the financial organization of public universities and colleges differed from that of private colleges, especially Catholic ones. During the winter of 1915–16, the college prepared a self-study and was visited by an accrediting team from the association. The sticking point was the matter of endowment. The college had very little, most of its resources being invested in buildings and faculty development. Sister Antonia worked to convince team members that the contributed services of the sisters constituted a considerable endowment.

Team member Charles Judd, a friend from the University of Chicago, seemed to understand the concept, for he wrote in his North Central report: "These teachers do not receive any pay and have no private contracts with the institution but are under the general control of the orders to which they belong. Many of the institutions undoubtedly receive in this way services that represent a large endowment."

But the larger commission did not at first accept the concept. Judd wrote to Sister Antonia: "The committee . . . is not including the name of your institution on the tentative list . . . on the grounds set forth in this report." She replied immediately, on March 18, 1916: "I note with complete satisfaction your just appreciation of the endowment question for Catholic schools. . . . With this matter settled in our favor, I am at a loss to know why our name is not included on your approved list, as I know we more than meet every other standard recommended by the Association."

The committee evidently reversed itself; the Spring 1916 *Ariston* crowed: "On Saturday, March 25, the announcement was made to us that our college had been placed upon its list of schools accredited by the North Central Association of Colleges." That year college recruitment ads replaced the line "accredited by the Minnesota State Board of Public Instruction and by several prominent universities" with "the only college for women in the Northwest belonging to the North Central Association, which places it educationally on a par with Vassar, Wellesley, and Smith."

Professional Educators

Indeed, the teaching services of the sisters constituted an extraordinary endowment. Sister Antonia had given high priority to the professional and cultural education of the faculty. The teaching sisters were to be as well educated as their equals at other colleges and universities. To Sister Antonia, that meant attending and receiving degrees at great universities in the United States as well as travel and study abroad, and the process had begun before the college opened. Sisters Hyacinth, who taught German, and Bridget, who taught music, had studied in France and Germany in 1903. Sister Antonia had begun her correspondence course at the University of Chicago, unheard of for Catholic sisters at the time. But with the cooperation of the superiors of the Sisters of St. Joseph, Sister Antonia sent many young sisters for further study as soon as they left the novitiate, conveniently constructed just east of the college in 1912. As they finished their graduate work, these sisters became the core of the St. Catherine faculty. Sometimes they started teaching before finishing their studies, working on dissertations in their free hours or while sitting up to check in residents returning from concerts and other events.

Sister Agnes Rita Lingl reflected: "To the horror of some people, sometimes bishops, Sister Antonia sent the sisters out to many non-Catholic or rather secular universities. . . . We studied at the University of Chicago, and [when the university] wanted to start a three-year master's program, they picked out a number of colleges—I think only thirty-seven across the country—St. Catherine's was the Catholic representative . . . the sisters from other communities were all being sent to the Catholic University or to Notre Dame."

• • •

With the well-educated sisters donating their teaching services, the college had little need for full-time lay teachers. The earliest years saw a succession of part-time teachers for subjects such as piano and violin, voice and elocution. Sister Antonia brought in competent part-time instructors from the University of Minnesota, St. Thomas and the St. Paul Seminary for areas in which the sisters were not yet prepared to teach. . . . George Klasse from the Minneapolis Symphony Orchestra also taught part-time. . . .

Among the most loved teachers from the University of Minnesota was author and scholar Mary Ellen Chase. She taught English at the college for three school years beginning in 1929 and for three additional summers. She devoted a chapter in her book *A Goodly Fellowship* to the college and the friends she made there, saying: "I have never seen happier people, or funnier for that matter, than the nuns at St. Catherine's. Many of them were Irish by inheritance, some by birth, and their sense of humor was inimitable. I have never known so much laughter elsewhere or such good, rich cause for it. I like the thought, which I learned first at St. Catherine's, that those virtues resulting in sainthood are, first of all, simplicity and joy in the Lord rather than meekness, humility, patience, and other less attractive forms of holiness. Knowledge of the saints was not encouraged in my Maine upbringing; but in the years since then I have had a great good time in reading of some of them, and they have added immeasurably to my enjoyment of life.

"St. Catherine's, so far as I know, never looked upon me as either a heretic or a heathen. I shared, in so far as my 'heresy' allowed me, in its life, from which I gained blessings immeasurable. I liked the peace of its chapel, the quiet of its garden, the friendliness and fun of its nuns, the good manners of its students. I liked the shuffling off of a hundred trivialities, the release of which seemed not only possible but inevitable within its gates . . . I liked the single-mindedness . . . the sense that religion was not something to be seized upon in uneasy moments, but natural, like one's hands and feet, and waiting only to be discovered.". . .

Religious, Humanistic, and Professional

. . . Sociology and social work curricula . . . developed remarkably in the 1920s and 1930s. The College Bulletin announced: "The new part that women must take in solving social problems makes it imperative that the department of social and political science furnish a standard of judgment, and include courses like 'Racial Backgrounds and Americanization'." To help meet the need for specially trained workers in the field of social service and to encourage students to become interested in social work, the department listed four senior courses in applied sociology, later called "social case work." The dean's report for June 1932 announced the addition of an organized course in social service work, leading to a social service major. The course consisted of one quarter of social psychology, one of social psychiatry, and one of supervised field work.

Interest in the social sciences on campus reflected the growing involvement of women in fields of social service in the United States. . . . Sister Marie Philip, later reflecting on social work experiences of students in the 1920s, said that a social worker named Ruby Boughman was teaching at the college during that period. She took students to visit a street along the Mississippi River called "The Levee": "There was something like a frame schoolhouse—just one room, as I can remember. And you would go in there and there would be . . . just the nicest Italian chefs and bakers—all men. The women didn't go out at night. . . . We were trying to teach them. Of course, we knew nothing about teaching English to foreigners—absolutely nothing. . . . But I remember those nights, the warmth of them and the gratitude of those men. . . . We kind of prepared them for Americanization. For citizenship papers you need to know a little civics. And we felt perfectly safe. Nobody worried about us walking from Seventh Street to the Levee and back."

New emphasis was also placed on educating teachers for preschool children. Particularly gifted in teaching young children, Sister Ann Harvey, who had earned a master's degree in childhood education at Columbia in 1930, took over the nursery school opened by Ruby Blackhurst in 1929, continuing until her retirement in 1974. Over the years she taught several thousand children, some of whom became prominent St. Paul professionals.

• • •

Of Buildings, Bucks, and Books

Increased enrollment and expanding programs necessitated buildings in addition to Derham Hall, and Sister Antonia had embarked on a large-scale construction program. With friends from the University of Chicago and elsewhere, Sister Antonia set out for New York more than once to submit proposals for new buildings to various funding institutions.

When Sister Antonia was appointed dean in 1914, work on a second major building for the college had already begun. With the Derham Hall dormitories filled to overflowing, some provision had to be made for housing. The November 12, 1912, *Catholic Bulletin* commented: "The excavation of the new building to be added to St. Catherine's College is about completed and work on the basement walls has begun. It will have a frontage of 198 feet on Randolph Street, near Prior, and will have a depth of 173 feet. It will be a brick building of reenforced concrete, and will have four stories and a basement." In the fall of 1914, College Hall (at first called simply "the other building"), for housing college students and college facilities, was opened. The central section of the first story was designated Music Hall, East Hall housed the art department, the west wing—Science Hall—housed home economics and science. The residence corridors could accommodate 250 students. Jeanne d'Arc Auditorium, an extension, soon welcomed students, teachers, and speakers, as well as music department concerts and dramatic productions.

Ecstatic about its lovely new building, members of the St. Catherine community watched the beginnings of war on the other side of the world. Sentiment was strong against U.S. involvement both across the country and on campus until, after some provocation, Congress voted to help France fight Germany, on April 2, 1917. Then, much of the discussion on campus turned towards how best to serve. The Summer 1917 *Ariston* included an editorial called "College Women and War" as well as poems such as "War Hymn to Mary" and "Flag of Peace." A later editorial countered a suggestion that the college close so students could work for the war effort. After all, well-trained minds would be needed to put the world back together: To continue school, pray for peace, and join the Red Cross effort seemed the better course.

The college stayed open. Sister Eleanore Michel worked to retain the teaching of German and build the department despite the growing regulation of German texts by the Minnesota Commission of Public Safety. Students variously put on war benefits or continued antiwar efforts, expressing their positions in poems and editorials. And though not all students and faculty members agreed on American involvement in the war, almost everyone on campus became involved in knitting or making dressings for the St. Paul Red Cross, setting up the Derham Hall dining room every Friday afternoon for the purpose. All were happy to hear "The Great War is Over" ringing through the hall at midday on Friday, November 8, 1918. A bit prematurely, Sister Antonia gave the rest of the day off, but on the following Monday, the armistice was signed.

Despite suggestions that college students go to work, the war had in fact brought enrollment up. On December 14, 1918, the *Catholic Bulletin* noted that "twenty music rooms have been converted into dormitories and thirty single rooms have been transformed into double rooms. The intention of young women to prepare themselves to fill positions of men who have gone to the front is thought to be one of the reasons for breaking all records." Sister Antonia was ready. To make her vision concrete, she had drawn up a complete building and landscape plan. The next step would be a building for the music department, to be named for the patron of music, St. Cecilia. She set out on one of several visits to George Vincent at the Rockefeller Foundation, returning from New York with the promise of financial help and advice to establish a board of trustees.

On January 27, 1919, the Board of Trustees of the College of St. Catherine met for the first time, in the "Alumnae Parlour" of College Hall. . . . The twelve-member board was to hold and invest endowment funds and to approve mortgages, indebtedness, purchase and sale of property, and the erection of buildings. . . . They appointed a committee to plan an endowment campaign to raise $200,000 as a match for a $100,000 grant from the Rockefeller Foundation and planned to entertain Wallace Buttrick, president of the foundation's General Education Board. At the next two meetings, they agreed with Buttrick on the terms of the grant, including that it not be used for theological instruction, and approved plans for the new music hall. . . . In the fall of 1921, Caecilian Hall opened with studios for the faculty, practice rooms for students, and a recital hall for performances.

The first college homecoming, sponsored by the St. Catherine Alumna Association in June 1923, marked the twentieth anniversary of the laying of the college cornerstone. . . . Also in 1923, the entire campus was enclosed by a wrought-iron fence with elaborate gates, and planning was initiated for a separate chapel. It would be large, Romanesque, and beautiful—from the high bell tower to the tiled roof and tile facing on interior walls and pillars. H. A. Sullwold was chosen as architect and Paul Steenberg as contractor. Sullwold was sent to Europe to visit Spanish and French medieval cathedrals so he would understand what the chapel should look like. He visited the Church of St. Trophime at Arles, France, which Sister Antonia had admired in 1922. She told him that with a few adaptations, the chapel at the college must follow suit.

Work on the chapel progressed rapidly, with many conferences among Sister Antonia, the architect, and the contractor. When the workers laying concrete for the floor were unable to finish before Thanksgiving of 1923, Sister Antonia promised to provide Thanksgiving dinner if they would work through the holiday to finish. And so they did. On another occasion, when the tile company did not want to work on Saturday, contractor Paul Steenberg persuaded the carpentry foreman and bricklayer foremen to lay tiles themselves. Sister Antonia was so pleased she gave each of them a box of cigars. Years later, Steenberg wrote: "I was much pleased with doing this chapel for many reasons. First, it was a place to worship God. It was a beautiful chapel, and I believe I had satisfied Sister Antonia's wish, which I was told could not be done. [She] was a woman who knew what she wanted and was pleased when she got a real job."

On October 7, 1924, the chapel was complete, and it was dedicated on the feast of Our Lady of Victory, for whom it was named. Three days earlier, the *Catholic Bulletin* had given fourteen pages almost exclusively to the college and its new chapel. Archbishop Dowling reportedly said: "Sister Antonia asked to build a chapel, but she built a cathedral." Sister Lioba, an enthusiastic observer, wrote to Sister Ste. Helene at Oxford University in England: "That great day dawned . . . summer sun, summer warmth, summer green on all sides—and through this loveliness of combined beauty there passed from College Hall to the Chapel of Our Lady of Victory, the procession of dedication—the Archbishop in Cappa Magna, monsignori in such a blaze of glory that it communicated itself to the entire line, priests to the number of at least seventy, the college student body, and people world without end . . . Father [Francis] Missia and the seminarians sang the litany all the way down the aisle, and the reverence of students and congregation can never be forgotten.

"Father [Aloysius] Ziskowsky presided in the sanctuary and his prowess in the church service kept things moving with both grace and precision, but with no sign of obtrusiveness . . . Some of the college girls were ushers in the true sense of the word, for they seated a throng which must have numbered 1,000. All the pews were full with six in a pew besides hundreds of chairs. Mr. [Leopold] Bruenner's Mass was divine—parts of it like the Agnus Dei really inspired—and never did Anna [Goulet] play nor the sisters sing as on last Tuesday. The seminarians sang the gradual and the proper of the Mass in Gregorian chant and the change from their voices to the choir was most affecting . . . there is no telling when [Anna] will again come down to foot locomotion." Sister Anna had first use of what the *Catholic Bulletin* described as: "a fine, three-manual organ . . . That this organ might thoroughly harmonize with the beautiful new building, the Reuter Organ Company sent their experts to St. Paul to go over the plans and details of the building with the architects . . . It . . . has character, one that is admirably well fitted for concert purposes as well as for chapel services."

With the dedication complete, faculty and staff helped move the library from Derham Hall to the ground floor of the new chapel. A new closed stack system meant that student assistants in large numbers paged books to waiting patrons. The library science department, at first called the "School of Library Science," moved there, too. Beginning in 1918 with a nine-credit course in school librarianship, the program had quickly grown. . . . In 1926 a principal sequence, distributed over the junior and senior years and leading to a bachelor's degree in library science, was offered.

• • •

In the meantime, Sister Antonia had attended to the construction of a new building for the sciences. A second grant of $100,000 from the Rockefeller Foundation in 1926 made possible the erection of Mendel Hall, named for the great Austrian biologist and discoverer of the laws of heredity. The *Catholic Bulletin* noted upon its opening in September 1927: "Mendel Hall is to be used exclusively by the science departments. It is a five-story building of variegated red and terra cotta brick . . . The building is divided by a tower, the center of which is ninety-four feet from the east end . . . The new hall was designed to hold approximately fifteen laboratories, as well as lecture rooms, study hall, and faculty office." But Mendel Hall soon accommodated the art department, the education department, and a Montessori child care facility as well. . . .

In 1929, the Rockefeller Foundation granted $300,000 to help develop the health program at the college. The new building, at first known as the Health Center and later as Fontbonne Hall, particularly was to provide space for training in basic sciences for nurses and in physical education for teachers. Sister Antonia, in the president's report for 1931–32, stated that the new Health Center, open that year, "embodies the complete realization . . . of the health unit in our expansion program." The burgeoning library school also moved to the Health Center. The new office for the department chair, a laboratory room for technical processes, and a large classroom there meant more room for the crowded library beneath the chapel.

Praise with Pots and Pans . . .

The care and maintenance of six buildings and the hundreds of students filling them demanded much of the nonteaching staff of the college. Among those working behind the scenes was Sister Georgia Morrisson, beloved friend and counselor of students living in Whitby Hall. She had greeted the first students arriving from St. Joseph's Academy in 1905. Among other responsibilities, she had charge of the laundry, which at that time meant washing all the students' clothes. Sister Georgia assigned each sister, including faculty members, a part of the laundry work according to her own estimate of the other's intelligence. When a task was not well done, she might say: "And you with your Ph.D.!"

• • •

Well known among students, too, were several Sisters of St. Joseph who had come to America from Ireland as lay missionaries. (The United States was considered mission territory until 1921.) The Irish sisters—Odelia Murphy, Jarlath Noonan, Candida Gallahue, Elerius Hennessy, and others—provided a warm, loving atmosphere, consoling many a homesick freshman with an extra cookie or piece of cake. Magdalen (later Sister Marie David) Schimanski, a student in the late 1930s, remembered: "Sister Odelia . . . used to provide our work-a-day spreads on a summer evening because we always stayed during summers and vacations . . . the painters, the electricians would have to work in the buildings, so we would move every month to a different building . . . I was very fond of all those kitchen sisters from Ireland: Sister Candida, Elerius, Jarlath. I remember them standing in the chapel—it would be the grand entrance to the chapel overlooking the Dew Drop. They'd be looking at the sunset there. I could almost draw them from memory—those silhouettes of those great big women. There was something beautiful about their peacefulness and their joy and the way they were friendly to us students."

Another admirer, Mary Ellen Chase, wrote in *A Goodly Fellowship*: "They praised the Lord with pots and pans as cymbals and harps and with good food. I used to go into their huge kitchen below the chapel cloister and talk with them as they beat, stirred, and kneaded. The four of them were ample women of great good humor. They wore large gray aprons over their black habits and usually had a touch of flour somewhere on their black veils. As they bustled about in their convent garb intent upon the means of existence, they somehow connected the religious life with the ageless, and surely religious, necessity of daily bread."

• • •

And Beyond

Sister Antonia oversaw the construction of five college buildings from 1914 to 1932, but her vision for the students reached beyond buildings, beyond campus, beyond city and nation. To her mind, one could not be fully educated without travel in Europe. She emphasized that basic to preparation for travel was intensive study of the appropriate language: "I am quite sure of this, that encouragement should be given to our young people in schools to acquire a language sense. They should be encouraged to learn at least one or two modern languages which they could use with facility—other than our mother tongue.

Many times I have had parents ask me, 'What is the good of learning French or German? Our daughter will not speak these languages here in America.' True, there is rare occasion for their use, but let us hope that most of our boys and girls will have a chance to visit the countries where these languages are spoken. Certainly it makes for cultural background in every way."

If students could not get to other countries, she found a way to bring other countries to them. One way to accomplish that was to offer scholarships to international students. Several students from Canada and one from Mexico had attended the college earlier, but the first European students were Lucienne and Angele Petit, at the college from 1918 to 1920. Emerging from the postwar devastation of France, they had had little preparation for the United States. Sister Mona Riley recalled: "I can remember them sitting with babushkas over their heads, not knowing any English, but they turned out beautifully. Lucienne finished at one of the universities—I think it was Columbia—and then she taught at Adelphi College on Long Island."

After these first two students from France, a steady stream of students—from Puerto Rico, Panama, Peru, and Brazil, from Germany, Hungary, Italy, Spain, Greece, the Philippines, Iraq, Israel, and Japan—registered at the college. In the 1970s and 1980s many students came from Africa—Kenya, Tanzania, Nigeria—and from the Orient—Japan, China, Malaysia, and Pakistan. . . . Sister Antonia also encouraged international-mindedness by inviting teachers from other countries as native speakers to help students improve their language skills.

• • •

Students unable to travel abroad learned much from international students and teachers on campus, as well as from other visitors and events of the day. In the vanguard of American women preparing for new participation in the world, they were independent in spirit and sometimes broke college rules designed to limit "radical behavior." Lucy Sanschagrin '25 (later Sister Marie Ursule), for instance, was almost expelled for bobbing her hair, and Mary O'Brien '27 (Sister Antonine's sister) was accused of "suffragetteism" for carrying a swagger stick. There seems to have been little activity related to women's suffrage (most students were not old enough to vote), but after women's right to vote was ratified in 1919, mock presidential elections were held. The first, apparently in response to the election of Calvin Coolidge, was described in the 1924 student yearbook: "Not to be outstripped by any other independent women in America, we of the College of St. Catherine decided to use our privilege of franchise and held our own election. It was with much agitation and anxiety that the girls gathered at eleven o'clock on a certain Wednesday morning in the auditorium. After several days electioneering the students met ready to assert their opinions and support their candidates. In fact, the meeting resembled a Republican caucus."

Then interest in social and political events grew, and with faculty members returning from study in other lands, the discussion of world issues flourished. . . . A *Wheel* editorial on April 12, 1935, discussed a speaker at the Woman's Club of Minneapolis: "Dame Rachel Crowdy, head of the humanitarian committee of the League of Nations, was scheduled to speak on 'Women in International Affairs.' She was astonished when told of her topic and said, 'I could not speak for five minutes on *women* in international affairs. There are none.' We, who are vitally interested in international peace, will some day answer Dame Crowdy's challenge and give her ample opportunity."

Some students combined artistic, entertainment and economic activities to good effect. Proceeds from a grassroots attempt to produce plays on campus were donated to a fund for a new elevator in Derham Hall in the early 1920s, for example. . . . Among the more formal musical and dramatic productions was *The Messiah,* presented by the Choral Club and assisted by the men of the St. Paul Municipal Chorus. On March 2, 1926, the *Lantern* (a weekly published by the sophomores for one year only) mentioned Austrian composer and pianist Percy Grainger's visit and the two programs he gave in Jeanne d'Arc Auditorium. Inspired by Edvard Grieg, he had collected English and Irish folksongs and arranged them for concert use. Sister Antonia's voice rang forth: "This event is one of the greatest privileges which are given to the students, probably a privilege which to some may not again be granted . . . It is your duty, girls, to let the public know of his coming and invite them."

• • •

Despite her many responsibilities, Sister Antonia kept in touch with the students, making sure the world of each was expanded through cultural activities outside the classroom. Sister Ann Harvey recalled: "Someone sent Mother Antonia four tickets to the symphony, and the seats were very good. She asked me if I wanted one and I said 'Yes,' because I was a poor little girl and did not have any money . . . a telephone call came from Mother Antonia about twenty minutes after she gave me the ticket, to please come to her office because she wanted to tell me what to wear, and how to look. She told me to wear a hat and bring my purse and wear gloves . . . In true Sister-Antonia-fashion, she waited up for us after the symphony and got our enthusiastic ideas on the music. It was my first symphony, and I thought I was in heaven."

According to Sister Antonia, the accumulation of knowledge was not the sole purpose of a college education. Character training or "the building of a life" was most often the subject of her assembly talks. Sister Marie Philip noted: "Wednesday after Wednesday she lashed us into a fairly homogeneous student group. She drove at practice, at homely virtues—honesty, cleanliness, industry, dependableness, a nice consideration for others. Who could ever forget her urging us to chisel our characters, to accomplish hard things, to be women of good sense? She taught us that the ideal of sound and strong Catholic womanhood is big, simple, noble, and practicable."

Mary Ellen Chase wrote in *A Goodly Fellowship:* " Sister Antonia went at the realization of St. Catherine's College with everything she had in her . . . *Laborare est orare* was sound doctrine to her . . . She saw architects and remade their plans; she sat on stone heaps and inspired workmen. She laid out grounds and planted trees . . . She had read widely and seemingly she had forgotten nothing that she had ever read. She was the best of teachers . . . Her feverish activity made her not only apparently omnipresent, but completely master of every scene and situation as well . . . In the chapel she could be intent upon her own devotions and aware of any lack of devotion in her girls . . . She was a handsome woman with an alert, eager face and a fine carriage. When she swept down the corridors of her college in her black habit on her way to the chapel, or the garden or the kitchen or the powerhouse, everyone upon her swift approach straightened head and shoulders."

In 1936, Sister Antonia became ill, suffering several strokes. In 1937 she resigned because of increasing disability, to live quietly in Whitby 106. Friends and alumnae still visited, and the honors poured in as before: President Herbert Hoover invited her to the White House Conference on Child Health and Protection. Pope Pius XI awarded her the *Pro Ecclesia et Pontifice* medal. She was elected president of the Association of Minnesota Colleges and awarded an honorary degree of Doctor of Laws by the University of Minnesota.

Sister Antonia McHugh died quietly on October 11, 1944. The Spring 1927 *Ariston* had written of her: "Sister Antonia succeeded in building up not only the physical plant but the curriculum and the faculty as well . . . Our development in every line is due to her farsightedness, her zeal in furthering the course of Catholic education in America. Under her wise guidance, courses of study have been organized and the college standardized until it is now recognized by the highest authorities. All the best in American universities, all the advantages, all the benefits of foreign travel, have been utilized . . . in the preparation of superior teachers."

Five years after her death, *Ariston* was still paying her tribute: "Always to her St. Catherine's has been a great college. Even when it was only a dream. Never just a building on a hill, it was a growing family of buildings: Caecilian, Mendel, the Health Center, the Chapel. All these she planned, built, and peopled in her mind long before the architects were ever summoned. The pews of Our Lady of Victory Chapel were filled with girls in cap and gown when the old chapel on fourth Derham was still adequate to the college needs. It is that vision for the future, that aspiration for excellence, and the creative power to convert vision into reality that has distinguished Mother Antonia's work." That vision of excellence was her legacy.

Adrienne Rich (1929–2012) was an American poet, essayist, feminist activist, and speaker. The following passage comes from On Lies, Secrets and Silence: Selected Prose 1966–1978 *(1979). Here Rich addresses a group of students gathered for a convocation at an all women's college. What key words does she define in this essay on the responsibility of women to be actively engaged in shaping their own education? For example, what is the difference between "claiming" and "receiving" here? What does this notion of "claiming an education" mean to you as a student at an all women's college?*

Claiming an Education

Adrienne Rich

For this convocation, I planned to separate my remarks into two parts: some thoughts about you, the women students here, and some thoughts about us who teach in a women's college. But ultimately, those two parts are indivisible. If university education means anything beyond the processing of human beings into expected roles, through credit hours, tests, and grades (and I believe that in a women's college especially it *might* mean much more), it implies an ethical and intellectual contract between teacher and student. This contract must remain intuitive, dynamic, unwritten, but we must turn to it again and again if learning is to be reclaimed from the depersonalizing and cheapening pressures of the present day academic scene.

The first thing I want to say to you who are students, is that you cannot afford to think of being here to *receive* an education; you will do much better to think of yourselves as being here to *claim* one. One of the dictionary definitions of the verb "to claim" is: *to take as the rightful owner; to assert in the face of possible contradiction.* "To receive" is *to come into possession of; to act as receptacle or container for; to accept as authoritative or true.* The difference is that between acting and being acted-upon, and for women it can literally mean the difference between life and death.

One of the devastating weaknesses of university learning, of the store of knowledge and opinion that has been handed down through academic training, has been its almost total erasure of women's experience and thought from the curriculum, and its exclusion of women as members of the academic community. Today, with increasing numbers of women students in nearly every branch of higher learning, we still see very few women in the upper levels of faculty and administration in most institutions. Douglass College itself is a women's college in a university administered overwhelmingly by men, who in turn are answerable to the state legislature, again composed predominantly of men. But the most significant fact for you is that what you learn here, the very texts you read, the lectures you hear, the way your studies are divided into categories and fragmented one from the other—all this reflects to a very large degree, neither objective reality, nor an accurate picture of the past, nor a group of rigorously tested observations about human behavior. What you can learn here (and I mean not only at Douglass but any college in any university) is how *men* have perceived and organized their experience, their history, their ideas of social relationships, good and evil, sickness and health, etc. When you read or hear about "great issues," "major texts," "the mainstream of Western thought," you are hearing about what men, above all white men, in their male subjectivity have decided is important.

Black and other minority peoples have for some time recognized that their racial and ethnic experience was not accounted for in the studies broadly labeled human; and that even the sciences can be racist. For many reasons, it has been more difficult for women to comprehend our exclusion, and to realize that even the sciences can be sexist. For one thing, it is only within the last hundred years that higher education has grudgingly been opened up to women at all, even to white, middle-class women. And many of us have found ourselves poring eagerly over books with titles like: *The Descent of Man; Man and His Symbols; Irrational Man; The Phenomenon of Man; The Future of Man; Man and the Machine; From Man to Man; May Man Prevail?; Man, Science and Society*; or *One-Dimensional Man*—books pretending to describe a "human" reality that does not include over one-half the human species.

Less than a decade ago, with the rebirth of a feminist movement in this country, women students and teachers in a number of universities began to demand and set up women's studies courses—to *claim* a woman-directed education. And, despite the inevitable accusations of "unscholarly," "group therapy," "faddism," etc., despite backlash and budget cuts, women's studies are still growing, offering to more and more women a new intellectual grasp on their lives, new understanding of our history, a fresh vision of the human experience, and also a critical basis for evaluating what they hear and read in other courses, and in the society at large.

But my talk is not really about women's studies, much as I believe in their scholarly, scientific, and human necessity. While I think that any Douglass student has everything to gain by investigating and enrolling in women's studies courses, I want to suggest that there is a more essential experience that you owe yourselves, one which courses in women's studies can greatly enrich, but which finally depends on you, in all your interactions with yourself and your world. This is the experience of *taking responsibility toward yourselves*. Our upbringing as women has so often told us that this should come second to our relationships and responsibilities to other people. We have been offered ethical models of the self-denying wife and mother; intellectual models of the brilliant but slapdash dilettante who never commits herself to anything the whole way, or the intelligent woman who denies her intelligence in order to seem more "feminine," or who sits in passive silence even when she disagrees inwardly with everything that is being said around her.

Responsibility to yourself means refusing to let others do your thinking, talking, and naming for you; it means learning to respect and use your own brains and instincts; hence, grappling with hard work. It means that you do not treat your body as a commodity with which to purchase superficial intimacy or economic security; for our bodies and minds are inseparable in this life, and when we allow our bodies to be treated as objects, our minds are in mortal danger. It means insisting that those to whom you give your friendship and love are able to respect your mind. It means being able to say, with Charlotte Bronte's *Jane Eyre*: "I have an inward treasure born with me, which can keep me alive if all the extraneous delights should be withheld or offered only at a price I cannot afford to give."

Responsibility to yourself means that you don't fall for shallow and easy solutions—predigested books and ideas, weekend encounters guaranteed to change your life, taking "gut" courses instead of ones you know will challenge you, bluffing at school and life instead of doing solid work, marrying early as an escape from real decisions, getting pregnant as an evasion of already existing problems. It means that you refuse to sell your talents and aspirations short, simply to avoid conflict and confrontation. And this, in turn, means resisting the forces in society which say that women should be nice, play safe, have low professional expectations, drown in love and forget about work, live through others, and stay in the places assigned to us. It means that we insist on a life of meaningful work, insist that work be as meaningful as love and friendship in our lives. It means, therefore, the courage to be "different"; not to be continuously available to others when we need time for ourselves and our work; to be able to demand of others—parents, friends, roommates, teachers, lovers, husbands, children—that they respect our sense of purpose and our integrity as persons. Women everywhere are finding the courage to do this, more and more, and we are finding that courage both in our study of women in the past who possessed it, and in each other as we look to other women for comradeship, community, and challenge. The difference between a life lived actively, and a life of passive drifting and dispersal of energies, is an immense difference. Once we begin to feel committed to our lives, responsible to ourselves, we can never again be satisfied with the old, passive way.

Now comes the second part of the contract. I believe that in a women's college you have the right to expect your faculty to take you seriously. The education of women has been a matter of debate for centuries, and old, negative attitudes about women's role, women's ability to think and take leadership, are still rife both in and outside the university. Many male professors (and I don't mean only at Douglass) still feel that teaching in a women's college is a second-rate career. Many tend to eroticize their women students—to treat them as sexual objects—instead of demanding the best of their minds. (At Yale a legal suit [*Alexander v. Yale*] has been brought against the university by a group of women students demanding a stated policy against sexual advances toward female students by male professors.) Many teachers, both men and women, trained in the male-centered tradition, are still handing the ideas and texts of that tradition on to students without teaching them to criticize its anti-woman attitudes, its omission of women as part of the species. Too often, all of us fail to teach the most important thing, which is that clear thinking, active discussion, and excellent writing are all necessary for intellectual freedom, and that these require *hard work*. Sometimes, perhaps in discouragement with a culture which is both anti-intellectual and anti-woman, we may resign ourselves to low expectations for our students before we have given them half a chance to become more thoughtful, expressive human beings. We need to take to heart the words of Elizabeth Barrett Browning, a poet, a thinking woman, and a feminist, who wrote in 1845 of her impatience with studies which cultivate a "passive recipiency" in the mind, and asserted that "women want to be made to *think actively*: their apprehension is quicker than that of men, but their defect lies for the most part in the logical faculty and in the higher mental activities." Note that she implies a defect which can be remedied by intellectual training; *not* an inborn lack of ability.

I have said that the contract on the student's part involves that you demand to be taken seriously so that you can also go on taking yourself seriously. This means seeking out criticism, recognizing that the most affirming thing anyone can do for you is demand that you push yourself further, show you the range of what you can do. It means rejecting attitudes of "take-it-easy," "why-be-so-serious," "why-worry-you'll-probably-get-married-anyway." It means assuming your share of responsibility for what happens in the classroom, because that affects the quality of your daily life here. It means that the student sees herself engaged *with* her teachers in an active, ongoing struggle for a real education. But for her to do this, her teachers must be committed to the belief that women's minds and experience are intrinsically valuable and indispensable to any civilization worthy of the name; that there is no more exhilarating and intellectually fertile place in the academic world today than a women's college—*if* both students and teachers in large enough numbers are trying to fulfill this contract. The contract is really a pledge of mutual seriousness about women, about language, ideas, methods, and values. It is our shared commitment toward a world in which the inborn potentialities of so many women's minds will no longer be wasted, raveled-away, paralyzed, or denied.

Jessica Lopez Lyman, as you will learn in the autobiographical essay, is a 2008 graduate of St. Kate's with a double major in English and Secondary Education. Born and raised in St. Paul, Lopez Lyman went on to earn her M.A. from the University of California Santa Barbara in Chicana and Chicano Studies and is now a doctoral candidate in the program. Her dissertation research brought her back to the Twin Cities, where she is exploring midwest regional identities, community organizing, and artists' networks through the poetry of the Palabristas Latin@ Spoken Word collective. In this piece, Lopez Lyman describes her experience as a Woman of Color at St. Kate's. Compare her experience with yours—do the same issues exist at St. Kate's today? What particular challenges do Women of Color and white allies confront in claiming an education in our community?

We Got Issues: Cultivating a Woman of Color Consciousness

Jessica Lopez Lyman

In third grade we were taught in Catholic school about Minnesota Native American history. As an awkwardly tall girl with long black hair and huge brown eyes I was elated to read for once about people that looked like me. While I knew I was not Dakato, the faces in the picture books we read mirrored my existence in ways that previous units on Laura Ingles Wilder and the pioneers had not. Growing up in an interracial home, I was constantly aware from a young age that I was different.

My parents came from working class families. My mother, a Chicana from California, and my father, a white German/Bohemian from Minnesota, met at San Diego State University, the first in both their immediate families to attend a four-year college. With a car and a few hundred dollars they moved to St. Paul after graduation in hopes of building a life together. Having been conditioned by the generation of groovy peace and love, my parents were less concerned with the racial politics of our home. Instead, Catholic practices of the golden rule became mantras, which my younger sister and I were meant to live by. However, the love thy neighbor philosophy failed to protect us from the harsh words and actions of others.

Due to my mixed identity it was difficult at times for most people to racially categorize me. They knew I was not white, but they could not label me, which resulted in the daily question, "what are you?"—a terrifying question for any young teenager negotiating hormonal adolescence to have to answer. Attending a predominantly white high school, I often felt isolated and tokenized by my peers and teachers. While we rarely talked about Mexican American history beyond the United Farm Workers and

Cesar Chavez, all eyes landed on me anytime race was discussed. At the same time my light skin and middle class status made me privy to conversations of racist banter among my peers who would later reply, "We're not talking about you. You're not like a normal Mexican." I learned early on to negotiate racial microaggressions.[1]

Full of rage and a depleting self-esteem that bordered on self-hatred, I filled notebooks with tearful poetry, hoping that in scribbling my experiences I could find an answer to the weighted question, "Who am I?" What saved me were the essays and poetry by U.S. Third World feminists of Color. Discussing race, class, gender and sexuality, their writing about negotiating multiple identities gave me language to articulate my experiences. Having combatted a deep loneliness for years, I found companionship through the work of Cherríe Moraga, Gloria Anzaldúa, Audre Lorde and others who gave voice to isolation and hopefulness for survival.[2] Reading anything I could get my hands on I graduated high school with a strong sense of self. I was a Chicana, a Woman of Color, a feminist.

With a new vocabulary and perspective I entered St. Kate's excited and ready to continue my learning at the university level. As a first year, enrolled as an Honors student, I longed to be immersed in an academic environment of radical thought. However, my fantasy quickly dissolved, as I once again was one of two Students of Color in The Reflective Women class. Childhood feelings of racial tension that I thought I had overcame quickly resurfaced. Not only were there very few Students of Color, many St. Kate's students were not familiar with urban life and were shocked by the race, class, gender and sexuality differences they were now experiencing. While I was ready to dive into theoretical ideas, students who were learning about difference of any kind for the first time impeded the classroom conversation. I often became frustrated and tired, feeling like I had to represent for all marginalized peoples, even those who were beyond my lived experience.

Living in the dorms only added to the turmoil. Taking my parents' advice to make friends, I attempted to build community on campus. My first semester I was introduced to a group of third and fourth year white lesbians who took me into their circle as one of their own. But I was not like them. While we found solidarity in our nerdy desires for non-conformity, my heterosexual privilege and their white privilege became places of contention. Even though we knew we needed to support one another, we did not know how to be allies to each other. For example, in an act of good intention the group started to call me m'ija, a term of endearment popular in Latin@ culture that elders use to refer to young people, often children, that they care about. This word had always played an integral part in my life. Fearing that my mother would be linguistically discriminated against for speaking Spanish, my grandparents never taught her the language. One of the only phrases that remained in her vocabulary however was the word m'ija, which she affectionately called my sister and me. Hearing my mother use the word, my friends, not aware of the cultural significance, usurped it as their own, turning it into a nickname loaded with mockery. While this was a step up from the nicknames of hot tamale and little Chihuahua that branded me during high school, the pain was the same.

Wanting to leave the university I was once again saved by Women of Color, but this time it came in the form of fellow students. During my second semester I was hired as a student worker in the Multicultural Programs and Services Office (MIPS). Under the mentorship of the MIPS staff I encountered a welcoming environment where, for the first time since arriving at St. Kate's, I felt that I could breath, relax, not have to explain myself to anyone. While working in the office I was introduced to other Students of Color. We informally began to have conversations about our lives. We discovered that despite several differences we shared similar experiences of isolation and discrimination while on and off campus. Under the direction of MIPS staff we were urged to formalize our meetings and think strategically about what we wanted to accomplish. Taking their advice, we resurrected Women of Color, a student group that once existed at St. Kate's but had in previous years diminished.

All self-identifying as Women of Color, we used the label to find connection and solidarity regardless of our heterogeneous backgrounds. As members we were Hmong, Black, Latina, Native American, Nepali, Gambian. We came from working class families, middle class families, single-parent households, and intergenerational households where grandparents, aunts and uncles aided in raising children. We were queers, dykes, bisexuals, heterosexuals and uncertain about our sexual desires. We spoke Spanish, Spanglish, Hmong, Hindi, Nepali, and English. We were vegetarians, meat loving carnivores, religious believers, and atheists. We were Democrats, Socialists, Maoists, Leftists, and undecided. Some of us had desires to have a family and become mothers one day, while others of us never wanted to have children. Some of us wanted to continue on to graduate school; others of us wanted to enter the workforce in the non-profit sector, or become artists, world travelers, poets. As a Women of Color collective we could bring our whole selves, our multiple identities, to the table because there was no shame, judgment or fear of being ostracized by one another. This is not to say that there were never conflicts. Our varying backgrounds and viewpoints made it difficult at times to determine how we wanted to move forward as a collective. What was essential to the collective, however, was our understanding of our multiple identities and our commitment to centralize our lived experiences, both of which became catalysts for creating change on and off campus.

In identifying as Women of Color we acknowledged that our identities were not fixed, but rather always in process and changing. For those who were international students this became particularly evident when moving to the United States. Where their previous home countries might have had color or ethnic hierarchies, arriving in the United States was an immersion into a racial paradigm that marked phenotype explicitly based upon a history of colonization that viewed race on a black/white color line.[3] Being treated as racially "Other," something that we as domestic Women of Color had experienced our entire lives within the United States, became an education for international women within the group who quickly learned through lived experience that their skin color, accent, clothing and food were signifiers that positioned them outside of mainstream white United States culture. While not all international students at St. Kate's accepted or acknowledged this shift in identity, for those within our group, adopting a Women of Color consciousness provided a language for articulating their racialized experiences within the United States. Beyond our racial consciousness the collective adopted a feminist consciousness. As women, our gendered experiences were integrally valid in understanding our worlds, and we cultivated a feminist consciousness that challenged patriarchal systems of oppression. Additional identity labels, our class, sexuality, religion, language, ableism, also became vital in understanding our multiple identities. Rather than seeing ourselves as fragmented, we recognized the importance of intersectionality—the overlapping, simultaneously existing connection of identities.[4] Multiple identities, thus, were relational for us, impacted by lived experience and social location.[5]

Understanding our multiple identities and honoring our lived experience, however, was not enough for the collective. As Women of Color feminists we realized that supporting one another was only the first step. We had to act. Under the mentorship of staff and faculty we created a campaign called We Got Issues, a multi-year venture to improve the racial climate on campus. The first meeting was an open invitation to all Students and Faculty of Color where people were able to express in a safe space their feelings, hopes and visions for enhancing the quality of life at St. Kate's. From these conversations we extrapolated key themes, and later, through additional meetings, determined a set of demands that included an increase of Administrators and Faculty of Color, expanded curriculums, racial justice training for staff, faculty and students, and more resources for Student of Color programming. We Got Issues culminated in a final presentation to the entire St. Kate's community. While our work alone cannot attest for the shift in racial climate—there were numerous staff and faulty who had been working for years to diversify St. Kate's—our organizing efforts affirmed an investment in Students of Color on campus. Our greatest victory was the increased financial support for Student of Color programming, an institutional change that would exist for years after we graduated.

Besides We Got Issues, during my senior year Women of Color expanded to form an additional group called WE—a collective that included white women allies. Unable to be an ally to my friends my first year at St. Kate's my evolving consciousness illuminated the necessity for coalitional building.[6] Any identity is valid and must be appreciated. However, working across differences sparked new possibilities for change.[7] While we did not spearhead a large campaign as many of us were graduating that year, WE taught us that to be an ally you must support and celebrate another person's identities and lived experiences not based on your own beliefs or perceptions, but on how that individual needs and wants support.

Since our time at St. Kate's, members from the Women of Color collective have moved to various places around the world. Some of us have enrolled in graduate programs; others of us have become freelance artists, worked for major news stations, non-profits or educational institutions; some have started families. Regardless of our distance, the memories, organizing, and solidarity work we experienced at St. Kate's impact the choices we make in our daily lives. As Women of Color we know that we will continue to encounter racism, sexism, homophobia and other oppressions. However, our racial and feminist consciousness paired with our deep commitment to coalition building fuels our move forward as we work to lead and influence our communities.

Notes

[1] Critical Race Theory scholars define microagressions as "subtle forms of racism that exist in daily life, which may be hard to pinpoint as racism, but cause harm nonetheless" (See Rita Kohli and Daniel G. Solórzano, "Teachers, please learn our names!:racial microagressions and the K-12 classroom," *Race Ethnicity and Education*, 15:4, 446).

[2] For more work by Women of Color U.S. Third World Feminists see Anzaldúa, Gloria and Cherríe Moraga eds. *This Bridge Called My Back: Writings by Radical Women of Color*. New York: Kitchen Table: Women of Color Press, 1981.

[3] DuBois, W. E. B. *The Souls of Black Folks.* Chicago: A.C. McClurg & CO., 1903.

[4] Crenshaw, Kimberlé, Neil Gotanda, Gary Peller, and Kendall Thomas, eds. *Critical Race Theory: The Key Writings That Formed the Movement*. New York: The New Press, 1995.

[5] Hurtado, Aída. "Understanding Multiple Identities." *Journal of Social Issues.* 1997, 299-328. Zavella, Patricia. "Reflections on Diversity among Chicanas." *Frontiers: A Journal of Women Studies*, 12. 2 (1991), pp. 73–85.

[6i] For work on coalition building see Carrillo Rowe, Aimee. *Power Lines: On the Subject of Feminist Alliances*. Durham: Duke University Press, 2008. Lugones, Maria. *Pilgrimages/Peregrinajes: Theorizing Coalition Against Multiple Oppressions.* Rowman & Littlefield Publishers, 2003.

[7] Anzaldúa, Gloria. "Now Let Us Shift . . . The Path of Conocimiento . . . Inner Work, Public Acts." In Gloria Anzaldúa and AnaLouise Keating eds. *This Bridge We Call Home: Radical Visions for Transformation*. New York: Routledge, 2002, 540–579.

Facebook 1

Hend al-Mansour
screen print
2013, 30 x 37-inches

Evelyn Alsultany is associate professor in the Program in American Culture at the University of Michigan. Co-editor of Arab and Arab American Feminisms *and of* Between the Middle East and the Americas, *she is also guest curator of* Reclaiming Identity: Dismantling Arab Stereotypes *(www.arabstereotypes.org). In the following essay (2002) Alsultany asks us to consider how our identities shape who we are, how others see us, and how we see those in our immediate and global communities. She uses personal narrative to challenge the idea of racial categories as a way to represent people and simplify their experiences. Can you identify your "moving selves?" What does Alsultany mean when she says her body becomes "marked by meaning" when she enters a public space?*

Los Intersticios: Recasting Moving Selves

Evelyn Alsultany

> *Ethnicity in such a world needs to be recast so that Our moving selves,can be acknowledged. . . . Who am I? When am I? The questions that are asked in the street, of my identity, mold me. Appearing in the flesh, I am cast afresh, a female of color—skin color, hair texture, clothing, speech, all marking, me in ways that I could scarcely have conceived of.*
>
> —Meena Alexander (66)

I'm in a graduate class at the New School in New York City. A white female sits next to me and we begin "friendly" conversation. She asks me where I'm from. I reply that I was born and raised in New York City and return the question. She tells me she is from Ohio and has lived in New York for several years. She continues her inquiry: "Oh, . . . well, how about your parents?" (I feel her trying to map me onto her narrow cartography; New York is not a sufficient answer. She analyzes me according to binary axes of sameness and difference. She detects only difference at first glance, and seeks to pigeonhole me. In her framework, my body is marked, excluded, not from this, country. A seemingly "friendly" question turns into a claim, to land and belonging,) "My father is Iraqi and my mother Cuban," I answer. "How interesting. Are you a U.S. citizen?"

I am waiting for the NYC subway. A man also waiting asks me if I too am Pakistani. I reply that I'm part Iraqi and part Cuban. He asks if I am Muslim, and I reply that I am Muslim. He asks me if I am married, and I tell him I'm not. In cultural camaraderie he leans over and says that he has cousins in Pakistan available for an arranged marriage if my family so desires. (My Cubanness, as well as my own relationship to my cultural identity, evaporates as he assumes that Arab plus Muslim equals arranged marriage. I can identify: he reminds me of my Iraqi relatives and I know he means well,) I tell him that I'm not interested in marriage but thank him for his kindness. (I accept his framework and respond accordingly, avoiding an awkward situation in which he realizes that I am not who he assumes I am, offering him recognition and validation for his [mis]identification.)

I am in a New York City deli waiting for my bagel to toast. The man behind the counter asks if I'm an Arab Muslim (he too is Arab and Muslim). I reply that yes, I am by part of my father. He asks my name, and I say, "Evelyn." In utter disdain, he tells, me that I could not possibly be Muslim; if I were truly Muslim I would have a Muslim name. What was I doing with such a name? I reply (after taking a deep breath and telling myself that it's not worth getting upset over) that my Cuban mother named me and that I honor my mother. He points to the fact that I'm wearing lipstick and have not changed my name, which he finds to be completely inappropriate and despicable, and says that I am a reflection of the decay of the Arab Muslim in America.

I'm on an airplane flying from Miami to New York. I'm sitting next to an Ecuadorian man. He asks me where I'm from. I tell him. He asks me if I'm more Arab, Latina, or American, and I state that I'm all of the above. He says that's impossible. I must be more of one ethnicity than another. He determines that I am not really Arab, that I'm more Latina because of the camaraderie he feels in our speaking Spanish.

I am in Costa Rica. I walk the streets and my brown skin and dark hair blend in with the multiple shades of brown around me. I love this first-time experience of blending in! I walk into a coffee shop for some café con leche, and my fantasy of belonging is shattered when the woman preparing the coffee asks me where I'm from. I tell her that I was born and raised in New York City by a Cuban mother and Arab father. She replies, "Que eres una gringa."

I am shocked by the contextuality of identity as gringa in Costa Rica, as Latina in some U.S. contexts, Arab in others, in some times and spaces not adequately Arab, or Latina, or "American," and in other contexts simply as *other*.

My body becomes marked with meaning as I enter public space.[1] My identity fractures as I experience differing dislocations in multiple contexts. Sometimes people otherize me, sometimes they identify with me. Both situations can be equally problematic. Those who otherize me fail to see a shared humanity, and those who identify with me fail to see difference; my Arab or Muslim identity negates my Cuban heritage. Identification signifies belonging or home, and I pretend to be at home for the mistaken person. It's my good deed for the day (I know how precious it can be to find a moment of familiarity with a stranger). The bridge becomes my back as I feign belonging, and I become that vehicle for others, which I desire for myself. Although it is illusory, I do identify with the humanity of the situation—the desire to belong in this world, to be understood. But the frameworks used to (mis)read my body, to disconnect me, wear on me. I try to develop a new identity. What should I try to pass for next time? Perhaps I'll just say I'm Cuban to those who appear to be Arab or South Asian. A friend suggests I say I'm an Italian from Brooklyn. I wonder if I could successfully pass for that. Ethnicity needs to be recast so that our moving selves can be acknowledged.

> *They would chop me up into little fragments and tag each piece with a label. Who, me confused? Ambivalent? Not so. Only your labels split me.*
>
> —Gloria Anzaldúa, "La Prieta" (205)

This Bridge Called My Back revolutionized how we saw ourselves as women of color. Our experiences—unacknowledged by the dominant culture and by feminist, ethnic, and/or queer movements—were finally named, This. *Bridge* insisted on a theory of the flesh through which to bridge the contradictions in our lives: "We do this bridging by naming ourselves and by telling our stories in our own words" (Moraga, 23). Bridge authors powerfully addressed the multiple displacements women of color often experience, or what Gloria Anzaldúa calls "los intersticios: 'Alienated from her mother culture,' 'alien' in the dominant culture, the woman of color does not feel safe within the inner life of her Self. Petrified, she can't respond, her face caught between los intersticios, the spaces between the different worlds she inhabits" (*Borderlands*, 20). Many multiethnic women identify strongly with this experience of being alienated in different ways from our various communities, trapped in a space of dislocation. Our complex selves can't be acknowledged as unified and whole.

When we're not acknowledged as complex unitary subjects, we become caught in los intersticios, haciendo caras to get by. Lisa Suhair Majaj, born to a Palestinian, father and a white American mother, growing up in Lebanon and Jordan, has spent much of her life in los intersticios: "I learned to live as if in a transitional state, waiting always for the time that, we would go to Palestine, to the United States, to a place where I would belong. But trips to Iowa and to Jerusalem taught me that once I got there, 'home' slipped away, inexplicably materializing again just beyond reach. If a sense of rootedness was what gave life meaning, as my parents' individual efforts to ward off alienation implied, this meaning seemed able to assume full import only in the imagination" ("Boundaries," 71). Majaj's lived experiences are not mapped out; there are no ready frameworks to understand her identity as complex and simultaneously Arab and American. She never felt like she fully belonged anywhere and found herself, searching for "home," a space of belonging. Yet she recurringly experienced belonging as deferment: "In my experience cultural marginality has been among the most painful of alienations. My childhood desire, often desperate, was not so much to be a particular nationality, to be American or Arab, but to be wholly one thing or another: to be *something* that I and the rest of the world could understand, categorize, label, predict" (79, author's emphasis).

We carry this pain with us as we live in los intersticios. To "belong," we must fragment and exclude particular parts of our identity. Dislocation results from the narrow ways in which the body is read, the rigid framerworks imposed on the body in public space. At the end of the day, I'm tired of wearing masks, being misunderstood, projected upon, otherized, erased. "I am tired of being afraid to speak who I am: American and Palestinian, not merely half one thing and half of another, but both at once—and in that inexplicable melding that occurs when two cultures come together, not quite either, so that neither American nor Arab find themselves fully reflected in me, nor I in them" (Majaj, "Boundaries," 68). Identity must be reconceptualized so that we can speak our own identities as we live and interpret them in multiple contexts. But how can we create a space for the articulation of multiethnic identities as unitary and whole rather than fragmented and dislocated? If we change the reading/framework/lens, we can transform dislocation into location. We must reconstruct "belonging" to embrace the experiences of all human beings. As Adrian Piper (a light-skinned African-American woman who grew up in los intersicios, alienated from the black community for her light skin complexion and alienated from the white community for her blackness) has stated, "the racial categories that purport to designate any of us are too rigid and oversimplified to fit anyone accurately. But then, accuracy was never their purpose" (110).

Racial categories' purpose has usually been geopolitical. In "Dislocated Identities: Reflections of an Arab Jew," Ella Shohat discusses how today's dominant frameworks do not account for her identity as an Arab Jew and illustrates the ways in which these categories have been recently constructed as antithetical. Such frameworks have a political function. For her grandmother's generation and for hundreds of prior generations, Jewishness was inextricably linked to Arabness; they were not binary categories but logically linked: an Arab could be Muslim, Jewish, Christian, or any other faith. It was when she arrived in Israel from Iraq (as a refugee) that her grandmother had to learn such imposed constructed distinctions. New cartographies were created within which her identity became dislocated: "For Middle Easterners, the operating distinction had always been 'Muslim,' 'Jew,' and 'Christian,' not Arab versus Jew. The assumption was that 'Arabness' referred to a common shared culture and language, albeit with religious differences." In the U.S. context this binarism between Arab and Jew operates, allowing for the narration of "a singular Jewish memory, i.e., a European one."

Shohat's experience points to the political nature of categorization. Meanings attached to identities shift not only over time and space but also according to political circumstance. That such meanings change indicates that we can alter them. We can create a new cartography. An inability to conceptualize multiethnic persons reflects a colonial ideology of categorization and separation based on a—"pure blood" criteria—a system constructed for the white colonists to maintain power. Rigid racial categories keep us separate. Multiethnic identity comes as a surprise and a danger within this framework as people attempt to place us, to make sense within the schemes available for understanding people and the world. Our identities transgress the constructed categories and become threatening. As Piper explains, "These incidents and others like them had a peculiar cognitive feel to them, as though, the individuals involved felt driven to make: special efforts to situate me in their, conceptual mapping of the world, not only by naming or indicating the niche in which they felt I belonged, but by seeking my verbal confirmation of it . . . [an attempt to] locate me within the rigid confines of [their] stereotype of black people" (83).

I seek to decolonize these essentialized frameworks, so that I can move through public space without strategizing a performance, selecting a mask for each scenario. I want to expand los intersticios, creating a space. for us all in our multiplicities to exist as unified subjects. It is a nonessentialist way of relating that creates a space to articulate multiple identifications and unlimited interpretations of those dimensions. This new space begins with a question: Ask me who I am. Don't project your essentialisms onto my body and then project hatred because I do not conform to your notions of who I'm supposed to be. There is no essentialized blueprint. Opening up the possibility of articulating the variety of ways we experience and negotiate our identities benefits everyone, not just the multiethnic. Recasting our moving selves begins with an openness and a willingness to listen, which leads to dialogue.

Notes

I would like, to thank Marisol Negrón, Alexandra Lang, María Helena Rueda, Ericka Beckman, Karina Hodoyan, Sara Rondinel, Jessi Aaron, and Cynthia María Paccacerqua for their feedback in our writing seminar at Stanford University with Mary Pratt. I would especially like to thank Mary Pratt for her invaluable feedback, and AnaLouise Keating and Gloria Anzaldúa for their thoughtful editing.

1. Although such episodes are not exclusive to "public space," I will not be dealing with the complex dynamics of "private space" in this piece.

Beverly Daniel Tatum, president of Spelman College, is a leading public intellectual and expert in the psychology of racism. She is author of several influential books, including Why are All the Black Kids Sitting Together in the Cafeteria, *from which this essay is taken. After earning her PhD in clinical psychology from the University of Michigan, Tatum taught at Westfield State University, University of California, Santa Barbara, and Mt. Holyoke College, where she served as professor, department chair, dean, and acting president. As you read her essay, pay particular attention to how she defines racism and prejudice as different from one another. How does this difference affect your understanding of how race operates in the United States? How does racism affect American identities? How does it lead to social injustice?*

Defining Racism
"Can We Talk?"

Beverly Daniel Tatum

Early in my teaching career, a White student I knew asked me what I would be teaching the following semester. I mentioned that I would be teaching a course on racism. She replied, with some surprise in her voice, "Oh, is there still racism?" I assured her that indeed there was and suggested that she sign up for my course. Fifteen years later, after exhaustive media coverage of events such as the Rodney King beating, the Charles Stuart and Susan Smith cases, the O. J. Simpson trial, the appeal to racial prejudices in electoral politics, and the bitter debates about affirmative action and welfare reform, it seems hard to imagine that anyone would still be unaware of the reality of racism in our society. But in fact, in almost every audience I address, there is someone who will suggest that racism is a thing of the past. There is always someone who hasn't noticed the stereotypical images of people of color in the media, who hasn't observed the housing discrimination in their community, who hasn't read the newspaper articles about documented racial bias in lending practices among well-known banks, who isn't aware of the racial tracking pattern at the local school, who hasn't seen the reports of rising incidents of racially motivated hate crimes in America—in short, someone who hasn't been paying attention to issues of race. But if you are paying attention, the legacy of racism is not hard to see, and we are all affected by it.

The impact of racism begins early. Even in our preschool years, we are exposed to misinformation about people different from ourselves. Many of us grew up in neighborhoods where we had limited opportunities to interact with people different from our own families. When I ask my college students, "How many of you grew up in neighborhoods where most of the people were from the same racial group as your own?" almost every hand goes up. There is still a great deal of social segregation in our communities. Consequently, most of the early information we receive about "others"—people racially, religiously, or socioeconomically different from ourselves—does not come as the result of firsthand experience. The secondhand information we do receive has often been distorted, shaped by cultural stereotypes, and left incomplete.

Some examples will highlight this process. Several years ago one of my students conducted a research project investigating preschoolers' conceptions of Native Americans.[1] Using children at a local day care center as her participants, she asked these three- and four-year-olds to draw a picture of a Native American. Most children were stumped by her request. They didn't know what a Native American was. But when she rephrased the question and asked them to draw a picture of an Indian, they readily complied. Almost every picture included one central feature: feathers. In fact, many of them also included a weapon—a knife or tomahawk—and depicted the person in violent or aggressive terms. Though this group of children, almost all of whom were White, did not live near a large Native American population and probably had had little if any personal interaction with American Indians, they all had internalized an image of what Indians were like. How did they know? Cartoon images, in particular the Disney movie *Peter Pan*, were cited by the children as their number-one source of information. At the age of three, these children already had a set of stereotypes in place. Though I would not describe three-year-olds as prejudiced, the stereotypes to which they have been exposed become the foundation for the adult prejudices so many of us have.

Sometimes the assumptions we make about others come not from what we have been told or what we have seen on television or in books, but rather from what we have *not* been told. The distortion of historical information about people of color leads young people (and older people, too) to make assumptions that may go unchallenged for a long time. Consider this conversation between two White students following a discussion about the cultural transmission of racism:

"Yeah, I just found out that Cleopatra was actually a Black woman."

"What?"

The first student went on to explain her newly learned information. The second student exclaimed in disbelief, "That can't be true. Cleopatra was beautiful!"

What had this young woman learned about who in our society is considered beautiful and who is not? Had she conjured up images of Elizabeth Taylor when she thought of Cleopatra? The new information her classmate had shared and her own deeply ingrained assumptions about who is beautiful and who is not were too incongruous to allow her to assimilate the information at that moment.

Omitted information can have similar effects. For example, another young woman, preparing to be a high school English teacher, expressed her dismay that she had never learned about any Black authors in any of her English courses. How was she to teach about them to her future students when she hadn't learned about them herself? A White male student in the class responded to this discussion with frustration in his response journal, writing "It's not my fault that Blacks don't write books." Had one of his elementary, high school, or college teachers ever told him that there were no Black writers? Probably not. Yet because he had never been exposed to Black authors, he had drawn his own conclusion that there were none.

Stereotypes, omissions, and distortions all contribute to the development of prejudice. *Prejudice* is a preconceived judgment or opinion, usually based on limited information. I assume that we all have prejudices, not because we want them, but simply because we are so continually exposed to misinformation about others. Though I have often heard students or workshop participants describe someone as not having "a prejudiced bone in his body," I usually suggest that they look again. Prejudice is one of the inescapable consequences of living in a racist society. Cultural racism—the cultural images and messages that affirm the assumed superiority of Whites and the assumed inferiority of people of color—is like smog in the air. Sometimes it is so thick it is visible, other times it is less apparent, but always, day in and day out, we are breathing it in. None of us would introduce ourselves as "smog-breathers" (and most of us don't want to be described as prejudiced), but if we live in a smoggy place, how can we avoid breathing the air? If we live in an environment in which we are bombarded with stereotypical images in the media, are frequently exposed to the ethnic jokes of friends and family members, and are rarely informed of the accomplishments of oppressed groups, we will develop the negative categorizations of those groups that form the basis of prejudice.

People of color as well as Whites develop these categorizations. Even a member of the stereotyped group may internalize the stereotypical categories about his or her own group to some degree. In fact, this process happens so frequently that it has a name, *internalized oppression*. Some of the consequences of believing the distorted messages about one's own group will be discussed in subsequent chapters.

Certainly some people are more prejudiced than others, actively embracing and perpetuating negative and hateful images of those who are different from themselves. When we claim to be free of prejudice, perhaps what we are really saying is that we are not hatemongers. But none of us is completely innocent. Prejudice is an integral part of our socialization, and it is not our fault. Just as the preschoolers my student interviewed are not to blame for the negative messages they internalized, we are not at fault for the stereotypes, distortions, and omissions that shaped our thinking as we grew up.

To say that it is not our fault does not relieve us of responsibility, however. We may not have polluted the air, but we need to take responsibility, along with others, for cleaning it up. Each of us needs to look at our own behavior. Am I perpetuating and reinforcing the negative messages so pervasive in our culture, or am I seeking to challenge them? If I have not been exposed to positive images of marginalized groups, am I seeking them out, expanding my own knowledge base for myself and my children? Am I acknowledging and examining my own prejudices, my own rigid categorizations of others, thereby minimizing the adverse impact they might have on my interactions with those I have categorized? Unless we engage in these and other conscious acts of reflection and reeducation, we easily repeat the process with our children. We teach what we were taught. The unexamined prejudices of the parents are passed on to the children. It is not our fault, but it is our responsibility to interrupt this cycle.

Racism: A System of Advantage Based on Race

Many people use the terms *prejudice* and *racism* interchangeably. I do not, and I think it is important to make a distinction. In his book *Portraits of White Racism,* David Wellman argues convincingly that limiting our understanding of racism to prejudice does not offer a sufficient explanation for the persistence of racism. He defines racism as a "system of advantage based on race."[2] In illustrating this definition, he provides example after example of how Whites defend their racial advantage—access to better schools, housing, jobs—even when they do not embrace overtly prejudicial thinking. Racism cannot be fully explained as an expression of prejudice alone.

This definition of racism is useful because it allows us to see that racism, like other forms of oppression, is not only a personal ideology based on racial prejudice, but a *system* involving cultural messages and institutional policies and practices as well as the beliefs and actions of individuals. In the context of the United States, this system clearly operates to the advantage of Whites and to the disadvantage of people of color. Another related definition of racism, commonly used by antiracist educators and consultants, is "prejudice plus power." Racial prejudice when combined with social power—access to social, cultural, and economic resources and decision-making—leads to the institutionalization of racist policies and practices. While I think this definition also captures the idea that racism is more than individual beliefs and attitudes, I prefer Wellman's definition because the idea of systematic advantage and disadvantage is critical to an understanding of how racism operates in American society.

In addition, I find that many of my White students and workshop participants do not feel powerful. Defining racism as prejudice plus power has little personal relevance. For some, their response to this definition is the following: "I'm not really prejudiced, and I have no power, so racism has nothing to do with me." However, most White people, if they are really being honest with themselves, can see that there are advantages to being White in the United States. Despite the current rhetoric about affirmative action and "reverse racism," every social indicator, from salary to life expectancy, reveals the advantages of being White.[3]

The systematic advantages of being White are often referred to as White privilege. In a now well-known article, "White Privilege: Unpacking the Invisible Knapsack," Peggy McIntosh, a White feminist scholar, identified a long list of societal privileges that she received simply because she was White.[4] She did not ask for them, and it is important to note that she hadn't always noticed that she was receiving them. They included major and minor advantages. Of course she enjoyed greater access to jobs and housing. But she also was able to shop in department stores without being followed by suspicious salespeople and could always find appropriate hair care products and makeup in any drugstore. She could send her child to school confident that the teacher would not discriminate against him on the basis of race. She could also be late for meetings, and talk with her mouth full, fairly confident that these behaviors would not be attributed to the fact that she was White. She could express an opinion in a meeting or in print and not have it labeled the "White" viewpoint. In other words, she was more often than not viewed as an individual, rather than as a member of a racial group.

This article rings true for most White readers, many of whom may have never considered the benefits of being White. It's one thing to have enough awareness of racism to describe the ways that people of color are disadvantaged by it. But this new understanding of racism is more elusive. In very concrete terms, it means that if a person of color is the victim of housing discrimination, the apartment that would otherwise have been rented to that person of color is still available for a White person. The White tenant is, knowingly or unknowingly, the beneficiary of racism, a system of advantage based on race. The unsuspecting tenant is not to blame for the prior discrimination, but she benefits from it anyway.

For many Whites, this new awareness of the benefits of a racist system elicits considerable pain, often accompanied by feelings of anger and guilt. These uncomfortable emotions can hinder further discussion. We all like to think that we deserve the good things we have received, and that others, too, get what they deserve. Social psychologists call this tendency a "belief in a just world."[5] Racism directly contradicts such notions of justice.

Understanding racism as a system of advantage based on race is antithetical to traditional notions of an American meritocracy. For those who have internalized this myth, this definition generates considerable discomfort. It is more comfortable simply to think of racism as a particular form of prejudice. Notions of power or privilege do not have to be addressed when our understanding of racism is constructed in that way.

The discomfort generated when a systemic definition of racism is introduced is usually quite visible in the workshops I lead. Someone in the group is usually quick to point out that this is not the definition you will find in most dictionaries. I reply, "Who wrote the dictionary?" I am not being facetious with this response. Whose interests are served by a "prejudice only" definition of racism? It is important to understand that the system of advantage is perpetuated when we do not acknowledge its existence.

Racism: For Whites Only?

Frequently someone will say, "You keep talking about White people. People of color can be racist, too." I once asked a White teacher what it would mean to her if a student or parent of color accused her of being racist. She said she would feel as though she had been punched in the stomach or called a "low-life scum." She is not alone in this feeling. The word *racist* holds a lot of emotional power. For many White people, to be called racist is the ultimate insult. The idea that this term might only be applied to Whites becomes highly problematic for after all, can't people of color be "low-life scum" too?

Of course, people of any racial group can hold hateful attitudes and behave in racially discriminatory and bigoted ways. We can all cite examples of horrible hate crimes which have been perpetrated by people of color as well as Whites. Hateful behavior is hateful behavior no matter who does it. But when I am asked, "Can people of color be racist?" I reply, "The answer depends on your definition of racism." If one defines racism as racial prejudice, the answer is yes. People of color can and do have racial prejudices. However, if one defines racism as a system of advantage based on race, the answer is no. People of color are not racist because they do not systematically benefit from racism. And equally important, there is no systematic cultural and institutional support or sanction for the racial bigotry of people of color. In my view, reserving the term *racist* only for behaviors committed by Whites in the context of a White-dominated society is a way of acknowledging the ever-present power differential afforded Whites by the culture and institutions that make up the system of advantage and continue to reinforce notions of White superiority. (Using the same logic, I reserve the word *sexist* for men. Though women can and do have gender-based prejudices, only men systematically benefit from sexism.)

Despite my best efforts to explain my thinking on this point, there are some who will be troubled, perhaps even incensed, by my response. To call the racially motivated acts of a person of color acts of racial bigotry and to describe similar acts committed by Whites as racist will make no sense to some people, including some people of color. To those, I will respectfully say, "We can agree to disagree." At moments like these, it is not agreement that is essential, but clarity. Even if you don't like the definition of racism I am using, hopefully you are now clear about what it is.

If I also understand how you are using the term, our conversation can continue—despite our disagreement.

Another provocative question I'm often asked is "Are you saying all Whites are racist?" When asked this question, I again remember that White teacher's response, and I am conscious that perhaps the question I am really being asked is, "Are you saying all Whites are bad people?" The answer to that question is of course not. However, all White people, intentionally or unintentionally, do benefit from racism. A more relevant question is what are White people as individuals doing to interrupt racism? For many White people, the image of a racist is a hood-wearing Klan member or a name-calling Archie Bunker figure. These images represent what might be called *active racism*, blatant, intentional acts of racial bigotry and discrimination. *Passive racism* is more subtle and can be seen in the collusion of laughing when a racist joke is told, of letting exclusionary hiring practices go unchallenged, of accepting as appropriate the omissions of people of color from the curriculum, and of avoiding difficult race-related issues. Because racism is so ingrained in the fabric of American institutions, it is easily self-perpetuating.[6] All that is required to maintain it is business as usual.

I sometimes visualize the ongoing cycle of racism as a moving walkway at the airport. Active racist behavior is equivalent to walking fast on the conveyor belt. The person engaged in active racist behavior has identified with the ideology of White supremacy and is moving with it. Passive racist behavior is equivalent to standing still on the walkway. No overt effort is being made, but the conveyor belt moves the bystanders along to the same destination as those who are actively walking. Some of the bystanders may feel the motion of the conveyor belt, see the active racists ahead of them, and choose to turn around, unwilling to go to the same destination as the White supremacists. But unless they are walking actively in the opposite direction at a speed faster than the conveyor belt—unless they are actively antiracist—they will find themselves carried along with the others.

So, not all Whites are actively racist. Many are passively racist. Some, though not enough, are actively antiracist. The relevant question is not whether all Whites are racist, but how we can move more White people from a position of active or passive racism to one of active antiracism? The task of interrupting racism is obviously not the task of Whites alone. But the fact of White privilege means that Whites have greater access to the societal institutions in need of transformation. To whom much is given, much is required.

It is important to acknowledge that while all Whites benefit from racism, they do not all benefit equally. Other factors, such as socioeconomic status, gender, age, religious affiliation, sexual orientation, mental and physical ability, also play a role in our access to social influence and power. A White woman on welfare is not privileged to the same extent as a wealthy White heterosexual man. In her case, the systematic disadvantages of sexism and classism intersect with her White privilege, but the privilege is still there. This point was brought home to me in a 1994 study conducted by a Mount Holyoke graduate student, Phyllis Wentworth.[7] Wentworth interviewed a group of female college students, who were both older than their peers and were the first members of their families to attend college, about the pathways that lead them to college. All of the women interviewed were White, from working-class backgrounds, from families where women were expected to graduate from high school and get married or get a job. Several had experienced abusive relationships and other personal difficulties prior to coming to college. Yet their experiences were punctuated by "good luck" stories of apartments obtained without a deposit, good jobs offered without experience or extensive reference checks, and encouragement provided by willing mentors. While the women acknowledged their good fortune, none of them discussed their Whiteness. They had not considered the possibility that being White had worked in their favor and helped give them the benefit of the doubt at critical junctures. This study clearly showed that even under difficult circumstances, White privilege was still operating.

It is also true that not all people of color are equally targeted by racism. We all have multiple identities that shape our experience. I can describe myself as a light-skinned, well-educated, heterosexual, able-bodied, Christian African American woman raised in a middle-class suburb. As an African American woman, I am systematically disadvantaged by race and by gender, but I systematically receive benefits in the other categories, which then mediate my experience of racism and sexism. When one is targeted by multiple isms—racism, sexism, classism, heterosexism, ableism, anti-Semitism, ageism—in whatever combination, the effect is intensified. The particular combination of racism and classism in many communities of color is life-threatening. Nonetheless, when I, the middle-class Black mother of two sons, read another story about a Black man's unlucky encounter with a White police officer's deadly force, I am reminded that racism by itself can kill.

The Cost of Racism

Several years ago, a White male student in my psychology of racism course wrote in his journal at the end of the semester that he had learned a lot about racism and now understood in a way he never had before just how advantaged he was. He also commented that he didn't think he would do anything to try to change the situation. After all, the system was working in his favor. Fortunately, his response was not typical. Most of my students leave my course with the desire (and an action plan) to interrupt the cycle of racism. However, this young man's response does raise an important question. Why should Whites who are advantaged by racism *want* to end that system of advantage? What are the *costs* of that system to them?

A *Money* magazine article called "Race and Money" chronicled the many ways the American economy was hindered by institutional racism.[8] Whether one looks at productivity lowered by racial tensions in the workplace, or real estate equity lost through housing discrimination, or the tax revenue lost in underemployed communities of color, or the high cost of warehousing human talent in prison, the economic costs of racism are real and measurable.

As a psychologist, I often hear about the less easily measured costs. When I ask White men and women how racism hurts them, they frequently talk about their fears of people of color, the social incompetence they feel in racially mixed situations, the alienation they have experienced between parents and children when a child marries into a family of color, and the interracial friendships they had as children that were lost in adolescence or young adulthood without their ever understanding why. White people are paying a significant price for the system of advantage. The cost is not as high for Whites as it is for people of color, but a price is being paid.[9] Wendell Berry, a White writer raised in Kentucky, captures this psychic pain in the opening pages of his book, *The Hidden Wound:*

> If white people have suffered less obviously from racism than black people, they have nevertheless suffered greatly; the cost has been greater perhaps than we can yet know. If the white man has inflicted the wound of racism upon black men, the cost has been that he would receive the mirror image of that wound into himself. As the master, or as a member of the dominant race, he has felt little compulsion to acknowledge it or speak of it; the more painful it has grown the more deeply he has hidden it within himself. But the wound is there, and it is a profound disorder, as great a damage in his mind as it is in his society.[10]

The dismantling of racism is in the best interests of everyone.

A Word about Language

Throughout this chapter I have used the term *White* to refer to Americans of European descent. In another era, I might have used the term *Caucasian*. I have used the term *people of color* to refer to those groups in America that are and have been historically targeted by racism. This includes people of African descent, people of Asian descent, people of Latin American descent, and indigenous peoples (sometimes referred to as Native Americans or American Indians).[11] Many people refer to these groups collectively as non-Whites. This term is particularly offensive because it defines groups of people in terms of what they are not. (Do we call women "non-men?") I also avoid using the term *minorities* because it represents another kind of distortion of information which we need to correct. So-called minorities represent the majority of the world's population. While the term *people of color* is inclusive, it is not perfect. As a workshop participant once said, White people have color, too. Perhaps it would be more accurate to say "people of more color," though I am not ready to make that change. Perhaps fellow psychologist Linda James Myers is on the right track. She refers to two groups of people, those of acknowledged African descent and those of unacknowledged African descent, reminding us that we can all trace the roots of our common humanity to Africa.

I refer to people of acknowledged African descent as Black. I know that *African American* is also a commonly used term, and I often refer to myself and other Black people born and raised in America in that way. Perhaps because I am a child of the 1960s "Black and beautiful" era, I still prefer *Black*. The term is more inclusive than *African American*, because there are Black people in the United States who are not African American—Afro-Caribbeans, for example—yet are targeted by racism, and are identified as Black.

When referring to other groups of color, I try to use the terms that the people themselves want to be called. In some cases, there is no clear consensus. For example, some people of Latin American ancestry prefer *Latino*, while others prefer *Hispanic* or, if of Mexican descent, *Chicano*.[12] The terms *Latino* and *Hispanic* are used interchangeably here. Similarly, there are regional variations in the use of the terms *Native American*, *American Indian*, and *Indian*. *American Indian* and *Native people* are now more widely used than *Native American*, and the language used here reflects that. People of Asian descent include Pacific Islanders, and that is reflected in the terms *Asian/Pacific Islanders* and *Asian Pacific Americans*. However, when quoting others I use whichever terms they use.

My dilemma about the language to use reflects the fact that race is a social construction.[13] Despite myths to the contrary, biologists tell us that the only meaningful racial categorization is that of human. Van den Berghe defines race as "a group that is socially defined but on the basis of *physical* criteria," including skin color and facial features.[14]

Racial identity development, a central focus of this book, usually refers to the process of defining for oneself the personal significance and social meaning of belonging to a particular racial group. The terms *racial identity* and *ethnic identity* are often used synonymously, though a distinction can be made between the two. An ethnic group is a socially defined group based on *cultural* criteria, such as language, customs, and shared history. An individual might identify as a member of an ethnic group (Irish or Italian, for example) but might not think of himself in racial terms (as White). On the other hand, one may recognize the personal significance of racial group membership (identifying as Black, for instance) but may not consider ethnic identity (such as West Indian) as particularly meaningful.

Both racial and ethnic categories are socially constructed, and social definitions of these categories have changed over time. For example, in his book *Ethnic Identity: The Transformation of White America*, Richard Alba points out that the high rates of intermarriage and the dissolution of other social boundaries among European ethnic groups in the United States have reduced the significance of ethnic identity for these groups. In their place, he argues, a new ethnic identity is emerging, that of European American.[15]

Throughout this book, I refer primarily to racial identity. It is important, however, to acknowledge that ethnic identity and racial identity sometimes intersect. For example, dark-skinned Puerto Ricans may identify culturally as Puerto Rican and yet be categorized racially by others as Black on the basis of physical appearance. In the case of either racial or ethnic identity, these identities remain most salient to individuals of racial or ethnic groups that have been historically disadvantaged or marginalized.

The language we use to categorize one another racially is imperfect. These categories are still evolving as the current debate over Census classifications indicates.[16] The original creation of racial categories was in the service of oppression. Some may argue that to continue to use them is to continue that oppression. I respect that argument. Yet it is difficult to talk about what is essentially a flawed and problematic social construct without using language that is itself problematic. We have to be able to talk about it in order to change it. So this is the language I choose.

Notes

1 C. O'Toole, "The effect of the media and multicultural education on children's perceptions of Native Americans" (senior thesis, Department of Psychology and Education, Mount Holyoke College, South Hadley, MA, May 1990).

2 For an extended discussion of this point, see David Wellman, *Portraits of White Racism* (Cambridge: Cambridge University Press, 1977), ch. 1.

3 For specific statistical information, see R. Farley, "The common destiny of Blacks and Whites: Observations about the social and economic status of the races," pp. 197–233 in H. Hill and J. E. Jones, Jr. (Eds.), *Race in America: The Struggle for Equality* (Madison: University of Wisconsin Press, 1993).

4 P. McIntosh, "White Priveledge: Unpacking the Invisible Knapsack," *Peace and Freedom* (July / August 1989): 10–12.

5 For further discussion of the concept of "belief in a just world," see M. J. Lerner, "Social Psychology of Justice and Interpersonal Attraction," in T. Huston (Ed.), *Foundations of Interpersonal Attraction* (New York: Academic Press, 1974).

6 For a brief historical overview of the institutionalization of racism and sexism in our legal system, see "Part V: How It Happened: Race and Gender Issues in U.S. law," in P. S. Rothenberg (Ed.), *Race, Class, and Gender in the United States: An Integrated Study*, 3rd. ed. (New York: St. Martin's Press, 1995).

[7] P. A. Wentworth, "The identity development of non-traditionally aged first-generation women college students: An exploratory study" (master's thesis, Department of Psychology and Education, Mount Holyoke College, South Hadley, MA, 1994).

[8] W. I. Updegrave, "Race and Money," *Money* (December 1989): 152–72.

[9] For further discussion of the impact of racism on Whites, see B. Bowser and R. G. Hunt (Eds.), *Impacts of Racism on White Americans* (Thousand Oaks, CA: Sage, 1981); P. Kivel, *Uprooting Racism: How White People Can Work for Racial Justice* (Philadelphia: New Society Publishers, 1996); and J. Barndt, *Dismantling Racism: The Continuing Challenge to White America* (Minneapolis: Augsburg Press, 1991).

[10] W. Berry, *The Hidden Wound* (San Francisco: North Point Press, 1989), pp. 3–4.

[11] It is important to note here that these groups are not necessarily mutually exclusive. For example, people of Latin America descent may have European, African, and Native American ancestors. The politics of racial categorization has served to create artificial boundaries between groups with shared ancestry.

[12] It is difficult to know which is the preferred term to use because different subgroups have different preferences. According to Amado Padilla, younger U.S.-born university-educated individuals of Mexican ancestry prefer *Chicano(a)* to *Mexican American* or *Hispanic*. On the other hand, *Latino* is preferred by others of Mexican ancestry or other Latin American origin. Those of Cuban ancestry may prefer *Cuban American* to *Latino*, wheras recent immigrants from Central America would rather be identified by their nationality (e.g., *Guatematecos* or *Salvadorenos*). A. Padilla (Ed.), *Hispanic Psychology* (Thousand Oaks, CA: Sage 1995).

[13] For an expanded discussion of the social construction of race, see M. Omi and H. Winant, *Racial Formation in the United States*, 2nd ed. (New York: Routledge, 1994).

[14] P. L. Van den Berghe, *Race and Racism* (New York: Wiley, 1967).

[15] See R. Alba, *Ethnic Identity: The Transformation of White America* (New Haven: Yale University Press, 1990).

[16] For a discussion of the census classification debate and the history of racial classification in the United States, see L. Wright, "One Drop of Blood," *The New Yorker* (July 25, 1994): 46–55.

Pamela R. Fletcher, a writer, editor, critic, and educator, is associate professor of English, co-director of the Interdisciplinary Program in Criminal Studies of Race and Ethnicity, and director of writing programs at St. Catherine University. Her story, "A Dream Deferred," appeared in Do You Know Me Now? An Anthology of Minnesota Multicultural Writings *(1993). She is also co-editor (with Buchwald and Roth) of* Transforming a Rape Culture, *frm which you can read an except in the GSJ section of this book. In this piece, Fletcher addresses issues of race, identity, self-knowledge, betrayal, and loss of innocence. What "dream" does her title refer to? What characterizes the loss of innocence she describes? How does her narrative express the complexity of the relationship between individual and community? How does it intersect with Tatum's explanation of racism or McIntosh's description of white privilege?*

A Dream Deferred[1]

Pamela Fletcher

Prancing on Seal Beach waves atop our slippery surfboards, we wiped out and choked on the foamy, pickled sea and giggled and pranced and wiped out and choked and giggled and pranced under a hot sun that browned B.K. like a chicken breast in a pan of sweet butter and blackened me like a filet of red snapper dusted with savory spices and fried over a high blue flame.

Occasionally B.K. and I took breaks to replenish our energy, eating sandwiches Mama Bindels made so lovingly with Wonder bread, margarine, and chocolate sprinkles. We also munched juicy black plums that Mama Bindels had picked from the plum tree in their backyard. To cool down, we drank enormous bottles of RC cola that I could barely swallow because the bubbly syrup stung my throat. B.K. and her older sisters glugged the liquid in large gulps and were instantly revived.

Mama and Papa Bindels waved at us with dark-shaded eyes and sun-lightened grins. Every now and then Papa Bindels swam quickly behind us, squealing and splashing and breaking our concentration when it appeared that we were about to ascend a giant wave. I adored him and his mischievous manner. He loved to tease and do pranks. Whenever I saw him, he gave me wholesome, warm hugs and tenderly patted my head. Most of the time I didn't completely understand his words when he talked to me because he spoke in a melodious Dutch accent that confused and delighted me. Yet I understood that he thought of me as his daughter and I felt quite special to have both him and my father care about me. I often wondered how it would feel to really be Mr. Bindels' daughter. He and my father were very different men, separated by age, color, and opportunity. I knew they were different, but at nine years old

I had no idea just how different their lives were. I wonder now just what it's like to be the daughter of a man who is not routinely beaten with a thick switch broken from a branch of the lynching tree.

B.K., blonde, tall, and Canadian, and I, dark, tall, and American, loved each other more than we loved our own sisters. In the summer of 1965, as in the previous two years, this love kept me afloat in the hostile suburban community of La Puente, located approximately thirty miles east of Watts where rebellion would soon erupt. I had no knowledge of what racism and discrimination meant; I never had heard the words before. But I was familiar with the slur "nigger" that the white and Mexican children fired like poison gas in my face and in the faces of my siblings. I vaguely remember hearing that Malcolm X was shot to death that year on February 21, the day of my brother's eighth birthday, but I didn't know who Malcolm X was and didn't know that I should even care. I also didn't understand the significance of the civil rights march that King and some thirty-five thousand national supporters had recently accomplished in Alabama. As far as I knew, Watts and Alabama were strange lands with voting rights violations, unfair housing, segregated schools, separate public accommodations, and police brutality that had nothing, whatsoever, to do with my life. Living in La Puente at nine years old, I had no idea what those problems meant at all. Besides, Mama and Daddy never mentioned them nor commented on the news. They moved us to San Gabriel Valley so we wouldn't have to worry about such things.

The Fletchers and the Bindels were oblivious to what was happening outside our suburban cocoon. All I cared about was how often B.K. and I would play together and how soon we would make up after a fight. About once a month we underwent a power struggle about some petty thing, nothing memorable. We had it down to a science: we screamed at each other, stomped our feet, and cried; then she ran away and I nervously awaited her return (sometimes it took a day or two), and then we hugged, laughed, and began anew. Our families did not understand our combative interaction, but these theatrics simply became our ritual for emotional adventure.

B.K. ran wild and barefooted, her straight hair swinging every which way. I didn't like getting my feet dirty so I wore tennis shoes, and since it was not proper for a colored girl to let her hair go its own direction, I captured its unruly nature in a ponytail. Once, while we played house, Valerie, my baby sister, attempted to braid B.K.'s hair but the ends would not stay. "It just won't act right," Valerie sighed, trying to braid B.K.'s hair as tightly as possible. As the braid unraveled, B.K. hunched her shoulders and we giggled, and left it up to God. This difference between our hair and hers mystified us sometimes. It struck me that while Mama permed our hair to straighten it, B.K.'s big sister, Bianca, permed her hair to curl it. I began to realize that girls spent a lot of time worrying about their hair, especially as they grew older. Bianca and her friends regularly changed their hair color and hair styles. B.K., though, liked her hair plain and natural. Once in a while she wore a ponytail, but she never wore braids. We colored girls kept our hair in bondage. Braiding it seemed to be the easiest way to create a presentable colored appearance. I envied B.K.'s nonchalance about hair; she never worried about being presentable. This child of Dutch ancestry, named after Queen Beatrix of Holland, had such confidence and spunk. I envied her rebellious spirit. She had the audacity to defy everyone, including her parents, especially Papa Bindels, who grounded her at every turn. But he never forbade us to see each other; somehow he knew that it would be cruel and unusual punishment. When he banished her to her room, I just moved in, and we often spent hours planning or replanning our next beach trip and laughing about the silly things we did the last time we went surfing.

In 1968 our elementary school years came to an abrupt end. One day, when we weren't looking, our bodies abandoned us and moved to some foreign land while our minds had yet to venture beyond the fifth grade. Feeling awkward and insecure, we began to experience things that we could not or would not mention to each other. For instance, although we didn't tell each other when we began to menstruate, I could tell her time had come because she acted guilty just like I acted once I began menstruating. Suddenly we discovered a horrible secret we didn't want anyone else to know. We no longer laughed easily. We walked with constraint and held our bodies close. We stopped wrestling, climbing trees, and playing house. We began to see through wide eyes that there was a direct correlation between our new external selves and how the world reacted to us. "Keep your legs shut!" Daddy said. "Stop rolling around out there on that grass like you somebody wild," Mama said. Men leered at us when we walked around the shopping center.

Yet, initially, I didn't see everything so clearly. I didn't see how much the world's reaction to our friendship would change our lives forever—until one certain day. That day we walked home from school together, talking and laughing just like our old selves. Suddenly B.K. startled me with a tone of voice that I hadn't heard before. It wasn't her angry I-will-never-speak-to-you-again voice; it was a voice that no longer recognized me.

"Quick! Get behind me. Walk behind me."

"Huh?" I said. "What do you mean?"

"Walk behind me," she repeated. But then she rushed ahead of me and walked away fast as if we weren't walking together. As she walked ahead, a car slowed, approaching us.

"Hey, B.K.! What cha doing?" a blonde girl yelled out of the car window.

"Hey, Cathy! You coming over later?"

"My mom says she might drop me off while she goes shopping. I'll call ya."

"Okay. See you guys later," B.K. waved as the car gained speed.

She maintained a safe distance from me until the car turned the corner and then she stopped and waited for me to catch up. B.K. resumed the conversation as if nothing had happened and I forced myself to withhold my riotous and jealous rage, though I did not know why. I may have been afraid of what I would have done if I released my fury; after all, I was not supposed to be this angry, so angry I could have killed her. Unlike most colored people, I was living the integrated dream of the late Martin Luther King and it was supposed to be good and equal, but over time I began to realize that it wasn't what my parents had expected and what they had led me to believe it would be. As we walked along that wide street together, I found that it didn't matter that for years B.K. and I lived in the same neighborhood on the same side of the street, one house away from each other, that we ate and slept in each other's homes, that we shared silly secrets and protected each other, that we went to the same schools and shopped in the same stores. Together. The fact that we were different colors still separated us.

King's recent death had touched so many people, including my family, and I began to pay close attention to what was happening around the country and what was happening to me as I was growing into someone brand new. The world exploded with talk about race and violence and civil rights, and I ascertained that society was forcing me to choose between being a person and being a "black" person. When I looked at B.K. then, she was no longer B.K.; she was now a "white" girl, representative of all the whites who had rejected and oppressed me. Although she walked beside me now, I realized that she had just relegated me to that "place" where black people are meant to placate or perish. As she assumed her privileged position in the white world, we were torn asunder. My best friend whom I considered my sister died right in front of my very eyes. And a piece of me died right along with her. Yet, my rage gave birth to an awareness that Watts and Alabama were not so distant from La Puente after all. It occurred to me that no matter where we lived, black people still had so much to overcome. While B.K. talked, I nodded my head for fear that if I opened my mouth, I would flood her with murderous grief. When we reached Barrydale Street, instead of stopping at her corner house as usual, I said good-bye with averted, teary eyes and walked away.

That afternoon I buried B.K. along with my innocent belief that love is a protective shield that saves one from being devoured by a world that eats the hearts of those who dare to be human and who dare to accept the humanity of someone else. B.K. and I had never discussed our blatant difference so I naively thought that for once it didn't matter. After having suffered loneliness for so long in La Puente, I thought I finally had found a friend who loved me regardless of how I looked, who loved me for my "character." Forever. I had never imagined that once we reached Edgewood Junior High our emotional points would no longer intersect simply because I was black and she was white. Although I had willed myself to forget that day, deep in my heart I was afraid I would never recover; I was afraid that I would continue to mourn the loss of the dream.

Yet, like the living dead who didn't die a timely death or get a proper burial, the dream can't rest. It's as alive as my vivid memory of B.K. and me prancing on those waves. Together.

Note

[1] Taken from a line in Langston Hughes' poem, "Dream Boogie."

Lucille Clifton, 1936–2010, was a widely published and influential American poet, winner of the Pulitzer Prize, a National Book Award and Ruth Lilly Poetry Prize. Clifton's themes include her African-American heritage, issues of race and identity in the U.S., and strong women confronting adversity. The following poem is included in Good Woman: Poems and A Memoir, 1969–1980 *(1987). How does Clifton use a woman's hips both literally and metaphorically in this poem—as both what they are and what they represent? In what way is "homage to my hips" an artistic expression of self?*

homage to my hips

Lucille Clifton

these hips are big hips.
they need space to
move around in.
they don't fit into little
petty places. these hips
are free hips.
they don't like to be held back.
these hips have never been enslaved,
they go where they want to go
they do what they want to do.
these hips are mighty hips.
these hips are magic hips.
i have known them
to put a spell on a man and
spin him like a top!

Kristina Anderson graduated from St. Kate's in 2000 with a double a major in English and philosophy. An exceptional student and gifted writer, she was invited to compose the following personal narrative for the 2002 edition of the TRW Reader. *A few years later, she added the postscript. In this essay, Anderson describes, with admirable honesty, her experience of coming to terms with her lesbian identity as a college student. Consider the ways Anderson includes both the pain and joy of self-discovery. How does she speak her truth even when it is difficult? In what ways has our community changed (or not) since Anderson's years here?*

Where I Belong

Kristina Anderson

I didn't even know what a lesbian was until I was twelve or thirteen. As I began to connect the word and its meaning with what I was feeling as a young adolescent, my world collapsed around me. Like many people in junior high and high school, the only references I heard to homosexuality were negative. "Dyke," "fag," "homo," and "fairy" were just a few of the hurtful words hurled at anyone a little different. I hid quietly, trying to blend into the crowd of ordinariness, hoping that no one could tell I might be a lesbian. I grasped early on that my confused sexual feelings must never be revealed, for I knew that homosexuality was not acceptable. In desperation and fear, I made an ultimatum with myself: if I discovered I truly was a lesbian, I would end my life. It sounded simple enough, and in many senses it comforted me to know that I could escape from what I perceived to be an unforgivable evil. I was certain that no one could live happily or productively as a lesbian, and if that turned out to be who I was, I had no choice but to die.

With time and the positive influence of others I reluctantly began to observe and even speak about my sexual orientation. I was still very much confused and filled with guilt and shame. Nonetheless, the more I dared to speak the more I came to understand that what I was feeling was not evil. The ultimatum I had made began to fade in my mind as I gained more confidence in myself. As high school came to an end, I knew I needed to find a college where I could openly discover myself in an environment that was both supportive and challenging.

I thought that by attending a women's college I would find the freedom to be myself, to be open about my sexual orientation. The College of St. Catherine was an immediate first choice because of its urban location, beautiful campus, and women-centered educational philosophy. I imagined St. Kate's to be a place where women, regardless of sexual orientation, were encouraged in their goals and dreams. The first day I arrived on campus St. Kate's seemed to be all I had imagined. As my family and I pulled into the parking lot of the dorm I was to live in, two women stood on the sidewalk holding hands. They appeared relaxed in their affection for one another, laughing and smiling. I stared at them from the window of the car, trying not to visibly display my excitement. "This is it!" I thought. These two women are being open about who they are, right in front of the first year dorm on moving in day. I felt a small sense of hope and excitement as I moved into the dorm, knowing I was not alone.

Within a few days I began to wonder if the lesbians I had seen on the sidewalk were not lesbians at all, or rather the only two such women who existed at St. Kate's. The first year dorm in which I resided was a stifling atmosphere of heterosexuality. I was inundated by glossy pictures of scantily clad male figures each time I entered the bathroom. It wasn't that I cared that many of the other residents enjoyed having male company while brushing their teeth, but rather that many women never considered the possibility that some of us were not attracted to men. Talk in the hallways and dorm rooms was not much better. Many of the women had boyfriends back home or were pursuing males they had met at parties. I began to feel resentful at the very sight of a woman and her boyfriend being able to express their affection for one another in the halls and lounges of the dorm.

One day after becoming exasperated by the hetero-ness on my floor, I decided to try a little experiment. If the bathroom had been claimed as heterosexual territory, then I was going to claim the walls of the elevator as a more woman friendly environment. I carefully searched through magazines that did not promote sexualized waifs and found pictures of strong, intelligent, beautiful women. There was nothing about these women that made them look dyke-ish; they were just women, sexual orientation undefined. I made several trips to the elevator throughout the day to check on the condition of the pictures taped to the walls. No more than four or five hours had passed before I found them torn from the walls, violently I imagined, and discarded in a crumpled heap on the floor. I did try again, cutting out more pictures and taping them up, just as determined as before. I was rewarded with the same results. I had expected this reaction from the beginning, but even so there still existed within me the tiniest bit of hope that no one would care. If we had to look at handsome men all the while brushing our teeth, could we not look at beautiful women while riding the elevator? You certainly do not have to be a lesbian to think women are beautiful. But somebody did not understand this. Someone was offended, perhaps disgusted, or maybe even frightened by their own reaction to the pictures.

The silence among my classmates was unnerving, as if I were walking around with some hideous malfunction that everyone pretended did not exist out of politeness. Some of the people around me were aware of my sexual orientation because I had found the courage to tell them, yet for whatever reason the subject was taboo. People rarely spoke about it directly to me, but rumors circulated freely. It was a strange feeling that people who knew nothing about me knew I was a lesbian. It didn't make much of a difference to them that I was active in campus groups striving for social justice, involved in campus ministry, that I loved outdoor activities, enjoyed writing poetry, or that my favorite thing to do on the weekends was watch movies. For some, none of these commonly shared activities made any difference because my sexual orientation was all they knew of me, perhaps all they allowed themselves to know. There was a certain group of students on campus, I discovered, who were deeply opposed to homosexuality. Someone within this group told me in confidence that I had been identified as a lesbian among these students; they had been informed not to have any contact with me. I was deeply hurt by this, and in many ways still am, because I have always been overly sensitive to the opinions of others. I try very hard to be liked by everyone. I am especially bothered when people do not like me before they truly know me. I felt ashamed any time I encountered these people around campus because I could only imagine what they were thinking of me (what I imagined them to be thinking were the same horrible things I had thought of my own self for so long). I am certain they held within their minds a negative notion of lesbianism and applied this to me. I wanted desperately to speak with them and let them know that lesbianism is only one part of my identity. And yet, I never really did. I stayed in my comfortable corner, as did they. This benefited neither of us. I was too frightened and intimidated to share other parts of myself with them, as were they to receive from me. I do not think it is my duty to prove to others that there is nothing wrong with homosexuality, but if no one takes the initiative to educate others about our common differences, divisions will remain. If I had been more comfortable with my own sexual orientation, perhaps I could have attempted to dispel the fears and myths this group had.

Even among some of my friends, people I should have felt comfortable and safe with, lesbianism was a topic rarely discussed. I *wanted* to talk about it. I wanted to know what people felt and thought. I wanted to tell people how excited and scared and confused and thrilled I was at the process of accepting a part of myself I had detested for so long. I wanted to share with my friends the amazing music, literature, poetry, films, and art that the LGBT (lesbian, gay, bisexual, transgender) community produced. Yet as long as my friends appeared accepting of my sexual orientation, few of them felt it necessary to ever discuss the matter or become involved in active support. I recall an incident in which I was telling one of my friends about an Indigo Girls concert that attracted protesters because of the musicians' sexual orientation. I was angry and discouraged by yet another attack on homosexuality. I went to my friend looking for some encouragement. Instead, she curtly replied, "Is that all you ever talk about?!?" It took all my energy not to scream at her and say, "I listen to you talk about your guy problems every night! Why is it that any time I mention anything having to do with lesbianism, which is not often, I am suddenly talking about it all the time?" She never questioned talking about guys and everything heterosexual because this was a privilege she took for granted. If I was a lesbian that was fine with her, as long as I did not talk about it.

One of my greatest struggles in dealing with my sexual orientation was how to do so in the academic arena. While there are many important aspects of college life, academics was always my top priority. I worked hard to receive good grades. I yearned for a student/professor relationship in which I could drop in during office hours and chat in depth about class discussions and related issues. Yet, I was fearful my emerging sexual orientation might jeopardize my grade or a relationship with a professor. I was a chameleon of sorts, changing attitudes and interests with each professor I met. It may seem trivial that professors ignore or refuse to acknowledge the possibility that some of their students may not be heterosexual, but it never felt trivial to me. If you have ever been the minority in a room of people praised and given attention to because of the color of their skin, religious beliefs, political affiliations, race, educational background, ability level, socioeconomic status, gender, age, or sexual orientation, you are familiar with the feeling of invisibleness. I felt invisible to a professor when she excluded me from class examples by using heterosexist language, knowing full well I was not heterosexual. I was not asking her, or anyone else, to accept my sexual orientation, simply to acknowledge it. I wanted to be seen and spoken to as a whole person. I did not want parts of my identity to be ignored. There is nothing more painful or life threatening than being invisible because of your mere creation.

It came as a great relief, a secret celebration, each time I found supportive students and professors in my classes. I always looked for professors' doors that were decorated with a sign or symbol indicating they were an ally of the LGBT community. Those signs were a friendly sight when walking down a hallway of dismally blank doors that showed no indication my whole self was welcome. Certainly many professors who do not display LGBT support are themselves supportive, but it is often difficult to discern this. I listened for subtle clues in class lectures that signaled to me a professor was okay with homosexuality. I remember the first time I was sitting in a class and the professor used the word "significant other" in place of boyfriend. My heart burst out of my chest upon hearing these two simple words. Finally, at last, my entire being had been acknowledged. My invisibility was beginning to melt away and the silence had been broken.

As I had yet to feel accepted in the residence halls, I reached outside of the dorm life and my straight friends to find what I thought I was looking for. I suppose it is like anyone who does not feel welcome in a community and turns elsewhere to find what it is they need. I met other lesbians on campus and tried to bring myself to be like them. Many of the women were what I considered to be very "out," both in appearance and attitude. Some were the stereotypical dyke in appearance with hair cut short and masculine attire. Some had freedom rings in their ears or eyebrows and others wore jewelry emblazoned with the black triangle, all symbols of pride in their sexual orientation. Some talked freely about their girlfriends, others questioned their like for women and even the necessity for labeling sexual orientation. They all appeared to have a confidence in themselves that allowed them to talk about their sexual orientation and say such words as "dyke" and "lesbian" in a positive, almost righteous way. I seemed to come in on the middle of this ongoing conversation because I could not yet utter such words, nor did I feel comfortable in the presence of those who could. I wanted to be "out," but I also wanted to be me. I felt as if these two identities were in conflict, especially since I was still figuring out who I was.

I knew I was a white girl who grew up in a middle class Christian family of rather conservative values. I knew the things I was hearing among the lesbians I met, and even the things I was feeling, were not in line with what I had been taught to believe. But somehow I wanted to embrace these things. I cut my hair short in the middle of the winter and began wearing a black triangle in my ear. I tried to be more assertive in counteracting the heterosexist language in classes, among my friends, and in the dorms. I thought that if I forced this upon myself it would eventually feel natural. There were times, however, when I didn't have the energy to notice the heterosexism, when I took my earring out around certain people, or when I didn't even correct people if they asked if I had a boyfriend. I was finding that I didn't feel like I belonged among the lesbians on our campus either. I questioned where I belonged.

It never occurred to me during my first years at St. Kate's that I did not have to give up my values, hobbies, taste in music, spiritual and religious beliefs, etc., to be a lesbian. I was so concerned with being a "real" lesbian that everything I valued and held to be true slipped away. I thought you had to look a certain way, act a certain way, dress a certain way, be a certain way to be a lesbian. As I tried to do all these things, I began to realize what little investment I had in *myself.* I simply wanted to fit in with a certain crowd, and if that meant being dishonest with myself, then I was willing to do this. However, I became increasingly unhappy as everything familiar and comforting was discarded for new ways of doing things. It wasn't that the new way was wrong or bad, it was simply different, and it wasn't always me. I do not know exactly what it was, perhaps the enormous amount of energy it took to be someone I was not, that made me realize I did not have to be a certain way to be a lesbian. I can be a lesbian who likes classical music, goes to church, reads literature, and goes fishing. As I again embraced those things that were important to me, while integrating some of my new interests, I became more confident among my lesbian and straight peers alike. First and foremost I discovered I am who I am, my sexual orientation is simply another element of my identity.

As time progressed, I began to create a place for myself at St. Kate's. I experimented with who I was and how I was going to portray myself to the world. I failed many times at this, made many mistakes, but always I found the courage and support to try again. I discovered I did not have to be like any other lesbian at St. Kate's, or any other lesbian in the world, to be a lesbian. I could be a self-described lesbian. I realized I could be a successful student, as well as an "out" lesbian. While this has never been easy, it has come to be less painful then pretending to be someone I am not. St. Kate's became what I made it: an environment in which to grow, discover, change, and voice opinions. This certainly did not come without great struggle and effort, but what St. Kate's offers, if you dare to find it, is a place to form definitions of who you are and find meaning in yourself, others, and the world.

2008 Postscript: Lesbian in Latin America

On September 1, 2001, almost a year after graduating from college, I boarded a plane headed for Guatemala to fulfill my childhood dream of working in missions and fighting for social justice for the poor and marginalized. I had been to Guatemala before as a student in a Global Search for Justice course and I had fallen in love with the Mayan people: their generosity and hospitality, their humility and simplicity, and their smiles, often toothless, radiating from dark faces even in times of hardship and suffering. I was going back to Guatemala for a three-year stint as a volunteer missionary with the dream of living and working among the poor. I was full of optimism and idealism as the plane bounced through the dark night sky, millions of blinking lights coming into view as we approached Guatemala City. I slipped a wisp of hair behind my ear, chewing a piece of tasteless gum with exaggerated force, and tried to ignore the anxiousness that was settling in the pit of my stomach. I was leaving behind everything and everyone I knew. No one I had previously made contact with in Guatemala knew anything about my sexual orientation, nor the years of struggle I had gone through to come to terms with myself. I was going to be working in a Catholic charitable hospital in a highly macho and conservative culture. It wasn't that I hadn't thought about this before; obviously I was hesitant and frightened about leaving behind the freedom I had found in finally accepting my sexual orientation and sharing it with others. Nevertheless, I had decided that if I had to choose between fulfilling my dream of working in missions or being an "out" lesbian, I would choose missions and go back into the closet. I didn't realize at that moment, as the plane came to a jolting stop on the runway, that my life was going to be jolted too, and that I was about to re-enter one of the darkest and loneliest closets of my life.

The first few months flew by in a sort of dreamlike reality. I was consumed with improving my Spanish in language school, learning the cultural customs of the Guatemalan people, and just trying to adjust to all the newness that surrounded me. Within the first few days of being in Guatemala I slipped back into my old role of pretending to be someone I was not. It became clear to me early on through conversations with Guatemalans that homosexuality was something not discussed, nor accepted, in fact, divulging one's sexual orientation could be dangerous within certain circles. I tried not to let this bother me. I was so focused on beginning my mission assignment that I let a lot of things go. I grimaced, yet remained quiet when Guatemalan men made sexist remarks towards women, or more specifically towards me—catcalling and whistling in the streets. I tried to disappear when sexually explicit language and jokes were told among my coworkers at the charitable hospital. Derogatory gay jokes or the use of the local vernacular for fag, *hueco* (coincidently the word *hueco* means hole in Spanish, like a hole in the ground, but it has become slang for a gay male in Guatemala) or *maricon*, peppered every conversation, especially when groups of men were together and a woman might be listening nearby. The jokes, the whistles and the comments were painful, but I found myself responding appropriately with a smile or smirk, never actually commenting or adding to a conversation, yet never speaking up either. I was a silent bystander with a fake smile pasted on my face and my silence was suffocating me. I didn't want to be noticed and I didn't want to be more different than I already was in this new country. I surprised even myself with my passivity. I thought I had traded it for assertiveness during my years at St. Kate's. I was ashamed by my cowardliness. The self-hatred I had worked so hard to kill was coming out of its hibernation and now it was hungry.

My work became my refuge and my salvation. I spent long hours in the operating room working as a translator for medical mission teams that came from North America, assisting them when they needed to communicate with the Guatemalan operating room staff. I also found a place for myself at the bedside of patients waiting for surgery. The majority of patients had come from small villages where no medical care was available to receive life-changing surgery at the hospital. Many of the patients were campesinos or indigenous that had never left their fields or remote villages, so the shock of being in a hospital was overwhelming. They were old men, brown and wrinkled like raisins waiting to have hernias the size of footballs removed from their bellies, fifty year-old women with deeply creased and cracked faces looking forward to the day they could walk without a prolapsed uterus hanging between their knees, and babies with dark eyes full of hope and love, their mouths grotesquely deformed by cleft lips waiting for a new smile: these were the people I spent my days with. Their graciousness and gratitude nourished me. In addition, I often visited the residential patients of the hospital, all of whom had some type of severe physical or mental disability. Many of them were tied into wheelchairs, adults and children alike, and spent the day in front of the droning television or sitting in a hallway. They lacked stimulation and would sometimes scream out or cry if they could not speak, hoping for some attention. I fell in love with the residential patients of the hospital. They desired nothing more than a hug, a listening ear, someone to hold their hand when they were in pain. I became that person for them, and in turn they did the same for me.

Most days my sexual orientation didn't even come to mind because my work was so consuming. After awhile it became a non-issue for me as it didn't even seem to be relevant when all around me people were struggling just to survive. I thought I could just let it go and be happy. Yet the constant denial of myself, making up excuses for why I didn't have a boyfriend, inventing boyfriends from the past to be part of a conversation, pretending I liked being gawked at and propositioned, it brought me down and began tearing me apart little pieces at a time. The joy and fulfillment I found in my work wasn't enough. While my sexual orientation is certainly not my defining feature as a person, it remains part of me, and denying that one part of my identity created chaos within me as a person. The closet I had chosen to re-enter was killing me. The darkness began to consume me and I couldn't see to get out. I didn't realize it until a few years later, but denying and lying about my sexual orientation actually caused me to fall into a profound depression.

There are many more stories about my time in Guatemala, both happy and sad, but what I came away learning from the whole experience is that truth is the greatest freedom, being honest about who you are and embracing and accepting that person is the first step on the path to happiness. I thought I had learned this while at St. Kate's, but my world changed so dramatically when I went to Guatemala that I threw away all I had learned. I was afraid; I was so fearful that I preferred crawling back into the darkness rather than risk rejection. I don't know what would have happened to me if I had been honest about my sexual orientation. A Guatemalan friend of mine, a woman in her early thirties, went through the coming out process while I was in Guatemala. Her family literally kicked her out of the house and disowned her when she told them she was a lesbian. They threatened her to the point that she sought and was granted asylum in the United States. After this experience I realized how fortunate and truly blessed I am to be from a more tolerant country and have the loving support of my family.

After a year and half reprieve and recovery in the United States, I am currently living in Colombia, where I teach English at a Catholic girls' school. I live in Bogota, the capital city, and have found that it is more open and tolerant of sexual orientation. I am able to have discussions about sexual orientation with my high school classes and I secretly cheer in my head when I hear my students talk about their gay friends. Nonetheless, I have to pick and choose with whom I share my life and I don't ever foresee being completely "out" while in this country. Some people might say I am a "sell-out," that I am embarrassed or ashamed of being a lesbian. I wonder and worry about this too, but I am proud to say the closet door is open. I am no longer trapped in the darkness and I think the experiences I have had are teaching me the importance of owning self-identity. I am a lesbian. I do not deny it, and in fact, I am learning to rejoice in who God has made me. It has not been an easy road, and I know it will never be, but it is a road I am choosing to take because it is the only road that will lead me to truth, freedom, and perhaps even a bit of happiness.

Amy Tan is the author of many works for children and adults, including the award-winning novels The Joy Luck Club *(1989) and* The Bonesetter's Daughter *(2001). Tan's parents emigrated to the U.S. from China in the late 1940s. Her personal experience as a first-generation Chinese-American informs the following text, which first appeared in* The Three-penny Review *(1990). In "Mother Tongue" Tan explores the complex and reciprocal relationship between language, culture, family, and identity through a personal narrative about her experience with what she calls several "different Englishes." How has Tan's experience with English affected her conception of self as well as her assessment of her own work as a fiction writer in English? How would you describe the relationship you perceive between the language(s) you use, the culture(s) and family(ies) you come from, and your identity?*

Mother Tongue

Amy Tan

I am not a scholar of English or literature. I cannot give you much more than personal opinions on the English language and its variations in this country or others.

I am a writer. And by that definition, I am someone who has always loved language. I am fascinated by language in daily life. I spend a great deal of my time thinking about the power of language—the way it can evoke an emotion, a visual image, a complex idea, or a simple truth. Language is the tool of my trade. And I use them all—all the Englishes I grew up with.

Recently, I was made keenly aware of the different Englishes I do use. I was giving a talk to a large group of people, the same talk I had already given to half a dozen other groups. The nature of the talk was about my writing, my life, and my book, *The Joy Luck Club*. The talk was going along well enough, until I remembered one major difference that made the whole talk sound wrong. My mother was in the room. And it was perhaps the first time she had heard me give a lengthy speech, using the kind of English I have never used with her. I was saying things like, "The intersection of memory upon imagination" and "There is an aspect of my fiction that relates to thus-and-thus"—a speech filled with carefully wrought grammatical phrases, burdened, it suddenly seemed to me, with nominalized forms, past perfect tenses, conditional phrases, all the forms of standard English that I had learned in school and through books, the forms of English I did not use at home with my mother.

Just last week, I was walking down the street with my mother, and I again found myself conscious of the English I was using, and the English I do use with her. We were talking about the price of new and used furniture and I heard myself saying this: "Not waste money that way." My husband was with us as well, and he didn't notice any switch in my English. And then I realized why. It's because over the twenty years we've been together I've often used that same kind of English with him, and sometimes he even uses it with me. It has become our language of intimacy, a different sort of English that relates to family talk, the language I grew up with.

So you'll have some idea of what this family talk I heard sounds like, I'll quote what my mother said during a recent conversation which I videotaped and then transcribed. During this conversation, my mother was talking about a political gangster in Shanghai who had the same last name as her family's, Du, and how the gangster in his early years wanted to be adopted by her family, which was rich by comparison. Later, the gangster became more powerful, far richer than my mother's family, and one day showed up at my mother's wedding to pay his respects. Here's what she said in part:

"Du Yusong having business like fruit stand. Like off the street kind. He is Du like Du Zong—but not Tsung-ming Island people. The local people call putong, the river east side, he belong to that side local people. That man want to ask Du Zong father take him in like become own family. Du Zong father wasn't look down on him, but didn't take seriously, until that man big like become a mafia. Now important person, very hard to inviting him. Chinese way, came only to show respect, don't stay for dinner. Respect for making big celebration, he shows up. Mean gives lots of respect. Chinese custom. Chinese social life that way. If too important won't have to stay too long. He come to my wedding. I didn't see, I heard it. I gone to boy's side, they have YMCA dinner. Chinese age I was nineteen."

You should know that my mother's expressive command of English belies how much she actually understands. She reads the *Forbes* report, listens to *Wall Street Week*, converses daily with her stockbroker, reads all of Shirley MacLaine's books with ease—all kinds of things I can't begin to understand. Yet some of my friends tell me they understand 50 percent of what my mother says. Some say they understand 80 to 90 percent. Some say they understand none of it, as if she were speaking pure Chinese. But to me, my mother's English is perfectly clear, perfectly natural. It's my mother tongue. Her language, as I hear it, is vivid, direct, full of observation and imagery. That was the language that helped shape the way I saw things, expressed things, made sense of the world.

Lately, I've been giving more thought to the kind of English my mother speaks. Like others, I have described it to people as "broken" or "fractured" English. But I wince when I say that. It has always bothered me that I can think of no way to describe it other than "broken," as if it were damaged and needed to be fixed, as if it lacked a certain wholeness and soundness.

I've heard other terms used, "limited English," for example. But they seem just as bad, as if everything is limited, including people's perceptions of the limited English speaker.

I know this for a fact, because when I was growing up, my mother's "limited" English limited *my* perception of her. I was ashamed of her English. I believed that her English reflected the quality of what she had to say. That is, because she expressed them imperfectly her thoughts were imperfect. And I had plenty of empirical evidence to support me: the fact that people in department stores, at banks, and at restaurants did not take her seriously, did not give her good service, pretended not to understand her, or even acted as if they did not hear her.

My mother has long realized the limitations of her English as well. When I was fifteen, she used to have me call people on the phone to pretend I was she. In this guise, I was forced to ask for information or even to complain and yell at people who had been rude to her. One time it was a call to her stockbroker in New York. She had cashed out her small portfolio and it just so happened we were going to go to New York the next week, our very first trip outside California. I had to get on the phone and say in an adolescent voice that was not very convincing, "This is Mrs. Tan."

And my mother was standing in the back whispering loudly, "Why he don't send me check, already two weeks late. So mad he lie to me, losing me money."

And then I said in perfect English, "Yes, I'm getting rather concerned. You had agreed to send the check two weeks ago, but it hasn't arrived."

Then she began to talk more loudly. "What he want, I come to New York tell him front of his boss, you cheating me?" And I was trying to calm her down, make her be quiet, while telling the stockbroker, "I can't tolerate any more excuses. If I don't receive the check immediately, I am going to have to speak to your manager when I'm in New York next week." And sure enough, the following week there we were in front of this astonished stockbroker, and I was sitting there red-faced and quiet, and my mother, the real Mrs. Tan, was shouting at his boss in her impeccable broken English.

We used a similar routine just five days ago, for a situation that was far less humorous. My mother had gone to the hospital for an appointment, to find out about a benign brain tumor a CAT scan had revealed a month ago. She said she had spoken very good English, her best English, no mistakes. Still, she said, the hospital did not apologize when they said they had lost the CAT scan and she had come for nothing. She said they did not seem to have any sympathy when she told them she was anxious to know the exact diagnosis, since her husband and son had both died of brain tumors. She said they would not give her any more information until the next time and she would have to make another appointment for that. So she said she would not leave until the doctor called her daughter. She wouldn't budge. And when the doctor finally called her daughter, me, who spoke in perfect English—lo and behold—we had assurances the CAT scan would be found, promises that a conference call on Monday would be held, and apologies for any suffering my mother had gone through for a most regrettable mistake.

I think my mother's English almost had an effect on limiting my possibilities in life as well. Sociologists and linguists probably will tell you that a person's developing language skills are more influenced by peers. But I do think that the language spoken in the family, especially in immigrant families which are more insular, plays a large role in shaping the language of the child. And I believe that it affected my results on achievement tests, IQ tests, and the SAT. While my English skills were never judged as poor, compared to math, English could not be considered my strong suit. In grade school I did moderately well, getting perhaps B's, sometimes B-pluses, in English and scoring perhaps in the sixtieth or seventieth percentile on achievement tests. But those scores were not good enough to override the opinion that my true abilities lay in math and science, because in those areas I achieved A's and scored in the ninetieth percentile or higher.

This was understandable. Math is precise; there is only one correct answer. Whereas, for me at least, the answers on English tests were always a judgment call, a matter of opinion and personal experience. Those tests were constructed around items like fill-in-the-blank sentence completion, such as, "Even though Tom was ____, Mary thought he was ____." And the correct answer always seemed to be the most bland combinations of thoughts, for example, "Even though Tom was shy, Mary thought he was charming," with the grammatical structure "even though" limiting the correct answer to some sort of semantic opposites, so you wouldn't get answers like, "Even though Tom was foolish, Mary thought he was ridiculous." Well, according to my mother, there were very few limitations as to what Tom could have been and what Mary might have thought of him. So I never did well on tests like that.

The same was true with word analogies, pairs of words in which you were supposed to find some sort of logical, semantic relationship—for example, "*Sunset* is to *nightfall* as ____ is to ____." And here you would be presented with a list of four possible pairs, one of which showed the same kind of relationship: *red* is to *stoplight, bus* is to *arrival, chills* is to *fever, yawn* is to *boring*. Well, I could never think that way. I knew what the tests were asking, but I could not block out of my mind the images already created by the first pair, "*sunset* is to *nightfall*"—and I would see a burst of colors against a darkening sky, the moon rising, the lowering of a curtain of stars. And all the other pairs of words—red, bus, stoplight, boring—just threw up a mass of confusing images, making it impossible for me to sort out something as logical as saying: "A sunset precedes nightfall" is the same as "a chill precedes a fever." The only way I would have gotten that answer right would have been to imagine an associative situation, for example, my being disobedient and staying out past sunset, catching a chill at night, which turns into feverish pneumonia as punishment, which indeed did happen to me.

I have been thinking about all this lately, about my mother's English, about achievement tests. Because lately I've been asked, as a writer, why there are not more Asian Americans represented in American literature. Why are there few Asian Americans enrolled in creative writing programs? Why do so many Chinese students go into engineering? Well, these are broad sociological questions I can't begin to answer. But I have noticed in surveys—in fact, just last week—that Asian students, as a whole, always do significantly better on math achievement tests than in English. And this makes me think that there are other Asian-American students whose English spoken in the home might also be described as "broken" or "limited." And perhaps they also have teachers who are steering them away from writing and into math and science, which is what happened to me.

Fortunately, I happen to be rebellious in nature and enjoy the challenge of disproving assumptions made about me. I became an English major my first year in college, after being enrolled as pre-med. I started writing nonfiction as a freelancer the week after I was told by my former boss that writing was my worst skill and I should hone my talents toward account management.

But it wasn't until 1985 that I finally began to write fiction. And at first I wrote using what I thought to be wittily crafted sentences, sentences that would finally prove I had mastery over the English language. Here's an example from the first draft of a story that later made its way into *The Joy Luck Club*, but without this line: "That was my mental quandary in its nascent state." A terrible line, which I can barely pronounce.

Fortunately, for reasons I won't get into today, I later decided I should envision a reader for the stories I would write. And the reader I decided upon was my mother, because these were stories about mothers. So with this reader in mind—and in fact she did read my early drafts—I began to write stories using all the Englishes I grew up with: the English I spoke to my mother, which for lack of a better term might be described as "simple"; the English she used with me, which for lack of a better term might be described as "broken"; my translation of her Chinese, which could certainly be described as "watered down"; and what I imagined to be her translation of her Chinese if she could speak in perfect English, her internal language, and for that I sought to preserve the essence, but neither an

English nor a Chinese structure. I wanted to capture what language ability tests can never reveal: her intent, her passion, her imagery, the rhythms of her speech and the nature of her thoughts.

Apart from what any critic had to say about my writing, I knew I had succeeded where it counted when my mother finished reading my book and gave me her verdict: "So easy to read."

Jan Oosting Kaminsky is a registered nurse who earned her PhD from John's Hopkins University in 2013. Her essay on choosing nursing as a career appears in Leading the Way: Young Women's Activism for Social Change *(2010). In it, Kaminsky charts her journey toward becoming a nurse and challenges the more traditional belief that nursing is "women's work," inferior to other more empowering fields of work for women. How does Kaminsky define "women's work" in this essay? What fields do you think of when you hear the term "women's work"? Has feminism influenced the profession of nursing or other female-dominated fields of work, particularly those taught here at St. Kate's? Has feminism affected your career choice?*

Choosing Nursing

A Feminist Odyssey

Jan Oosting Kaminsky

> *"Nursing . . . has faced the paradox of being women's work—invisible, devalued, underpaid—and yet a critical necessity to society."*
>
> —Andrist et al., *A History of Nursing Ideas*

For many middle-class women in our mother and grandmother's generations, the question was simply "Will you be a teacher or a nurse?" Young women expected to limit their aspirations to traditionally female careers with the understanding that they would limit or leave work when their children were born. Nursing has traditionally been seen as women's work; therefore, the history of nursing is directly tied to the evolution of the feminist movement. Our generation has been given the gift of choice to expand our possibilities, to embrace careers in the highest echelons of medicine, law, and business. Why, then, would any intelligent young Generation Y woman with these possibilities open to her choose nursing? My father asked me that very question when I told him that I was considering rejecting other career paths in favor of nursing. With the world at our feet, young educated women have choices. However, by the hundreds of thousands, young intelligent women (and men) *are* choosing this expanding occupation.

My road to the nursing profession was definitely nontraditional. During a college study-abroad semester in South Africa, I worked as an intern with a nongovernmental organization (NGO) that distributed health information to women in rural areas. We educated women of all ages about their rights under the relatively new Constitution. We handed out copies of a new women's health handbook that had been developed by NGOs working in the area to answer questions on issues ranging from divorce to reproductive rights and HIV/AIDS prevention and treatment. I began to realize that changing lives through health education and preventative treatment was a perfect match for my activist background and presented the excitement of a challenge. My experience during this internship was deeply influential in my decision to pursue a career in health care.

I graduated from college in May of 2001 and moved immediately to New York City to start my career as a research assistant at a major health care institution. Just four short months later, our country seismically shifted when terrorism hit home. The events of 9/11 caused many people to reevaluate their lives, and I was no exception. I realized that I had only so much time in my life to define and pursue my goals. As my first few months of independent young adulthood coincided with these horrific events, a new imperative that I had not felt before convinced me that "meaningful work" would need to define my career. At that time, I began to search for a field of work that would give me that chance, along with the job security and opportunities for growth that I knew were important to me.

After surveying several options in health care careers, I, like many of my colleagues, decided on nursing because of my deep interest in helping people get through times when they are less able to care for themselves. I explored my educational options and discovered programs for second-degree students in nursing. I immediately knew that this would be the perfect option for me. I chose the Johns Hopkins University School of Nursing and moved to Baltimore for an intensive accelerated program that would result in a bachelor's of science in nursing. For a little more than a year, I immersed myself in the culture of hospitals and health care, received my degree, and returned to New York to work. The nursing shortage was already in full swing, and I was hard at work at my first nursing job within two weeks of graduation. Because I have always had a rapport with children, a natural place for me seemed to be pediatrics. I accepted a position in a pediatric intensive care unit (ICU) close to my home in Brooklyn.

The most unexpected part of my early career as a novice pediatric ICU nurse was being invited so immediately into the most intimate details of the lives of the families for whom I was caring. As a new graduate, I did not fully understand the sheer humanity of the process. This aspect of nursing was, and continues to be, profoundly moving. Each day that I am at the bedside of a critically ill child with that child's family, I marvel at the strength and love that families are able to show despite the desperation they must feel. I have had the same experience from the other side in several circumstances with recent family illnesses, and I have experienced firsthand the importance of high quality nursing care and evidence-based practice. Having a career where you are so significant in the life experience of a stranger is stressful at times but often exhilarating as patients progress from illness to health.

I have a unique perspective on the nursing profession because my original undergraduate degree was in women's studies and history. Since I began nursing, my professional experience has been colored with those gendered lenses as I explore the connections between women's experiences in American society and within the field of nursing. In many ways, nursing and feminism have been two ships that passed in the night, with nursing still viewed by many traditional feminists as inferior to other fields. However, nursing has been influenced by feminism in ways both large and small, including the change of nursing uniforms from starched white skirts and pinned hats to gender-neutral scrubs in most places. The incursion of female physicians and male nurses has also had an influence as roles traditionally based on gender have evolved to be roles based on other types of hierarchy, which can have both positive and negative implications.

On the positive side, there has been a huge shift in the relationship between physicians and nurses. Gone are the days when (female) nurses would carry charts for (male) physicians or stand when physicians entered a room in the "hospital salute." This is due in part to the technology with which we work. Often a nurse is more familiar with a frequently used piece of equipment and is able to educate the physician. In general, nurses and doctors must work well together to reap the greatest benefit for the patient. It is essential that there be a level playing field on which all health care workers can come together to promote healing. Most health care professionals realize this, and in my experience there has been great professional collaboration, with due respect given for the ideas of all parties.

In the hospital setting, nurses and physicians work together on a minute-to-minute basis, and effective communication is required. Although the number of women physicians is now approaching 50 percent, many hospital-based positions are still filled by male doctors. The interaction between nurses and physicians has changed over the years as gender shifts have occurred. However, the leader–follower structure of the physician giving orders and the nurse carrying them out has a distinctly gendered feeling. In my experience in two different hospitals and seven different units, I have found most physicians to be respectful of the nursing role. The nurse is seen as the essential final link in the chain of care for the patient and is usually treated as such. Of course some physicians do not value the role of nurses and retain the old standards of seeing the nurse as not worthy of participation in the interdisciplinary health care team.

The interconnection of feminism and nursing has also had a complicated history. Since the 1970s, nursing and other female-dominated fields have been denigrated by many feminists who wanted young, educated women to embrace traditionally male-dominated professions. Women were encouraged by the so-called second wave to reject "women's work" and to become doctors, lawyers, and business leaders. They heeded this call in large numbers, causing important societal shifts in perceptions of the value of women's work in general and nursing in particular. Some of the women who would have taken these jobs in the past did not, leaving a gaping generational hole in the nursing profession. At the same time, hospitals were seeing more and sicker patients, and patients were living longer and requiring more nursing care due to improvements in technology, medications, and other therapies. Third-wave feminism has not taken a stance on nursing specifically, but this generation of feminists in general is more inclusive of women making radical or traditional decisions for themselves, including the decision to choose a field of work that is still dominated by women.

Nursing remains a women-centered profession, with men holding 6 percent of nursing jobs. Nursing is one of the few health care fields in which the number of women in academic positions is disproportional to the number of men; women hold greater than 95 percent of academic jobs in nursing. Of the top ten schools of nursing, ranked by the National Institutes of Health (NIH) in order of amount of funding, all ten are led by distinguished women deans. This imbalance should encourage men to come into the nursing profession, but we should also see it as an aspect of nursing to be celebrated. Women are in powerful, decision-making positions in all areas of nursing, and we should see this as empowering.

Nurses have been activists since the origins of the profession, caring for patients whose families refused to or were unable to. Nurse pioneers such as Florence Nightingale, Dorothea Dix, and Margaret Sanger believed that nurses were obligated to improve the lives of individuals and communities through their activism and public health improvements. Nurses were among the most prominent members of the antislavery movement and were active during the Civil War, before formal nursing education appeared in universities and hospitals. Louisa May Alcott, Harriet Tubman, and Sojourner Truth all nursed during the Civil War.[1] Nightingale herself was partially responsible for the evolution of nursing as a job for women. She believed that nursing was nurturing, an extension of women's role in the home, and she discouraged men from filling nursing positions. Unfortunately, her advocacy in this direction may have helped to lower the societal value of nurses as well as the level of compensation.

Since the Civil War, nursing has evolved exponentially. No longer are nurses the handmaidens of physicians; instead we are an integral part of the health care team, making interdisciplinary decisions to improve patient care. Young women and men now come to the nursing profession prepared for a challenging, technology-based, science-oriented curriculum. Every day we care for people being kept alive by machines and medications that were unimaginable even a generation ago. These technologies require caregivers with technological expertise and the ability to recognize subtle changes before they have consequences for the patient. Nurses are challenged scientifically in school, and this continues in the workplace with new technology information every day balanced with patient care and safety.

Many nurses have autonomy now that could only have been dreamt of in previous generations. Nurse practitioners (NPs) now number more than fifty thousand nationwide. In many states, they have full prescription privileges and can even admit patients to the hospital, but NPs have quite limited privileges in other states and must only work under the license of a physician. NPs are becoming a growing trend for many reasons, including the ability for insurance companies to cut costs for well-patient care using this option. Both salaries and malpractice insurance costs are lower for NPs than for physicians. Nurses have autonomy as well in the area of nurse midwifery and, through relationships with physicians and hospitals, offer women alternatives to the soaring cesarean section and epidural rates. There are departments of nursing at many prestigious Ivy League colleges and universities turning out nurses prepared at the master's and doctoral levels, primed for leadership positions at the helms of hospitals, businesses, and universities. Legal nurse consultants advise lawyers on health care–related cases, and nurse anesthetists are used frequently in critical care settings in many states. Nurses are valued across many disciplines for the "in the trenches" knowledge that they possess in the area of patient care and safety.

Nurses are well paid compared with many other entry-level/college graduate positions, with average starting salaries ranging from $45,000 in rural or outlying areas to more than $80,000 in some urban areas. The Bureau of Labor Statistics (BLS) reports the 2007 median wage for registered nurses in New Jersey to be $78,510.00.[2] Nursing offers the prospect of being paid well and treated as a professional while caring for and nurturing others during the most difficult times of their lives. Many nursing jobs offer flexible work schedules, such as working three twelve-hour shifts per week. This can be an extremely convenient schedule when raising children or attending graduate school to further your education. I did not have children when I made the decision to become a nurse, but now that I have two sons I have reaped the benefits of flexible scheduling, shift work, and the ability for work–personal balance that is missing from so many fields. This has been essential in my ability to both work full-time and dedicate to my children the time that they so richly deserve.

Bedside nurses play a central role in the health care structure caring most intimately for individual patients. I have been privileged to be a pediatric intensive care nurse, and I have seen the vital importance of safe staffing levels, a central problem facing our health care system today. Currently there is an acute state and national nursing shortage. In New Jersey alone, it is projected that there will be a shortage of more than 37,000 nurses statewide by the year 2020, the equivalent of 43 percent (out of a total of 100 percent) of needed nurses, according to the Bureau of Health Professions, Health Resources and Services Administration.[3] The Bureau of Labor Statistics estimates that more than one million new nurses must be attracted to the profession by the year 2012 to replace retiring nurses and meet the health care needs of an aging population.[4] According to the BLS, nursing leads all other professions in the projected need for workers in the years to come.

This shortage helps to give nurses a louder voice when advocating for improvements in working conditions and pay. Many states and individual hospital systems have strong nursing unions in place. These groups work to support the nursing role at the hospital and state levels, advocating for safe staffing levels and good salaries and benefits in this demanding career. Nurses have successfully lobbied for causes that affect all of American society, including staff-to-patient ratios, medication administration safety, and nonpunitive reporting of medical errors. Lobbying by organizations such as the American Nurses Association is essential in the improved health care of all Americans.

This year I will be starting in a doctoral program in nursing that I hope will guide me to influence the future of the profession, leading it through the increasing crises of personnel shortages, multiplying health care costs, and spiraling numbers of chronically ill patients. My graduate education will be fully funded by the Jonas Foundation, which has been established by the Jonas family, New York philanthropists who enable young nursing leaders to continue their educations in order to enter nursing academia, where there is a "shortage within a shortage." I have been incredibly fortunate to receive this fellowship, without which I would be unable to pursue an advanced degree. In today's nursing shortage, nurses have become that much more valuable. With increased demand come greater influence and a higher "value" placed on nursing. Nurses are no longer invisible as we reach for higher levels of autonomy and education, and we need to continue to advocate for appropriate wages, safe nurse to patient ratios, and quality health care for all.

In my doctoral research work, I will be studying the impact of domestic violence on children in the home, working with the New York City Mayor's Office to Combat Domestic Violence. I will have many opportunities to interact with people at their most vulnerable, and I have a responsibility to guide them well. This research topic suits me because it connects my women's studies background and nursing work with pediatric populations to advance families and affect public health for a large group of people.

I am fortunate that I became a nurse at the beginning of its current resurgence, when there were empty places to fill in nursing schools. Now large numbers of young women and men are choosing to enter nursing, but hundreds of thousands of qualified students are being turned away every year due to lack of nursing faculty to teach them. Additionally, the number of nurses retiring in the next few years far surpasses the number of new graduates projected to enter the field. To make matters even worse, the number of aging Americans who require more advanced health care is steadily rising, increasing the need for qualified nursing staff. Philanthropic and government money is being allocated to help nursing schools meet their needs. My doctoral scholarship will enable me to be trained not only as a researcher but also as a teacher, and I plan to be part of the solution to the problem of the faculty shortage in years to come.

Young women entering nursing will be replacing nurses of the baby boomer generation who are expected to begin to retire in the next few years. Young nurses will have unprecedented opportunities to lead and to steer the field of nursing toward future ports. Some feminists and women leaders have turned away from nursing in the past, seeing it as traditionally women's work. This view undermines nursing and indeed is counterintuitive; nursing should be valued that much more *because* of its history as a women's profession. As more men become involved in nursing, the entire field will benefit as men push for autonomy and competitive salaries alongside women. Feminists and all women should see nursing care for its power to heal physically and emotionally, and as a field in which women have always held sway and will continue to do so. We should embrace women's work as highly valuable when it is the choice of the individual woman to perform it. If the nursing profession is held up as a valued and interesting option for young, intelligent women of my generation, society as a whole will benefit from high-quality care and better health care outcomes.

Notes

Epigraph: Linda C. Andrist, Patrice K. Nicholas, and Karen A. Wolf, *A History of Nursing Ideas* (Sudbury, MA: Jones & Bartlett Publishers, 2005).

1 Ibid.

2 Bureau of Labor Statistics, "Occupational Employment and Wages, May 2007: 29-1111 Registered Nurses," September 30, 2008. http://www.bls.gov/OES/current/ 0es2911n.htm.

3 "National Advisory Council on Nurse Education and Practice: Second Report to the Secretary of Health and Human Services and the Congress," Health Resources and Services Administration, U.S. Department of Health and Human Services. http://bhpr.hrsa.g0v/nursing/NACNEP/reports/second/3.htm.

4 Bureau of Labor Statistics.

Brian E. Fogarty, professor of sociology at St. Kate's, came of age during the turbulent '60s—amid the Cold War, Beatlemania, and Vietnam. Born to a solidly working-class family, his college education opened up a world of ideas and interests that had previously been unknown or unappreciated. Besides teaching at St. Kate's, he is a writer of opera and a supporter of the arts. Fogarty asks us "why learn about the arts?" and gives us compelling reasons why we should. Do you agree with Fogarty's reasoning that art matters? He says artistic expression both conveys truths and is a way to explore truths. Can art do what words cannot? Do you agree or disagree that "to reject 'difficult' art in favor of what we like and are comfortable with is to reject a message"?

Art Matters

Brian E. Fogarty

The study of the arts is not new to any of us. We have taken "art class" since kindergarten, starting with finger painting and flower-pressing activities, and gradually gaining artistic sophistication through our school years. But one thing has remained consistent throughout our academic experience with art: for most of us, it has always been a less serious, non-academic class. Art class is fun; a break from books and tests. It's a chance for self-expression, unfettered by too much thinking or scholarly principles. In fact, one might argue that art is the course taken least seriously by students and school authorities alike. Even physical education classes involve a certain amount of exertion at least, and the importance placed in American society on fitness and competition is surely reflected in the authority of the PE coach. By the time we are in high school, only art retains its playful, non-serious status among our classes.

It's no wonder, then, that by the time we enter college, we might question the importance of art to the serious education we seek. Although our previous experience of the arts has been a break from the more serious routine of learning things, at least that education was free for most of us. We could afford the luxury of dabbling in something we had no real need to learn about, and besides, our younger years were less serious anyway. Today the stakes are higher: as college students we are motivated to learn something useful; we may even have specific career goals in mind—and college is expensive. In the end, it seems worthwhile to ask: why should we commit this kind of money and effort to something that seems recreational? Why *learn* about the arts?

I'd like to make the case that learning about the arts and about aesthetics in general is as important and as worthwhile as the learning you'll do about biology or literature or political science. Nor do I mean that it is important in some unspecified, vague way, perhaps because it will make you a better citizen, or because it will enrich your middle age when the pursuits of youth become less interesting. On the contrary, the study of aesthetics will make you a more skilled, more perceptive student right away, and it will make you a better qualified graduate. Whether you aspire to become a business executive, nurse, physicist, sociologist, or something else, the study of aesthetics will better qualify you for a career, and it will help that career advance more rapidly than it otherwise would. In short, *art matters,* and the study of art matters is an important part of serious higher education.

I don't mean to suggest that thinking a little about aesthetic values in *The Reflective Woman* or taking a course in art history or jewelry design will turn you from an intellectual ugly duckling into a magnificent swan. No single course or body of knowledge does that. I do believe, though, that learning about the arts is at least as useful as learning any other body of knowledge; say, chemistry or history or accounting. Here are some reasons why.

1. Art is another form of communication. We know that college work (and, by the way, the work of most professions as well) involves communicating ideas to people and understanding communications from others, usually through writing or speaking. And many of the ideas we deal with are fairly mundane ones. Ordinary words, in the form of essays, research reports, memos, and letters are usually good enough communications devices in these instances. But what happens when you need to express some subtle and complex idea about love, or faith, or freedom, or oppression? How many pages would it take for your essay to describe a strong feeling or passion about one of these ideas? At some point, you might depart from prose and write a poem, or perhaps words would simply fail altogether.

Yet music, film, painting, dance, even architecture—all the arts are exactly geared to expressing those very ideas and values that words fail to express. We are often "left speechless" by a work of art or music for precisely that reason—the work expresses something for which words are inadequate. After all, if words could be used to describe the ideas conveyed, we wouldn't need the art in the first place.

This is hardly a twentieth-century discovery, by the way. I once heard a lecture by an expert on Chartres cathedral, in which he demonstrated how its stained-glass windows were used to express the metaphorical subtleties of holy scripture. Each main window, it turns out, is actually a pair of windows: one side tells a New Testament story, while the other side shows the Old Testament parallel to it. The "language" of the images is capable of expressing the thematic similarities and contrasts between the two sources far more subtly and more efficiently than words could do—and this was just as well, since almost no one could read in the thirteenth century anyway. What an irony that the lowest serf of the middle ages may have understood the Bible in a more subtle way than we literate moderns do!

Art also has the advantage of speaking "below the surface" of consciousness. One doesn't always have to be trying to "read" a piece of art in order for it to communicate to us. For example, the U.S. Capitol building probably expresses both majesty and democracy, even to the casual visitor, better than reams of written material or lofty speeches. Try imagining a modern steel-and-glass capitol instead, or a gothic one, or a square one of red brick, and the impact of architecture becomes clear. And speaking of Washington, doesn't the starkness of the Vietnam memorial speak as clearly about the legacy of that war than all the heroic statuary we see commemorating World War II?

The trouble is, art is by nature subtle and it requires some effort to understand. Thus, our previous non-serious training in the arts—not only in school but throughout our experience—encourages us to reject a lot of difficult art, because it doesn't give pleasure right away, or sometimes not at all. This has a serious implication for our intellectual and professional development: that to reject "difficult" art in favor of what we like and are comfortable with is to reject a message. It's a little like deciding to read at only a fifth-grade level because all the stories are easy, happy ones. And this, of course, is nothing more than opting for ignorance. Shouldn't the task of higher education be to discourage this?

People are trying to communicate with us; to tell us things we can't understand any other way. They are artists, musicians, dancers, playwrites, poets, architects. And in fact, the more complex and subtle the idea being communicated, the more "difficult" the art is. The ability to participate in this sort of communication may not be very important to those in careers that don't involve subtleties. But people who make decisions for a living, who work at non-routine and complex jobs, are at a serious disadvantage if they haven't developed the skill to get something from a poem or painting or dance.

2. Art provides an analytical workout. I was a teenager in the summer of 1964 when the "British invasion" of rock music arrived on American shores. Literally dozens of recordings would be released by these new English groups every week. I remember a promotional contest that my local radio station ran at the time: they would play a new release from one of the new groups, and you would have to guess whether or not it was the Beatles. Sometimes it was, but often it was the Dave Clark Five, or Jerry and the Pacemakers or the Zombies or somebody else. Since nobody had heard the new release before, there was an interesting analytical task involved: you had to develop some concepts for determining whether the new song had the *sound* of the Beatles, or whether it was some other group. What made up the Beatles' sound? Were there certain characteristics of the melodies, or the lyrics, or the arrangements, that made them Beatles songs? I became very good at this by the end of the summer—though I can't put into words what rules or concepts or theories I used to distinguish the Beatles from the others.

A few years later I found myself in a large college lecture hall, trying to do the same thing with Beethoven and Mozart. As a matter of fact, the "game" hadn't changed much: the final exam consisted of listening to short recorded musical passages; we'd have to write down the composer's name for each one. Now, the hard way to approach this was to try to memorize which composer went with which recording. They were all on reserve at the library and we were to spend our evenings there drumming into our brains various tricks for linking them together ("It's a bird, it's a plane, it's a Mozart," sung to the tune of the Mozart piece that would be on the quiz, was one device). The smart students figured out the better tactic: to try to develop some analytic concepts for distinguishing Beethoven's sound from Mozart's—and Stravinsky's, Prokofiev's and Britten's and all the others.

The funny things is, while I had become adept at distinguishing very readily the Stones from the Beatles, I had great difficulty distinguishing the various symphonic composers from one another. And this was remarkable, since I'm sure that Beethoven's music was in its day considered as great a departure from Mozart as Pearl Jam is from Frank Sinatra. But to an eighteen-year-old whose experience had included little of this, it all sounded the same—the way that, say, traditional Japanese music still does to my unschooled ear.

The study of aesthetics thus affords us an opportunity to exercise our analytical powers in ways that are not always tapped by other academic work, and this is probably a worthwhile thing in itself. But still, what reason do we have to believe this exercise to be beneficial in a pragmatic way? Put bluntly, how will it make one a better physical therapist, or lawyer, or insurance underwriter? The answer is that these same analytical skills are the ones that professional people put to use every day. They are the mental faculties by which we make subtle decisions based on scanty information. The care of a patient, the handling of a personnel dispute, the tone of a memo, the design of a lesson plan—they all involve reading the subtle cues of a situation, forming categories and concepts, and applying them to a decision. They are the kind of skills that people might say "can't be taught" but rather are innate or acquired through long experience. People who possess these skills are simply considered "smart" people. But the fact is, they *can* be taught—you can learn them through study of the arts.

3. Art expresses political realities that must be reckoned with. The arts have a curious and ambivalent character regarding politics and morals. On the one hand, the arts tend to be at the forefront of avant-garde thinking, and seem to endorse and celebrate new lifestyles, challenge traditional values, and elevate the bohemian to the artistic elite. But on the other hand, the arts also express the traditions of a society, not only in what is portrayed but in who portrays it. A walk through your local art museum or a visit to Orchestra Hall will make the point: even now, there is a stunning overrepresentation of Europeans and men among the painters, composers, and performers. This is not simply to say that there is a conspiracy of white men at the "top" of the art world, although many will make that point persuasively. Rather, these biases of representation show us something more fundamental about our culture: that the dominance of one race and one gender runs deep in American society. I'd say, in fact, that they show precisely that this dominance is *not* a matter of the conspiracy of a few, but rather a deeply-rooted element of our national character. Frankly, this is much more difficult to swallow than a simplistic conspiracy theory, but it fits better with the facts.

At the same time, we often see in a typical visit to the museum a special exhibit of "Emerging African-American Artists" or "Women of the Arts and Crafts Movement," or "Caribbean Carnival Costume," each giving voice and exposure to a heretofore neglected cultural tradition. And this tells us something, too: that these groups are emerging, gaining force and recognition within the artistic community, finding their way into the public consciousness. Such exhibits were not so common fifty years ago, and it is a measure of social change that we see them in established museums and galleries today.

And it's not only the authorship of the arts that conveys political and social realities. The content of the paintings, photographs, and music also tells us something. How are women represented in 19th-century painting? Are they action figures, suffering saints, sex objects? What does Puccini's opera *Madama Butterfly* say about encounters between the industrialized world and the traditional one? Or about encounters between men and women? Or about Western stereotypes of Asians?

What is considered "acceptable" art in a certain place in a certain time tells us much about the values and ideals of the society that produced it—keeping in mind that art is a production not just of the artist but of the publishers, critics, and viewing or listening public as well. In the 1930's the Nazi regime banned "degenerate" art—that is, modern, Jewish, or politically critical art—allowing only heroic and representational works to be publicly displayed. It's easy for us today to see how wrong that was. But what's our own reaction to gay literature, or anti-American films, or avant-garde music? What does art and our response to it say about us as a people?

All of this aside, we must still address the question of how understanding the political and social realities we learn from art can help us in the "real" world. The answer, of course, is that the real world is full of the very people we've been talking about! Our workplaces are made up of people of different races, genders, sexual identities, political stripes. Even looking at it from a strictly pragmatic standpoint, is it good for our careers to remain ignorant of how things look and sound and feel to our colleagues, clients, patients, students, customers?

4. Art is a window to culture. We are told incessantly that we now live in a global society, and that we shall have to understand the values and beliefs of other cultures in order to be successful in our lives. This may not seem very relevant to us today, because American culture seems so pervasive throughout the world. But this won't last forever. There will come a time when Americans will have to compete in that global marketplace—and not only for resources and markets, but also in terms of language and ideas and values and traditions. What then? We shall have to understand deeply the meanings things have for people of other cultures—what ideals are important, what constitutes beauty, what is considered the best way to live. Our study of aesthetics will help us perceive these diverse points of view, especially if our studies include diverse aesthetic traditions.

But perhaps more important, the arts connect one deeply to one's *own* culture, and that is a fundamental human need. My total immersion in rock music as a teenager was the main way that I *was* a teenager. And we all take on and proclaim our cultural identity all the time through attending concerts, buying records, going to movies, buying clothes, and many other aesthetic activities. My aesthetic choices are a part of who I am—that is, my identification with a community—and it helps both to make me who I am and to communicate it to others. When those medieval serfs looked up at the impossibly soaring and airy space of Chartres cathedral and read the stained-glass windows, they must have felt a profound sense of belonging to something, and of understanding their own identity. These feelings cannot be imparted by words—they require forms of understanding that lie underneath the verbal realm we usually operate in. They require artistic expression and perception.

In the end, the study of aesthetics is the study of the meanings and ideas that make up one's own community, and to understand and appreciate the arts is to understand that community more deeply. I believe one reason many people—and not just students—chafe at understanding the arts is that much of the art we are shown seems to represent a community other than our own. We have already seen that this is true to some extent for people of color, women, and others who are underrepresented or under-appreciated overall in American society. But this hardly argues for a rejection of the study of art, for a retreat to ignorance. In fact, one could argue that this inequity alone justifies a serious effort to learn about the aesthetic dimension of life, simply because it reflects so well the position of various cultural groups in a society.

But curiously, there is a strong tendency even among Euro-Americans to reject learning about their own aesthetic traditions. There is a feeling that the art found in the museums and in the texts is of some other community than one's own, and that it is "shoved down the throats" of students by their professors. I know I experienced it as a younger man; I had to be dragged kicking and screaming to Picasso and Mozart by my professors too. In a sense, they really did represent a community foreign to me; one that I had little interest in and no claim to. But the fact is, so did all the other things I learned in college—the literature, the biology, the math, the philosophy, the political science. They were *all* part of a different world than the one I had inhabited until then: the world of the educated person. To incorporate that knowledge and to study those ideas would be to enter that community—and it would mean changing who I was.

Most of us like ourselves just fine the way we are, and I think the prospect of change in one's identity is a large part of the resistance to learning about the arts. It's more comfortable to hold on to one's own tastes and resist the new because in doing so we can remain our old familiar selves. In fact, this resistance to change tells us all by itself how important the arts are—they help us define and know ourselves. It's difficult to open up to new aesthetic tastes. In fact, we are more willing to explore new ideas about science or politics or ethics or even religion than we are to explore new aesthetic preferences, because they are in some ways more fundamental to our identity.

But do we come to college to stay the way we are? Isn't this supposed to be a period of exploration and growth? I believe that college is meant to be a life-changing experience; that we are supposed to emerge from our education with a somewhat different identity than the one we entered with. Any less wouldn't be worth the expense. Frankly, I am a different person than the one I was when I entered college, and I don't regret it. Nor have I really had to give anything up; for example, I never did lose my taste for rock music of the 60's and 70's. I've simply gained new interests that I didn't have then. In fact, "It's a bird, it's a plane, it's a Mozart" (Symphony No. 40) is a particular favorite.

Nancy A. Heitzeg, professor of sociology and co-director of the interdisciplinary program in critical studies of race and ethnicity at St. Kate's, is a leader in social justice advocacy in our community and beyond. She has published widely on issues of inequality and their intersection. In this essay, she presents us with certain facts about human society and asks us if they are justice issues. How do we decide what is right or just? We don't often consciously recognize the sources of our belief systems or the assumptions we are making. Heitzeg's analysis of the sources, standards, and scope of justice frameworks helps us to see different disciplinary approaches to justice. What are the sources of your sense of justice? Which framework provides the best guide for thinking about justice in your field of study and work?

Searching for Truths, Searching for Justice

Nancy A. Heitzeg

Facts, Values, Truths and Justice

"the earthen vessel may hold the sweet wine
the handwrought silver goblet—gall
the tattered cover—words of wisdom
the gold-edged leaf—the cruelest lie
stumbling words—love's true oath
the silver tongue—a razor's edge
the truth arrives disguised,
therein the sorrow lies"

—Jimmy Glass, 1984
Executed in Louisiana 1987[1]

Consider the following points:

- The richest 400 Americans—all billionaires—have a net worth of over $2 trillion, which is more than 1,000 times greater than the net worth of the 47 million poorest Americans. (Forbes 2013; Census Bureau 2012)
- Only 31 women are listed among the 400 richest Americans. The overwhelming majority directly inherited their wealth. Oprah Winfrey is one of two African Americans on the list and the only "rags to riches" story of the Forbes 400. (Forbes 2013)
- Nearly 47 million Americans live in official poverty (i.e., annual income of approximately $12,000 for a single person, $15,000 for a two-person household, and $23,000 for a family of four). A more accurate

indicator (i.e., relative poverty) would count over 60 million Americans as poor. (Census Bureau 2012)

- People of color, women, and children are disproportionately in poverty. Female-headed single-parent households represent 60% of the poor, and one-third of all female-headed households, one-third of racial/ethnic minorities, over 50% of children of color, and 22% of all children in the U.S. live in official poverty. (Census Bureau 2012)
- The U.S. has the second highest rate of child poverty, and the greatest extremes of income/wealth inequality, of any First World country. (United Nations Children's Fund, 2013)
- Anywhere from 1.5 to 3 million Americans are homeless at some point during the course of a year. Over 50% percent are families with children; 10 percent are over 65 years of age. (National Coalition for the Homeless, 2012)
- An estimated 14.5 percent of American households were food insecure at least some time during the year in 2012, meaning they lacked access to enough food for an active, healthy life for all household members. (Coleman-Jensen, Nord, and Singh, 2013)
- 23.5 million Americans live in food deserts, i.e. urban neighborhoods (1 mile radius) and rural towns (10 mile radius) without ready access to fresh, healthy, and affordable food. (USDA's Economic Research Service, 2013)
- Over 50% of the U.S. adult poor are working. Federal minimum wage is $7.25 an hour, although most independent estimates suggest that a living wage is may be $18 per hour. (U.S. Bureau of Labor Statistics, 2011; Living Wage Calculator 2013)
- Women, on average, still earn only 81 cents for every dollar men make. in 2012, Asian women earned 73 percent of Asian men's earnings; Black women, 90 percent of Black men's earnings; and Hispanic women, 88 percent of Hispanic men's earnings. White women earned 81 percent of White men's earnings.(Corbett and Hill, 2013; U.S. Bureau of Labor Statistics, 2013)
- The typical woman with a Ph.D. degree earns less than the typical male with a B.A. degree. (Corbett and Hill, 2013)
- There are no Federal Civil Rights protections in the U.S. for GLBT persons and only 15 states offer full protection against any discrimination based on sexual orientation and gender.(American Civil Liberties Union [ACLU], 2013; Human Rights Campaign [HRC], 2013)
- The U.S. has more than 2.4 million persons in prison; this is the highest incarceration rate in the world as the U.S. has 5% of the world's population and 25% of all inmates. The majority of inmates are serving

time for non-violent property and drug offenses. (Bureau of Justice Statistics, 2012; Snetencingproject 2013)

- Corporate "crime results in 5 times more deaths and at least 10 times more economic loss every year than "street crime". (Simon, 2011; Federal Bureau of Investigation [FBI], 2012)
- Although there are no racial differences in participation in crime, African Americans and Latinos are approximately 10 times more likely to be arrested and more than 7 times more likely to be incarcerated than whites. (Walker, Spohn, and DeLone, 2012)
- There are more than 3100 prisoners on death rows federally and in the 32 states that allow for capital punishment. African Americans and Latinos comprise 25% of the U.S population, but account for nearly 60% of death row inmates. (Death Penalty Information Center, 2013)
- Women do nearly 70% of the world's unpaid labor. (Miranda, 2011)
- Nearly a billion people entered the 21st century unable to read a book or sign their names. Two of every three of these illiterate people are women. (United Nations Statistics Division, 2012)
- One half of the world's 7 billion people live on the equivalent of $2 per day. (United Nations Statistics Division, 2012)
- Every 3.6 seconds, some dies of hunger. (United Nations Statistics Division, 2012)
- 80% of the grain produced in the U.S. each year is fed to livestock and 70% of all antibiotics produced annually are used for the production of meat. (United Nations Environmental Programme 2010; National Resource Defense Council, 2012)
- Over 32 billion animals are killed in the U.S each year for food. More than 100 million more are killed for fur, laboratory research or in the course of providing entertainment. (Mohr 2012; People for the Ethical Treatment of Animals [PETA], 2012)
- Agriculture, particularly meat and dairy products, accounts for 70% of global freshwater consumption, 38% of the total land use and 19% of the world's greenhouse gas emissions. (United Nations Environmental Programme 2010)
- The U.S. represents 5% of the world's population and consumes over 25% of all fossil fuels, 20% of metals and 33% of paper. The U.S. is responsible for the creation of nearly 75% of the world's hazardous waste every year. (Shah, 2013)
- Humans have destroyed more than 30 percent of the natural world since 1970. (Shah, 2013)

All of the preceding points are "facts"; they are empirically measurable by scientists and social scientists using multiple methods, both quantitative and qualitative. Many of these facts are also long-standing; for example, extremes of wealth and poverty in the U.S. and the world represent patterns that have remained relatively unchanged for hundreds of years. There are minor fluctuations, some small movement and minor change over time, but the general pattern remains. Consequently, these statistics are widely accepted as accurate, as factual, as "true."

Unlike the truths of the natural world, however, these truths are socially constructed, i.e. they are the result of human activity, of social interaction, of institutional and organizational arrangements, of social structures and status inequality, of public policy, political decisions and economic endeavors. These "truths" are created by social action and, as such, they can also be changed by social action. And unlike the truths of the natural and mathematical sciences, these social facts of poverty and racism and sexism and more evoke an evaluative response. It is unlikely that "$e=mc^2$" or the Pythagorean Theorem calls us to an emotional response, or to a judgment. We do not assess them as morally "right" or "wrong," "fair" or "unfair"—they simply are. But the social truths cited above raise these very questions for us—we are left asking about fairness, about equity, about values. We are left asking about justice.

And are these justice issues? It is likely that most of us would answer yes. When pressed, however, to elaborate as to why, and how, and for what reasons, we may have more difficulty responding. Justice, it seems, is easy to intuitively acknowledge, but more difficult to articulate. Justice for whom? By what standards? According to which perspectives—social, economic, political, legal, theological, philosophical, ecological? To what end? What exactly do fairness, equality and freedom mean? What rights do we have? What rights should we have? And what are our obligations?

Fortunately we are not alone in our questioning or our search for answers. Debates over justice are timeless and as varied as historical experience. Questions of justice have been raised and disputed, asked, answered and re-asked by theologians, philosophers, political theorists, economists, sociologists, biologists and grassroots activists as well. All of the disciplines of the Liberal Arts and Sciences offer us either explicit or implicit perspectives on justice, and offer us some guidance in discussing justice and action. (See Appendix.) Poets and artists, philosophers and theologians, social and natural scientists have all explored the truths of human society and the human experience in the socially constructed and perhaps, unjust, world.

Often these discussions are explicit, expressly directed towards defining justice. Such is the case with many religious tracts, political treatises, and philosophical essays. Similarly, analyses of justice are also found in the writings of sociologists, anthropologists, historians and political scientists, among others. Issues of justice also form the foundation for many areas of interdisciplinary studies, which emphasize the vantage point of disenfranchised groups. Women's Studies, GLBT Studies, Racial/Ethnic Studies and Post-Colonial Studies are all cases in point. In all of these areas, issues of justice are at the fore; indeed, a primary goal of the discipline is to advance discourse on issues of justice.

On other occasions, perspectives on justice are emergent, less overtly articulated, but present nonetheless. Some of these are implicit in the theoretical perspectives and applications of various disciplines of the humanities—literature, art, music and theater, and in the social and natural sciences as well. Here, notions of equity, of balance, of resource allocation provide a seminal justice/action framework. Other emergent views of justice and action emanate from the grass roots, from every day understandings of the world, from patterns of interaction with others, nature and the unseen. These are worldviews, ways of life which are based on a taken for granted notion of what constitutes justice and right action. Grassroots perspectives on justice and action also arise under duress, from spontaneous collective responses (e.g. demonstrations, riots, and revolt) to perceived injustice. These latent definitions of justice may become manifest in the face of oppression, and what was unclear becomes certain as the people respond. In other words, notions of justice and also, of action, may be embedded in ways of thinking and being; these are implied rather than explicitly stated, but become apparent under closer examination.

Questions of truth, questions of justice are complex. Their exploration requires a critical examination of our values and those of the societies we live in. This exploration also requires critical analysis of evidence and argument and ultimately, it calls us to decide. What follows is an overview of general themes and considerations that can guide our analysis and our understanding.

Justice Frameworks

"The arc of the moral universe is long, but it bends towards justice..."

—Rev. Dr. Martin Luther King, Jr., 1968 [2]

While justice has been approached from many disciplinary perspectives, there are common themes. These themes serve as a framework for analyzing issues of justice and comparing possible responses; they offer a way of organizing and evaluating the common threads that are woven through most considerations of justice.

First of all, justice is ultimately a collective, rather than individual concern. Justice issues are issues of community, accountability, and right relationship. Justice issues have a broad impact, and even seemingly isolated incidents often have global connections. Many grassroots actions for justice emerge at the local level only to uncover links with global goals. Consider Lois Gibbs and Love Canal. In 1978, Lois Gibbs was a lower-middle-class housewife in Niagara Falls, who, with other women in her neighborhood, "became politicized by the life and death issues directly affecting their children and their homes." (Merchant, 2005, pp. 192–193) Gibbs and other members of the Love Canal Homeowners Association conducted studies documenting the health problems associated with the Hooker Chemical and Plastic waste site and succeeded in obtaining redress from the state of New York. As the involvement of these women deepened, they came to realize that the hazardous waste was not an isolated local problem. Similar action by women globally linked them together as ecofeminists—i.e., women who connect the liberation of women with that of nature As Carolyn Merchant (2005) writes, "From initial Not In My Back Yard (NIMBY) concerns, the movement has changed to Not In Anybody's Back Yard (NIABY) to Not On Planet Earth (NOPE)." (p. 193)

Secondly, justice issues are often systemic issues, i.e. they reflect larger structural patterns of inequality and disparity. All of the aforementioned statistics reveal structured inequality both globally and nationally. They all represent the consequences of systemic and institutionalized classism, racism, sexism, heterosexism, ageism, abelism, speciesism, and anthropocentrism. Consideration of justice issues as systemic requires distinguishing between what sociologist C. Wright Mills (1959) calls "personal troubles and social issues." (p. 45) If, for example, someone becomes poor due to laziness, bad habits, and inertia, that is a personal trouble. When, however, more than 47 million people (most of them women, children, persons of color, and senior citizens) live in absolute poverty in the richest nation in the world, this can no longer be attributed to personal failing. That is an issue of structured inequality, an issue of justice.

Thirdly, justice issues imply, indeed, impel action. Justice and action are inextricably linked. In fact some such as Gandhi argue that questions of justice and action are inseparable; "I would say means are after all everything. As the means, so the end." (Murton, 1964, p. 28) While our primary concern here is the analysis of justice issues, justice claims are more often than not, accompanied by calls to action. Conversely, spontaneous action is often later linked to broader justice issues. The Stonewall riots provide an example. On the fringes of the emerging gay liberation movement, the gay men, lesbians and transgender patrons who frequented the Stonewall Inn (a Greenwich Village bar) wanted merely to dance and socialize. But a night in late June 1969 changed all that. Fed up with perpetual police harassment and arrests, the patrons fought back as yet another police raid unfolded. The officers were outnumbered, and three days of street fights and skirmishes ensued. The event, now referred to as the Stonewall Riots, is widely regarded as the symbolic beginning of the gay liberation movement. Action led to activism (out of the closets and into the streets . . .) and many disenfranchised Stonewall patrons became part of the general movement for GLBT rights. (Duberman, 1993) What was initially a very specific response to perceived injustice became linked with general justice issues and broader goals, and in many respects, became a symbolic rallying point.

Finally, justice and action, despite their complexities and often, emotional overtones, can be critically analyzed. That is our primary objective here, to identify general themes and common threads that link the wide range of perspectives on justice and eventually lead us to imagine corresponding action. In general, discussions of justice share also these central features: all emerge from specific sources that frame the nature of the discussion and the criterion for evaluating justice; all identify standards by which justice/injustice is measured and meted out, and all, in varying degree, address the scope of justice—the range of Beings to which the standards apply. And finally, all, directly or indirectly suggest actions appropriate for achieving justice. Each will be considered in turn.

Sources

> *The white fathers told us: I think, therefore I am. The Black mother within each of us—the poet—whispers in our dreams: I feel therefore I can be free...*
>
> *For there are no new ideas. There are only new ways of making them felt. . . ."*
>
> —Audre Lorde, 1977[3]

Justice frameworks may be most immediately analyzed with reference to their inspirational sources. Perspectives on justice or conversely, injustice began with a particular worldview, a vantage point from which to gauge and assess. One of the most important steps in searching for truths and justice involves the identification of the source of the claims. The source reveals the types of arguments and evidence offered as well as the methods for arriving at an understanding of justice.

Historically and currently, justice has been defined from several perspectives: religious/spiritual, philosophical, political, and scientific—both natural and social. These sources continue to frame most discussions of justice.

The world's religions provide some of the oldest and most diverse perspectives on justice. Here justice is divinely revealed as absolute. All of the major world religions as well as nature-based perspectives of indigenous peoples include notions of duties, rights and standards of conduct. These outline just relationships between humans, the divine, and nature. Often, religious perspectives on justice have both sacred and secular implications. Divinely

Justice Frameworks

Sources

- Theological/spiritual
  (e.g., Catholic, Protestant, Judaic, Islamic, Eastern, Native American spirituality, feminist theology, revitalization)
- Political
  (e.g., Nationalist, Democratic/Pluralist, Socialist/Communist, Anarchist, international accords)
- Philosophical/Cosmological
  (e.g., idealism, materialism, utilitarianism, libertarian, communitarian, existentialism, feminist philosophy, post-modernism, Eastern philosophies, indigenous worldviews)
- Natural/Social Scientific
  (e.g., ecological, biological, psychological, anthropological, sociological, economic, demographic)

Standards

- universalism/absolutism
- relativism/particularism

- distributive
- commutative
- retributive
- restorative

- merit or need
- liberty or equality

Scope

- human-centered
  (e.g., exclusion/inclusion based on class, race/ethnicity, gender, sexual orientation, age, ability, religion, and nationality)
- eco-centered
  (e.g., earth-based religious/political movements, animal rights and green movements, Gaia hypothesis

Figure 1. Justice Frameworks

inspired justice should pervade this world as well as the next. (Catholic Social Teaching provides an excellent example of this and is discussed in detail in Dr. Connors' article later in this text). Indeed, for much of human history, sacred justice was synonymous with secular justice; it was "on Earth as it is in Heaven." (Connors, 2000; Ishay, 1997, 2004; Klass, 1995)

Of course, philosophy is an equally significant source regarding justice. From the early Greeks to the present day, explicit discussions of justice remain a central topic of philosophical debate. Philosophical views of the common good, universal rights and ethics, just distribution, and retribution have shaped both political and scientific views of justice. (Ishay, 2004; Shute and Hurley, 1993)

Political theorists, governmental legal systems and international bodies offer secular views of justice in treaties, constitutions, documents and accords. The common sense understandings that many hold regarding justice and the relationship between citizens and the state, civil rights and liberties, access to resources and just law and punishment derive from these legal/political documents. Originally, political notions of justice were most often discussed relative to the nation state. Many current political discussions of justice, however, are global; these emerge from international bodies such as the United Nations or transnational non-governmental organizations (NGO's) such as Amnesty International and Human Rights Watch.

The sciences, both natural and social, are less explicit sources on the topic of justice. Like political sources, earlier philosophical perspectives often inform these views. Although the term "justice" itself is rarely used, perspectives on justice are embedded in analyses of the social institutions and arrangements, the psyche and the natural world. The conflict paradigm in sociology for example, presents a clear commentary on structured inequality and its correlation with classism, racism, sexism, heterosexism, and ageism. (Collin, 1994) Similarly, ecology incorporates mechanistic models of science into a holistic view that emphasizes balance, biodiversity and sustainability. (Merchant, 2005) All the previous justice questions regarding distribution, rights, responsibilities and equity are implicit in these approaches.

It is crucial to note that these sources do not provide unified provide perspectives on justice. These sources of justice, in fact, are neither internally consistent nor mutually exclusive. There are vast disagreements within categories as well as points of congruence between them. Philosophers, for example, have debated for centuries over the nature of justice—is it an absolute ideal or a construct relative to socio-cultural circumstances? Is justice best represented by "the greatest good for the greatest number" or "from each according to his/her ability to each according to his/her need"? Is liberty, equal treatment, or equal opportunity the standard? (Ishay 2004; Lebacqz, 1986) Such is also the case with religious, political, and scientific sources; they share a certain starting point for framing justice, but diverge on its precise meaning.

There are, on the other hand, many similarities that exist between the different sources. Indeed some of the most compelling justice arguments are made by relying on. multiple sources to make the same central case. Perhaps one of the most striking examples of this congruency can be found in the life and work of Dr. Martin Luther King Jr. As a minister, president of the Southern Christian Leadership Conference, and a leader in the struggle for civil rights, he moved with ease from framing justice religiously and politically. Full civil rights for African Americans, he argued, must be granted for moral and political reasons. Legal segregation on the basis of race was both a sin and an affront to the Constitution of the United States. The Bible and the Bill of Rights both spoke to the issue, and, for King, were completely compatible sources on justice. (Carson et. al., 1991; Washington, 1992)

Sister Helen Prejean, CSJ, provides another excellent example of drawing upon the congruencies among justice frameworks. The author of *Dead Man Walking* (1993), *The Death of Innocents* (2005) and presenter at a CSC Core convocation in the fall of 1999, Sister Helen opposes the death penalty on several grounds: moral/theological, philosophical and political. As honorary chair of Moratorium 2000, a global grassroots campaign that aims towards the ultimate abolition of capital punishment, Sister Helen Prejean eloquently opposes the death penalty, first on the basis of Catholic social teaching on life. She also notes high financial and political costs, the issue of incompetent legal representation for poor defendants, the question of error and the execution of innocents, the question of cruelty in method of execution, and the race and class disparities in prosecution and conviction. All suggest U.S. constitutional violations of due process and equal protection as well as violations of standards set by the U.N. Commission on Human Rights.

These interconnections among seemingly disparate sources are closely related to questions of justice standards and scope. What constitutes justice? Who is justice for?

Standards

> *"What would the coal in the mines be worth if you did not work to take it out?*
>
> *You create its wealth, so I say let the fight go on . . ."*
>
> —Mary Harris "Mother" Jones, 1914[4]

The sources for framing justice arguments are only a starting point. The issue of how justice might be measured—what are the standards for justice—is at the heart of all discussions. Again, there are many questions and no definitive answers.

Three general dimensions of justice standards will be considered here. First of all, justice standards may be construed as universal or relative. Are there universal standards of justice that apply to everyone at all times and places? The relativists and subjectivists would say no. They argue that justice standards emanate from particular historical circumstances, perspectives or cultures. We cannot judge what works for others in the context of their culture, their time, their experience. This perspective is often rooted in a critique of supposedly universal standards as non-inclusive, and proceeds from the perspective of excluded groups. Relativistic standards of justice are explicitly expressed in strands of existential and feminist philosophy, in some variations of identity politics of racial/ethnic minorities, women, GLBT persons, and Third World nationalists; in the standpoint critiques of theory in the social sciences, the interdisciplinary approaches of women's, multicultural, and GLBT studies and in the religious/political agendas of liberation movements. (Ishay, 2004; Hill Collins, 1990; hooks, 1984; Cruikshank, 1992) Perhaps, the anthropological debate over "cultural relativism" represents one of the clearest discussions of relativistic views of justice in the social sciences. From this perspective, cultures can only be observed and described—they cannot be judged by any standards outside their own particular context (Ward, 1999; Walker A., 1992).

Proponents of the universalist position argue that justice standards are universally applicable, transcending time, culture, and social context—and often absolute. Until recently, the universalist approach has characterized most theological, philosophical, political and scientific views of justice. Discussions of divine and natural law, "the inalienable rights of citizens", and universal human rights as set forth by the United Nations all suggest universal standards. (Declaration of Independence, United Nations—See GSJ Resources, 644) The majority of explicit theological, philosophical, and political justice tracts are grounded in universal standards. So, too, are many of the more implicit justice perspectives that emerge from the sciences and the humanitarians as well as indigenous religions, and grassroots social movements.

One of the most heated debates over universal/relative justice standards is centered on the practice of female genital mutilation (FGM), which involves the removal of all or part of the external female genitalia without anesthetic. While FGM is practiced in other regions of the world, it is most widely practiced in Northern Africa, where over 100 million women have undergone the procedure. First brought to Western attention in the work of Alice Walker (i.e. *Possessing the Secret of Joy,* 1992 and *Warrior Marks,* 1999), FGM clearly illustrates the tension between universal and relative views of justice. Proponents contend that it is a cultural tradition that can only be understood and addressed from within. (Cohn, 2007) Opponents cite a long list of physical complications (e.g. infection, pain-induced shock, urine and menstrual retention, damage to the urethra, painful intercourse, greater risk of STD infection, and obstructed labor) and maintain that FGM is a civil rights issue for women, human rights violation and grounds for political asylum. (Cohn, 2007; Seager, 1997 pp. 52–53) As a result, the practice is increasingly banned in many regions of the world. The universal perspective on rights has largely prevailed here; Alice Walker (Walker and Parmar, 1999) so succinctly puts it, "Torture is not culture." (p. 95)

Discussions of the general or specific applicability of justice standards are closely intertwined with the universalism/relativism debate. Here, the debate centers on the extent to which justice standards apply to all areas of social life or are limited to certain select concerns. Philosophers and political theorists have provided most of the explicit discourse, here often dividing justice into four areas: distributive (i.e. distribution of rewards and resources), commutative (i.e. justice in exchange), retributive (i.e. justice in punishment), and restorative (i.e. justice in compensation). (LeBacqz, 1986) Perspectives on justice may encompass some or all of these. Many theological and political perspectives often encompass all four, as part of divinely sacred and secular justice. (Ishay, 2004)

Certain political perspectives and grass roots movements, on the other hand, narrow the focus. Libertarians, for example, emphasize commutative justice in exchange, arguing that the only just government intervention involves minimal regulation of the economy to insure equitable exchange. (Lebacqz, 1986; Ishay, 1997) In contrast, civil rights movements of disenfranchised groups often argue for distributive justice. Globally, for example, women perform nearly 70% of the world's unpaid labor, are more likely than men to live in poverty, and earn less than 80% of what men make for comparable work. Women are over-represented in the lower wage sectors of economies, and are disproportionately employed in the unprotected enterprise zones of the global economy. (Mather, 2011) These are clearly issues of distributive justice.

Retributive and restorative justice are concerns for groups who focus on issues related to the criminal, civil, and administrative law, such as racial profiling, incarceration, capital punishment, political prisoners, calls for compensation and reparations (Davis, 2003; Magnani and Wray, 2006; Walker, Spohn and DeLone, 2005) Supporters of retribution make the claim that it is just to punish and often to punish harshly with long imprisonment or death. Others argue that justice requires a restored balance—the righting of a wrong—whether it be to a victim of crime or a group that has been harmed by practices of the past. Victim—offender mediation programs, restitution, and the call for reparations—to the descendants of slaves, the survivors of the Holocaust or Native Americans who have been robbed of lands—are all examples of restitutive or restorative justice. (Winsbush, 2003; Robinson, 2000)

The final dimension relative to justice standards is the hallmark, the ultimate measure of justice. How old we measure justice? What is the central, essential feature? This is the subject of much debate within and between all the perspectives on justice and is at the heart of much theological, philosophical, and political literature on justice. In general, discussions of justice often make reference to key concepts such as merit and/or need, liberty and/or equality. Again, these are illusive concepts, which are variously defined in religious documents, philosophical tracts and the constitutions of nation states. (Ishay, 1997, 2004; Shute and Hurley, 1993)

Most national constitutions for example, enumerate the rights and freedoms available to all or particular groups of citizens. The United Nations Universal Declaration of Human Rights, however, lists rights that seem applicable to everyone regardless of nationality; ". . . recognition of the inherent dignity and of the equal and inalienable rights of all members of the human family is the foundation of freedom, justice and peace in the world." (United Nations, 1999, p.21) (See Appendix.)

More importantly, however, is the prioritizing of these standards. Liberals, particularly in capitalist Western democracies, tend to hold freedom and liberty central to justice. This often refers to a "free-market" where there are limited governmental interventions in the economy. The rights of individuals, then, especially those safeguarding freedoms, take precedent over equality. The rights of free speech, to keep and bear arms, to own/accumulate private property, to pursue happiness, are supposedly universal standards of justice. In the U.S. however, the emphasis on liberty in law and public opinion, however, leads to a limited definition of equality. Equal access to all social resources, in most liberal analyses of justice, is a lesser hallmark of justice that is limited by individual merit, rights, and liberties. (LeBacqz, 1986; Ishay, 2004) Equality, then, is frequently defined in the most minimal of terms, as equal protection under the law. It has, rarely meant equal access to rewards and resources, a point that is painfully clear to the poor, people of color and women. This prioritizing of liberty over equality helps us understand the high rates of poverty and homelessness in the richest nation on earth.

Socialists/Marxists, on the other hand, regard economic equality and freedom from economic oppression as the precondition for justice. Need, not merit, is the measure; the famed Marxian dictum speaks directly to this point—"from each according to their ability to each according to their need" (Tucker, 1972, p. 383). Further, individual freedoms, especially those related to material accumulation, are defined as lesser considerations subject to restraint in pursuit of the higher standard and the communal good. (Marx and Engels, 1948; Tucker, 1972; Shiva, 1997, 2000) Consequently, the socialist democracies of western Europe and elsewhere take for granted that citizens will have the right to free education, adequate housing, multiple employment benefits and universal health care—issues that are often highly contested in the U.S. Indeed, much historical conflict over the ideologies of capitalism and socialism / communism revolve around the standards of justice and the value of freedom vs. equality, merit vs. need, the right to accumulate wealth vs. the right to basic necessities of survival.

Finally, the definitions of justice standards such as freedom, equality, and rights are shaped by considerations of the scope of justice, i.e. justice for whom and why? To whom do these standards apply? Who has standing to receive justice?

Scope

> *"I saw the whole globe symbolized at Auschwitz, and it was covered in blood: people being manipulated and used; animals tortured in useless experiments; men hunting helpless, vulnerable creatures for "thrill"; human beings ground down by inadequate housing and medical care and by not having enough to eat; men abusing women and children; people polluting the earth, filling it with poisons that foul the air, the soil, and the water; the imprisonment of dissident voices; the elimination of people of opposing political views; the oppression of those who look, act or feel differently."*
>
> —Judy Chicago, 1993[5]

Questions of scope are significant considerations in all discussions of justice. Scope, here, refers to the range of persons and / or beings to which justice standards apply. It refers to considerations of inclusion and, conversely, discrimination, as well as human-centered and eco-centered claims.

Perspectives on justice—from all sources—have long held that justice was a concept applicable and available to humans. On closer examination, however, it is clear that historical and contemporary perspectives have frequently narrowed the concept of justice, which permits the exclusion of certain categories of persons.

Prior to the twentieth century, the classical philosophical, theological, and political perspectives of the West have limited justice to those who were deemed "deserving" by nature or "reason", or nationality or "morality". Almost invariably, this led to the dehumanization and subsequent oppression of persons who allegedly failed to meet these standards. As Richard Rorty (1993) notes, "For most white people, until very recently, black people did not so count. For most Christians, up until the seventeenth century or so, most heathens did not so count. For the Nazis, Jews did not so count. For most males, in countries where the average annual income is under $4000, most females still do not so count. Whenever tribal and national rivalries become important, members of rival tribes and nations will not so count." (p. 263)

Philosophically and theologically, such a narrow scope of justice allowed seemingly "righteous" and "reasonable" men to endorse slavery, conduct inquisitions, colonize, and exterminate indigenous peoples globally, brutalize women and children in the name of discipline and property rights, and execute anyone who deviated from proscribed norms of sexual conduct. (Golden et. al., 1991)

Politically, this constricted view of personhood allowed even the "enlightened" Western democracies to limit those so-called universal and "inalienable" rights to white men who owned property. At the time of its writing, the rights and freedoms enumerated in the U.S. Constitution were only available to white, adult, property owning males. Native Americans—the only indigenous Americans—are mentioned in the Declaration of Independence as the "merciless Indian savages, whose known rule of warfare, is an undistinguished destruction of all ages, sexes, and conditions." (Declaration of Independence, p.7) African Americans, then enslaved, were counted as three-fifths of a person for purposes of determining state population size and subsequent representation. They remained property (a point reinforced by several Supreme Court decisions) until the ratification of the Thirteenth Amendment in 1865. (Constitution of the United States, pp. 14, 42) Women, of course, were not citizens either and were, for all intents and purposes, the property of their parents or husbands. Full Constitutional rights were finally extended to women with the passage of the Nineteenth Amendment in 1920. (Constitution of the United States, p. 48)

Constricted views of personhood and consequently justice are not limited to the past. In the U.S., federal law did not prohibit discrimination against racial/ethnic minorities, women, the differently abled, and senior citizens until the mid-1960s. GLBT persons and those under eighteen still do not have the full rights of citizenship here, and GLBT persons, in particular, are denied federal civil rights protections against discrimination in several areas including employment, housing, family relationships, the military, security clearances, and matters of the criminal law. (ALCU, 2007; HRC, 2007) In addition, many contend that the theoretical inclusion of formerly disenfranchised groups in constitutional claims of justice does not necessarily translate into justice in practice. As noted before, equal protection under the law does not translate into equal access to social resources. The persistence of institutionalized classism, racism, sexism, heterosexism and ageism is well documented and continues to be regarded as just by certain groups of religious and political conservatives. (Feagin, 2014; Bonilla-Silva, 2013)

Globally, the scope of justice also continues to be narrowly construed. Despite the broadly based universal human rights outlined in a series of international accords, a variety of explicit and implicit theological, philosophical, and socio-political perspectives exclude certain persons from the purview of justice. Race/ethnicity, gender, sexual orientation, age, and religion remain the source of devalued status in many regions of the world.

The system of apartheid in South Africa remained legal until 1992, and the ill effects are still felt by the black majority. (Bratton, 1998) Similarly, post-colonial religious and ethnic conflict rages from Bosnia to Iraq, throughout the continent of Africa to Indonesia to beyond. Women are still denied social and legal rights in many areas of the world. They remain the property of men, are denied access to education, restricted in their movements, are bought, sold, beaten, mutilated, forced to labor, raped and killed at will. So, too, in most of the world, GLBT persons and children are often excluded from the scope of justice. Same-sex activity is still illegal in most nations of the world, and GLBT persons continue to be religiously and politically persecuted. Children are parental property and, in spite of international standards to the contrary, over 75 million children under fifteen labor, often in sweatshop conditions. (Seager, 1997; Population Reference Bureau [PRB], 2006)

The scope of justice is not always so narrow. More inclusive perspectives flourish as well. Historically, these can be found in some strands of early Greek philosophy, and the nature-based religions of many indigenous peoples, the universal tenets of Buddhism, which extend to all sentient beings; and the informal, non-stratified political arrangements of foraging bands. (Ishay, 2004; LaDuke, 1999; Ward, 1999) Some of these perspectives are supported by extensive writings; others are reported in the anthropological and historical literature. All, however, limit social differentiation and inequality and extend the scope of justice at minimum, to all humans.

Several Western-based theological, philosophical, and political perspectives also broaden the scope. Progressive interpretations of Christianity include all people and often advocate for secular justice for all, as well. Many Catholic and Protestant theologians have been involved in the struggle for civil rights, economic justice, and women's rights on religious as well as political grounds. Catholic social teaching holds up the dignity of every person and the preference for the poor as key tenets. (Connors, 2000; Hennelly, 1990) Feminist theology has also expanded traditional interpretations of Christianity to be more inclusive of the role(s) of women, both spiritually, and in institutional roles on the church. (Johnson, 1993) Johnson does not appear in your reference list.

In the past 150 years, the identity politics of disenfranchised groups have staked both explicit and implicit claims for inclusion within justice frameworks. The poor, racial/ethnic minorities, women, religious sects, senior citizens, the differently abled, and GLBT persons through social action and interdisciplinary writings have continued to push the margins of justice debates. Much of this work is rooted in a critique of the narrow Eurocentric patriarchal view of justice held by many Western political and philosophical frameworks. A vast array of work is included here: socialist critique of capitalism ranging from Marx to the present; feminist and post-colonial philosophy, political theory; critical, conflict, and standpoint theory in sociology; multicultural and feminist perspectives in a variety of disciplines, and political demands for inclusion that range from abolition and Seneca Falls, to the Civil Rights era and beyond. (Ishay, 1997, 2004; Tucker, 1972; Burns, 1990) The common feature of all is a broad-based scope of justice that seeks to include all persons within existing socio-political parameters of justice or abandon them in favor of non-discriminatory alternatives.

At the heart of all these claims are several key points. Oppressions intersect; class, race, gender, sexual orientation and age are sources of interrelated disadvantages and subsequent injustice. Further, justice is not a commodity that can be parceled out to some and not all. It is an all or nothing proposition. As Martin Luther King Jr. (Washington, 1992) so aptly noted in Letter From A Birmingham Jail: "Injustice anywhere is a threat to justice everywhere. We are caught in an inescapable network of mutuality tied in a single garment of destiny." (p. 85) Whatever affects one directly affects all indirectly.

Finally, the scope of justice may be extended to non-human species and, in fact, the entire planet. Eco-centered perspectives on justice contend that the classical Western views of justice limit the scope to human centered concerns, thus overlooking a range of beings who may also be entitled to rights, freedoms and equality. While some of eco-centered justice arguments are centuries old, many have emerged in the late 20th century in conjunction with the ecology and animal rights movements. (Merchant, 2005; Finsen and Finsen, 1994)

Historically, eco-centric views of justice are found in non-Western religions such Buddhism, Hinduism and Native American spirituality. In fact, according to anthropological evidence indigenous animistic religions are the oldest in the world. Many still persist and, in the U.S., Native American spirituality continues to inform both the religious and ecological positions of many Native Americans. In *All Our Relations*, Winona LaDuke (1999) makes this observation, "Native American teachings describe the relations all around—animals, fish, trees, and rocks—as our brothers, sisters, uncles, and grandpas . . . Our relations to each other, our prayers whispered across generations to our relatives, are what bind our cultures together. These relations are honored in ceremony, song, story, and life that keeps the relations close—to buffalo, sturgeon, salmon, turtles, bears, wolves, and panthers. These are our elder relations—the ones that came before and taught us how to live." (p. 2)

More recently, eco-centered conceptions of justice have begun to be included in Western theological thought. Feminist theology in particular, is a key contributor here. Elisabeth Johnson CSJ, in *Women, Earth, and Creator Spirit* (1993?) argues for an ecofeminist reconsideration of "hierarchical dualism" which has relationships between God/Man, Man/Woman, and

Man/Nature. Johnson writes, "Hierarchical dualism . . . places the privileged, so-called rational man apart from and above other persons such as the poor and people of color . . . Feminist analysis insists that the devastating ecological consequences of this two-tiered vision cannot be fully addressed until we face it as a whole . . . We need to realize that the natural environment is oppressed, manipulated and abused in ways analogous to the patriarchal use of women." (pp. 11–12)

Eco-inclusive perspectives on justice extend beyond theology. Philosophy has made significant contributions including further development of ecofeminist ideas. Perhaps, most importantly, philosophy paved the way for continued challenges to human-centered views of justice on several fronts. From the "land ethic" of Aldo Leopold (1966) to the "deep ecology" of Norwegian philosopher Arne Naess (1989), philosophers have extended claims of justice to the natural environment—"that land is a community is the basic concept of ecology, but that land is to be loved and respected is an extension of ethics." (Leopold, 1966, p. 239) The Philosophers were also among the first to critique speciesism and make the case for animal rights. In particular, Peter Singer (drawing on the classical writings of Jeremy Bentham) and Tom Regan inspired the contemporary animal rights movement with their respective works, *Animal Liberation* (1975), and *The Case for Animal Liberation* (1985).

Several perspectives found in the natural and social sciences comparably widen the scope of justice. Physicists, biologists, and chemists have begun to question the predominance of the Western mechanistic view of science. (Merchant, 2005; Sheldrake, 1981; Shiva 1997, 2000) Holistic approaches, which view the earth as an ecosystem or a complex organism, itself, imply that balance, equality, and in fact, justice, require a consideration of non-human nature. In fact, one scientific approach—the Gaia hypothesis—contends that the entire earth itself is a complex organism that should receive consideration as such. (Lovelock, 1979)

The social sciences and interdisciplinary areas of study have also begun to expand their scope of inquiry to the environment and other species. Increasingly, sociology, psychology, women's studies, and racial/ethnic studies have considered the relationship between social and environmental inequality. The sociological interest in the green and animal rights movements, eco-psychology, and the study of environmental racism, sexism, and classism are all cases in point. (Bullard, 1993, 2005; Roszak, 1992; Finsen and Finsen, 1994; Patterson, 2001)

Finally, more inclusive, eco-centered views of justice have emerged from political thought and practice. Rudimentary notions of eco-justice can be found in the socialist writings of Marx and Engels, as well as the early anarchists. (Merchant, 2005) Both critique economic and political relations as oppressive and exploitive to humans as well as the environment. These perspectives have informed much of the green movement in the

U.S. as well as indigenous efforts globally to maintain ecologically sound practices. (LaDuke, 1999; Shiva, 2000)

National legislation and international treaties have also begun to reflect more expansive views of justice. Animals and the environment have limited legal protection here, and there is continued lobbying and political pressure to expand our legal notions of animal and environmental rights. Political proponents are for a variety of changes in our legal system including enhanced penalties for animal cruelty, the abolition of animal experimentation and factory farming, and moratoria on nuclear energy, urban sprawl, and the use of fossil fuels. (Bullard, 1993, 2005; Merchant, 2005; Newkirk, 2005) In addition, international bodies and agencies are increasingly called upon to consider the environment and other species in political treaties and agreements. Pressures from indigenous peoples and environmental groups globally have led to agreements on sustainable development, pollution reduction, responses to the climate crisis, and endangered species protection. Examples include the inaugural Earth Summit held in Rio de Janeiro in 1992, the United Nations Declaration of Indigenous People's Rights, and the international climate meetings from Kyoto 1992 to Warsaw 2013. (Merchant. 2005; UN, 2010) While many such documents are motivated by human-based concerns, they do nonetheless extend the concept of justice, rights, and protections to non-humans as well.

Truths, Justice and Action

"The philosophers have only interpreted the world in various ways—the point, however, is to change it."

—Karl Marx. 1845[6]

The truths created by the social world call out for evaluation, for analysis, for judgment. They call for a critical analysis of justice. Justice frameworks—those common threads among a multiplicity of experiences and perspectives—provide this analytical basis from which to identify and evaluate justice arguments. Justice frameworks may be characterized by their implicit or explicit definitions of justice—its source, standards and scope. As the all of foregoing suggests, even this rudimentary classification scheme quickly becomes complicated with both comparisons and caveats, and, at best, serves as a rough guide to the intricacies of justice.

And yet, this is only half the story. The rest will be fully explored another day. For now, know that this is just the start of the journey—issues of justice are also calls to action. Once justice has been conceptualized, its realization inevitably comes into question. Justice without action is mere intellectual exercise; the circumstances of everyday life, our inevitable connection to community, and our obligation as engaged citizens demand much more.

Epilogue/The Past Is Prologue

"First they came for the Socialists and I did not speak out—
because I was not a Socialist.
Then they came for the Trade Unionists, and I did not speak out-
because I was not a Trade Unionist.
Then they came for the Jews, and I did not speak out-
because I was not a Jew.
Then they came for me—and there was no one left to speak for me."

—Pastor Niemöller. 1955[7]

Notes

[1] Jimmy L. Glass (1962–1987) quoted on the inscription page of Prejean, H. (2005). *The Death of Innocents: An Eyewitness Account of Wrongful Executions*. NY: Random House. Glass, along with co-defendant Jimmy Wingo, was executed in the Louisiana electric chair (aka "Gruesome Gertie") for two murders committed on a prison escape. Glass is best known for his writ of certiorari to the U.S. Supreme Court. In Glass v. Louisiana, 471 U.S. 1080 (1985), he argued that the use of the electric chair constituted cruel and unusual" punishment in violation of the 8th Amendment. His petition was denied despite strong dissent from Justices Brennan and Marshall.—"For the reasons set forth above, there is an ever-more urgent question whether electrocution in fact is a "humane" method for extinguishing human life or is, instead, nothing less than the contemporary technological equivalent of burning people at the stake." Louisiana —and most states that retain capital punishment—abandoned the use of the electric chair in 1993 in favor of lethal injection. Ironically, this method of execution is under similar 8th Amendment constitutional challenges at the time of this writing.

[2] Reverend Dr. Martin Luther King Jr. (1929–1968) from the speech delivered at the National Cathedral, Washington, D.C., on 31 March 1968—Remaining Awake Through a Great Revolution. Retrieved January 15 2008 http://www.africanamericans.com/MLK RemainingAwakeThroughGreatRevolution.htm. King is unarguably the most famous of a series of great Civil Rights leaders—Ella Baker, Fannie Lou Hamer, Malcolm X, Rev. Ralph Abernathy, Rosa Parks, Huey P. Newton and many more. He was the youngest recipient of the Nobel Peace Prize, and is the only U.S. citizen who was not a President to have a National Holiday declared in his honor. Following the passage of the Civil Rights Act of1964 and the Voting Rights Act of 1965, Dr. King turned his attention to combating issues of poverty via The Poor People's Campaign, and questioning the U.S. role in Vietnam. He was assassinated in Memphis on April 4 1968, while working to end a sanitation workers strike.

[3] Audre Lorde (1934–1992) quotation from "Poetry is not a Luxury" in Lorde, A. (1984) *Sister Outsider: Essays and Speeches*. Freedom, CA: Crossing Press. Black, Woman, lesbian, immigrant, mother, survivor, warrior poet, Audre Lorde is widely credited with ushering in the Third Wave of feminism. Her attention to intersecting oppressions, the voices of marginalized women, and her call to speak out and to make our differences strengths were all ground-breaking contributions to the both women's movement and scholarly feminist analysis.

[4] Mary Harris "Mother" Jones (1837–1930) from a speech to striking coal miners following the Ludlow Massacre (Colorado) of 1914, quoted in Zinn, H. (2004). *Let the people speak*. New York: Perennial. Jones was 82 at the time Jones was a prominent U.S. labor organizer, Socialist, United Mine Workers, and member of the I.W.W. The progressive magazine *Mother Jones* is named as a tribute to her tireless efforts for the workers. Her most famous quote is this—"Pray for the dead—but fight like hell for the living."

[5] Judy Chicago (1939–) quoted in commentary about the *Holocaust Project: From Darkness into Light* http://www.throughtheflower. org/page.php?p= 13&n=2. Judy Chicago is a feminist artist, educator, and author who is best known for her art installation projects including *The Dinner Party* (1974–79) (an homage via a place setting for 39 famous women of history), *The Birth Project* (1980–85) and the *Holocaust Project* (1993). She is the founder of Through the Flower (1978), a non-profit feminist art organization devoted to education, collaboration, and change.

[6] Karl Marx (1818–1883) the last line from the "Thesis on Feuerbach" quoted in Tucker, R, (1972). *The Marx–Engels Reader*. NY: W. W. Norton. These words are also inscribed on his tombstone at Highgate Cemetery in London. A philosopher, political theorist, economist, sociologist, founder of the Communist Party and revolutionary, Marx was one of the most influential thinkers of all time. The opening line of The Communist Manifesto (1948)—"The history of all hitherto existing society is the history of class struggle"—sums up the central theme of his voluminous body of work. His epitaph illustrates his life-long commitment to praxis—the union of theory and action—to seek justice in an unequal world.

[7] Pastor Martin Niemöller (1892–1984) credited to post-War writings and speeches. There are various versions of this poem—the version cited is inscribed at the U.S. Holocaust Museum in Washington, DC http://www.ushmm.org/. Niemöller was a Lutheran Minster, and an early supporter of Hitler who became a vocal critic of the Nazi regime. He spent 7 years in concentration camps, and survived to be a leader in reconciliation in post-war Germany. This quote is often cited as a reminder of the dangers of apathy as well as the deep connections between justice issues and situations of oppression.

Appendix

Liberal Arts: Disciplines, Subject Matter, and Methods

Humanities	Social Sciences	Natural Sciences
• The Fine Arts, Foreign Languages, History, Literature in English, Philosophy, Theology	• Anthropology, Economics, Geography, Political Science, Psychology, Sociology	• Biology, Chemistry, Physics, Mathematics and all related sub-fields of study
• Emphasis on symbolic communication and expression, interpretation, and questions of meaning, experience, existence, metaphysics, and cosmology	• Emphasis on empirical examination of human interaction with the environment, culture, economic and political arrangements and activity, the self and society	• Emphasis on the observable, empirical underpinnings, and unchanging principles of the physical world, including human existence
• Rules and norms of grammar, logic and composition/Multiple paradigms, and schools of theory and practice/Qualitative methods—reliance on critical thinking and a degree of methodological "subjectivity" in interpretation of historical, philosophical and religious texts, works of art, literature, and music	• Standard methodologies that span disciplines/Multiple paradigms within disciplines with common historical and theoretical roots/Use of both qualitative and quantitative methods—emphasis on empirically measurable variables, correlation, and a degree of "objectivity" in examining human activity	• Standard methodologies that span disciplines/Tendencies towards single paradigms that stand until "disproved"/Use of quantitative methods—emphasis on mathematical formulas, theorems, the experiment, causation, "proof," and "objectivity" in the examination of empirical data

References

American Civil Liberties Union (2013). Lesbian-Gay Rights. Retrieved October 14, 2013 from http://www.aclu.org/lgbt/ relatedinformation_fact_sheets.html

Amnesty International. (1998). *United States of America: Rights For All*. NY: Amnesty International.

Amnesty International. (2006). *Amnesty Report 2006*. NY: Amnesty International.

Bonilla-Silva, E. (2013). *Racism without racist: Color-blind racism and the persistence of racial inequality in the United States*. 4E. New York: Rowman and Littlefield.

Bratton, M. (1998). After Mandela's Miracle in South Africa. *Current History* 97: 214–219.

Bullard, R. (1993).*Confronting Environmental Racism: Voices from the Grassroots*. Boston, MA: South End Press.

Bullard, R.(2005). *Environmental Justice in the 21st Century*. Retrieved December 15, 2007, from http://www.ejrc.cau.edu/ ejinthe21century.htm at the Environmental Justice Resource Center.

Bureau of Justice Statistics. (2012). *Prison Statistics*. Retrieved November 8, 2013, from http://www.ojp.usdoj.gov/bjs/prisons.htm

Bureau of Labor Statistics Report (2012) *A Profile of the Working Poor, 2011* Retrieved November 28, 2013 from http://www.bls.gov/cps/ cpswp2011.pdf

Bureau of Labor Statistics Report (2013) *The Economic Status of Women of Color: A Snapshot*. Retreived November 25. 2013 from http:// www.dol.gov/wb/media/reports/WB_WomenColorFactSheet.pdf

Burns, Stewart. (1990). *Social Movements of the 1960s: Searching for Democracy*. New York, NY: Twayne.

Carson, Claybonne, Jarnow, David J., Gill, Gerald, Hardy, Vincent, & Hine, Darlen Clark. (Eds.) (1991). *The Eyes on the Prize Civil Rights Reader: Documents, Speeches and Firsthand Accounts from the Black Freedom Struggle*. New York, NY: Penguin Books.

Collins, R. (1994). *Four Sociological Traditions*. NY: Oxford University Press.

Connors, R. (2000). Catholic Social Teaching—Convictions and Connections. In College of St Catherine, (2004). *Global Search for Justice Reader* 2E. Acton, MA: Copley Custom: 58–88.

Cohn, D. (2007). The Campaign Against Female Genital Cutting: New Hope, New Challenges. *Population Reference Bureau*. Retrieved January 5, 2008 from http://www.prb.org/Articles/2007/CampaignAgainstFemaleGenitalCutting.aspx

Coleman-Jensen, Alisha, Mark Nord, and Anita Singh. *Household Food Security in the United States in 2012,* ERR-155, U.S. Department of Agriculture, Economic Research Service, September 2013.Retreived Novemebr 1. 2013 from http://www.ers.usda.gov/publications/err-economic-research-report/err155.aspx#.UpgS5z-uoVA

Corbett, Christina and Catherine Hill (2013), *Graduating to a Pay Gap.* Washington, D.C.: American Association of University Women.

Cruikshank, M. (1992). *The Gay and Lesbian Liberation Movement.* New York, NY: Routledge, Chapman and Hall.

Declaration of Independence and the Constitution of the United States, The. (1995). New York, NY: Penguin.

Davis, A. (2003). *Are prisons obsolete?* New York: Seven Stories Press.

Death Penalty Information Center (2013) *Facts About the Death Penalty.* Retrieved November 26, 2013 from http://www.deathpenaltyinfo.org/documents/FactSheet.pdf

DeNavas-Walt, C., Proctor, B. D., & Smith, J. (2013). *Income, Poverty, and Health Insurance Coverage in the United States, 2012.* U.S. Census Bureau. Current Population Reports, P60–233. Washington, DC: U.S. Government Printing Office.

Duberman, Martin. (1993). *Stonewall.* New York, NY: Plume,.

Feagin, J. R. (2014). *Racist America: Roots, realities, and future reparations.3E* New York: Routledge.

Farm Sanctauary. (2013). Factory Farming: The Issues. Retrieved November 17, 2013 from http://www.farmsanctuary.org/issues/factoryfarming/

FBI and U.S. Department of Justice (2013). *Crime in the United States 2012* Retreived November 20 2013 http://www.fbi.gov/about-us/cjis/ucr/crime-in-the-u.s/2012

Finsen, L. and S. Finsen (1994).*The Animal Rights Movement in the United States.* NY: Twayne.

Forbes. (2013). The Forbes 400: Rich Lists. Retrieved October 12, 2013 from http://www.forbes.com/sites/luisakroll/2013/09/16/inside-the-2013-forbes-400-facts-and-figures-on-americas-richest/

Glass v. Louisiana, 471 U.S. 1080 (1985).

Golden, R.,McConnell, M, Mueller, P, Popper, C, & Turkovic, M (1991). *Dangerous Memories: Invasion and Resistance Since 1492.* Chicago, IL: Chicago Religions Task Force on Central America.

Hennelly, A. (Ed.).(1990). *Liberation Theology: A Documentary History.* Maryknoll, NY: Orbis,

Hill Collins, P. (1990).*Black Feminist Thought: Knowledge, Consciousness and the Politics of Empowerment.* Boston, MA: Unwin Hyman.

hooks, b. (1984). *Feminist Theory from Margin to Center.* Boston, MA: South End Press.

Human Rights Campaign. (2013). GLBT Issues. Retrieved October 5, 2013, from http://www.hrc.org/issues/index.htm

Human Rights Watch. (2007). Defending Human Rights Worldwide..Retreived January 12, 2008, from http://www.hrw.org/

Ishay, M. (Ed.). (1997).*The Human Rights Reader: Major Political Essays, Speeches and Documents from the Bible to the Present.* New York, NY: Routledge.

Ishay, M. (2004). *The History of Human Rights.* Berkeley: University of California Press.

Johnson, Elizabeth A. CSJ. (1993). *Women, Earth, and Creator Spirit.* Mahwah, NJ: Paulist Press.

Klass, M. (1995).*Ordered Universes: Approaches to the Anthropology of Religion.* Boulder, CO: Westview.

King, M. L. Jr. (1968, March 31) Remaining Awake from a Great Revolution. Retrieved January 15, 2008, from http://www. africanamericans.com/ MLKRemainingAwakeThrough GreatRevolution.htm

King, M. L. Jr. (1963). Letter from a Birmingham Jail. In J. Washington (Ed.). (1992) *I Have a Dream: Writing and Speeches That Changed the World/Martin Luther King Jr.* New York, NY: Harper Collins.

LaDuke, W. (1999). *All Our Relations: Native Struggles for Land and Life.* Cambridge, MA: South End Press.

Lebacqz, K. (1986). *Six Theories of Justice.* Minneapolis, MN: Augsburg Publishing House.

Leopold, A. (1966). *A Sand County Almanac.* NY: Ballantine.

Living Wage Calculator. (2013). Retrieved October 20, 2013 form http://livingwage.mit.edu/

Lorde, Audre. (1984). *Sister Outsider: Essays and Speeches.* Freedom, CA: Crossing Press.

Lovelock, J. (1979). *Gaia: A New Look at Life on Earth*. NY: Oxford University Press.

Magnani, L.& Wray, H. (2006).*Beyond Prisons*. Minneapolis, MN: Fortress Press.

Marx, K. & Engels, F. (1948). *The Communist Manifesto*. London: International Publishers.

Merchant, C. (2005). *Radical Ecology*. 2E. NY: Routledge.

Mills, C. W. (1959). *The Sociological Imagination*. NY: Oxford University Press.

Miranda, V. (2011), "Cooking, Caring and Volunteering: Unpaid Work Around the World", *OECD Social, Employment and Migration Working Papers*, No. 116, OECD Publishing. doi: 10.1787/5kghrjm8s142-en

Murton, T. (1965). *Gandhi on Non-Violence*. New York, NY: New Directions.

Naess, A. (1989). *Ecology, Community, and Lifestyle*. Cambridge: Cambridge University Press.

National Coalition for Homeless. (August 2009). Factsheets on the Homeless. Retrieved January 15, 2013, from http://www.nationalhomeless.org/publications/facts.html

Newkirk, I. (2005). *Making Kind Choices*. NY: St. Martins Griffin.

Patterson, C. (2001). *Eternal Treblinka: The Holocaust and Our Treatment of Animals*. NY: Lantern.

People for the Ethical Treatment of Animals. (2013). Why Animal Rights? Retrieved October 10, 2013, from http://www.peta.org/about/WhyAnimalRights.asp

Population Reference Bureau (February 2007) Worlds'Youth Data Sheet. Retrieved January 10, 2008, from http://www.prb.org/pdf06/WorldsYouth2006DataSheet.pdf

Prejean, H. (1999). *Dead Man Walking*. NY: Vintage.

Prejean, H. (2005). *The Death of Innocents: An Eyewitness Account of Wrongful Executions*. NY: Random House.

Rashid, Ahmed. (2000). *Taliban: Militant Islam, Oil, and Fundamentalism in Central Asia*. New Haven, CT: Yale University Press,

Regan, T. (1985).*The Case for Animal Rights*. Berkeley: University of California Press.

Robinson, R. (2000). *The Debt*. NY: Plume.

Rorty, R. (1993). Human rights, rationality, and sentimentality.In M. Ishay (ed.) (1997).*The Human Rights Reader: Major Political Essays, Speeches and Documents from the Bible to the Present.* New York, NY: Routledge: 253–265.

Roszak, T. (Ed.).(1992) *The Voice of the Earth.* NY: Touchstone.

Schlosser, E. (2001). *Fast Food Nation,* Boston: Houghton Mifflin.

Seager, J. (1997). *The State of Women in the World Atlas.* New York, NY: Penguin.

Sentencing Project (2013) Trends in U.S. Corrections. Retrieved October 30, 2023 from http://sentencingproject.org/doc/publications/inc_Trends_in_Corrections_Fact_sheet.pdf

Shah, A. (2013). Global Issues. Social, Political, Economic and Environmental Issues That Affect Us All. Retrieved October 12, 2013, from http://www.globalissues.org/

Sheldrake, R, (1981) A New Science of Life. LA: Jeremy P. Tarcher.

Sheldrake, R., T. McKenna and R. Abraham (1992). *Chaos, Creativity and Consciousness.* Rochester, VT: Park Street Press.

Shiva, V. (1997).Staying Alive: Development, Ecology and Women. In *The Human Rights Reader: Major Political Essays, Speeches and Documents from the Bible to the Present.* In M. Ishay. (Ed.) New York, NY: Routledge. 253–263.

Shiva, V. (2000). *Stolen Harvest.* Boston, MA: South End Press.

Shute, S. & Hurley, S. (Ed.). (1993).*On Human Rights: Oxford Amnesty Lectures.* New York, NY. Basic Books.

Simon, D. (2011). *Elite Deviance.* 10E. Boston: Allyn and Bacon.

Singer, P. (1975). *Animal Liberation.* Berkeley: University of California Press.

Tanzey, G. & D'Silva, J. (Eds.).(2000). *The Meat Business.* London: Earthscan.

Tucker, R. (1972). *The Marx-Engels Reader.* NY: W.W. Norton.

United Nations. (1999). *Human Rights: A Compilation of International Instruments.* Vol. 1. New York, NY United Nations Publications.

United Nations Children's Fund (2013). *Millennium Development Goals.* Retrieved November 35. 2023 from http://www.unicef.org/mdg/poverty.html

United Nations Statistical Division (2007) *Statistical Annex: Millennium Development Goals, Targets and Indicators*. Retrieved on December 20, 2007, from http://unstats.un.org/unsd/mdg/ Host.aspx?Content= Data/Trends.htm

United Nations Environmental Programme (2010) *Assessing the Environmental Impacts of Consumption and Production: Priority Products and Materials, A Report of the Working Group on the Environmental Impacts of Products and Materials to the International Panel for Sustainable Resource Management*. Retrieved November 28, 2013 from http://www.unep.fr/shared/publications/pdf/ DTIx1262xPA-PriorityProductsAndMaterials_Report.pdf

United States Department of Agriculture (2013). Food Deserts. Retieved October 15. 2013 from http://apps.ams.usda.gov/fooddeserts/ foodDeserts.aspx

Walker, A. (1992).*Possessing the Secret of Joy*. New York, NY: Harcourt Brace Jovanovich.

Walker, A. & Parmar, P.(1993). *Warrior Marks: Female Genital Mutilation and the Sexual Blinding of Women*. New York, NY: Harcourt Brace Jovanovich.

Walker, S., Spohn, C., & DeLone, M. (2012). *The color of justice: Race, ethnicity and crime in America*, 5E. Belmont, CA: Wadsworth.

Ward, M. C. (1999). *A World Full of Women*. 2nd ed. Boston, MA: Allyn and Bacon.

Washington, J. (Ed.). (1992). *I Have a Dream: Writing and Speeches That Changed the World/Martin Luther King Jr.* New York, NY: Harper Collins

Winbush, R. (2003). *Should America Pay? Slavery and the Raging Debate on Reparations*. NY: Amistad.

World Resources Institute (2007) *Climate Change and Developing Countries*. Retrieved January 11, 2008, from http://archive.wri.org/ item_detail.cfm?id=1284§ion=climate&page=project_content_tex t&z=?

World Wildlife Federation. (2006). *The Living Planet Report 2006*. Retrieved January 2, 2008, from http://assets.panda.org/ downloads /living_planet_report.pdf

Zinn, H. (2004). *Let the people speak.* New York: Perennial.

William Andrew Myers is professor emeritus of St. Kate's, where he taught philosophy for more than thirty years. Most of his courses have been in ethics, political philosophy, history of philosophy, philosophy of science, and philosophy of the arts. He also is a printmaker and book artist on the faculties of Minnesota Center for Book Arts and the Grand Marais Art Colony. In this essay Myers describes the standards that govern modern scientific practices and shows why examples of three other belief systems are not scientific. What reasons can you give for accepting the results of a scientific research project? Does the fact that a belief is not supportable scientifically make it false? What position is he taking when Myers says that he does not know if the claims of astrology are true or false?

Evidence and the Projects of Rationality

William Andrew Myers

The ideal of rational objectivity used as a standard to guide inquiries into truth is one of the hallmarks of Western Civilization. Our sciences, medical practices, legal processes, and many academic fields of study depend for their credibility and practical success on some version of this standard. Critics of the concepts of rationality and of objectivity have in general complained that these are fictional standpoints, culturally relative and no different in principle from other perspectives on truth. But to understand such criticisms we have to know something of the history and practice of rational objectivity. This essay will provide a sketch of the standpoint as it is expressed in the sciences and show its applications in a few selected areas.

I. The Fixation of Belief

The American philosopher Charles Sanders Peirce (1839–1914) wrote an important essay called "The Fixation of Belief" (1887) in which he discusses the ways in which people typically form their own beliefs. "Fixation" here means taking an idea to be settled and adopting it as your own. Peirce (note the spelling—it is pronounced "purse") observes that people tend to engage in thinking when they are prodded by doubt or uncertainty about some issue. Doubt is uncomfortable, and when we encounter it we "struggle to free ourselves and pass into the state of belief."[1] He then describes four ways in which people typically settle on their beliefs.

First, some people deal with the discomfort of uncertainty by walling it off from their sight. They concentrate on all the ideas that seem to support their view, and they treat with contempt or just ignore anything that might look like a contrary idea. Their minds are made up, and their minds are closed. Peirce calls this the *method of tenacity*.[2] It has the advantage that employing this method will insulate you from the discomfort of uncertainly and enable you to avoid the hard work of research, actual thinking. But, he says, it has the disadvantages that unless you are a hermit you will encounter alternative beliefs which can be just as well supported as your own, and unless you simply refuse to discuss anything or read or listen to anything that might challenge your belief, doubt is going to creep in at some point.

Second, opinions might be established for the community as a whole by government, religious authority, or a political party. For some people it is very comforting to accept what others have established as the true belief. Peirce calls this the *method of authority*.[3] Once again it has the advantage that it helps avoid the discomfort of uncertainty and the labor of investigation. But it has the disadvantage that if you look at others' beliefs, for example those of citizens of other countries, you might conclude that your beliefs established by authority are rather arbitrary, an accident of where you grew up. And if you dwell on that fact, doubt can slip in and you can lose the comfort of established opinions.

Third, we might accept only beliefs that fit in with what we already do believe. He calls this the *a priori method*[4] of establishing belief. This is a way of avoiding the arbitrariness of the first two methods and it has the advantage that, if we think logically, we will avoid any contradictions in our thought, and we will have a coherent system of beliefs. But in fact, Peirce says, this method does not differ much from the method of authority; it simply trades the authority of the government or the church for the authority of whatever happens to be in our minds that new knowledge must conform to. It makes the establishment of belief rather like the establishment of taste in fashions or the like.

Notice that for all three of the methods Peirce has described so far one's beliefs may be true, or they may be false. The problem with them is not just the psychological one that they ultimately fail to make your beliefs stand still, but that as methods they have nothing to do with establishing the actual truth of an idea. That, he thinks, comes with the fourth method, which he calls the *method of science*.[5]

Now Peirce regards scientific method not merely as a set of formal procedures used in a laboratory or observatory, but as what we all do when we pay proper attention to reality and investigate it. Starting from what we know to be true we can investigate and reason to new knowledge that is grounded in evidence. Peirce, as a philosopher of science, knew that scientific investigation was always fallible—further investigation might overturn the settled beliefs of today. But he says that, of the four methods he describes, this is the only one that pays proper attention to whether a belief conforms to observations repeatable by members of a community investigating the same questions.

I take the importance of Peirce's article to be the propositions that, (1) though there are a number of ways of creating opinions, most of them boil down to arbitrary or ideological ways to block inquiry. This is the closed mind, and on a larger scale the closed society. And (2) an openness to new evidence and new thinking, the willingness to rethink our opinions while looking for better ways to support them, is the practice of the reasonable person who cares more about finding out what is true than about being comfortable.

II. The Methods of Science

Ancient Greek thinkers had considerable success understanding and manipulating the physical world. Thales, credited with being the first philosopher, accurately predicted the year (585 B.C.E.) of a solar eclipse and engineered a way to split the course of a large river so that an army could cross the resulting shallower streams. Aristarchus of Samos taught that the sun was the center of the universe with the earth orbiting it, and he and other natural philosophers made reasonable estimates of the size (and shape) of the earth and the distance to the moon. The Hippocratean school of medicine developed the first systematic observations of diseases in the West. The Greek physician, or *iatros*, used most of his senses in examining a patient, and most important for developing medicine as a science in our modern sense, he kept careful records of those observations. These records formed a body of case studies that showed that symptoms and diseases followed regular patterns. Getting sick wasn't just a visitation of some angry god, but a rationally understandable process. Through the concepts of *diagnosis* (literally, "knowing-through") and *prognosis* ("knowing ahead") the Greek physician could identify what was wrong with a patient and predict what was likely to happen.

Greek science was certainly limited. It never developed an idea of systematic experiment to go along with observations, and medicine was shackled to an unfortunate belief system about the human body—the doctrine of the four humors—that still held sway as late as the nineteenth century. And there wasn't much the *iatros* could do by way of intervention; diseases like tetanus and diabetes, for instance, were common and invariably fatal. Yet the recognition of common patterns to disease that could be understood rationally is one of the foundations of a more general Western approach to nature that we today have inherited. That approach holds as its basic tenet the belief that the universe is rational, and that since human beings are rational, we can understand it. Close observation of physical evidence is the basic practice that gives life to this belief.

III. The Beginnings of Modern Scientific Practice

Science as we know it is a product of European philosophers and scientists who worked to build a system for investigating nature that would be rational, independent of dogma, especially religious dogma, and reliable—they wanted it to work. In the landmark year 1543 Nicolaus Copernicus, a Polish mathematician and monk, published a book hypothesizing that the planets orbited the sun, not the earth, thus threatening the entrenched Medieval belief in the cosmology of Aristotle, which located earth at the center. And in the same year Andreas Vesalius published an anatomy textbook with woodcuts showing with unprecedented detail and accuracy the workings of the human body. Both works inspired a tremendous amount of scientific observation and experiment. In the following century, Galileo's use of the newly invented telescope to support the Copernican world view and Van Leuwenhoek's use of his invention, the microscope, to discover a previously unsuspected world of microbes, continued what the works of Copernicus and Vesalius started: what we now call the Scientific Revolution.

As is well known, Galileo also discovered the principle of the pendulum and rolled balls down ramps to measure the force of gravity. (It is not actually certain that he ever dropped balls off the Leaning Tower in Pisa.) Although his publications led to his trial for heresy and a sentence of perpetual house arrest, he probably did more than any single person to create the standards of the new science. Three major principles have animated the physical sciences from Galileo's time until ours.

First, hypotheses—those initial guesses we make about how to explain something—must be *testable*. Sir Karl Popper, a major Twentieth Century philosopher of science, says that "the criterion of the scientific status of a theory is its falsifiability, or refutability, or testability."[6] If no evidence in principle will count against a theory, then the theory is not scientific. The search for life on Mars can be a scientific quest because the hypothesis that life once existed there is testable (though with difficulty and at great expense). Given certain definitions of what counts as a living organism and theories about how such organisms might show up even if long dead, we can send space craft equipped to look for evidence of life. However, to revive an old cliché about arguments in Medieval philosophy, a hypothesis about the number of angels that will fit on the head of a pin is untestable because current methods of investigation give us no way to observe and count angels. Ideological commitments and religious beliefs tend to be untestable by observation or experiment. If evidence or observation would count as a disproof of a hypothesis, then the hypothesis is outside the range of application of scientific method. That does not in itself mean the hypothesis is false. It simply means that if it is worth believing, the grounds for that belief will not be scientific.

Second, the phenomena under study must be *measurable*. Galileo once wrote, "The Book of Nature is written in the language of mathematics." The lack of accurate clocks (let alone stopwatches!) in his time hampered Galileo's own measurements, but he used ingenious methods to get around this barrier. The ramps he rolled balls down had the effect of slowing their fall so it could be observed more precisely (watching something fall through the air, it is quite difficult to say just exactly when it passes a certain point). And he is said to have used his own pulse as a clock to measure the swing of a lamp (or perhaps an incense sensor—stories conflict) in the cathedral in Pisa. However he did his work, Galileo's belief in measuring the phenomena as precisely as possible became a foundation stone for modern scientific practice.

The third major principle is that observations and experiments must be *repeatable by others*. It is all well and good for Galileo to point his telescope at Jupiter and claim he saw "little stars" orbiting close to the planet. But only if others could see them too could it be known that Galileo was observing something real in the sky, and not dirt on the lens or some apparition inside the tube. (With low power binoculars on a clear night you can make the same observations he did. The "little stars" he saw are now called the Galilean moons of Jupiter.)

These ideas, *testability, exact measurement,* and *repeatability of observations,* are the basis for scientific practice in our time. A fourth important idea, *peer review,* operates in a practical way for scientists today to connect their work to a community of practice—other scientists pursuing the same or similar questions. The old film stereotype of the solitary genius in a private laboratory discovering "breakthroughs" is quite contrary to the communal nature of actual scientific practice. Up front, applications for research grants are reviewed and critiqued by others in the field before funding is approved. For research involving human subjects, for instance in psychology, groups usually called Institutional Review Boards (there's one at St. Kate's) examine the research design for ethical problems. And then, before results can be published in scientific journals they are reviewed by peers as well. Though the process of peer review is not without problems (we are talking about the activities of actual human beings, after all), it does help to ensure that scientific results are reliable and conform to the basic standards of experimentation in that field.

As criteria, testability, measurement, repeatability, and peer review provide a way of separating practices and beliefs that are scientific from those that are not. But how are they applied in actual research work? How do peer reviewers know—in detail—that a study fits the criteria for research in its specific field?

IV. The Paradigm of Science

One of the most influential answers to these questions was provided by Thomas Kuhn in his 1962 book *The Structure of Scientific Revolutions*.[7] This thin little volume is one of the landmarks of twentieth century philosophy. Kuhn studied the Copernican Revolution and the tortuous evolution of chemistry out of Medieval alchemy, and he proposed that the contents and methods of individual sciences like astronomy and chemistry are the result of the formation of *paradigms*. He argued that most of the time a science has a settled content and methodology that guides its practitioners in their work. He called these periods of stability *normal science*. Scientific progress is not a matter of adding more and more facts to a body of learning. Instead, it takes the form of occasional radical changes in the understanding of what questions to ask of Nature and how to attempt to answer them. When a revolution in scientific understanding occurs, Kuhn said, it looks like a thorough revision of what counts as doing science at all. He called these events paradigm shifts.

Unfortunately for our understanding of Kuhn, the phrase "paradigm shift" has entered the common vocabulary, becoming a piece of organizational jargon. It has been watered down to mean any change of thinking. But Kuhn was referring to something momentous. After the discovery of electricity, of x-rays, of oxygen, the relevant sciences were changed from top to bottom. Take the theory of combustion: right down to the eighteenth century people had only a sketchy sense of what actually happened when something burned. They had invented an explanation based on a substance called phlogiston. The presence of this substance in a material such as wood or coal is what made it flammable. The process of combustion was thought to be simply the process of *phlogiston* leaving the substance. Wood and coal were claimed to be mostly phlogiston, so when they were, in the term of the time, dephlogisticated, they mostly disappeared. An elaborate set of theories developed around the hypothesis of phlogiston, and they went along with another idea common in that era, that heat was a substance that flowed through materials. That substance was called *caloric*. Chemists of the time (this would be the mid-1700s) were thus working within a paradigm that included phlogiston and caloric as part of their basic understanding, a paradigm that guided them in designing experiments and thinking up what questions they wanted their experiments to answer. All this changed, over the course of a couple of years, when a number of scientists independently in Sweden, England, and France isolated a gas that came to be called *oxygen* and figured out that it was one of the main constituents of air. Antoine Lavoisier through carefully quantified experiments (precise weighing of samples before and after combustion) showed that combustion was the process of oxygen combining with other substances. In time the new theory of combustion based on oxygen generated completely new questions and experimental designs. Phlogiston disappeared from the scientific vocabulary, only to be referred to henceforth by historians and philosophers of science who like the feel of the word on the tongue.

From phlogiston to oxygen was such a fruitful shift in understanding, uniting disparate phenomena—it wasn't long before scientists figured out that oxygen had an essential role to play in supporting life—that it changed the very meaning of doing chemistry. Questions that had been asked before were no longer relevant to anything, and brand new questions that were unimaginable before became the basis for normal science. A paradigm shift had occurred. And a young student learning how to be a chemist would be introduced to a completely different science than had existed before. This is one example among many of fundamental changes in scientific understanding during the last 250 years that confirm Kuhn's approach. There are numerous other examples: relativity theory and quantum mechanics did not merely add to the sum of knowledge in physics, but changed what it meant to be doing physics at all.

Kuhn's book generated a lot of critique, especially as he was initially not as clear as he might have been about the definition of a paradigm. We might generalize Kuhn's refinement of the concept in later essays in this way: a scientific paradigm is a shared communal understanding of the meaning of a certain kind of research. It contains rules of methodology—including the symbolic language practitioners use, such as chemical formulas and statistical charts; basic ideas about what questions should be investigated; and, most important, a definition of the boundaries that define the discipline.[8] One of the strengths of Kuhn's work is that it locates the paradigm within the practices and shared understandings of scientists themselves. Thus paradigms are always relative to a community of practice in a given era. In this discussion I have emphasized physics, chemistry, and biology, because Kuhn takes his examples from those fields. But exactly the same points can be made about the social sciences as well. Psychology, sociology, political science, etc., likewise operate on shared paradigms imbedded in the practices of their respective fields.

This leads to a major point of this essay. Though Kuhn emphasizes the existence of discipline-specific paradigms, the ones that guide individual sciences, he recognized that there is a large scale paradigm of what counts as scientific research in general.[9] This large scale paradigm of scientific research is what I was describing when I talked about testability, measurement, repeatability of observations, and peer review.

V. Science and Non-Science

The large scale paradigm expresses the scientific community's understanding of its work today. This matters because the role of scientific knowing in contemporary American society is a contested issue. To illustrate I will consider three areas: astrology; the New Age belief in ley lines;

and creationism. In selecting these examples from among many possibilities I looked for areas that have many adherents and that clearly do not fit the general paradigm of science as it stands today.

A. The Persistence of Astrology

Astrology is a system of understanding that connects human lives to astronomical phenomena, chiefly the motions of the planets. It is very ancient: archeologists have found horoscopes scratched on buried walls in Greece, and there are astrological texts in every major civilization we know of, from ancient Babylon and China to the pre-conquest people of Mesoamerica. There are basically two sides to the astrological understanding: first there is the calculation of the positions of the sun, earth's moon, and the planets measured against the background of the constellations lying along the ecliptic, for a particular time, normally a person's time of birth.* This information is really astronomical in the sense that it depends on observation and measurement of the skies, and it is what ancient systems of astrology had in common; that is, Greek and Arab and Chinese systems tended to agree on where things were in the skies (within broad limits, given the lack of precise measuring tools) because they were seeing the same motions. The second part of astrological understanding is the interpretation of the meaning of these motions for the formation of individual personality and fate. These interpretations are the part of astrology that is handed down as a system of traditional lore. An astrologer casting an individual's horoscope uses many calculations of positions of planets and the angles between them; these measurements and their interpretations for a person's life are quite complex and detailed. (It should be clear from this that the fanciful astrology columns in the newspapers have little to do with the serious practice of casting horoscopes. That's why they typically are printed on the comics pages!)

Though some advocates of astrology attempt to compare it favorably with scientific method, these efforts tend to be based on faulty analogies. For instance, in his *Encyclopedia of Astrology* James R. Lewis says,

> We cannot touch, taste, or see astrological forces, but neither can we touch, taste, or see gravity. Gravity is perceived only indirectly—in terms of its effects. Astrological forces are also perceived indirectly—in terms of their impact on human beings and worldly events.

* The ecliptic is an imaginary line across the sky near which most of the planets in the solar system appear. It is a line because most of the planets orbit the sun in the same plane, so throughout the year we always see them against the background of the same constellations. The ecliptic passes through twelve ancient constellations, known as the zodiac.

He goes on to note that statistical studies have been done "which have yielded significant correlations between career choices and the prominence of certain planets in the natal chart."[10] Now it may well be that well-designed research programs in psychology will come to verify statistically some of the findings of astrology. But that is beside the point. Psychological research operates from a scientific paradigm in which careful measurement and repeatability of observations are basic. Astrologers cast horoscopes using interpretive methods and a complex system of meanings which are not the result of application of scientific methods. And the analogy between astrological forces and gravity is weak, though certainly there are plenty of forces and entities studied by physicists, chemists, etc., that are known only through their effects. The point is not whether what is studied is effects of unobserved forces, but the *methods* by which those effects are studied.

It makes perfect sense for someone like Lewis, writing a comprehensive encyclopedia of his field, to be somewhat defensive about the place of astrology in contemporary culture. As he says,

> Since the Enlightenment, the Western world has been home to a vocal group of scientists and science believers who have railed against religion and anything else that dared suggest the human being is anything more than a physical-chemical organism. Astrology has been lumped in the category of irrational superstition, along with anything else that does not fall within a narrow definition of science.[11]

He is correct that there are many people who regard astrology as irrational superstition. But the counter to that misconception is not to try to pretend that astrology is more scientific than it actually is, but to recognize that it is a body of self-consistent traditional lore, with its own methods and practices. It may not be stretching Kuhn's meaning too much to say that astrology has its own paradigm of practice. Indeed, Lewis's encyclopedia attempts to be a comprehensive account of this paradigm and to serve as a textbook as well. Still, the extensive body of knowledge that forms the system of astrological interpretation was not developed from within a paradigm of *scientific* research. Contemporary astrology still relies on astronomy—more precisely, celestial mechanics—in calculating positions of planets, moon, and sun, and it is interesting that various asteroids, which were not known to ancient observers, have now been incorporated in the calculations. But it is the system of interpretation that makes these calculations applicable to human lives, and these, again, have not been developed via scientific methodology. Take this example, again from Lewis:

> Of particular importance are the four elements—earth, water, air, and fire—which represent certain basic personality orientations. Earth represents practicality; water, emotional sensitivity; air, a mental orientation; and fire,

> activity. So for people whose charts are comprised primarily of water signs (Cancer, Scorpio, and Pisces), feelings are what are most *real* in life; for a predominance of air signs (Gemini, Libra, and Aquarius), ideas are most valued; for earth (Taurus, Virgo, and Capricorn), practical concerns; and for fire (Aries, Leo, and Sagittarius), activity.[12]

We can perhaps imagine an experimental design that would test these correlations, but *they themselves are not the result of scientific experiment.* They have been handed down through ages of tradition. To the extent that the system is self-coherent, that is, does not contain within itself any contradictions, it is not irrational. I do not know whether the central claim of astrology, that the positions of the planets, moon and sun at the time of one's birth influence one's personality and life's path, is true. But I do know that this claim is not a scientific one.*

B. Ley Lines

In 1922 Alfred Watkins (1855–1935) published a book in which he described a number of straight lines linking ancient sites on a map of Blackwardine, England.[13] He thought they represented trade routes constructed by prehistoric Britons. In his second book on his discovery, he said

> Imagine a fairy chain stretched from mountain peak to mountain peak, as far as the eye could reach, and paid out until it reached the 'high places' of the earth at a number of ridges, banks, and knowls [sic]. Then visualize a mound, circular earthwork, or clump of trees, planted on these high points, and in low points in the valley other mounds ringed around with water to be seen from a distance. Then great standing stones brought to mark the way at intervals, . . .[14]

Watkins extended his search for straight lines on maps to other parts of Great Britain and Europe, and named the lines he could draw between sites "Ley lines," apparently because a number of them passed through present day places with names ending in –ley, a common British place name ending. It wasn't long before Watkins's readers noted that some of the supposed trade routes would have required travelers to ascend vertical cliffs, and another explanation for the lines emerged, one that enjoys considerable popularity today. This is the thesis that the lines are "sources of power or energy," and by some accounts are used as navigational guides by UFOs.

* The basic belief of astrology, that human lives are influenced by the positions of planets, etc., at the time of birth, also raises the issue of determinism, that is, it calls into question the degree to which people have free will and can choose their own destiny. This consequence of the system may lead it into conflict with other systems of belief, for instance some forms of Christianity, but that in itself does not bear on whether the claim is true or not.

New Age occultists believe that there are certain sites on the earth which are filled with special "energy." Stonehenge, Mt. Everest, Ayers Rock in Australia, Nazca in Peru, the Great Pyramid at Giza, Sedona (Arizona), Mutiny Bay, among other places, are believed to be places of special energy.[15]

I can add to this list Machu Picchu in Peru and the cathedral in Kracow, Poland, where so many people came to put their hands on a particular outside wall of the building to feel the energy alleged to be emanating from a sacred stone underneath the cathedral that the Bishop of Kracow had that section of wall roped off, and posted a sign there debunking the belief.[16]

In 1987 in Seattle an environmental art organization called the Geo Group received funding from the city's Arts Commission to produce a ley line map of the city. The method of creating the map was described by Chuck Pettis.

I created the map by using a brass pendulum to map dowse a large four-by-eight foot Seattle road map for ley lines. Then, we verified the ley-line power centers by visiting the sites and dowsing the exact location of the power center.[17]

Dowsing is the process by which some people are able, using forked sticks or other tools, to discover subterranean water or, in this case, "electromagnetic energy fields emanating from the Earth."[18] Pettis describes the results of this process:

60 ley lines and 44 power centers were identified within Seattle city limits. Ley lines are a network of energy lines that crisscross the Earth. Ley lines originate at power centers. Ancient monuments such as pyramids, stone circles, medicine wheels, shrines, cathedrals and other sacred architectural structures have traditionally been located on power centers. Power centers are significant because they can affect consciousness and uplift the human condition, the time-honored missions of art.[19]

As an artwork the resulting map is quite intriguing, a satellite image with a network of lines superimposed. But what is behind the whole concept of the map is a belief system that has at its center a concept that cannot be verified within the methodologies of the physical sciences. Though people like Chuck Pettis use terms like "electromagnetic energy," if the power centers actually emanated *electromagnetic* energy, one would not need to dowse to detect it: there are any number of actual measuring devices that could do the job. The uses of the word "energy" in New Age beliefs would make an interesting scholarly study on its own, but for my purposes here, suffice it to say that energy for a practitioner of New Age spirituality is most likely not the same thing as energy for a physicist.

This point is one basis for my conclusions about belief in ley lines. First, it is not impossible that mapped ley lines represent a real phenomenon that our scientific methods are at present unable to detect. After all, at the time of their discovery x-rays, "energy" that could pass through walls and metal cabinets to fog photographic plates, were quite incredible. But second, belief in ley lines remains unscientific, for the straightforward reason that the methods of detecting them do not fit the current paradigm of scientific research. I conclude that ley lines may be perfectly real (I don't know), but if you believe in them you are doing so outside the paradigm of scientific investigation that prevails at this time.

C. Creationism

In an essay of the scope of this one I cannot hope to give more than a cursory account of the anti-evolution controversy in the United States. But I think it is worth risking oversimplification in order to put in front of you an important debate about the place of the sciences in contemporary society. Recently, the paradigm of scientific research in biology itself has been challenged as creationists attempted to borrow some of the prestige of the word "science" by asserting a new model of research called "creation science." Along with the doctrine of intelligent design, proponents of creation science have tried to shift the grounds of the debate about evolution. In no other area is the line between science and non-science more important. First, some background.

In the nineteenth century two major and interrelated scientific revolutions took place, one in geology and one in biology. Naturalists of the period had for a long time puzzled over the fossil remains of fish found in landlocked limestone quarries in England. Many people interpreted these as accidental freaks of nature. But in 1830 Charles Lyell published the first volume of his *Principles of Geology*, in which he established the science of paleontology based on analysis of rock strata. On the basis of Lyell's work it became possible to interpret fossils as evidence of ancient seas. Real fish had died and their shapes had been preserved in sedimentary deposits that later hardened to stone. If that was correct, then the processes of fossilization required lots more time than the prevailing opinion allowed. That opinion held that the universe, including the earth and all its species of life, was created complete and whole on Sunday, October 23, in the year 4004 B.C.E. This rather precise calculation came from an intrepid Biblical and Near Eastern scholar named James Ussher, an Irish archbishop, who in 1650 published a book called *The Annals of the World*. He used evidence within the text of the Bible correlated with other accounts of the history of the ancient Near East in calculating his chronology. In 1701 Ussher's dating of the creation and many other events was included in an authorized printing of the Bible, and thereafter came to be regarded as being nearly as authoritative as the scriptures themselves. The tradition of printing Ussher's dates alongside scripture has continued well into our own time, though more contemporary translations of the Bible omit it. Ussher's book lives on: an English translation of the *Annals* published in 2003 has been praised as a major support for present day creationists.[20]

But Lyell's work provided the evidence for dating the earth as much older than Ussher's chronology allowed, and provided an essential framework for the work of Lyell's friend, Charles Darwin.

Darwin published *On the Origin of Species* in 1859. In it he advanced two ideas to explain observations he made as a naturalist voyaging in the southern hemisphere in the early 1830s on a British naval vessel, the Beagle. Attempting to explain differences in the weight and shape of the beaks of Galapagos Finches on different islands, he noted that the food available to them differed in a way that correlated exactly with beak shape. Darwin hypothesized that these variations were adaptations to local conditions, changes that allowed the birds to be more successful in feeding, and therefore more successful in reproducing. Chance mutation in the genetic makeup of the birds met with a favorable environment and so was passed on to progeny who were similarly successful in that environment. Darwin called this process natural selection. He began to find examples of it in other species. And he further hypothesized that species themselves are the product of the age-long working out of these two principles: chance mutation and natural selection.

Darwin knew his work would be controversial, and it was, especially as the new explanation of how members of biological species come to have the form they do began to be applied to human beings. From ancient times to Darwin's there were powerful traditions regarding humans as unique in the universe. For Aristotle, we were the only reasoning beings, the only ones with language. For Medieval thinkers, we were the only beings with souls, placed by God just below the angels in the Great Chain of Being. The Darwinian revolution in biology seemed to challenge the imbedded idea of the uniqueness of humans, particularly our distinctness from other primates, and it is that challenge today to which creationists respond.

Creationist beliefs have themselves changed over time. Followers of Archbishop Ussher's chronology or similar calculations of the age of the earth are called Young Earth Creationists, and they typically hold that the earth is between 6,000 and 10,000 years old.[21] This belief requires denying multiple independent sources of evidence for a very much older earth and universe. Logically, one cannot disprove the hypothesis that God created the earth in 4004 B.C., created it complete with the fossil record and all the other evidence of much longer existence. I think it was Bertrand Russell who pointed out that you cannot positively disprove the hypothesis that the whole universe and everything in it, including us, was created five minutes ago, complete with all our memories, etc. His point was that though it cannot be positively disproved, no reasonable person would believe it, because all the evidence is against it. The same logic applies to the major belief of Young Earth Creationists, except that a lot of people do seem to believe it. Still, divine creation (at any time) is not a scientifically testable belief.

Recently some creationists have shown a willingness to accept a much older age for the earth. A new orientation to creationism has emerged with two facets to it: one, called creation science, applies scientific methodology to the project of critiquing the findings of evolutionary biology and the methods used to date the earth. The other, called the theory of intelligent design, uses the fact of the orderliness of life to argue for a designer, that is, an intelligence who created it. Intelligent design theory is a contemporary version of one of the classic arguments for the existence of God, the Argument from Design, and it suffers some of the same problems that argument has. One of them is that though it may be difficult to comprehend how the apparent orderliness of the world could have arisen entirely by chance, nothing *logically* prohibits chance from being the true origin of our observed world. Improbability is not the same as impossibility. But second, even if we accept the argument as proving the existence of a designer, nothing in the argument requires us to conclude that the designer is of divine origin. In fact, there is an international group of people, the Raëlian Movement, who believe that life on earth is the product of the intervention of extraterrestrial beings who are the intelligent designers. The Raëlians are a religious movement and, like creationists, oppose evolution. They accept the thesis of intelligent design, but they hold "that intelligent aliens landed here millennia ago in spaceships and formed all of life on earth, including human beings, using highly advanced genetic engineering."[22]

A counter to the thesis of alien intelligent designers might be that the orderliness of things extends to the structures of the universe itself and its natural laws. It isn't just the presence of *life* on earth that is to be explained, but the presence of order itself in the cosmos. Still, as the philosopher David Hume pointed out in the eighteenth century, even if the argument works to establish that the apparent orderliness of the cosmos is the product of a intelligent designer, it does not establish that the designer has the characteristics, such as perfection, typically attributed to the Christian God.[23] As a result, the Argument from Design has been regarded by many as giving only probable grounds for its conclusion. Many people accept the argument as giving a measure of rational support to their belief in the existence of God, but their belief is actually grounded on faith. Creationists, because they want to challenge evolution as the basis for the prevailing paradigm of research in the sciences, attempt to go beyond faith in the field called creation science.

The Institute for Creation Research (ICR) is one of a number of organizations whose work is to foster research supporting a creationist conception of the world and human life. Under "Creation Scientists" its website says,

> Scientists who are creationists repudiate any form of molecules-to-man evolution in their analysis and use of scientific data. Creation scientists and the work they conduct are at the heart of ICR's mission to defend biblical truth with scientific evidences, particularly on the issue of origins.[24]

To explain why this approach to science fails to fit the current general paradigm of research, I'll return to some ideas of Karl Popper. Opponents of evolution often say, "It's just a theory—it hasn't been proven." This comment reveals a mistake about the way the sciences work. First, every scientific claim is a theory, or more precisely a hypothesis. The word "theory" in science does not carry the connotation that it has in common language, of being uncertain or unsure. A theory is simply a hypothesis offered for testing. At first, the truth of a hypothesis is unknown. If it were known, there would be no reason to test it. Over time, some theories come to be more thoroughly tested than others. Popper wrote that a good experiment does not attempt to prove that a theory is true—in most cases that is nearly impossible. It attempts to prove that the theory is false. If an experiment does not prove the theory to be false, then belief in its truth is just that little bit more justified. But you should keep trying to *dis*prove it. If you succeed, then you know the claim is false and you can move on. And you have learned something. Each time a serious program of research *fails* to *dis*prove a hypothesis, belief in the truth of the theory is that much more justified. That's Popper's idea of scientific progress. It takes a lot of time and the work of many people experimenting, observing, and measuring to arrive at a consensus that a theory is well established, worthy of belief.[25]

Evolution by natural selection is one of those now well established theories. Natural selection has been observed in birds, fruit flies, and bacteria.* Chance mutation plus natural selection has proved such a fruitful framework for understanding biological phenomena that that it has become part of the paradigm for research in the biological sciences, tested over and over again in multiple, independent research programs. We have abundant good reasons to accept evolution as explaining the phenomena it applies to. By contrast, creation science starts from a standpoint that is essentially religious and political, and attempts not to disprove its hypotheses but to find evidence that can be described as proving their point of view. To propose a hypothesis explaining some observed phenomena and then to design rigorous research to test that hypothesis is the essence of scientific practice. Scientists have to follow the evidence where it leads and have to be willing to accept that their hypotheses may be wrong. On the other hand, to engage in research to prove a thesis one has already arrived at through other means, especially the religious thesis of creationism, is to engage in the pretense of doing science without the nec-

* Indeed, the present day problem of antibiotic resistant strains of microbes is an eloquent demonstration of natural selection at work.

essary commitment to the openness of scientific methods, acceptance of the possibility of completely new insights and surprise endings.

The mark of an ideology is that people who hold it regard it as impervious to critique; no evidence is allowed to count against it. That is Peirce's Method of Tenacity in action. Could the paradigm of evolutionary biology ever change or be replaced? Certainly. For one thing there are disputes among biologists and paleontologists about different models of evolution, and it is probable that one or another of these will stand up to testing better than the others.[26] Also, a follower of Popper would say that *no* theory is ever provable beyond any possibility of refutation. And it is possible that an entirely different understanding of biological species and the prehistory of human life will emerge in time from the work of scientists. We cannot predict what that new understanding might look like any more than an early nineteenth century thinker could have predicted quantum physics. But if there is such a paradigm shift, it will almost certainly emerge from work being done within the prevailing scientific paradigm, not from the work of religious ideologues.

The paleontologist and historian of science, Stephen Jay Gould, one of the major figures in the development of contemporary evolutionary theory, wrote a book toward the end of his too-short life in which he argued that science and religion should never come into conflict. His idea was that the domains of the two areas were so different that though they might illuminate each other they cannot "be unified, or even synthesized, under any common scheme of explanation or analysis."[27] He hoped for something called "respectful noninterference":

> Science tries to document the factual character of the natural world, and to develop theories that coordinate and explain these facts. Religion, on the other hand, operates in the equally important, but utterly different, realm of human purposes, meanings, and values—subjects that the factual domain of science might illuminate, but can never resolve. Similarly, while scientists must operate with ethical principles, some specific to their practice, the validity of these principles can never be inferred from the factual discoveries of science.[28]

I agree with Gould that in principle there should not be a conflict: science does not do its work *versus* religion, and religious believers should not be threatened by the findings of the sciences. The debate about evolution in the U.S., which is essentially political, does try to set up a rigid dichotomy between the two, which is unfortunate. Paying attention to the demarcation between the sciences and areas whose truths have a non-scientific basis should help us understand the grounds for inquiry and belief in different fields.

The sciences have fostered important human goods, both in terms of individual life expectancy and in terms of the quality of lives lived. Examples are abundant: organ transplants, antibiotics, and synthetic human insulin harvested from genetically engineered *e. coli* bacteria quickly come to mind. Millions of people have benefited from these products of scientific method. Still, there are many criticisms of our dependency on the technologies that have resulted from applications of scientific research. Antibiotics have been overused, so that we may be facing a time when they will no longer be as effective as they have been in controlling infections. Distribution of medicines is controlled by large for-profit corporations, so that many in the world cannot afford the benefits of current medical understanding. And much scientific work throughout history has been devoted not to fostering the quality of human life but to technologies of warfare. Yet these are criticisms not of the paradigms of scientific research itself, but of the societies in which scientific practice is imbedded.

Conclusion

The English mystery novelist Josephine Tey, active in the 1940s and '50s, once wrote,

> There is a little phrase commonly used in police work that says, 'in accordance with the evidence.' You say that over six times a day as a grace before and after meals, and perhaps it will keep your feet on the ground and stop you ending up thinking you're Frederick the Great or a hedgehog or something.

I think this succinctly expresses an attitude that is basic to the rationalist orientation. You can of course believe anything you want to and you can use any method you wish—or no method at all—to establish your beliefs. But paying scrupulous attention to evidence and its analysis has proved to provide a fruitful standpoint for inquiry in areas where beliefs can be fixed by such methods.

There is a dogma called "scientism" according to which it is irrational to believe anything that has not been established by the empirical methods of the sciences. I hope this essay is not read as an exercise in scientism. There are a few useful guide dogmas, but scientism is not one of them. My purpose has been to show in a general way where the line is drawn between the paradigms of scientific inquiry and other ways of establishing beliefs. Like Peirce, I do think that some methods of fixing belief are better than others in the long run in getting us the truths we can live by. But I am also convinced that no single orientation to truth seeking will completely satisfy our human drive to understand the world and ourselves in it.

Notes

[1] Charles Sanders Peirce, "The Fixation of Belief," in *Philosophical Writings of Peirce*, ed. Justus Buchler (New York: Dover, 1955), 10.

[2] Ibid., 12.

[3] Ibid., 14.

[4] Ibid., 17.

[5] Ibid., 18.

[6] Karl R. Popper, *Conjectures and Refutations* (New York: Basic Books, 1962), 37.

[7] Thomas S. Kuhn, *The Structure of Scientific Revolutions* (2d. ed. Chicago: University of Chicago Press, 1970).

[8] Ibid., "Postscript," 174–210.

[9] Ibid., 42.

[10] James R. Lewis, *Encyclopedia of Astrology* (Detroit: Gale Research, 1994), xvi.

[11] Ibid.

[12] Ibid., xxii.

[13] Alfred Watkins, *Early English Trackways,* (1922).

[14] Ibid., *The Old Straight Track* (1925), quoted in http://whitcomb.sbc.edu/earthmysteries/EMLeyLines.html (Jan. 15, 2008).

[15] http://skepdic.com/leylines.html (Jan. 15, 2008).

[16] This was as of my visit there in 2001.

[17] http://geo.org/qa.htm#tof (revised Feb. 14, 2000, accessed Jan. 15, 2008).

[18] Ibid.

[19] Ibid.

[20] James Ussher, *Annals of the World: James Ussher's Classic Survey of World History,* Larry Pierce and Marion Pierce, eds. (Master Books, 2003).

[21] Robert T. Pennock, *Tower of Babel: The Evidence Against the New Creationism* (Cambridge, MA: MIT Press, 1999), 216 ff.

[22] Ibid., 234.

[23] David Hume, *Dialogues Concerning Natural Religion* (1779).

[24] http://www.icr.org/research (accessed January 25, 2008).

[25] Popper, Ch. 1.

[26] See, for instance, Stephen Jay Gould, "Bushes and Ladders in Human Evolution," in *Ever Since Darwin* (New York: W.W. Norton, 1977) 56–62.

[27] Stephen Jay Gould, *Rocks of Ages; Science and Religion in the Fullness of Life* (New York: Ballantine, 1999), 4.

[28] Ibid., 4–5.

Anita Ho is a philosopher of medical ethics who taught at St. Kate's for several years and is now associate professor at the W. Maurice Young Centre for Applied Ethics at the University of British Columbia and director of ethics services at Providence Health Care. In this piece written in 2002 for the TRW Reader, Ho asks us to consider the philosophical nature of moral truth. Are there any absolute or universal moral standards? What are the ramifications of thinking there are or are not? Raised in Hong Kong, educated and teaching in Canada, Ho is well positioned to address both cultural and individual differences in customs and beliefs. She critically evaluates arguments for and against ethical relativism and subjectivism. Does this help you to clarify your own values? In the end, do you agree with Ho that a universal approach to morality does not imply ethnocentrism?

"It's So Judgmental!"
A Lesson on Subjectivity and Relativism

Anita Ho

"I wouldn't do it, but how can I tell you that you can't do it either?" one of my students comments on the issue of slavery. "I believe in equality, and I think it is wrong for me to own slaves. But who am I to tell you that you shouldn't own slaves? That's your decision to make, not mine!" Other students from the class start to get into the discussion. One of them says, "I agree. We should just mind our own business. How can we tell others what to do and what not to do? It's so judgmental!"

Yes, we are talking about relativism and subjectivism. We are trying to figure out if there are any absolute or universal moral standards that each and every one of us should follow. We are wondering if there are certain things that people should simply never do to another human being. Almost all my students say that there is no such universal moral standard. Each culture has its own custom, and people outside of that culture should not interfere. As a matter of fact, some students believe that each person has his or her own moral beliefs, and people should not tell others that they are wrong.

Our discussion moves from slavery to the Holocaust. I ask, "What about the Nazis? Can't we say that it was absolutely wrong for them to kill six million Jews?"

Everyone looks at each other. A couple of them gently nod, but still say that they cannot tell the Nazis what to do. One of them says that it was horrible that the Nazis killed these people. She says she hopes that nobody would ever do this again. However, she understands why they did it. She says, "These people were taught to believe that the Jewish people were subhuman. Obviously, I don't believe in that. But it is easy for me to say that, because we don't have Hitler here. But if these people were brought up in that environment, it is unfair for outsiders to judge them."

Other students make similar remarks. They say that the concentration camps were terrible, but they refuse to say that it was morally wrong for the Nazi Germans to kill all those people.

What's happening here? Really, can we not say that ethnic cleansing and slavery are absolutely wrong, no matter who you are, where you live, and when you live? Do these students really believe that we should not judge these actions, even though they also think that they themselves should not engage in these practices? Is it really so bad to be judgmental on some issues? I know some of these students are working in various volunteering projects to promote social justice, so why do they somehow deny that there is fundamental injustice in some practices? Are they simply confused about what they believe in?

Students often say that there is no such thing as a "universal moral standard." They insist that morality is simply a matter of one's own personal opinion. You have your opinion, and I have mine. You cannot tell me that I am wrong, and I also cannot tell you that you are wrong. They worry that believing in universal moral standards means that they are arrogant and are trying to impose their viewpoints on others. As Robert Simon says, students often think that any criticism of another culture's practices or ideologies is a kind of cultural imperialism.[1] There is the belief that if a practice is part of some people's cultural or moral belief, and if it has worked for them, then others should not pass judgment or interfere.

Worrying about being called judgmental and arrogant, many students say that they are *relativists*. They use the word in many different ways, but in general, they think that ethical beliefs or viewpoints are relative to societies and cultures. If your culture believes in footbinding, it is correct for your culture. If it does not, it is incorrect for your culture. Other cultures may have different ideas than your culture, and they can judge the rightness of this practice according to their own cultural beliefs. However, they cannot judge *your* culture's ideology, but can only determine for *themselves* what is right and wrong. If the Nazi Germans believe that ethnic cleansing was acceptable in their culture, contemporary Americans like my students simply cannot judge them, even if my students would not want that to happen here.

What is interesting in our discussion about relativism is that, students seem to believe that not only are cultures entitled to their traditions and beliefs, but so are individuals. When we start talking about whether it is absolutely wrong for an American today to own slaves, most students are still reluctant to say yes. I ask, "If you find out that your neighbor has a slave, you still don't think that is wrong?" One student says, "Well, I don't think I can tell anyone what to do. Of course I wouldn't own slaves, but what he does is not my business." In other words, it seems that my students believe that each and every individual is the only one who can decide what is right for himself or herself.

Surprised by the unanimous agreement among my students who almost never agree on anything, I proceed with the most awful and shocking example I can think of: "Suppose there is a group of people who believe that burning babies just for fun is acceptable." One student whispers, "Oh my god!" Another student quietly says, "Yuck!" Almost all of them give me a big, long, and disgusted stare. I realize that I am on dangerous ground, but I am hoping that a shocking and extreme example can get my students to rethink their position. I cautiously ask, "Can we tell them that it is absolutely wrong for them to do that? Can we say that it does not matter what their preference of entertainment may be, it is simply wrong for anyone to burn babies for fun?"

By the look of disbelief and shock on my students' faces, I start to think that they may be seriously questioning their position.

A few seconds lapse, and then I hear a quiet voice, "I guess it is awful for anyone to do that." A couple other nods follow.

I secretly think, *I am getting somewhere.*

Then, I hear a voice, "Yeah, but I still don't think we can make such a blank statement to say that it is wrong for anyone to do this. Sure, I think it is gross and everything, and like I said about slavery, I wouldn't do this myself. But again, I don't think I can tell these people what to do. I don't think we should be judgmental about what others do. I am not God. I can't tell others what is right and what is wrong."

Another voice follows, "I agree. I'm sitting here thinking, would I want others to tell me that what I do in my private life is wrong? No! I should be allowed to do whatever I believe in. I don't need to explain anything to other people. It's my life!"

Do students really believe that? Why do even the best students think that we can never say that there are things that are simply wrong?

When I probe the matter further, I realize that these students seem not only to be ethical relativists, but also subjectivists. They say that whether something is right or wrong depends solely on what you subjectively believe. For example, if I believe burning babies is a cruel and illegitimate way to derive pleasure, then it is wrong for me. If you believe it is the best form of entertainment, then it is right for you. People have different perspectives, and no one can say that one perspective is objectively better than another.

This is a worrying position. If everything is "free for all" and people can do whatever they want, wouldn't we have chaos? Why would our students believe in such a position?

Arguments for Ethical Relativism and Subjectivism

There are a few reasons why students are or at least think they are ethical relativists and subjectivists. "Evidence" of diversity is overwhelming. People of different times and places have vastly different or even conflicting ideologies and experiences. Anthropologists such as Ruth Benedict have given us numerous examples to show that it is not unusual for one society to approve of an act that is held to be abnormal or immoral by another.[2] When people around the world have vastly different customs and beliefs, it is unclear how we can evaluate them objectively. Some cultures avoid eating certain types of animals, while others use different kinds of animals for celebration. Some cultures avoid using certain numbers (e.g., "7" in the Chinese culture), while other societies think of the same number as lucky. Certain societies believe that female circumcision is an important element of cultural identity, while others believe that such practice is oppressive and barbaric. Some cultures require women to wear head-to-toe burkas, while other societies allow women to wear bikinis or even go to nude beaches.

On an individual level, there are also different ideas of the morality of practices such as abortion, capital punishment, and cloning. In the face of diversity, it is doubtful that we have any one custom or practice that is embraced by all. It is also unclear if anyone has a legitimate basis for interfering with customs and practices that are different from their own.

Ethical relativism and subjectivism also seem more plausible when we consider how there are various perspectives even among academics who are supposedly "experts" on ethics. They disagree on all the aforementioned ethical issues. If there is disagreement even among experts on the morality of various practices, it seems unlikely that there can be any absolute moral standard governing everyone. As one of my students says, "If these so-called experts can't straighten everything out for us, I doubt we can ever come to agreement anywhere else."

Another reason why many embrace ethical relativism and subjectivism is that they are uncertain if any culture or person should have the authority to determine for everyone else what is moral and immoral. As my students ask, who can be the judge, and how can we force others who have different ideologies to adopt our values? They claim that people of various societies should respect each other and not interfere with their culture and customs. They sometimes also say that whatever happens within a culture or society, it is a "domestic" or "private" matter of that society, and people outside of that society have no right to criticize its "domestic affairs." If certain societies require their women to wear a burka, we should simply respect their custom.

Foreign diplomats have said similar things. Chinese officials, for example, have repeatedly criticized the United States and other countries for trying to interfere with their domestic policies, such as how they deal with dissidents and criminal defendants. They argue that other countries have no right to impose their values on China. They insist that other countries that try to interfere with their internal affairs are claiming moral superiority and are therefore ethnocentric. In a speech regarding the China–U. S. relationship, President Jiang Zemin of The Republic of China argues that friendly relations and cooperation can only exist on the principles of "mutual non-aggression" and "non-interference in each other's internal affairs."[3] He insists that the United States cannot legitimately ask all countries to institute the same political system or to judge the various choices made by people of other countries according to their own values.

Many people also think that we can only have a harmonious society if we respect different ideologies. They worry that allowing some people to make decisions for everyone else will inevitably lead to an oppressive and totalitarian regime. This is especially an important concern for democratic societies like the United States, since we cannot consistently argue for democracy and at the same time impose certain beliefs on other cultures or even our own citizens. After all, democracy requires that all rational human beings be allowed to determine for themselves their way of life and personal values. It requires that others do not authoritatively impose their view as absolute and coerce everyone else to follow it. When there are different moral standards, we cannot simply ignore the perspectives of certain individuals. Imposing one's moral standard on others ignores people's ability to make decisions for themselves and violates their autonomy. As some of my students say, it seems to be pure arrogance for us to exalt our own morality as the only true one and dismiss all other ideas as false or inferior.

Responses to Ethical Relativists and Subjectivists

It is admirable that students want to respect different perspectives. But does respect require that we can never say that certain practices are illegitimate? Students are correct that there are many different beliefs in the world, and it is often difficult to find one right answer for any ethical dilemma. There are usually many complex issues involved in each case, and sometimes there is no simple way to reach an answer. In many instances, even after reflecting on various possible perspectives, we may still not know which perspective is the best one.

However, admitting the difficulty to determine which of the various perspectives is best is different from claiming that each perspective is equally valid, or that we cannot critically evaluate them. Just because there are numerous perspectives or ethical positions does not mean that everything reduces to cultural or personal opinions, or that there is no right or wrong answer to anything. While it is often difficult to find the right answer, we do not have to immediately reject the possibility that some perspectives have *more* validity than others. Although it is difficult to find *one* idea that will be agreeable for all, it is often possible for us to find out which viewpoints are at least more plausible than others. Sometimes even when we do not know what the best answer may be, we can still say that there are certain perspectives that are clearly objectionable. For example, although it is difficult to find a simple answer to the question of how we should treat other human beings, it is clear that there are good reasons to reject the idea that we can kill others whenever we want. Killing each other is a less plausible perspective *in any society* partly because life will become "nasty, brutish, and short," to use the philosopher Thomas Hobbes' phrase.[4]

It is admirable that students want to listen to and respect different perspectives. I agree that we need to refrain from assuming that there is always only one answer to each problem. There are times when there may be various plausible approaches to deal with an ethical issue. I also agree that we should not assume that we are always correct, and that dissenting viewpoints are automatically inferior or wrong. However, the argument that some perspectives are objectively better than others does not imply that one is presuming her moral superiority. Rather, the universal approach to morality only says that there are certain perspectives that are objectively more valid than others, and that these perspectives should apply to everyone. Our job is to *consider various perspectives carefully,* and then find out which ones are better than the rest, and why they are better. It is consistent for one to argue that some perspectives are better and deny that one actually is holding the better perspective. When we question the legitimacy of relativistic positions, we are not saying that we have to condemn *other* people's values. What we are saying is that we need to critically evaluate every perspective, *including our own.* Such a task acknowledges the possibility that we may be holding the wrong perspective.

In other words, it is a mistake to think that a universal approach to morality implies ethnocentrism. It is also a mistake to think that relativistic positions only ask us to withhold judgment of other people's cultural and personal beliefs. Relativism and subjectivism actually permit us to not even judge or evaluate our own beliefs. After all, under these relativistic positions, you do not need to question your beliefs. As one of my students says, she does not want anyone to tell her that she may be wrong, because she thinks she should be allowed to do whatever she believes in.

Her idea is that, whatever you believe in is right for you. You do not have to explain or justify to others why you believe in certain things, and others have no right to impose their standard on you. In other words, there is no need for you to give reasons for your actions.

In this way, it is not the universal approach to morality that leads to ethnocentrism and unwillingness to question one's own beliefs. Rather, it is when we adopt a relativistic approach that we may fall into the idea that we are always correct in holding our own beliefs, so that we do not need to critically examine or correct our own belief. After all, if we are all correct in our opinions, we never have to question whether our sense of morality is distorted. Ironically, it seems that by adopting the universal approach to morality, we can have a better chance of questioning our own beliefs.

It is admirable that students want to withhold judgment of other cultures and people. Certainly, people from different cultural and social backgrounds may not understand each other's viewpoint, and without such understanding it is arrogant to impose our views on others. Some societies have long-established traditions, and it may be difficult and traumatic to make them change their ways of life, since people may feel that they are losing their cultural identity. When we are non-judgmental, we can learn from each other and improve our understanding of others' viewpoints. Such a tolerant attitude can help us to live harmoniously in a morally and culturally diverse society.

Moreover, it is only when we all respect others and remain tolerant that those of minority opinions have a fair chance to express their views. One of the reasons why democratic societies are appealing is that everyone has a legal right to express his or her ideas, even when his or her views are in the minority.[5] Maintaining such a tolerant attitude ensures that unpopular views are not being unfairly suppressed.

While these are all good reasons for us to keep an open mind, commitments to respect others and keep an open mind do not imply that ethical relativism and subjectivism are correct. While some customs and practices are relatively innocent and people should have a right to engage in them, not all practices fall into this category. Certainly, worshipping, burning incense, or not eating certain animals do not negatively affect the lives of others, and there is little reason to reject such practices even if we do not agree with them. However, it seems that there are limits on what people can do in the name of customs or personal beliefs. When one's action harms another person, as in the examples of ethnic cleansing and slavery, it is unclear if one can justify it simply by claiming that it is one's cultural or personal belief. It is also unclear if people can deny the legitimacy of criticism or interference in the convenient name of "internal affairs" or "private matters."

John Stuart Mill's idea of liberty may be helpful here. As a moral philosopher who values liberty, Mill argues that the only justification for interfering with liberty is to prevent harm to others.[6] Mill acknowledges that people have different beliefs, and we need to have open dialogues to discuss such beliefs. He argues that freedom of expression should be allowed, since it is only when we have such freedom that we can fairly evaluate various perspectives and get closer to the truth. Mill also values diversity and originality. He argues that we should not try to shape people after one model, but should allow them to develop in their own ways. He argues that we should resist "forcing improvements on an unwilling people," since "the only unfailing and permanent source of improvement is liberty."[7] Mill argues that even when we disagree with each other's choices, *if such choices do not harm others,* we cannot interfere.

This last point is important. Mill treasures liberty and autonomy, and he thinks that we need to allow rational adults to express their own views and act on their own ideologies. However, he does not think that respect for others implies that we have to allow absolute freedom. There can still be limits to what people can do. As Mill says, "the fact of living in society renders it indispensable that each should be bound to observe a certain line of conduct towards the rest."[8] For example, people cannot injure the interests of another. After all, one cannot consistently argue for one's own freedom but harm another. In this way, respect for freedom does not imply that people should never be accountable for their actions. We can argue that people can engage in various activities in accordance with their cultural and personal ideology, *so long as their actions do not harm another human being's well being or violate another's freedom.* For example, ethnic cleansing and killing infants for entertainment purposes cannot be justified by cultural and personal ideologies, because they harm other people.

More Problems for Ethical Relativists and Subjectivists

Mill's "harm principle" brings out another inadequacy of ethical relativism and subjectivism. When pushed to the extreme, relativistic views run into trouble. Their view that morality is relative to one's cultural or individual beliefs makes it impossible for anyone to condemn or correct even the most atrocious practices. Ethical relativists and subjectivists do not distinguish between innocent customs and unethical practices. They seem to think that they are morally equivalent, i.e., they are all correct if you believe in them. Their failure to see the distinction may have led them to deny the legitimacy of condemning practices that are harmful to others. This is perhaps why many students refuse to say that the Nazi Germans were absolutely wrong in killing six million Jews. After all, we cannot condemn ethnic cleansing unless we accept the view that these practices are not "simply domestic affairs," and that they are wrong regardless of people's personal or cultural beliefs.

One may ask, does it matter whether one believes in relativism or subjectivism? What is the big deal? If we simply allow people to do what they believe in, can't we get along better?

No. I don't think we can get along better by being relativists. Yes. It is a big deal if people believe in relativism. It has enormous implications for social policies and justice issues. After all, we cannot do anything to "correct" injustice unless we can truly say that certain things that happened to people in the past were wrong. If we adopt a relativistic approach, we will be rejecting some of the most important ideas, such as the notion of human rights. Human rights are supposed to apply to all human beings regardless of who they are, where they live, and when they are born. No society or individual is allowed to violate these rights, regardless of their cultural or personal beliefs.

What will happen if we all become relativists? As shown in my class discussion, we will not be able to say that people were wrong in owning slaves, because they lived in a different time in which such practice was allowed. We also will not be able to talk intelligently about international tribunals prosecuting war crimes. If the Nazi Germans believed that it was morally legitimate to kill Jewish people, then according to ethical relativism, it was right for them to do so. It makes no difference that other societies thought or continue to think that it was wrong for the Nazis to kill innocent people. We also cannot criticize the Taliban regime in Afghanistan, even though they publicly kill women who go outside without a male relative or a burka. If we accept relativism, we will have to say that all these actions are morally right for those who believe in them. If we disagree with such actions, all that means is that we will not condone it in our own society. However, acceptance of ethical relativism implies that we cannot interfere with or even intelligently criticize the Taliban's policies.

In the end, we will not act against injustice. If we cannot even say that certain things are morally wrong, of course we will not do anything to prevent or correct the wrong. We also do not need to strive for better societies. If the belief that we are entitled to our opinions implies that we are all correct in holding our opinions, then there is no point of questioning or improving ourselves. We will always be right! Ethical relativism and subjectivism seem to give us a convenient justification never to question our own viewpoints. It also provides justification for us to sit by and do nothing even when we have fundamental disagreement on moral matters.

It is no surprise that many proponents of ethical relativism, such as China and other regimes in the Middle East, have been the most flagrant violators of human rights. After all, if various cultures are entitled to their own moral standard and call their practices "domestic policies," other cultures cannot judge them or interfere with their policies. They are automatically immune from scrutiny. Feminists have criticized how many abuses of women are tolerated in the name of privacy and family autonomy. Women who suffer from abuse and other forms of inequality and violence often are not protected under relativistic positions, because what happens in a household or society is considered a private or domestic matter. Such matters cannot be interfered with, even if others may not agree with them. After all, under ethical relativism and subjectivism, whatever people believe is right for them.

What is most startling about ethical relativism and subjectivism is that, according to these doctrines, we can hold contradictory views and all be correct at the same time! According to relativism and subjectivism, part of the reason why we cannot criticize and interfere with each other's position is that we are each correct in holding our individual views! If I believe that physical assault is the right way to teach my spouse about his household duties, it is right for me to do so. If you are against such practice, your view is right for you. In the end, we are both right![9] This means that it is impossible for any culture to condone the wrong practice, or for any individual to believe in the wrong thing.

This is certainly a convenient but troubling position. If we accept the subjectivist idea and believe that we are each correct in believing contradicting positions, it is unclear if any society can legitimately have laws. It appears that under subjectivism, laws are inherently discriminatory, since they treat certain moral beliefs unfavorably. After all, laws that prohibit people from killing others or beating their spouses impose a standard on those who may have different beliefs. They prohibit these people to act on their beliefs.

Certainly, ethical relativists may argue that we need laws for practical reasons, since chaos will result if people can do anything that they "believe" in. However, the fact that we need laws to prevent chaos already shows that ethical relativists and subjectivists are mistaken. Contrary to what they believe, we simply cannot have a harmonious world or safe society if we take these relativistic positions seriously and allow people to do whatever they believe.

Putting aside the problem of chaos in accepting ethical relativism and subjectivism, it seems absurd that the correctness of a position depends on whether one believes in it. My students seem to think that whether slavery is wrong depends on whether people who own slaves believe in such a practice. (Of course, these students are not thinking about whether the slaves agree with such a practice!) But this makes all moral judgments arbitrary. If a culture or an individual happens to believe that owning slaves is wrong, it is wrong. However, if this culture or individual happens to hold the opposite belief, then owning slaves is moral. It does not ask *why* a certain culture or individual believes in various practices. It only asks *if* this culture or individual believes them.

However, it is unclear how my believing in certain things automatically makes it right. Relativistic positions do not require us to give independent reasons or logical arguments for holding such beliefs. They seem to believe that what we *think* is right is the same with what *is* right. The fact that some people believe in ethnic cleansing is sufficient to make it right for them. They do not need to provide any other supporting arguments to show *why* they believe such a practice is right. If another group of people believe the opposite, they also do not need to explain why they hold such position.

If ethical relativism and subjectivism are true, moral dialogues or arguments will be meaningless. As I ask my students who are reluctant to say that anything is morally wrong, what is the point of studying ethics, if we are all correct in believing in whatever opinion we happen to hold? There is no point of evaluating different moral positions. And what is the point of trying to teach our children to become "moral citizens"? They can simply do whatever they want, and they will automatically be right! Moreover, what is the point of convincing others or even ourselves that our point of view may have merits? After all, others are also equally correct in holding their viewpoints.

When everyone is automatically right at all times, the whole notion of moral progress is also meaningless. Moral progress means an improvement from worse to better, and it implies an acknowledgement that certain ideologies are better than others. According to relativistic positions, however, we cannot say that the society we are living in right now is better than the one that allowed slavery. We cannot say that various anti-discriminatory practices enforced in the United States today are better than the discriminatory ones that resulted in the deaths of millions in Germany in the 1940s.

It is difficult to balance tolerance and a critical perception of various cultural and individual ideologies. On the one hand, we need to be open-minded and allow other rational beings to reach moral judgements on their own. On the other hand, we also need to keep in mind that being open-minded does not mean that we cannot be critical of various ideas, or that every idea is equally valid. In other words, while we need to keep an open mind, we can still reject ethical relativism or subjectivism. Certainly, we need to be extremely careful in evaluating various views and imposing our views on others. We may be wrong, or there may be practical difficulties in imposing our views on others. However, a commitment to respect others and to keep an open mind does not imply that we can never make judgments about right and wrong. When we keep an open mind, we have a greater chance of understanding each other's viewpoints. At the same time, we will also be more equipped in critically evaluating various positions, including our own. Respect of others only requires that we carefully evaluate different perspectives, and give people of different ideologies an equal chance to explain and defend their respective positions. It requires that we do not assume authority on moral matters and automatically judge others' perspectives as inferior to ours. However, ethical relativism and subjectivism are not the best ways to keep us open-minded and respectful of others. In fact, they prevent us from understanding different viewpoints. The idea that there are universal moral standards may give us a better chance to evaluate critically various ideologies. The universal approach to morality does not argue that we are the ones who always have the right answer, and that others who have different ideologies are inferior. Rather, it requires that we all accept the possibility that everyone is susceptible to mistakes, and we all have to be patient and careful in investigating various moral positions.

I discuss all these issues with my students. Are they convinced? One of them says, "I guess I was wrong in thinking that I am a relativist. I am still not sure when we can impose our ideas on others, but I do think our laws prohibiting slavery and killing are right, and those who commit these acts should be punished." Another says, "I never thought that relativism might give people the perfect reason to sit by and watch injustice happening in the world, but I guess it inevitably leads to that." A few more students nod. As we are ready to leave the class, one student says, "Well, I guess that's your opinion. I still don't buy it." I respond, "And you can't tell me I am wrong."

Notes

[1] Robert Simon, "The Paralysis of Absolutophobia," *The Chronicle of Higher Education*, 27 June 1997, 85–86.

[2] Ruth Benedict, "Ethics Are Relative," in *Classical Philosophical Questions* 9th ed., ed. J. A. Gould (Upper Saddle River, NJ: Prentice Hall, 1998), 159–167.

[3] For the complete speech made by President Jiang, please see http://www.ncuscr.org/articles%20and%20speeches/jiang.speech.html

[4] Thomas Hobbes, *Leviathan* (1651; reprint, Harmondsworth, Middlesex: Penguin Books, 1975), 186.

[5] There are often other barriers to minorities actually voicing their opinions, even when they have the legal right to do so. For example, minorities may worry about the "tyranny of the majority." They may worry that even when they have the "right" to voice their opinions, their unpopular views will still go unnoticed or be intentionally ignored. However, for the purpose of this essay, I will put aside this issue.

[6] John Stuart Mill, *On Liberty* (1859; reprint, London: Penguin Books, 1985).

[7] Mill, 136.

[8] Mill, 141.

[9] The ironic result of ethical relativism and subjectivism is that their proponents cannot prove that I am wrong. They cannot even try to convince me that they are correct. If I believe that there are universal moral standards, according to subjectivism, I am automatically correct! In the end, ethical relativism, subjectivism, and a universal approach to morality are all correct!

Kenneth R. Miller is professor of biology and Royce Family Professor for Teaching Excellence at Brown University. As a public intellectual, a scientist and a Catholic, he has argued widely for the compatibility of religion with Darwin's theory of evolution. In this article from the Brown University Alumni Magazine *(1999), which summarizes some of his points in his book* Finding Darwin's God *(1999), he connects a theological way of knowing with that of science. A key tenet of the Catholic intellectual tradition is that faith and reason are not at odds—a viewpoint that Miller shares. Why is it, according to Miller, that creationist thinking (which holds a literalist interpretation of the Bible and denies evolution) is much more dangerous to religion than to science? What does he mean that the creationists have sought God in darkness? Miller also addresses our uneasiness with the indeterminate nature of evolution and its implications for the nature of human existence. Does his answer to this work for you? Would you agree that Miller's analysis provides us with a way to reconcile two ways of knowing: scientific and religious?*

Finding Darwin's God

Kenneth R. Miller

The great hall of the Hynes Convention Center in Boston looks nothing like a church. And yet I sat there, smiling amid an audience of scientists, shaking my head and laughing to myself as I remembered another talk, given long ago, inside a church to an audience of children.

Without warning, I had experienced one of those moments in the present that connects with the scattered recollections of our past. Psychologists tell us that things happen all the time. Five thousand days of childhood are filed, not in chronological order, but as bits and pieces linked by words, or sounds, or even smells that cause us to retrieve them for no apparent reason when something "refreshes" our memory. And just like that, a few words in a symposium on developmental biology had brought me back to the day before my first communion. I was eight years old, sitting with the boys on the right side of our little church (the girls sat on the left), and our pastor was speaking.

Putting the finishing touches on a year of preparation for the sacrament, Father Murphy sought to impress us with the reality of God's power in the world. He pointed to the altar railing, its polished marble gleaming in sunlight, and firmly assured us that God himself had fashioned it. "Yeah, right," whispered the kid next to me. Worried that there might be the son or daughter of a stonecutter in the crowd, the good Father retreated a bit. "Now, he didn't carve the railing or bring it here or cement it in place . . .

but God himself *made* the marble, long ago, and left it for someone to find and make into part of our church."

I don't know if our pastor sensed that his description of God as craftsman was meeting a certain tide of skepticism, but no matter. He had another trick up his sleeve, a can't-miss, sure-thing argument that, no doubt, had never failed him. He walked over to the altar and picked a flower from the vase.

"Look at the beauty of a flower," he began. "The Bible tells us that even Solomon in all his glory was never arrayed as one of these. And do you know what? Not a single person in the world can tell us what makes a flower bloom. All those scientists in their laboratories, the ones who can split the atom and build jet planes and televisions, well, not one of them can tell you how a plant makes flowers." And why should they be able to? "Flowers, just like you, are the work of God."

I was impressed. No one argued, no one wisecracked. We filed out of the church like good little boys and girls, ready for our first communion the next day. And I never thought of it again, until this symposium on developmental biology. Sandwiched between two speakers working on more fashionable topics in animal development was Elliot M. Meyerowitz, a plant scientist at Caltech. A few of my colleagues, uninterested in research dealing with plants, got up to stretch their legs before the final talk, but I sat there with an ear-to-ear grin on my face. I jotted notes furiously; I sketched the diagrams he projected on the screen and wrote additional speculations of my own in the margins. Meyerowitz, you see, had explained how plants make flowers.

The four principal parts of a flower—sepals, petals, stamens, and pistils—are actually modified leaves. This is one of the reasons why plants can produce reproductive cells just about anywhere, while animals are limited to a very specific set of reproductive organs. Your little finger isn't going to start shedding reproductive cells anytime soon. But in springtime, the tip of any branch on an apple tree may very well blossom and begin scattering pollen. Plants can produce new flowers anywhere they can grow new leaves. Somehow, however, the plant must find a way to "tell" an ordinary cluster of leaves that they should develop into floral parts. That's where Meyerowitz's lab took over.

Several years of patient genetic study had isolated a set of mutants that could only form two or three of the four parts. By crossing the various mutants, his team was able to identify four genes that had to be turned on or off in a specific pattern to produce a normal flower. Each of these genes, in turn, sets off a series of signals that "tell" the cells of a brand new bud to develop as sepals or petals rather than ordinary leaves. The details are remarkable, and the interactions between the genes are fascinating. To me, sitting in the crowd thirty-seven years after my first communion, the scientific details were just the icing on the cake. The real message was "Father Murphy, you were wrong." God doesn't make a flower. The floral induction genes do.

Our pastor's error, common and widely repeated, was to seek God in what science has not yet explained. His assumption was that God is best found in territory unknown, in the corners of darkness that have not yet seen the light of understanding. These, as it turns out, are exactly the wrong places to look.

Searching the Shadows

By pointing to the process of making a flower as proof of the reality of God, Father Murphy was embracing the idea that God finds it necessary to cripple nature. In his view, the blooming of a daffodil requires not a self-sufficient material universe, but direct intervention by God. We can find God, therefore, in the things around us that lack material, scientific explanations. In nature, elusive and unexplored, we will find the Creator at work.

The creationist opponents of evolution make similar arguments. They claim that the existence of life, the appearance of new species, and, most especially, the origins of mankind have not and cannot be explained by evolution or any other natural process. By denying the self-sufficiency of nature, they look for God (or at least a "designer") in the deficiencies of science. The trouble is that science, given enough time, generally explains even the most baffling things. As a matter of strategy, creationists would be well-advised to avoid telling scientists what they will never be able to figure out. History is against them. In a general way, we really do understand how nature works.

And evolution forms a critical part of that understanding. Evolution really does explain the very things that its critics say it does not. Claims disputing the antiquity of the earth, the validity of the fossil record, and the sufficiency of evolutionary mechanisms vanish upon close inspection. Even to the most fervent anti-evolutionists, the pattern should be clear—their favorite "gaps" are filling up: the molecular mechanisms of evolution are now well-understood, and the historical record of evolution becomes more compelling with each passing season. This means that science can answer their challenges to evolution in an obvious way. Show the historical record, provide the data, reveal the mechanism, and highlight the convergence of theory and fact.

There is, however, a deeper problem caused by the opponents of evolution, a problem for religion. Like our priest, they have based their search for God on the premise that nature is *not* self-sufficient. By such logic, only God can make a species, just as Father Murphy believed only God could make a flower. Both assertions support the existence of God *only* so long as these assertions are true, but serious problems for religion emerge when they are shown to be false.

If we accept a *lack* of scientific explanation as proof for God's existence, simple logic would dictate that we would have to regard a successful scientific explanation as an argument *against* God. That's why creationist reasoning, ultimately, is much more dangerous to religion than to science. Elliot Meyerowitz's fine work on floral induction suddenly becomes a threat to the divine, even though common sense tells us it should be nothing of the sort. By arguing, as creationists do, that nature cannot be self-sufficient in the formation of new species, the creationists forge a logical link between the limits of natural processes to accomplish biological change and the existence of a designer (God). In other words, they show the proponents of atheism exactly how to disprove the existence of God—show that evolution works, and it's time to tear down the temple. This is an offer that the enemies of religion are all too happy to accept.

Putting it bluntly, the creationists have sought God in darkness. What we have not found and do not yet understand becomes their best—indeed their only—evidence for the divine. As a Christian, I find the flow of this logic particularly depressing. Not only does it teach us to fear the acquisition of knowledge (which might at any time disprove belief), but it suggests that God dwells only in the shadows of our understanding. I suggest that, if God is real, we should be able to find him somewhere else—in the bright light of human knowledge, spiritual and scientific.

Faith and Reason

Each of the great Western monotheistic traditions sees God as truth, love, and knowledge. This should mean that each and every increase in our understanding of the natural world is a step toward God and not, as many people assume, a step away. If faith and reason are both gifts from God, then they should play complementary, not conflicting, roles in our struggle to understand the world around us. As a scientist and as a Christian, that is exactly what I believe. True knowledge comes only from a combination of faith and reason.

A nonbeliever, of course, puts his or her trust in science and finds no value in faith. And I certainly agree that science allows believer and nonbeliever alike to investigate the natural world through a common lens of observation, experiment, and theory. The ability of science to transcend cultural, political, and even religious differences is part of its genius, part of its value as a way of knowing. What science cannot do is assign either meaning or purpose to the world it explores. This leads some to conclude that the world as seen by science is devoid of meaning and absent of purpose. It is not. What it does mean, I would suggest, is that our human tendency to assign meaning and value must transcend science and, ultimately, must come from outside it. The science that results can thus be enriched and informed from its contact with the values and principles of faith. The God of Abraham does not tell us which proteins control the cell cycle. But he does give us a reason to care, a reason to cherish that understanding, and above all, a reason to prefer the light of knowledge to the darkness of ignorance.

As more than one scientist has said, the truly remarkable thing about the world is that it actually does make sense. The parts fit, the molecules interact, the darn thing works. To people of faith, what evolution says is that nature is complete. Their God fashioned a material world in which truly free and independent beings could evolve. He got it right the very first time.

To some, the murderous reality of human nature is proof that God is absent or dead. The same reasoning would find God missing from the unpredictable branchings of an evolutionary tree. But the truth is deeper. In each case, a deity determined to establish a world that was truly independent of his whims, a world in which intelligent creatures would face authentic choices between good and evil, would have to fashion a distinct, material reality and then let his creation run. Neither the self-sufficiency of nature nor the reality of evil in the world mean God is absent. To a religious person, both signify something quite different—the strength of God's love and the reality of our freedom as his creatures.

The Weapons of Disbelief

As a species, we like to see ourselves as the best and brightest. We are the intended, special, primary creatures of creation. We sit at the apex of the evolutionary tree as the ultimate products of nature, self-proclaimed and self-aware. We like to think that evolution's goal was to produce us.

In a purely biological sense, this comforting view of our own position in nature is false, a product of self-inflating distortion induced by the imperfect mirrors we hold up to life. Yes, we are objectively among the most complex of animals, but not in every sense. Among the systems of the body, we are the hands-down winners for physiological complexity in just one place—the nervous system—and even there, a nonprimate (the dolphin) can lay down a claim that rivals our own.

More to the point, any accurate assessment of the evolutionary process shows that the notion of one form of life being more highly evolved than another is incorrect. Every organism, every cell that lives today, is the descendant of a long line of winners, of ancestors who used successful evolutionary strategies time and time again, and therefore lived to tell about it—or, at least, to reproduce. The bacterium perched on the lip of my coffee cup has been through as much evolution as I have. I've got the advantage of size and consciousness, which matter when I write about evolution, but the bacterium has the advantage of numbers, of flexibility, and most especially, of reproductive speed. That single bacterium, given the right conditions, could literally fill the world with its descendants in a matter of days. No human, no vertebrate, no animal could boast of anything remotely as impressive.

What evolution tells us is that life spreads out along endless branching pathways from any starting point. One of those tiny branches eventually led to us. We think it remarkable and wonder how it could have happened, but any fair assessment of the tree of life shows that our tiny branch is crowded into insignificance by those that bolted off in a thousand different directions. Our species, *Homo sapiens*, has not "triumphed" in the evolutionary struggle any more than has a squirrel, a dandelion, or a mosquito. We are all here, now, and that's what matters. We have all followed different pathways to find ourselves in the present. We are all winners in the game of natural selection. *Current* winners, we should be careful to say.

That, in the minds of many, is exactly the problem. In a thousand branching pathways, how can we be sure that one of them, historically and unavoidably, would lead for sure to us? Consider this: we mammals now occupy, in most ecosystems, the roles of large, dominant land animals. But for much of their history, mammals were restricted to habitats in which only very small creatures could survive. Why? Because another group of vertebrates dominated the earth—until, as Stephen Jay Gould has pointed out, the cataclysmic impact of a comet or asteroid drove those giants to extinction. "In an entirely literal sense," Gould has written, "we owe our existence, as large and reasoning animals, to our lucky stars."

So, what if the comet had missed? What if our ancestors, and not dinosaurs, had been the ones driven to extinction? What if, during the Devonian period, the small tribe of fish known as rhipidistians had been obliterated? Vanishing with them would have been the possibility of life for the first tetrapods. Vertebrates might never have struggled onto the land, leaving it, in Gould's words, forever "the unchallenged domain of insects and flowers."

Surely this means that mankind's appearance on this planet was *not* preordained, that we are here not as the products of an inevitable procession of evolutionary success, but as an afterthought, a minor detail, a happenstance in a history that might just as well have left us out. What follows from this, to skeptic and true believer alike, is a conclusion whose logic is rarely challenged—that no God would ever have used such a process to fashion his prize creatures. How could he have been sure that leaving the job to evolution would lead things to working out the "right" way? If it was God's will to produce us, then by showing that we are the products of evolution, we would rule God as Creator. Therein lies the value or the danger of evolution.

Not so fast. The biological account of lucky historical contingencies that led to our own appearance on this planet is surely accurate. What does not follow is that a perceived lack of inevitability translates into something that we should regard as incompatibility with a divine will. To do so seriously underestimates God, even as this God is understood by the most conventional of Western religions.

Yes, the explosive diversification of life on this planet was an unpredictable process. But so were the rise of Western civilization, the collapse of the Roman Empire, and the winning number in last night's lottery. We do not regard the indeterminate nature of any of these events in human history as antithetical to the existence of a Creator; why should we regard similar events in natural history any differently? There is, I would submit, no reason at all. If we can view the contingent events in the families that produced our individual lives as consistent with a Creator, then certainly we can do the same for the chain of circumstances that produced our species.

The alternative is a world where all events have predictable outcomes, where the future is open neither to chance nor to independent human action. A world in which we would always evolve is a world in which we would never be free. To a believer, the particular history leading to us shows how truly remarkable we are, how rare is the gift of consciousness, and how precious is the chance to understand.

Certainty and Faith

One would like to think that all scientific ideas, including evolution, would rise or fall purely on the basis of the evidence. If that were true, evolution would long since have passed, in the public mind, from controversy into common sense, which is exactly what has happened within the scientific community. This is, unfortunately, not the case—evolution remains, in the minds of much of the American public, a dangerous idea, and for biology educators, a source of never-ending strife.

I believe much of the problem is the fault of those in the scientific community who routinely enlist the findings of evolutionary biology in support their own philosophical pronouncements. Sometimes these take the form of stern, dispassionate pronouncements about the meaninglessness of life. Other times we are lectured that the contingency of our presence on this planet invalidates any sense of human purpose. And very often we are told that the raw reality of nature strips the authority from any human system of morality.

As creatures fashioned by evolution, we are filled, as the biologist E. O. Wilson has said, with instinctive behaviors important to the survival of our genes. Some of these behaviors, though favored by natural selection, can get us into trouble. Our desires for food, water, reproduction, and status, our willingness to fight, and our tendencies to band together into social groups, can all be seen as behaviors that help ensure evolutionary success. Sociobiology, which studies the biological basis of social behaviors, tells us that in some circumstances natural selection will favor cooperative and nurturing instincts—"nice" genes that help us get along together. Some circumstances, on the other hand, will favor aggressive self-centered behaviors, ranging all the way from friendly competition to outright homicide. Could such Darwinian ruthlessness be part of the plan of a loving God?

Yes, it could. To survive on this planet, the genes of our ancestors, like those of any other organism, had to produce behaviors that protected, nurtured, defended, and ensured the reproductive successes of the individuals that bore them. It should be no surprise that we carry such passions within us, and Darwinian biology cannot be faulted for giving their presence a biological explanation. Indeed, the Bible itself gives ample documentation of such human tendencies, including pride, selfishness, lust, anger, aggression, and murder.

Darwin can hardly be criticized for pinpointing the biological origins of these drives. All too often, in finding the sources of our "original sins," in fixing the reasons why our species displays the tendencies it does, evolution is misconstrued as providing a kind of justification for the worst aspects of human nature. At best, this is a misreading of the scientific lessons of sociobiology. At worst, it is an attempt to misuse biology to abolish any meaningful system of morality. Evolution may explain the existence of our most basic biological drives and desires, but that does not tell us that it is always proper to act on them. Evolution has provided me with a sense of hunger when my nutritional resources are running low, but evolution does not justify my clubbing you over the head to swipe your lunch. Evolution explains our biology, but it does not tell us what is good, or right, or moral. For those answers, however informed we may be by biology, we must look somewhere else.

What Kind of World?

Like it or not, the values that any of us apply to our daily lives have been affected by the work of Charles Darwin. Religious people, however, have a special question to put to the reclusive naturalist of Down House. Did his work ultimately contribute to the greater glory of God, or did he deliver human nature and destiny into the hands of a professional scientific class, one profoundly hostile to religion? Does Darwin's work strengthen or weaken the idea of God?

The conventional wisdom is that whatever one may think of his science, having Mr. Darwin around certainly hasn't helped religion very much. The general thinking is that religion has been weakened by Darwinism and has been constrained to modify its view of the Creator in order to twist doctrine into conformity with the demands of evolution. As Stephen Jay Gould puts it, with obvious delight," Now the conclusions of science must be accepted *a priori,* and religious interpretations must be finessed and adjusted to match unimpeachable results from the magisterium of natural knowledge!" Science calls the tune, and religion dances to its music.

This sad specter of a weakened and marginalized God drives the continuing opposition to evolution. This is why the God of the creationists requires, above all, that evolution be shown not to have functioned in the past and not to be working now. To free religion from the tyranny of Darwinism, creationists need a science that shows nature to be incomplete; they need a history of life whose events can only be explained as the result of supernatural processes. Put bluntly, the creationists are committed to finding permanent, intractable mystery in nature. To such minds, even the most perfect being we can imagine would not have been perfect enough to fashion a creation in which life would originate and evolve on its own. Nature must be flawed, static, and forever inadequate.

Science in general, and evolutionary science in particular, gives us something quite different. It reveals a universe that is dynamic, flexible, and logically complete. It presents a vision of life that spreads across the planet with endless variety and intricate beauty. It suggests a world in which our material existence is not an impossible illusion propped up by magic, but the genuine article, a world in which things are exactly what they seem. A world in which we were formed, as the Creator once told us, from the dust of the earth itself.

It is often said that a Darwinian universe is one whose randomness cannot be reconciled with meaning. I disagree. A world truly without meaning would be one in which a deity pulled the string of every human puppet, indeed of every material particle. In such a world, physical and biological events would be carefully controlled, evil and suffering could be minimized, and the outcome of historical processes strictly regulated. All things would move toward the Creator's clear, distinct, established goals. Such control and predictability, however, comes at the price of independence. Always in control, such a Creator would deny his creatures any real opportunity to know and worship him—authentic love requires freedom, not manipulation. Such freedom is best supplied by the open contingency of evolution.

One hundred and fifty years ago it might have been impossible not to couple Darwin to a grim and pointless determinism, but things look different today. Darwin's vision has expanded to encompass a new world of biology in which the links from molecule to cell and from cell to organism are becoming clear. Evolution prevails, but it does so with a richness and subtlety its original theorist may have found surprising and could not have anticipated.

We know from astronomy, for example, that the universe had a beginning, from physics that the future is both open and unpredictable, from geology and paleontology that the whole of life has been a process of change and transformation. From biology we know that our tissues are not impenetrable reservoirs of vital magic, but a stunning matrix of complex wonders, ultimately explicable in terms of biochemistry and molecular biology. With such knowledge we can see, perhaps for the first time, why a Creator would have allowed our species to be fashioned by the process of evolution.

If he so chose, the God whose presence is taught by most Western religions could have fashioned anything, ourselves included, *ex nihilo*, from his wish alone. In our childhood as a species, that might have been the only way in which we could imagine the fulfillment of a divine will. But we've grown up, and something remarkable has happened: we have begun to understand the physical basis of life itself. If a string of constant miracles were needed for each turn of the cell cycle or each flicker of a cilium, the hand of God would be written directly into every living thing—his presence at the edge of the human sandbox would be unmistakable. Such findings might confirm our faith, but they would also undermine our independence. How could we fairly choose between God and man when the presence and the power of the divine so obviously and so literally controlled our every breath? Our freedom as his creatures requires a little space and integrity. In the material world, it requires self-sufficiency and consistency with the laws of nature.

Evolution is neither more nor less than the result of respecting the reality and consistency of the physical world over time. To fashion material beings with an independent physical existence, any Creator would have had to produce an independent material universe in which our evolution over time was a contingent possibility. A believer in the divine accepts that God's love and gift of freedom are genuine—so genuine that they include the power to choose evil and, if we wish, to freely send ourselves to Hell. Not all believers will accept the stark conditions of that bargain, but our freedom to act has to have a physical and biological basis. Evolution and its sister sciences of genetics and molecular biology provide that basis. In biological terms, evolution is the only way a Creator could have made us the creatures we are—free beings in a world of authentic and meaningful moral and spiritual choices.

Those who ask from science a final argument, an ultimate proof, an unassailable position from which the issue of God may be decided will always be disappointed. As a scientist I claim no new proofs, no revolutionary data, no stunning insight into nature that can tip the balance in one direction or another. But I do claim that to a believer, even in the most traditional sense, evolutionary biology is not at all the obstacle we often believe it to be. In many respects, evolution is the key to understanding our relationship with God.

When I have the privilege of giving a series of lectures on evolutionary biology to my freshman students, I usually conclude those lectures with a few remarks about the impact of evolutionary theory on other fields, from economics to politics to religion. I find a way to make clear that I do not regard evolution, properly understood, as either antireligious or antispiritual. Most students seem to appreciate those sentiments. They probably figure that Professor Miller, trying to be a nice guy and doubtlessly an agnostic, is trying to find a way to be unequivocal about evolution without offending the University chaplain.

There are always a few who find me after class and want to pin me down. They ask me point-blank: "Do you believe in God?"

And I tell each of them, "Yes."

Puzzled, they ask: "What kind of God?"

Over the years I have struggled to come up with a simple but precise answer to that question. And, eventually I found it. I believe in Darwin's God.

Emily Dickinson (1830–1886), now one of the most renowned American poets, was not well known in her lifetime. In fact, she rarely left her home in Amherst, Massachusetts. But her works conveyed such an unwavering understanding of the human condition that their universal themes gained popularity over the course of the twentieth century. More 1,700 of her poems have been published since her death. In this poem, Dickinson is asking us to consider how best to tell the truth, and she implies that the recipient of our truth-telling may be vulnerable or have some difficulty understanding if our truth is rushed or not shared carefully. Do you agree? How do you share your truths?

Tell All the Truth

Emily Dickinson

Tell all the truth but tell it slant,
Success in circuit lies,
Too bright for our infirm delight
The truth's superb surprise;

As lightning to the children eased
With explanation kind,
The truth must dazzle gradually
Or every man be blind.

Jayne Cortez (1934–2012) was born Sallie Jayne Richardson, and claimed Cortez, her maternal grandmother's maiden name, for her artistic career. That career spanned decades and included spoken-word performance art, jazz poetry, activism, and publishing. Inspired by Josephine Baker, Langston Hughes, and Henry Dumas, she often wrote confrontational poetry about race, sex and homophobia. In this poem, Cortez is asking the reader to embrace challenging truth. What truth is Cortez asking us to consider? What does she suggest are the consequences if we don't face difficult truths?

There It Is

Jayne Cortez

And if we don't fight
if we don't resist
if we don't organize and unify and
get the power to control our own lives
then we will wear
the exaggerated look of captivity
the stylized look of submission
the bizarre look of suicide
the dehumanized look of fear
and the decomposed look of repression
forever and ever and ever
And there it is . . .

Sandra Marie Schneiders, IHM, is professor emerita at the Jesuit School of Theology at the Graduate Theological Union at Berkeley. She is a lecturer on women and religious life and the author of several books. Although this essay was written thirty years ago, the ideas expressed may be new to you. Many of us in our spiritual life actually get very little exposure to a theological approach to questions of faith. This selection from Women and the Word *(1986) illustrates what it means to address religious doctrine theologically and also how what we "know," even in a faith tradition, is influenced by culture. It makes us ponder, how is the truth of faith derived? Do you find Schneiders' argument persuasive? Why or why not?*

from Women and the Word
The Gender of God in the New Testament and the Spirituality of Women

Sandra Marie Schneiders

I. The Question about the Gender of God

A. The Modernity of the Question

. . . At the outset of this discussion it is important to be aware that the question of the gender of God is a thoroughly modern issue. No matter how entrenched in the imagination of the average Christian the image of a male God might be, theological tradition has never assigned sex to God.[1] St. Gregory of Nazianzus well represented the tradition when he affirmed that the terms "Father" and "Son" as applied to the persons of the Trinity were not names of natures or essences but of relations[2] and even in this case the terms are used metaphorically. In other words, God is neither a father nor a son but the first person of the Trinity is related to the second person as origin is related to that which is originated. Because the ancients believed that God was indeed personal, and because their defective biology ascribed all agency in procreation or personal originating activity to the male partner, their choice of "father" for the originating person of the Trinity was logical enough. And since they wished to affirm the absolute likeness and equality of the one originated to the divine principle they called the second person the "son." They were, however, quite aware of the metaphorical nature of their language and never intended to impute actual sexuality to the God whom Scripture affirms is pure Spirit (cf. Jn 4:24).

Second, theological tradition has virtually always maintained that the maleness of Jesus is theologically, christologically, soteriologically, and sacramentally irrelevant.[3] It has been suggested, not without reason, that the attempt of the Vatican's Congregation for the Doctrine of the Faith in its "Declaration on the Question of the Admission of Women to the Ministerial Priesthood" (*Inter Insignores*)[4] to assign theological significance to the sex of Jesus by maintaining that women Christians, because they are female, do not resemble Christ is not only non-traditional but also at least theologically confused if not strictly heretical.[5] As patristics scholar R. A. Norris states,

> The argument [against the ordination of women on the grounds that male sex is required for likeness to Christ] is virtually unprecedented. It does not in fact state any of the traditional grounds on which ordination to the presbyterate or episcopate has been denied to women. To accept this argument and its practical consequences, therefore, is not to maintain tradition but to alter it by altering its meaning.[6]

More important, however, than its non-traditionality is the threat it raises to a central theological affirmation about the incarnation, namely, that as Gregory of Nazianzus and numerous other Fathers of the Church have maintained, "*Tò gàr àprósleptou àtherápeuton,*" i.e., "What is not assumed is not redeemed."[7] The Vatican argument attempts to make the maleness of Jesus a necessary precondition to his being who he is, God-with-us, and doing what he does, redeeming us by his paschal mystery. To do so, as Norris says, "is to qualify or deny the universality of his redemption."[8]

In short, the theological tradition of the Church never assigned sex to God and almost never (until the theologically faulty 1977 document) assigned any theological significance to the sex of Jesus. Why, then, is the gender of God such a troubling question for contemporary Christians, especially for women whose consciousness has been raised by the women's movement in our time?

B. The Dilemma for Women

As women have become aware of their inferior status and actual oppression in family, society, and Church, they have also become aware that the gender of God, God's presumed masculinity, has functioned as the ultimate religious legitimation of the unjust social structures which victimize women. First, the maleness of Jesus has been used in Christian cultures as a support from divine revelation for the age-old claim that maleness is normative for humanity and that men are superior to women. Most western languages themselves, in which the generic human is always masculine, testify incessantly to the misconception that humanity is originally and normatively male and that women are a derivative and subordinate, if not actually misbegotten, version of the essentially male species. Male privilege, based on this erroneous assumption of male superiority, is firmly entrenched in virtually every sector of human life.

Second the "fatherhood" of God has been used to justify patriarchy or father-rule, the social system which sacralizes male domination and legitimates virtually all forms of oppression of the weak by the strong. We will return to the topic of patriarchy shortly.

Third, the masculinity of God and of Jesus has been used, in the practical sphere, to deny the likeness of women to God and to Christ and to exclude them from full participation in the life of the Church. Whether this spiritual degradation takes the relatively mild form of excluding little girls from serving at the altar or the more serious forms of exclusion of women from decision-making positions in the Church and enforcement of their sacramental dependence on men, it has a destructive effect on women's spiritual self-image and perverts their relationships with male Christians and with God.

The masculinity of God, in other words, is not primarily an issue in speculative theology. It can easily be established that the God of Judaeo-Christian revelation and Christian theological tradition is not male and that Jesus' maleness is theologically irrelevant. This helps very little, however, because the real problem is not in the area of systematic theology but in the area of religious experience or spirituality.[9] How women experience themselves in relation to God, Christ, and Church is profoundly affected by the imputed masculinity of God which is operative in the imaginations of both male and female believers.

Once their consciousness is raised, women Christians can find themselves impaled on the horns of a dilemma. Either they can continue as Christians, accepting the spiritual consequences of their lack of resemblance to God and Christ and their consequent inferiority to and spiritual dependence on men in the Church (the position advocated by the Vatican Declaration despite its protestations to the contrary), or they can abandon Christianity as a hopelessly patriarchal religion and seek their spiritual home in a religious tradition in which women and women's experience are central and valued.[10] Unless educated and aware women can find a creative and liberating understanding of God and of Jesus, one which does not glorify masculinity at the expense of femininity and does not justify the oppression of women by men, they have no future in institutional Christianity.

II. Preliminary Clarifications

Before undertaking an exploration of the problem of God's "masculinity" and women's spirituality two clarifications are necessary. First, we must distinguish clearly between sex and gender because, as we will see, it is the *gender* of God and the *sex* of Jesus which are the real problems. Second, we have to distinguish between patriarchy (and paternalism) on the one hand and paternity or fatherhood on the other because it is only the former which is problematic. Fatherhood as such, provided that it is not used exclusively, is one appropriate metaphor for God.

A. Sex and Gender

Sex refers to biological identity, the possession of male or female sexual organs and the proportionate activity of male or female hormones which grounds the distinctive roles of men and women in the reproductive process. Gender, however, refers to the experience of self and others in terms of sexual identity. Although sex and gender normally coincide in humans, i.e., females experience themselves and are experienced by others as feminine and males as masculine, this is not always the case, nor is the experience always totally dichotomous. Thus, someone who is biologically a male might experience himself as feminine and might be experienced that way by others. And persons are sometimes experienced as both feminine and masculine, or androgynous. The point is that while sex is biologically determined by observation of empirically available data, gender refers to the way one experiences oneself or others.[11]

God, as we have said, is neither male nor female, i.e., God does not have a body and therefore does not have sex. But because all human persons have gender and we experience God as personal we tend to experience God anthropomorphically as either masculine or feminine or both, i.e., as male and female successively, or as androgynous. Our God-image, as we will explain below, is a function of the imagination, and the Christian religious imagination is deeply influenced by the belief in the personal nature of God, by the overwhelmingly male God-language in the Bible, and by the incarnation of God in the concrete humanity of a male human being, Jesus. Until very recently many if not most Christians, including those who were theologically convinced that God is Spirit, experienced God as almost exclusively masculine. Theologically well-informed people of both sexes have insisted vehemently on the maintenance of exclusively male language for God in public prayer.[12] To a large extent this insistence has more to do with maintaining male dominant power arrangements in family, society, and Church than with theological issues. But for many people the problem is genuinely religious. Their problem is a paralysis of the religious imagination. To imagine God or speak to God as feminine does not simply change the God image for these people; it destroys it.

If God is pure spirit, the same cannot be said about Jesus who was actually a male. However, although biologically male and masculine in gender, Jesus has also been experienced as distinctly feminine in many ways. Sentimental art provides a perverted testimony to this fact, but the motherhood of Jesus and of Christ is a consistent theme in medieval mystical literature. Bernard of Clairvaux, Julian of Norwich, Anselm of Canterbury, Gertrude of Helfta, Mechtild of Hackeborn, and Mechtild of Magdeburg are among the spiritual writers whose works are explored by medieval scholar Caroline Walker Bynum in her 1982 volume, *Jesus as Mother*.[13] The Gospel portrays Jesus as non-aggressive, non-competitive, meek and humble of heart, a nurturer of the weak, and a friend of the outcast. He manifested and preached a spirituality that was characterized by stereotypically feminine rather than masculine virtues. This femininity of Jesus has often enough proven difficult for men to assimilate, but it has always supported the spirituality of women. For women, the problem is not the gender of Jesus, his masculinity which is so inclusively feminine, but his sex. It is the biological fact that Jesus, by being a man rather than a woman, is irreducibly and irrevocably different from women that seems to exclude women from the fullness of identity with him. Furthermore, the maleness of Jesus cannot help but intensify the experience of God as masculine and of maleness as normative, i.e., as the best and fullest way to be human.

B. Patriarchy and Paternity

A second distinction important for our purposes is that between paternity on the one hand and patriarchy / paternalism on the other. Patriarchy is a social system based on the *patria potestas*, i.e., the absolute and unaccountable power over wives and concubines, children, servants, slaves, animals and real property enjoyed by the *paterfamilias*, i.e., the father who is head of the family, tribe, or clan. To the father of the family belonged, as property, all members of the extended household and all goods. In classical Greek and Roman societies this authority of ownership extended even to the power of life and death. Children, especially girls, were often deemed valueless to the father and left to die. Insubordinate wives or slaves could be sold or killed.[14] While sons, when they became adults, were emancipated and became patriarchs in their own right, daughters were passed, with or without their consent, from the control of the father to that of a husband,[15] i.e., from one patriarch to another.

In the patriarchal system authority and power were strictly coterminous and belonged totally and exclusively to the head of the household unless he delegated it to another. The authority and power of the *paterfamilias* were considered as divinely established, and thus the patriarchal system was unalterable and rebellion against the father was rebellion against God. Furthermore, even though in the absence of a man patriarchal power might sometimes be exercised by a woman, e.g., by a mother or a queen, and unemancipated males, e.g., minor sons and slaves, were as subject to the father's dominion as were females in the family, there is a vital connection in the patriarchal system among power, authority, property, and maleness. Conversely, powerlessness, exclusion from authority, dependence, and femaleness are closely linked. And the entire system is understood as the product and expression of the will of God.

For two reasons patriarchy is not just one social system among others. First, patriarchy is the basic principle of all major relational systems in the western world. As the former president of the World Council of Churches, Dr. W. A. Visser't Hooft, expressed it:

> . . . the patriarchal spirit and the doctrine upon which it is based have had an astonishingly wide influence, penetrating into many different spheres of life. Indeed, it has not been merely one of the many facets of society, but has rather formed its general pattern. . . . [Thus] emancipation [from patriarchy] concerns not only developments in family life, but also those in the state, the church and even in international relations.[16]

Visser't Hooft, like Rosemary Ruether, has pointed out that patriarchy is the basic principle underlying not only the subordination of women to men, but of one race to another, of colonies to master nations, of children to adults, of nations to divine right monarchs, of believers to clergy. In other words, patriarchy is the nerve of racism, ageism, classism, colonialism, and clericalism well as of sexism.[17] Patriarchy is fundamentally a masculine power in which all relationships are understood in terms of superiority and inferiority and social cohesion is assured by the exercise of dominative power.

The second reason why patriarchy is not just one system among others is that patriarchy is essentially hierarchy, i.e., the power and authority exercised over subordinates is believed to derive from the will of God and is exercised in the name of God. The patriarchal structure of the family was understood as divinely established for the good of all. When this structure was extended to other situations they were seen as quasi-families in which there is one adult and all others are minors. The feudal lord, the abbot in his monastery, the divine right monarch, the priest in his parish, the white European in the colonies, the husband in relation to his wife, the slave-holder with his "darkies," the Pope, were all father-figures caring for the "children" over which God had placed them. The difference, of course, between these extensions of patriarchy and its original locus, the family, is that these "children" are adults and, unlike real children, they are expected never to grow up. Thus, in a patriarchal system most people will remain subordinates all their lives and they cannot protest against this arrangement without challenging God "himself" who is the first patriarch and the legitimator of all others.

While not all men are patriarchs, women never are. Where patriarchy reigns women are subject to men. The man may be father, husband, slave-holder, priest, or Pope but the woman is always a minor. It is not surprising, then, that women, once they have analyzed the situation, repudiate patriarchy as the universal social structure and especially its claims to divine legitimacy. A patriarchal God, to feminist women, is at least a legitimator of women's victimization by men if not "himself" the very personification of the oppression of women.

However, it is important to distinguish sharply between patriarchy (including its more benign expression as paternalism) on the one hand, and paternity or fatherhood on the other. The association of fatherhood with patriarchy is so long-standing and widespread that the equation of the two is quite understandable and very often perfectly accurate. However, it is possible for a man to be a father to his minor children without assuming absolute power over them and to remain a father in relation to adult children whose autonomy and equality with himself he fully accepts. Likewise, it is possible for God to be experienced as paternal without being experienced as a patriarch. And a father-God who is not experienced as a patriarch can equally well be experienced as a mother-God without loss of status.

III. Imagination and Spirituality

In what has been said so far I have attempted to locate with some accuracy the problem of the gender of God. The problem is not the sex of God (which does not exist) but our experience of God as masculine; and it is not the masculinity of Jesus (who is anything but a glorification of machismo) but his male sex. However, the reason Jesus' male sex is a problem is because it is seen as a revelatory confirmation of the masculinity of God and therefore of the divinity of maleness. Jesus, the man, is the incarnation of the Son of the Father. Consequently, our primary concern must be with the experienced masculinity of God.

• • •

The tenacity of the patriarchal God-image is such that many feminists have decided that the only course open to women whose self-image has been healed of gender inferiority and whose world-image has been healed of hierarchy in general and patriarchy in particular is to abandon the Christian God altogether. I would like to suggest that just as the self and world images can be healed, so can the God-image. It cannot be healed, however, by rational intervention alone. Repeating the theological truth that God is Spirit may correct our ideas but a healthy spirituality requires a healing of the imagination which will allow us to think not only differently about God but to experience God differently. The imagination is accessible not primarily to abstract ideas but to language, images, interpersonal experience, symbolism, art—all the integrated approaches which appeal simultaneously to intellect, will, and feeling. What must be undertaken is a therapy of the religious imagination, first in regard to God and then in regard to our relationship with Jesus Christ.

• • •

IV. The "Maleness" of God in the Old Testament

• • •

B. Old Testament Metaphors for God[18]

In the Old Testament there are numerous metaphors for God derived from human relationships. The vast majority, although not all, of the vehicles in these metaphors either are necessarily male, e.g., father or husband, or denote roles or activities which were virtually exclusively exercised by males in Israelite society. In the New Testament Jesus frequently used one of these metaphors, namely, father, at least in speaking to God and probably also in speaking about God. Fairly early in Christian history the father metaphor was literalized in religious imagination. The literalized metaphor, it must be remembered, no longer carries its "is not" but simply transfers to the referent all the characteristics of the vehicle. Thus, God the "father" came to be imagined as literally male. All the male metaphors for God in the Old Testament then tended to be drawn into this one metaphor. Since many of the Old Testament God-metaphors such as warlord and king were patriarchal the metaphorical fatherhood of God was not only literalized but patriarchalized. As both theologian Sallie McFague and biblical scholar Johanna Bos have pointed out, the literalized father metaphor for God has not only died but, in its ascription of maleness to God, it has become actually idolatrous.[19] We have created a false god and substituted "him" for the true God of Judaeo-Christian revelation.

It is highly enlightening, then, to examine the father metaphor as it actually occurs in the Old Testament. The most striking characteristic of this metaphor is how seldom it occurs. God is actually referred to as father only twelve times in the Hebrew Scriptures and never in direct address. Father is not a name for God but "a pointer to the free presence of God, which cannot be encapsulated in or manipulated by names."[20] Five of the references to God as father concern the special relation of God to the king. (2 Sam 7:14; 1 Chr 17:13; Ps 89:26; 1 Chr 22: 10; 28:6) and thus do not apply to the ordinary person. The other seven references (Ps 103:13; Dt 32:6, 18; Jer 3:4–5; 31:9; Is 63:16; Mal 1:6) all refer to God in the context of Israel's sin, repentance, and restoration and God's endless forgiveness.[21] The father metaphor in the Old Testament is nowhere used to present God as a patriarch dominating the people or exercising coercive power over them. On the contrary, the father metaphor is evoked precisely to describe the compassionate love of God who is like a parent spurned by ungrateful children but who is endless in patience and loving-kindness toward a rebellious people. The God who is presented as father in the Old Testament is like the father in the New Testament parable of the prodigal son, a paternal rather than patriarchal figure who is in no way a model for or a legitimation of patriarchy.

A second important point about the parental metaphor in the Old Testament is that it is not exclusively masculine. When Israel is referred to as a child the implied parent is sometimes masculine as in Deuteronomy 1:31 where Israel is reminded that "God bore you as a man bears his son." But at other times it is feminine as in Numbers 11:12 where the exasperated Moses demands of God, "Did I conceive all this people? Did I bring them forth, that thou should say to me, 'Carry them in thy bosom . . . ?'" clearly implying that God is the true mother of this people. At other times the metaphor is both masculine and feminine as in Hosea 11: 1–4:

> When Israel was a child, I loved him, and out of Egypt I called my son. The more I called them the more they went from me; they kept sacrificing to Baals, and burning incense to idols. Yet it was I who taught Ephraim to walk, I took them up in my arms; but they did not know that I healed them. I led them with cords of compassion, with the bands of love, and I became to them as one who eases the yoke on their jaws, and I bent down to them and fed them.

Thus, it is to be noted that, while they are not as frequent as even the infrequent paternal metaphors, there are clear maternal metaphors for God in the Old Testament as well as a pervasive maternal climate evoked by imagery based on the womb. In Deuteronomy 32:18 God clearly refers to herself, in feminine language, as "the God who gave you birth." In Isaiah 49:15 Israel is assured that God cherishes her people with a mother's love. In Isaiah 66:13 God says to Israel, "As one whom his mother comforts so will I comfort you." In Psalm 131:2 the psalmist says of reliance on God, "I have calmed and quieted my soul, like a child quieted at its mother's breast." As Phyllis Trible has pointed out[22] the typical Old Testament word for the compassion of God seems to be drawn from *rehem* the Hebrew word for womb, suggesting that God's tenderness is that of a mother for the child to whom she has given birth (cf. Is 63:15; Ex 34:6).[23] In Isaiah 42:14 God compares the divine anguish to that of a woman in the pangs of childbirth.[24]

In sum, an examination of the Old Testament father metaphor reveals that it was by no means a common, much less the preferred or only, metaphor for God, that it was never used to portray God as a patriarch in relation to the people, and that it is complemented by maternal imagery and metaphors which assure us that in no sense was the father metaphor meant to suggest that God is male[25] or that the divine parenthood is exclusively paternal.

Besides the father metaphor which, because of Jesus' use of it, exerted a powerful influence on the Christian imagination, there is one other Old Testament male metaphor for God which has had a major impact on the Christian God-image, namely, the spousal metaphor. Like the paternal metaphor which has been distorted into an exclusive and literalized support for male supremacy and patriarchy, the spousal metaphor has also exercised a perverse influence on the Christian imagination as a degradation of feminine sexuality and a justification of patriarchal marriage.

In some of the prophets, especially Jeremiah and Hosea, the relationship between God and Israel is depicted as marital union. God is the husband and Israel the wife in a marriage founded on love rather than on patriarchal authority and power. The extended metaphor is used, however, to describe the unfaithfulness of Israel to its faithful God. Israel, the wife, is a harlot. As feminist scholars have rightly pointed out, in this metaphor female sexuality is objectified and demonized. The male is assimilated to God and the female to sinful humanity.[26]

However, it must be realized that in the patriarchal culture of ancient Israel a husband could not really sin against his wife since he could do to her with impunity what he willed.[27] Marital fidelity was never absolutely required of men whereas a woman's infidelity was considered an offense against her husband's property rights. In such a culture, therefore, this metaphor could not have been structured in any other way. To make the point that God took the free initiative in choosing Israel, that God entered into a relationship of intimate love with Israel, and that Israel was unfaithful to that covenant, God had to be imaged as the husband who alone could act this way. However, in the husband role God acts not as a patriarch would have acted but as a wife would have acted. A husband who had been betrayed by his wife would at least have divorced her if he had not had her executed. A wife who had been betrayed would be expected, nevertheless, to be faithful and loving. God, in the marital metaphor, is a faithful lover who continually seeks reconciliation through the offer of forgiveness. In other words, the patriarchy of the metaphor is assumed because of the culture, but the message of the metaphor subverts patriarchy.

• • •

This brief exploration of the Old Testament language about God and the way this language has been used suggests several conclusions. God is not presented in the Old Testament in exclusively male terms. Even the two necessarily male metaphors, father and husband, are balanced by maternal imagery and the presentation of marital love as a relation of mutuality between equals. It is true that male imagery for God predominates, but this should serve to draw our attention to the unexpected feminine imagery which is perhaps more revelatory precisely because it cannot be adequately explained by the culture. In any case, any literalizing of God metaphors results not only in an impoverishment and distortion of the religious imagination but in a blasphemous assimilation of God to human categories and an idolatrous divinizing of human maleness.

Notes

[1] See Elizabeth A. Johnson, "The Incomprehensibility of God and the Image of God Male and Female," *Theological Studies* 45 (1984) 441–465.

[2] Gregory of Nazianzus, "The Third Theological Oration—on the Son," *Christology of the Later Fathers,* Vol. III, ed. E. R. Hardy (Philadelphia: Westminster, 1954), p. 171. Migne, *Patrologia Graeca* 36:93–96.

[3] The argument that priests had to be male to represent Christ is found in Bonaventure. See J. Rézette, "Le sacerdoce et la femme chez Saint Bonaventure," *Antonianum* 51 (1976) 520–527.

[4] *Acta Apostolicae Sedis* 69 (1977) 98–116; E. T. *Women Priests: A Catholic Commentary on the Vatican Declaration,* ed. L. and A. Swidler (New York: Paulist, 1977), pp. 37–49.

[5] See the excellent article by R. A. Norris, Jr., "The Ordination of Women and the 'Maleness' of Christ," *Supplementary Series of the Anglican Theological Review* 6 (June 1976) 69–80.

[6] Norris, "The Ordination of Women," p. 70.

[7] Gregory of Nazianzus, "Epistle 101," Hardy, *Christology,* p. 218. Migne, *P. G.* 37: 181.

[8] Norris, "The Ordination of Women," p. 74.

[9] See Gail R. Schmidt, "De Divinis Nominibus: The Gender of God," *Worship* 56 (1982) 117–131, for a discussion of how male God language affects liturgical experience.

[10] See, for example, the article by Carol P. Christ, "Why Women Need the Goddess: Phenomenological, Psychological, and Political Reflections," in *Womanspirit Rising: A Feminist Reader in Religion,* ed. C. P. Christ and J. Plaskow (San Francisco: Harper and Row, 1979), 273–287.

[11] Cf. Suzanne J. Kessler and Wendy McKenna, *Gender: An Ethnomethodological Approach* (Chicago: University of Chicago, 1985).

[12] On this subject, see Mary Collins, "Naming God in Public Prayer," *Worship* 59 (1985) 291–304.

[13] Caroline W. Bynum, *Jesus as Mother* (Berkeley: University of California, 1982).

[14] See R. Hamerton-Kelly, *God the Father: Theology and Patriarchy in the Teaching of Jesus* (Philadelphia: Fortress, 1979), pp. 55–60, for a good description of patriarchy in the Judaism of Jesus' time as well as in the Greco-Roman world of first century Christianity.

[15] See W. A. Visser't Hooft, *The Fatherhood of God in an Age of Emancipation* (Geneva: World Council of Churches, 1982), esp. chapters one to three, for a fuller description of this social system.

[16] Visser't Hooft, *Fatherhood,* p. 2.

[17] See Rosemary Ruether, "Feminists Seek Structural Change," *National Catholic Reporter* 20 (April 13, 1984) 4–6.

[18] I am indebted to my colleague, Dr. John Endres, and to Dr. Alice Laffey of Holy Cross College, Worcester, Massachusetts for their help on the Old Testament section of this paper.

[19] Cf. McFague, *Metaphorical Theology*, pp. 145–192; Bos, "When You Pray," p. 12.

[20] Bos, "When You Pray," p. 12.

[21] Cf. Diane Tennis, *Is God the Only Reliable Father?* (Philadelphia: Westminster, 1985), esp. pp. 82–83.

[22] See Phyllis Trible, *God and the Rhetoric of Sexuality* (Philadelphia: Fortress, 1978), pp. 34–56, and "Feminist Hermeneutics and Biblical Studies," *The Christian Century* 99 (Feb. 3–10, 1982)116–118.

[23] Mayer I. Gruber, in "The Motherhood of God in Second Isaiah," *Revue Biblique* 90 (1983) 351–359, challenges Trible's interpretation.

[24] It is interesting that John Paul II in his encyclical *Dives in Misericordia* (Nov. 13, 1980) has a long footnote (#52) in which he explores the feminine significance of *rahamim*.

[25] Cf. Bos, "When You Pray," p. 12.

[26] Cf. T. Drorah Setel, "Prophets and Pornography: Female Sexual Imagery in Hosea," *Feminist Interpretation of the Bible*, ed. Letty M. Russell (Philadelphia: Westminster, 1985) 86–95.

[27] See Phyllis Trible, *Texts of Terror: Literary Feminist Readings of Biblical Narratives* (Philadelphia: Fortress, 1984) for evidences of the male attitude toward women and their rights.

"The Oppositional Gaze: Black Female Spectators" is a chapter in bell hooks' Black Looks: Race and Representation. *Born Gloria Jean Watkins, she took "bell hooks" as a pen name for the many books of cultural criticism and feminist thinking that have made her one of the U.S.'s leading voices for social change. Overall, this book is complicated, and this chapter is a subset of its complexity. Here she theorizes about white and male control over black female representation in the U.S. media, then calls for Black female subjectivity in films. This shift would disrupt the traditional norm of the woman as object for masculine spectatorship—"the male gaze," as feminist film criticism describes it. Over twenty years later, what is the state of Black female subjectivity in Hollywood films and on television? Have we, as hooks hoped, imagined new, authentic ways of looking and knowing? Can you find contemporary examples of the oppositional gaze?*

The Oppositional Gaze: Black Female Spectators

bell hooks

When thinking about black female spectators, I remember being punished as a child for staring, for those hard intense direct looks children would give grown-ups, looks that were seen as confrontational, as gestures of resistance, challenges to authority. The 'gaze' has always been political in my life. Imagine the terror felt by the child who has come to understand through repeated punishments that one's gaze can be dangerous. The child who has learned so well to look the other way when necessary. Yet, when punished, the child is told by parents, 'Look at me when I talk to you.' Only, the child is afraid to look. Afraid to look, but fascinated by the gaze. There is power in looking.

Amazed the first time I read in history classes that white slave-owners (men, women, and children) punished enslaved black people for looking, I wondered how this traumatic relationship to the gaze had informed black parenting and black spectatorship. The politics of slavery, of racialized power relations, were such that the slaves were denied their right to gaze. Connecting this strategy of domination to that used by grown folks in southern black rural communities where I grew up, I was pained to think that there was no absolute difference between whites who had oppressed black people and ourselves. Years later, reading Michel Foucault, I thought again about these connections, about the ways power as domination reproduces itself in different locations employing similar apparatuses, strategies, and mechanisms of control. Since I knew as a child that the dominating power adults exercised over me and over my gaze was never so absolute that I did not dare to look, to sneak a peep, to stare dangerously, I knew that the slaves had looked. That all attempts to repress our black peoples' right to gaze had produced in us an overwhelming longing to look, a rebellious desire, an oppositional gaze. By courageously looking, we defiantly declared: 'Not only will I stare. I want my look to change reality.' Even in the worse circumstances of domination, the ability to manipulate one's gaze in the face of structures of domination that would contain it, opens up the possibility of agency. In much of his work, Michel Foucault insists on describing domination in terms of 'relations of power' as part of an effort to challenge the assumption that 'power is a system of domination which controls everything and which leaves no room for freedom.' Emphatically stating that in all relations of power 'there is necessarily the possibility of resistance,' he invites the critical thinker to search those margins, gaps, and locations on and through the body where agency can be found.

Stuart Hall calls for recognition of our agency as black spectators in his essay 'Cultural Identity and Cinematic Representation.' Speaking against the construction of white representations of blackness as totalizing, Hall says of white presence: 'The error is not to conceptualize this "presence" in terms of power, but to locate that power as wholly external to us—as extrinsic force, whose influence can be thrown off like the serpent sheds its skin. What Franz Fanon reminds us, in *Black Skin, White Masks*, is how power is inside as well as outside:

> . . . the movements, the attitudes, the glances of the Other fixed me there, in the sense in which a chemical solution is fixed by a dye. I was indignant; I demanded an explanation. Nothing happened. I burst apart. Now the fragments have been put together again by another self. This 'look,' from—so to speak—the place of the Other, fixes us, not only in its violence, hostility and aggression, but in the ambivalence of its desire.

Spaces of agency exist for black people, wherein we can both interrogate the gaze of the Other but also look back, and at one another, naming what we see. The 'gaze' has been and is a site of resistance for colonized black people globally. Subordinates in relations of power learn experientially that there is a critical gaze, one that 'looks' to document, one that is oppositional. In resistance struggle, the power of the dominated to assert agency by claiming and cultivating 'awareness' politicizes 'looking' relations—one learns to look a certain way in order to resist.

When most black people in the United States first had the opportunity to look at film and television, they did so fully aware that mass media was a system of knowledge and power reproducing and maintaining white supremacy. To stare at the television, or mainstream movies, to engage its images, was to engage its negation of black representation. It was the oppositional black gaze that responded to these looking relations by developing independent black cinema. Black viewers of mainstream cinema and television could chart the progress of political movements for racial equality *via* the construction of images, and did so. Within my family's southern black working-class home, located in a racially segregated neighborhood, watching television was one way to develop critical spectatorship. Unless you went to work in the white world, across the tracks, you learned to look at white people by staring at them on the screen. Black looks, as they were constituted in the context of social movements for racial uplift, were interrogating gazes. We laughed at television shows like *Our Gang* and *Amos 'n Andy*, at these white representations of blackness, but we also looked at them critically. Before racial integration, black viewers of movies and television experienced visual pleasure in a context where looking was also about contestation and confrontation.

Writing about black looking relations in 'Black British Cinema: Spectatorship and Identity Formation in Territories,' Manthia Diawara identifies the power of the spectator: 'Every narration places the spectator in a position of agency; and race, class and sexual relations influence the way in which this subjecthood is filled by the spectator.' Of particular concern for him are moments of 'rupture' when the spectator resists 'complete identification with the film's discourse.' These ruptures define the relation between black spectators and dominant cinema prior to racial integration. Then, one's enjoyment of a film wherein representations of blackness were stereotypically degrading and dehumanizing co-existed with a critical practice that restored presence where it was negated. Critical discussion of the film while it was in progress or at its conclusion maintained the distance between spectator and the image. Black films were also subject to critical interrogation. Since they came into being in part as a response to the failure of white-dominated cinema to represent blackness in a manner that did not reinforce white supremacy, they too were critiqued to see if images were seen as complicit with dominant cinematic practices.

Critical, interrogating black looks were mainly concerned with issues of race and racism, the way racial domination of blacks by whites overdetermined representation. They were rarely concerned with gender. As spectators, black men could repudiate the reproduction of racism in cinema and television, the negation of black presence, even as they could feel as though they were rebelling against white supremacy by daring to look, by engaging phallocentric politics of spectatorship. Given the real life public circumstances wherein black men were murdered/lynched for looking at white womanhood, where the black male gaze was always subject to control and/or punishment by the powerful white Other, the private realm of television screens or dark theaters could unleash the repressed gaze. There they could 'look' at white womanhood without a structure of domination overseeing the gaze, interpreting, and punishing. That white supremacist structure that had murdered Emmet Till after interpreting his look as violation, as 'rape' of white womanhood, could not control black male responses to screen images. In their role as spectators, black men could enter an imaginative space of phallocentric power that mediated racial negation. This gendered relation to looking made the experience of the black male spectator radically different from that of the black female spectator. Major early black male independent filmmakers represented black women in their films as objects of male gaze. Whether looking through the camera or as spectators watching films, whether mainstream cinema or 'race' movies such as those made by Oscar Micheaux, the black male gaze had a different scope from that of the black female.

Black women have written little about black female spectatorship, about our moviegoing practices. A growing body of film theory and criticism by black women has only begun to emerge. The prolonged silence of black women as spectators and critics was a response to absence, to cinematic negation. In The 'Technology of Gender,' Teresa de Lauretis, drawing on the work of Monique Wittig, calls attention to 'the power of discourses to "do violence" to people, a violence which is material and physical, although produced by abstract and scientific discourses as well as the discourses of the mass media.' With the possible exception of early race movies, black female spectators have had to develop looking relations within a cinematic context that constructs our presence as absence, that denies the 'body' of the black female so as to perpetuate white supremacy and with it a phallocentric spectatorship where the woman to be looked at and desired is 'white.' (Recent movies do not conform to this paradigm but I am turning to the past with the intent to chart the development of black female spectatorship.)

Talking with black women of all ages and classes, in different areas of the United States, about their filmic looking relations, I hear again and again ambivalent responses to cinema. Only a few of the black women I talked with remembered the pleasure of race movies, and even those who did, felt that pleasure interrupted and usurped by Hollywood. Most of the black women I talked with were adamant that they never went to movies expecting to see compelling representations of black femaleness. They were all acutely aware of cinematic racism—its violent erasure of black womanhood. In Anne Friedberg's essay 'A Denial of Difference: Theories of Cinematic Identification' she stresses that 'Identification can only be made through recognition, and all recognition is itself an implicit confirmation of the ideology of the status quo.' Even when representations of black women were present in film, our bodies and being were there to serve—to enhance and maintain white womanhood as object of the phallocentric gaze.

Commenting on Hollywood's characterization of black women in *Girls on Film,* Julie Burchill describes this absent presence:

> Black women have been mothers without children (Mammies—who can ever forget the sickening spectacle of Hattie MacDaniels waiting on the simpering Vivien Leigh hand and foot and enquiring like a ninny, 'What's ma lamb gonna wear?') . . . Lena Horne, the first black performer signed to a long

> term contract with a major (MGM), looked gutless but was actually quite spirited. She seethed when Tallulah Bankhead complimented her on the paleness of her skin and the non-Negroidness of her features.

When black women actresses like Lena Horne appeared in mainstream cinema most white viewers were not aware that they were looking at black females unless the film was specifically coded as being about blacks. Burchill is one of the few white women film critics who has dared to examine the intersection of race and gender in relation to the construction of the category 'woman' in film as object of the phallocentric gaze. With characteristic wit she asserts: 'What does it say about racial purity that the best blondes have all been brunettes (Harlow, Monroe, Bardot)? I think it says that we are not as white as we think.' Burchill could easily have said 'we are not as white as we want to be,' for clearly the obsession to have white women film stars be ultra-white was a cinematic practice that sought to maintain a distance, a separation between that image and the black female Other; it was a way to perpetuate white supremacy. Politics of race and gender were inscribed into mainstream cinematic narrative from *Birth of a Nation* on. As a seminal work, this film identified what the place and function of white womanhood would be in cinema. There was clearly no place for black women.

Remembering my past in relation to screen images of black womanhood, I wrote a short essay, 'Do you remember Sapphire?' which explored both the negation of black female representation in cinema and television and our rejection of these images. Identifying the character of 'Sapphire' from *Amos 'n Andy* as that screen representation of black femaleness I first saw in childhood, I wrote:

> She was even then backdrop, foil. She was bitch—nag. She was there to soften images of black men, to make them seem vulnerable, easygoing, funny, and unthreatening to a white audience. She was there as man in drag, as castrating bitch, as someone to be lied to, someone to be tricked, someone the white and black audience could hate. Scapegoated on all sides. She was not us. We laughed with the black men, with the white people. We laughed at this black woman who was not us. And we did not even long to be there on the screen. How could we long to be there when our image, visually constructed, was so ugly. We did not long to be there. We did not long for her. We did not want our construction to be this hated black female thing—foil, backdrop. Her black female image was not the body of desire. There was nothing to see. She was not us.

Grown black women had a different response to Sapphire; they identified with her frustrations and her woes. They resented the way she was mocked. They resented the way these screen images could assault black womanhood, could name us bitches, nags. And in opposition they claimed Sapphire as their own, as the symbol of that angry part of themselves white folks and black men could not even begin to understand.

Conventional representations of black women have done violence to the image. Responding to this assault, many black women spectators shut out the image, looked the other way, accorded cinema no importance in their lives. Then there were those spectators whose gaze was that of desire and complicity. Assuming a posture of subordination, they submitted to cinema's capacity to seduce and betray. They were cinematically 'gaslighted.' Every black woman I spoke with who was/is an ardent moviegoer, a lover of the Hollywood film, testified that to experience fully the pleasure of that cinema they had to close down critique, analysis; they had to forget racism. And mostly they did not think about sexism. What was the nature then of this adoring black female gaze—this look that could bring pleasure in the midst of negation? In her first novel, *The Bluest Eye,* Toni Morrison constructs a portrait of the black female spectator; her gaze is the masochistic look of victimization. Describing her looking relations, Miss Pauline Breedlove, a poor working woman, maid in the house of a prosperous white family, asserts:

> The onliest time I be happy seem like was when I was in the picture show. Every time I got, I went, I'd go early, before the show started. They's cut off the lights, and everything be black. Then the screen would light up, and I's move right on in them picture. White men taking such good care of they women, and they all dressed up in big clean houses with the bath tubs right in the same room with the toilet. Them pictures gave me a lot of pleasure.

To experience pleasure, Miss Pauline sitting in the dark must imagine herself transformed, turned into the white woman portrayed on the screen. After watching movies, feeling the pleasure, she says, 'But it made coming home hard.'

We come home to ourselves. Not all black women spectators submitted to that spectacle of regression through identification. Most of the women I talked with felt that they consciously resisted identification with films—that this tension made moviegoing less than pleasurable; at times it caused pain. As one black woman put, 'I could always get pleasure from movies as long as I did not look too deep.' For black female spectators who have 'looked too deep' the encounter with the screen hurt. That some of us chose to stop looking was a gesture of resistance, turning away was one way to protest, to reject negation. My pleasure in the screen ended abruptly when I and my sisters first watched *Imitation of Life.* Writing about this experience in the 'Sapphire' piece, I addressed the movie directly, confessing:

> I had until now forgotten you, that screen image seen in adolescence, those images that made me stop looking. It was there in *Imitation of Life,* that comfortable mammy image. There was something familiar about this hard-working black woman who loved her daughter so much, loved her in a way that hurt. Indeed, as young southern black girls watching this film, Peola's another reminded us of the hardworking, churchgoing, Big Mamas we knew

> and loved. Consequently, it was not this image that captured our gaze; we were fascinated by Peola.

Addressing her, I wrote:

> You were different. There was something scary in his image of young sexual sensual black beauty betrayed—that daughter who did not want to be confined by blackness, that 'tragic mulatto' who did not want to be negated. 'Just let me escape this image forever,' she could have said. I will always remember that image. I remembered how we cried for her, for our unrealized desiring selves. She was tragic because there was no place in the cinema for her, no loving pictures. She too was absent image. It was better then, that we were absent, for when we were there it was humiliating, strange, sad. We cried all night for you, for the cinema that had no place for you. And like you, we stopped thinking it would one day be different.

When I returned to films as a young woman, after a long period of silence, I had developed an oppositional gaze. Not only would I not be hurt by the absence of black female presence, or the insertion of violating representation, I interrogated the work, cultivated a way to look past race and gender for aspects of content, form, language. Foreign films and US independent cinema were the primary locations of my filmic looking relations, even though I also watched Hollywood films.

From 'jump,' black female spectators have gone to films with awareness of the way in which race and racism determined the visual construction of gender. Whether it was *Birth of a Nation* or Shirley Temple shows, we knew that white womanhood was the racialized sexual difference occupying the place of stardom in mainstream narrative film. We assumed white women knew it too. Reading Laura Mulvey's provocative essay, 'Visual Pleasure and Narrative Cinema,' from a standpoint that acknowledges race, one sees clearly why black women spectators not duped by mainstream cinema would develop an oppositional gaze. Placing ourselves outside that pleasure in looking, Mulvey argues, was determined by a 'split between active/male and passive/female.' Black female spectators actively chose not to identify with the film's imaginary subject because such identification was disenabling.

Looking at films with an oppositional gaze, black women were able to critically assess the cinema's construction of white womanhood as object of phallocentric gaze and choose not to identify with either the victim or the perpetrator. Black female spectators, who refused to identify with white womanhood, who would not take on the phallocentric gaze of desire and possession, created a critical space where the binary opposition Mulvey posits of 'woman as image, man as bearer of the look' was continually deconstructed. As critical spectators, black women looked from a location that disrupted, one akin to that described by Annette Kuhn in *The Power of The Image*:

> . . . the acts of analysis, of deconstruction and of reading 'against the grain' offer an additional pleasure—the pleasure of resistance, of saying 'no': not to 'unsophisticated' enjoyment, by ourselves and others, of culturally dominant images, but to the structures of power which ask us to consume them uncritically and in highly circumscribed ways.

Mainstream feminist film criticism in no way acknowledges black female spectatorship. It does not even consider the possibility that women can construct an oppositional gaze via an understanding and awareness of the politics of race and racism. Feminist film theory rooted in an ahistorical psychoanalytic framework that privileges sexual difference actively suppresses recognition of race, reenacting and mirroring the erasure of black womanhood that occurs in films, silencing any discussion of racial difference—of racialized sexual difference. Despite feminist critical interventions aimed at deconstructing the category 'woman' which highlight the significance of race, many feminist film critics continue to structure their discourse as though it speaks about 'women' when in actuality it speaks only about white women. It seems ironic that the cover of the recent anthology *Feminism and Film Theory* edited by Constance Penley has a graphic that is a reproduction of the photo of white actresses Rosalind Russell and Dorothy Arzner on the 1936 set of the film *Craig's Wife* yet there is no acknowledgment in any essay in this collection that the woman 'subject' under discussion is always white. Even though there are photos of black women from films reproduced in the text, there is no acknowledgment of racial difference.

It would be too simplistic to interpret this failure of insight solely as a gesture of racism. Importantly, it also speaks to the problem of structuring feminist film theory around a totalizing narrative of woman as object whose image functions solely to reaffirm and reinscribe patriarchy. Mary Ann Doane addresses this issue in the essay 'Remembering Women: Psychical and Historical Construction in Film Theory':

> This attachment to the figure of a degeneralizible Woman as the product of the apparatus indicates why, for many, feminist film theory seems to have reached an impasse, a certain blockage in its theorization . . . in focusing upon the task of delineating in great detail the attributes of woman as effect of the apparatus, feminist film theory participates in the abstraction of women.

The concept 'Woman' effaces the difference between women in specific socio-historical contexts, between women defined precisely as historical subjects rather than as a psychic subject (or non-subject). Though Doane does not focus on race, her comments speak directly to the problem of its erasure. For it is only as one imagines 'woman' in the abstract, when woman becomes fiction or fantasy, can race nor be seen as significant. Are we really to imagine that feminist theorists writing only about images of white women, who subsume this specific historical subject under the totalizing category 'woman,' do not 'see' the whiteness of the image? It may very well be that they engage in a process of denial that eliminates the necessity of revisioning conventional ways of thinking about psychoanalysis as a paradigm of analysis and the need to rethink a body of feminist film theory that is firmly rooted in a denial of the reality that sex/ sexuality may not be the primary and/or exclusive signifier of difference. Doane's essay appears in a very recent anthology, *Psychoanalysis and Cinema* edited by E. Ann Kaplan, where, once again, none of the theory presented acknowledges or discusses racial difference, with the exception of one essay, 'Not Speaking with Language, Speaking with No Language,' which problematizes notions of orientalism in its examination of Leslie Thornton's film *Adynata*. Yet in most of the essays, the theories espoused are rendered problematic if one includes race as a category of analysis.

Constructing feminist film theory along these lines enables the production of a discursive practice that need never theorize any aspect of black female representation or spectatorship. Yet the existence of black women within white supremacist culture problematizes, and makes complex, the overall issue of female identity, representation, and spectatorship. If, as Friedberg suggests, 'identification is a process which commands the subject to be displaced by an other; it is a procedure which breeches the separation between self and other, and, in this way, replicates the very structure of patriarchy.' If identification 'demands sameness, necessitates similarity, disallows difference'—must we then surmise that many feminist film critics who are 'over-identified' with the mainstream cinematic apparatus produce theories that replicate its totalizing agenda? Why is it that feminist film criticism, which has most claimed the terrain of woman's identity, representation, and subjectivity as its field of analysis, remains aggressively silent on the subject of blackness and specifically representations of black womanhood? Just as mainstream cinema has historically forced aware black female spectators not to look, much feminist film criticism disallows the possibility of a theoretical dialogue that might include black women's voices. It is difficult to talk when you feel no one is listening, when you feel as though a special jargon or narrative has been created that only the chosen can understand. No wonder then that black women have for the most part confined our critical commentary on film to conversations. And it must be reiterated that this gesture is a strategy that protects us from the violence perpetuated and advocated by discourses of mass media. A new focus on issues of race and representation in the field of film theory could critically intervene on the historical repression reproduced in some arenas of contemporary critical practice, making a discursive space for discussion of black female spectatorship possible.

When I asked a black woman in her twenties, an obsessive moviegoer, why she thought we had not written about black female spectatorship, she commented: 'We are afraid to talk about ourselves as spectators because we have been so abused by "the gaze".' An aspect of that abuse was the imposition of the assumption that black female looking relations were not important enough to theorize. Film theory as a critical 'turf' in the United States has been and continues to be influenced by and reflective of white racial domination. Since feminist film criticism was initially rooted in a women's liberation movement informed by racist practices, it did not open up the discursive terrain and make it more inclusive. Recently, even those white film theorists who include an analysis of race show no interest in black female spectatorship. In her introduction to the collection of essays *Visual and Other Pleasures,* Laura Mulvey describes her initial romantic absorption in Hollywood cinema, stating:

> Although this great, previously unquestioned and unanalyzed love was put in crisis by the impact of feminism on my thought in the early 1970s, it also had an enormous influence on the development of my critical work and ideas and the debate within film culture with which I became preoccupied over the next fifteen years or so. Watched through eyes that were affected by the changing climate of consciousness, the movies lost their magic.

Watching movies from a feminist perspective, Mulvey arrived at that location of disaffection that is the starting point for many black women approaching cinema within the lived harsh reality of racism. Yet her account of being a part of a film culture whose roots rest on a founding relationship of adoration and love indicates how difficult it would have been to enter that world from 'jump' as a critical spectator whose gaze had been formed in opposition.

Given the context of class exploitation, and racist and sexist domination, it has only been through resistance, struggle, reading, and looking 'against the grain,' that black women have been able to value our process of looking enough to publicly name it. Centrally, those black female spectators who attest to the oppositionality of their gaze deconstruct theories of female spectatorship that have relied heavily on the assumption that, as Doane suggests in her essay, 'Woman's Stake: Filming the Female Body,' 'woman can only mimic man's relation to language, that is assume a position defined by the penis-phallus as the supreme arbiter of lack.' Identifying with neither the phallocentric gaze nor the construction of white womanhood as lack, critical black female spectators construct a theory of looking relations where cinematic visual delight is the pleasure of interrogation. Every black woman spectator I talked to, with rare exception, spoke of being 'on guard' at the movies. Talking about the way being a critical spectator of Hollywood films influenced her, black woman filmmaker Julie Dash exclaims, 'I make films because I was such a spectator!' Looking at Hollywood cinema from a distance, from that critical politicized standpoint that did not want to be seduced by narratives reproducing her negation, Dash watched mainstream movies over and over again for the pleasure of deconstructing them. And of course there is that added delight if one happens, in the process of interrogation, to come across a narrative that invites the black female spectator to engage the text with no threat of violation [. . .]

Talking with black female spectators, looking at written discussions either in fiction or academic essays about black women, I noted the connection made between the realm of representation in mass media and the capacity of black women to construct ourselves as subjects in daily life. The extent to which black women feel devalued, objectified, dehumanized in this society determines the scope and texture of their looking relations. Those black women whose identities were constructed in resistance, by practices that oppose the dominant order, were most inclined to develop an oppositional gaze. Now that there is a growing interest in films produced by black women and those films have become more accessible to viewers, it is possible to talk about black female spectatorship in relation to that work. So far, most discussions of black spectatorship that I have come across focus on men. In 'Black Spectatorship: Problems of Identification and Resistance' Manthia Diawara suggests that 'the components of "difference" ' among elements of sex, gender, and sexuality give rise to different readings of the same material, adding that these conditions produce a 'resisting' spectator. He focuses his critical discussion on black masculinity.

The recent publication of the anthology *The Female Gaze: Women as Viewers of Popular Culture* excited me, especially as it included an essay, 'Black Looks,' by Jacqui Roach and Petal Felix that attempts to address black female spectatorship. The essay posed provocative questions that were not answered: Is there a black female gaze? How do black women relate to the gender politics of representation? Concluding, the authors assert that black females have 'our own reality, our own history, our own gaze—one which sees the world rather differently from "anyone else." ' Yet, they do not name/describe this experience of seeing 'rather differently.' The absence of definition and explanation suggests they are assuming an essentialist stance wherein it is presumed that black women, as victims of race and gender oppression, have an inherently different field of vision. Many black women do not 'see differently' precisely because their perceptions of reality are so profoundly colonized, shaped by dominant ways of knowing. As Trinh T. Minh-ha points out in 'Outside In, Inside Out': 'Subjectivity does not merely consist of talking about oneself . . . be this talking indulgent or critical.'

Critical black female spectatorship emerges as a site of resistance only when individual black women actively resist the imposition of dominant ways of knowing and looking. While every black woman I talked to was aware of racism, that awareness did not automatically correspond with politicization, the development of an oppositional gaze. When it did, individual black women consciously named the process. Manthia Diawara's 'resisting spectatorship' is a term that does not adequately describe the terrain of black female spectatorship. We do more than resist. We create alternative texts that are not solely reactions. As critical spectators, black women participate in a broad range of looking relations, contest, resist, revision, interrogate, and invent on multiple levels. Certainly when I watch the work of black women filmmakers Camille Billops, Kathleen Collins, Julie Dash, Ayoka Chenzira, Zeinabu Davis, I do not need to 'resist' the images even as I still choose to watch their work with a critical eye.

Black female critical thinkers concerned with creating space for the construction of radical black female subjectivity, and the way cultural production informs this possibility, fully acknowledge the importance of mass media, film in particular, as a powerful site for critical intervention. Certainly Julie Dash's film *Illusions* identifies the terrain of Hollywood cinema as a space of knowledge production that has enormous power. Yet, she also creates a filmic narrative wherein the black female protagonist subversively claims that space. Inverting the 'real-life' power structure, she offers the black female spectator representations that challenge stereotypical notions that place us outside the realm of filmic discursive practices. Within the film she uses the strategy of Hollywood suspense films to undermine those cinematic practices that deny black women a place in this structure. Problematizing the question of 'racial' identity by depicting passing, suddenly it is the white male's capacity to gaze, define, and know that is called into question.

When Mary Ann Doane describes in 'Woman's Stake: Filming the Female Body' the way in which feminist filmmaking practice can elaborate 'a special syntax for a different articulation of the female body,' she names a critical process that 'undoes the structure of the classical narrative through an insistence upon its repressions.' An eloquent description, this precisely names Dash's strategy in *Illusions,* even though the film is not unproblematic and works within certain conventions that are not successfully challenged. For example, the film does not indicate whether the character Mignon will make Hollywood films that subvert and transform the genre or whether she will simply assimilate and perpetuate the norm. Still, subversively, *Illusions* problematizes the issue of race and spectatorship. White people in the film are unable to 'see' that race informs their looking relations. Though she is passing to gain access to the machinery of cultural production represented by film, Mignon continually asserts her ties to black community. The bond between her and the young black woman singer Esther Jeeter is affirmed by caring gestures of affirmation, often expressed by eye-to-eye contact, the direct unmediated gaze of recognition. Ironically, it is the desiring objectifying sexualized white male gaze that threatens to penetrate her 'secrets' and disrupt her process. Metaphorically, Dash suggests the power of black women to make films will be threatened and undermined by that white male gaze that seeks to reinscribe the black female body in a narrative of voyeuristic pleasure where the only relevant opposition is male/female, and the only location for the female is as a victim. These tensions are not resolved by the narrative. It is not at all evident that Mignon will triumph over the white supremacist capitalist imperialist dominating 'gaze.'

Throughout *Illusions,* Mignon's power is affirmed by her contact with the younger black woman whom she nurtures and protects. It is this process of mirrored recognition that enables both black women to define their reality, apart from the reality imposed upon them by structures of domination. The shared gaze of the two women reinforces their solidarity. As the younger subject, Esther represents a potential audience for films that Mignon might produce, films wherein black females will be the narrative focus. Julie Dash's recent feature-length film *Daughters of the Dust* dares to place black females at the center of its narrative. This focus caused critics (especially white males) to critique the film negatively or to express many reservations. Clearly, the impact of racism and sexism so over-determine spectatorship—not only what we look at but who we identify with—that viewers who are not black females find it hard to empathize with the central characters in the movie. They are adrift without a white presence in the film.

Another representation of black females nurturing one another *via* recognition of their common struggle for subjectivity is depicted in Sankofa's collective work *Passion of Remembrance.* In the film, two black women friends, Louise and Maggie, are from the onset of the narrative struggling with the issue of subjectivity, of their place in progressive black liberation movements that have been sexist. They challenge old norms and want to replace them with new understandings of the complexity of black identity, and the need for liberation struggles that address that complexity. Dressing to go to a party, Louise and Maggie claim the 'gaze.' Looking at one another, staring in mirrors, they appear completely focused on their encounter with black femaleness. How they see themselves is most important, not how they will be stared at by others. Dancing to the tune 'Let's get Loose,' they display their bodies not for a voyeuristic colonizing gaze but for that look of recognition that affirms their subjectivity—that constitutes them as spectators. Mutually empowered they eagerly leave the privatized domain to confront the public. Disrupting conventional racist and sexist stereotypical representations of black female bodies, these scenes invite the audience to look differently. They act to critically intervene and transform conventional filmic practices, changing notions of spectatorship. *Illusions, Daughters of the Dust,* and *A Passion of Remembrance* employ a deconstructive filmic practice to undermine existing grand cinematic narratives even as they retheorize subjectivity in the realm of the visual. Without providing 'realistic' positive representations that emerge only as a response to the totalizing nature of existing narratives, they offer points of radical departure. Opening up a space for the assertion of a critical black female spectatorship, they do not simply offer diverse representations, they imagine new transgressive possibilities for the formulation of identity.

In this sense they make explicit a critical practice that provides us with different ways to think about black female subjectivity and black female spectatorship. Cinematically, they provide new points of recognition, embodying Stuart Hall's vision of a critical practice that acknowledges that identity is constituted 'not outside but within representation,' and invites us to see film 'not as a second-order mirror held up to reflect what already exists, but as that form of representation which is able to constitute us as new kinds of subjects, and thereby enable us to discover who we are.' It is this critical practice that enables production of feminist film theory that theorizes black female spectatorship. Looking and looking back, black women involve ourselves in a process whereby we see our history as) counter-memory, using it as a way to know the present and invent the future.

References

Burchill, Julie, *Girls on Film* (New York: Pantheon, 1986).

Diawara Manthia, 'Black Spectatorship: Problems of Identification and Resistance'. *Screen,* Vol. 29, No. 4 (1988).

Diawara, Manthia, 'Black British Cinema: Spectatorship and Identity Formation in Territories'. *Public Culture,* Vol. 1, No. 3 (Summer 1989).

Doane, Mary Ann, 'Woman's Stake: Filming the Female Body'. In *Feminism and Film Theory,* edited by Constance Penley (New York: Routledge, 1988).

Doane, Mary Ann, 'Remembering Women: Psychical and Historical Constructions in Film Theory'. In *Psychoanalysis and Cinema,* edited by E. Ann Kaplan (London: Routledge, 1990).

Fanon, Franz, *Black Skin, White Masks* (New York: Monthly Review, 1967).

Friedberg, Anne, 'A Denial of Difference: Theories of Cinematic Identification'. In *Psychoanalysis and Cinema,* edited by E. Ann Kaplan (London: Routledge, 1990).

Gamman, Lorraine and Marshment, Margaret (eds), *The Female Gaze: Women as Viewers of Popular Culture* (London: The Women's Press, 1988).

Hall, Stuart, 'Cultural Identity and Diaspora'. In *Identity: Community, Culture, Difference,* edited by Jonathan Rutherford (London: Lawrence & Wishart, 1990).

hooks, bell, 'Do You Remember Sapphire?'. In hooks, *Talking Back: Thinking Feminism, Thinking Black* (Boston: South End Press, 1989).

Kuhn, Annette, *The Power of the Image: Essays on Representation and Sexuality* (New York: Routledge, 1985).

Minh-ha, Trinh T., 'Outside In, Inside Out'. In *Questions of Third Cinema,* edited by Jim Pines (London: British Film Institute, 1989).

Morrison, Toni, *The Bluest Eye* (New York: Holt, Rinehart and Winston, 1970).

Mulvey, Laura, 'Visual Pleasure and Narrative Cinema'. *Screen* Autumn 1975, Vol. 16, No. 3, pp. 6-18.

Mulvey, Laura, *Visual and Other Pleasures* (Bloomington: University of Indiana Press, 1989).

Peggy McIntosh is a professor and the associate director of the Wellesley College Center for Research on Women, and is founder and co-director of the national S.E.E.D. (Seeking Educational Equity and Diversity) Project on Inclusive Curriculum. Her many articles have examined different aspects of race and the integration of feminist theories into traditional curricula. In the following essay (1988) McIntosh is careful to say that this text is more of a personal record of her observations than a scholarly analysis. She uses the metaphor of an "invisible weightless knapsack" to specify the nature of white privilege. Can you explain how this metaphor works? How does she relate white privilege to male privilege? Why does she do this? What does she mean by hegemony? Systemic racism? Meritocracy? Taboos? How do McIntosh's ideas correspond to other texts in this unit, in particular to Rich's "Claiming an Education"?

White Privilege and Male Privilege

A Personal Account of Coming to See Correspondences through Work in Women's Studies

Peggy McIntosh

Through work to bring materials and perspectives from Women's Studies into the rest of the curriculum, I have often noticed men's unwillingness to grant that they are overprivileged in the curriculum, even though they may grant that women are disadvantaged. Denials that amount to taboos surround the subject of advantages that men gain from women's disadvantages. These denials protect male privilege from being fully recognized, acknowledged, lessened, or ended.

Thinking through unacknowledged male privilege as a phenomenon with a life of its own, I realized that since hierarchies in our society are interlocking, there was most likely a phenomenon of white privilege that was similarly denied and protected, but alive and real in its effects. As a white person, I realized I had been taught about racism as something that puts others at a disadvantage, but had been taught not to see one of its corollary aspects, white privilege, which puts me at an advantage.

I think whites are carefully taught not to recognize white privilege, as males are taught not to recognize male privilege. So I have begun in an untutored way to ask what it is like to have white privilege. This paper is a partial record of my personal observations and not a scholarly analysis. It is based on my daily experiences within my particular circumstances.

I have come to see white privilege as an invisible package of unearned assets that I can count on cashing in each day, but about which I was "meant" to remain oblivious. White privilege is like an invisible weightless knapsack of special provisions, assurances, tools, maps, guides, codebooks, passports, visas, clothes, compass, emergency gear, and blank checks.

Since I have had trouble facing white privilege, and describing its results in my life, I saw parallels here with men's reluctance to acknowledge male privilege. Only rarely will a man go beyond acknowledging that women are disadvantaged to acknowledging that men have unearned advantage, or that unearned privilege has not been good for men's development as human beings, or for society's development, or that privilege systems might ever be challenged and *changed*.

I will review here several types or layers of denial that I see at work protecting, and preventing awareness about, entrenched male privilege. Then I will draw parallels, from my own experience, with the denials that veil the facts of white privilege. Finally, I will list forty-six ordinary and daily ways in which I experience having white privilege, by contrast with my African American colleagues in the same building. This list is not intended to be generalizable. Others can make their own lists from within their own life circumstances.

Writing this paper has been difficult, despite warm receptions for the talks on which it is based.[1] For describing white privilege makes one newly accountable. As we in Women's Studies work reveal male privilege and ask men to give up some of their power, so one who writes about having white privilege must ask, "Having described it, what will I do to lessen or end it?"

The denial of men's overprivileged state takes many forms in discussions of curriculum change work. Some claim that men must be central in the curriculum because they have done most of what is important or distinctive in life or in civilization. Some recognize sexism in the curriculum but deny that it makes male students seem unduly important in life. Others agree that certain *individual* thinkers are male oriented but deny that there is any *systemic* tendency in disciplinary frameworks or epistemology to overempower men as a group. Those men who do grant that male privilege takes institutionalized and embedded forms are still likely to deny that male hegemony has opened doors for them personally. Virtually all men deny that male overreward alone can explain men's centrality in all the inner sanctums of our most powerful institutions. Moreover, those few who will acknowledge that male privilege systems have overempowered them usually end up doubting that we could dismantle these privilege systems. They may say they will work to improve women's status, in the society or in the university, but they can't or won't support the idea of lessening men's. In curricular terms, this is the point at which they say that they regret they cannot use any of the interesting new scholarship on women because the syllabus is full. When the talk turns to giving men less cultural room, even the most thoughtful and fair-minded of the men

I know will tend to reflect, or fall back on, conservative assumptions about the inevitability of present gender relations and distributions of power, calling on precedent or sociobiology and psychobiology to demonstrate that male domination is natural and follows inevitably from evolutionary pressures. Others resort to arguments from "experience" or religion or social responsibility or wishing and dreaming.

After I realized, through faculty development work in Women's Studies, the extent to which men work from a base of unacknowledged privilege, I understood that much of their oppressiveness was unconscious. Then I remembered the frequent charges from women of color that white women whom they encounter are oppressive. I began to understand why we are justly seen as oppressive, even when we don't see ourselves that way. At the very least, obliviousness of one's privileged state can make a person or group irritating to be with. I began to count the ways in which I enjoy unearned skin privilege and have been conditioned into oblivion about its existence, unable to see that it put me "ahead" in any way, or put my people ahead, overrewarding us and yet also paradoxically damaging us, or that it could or should be changed.

My schooling gave me no training in seeing myself as an oppressor, as an unfairly advantaged person, or as a participant in a damaged culture. I was taught to see myself as an individual whose moral state depended on her individual moral will. At school, we were not taught about slavery in any depth; we were not taught to see slaveholders as damaged people. Slaves were seen as the only group at risk of being dehumanized. My schooling followed the pattern which Elizabeth Minnich has pointed out: whites are taught to think of their lives as morally neutral, normative, and average, and also ideal, so that when we work to benefit others, this is seen as work that will allow "them" to be more like "us." I think many of us know how obnoxious this attitude can be in men.

After frustration with men who would not recognize male privilege, I decided to try to work on myself at least by identifying some of the daily effects of white privilege in my life. It is crude work, at this stage, but I will give here a list of special circumstances and conditions I experience that I did not earn but that I have been made to feel are mine by birth, by citizenship, and by virtue of being a conscientious law-abiding "normal" person of goodwill. I have chosen those conditions that I think in my case *attach somewhat more to skin-color privilege* than to class, religion, ethnic status, or geographical location, though these other privileging factors are intricately intertwined. As far as I can see, my Afro-American co-workers, friends, and acquaintances with whom I come into daily or frequent contact in this particular time, place, and line of work cannot count on most of these conditions.

1. I can, if I wish, arrange to be in the company of people of my race most of the time.
2. I can avoid spending time with people whom I was trained to mistrust and who have learned to mistrust my kind or me.
3. If I should need to move, I can be pretty sure of renting or purchasing housing in an area which I can afford and in which I would want to live.
4. I can be reasonably sure that my neighbors in such a location will be neutral or pleasant to me.
5. I can go shopping alone most of the time, fairly well assured that I will not be followed or harassed by store detectives.
6. I can turn on the television or open to the front page of the paper and see people of my race widely and positively represented.
7. When I am told about our national heritage or about "civilization," I am shown that people of my color made it what it is.
8. I can be sure that my children will be given curricular materials that testify to the existence of their race.
9. If I want to, I can be pretty sure of finding a publisher for this piece on white privilege.
10. I can be fairly sure of having my voice heard in a group in which I am the only member of my race.
11. I can be casual about whether or not to listen to another woman's voice in a group in which she is the only member of her race.
12. I can go into a book shop and count on finding the writing of my race represented, into a supermarket and find the staple foods that fit with my cultural traditions, into a hairdresser's shop and find someone who can deal with my hair.
13. Whether I use checks, credit cards, or cash, I can count on my skin color not to work against the appearance that I am financially reliable.
14. I could arrange to protect our young children most of the time from people who might not like them.
15. I did not have to educate our children to be aware of systemic racism for their own daily physical protection.
16. I can be pretty sure that my children's teachers and employers will tolerate them if they fit school and workplace norms; my

chief worries about them do not concern others' attitudes toward their race.

17. I can talk with my mouth full and not have people put this down to my color.
18. I can swear, or dress in secondhand clothes, or not answer letters, without having people attribute these choices to the bad morals, the poverty, or the illiteracy of my race.
19. I can speak in public to a powerful male group without putting my race on trial.
20. I can do well in a challenging situation without being called a credit to my race.
21. I am never asked to speak for all the people of my racial group.
22. I can remain oblivious to the language and customs of persons of color who constitute the world's majority without feeling in my culture any penalty for such oblivion.
23. I can criticize our government and talk about how much I fear its policies and behavior without being seen as a cultural outsider.
24. I can be reasonably sure that if I ask to talk to "the person in charge," I will be facing a person of my race.
25. If a traffic cop pulls me over or if the IRS audits my tax return, I can be sure I haven't been singled out because of my race.
26. I can easily buy posters, postcards, picture books, greeting cards, dolls, toys, and children's magazines featuring people of my race.
27. I can go home from most meetings of organizations I belong to feeling somewhat tied in, rather than isolated, out of place, outnumbered, unheard, held at a distance, or feared.
28. I can be pretty sure that an argument with a colleague of another race is more likely to jeopardize her chances for advancement than to jeopardize mine.
29. I can be fairly sure that if I argue for the promotion of a person of another race, or a program centering on race, this is not likely to cost me heavily within my present setting, even if my colleagues disagree with me.
30. If I declare there is a racial issue at hand, or there isn't a racial issue at hand, my race will lend me more credibility for either position than a person of color will have.

31. I can choose to ignore developments in minority writing and minority activist programs, or disparage them, or learn from them, but in any case, I can find ways to be more or less protected from negative consequences of any of these choices.
32. My culture gives me little fear about ignoring the perspectives and powers of people of other races.
33. I am not made acutely aware that my shape, bearing, or body odor will be taken as a reflection on my race.
34. I can worry about racism without being seen as self-interested or self-seeking.
35. I can take a job with an affirmative action employer without having my co-workers on the job suspect that I got it because of my race.
36. If my day, week, or year is going badly, I need not ask of each negative episode or situation whether it has racial overtones.
37. I can be pretty sure of finding people who would be willing to talk with me and advise me about my next steps, professionally.
38. I can think over many options, social, political, imaginative, or professional, without asking whether a person of my race would be accepted or allowed to do what I want to do.
39. I can be late to a meeting without having the lateness reflect on my race.
40. I can choose public accommodation without fearing that people of my race cannot get in or will be mistreated in the places I have chosen.
41. I can be sure that if I need legal or medical help, my race will not work against me.
42. I can arrange my activities so that I will never have to experience feelings of rejection owing to my race.
43. If I have low credibility as a leader, I can be sure that my race is not the problem.
44. I can easily find academic courses and institutions that give attention only to people of my race.
45. I can expect figurative language and imagery in all of the arts to testify to experiences of my race.
46. I can choose blemish cover or bandages in "flesh" color and have them more or less match my skin.

I repeatedly forgot each of the realizations on this list until I wrote it down. For me, white privilege has turned out to be an elusive and fugitive subject. The pressure to avoid it is great, for in facing it I must give up the myth of meritocracy. If these things are true, this is not such a free country; one's life is not what one makes it; many doors open for certain people through no virtues of their own. These perceptions mean also that my moral condition is not what I had been led to believe. The appearance of being a good citizen rather than a troublemaker comes in large part from having all sorts of doors open automatically because of my color.

A further paralysis of nerve comes from literary silence protecting privilege. My clearest memories of finding such analysis are in Lillian Smith's unparalleled *Killers of the Dream* and Margaret Andersen's review of Karen and Mamie Fields' *Lemon Swamp*. Smith, for example, wrote about walking toward black children on the street and knowing they would step into the gutter; Andersen contrasted the pleasure that she, as a white child, took on summer driving trips to the south with Karen Fields' memories of driving in a closed car stocked with all necessities lest, in stopping, her black family should suffer "insult, or worse." Adrienne Rich also recognizes and writes about daily experiences of privilege, but in my observation, white women's writing in this area is far more often on systemic racism than on our daily lives as light-skinned women.[2]

In unpacking this invisible knapsack of white privilege, I have listed conditions of daily experience that I once took for granted, as neutral, normal, and universally available to everybody, just as I once thought of a male-focused curriculum as the neutral or accurate account that can speak for all. Nor did I think of any of these perquisites as bad for the holder. I now think that we need a more finely differentiated taxonomy of privilege, for some of these varieties are only what one would want for everyone in a just society, and others give license to be ignorant, oblivious, arrogant, and destructive. Before proposing some more finely tuned categorization, I will make some observations about the general effects of these conditions on my life and expectations.

In this potpourri of examples, some privileges make me feel at home in the world. Others allow me to escape penalties or dangers that others suffer. Through some, I escape fear, anxiety, insult, injury, or a sense of not being welcome, not being real. Some keep me from having to hide, to be in disguise, to feel sick or crazy, to negotiate each transaction from the position of being an outsider or, within my group, a person who is suspected of having too close links with a dominant culture. Most keep me from having to be angry.

I see a pattern running through the matrix of white privilege, a pattern of assumptions that were passed on to me as a white person. There was one main piece of cultural turf; it was my own turf, and I was among those who could control the turf. I could measure up to the cultural standards and take advantage of the many options I saw around me to make what the culture would call a success of my life. *My skin color was an asset for any move I was educated to want to make.* I could think of myself as "belonging" in major ways and of making social systems work for me. I could freely disparage, fear, neglect, or be oblivious to anything outside of the dominant cultural forms. Being of the main culture, I could also criticize it fairly freely. My life was reflected back to me frequently enough so that I felt, with regard to my race, if not to my sex, like one of the real people.

Whether through the curriculum or in the newspaper, the television, the economic system, or the general look of people in the streets, I received daily signals and indications that my people counted and that others *either didn't exist or must be trying, not very successfully, to be like people of my race.* I was given cultural permission not to hear voices of people of other races or a tepid cultural tolerance for hearing or acting on such voices. I was also raised not to suffer seriously from anything that darker-skinned people might say about my group, "protected," though perhaps I should more accurately say *prohibited,* through the habits of my economic class and social group, from living in racially mixed groups or being reflective about interactions between people of differing races.

In proportion as my racial group was being made confident, comfortable, and oblivious, other groups were likely being made unconfident, uncomfortable, and alienated. Whiteness protected me from many kinds of hostility, distress, and violence, which I was being subtly trained to visit in turn upon people of color.

For this reason, the word "privilege" now seems to me misleading. Its connotations are too positive to fit the conditions and behaviors which "privilege systems" produce. We usually think of privilege as being a favored state, whether earned, or conferred by birth or luck. School graduates are reminded they are privileged and urged to use their (enviable) assets well. The word "privilege" carries the connotation of being something everyone must want. Yet some of the conditions I have described here work to systemically overempower certain groups. Such privilege simply *confers dominance,* gives permission to control, because of one's race or sex. The kind of privilege that gives license to some people to be, at best, thoughtless and, at worst, murderous should not continue to be referred to as a desirable attribute. Such "privilege" may be widely desired without being in any way beneficial to the whole society.

Moreover, though "privilege" may confer power, it does not confer moral strength. Those who do not depend on conferred dominance have traits and qualities that may never develop in those who do. Just as Women's Studies courses indicate that women survive their political circumstances to lead lives that hold the human race together, so "underprivileged" people of color who are the world's majority have survived their oppression and lived survivors' lives from which the white global minority can and must learn. In some groups, those dominated have actually become strong through *not* having all of these unearned advantages, and this gives them a great deal to teach the others. Members of so-called privileged groups can seem foolish, ridiculous, infantile, or dangerous by contrast.

I want, then, to distinguish between earned strength and unearned power conferred systemically. Power from unearned privilege can look like strength when it is, in fact, permission to escape or to dominate. But not all of the privileges on my list are inevitably damaging. Some, like the expectation that neighbors will be decent to you, or that your race will not count against you in court, should be the norm in a just society and should be considered as the entitlement of everyone. Others, like the privilege not to listen to less powerful people, distort the humanity of the holders as well as the ignored groups. Still others, like finding one's staple foods everywhere, may be a function of being a member of a numerical majority in the population. Others have to do with not having to labor under pervasive negative stereotyping and mythology.

We might at least start by distinguishing between positive advantages that we can work to spread, to the point where they are not advantages at all but simply part of the normal civic and social fabric, and negative types of advantage that unless rejected will always reinforce our present hierarchies. For example, the positive "privilege" of belonging, the feeling that one belongs within the human circle, as Native Americans say, fosters development and should not be seen as privilege for a few. It is, let us say, an entitlement that none of us should have to earn; ideally it is an *unearned entitlement*. At present, since only a few have it, it is an *unearned advantage* for them. The negative "privilege" that gave me cultural permission not to take darker-skinned Others seriously can be seen as arbitrarily conferred dominance and should not be desirable for anyone. This paper results from a process of coming to see that some of the power that I originally saw as attendant on being a human being in the United States consisted in *unearned advantage* and *conferred dominance*, as well as other kinds of special circumstance not universally taken for granted.

In writing this paper I have also realized that white identity and status (as well as class identity and status) give me considerable power to choose whether to broach this subject and its trouble. I can pretty well decide whether to disappear and avoid and not listen and escape the dislike I may engender in other people through this essay, or interrupt, answer, interpret, preach, correct, criticize, and control to some extent what goes on in reaction to it. Being white, I am given considerable power to escape many kinds of danger or penalty as well as to choose which risks I want to take.

There is an analogy here, once again, with Women's Studies. Our male colleagues do not have a great deal to lose in supporting Women's Studies, but they do not have a great deal to lose if they oppose it either. They simply have the power to decide whether to commit themselves to more equitable distributions of power. They will probably feel few penalties whatever choice they make; they do not seem, in any obvious short-term sense, the ones at risk, though they and we are all at risk because of the behaviors that have been rewarded in them.

Through Women's Studies work I have met very few men who are truly distressed about systemic, unearned male advantage and conferred dominance. And so one question for me and others like me is whether we will be like them, or whether we will get truly distressed, even outraged, about unearned race advantage and conferred dominance and if so, what we will do to lessen them. In any case, we need to do more work in identifying how they actually affect our daily lives. We need more down-to-earth writing by people about these taboo subjects. We need more understanding of the ways in which white "privilege" damages white people, for these are not the same ways in which it damages the victimized. Skewed white psyches are an inseparable part of the picture, though I do not want to confuse the kinds of damage done to the holders of special assets and to those who suffer the deficits. Many, perhaps most, of our white students in the United States think that racism doesn't affect them because they are not people of color; they do not see "whiteness" as a racial identity. Many men likewise think that Women's Studies does not bear on their own existences because they are not female; they do not see themselves as having gendered identities. Insisting on the universal "effects" of "privilege" systems, then, becomes one of our chief tasks, and being more explicit about the *particular* effects in particular contexts is another. Men need to join us in this work.

In addition, since race and sex are not the only advantaging systems at work, we need to similarly examine the daily experience of having age advantage, or ethnic advantage, or physical ability, or advantage related to nationality, religion, or sexual orientation. Professor Marnie Evans suggested to me that in many ways the list I made also applies directly to heterosexual privilege. This is a still more taboo subject than race privilege: the daily ways in which heterosexual privilege makes some persons comfortable or powerful, providing supports, assets, approvals, and rewards to those who live or expect to live in heterosexual pairs. Unpacking that content is still more difficult, owing to the deeper imbeddedness of heterosexual advantage and dominance and stricter taboos surrounding these.

But to start such an analysis I would put this observation from my own experience: the fact that I live under the same roof with a man triggers all kinds of societal assumptions about my worth, politics, life, and values and triggers a host of unearned advantages and powers. After recasting many elements from the original list I would add further observations like these:

1. My children do not have to answer questions about why I live with my partner (my husband).
2. I have no difficulty finding neighborhoods where people approve of our household.
3. Our children are given texts and classes that implicitly support our kind of family unit and do not turn them against my choice of domestic partnership.
4. I can travel alone or with my husband without expecting embarrassment or hostility in those who deal with us.
5. Most people I meet will see my marital arrangements as an asset to my life or as a favorable comment on my likability, my competence, or my mental health.
6. I can talk about the social events of a weekend without fearing most listeners' reactions.
7. I will feel welcomed and "normal" in the usual walks of public life, institutional and social.
8. In many contexts, I am seen as "all right" in daily work on women because I do not live chiefly with women.

Difficulties and dangers surrounding the task of finding parallels are many. Since racism, sexism, and heterosexism are not the same, the advantages associated with them should not be seen as the same. In addition, it is hard to isolate aspects of unearned advantage that derive chiefly from social class, economic class, race, religion, region, sex, or ethnic identity. The oppressions are both distinct and interlocking, as the Combahee River Collective statement of 1977 continues to remind us eloquently.[3]

One factor seems clear about all of the interlocking oppressions. They take both active forms that we can see and embedded forms that members of the dominant group are taught not to see. In my class and place, I did not see myself as racist because I was taught to recognize racism only in individual acts of meanness by members of my group, never in invisible systems conferring racial dominance on my group from birth. Likewise, we are taught to think that sexism or heterosexism is carried on only through intentional, individual acts of discrimination, meanness, or cruelty, rather than in invisible systems conferring unsought dominance on certain groups. Disapproving of the systems won't be enough to change them. I was taught to think that racism could end if white individuals changed their attitudes; many men think sexism can be ended by individual changes in daily behavior toward women. But a man's sex provides advantage for him whether or not he approves of the way in which dominance has been conferred on his group. A "white" skin in the United States opens many doors for whites whether or not we approve of the way dominance has been conferred on us. Individual acts can palliate, but cannot end, these problems. To redesign social systems, we need first to acknowledge their colossal unseen dimensions. The silences and denials surrounding privilege are the key political tool here. They keep the thinking about equality or equity incomplete, protecting unearned advantage and conferred dominance by making these taboo subjects. Most talk by whites about equal opportunity seems to me now to be about equal opportunity to try to get into a position of dominance while denying that *systems* of dominance exist.

Obliviousness about white advantage, like obliviousness about male advantage, is kept strongly inculturated in the United States so as to maintain the myth of meritocracy, the myth that democratic choice is equally available to all. Keeping most people unaware that freedom of confident action is there for just a small number of people props up those in power and serves to keep power in the hands of the same groups that have most of it already. Though systemic change takes many decades, there are pressing questions for me and I imagine for some others like me if we raise our daily consciousness on the perquisites of being light-skinned. What will we do with such knowledge? As we know from watching men, it is an open question whether we will choose to use unearned advantage to weaken invisible privilege systems and whether we will use any of our arbitrarily awarded power to try to reconstruct power systems on a broader base.

Notes

1 This paper was presented at the Virginia Women's Studies Association conference in Richmond in April, 1986, and the American Educational Research Association conference in Boston in October, 1986, and discussed with two groups of participants in the Dodge seminars for Secondary School Teachers in New York and Boston in the spring of 1987.

2 Andersen, Margaret, "Race and the Social Science Curriculum: A Teaching and Learning Discussion." *Radical Teacher*, November, 1984, pp. 17–20. Smith, Lillian, *Killers of the Dream*, New York: W. W. Norton, 1949.

3 "A Black Feminist Statement," The Combahee River Collective, pp. 13–22 in G. Hull, P. Scott, B. Smith, Eds., *All the Women Are White, All the Blacks Are Men, But Some of Us Are Brave: Black Women's Studies*, Old Westbury, NY: The Feminist Press, 1982.

White People Facing Race
Uncovering the Myths That Keep Racism in Place

Peggy McIntosh

Foreword by The Saint Paul Foundation

Through its **Facing Race** *We're all in this together*™ anti-racism initiative, The Saint Paul Foundation encourages constructive conversations on the tough issue of racism. Peggy McIntosh's 1989 seminal article, "White Privilege: Unpacking the Invisible Knapsack," is a critical tool that has been used with conversation participants to raise awareness of racism and white privilege.

For many white people, discussions about racism and privilege can engender fear, shame and anger. In this article, "White People Facing Race: Uncovering the Myths That Keep Racism in Place," Dr. McIntosh explores the reasons why these conversations are so difficult. She addresses five myths that preserve white privilege and also discusses the rich rewards that actually facing race can bring.

It is an honor that Dr. McIntosh chose to work with The Saint Paul Foundation on this new article. The Foundation appreciates the opportunity to support her efforts to dismantle racism and to help build a community where everyone feels safe, valued and respected.

"A hard or scary thing about talking about racism is. . . ." As Victor Lewis, Hugh Vasquez and I start our workshops on race across the United States, we ask everyone in the participant group to pair up with another person and finish this oral prompt as many times as possible in one minute. Each person speaks uninterrupted.

This is a remarkable way of getting fear and resistance into the open, as people speak for themselves. Here are some of the responses we have heard from white participants:

- You don't want to be called a racist.
- I am afraid I may be blamed.
- I may be ashamed.
- I may make a fool of myself.
- My racism may show.
- I'm afraid I may shut down.
- I may get hopeless.
- Someone will get angry at me.

- I could hurt someone.
- I may find out I have a lot to learn about myself.
- I may have to say I'm part of the problem.

In these responses from white people, I hear two fears—that of saying a "wrong" or hurtful thing, and that of losing self-esteem. I've concluded that these responses are rooted in our desire to feel good about ourselves and preserve our images of ourselves and our relationships in the world. We seem to know there is something to be feared, that may get us into trouble with others if we open the lid and speak about racism in the United States.

Resistance, Privilege and Governing Myths

I see the desire to keep our image of ourselves "clean" as part of white privilege. Those of us who are white people in the United States feel entitled to feel good about ourselves because we have been shielded from the negative aspects of white history. We have received assurances that we are normal, admirable and deserving, and that we have better values and behavior than people of color here and around the world. These teachings most often come to us subliminally from our families, educational systems and the media. We resist looking at racism because we fear damage to our perception of ourselves as "good people" in the greatest country" in the world.

I think it is natural that we resist anything that might cloud our image of our goodness. But I suggest we ask ourselves why that image hasn't already been clouded. How have whites kept such a strong sense of pride and deservedness? The answer, I think, is that white people are raised on five strong cultural myths: meritocracy, manifest destiny, white racelessness, monoculture and white moral elevation. These lay the foundation for our feeling good about ourselves as white people, and they work in us to override and discredit counter-evidence. They also deter us from entering into serious discussions of racism. One of the central elements of white privilege is not having to take the subject of racism seriously.

The **myth of meritocracy** is the myth that the individual is the only unit of society, and that whatever a person ends up with must be what he or she individually wanted, worked for, earned and deserved. This myth rests on the assumption that what people experience; how they see, feel, think and behave; and what they are capable of accomplishing are not influenced by any social system or circumstance. The myth of meritocracy acknowledges no systems of oppression or privilege that, for various people and in various situations, could make life arbitrarily more, or less, difficult.

The **myth of manifest destiny** includes the idea that white people were intended by God to take the lands of indigenous people and others in order to possess the whole of what is now the continental United States. Under this myth, whites do not have to allow into their moral or ethical awareness the fact that we live on land taken from those who were here before us, and whose cultures and physical existences white people attempted to destroy. Believing explicitly or implicitly that God intended white people to settle North America has excused many whites from seeing white settlement as a matter of racial oppression in which they are the evildoers.

The **myth of white racelessness** is the notion that white people do not have race or racial experience. In this view, we are just "normal." Others have race, which we are led to believe makes problems for them, or us. We who are "normal" are racially unmarked, and we set the standard for what it is to be human. The participation of white people in systems of dominance or oppression is not seen as racial.

The **myth of monoculture** is that there is one American culture and that we all experience it more or less the same way. Anyone who is having trouble with American culture is not seeing accurately or behaving appropriately. The myth of monoculture imposes an assumption and a requirement on people of color. It requires them to see and feel and behave like white people ("normal" people)—that is, to assimilate into white culture—and it assumes that they have nothing to lose by forsaking their cultures of origin, and a great deal to gain from fitting into the one "normal" culture. Under the myth of monoculture, *E pluribus unum* (Out of many, one) is understood as an ideal, but not its converse, *Intra unum plures* (Within one, many).

When white people receive these key beliefs and assumptions from their families, the educational systems and the media, they absorb the idea that white people are superior to others. This is not said in so many words. Instead, the assumption that it is natural for us to be in charge of the world and its affairs, and that only a very unusual person of color, unlike others of his or her kind, can be trusted with power, gets instilled in the subconscious minds of whites. This, finally, is the **myth of white moral elevation,** also called internalized superiority.

It is important to recognize how strong a part this cluster of myths plays in creating the psychological underpinnings for white refusal to face racism. The myths have been taught to white people in the United States, usually at a subconscious level, for centuries. Each of these five myths rests in part on white privilege and creates resistance in the hearts and minds of white people to facing race. Elements of the myths can be heard in the most common statements of resistance to discussing race or even raising the subject:

- Why can't we just get along? There aren't any racial problems if people don't create them.
- We're all the same.
- I'm not prejudiced.

- I don't see color. I just see people.
- Why make waves?
- Don't make people angry.
- Look on the bright side. We all have problems: People with character overcome them. Opportunity is there for everyone.
- Some people just don't know how to fit in.
- If they're going to live here they ought to speak English. They are lucky to even be here.
- They are just ungrateful.
- They spoil this community—this country.

To face race is to be willing to critically examine the five myths underlying these statements. White people's resistance is natural. Raised in an environment that accepts these five myths as truth, why would those of us who are white not resist upsetting our egos, our perceptions of our family and ancestors, and our ideas about this nation? Will a new awareness of our racial history and of the present improve our lives? I feel strongly that the answer is yes. But raising our awareness is not easy because the process works against so much of what we have been led to believe.

K–12 Education

The messages delivered in my schooling with regard to public life in the United States went like this: Things are as they should be. It is all working out. The United States is an example to the rest of the world. We won the big wars, and other people want to come here. Life is good. We (white) Americans are normal people and good people.

This closed system of reassurances reinforced my sense of social stability and managed to stave off my most terrifying visions of war and threat. But now, decades later, I have come to see that these messages also created resistance in me to understanding any history that did not paint me and my white ancestors in a positive light.

Probably more important than the actual content of schooling is the fact that education at all levels in all subject areas in the U.S. discourages students from seeing beyond individuals to the power systems already in place in the worlds we are born into. It discourages students from recognizing systems of both discrimination and advantage, or privilege, and from seeing that our opportunities for choice are in part determined by the systems of power in our society.

The self-affirming view of whites in education helps to explain some of whites' resistance to facing racism, or any other source of injustice. To pay attention to a larger landscape raises doubts about whether, in Browning's words, "God's in his heaven/All's right with the world." It is natural that people who don't have to grapple with this kind of doubt would choose to avoid doing so. It is easier and more comfortable for the more empowered individuals in our culture to believe that all impediments to the good life can be resolved at the individual level.

Media

The public media mirror and increase our resistance to facing race. For example, the media give us glimpses of stories of individuals but do not connect these stories to one another historically. They do not construe race as bearing on the war in Iraq or the Vietnam War, or connect the World War II internment of Japanese people—and not Germans—with race. Even moderately liberal newspaper writers avoid words like *patriarchy, white privilege* or *heterosexism* that imply the existence of large systems of power. Talk show hosts back off from systemic comments made by feminist authors and men and women of color. They retreat to individual questions about individual people. In this way they avoid, and teach listeners to avoid, a systemic analysis of injustice in the U.S. that includes an understanding of both oppression and privilege.

Until recent elections, we saw a reluctance on the part of the media and the U.S. white population to have serious discussions on race, culture and the experiences of people of color in the United States. Even when the candidates themselves gave serious speeches on race relations, white writers and pundits did not follow up on the content of what they said. Instead they focused on the horse race: Who was winning? People working in the media have received the same cultural education as the rest of us. Therefore, they lack the skills to see the systemic workings of race and gender hierarchies. The media will report on the interesting ways that people negotiate their situations, but they resist connecting the dots between the larger systems and the bits and pieces of news they report about individuals.

White People's Stakes in Facing Race

Resistance to work on race also comes in a familiar, natural and very personal way from people fearing what they are getting themselves into if they take racism seriously and work against it. Natural questions are: What will it require of us? Consistency? Commitment? How much time and attention will race work cost us? How much money? What obligations? How many changes am I going to have to make? Am I going to be made to feel bad about myself? Am I meant to become a member of the "PC police"? How will I handle social events where my friends and family start to tell racist jokes? Will I lose my popularity or my place? Is all this race talk leading to talk of reparations for slavery? Am I going to lose my job to a person of color?

I think my own biggest fear about facing race was that the universe as I knew it would be utterly changed if I did so. And my place in the universe would be changed. And so it has been, but in a good way.

Resistance in Organizations and Institutions

I have observed that organizations and institutions act like individuals in resisting facing race. Although they have public profiles and policies, and effects on a far larger scale than individuals, I think their fears are similar. They fear that if they examine their histories and try to remedy past inequity, they will lose power, prestige, profit, security, pride, reputation, freedom and the ability to do whatever they want.

Large corporations for many decades have resisted racial diversification of their leadership. Now, many of them have realized that it may not be in their self-interest to remain monocultural in a time of globalization. It may put them out of touch with reality and damage their credibility, growth and profits. As a result, there is a certain amount of diversity work now done in and by corporations. Most of it is done to improve the bottom line. Still, it may do some good, if it introduces employees to the concepts and realities of institutionalized privilege and oppression.

University Systems

I think that it is very difficult for a white person to get a good education in race and gender in our colleges and universities. The habits of exclusion in the knowledge system and in scholars' individual egos are deeply ingrained. Knowledge is seen as a white person's realm still, and as largely a male realm. But where are we to raise students' awareness of wider social reality if not in the institutions that claim to work toward transmission of accurate knowledge from one generation to another? Colleges and universities should continue their work to try to make good on the claim of historical accuracy, which always entails multicultural and gendered perspectives. People outside of academic institutions have done some of the strongest work to build awareness ·and visibility of equity and diversity. In doing so they have increased racial and gender awareness and developed insights that are needed for the improvement of thinking in academic institutions.

Overcoming Resistance

Those who want to do their homework on race relations must give up the sunny view of monoculture, that we are all in the same system and experiencing it the same way. They must learn to pluralize their minds. They must give up the myth of meritocracy and the assumption that whites should be in charge. The more-accurate frameworks allow one to perceive and recognize the diseases of racism and other societal ills even if one is not suffering as an obvious victim. Developing more-accurate frameworks in the minds of students or citizens requires developing six skills that are seldom taught in American schools:

- the ability to see that the circumstances of our birth give us starting orientations within many kinds of existing social, linguistic, cultural and political systems
- the ability to see how our locations in those systems influence our experience and understanding of ourselves and the world
- the ability to recognize that systemic hierarchies have created discrimination and disempowerment, which all of us experience to a degree
- the ability to recognize that the hierarchies have also created unearned advantage, or privilege, which all of us experience to a degree
- the ability to work effectively and reflectively within or despite these hierarchies, in order to limit harm and increase the common good

In the monocultural, single-system world I was living in before I learned to see other systems, I was looking fine. But in the multicultural world that I actually live in, the truth of my history is that I am a member of both oppressive and oppressed groups. To acknowledge the oppressive part of my ancestral history is to reposition myself in the social and political world more as part of the problem than as part of the solution. I was fearful of this repositioning; I feared loss of centrality, certainty, self-esteem, confidence, entitlement, power, self-satisfaction, self-respect, pride, the sense of superiority, the sense of protection, the sense of competence and the familiar landscape of my psyche. Like most white people, I resisted looking at race.

What can help overcome that resistance? Processes of group discussion that value and honor the stories of each person in the group are the best way I know. We are all arbitrarily placed in systems, but we all have our individual essences, which I feel are our sacred centers. When white people tell deep, honest stories of knowing both oppression and privilege, and when these stories are honored, my experience is that white people can open themselves to facing race, without blame, shame or guilt. They can exchange their resistance for a profound new understanding that sustains rather than destroys the psyche and the social fabric.

At our workshops on race, after the first prompt has allowed people to acknowledge what is hard and scary in talking about race, we ask the pairs of participants to take a minute each to respond to another prompt: "A good thing about talking about racism is . . . ." When we repeat this session, we hear from white people responses like these:

- It is such a relief to get it out in the open.
- I've never just sat and listened to people of color talking about their lives before.
- I had no idea our lives were so different—and we work in the same building.
- I learned I was dreaming that we are "all living in the same world."
- I was sure I could be heard here.
- I know I am not being blamed here.
- Talking about race showed me to myself in a hard but good new way.
- I think I will be a better person now.
- Learning about privilege is changing everything for me.
- I can learn how to work against racism in myself and others.
- I have longed for interracial community; now I think there is hope for it.
- I am feeling healed of my fear of people of color.
- I know I am white and this has untied so many knots for me.
- I never realized I had personal power to weaken the system of white privilege.

These responses reflect my own experience. Being known and heard while telling one's experience, and listening to the experiences of others, can be transformational. It lessens resistance to facing the grievous injustice that has distorted all of us and produced social myths. It lessens fear and increases compassion and empathy. It helps white people see more clearly who we are and where we came from, and makes us better at seeing how our learning of what we were taught has distorted and disempowered us, too.

"Deeply personal group work" is the name I have given to the format of work in the National SEED Project, which I founded in 1986 to help K–12 teachers put their teaching and self-knowledge on a more inclusive base. The project does transformational change, and for the participants who are white, it overcomes the sad, sick, resentful and fearful feeling that whites often harbor as they resist facing race. In that frame, white people see "race" as belonging to those "other than us." A healing understanding is that all of us are racialized and that race is in us as well as around us, that whites were taught not to know this, and that we can undo that ignorance and use our newly recognized power constructively.

Support for overcoming my resistance to facing race came from some of the most compelling authors I have read: Frantz Fanon, Paulo Freire, Lillian Smith, Virginia Woolf, Barbara Smith, Will Gravely, Tillie Olsen, Akasha Hull, Sylvia Ashton-Warner and Alice Walker. It also came from work with my colleagues Victor Lewis and Hugh Vasquez of the film The *Color of Fear*, people in the film *Mirrors of Privilege*, people in women's studies around the world and colleagues in the SEED Project of the Wellesley Centers for Women, especially Brenda Flyswithhawks and Emily Style. These companions have provided me with the sense that we are not alone and that we are all hurt by the systems we are in.

Facing race, I have learned, opens new doors to possibility and connection. My life has been transformed by walking through those doors. A glimpse of the potential for transformation can help to overcome whites' resistance to facing race.

Facing race,
I have learned,
opens new doors to
possibility and
connection.

Dr. Martin Luther King, Jr. (1929–1968) was a leader of the United States Civil Rights Movement during the 1950s and 1960s and a proponent of nonviolent resistance. At the age of thirty-five, he was the youngest man to have ever received the Nobel Peace Prize. King was assassinated in 1968. One example of King's powerful legacy is the following letter, written April 12, 1963 after his arrest at a non-violent protest against segregation. It is a response to criticism of his tactics by some Birmingham clergy, who argued that segregation should be fought in the courts, not in the streets. King replies that we are not only justified but also morally responsible to break unjust laws; he argues that civil disobedience is particularly effective in bringing change. How does he make this argument, and how effective is it? Do you think it is possible for words to lead to actions? What principles should be used in selecting actions in the pursuit of social justice? Do the ends ever justify the means? Are the means connected in some way to the ends we desire and achieve?

Letter from a Birmingham Jail

Martin Luther King Jr.

Birmingham City Jail
April 16, 1963

Bishop C. C. J. Carpenter
Bishop Joseph A. Durick
Rabbi Milton L. Grafman
Bishop Paul Hardin
Bishop Nolan B. Harmon
The Reverend George M. Murray
The Reverend Edward V. Ramage
The Reverend Earl Stallings

My dear Fellow Clergymen,

While confined here in Birmingham City jail, I came across your recent statement calling our present activities "unwise and untimely." Seldom, if ever, do I pause to answer criticism of my work and ideas. If I sought to answer all of the criticisms that cross my desk, my secretaries would be engaged in little else in the course of the day and I would have no time for constructive work. But since I feel that you are men of genuine good will and your criticisms are sincerely set forth, I would like to answer your statement in what I hope will be patient and reasonable terms.

I think I should give the reason for my being in Birmingham, since you have been influenced by the argument of "outsiders coming in." I have the honor of serving as president of the Southern Christian Leadership Conference, an organization operating in every Southern state with headquarters in Atlanta, Georgia. We have some eighty-five affiliate organizations all across the South—one being the Alabama Christian Movement for Human Rights. Whenever necessary and possible we share staff, educational, and financial resources with our affiliates. Several months ago our local affiliate here in Birmingham invited us to be on call to engage in a nonviolent direct action program if such were deemed necessary. We readily consented and when the hour came we lived up to our promises. So I am here, along with several members of my staff, because we were invited here. I am here because I have basic organizational ties here. Beyond this, I am in Birmingham because injustice is here. Just as the eighth century prophets left their little villages and carried their "thus saith the Lord" far beyond the boundaries of their home town, and just as the Apostle Paul left his little village of Tarsus and carried the gospel of Jesus Christ to practically every hamlet and city of the Graeco-Roman world, I too am compelled to carry the gospel of freedom beyond my particular home town. Like Paul, I must constantly respond to the Macedonian call for aid.

Moreover, I am cognizant of the interrelatedness of all communities and states. I cannot sit idly by in Atlanta and not be concerned about what happens in Birmingham. Injustice anywhere is a threat to justice everywhere. We are caught in an inescapable network of mutuality tied in a single garment of destiny. Whatever affects one directly affects all indirectly. Never again can we afford to live with the narrow, provincial "outside agitator" idea. Anyone who lives inside the United States can never be considered an outsider anywhere in this country.

You deplore the demonstrations that are presently taking place in Birmingham. But I am sorry that your statement did not express a similar concern for the conditions that brought the demonstrations into being. I am sure that each of you would want to go beyond the superficial social analyst who looks merely at effects, and does not grapple with underlying causes. I would not hesitate to say that it is unfortunate that so-called demonstrations are taking place in Birmingham at this time, but I would say in more emphatic terms that it is even more unfortunate that the white power structure of this city left the Negro community with no other alternative.

In any nonviolent campaign there are four basic steps: (1) collection of the facts to determine whether injustices are alive; (2) negotiation; (3) self-purification; and (4) direct action. We have gone through all of these steps in Birmingham. There can be no gainsaying of the fact that racial injustice engulfs this community. Birmingham is probably the most thoroughly segregated city in the United States. Its ugly record of police brutality is known in every section of this country. Its unjust treatment of

Negroes in the courts is a notorious reality. There have been more unsolved bombings of Negro homes and churches in Birmingham than any city in this nation. These are the hard, brutal, and unbelievable facts. On the basis of these conditions Negro leaders sought to negotiate with the city fathers. But the political leaders consistently refused to engage in good faith negotiation.

Then came the opportunity last September to talk with some of the leaders of the economic community. In these negotiating sessions certain promises were made by the merchants—such as the promise to remove the humiliating racial signs from the stores. On the basis of these promises Rev. Shuttlesworth and the leaders of the Alabama Christian Movement for Human Rights agreed to call a moratorium on any type of demonstrations. As the weeks and months unfolded we realized that we were the victims of a broken promise. The signs remained. As in so many experiences of the past we were confronted with blasted hopes, and the dark shadow of a deep disappointment settled upon us. So we had no alternative except that of preparing for direct action, whereby we would present our very bodies as a means of laying our case before the conscience of the local and national community. We were not unmindful of the difficulties involved. So we decided to go through a process of self-purification. We started having workshops on nonviolence and repeatedly asked ourselves the questions, "Are you able to accept blows without retaliating?" "Are you able to endure the ordeals of jail?"

We decided to set our direct action program around the Easter season, realizing that with the exception of Christmas, this was the largest shopping period of the year. Knowing that a strong economic withdrawal program would be the by-product of direct action, we felt that this was the best time to bring pressure on the merchants for the needed changes. Then it occurred to us that the March election was ahead, and so we speedily decided to postpone action until after election day. When we discovered that Mr. Connor was in the runoff, we decided again to postpone action so that the demonstrations could not be used to cloud the issues. At this time we agreed to begin our nonviolent witness the day after the runoff.

This reveals that we did not move irresponsibly into direct action. We too wanted to see Mr. Connor defeated; so we went through postponement after postponement to aid in this community need. After this we felt that direct action could be delayed no longer.

You may well ask, "Why direct action? Why sit-ins, marches, etc.? Isn't negotiation a better path?" You are exactly right in your call for negotiation. Indeed, this is the purpose of direct action. Nonviolent direct action seeks to create such a crisis and establish such creative tension that a community that has constantly refused to negotiate is forced to confront the issue. It seeks so to dramatize the issue that it can no longer be ignored. I just referred to the creation of tension as a part of the work of the nonviolent resister. This may sound rather shocking. But I must confess that I am not afraid of the word tension. I have earnestly worked and preached against violent tension, but there is a type of constructive nonviolent tension that is necessary for growth. Just as Socrates felt that it was necessary to create a tension in the mind so that individuals could rise from the bondage of myths and half-truths to the unfettered realm of creative analysis and objective appraisal, we must see the need of having nonviolent gadflies to create the kind of tension in society that will help men rise from the dark depths of prejudice and racism to the majestic heights of understanding and brotherhood. So the purpose of the direct action is to create a situation so crisis-packed that it will inevitably open the door to negotiation. We, therefore, concur with you in your call for negotiation. Too long has our beloved Southland been bogged down in the tragic attempt to live in monologue rather than dialogue.

One of the basic points in your statement is that our acts are untimely. Some have asked, "Why didn't you give the new administration time to act?" The only answer that I can give to this inquiry is that the new administration must be prodded about as much as the outgoing one before it acts. We will be sadly mistaken if we feel that the election of Mr. Boutwell will bring the millennium to Birmingham. While Mr. Boutwell is much more articulate and gentle than Mr. Connor, they are both segregationists dedicated to the task of maintaining the status quo. The hope I see in Mr. Boutwell is that he will be reasonable enough to see the futility of massive resistance to desegregation. But he will not see this without pressure from the devotees of civil rights. My friends, I must say to you that we have not made a single gain in civil rights without determined legal and nonviolent pressure. History is the long and tragic story of the fact that privileged groups seldom give up their privileges voluntarily. Individuals may see the moral light and voluntarily give up their unjust posture; but as Reinhold Niebuhr has reminded us, groups are more immoral than individuals.

We know through painful experience that freedom is never voluntarily given by the oppressor; it must be demanded by the oppressed. Frankly I have never yet engaged in a direct action movement that was "well timed," according to the timetable of those who have not suffered unduly from the disease of segregation. For years now I have heard the word "Wait!" It rings in the ear of every Negro with a piercing familiarity. This "wait" has almost always meant "never." It has been a tranquilizing thalidomide, relieving the emotional stress for a moment, only to give birth to an ill-formed infant of frustration. We must come to see with the distinguished jurist of yesterday that "justice too long delayed is justice denied." We have waited for more than three hundred and forty years for our constitutional and God-given rights. The nations of Asia and Africa are moving with jet-like speed toward the goal of political independence, and we still creep at horse and buggy pace toward the gaining of a cup of coffee at a lunch counter.

I guess it is easy for those who have never felt the stinging darts of segregation to say wait. But when you have seen vicious mobs lynch your mothers and fathers at will and drown your sisters and brothers at whim; when you have seen hate-filled policemen curse, kick, brutalize, and even kill your black brothers and sisters with impunity; when you see the vast majority of your twenty million Negro brothers smothering in an airtight cage of poverty in the midst of an affluent society; when you suddenly find your tongue twisted and your speech stammering as you seek to explain to your six-year-old daughter why she can't go to the public amusement park that has just been advertised on television, and see tears welling up in her little eyes when she is told that Funtown is closed to colored children, and see the depressing clouds of inferiority begin to form in her little mental sky, and see her begin to distort her little personality by unconsciously developing a bitterness toward white people; when you have to concoct an answer for a five-year-old son asking in agonizing pathos: "Daddy, why do white people treat colored people so mean?"; when you take a cross-country drive and find it necessary to sleep night after night in the uncomfortable corners of your automobile because no motel will accept you; when you are humiliated day in and day out by nagging signs reading "white" men and "colored"; when your first name becomes "nigger" and your middle name becomes "boy" (however old you are) and your last name becomes "John," and when your wife and mother are never given the respected title "Mrs."; when you are harried by day and haunted by night by the fact that you are a Negro, living constantly at tip-toe stance never quite knowing what to expect next, and plagued with inner fears and outer resentments; when you are forever fighting a degenerating sense of "nobodiness";—then you will understand why we find it very difficult to wait. There comes a time when the cup of our endurance runs over, and men are no longer willing to be plunged into an abyss of injustice where they experience the bleakness of a corroding despair. I hope, sirs, you can understand our legitimate and unavoidable impatience.

You express a great deal of anxiety over our willingness to break laws. This is certainly a legitimate concern. Since we so diligently urge people to obey the Supreme Court's decision of 1954 outlawing segregation in the public schools, it is rather strange and paradoxical to find us consciously breaking laws. One may well ask, "How can you advocate breaking some laws and obeying others?" The answer is found in the fact that there are two types of laws. There are *just* laws and there are *unjust* laws. I would be the first to advocate obeying just laws. One has not only a legal but moral responsibility to obey just laws. Conversely, one has a moral responsibility to disobey unjust laws. I would agree with Saint Augustine that "An unjust law is no law at all."

Now what is the difference between the two? How does one determine when a law is just or unjust? A just law is a man-made code that squares with the moral law or the law of God. An unjust law is a code that is out of harmony with the moral law. To put it in the terms of Saint Thomas Aquinas, an unjust law is a human law that is not rooted in eternal and natural law. Any law that uplifts human personality is just. Any law that degrades human personality is unjust. All segregation statutes are unjust because segregation distorts the soul and damages the personality. It gives the segregator a false sense of superiority and the segregated a false sense of inferiority. To use the words of Martin Buber, the great Jewish philosopher, segregation substitutes an "I-it" relationship for the "I-thou" relationship, and ends up relegating persons to the status of things. So segregation is not only politically, economically, and sociologically unsound, but it is morally wrong and sinful. Paul Tillich has said that sin is separation. Isn't segregation an existential expression of man's tragic separation, an expression of his awful estrangement, his terrible sinfulness? So I can urge men to obey the 1954 decision of the Supreme Court because it is morally right, and I can urge them to disobey segregation ordinances because they are morally wrong.

Let us turn to a more concrete example of just and unjust laws. An unjust law is a code that a majority inflicts on a minority that is not binding on itself. This is *difference* made legal. On the other hand a just law is a code that a majority compels a minority to follow that it is willing to follow itself. This is *sameness* made legal.

Let me give another explanation. An unjust law is a code inflicted upon a minority which that minority had no part in enacting or creating because they did not have the unhampered right to vote. Who can say the legislature of Alabama which set up the segregation laws was democratically elected? Throughout the State of Alabama all types of conniving methods are used to prevent Negroes from becoming registered voters and there are some counties without a single Negro registered to vote despite the fact that the Negro constitutes a majority of the population. Can any law set up in such a state be considered democratically structured?

These are just a few examples of unjust and just laws. There are some instances when a law is just on its face but unjust in its application. For instance, I was arrested Friday on a charge of parading without a permit. Now there is nothing wrong with an ordinance which requires a permit for a parade, but when the ordinance is used to preserve segregation and to deny citizens the First Amendment privilege of peaceful assembly and peaceful protest, then it becomes unjust.

I hope you can see the distinction I am trying to point out. In no sense do I advocate evading or defying the law as the rabid segregationist would do. This would lead to anarchy. One who breaks an unjust law must do it *openly, lovingly* (not hatefully as the white mothers did in New Orleans when they were seen on television screaming "nigger, nigger, nigger") and with a willingness to accept the penalty. I submit that an individual who breaks a law that conscience tells him is unjust, and willingly accepts the penalty by staying in jail to arouse the conscience of the community over its injustice, is in reality expressing the very highest respect for law.

Of course there is nothing new about this kind of civil disobedience. It was seen sublimely in the refusal of Shadrach, Meshach, and Abednego to obey the unjust laws of Nebuchadnezzar because a higher moral law was involved. It was practiced superbly by the early Christians who were willing to face hungry lions and the excruciating pain of chopping blocks, before submitting to certain very unjust laws of the Roman Empire. To a degree our academic freedom is a reality today because Socrates practiced civil disobedience.

We can never forget that everything Hitler did in Germany was "legal" and everything the Hungarian freedom fighters did in Hungary was "illegal." It was "illegal" to aid and comfort a Jew in Hitler's Germany. But I am sure that, if I had lived in Germany during that time, I would have aided and comforted my Jewish brothers even though it was illegal. If I lived in a communist country today where certain principles dear to the Christian faith are suppressed, I believe I would openly advocate disobeying these antireligious laws.

I must make two honest confessions to you, my Christian and Jewish brothers. First I must confess that over the last few years I have been gravely disappointed with the white moderate. I have almost reached the regrettable conclusion that the Negroes' great stumbling block in the stride toward freedom is not the White Citizens' "Councilor" or the Ku Klux Klanner, but the white moderate who is more devoted to "order" than to justice; who prefers a negative peace which is the absence of tension to a positive peace which is the presence of justice; who constantly says "I agree with you in the goal you seek, but I can't agree with your methods of direct action"; who paternalistically feels that he can set the timetable for another man's freedom; who lives by the myth of time and who constantly advises the Negro to wait until a "more convenient season." Shallow understanding from people of good will is more frustrating than absolute misunderstanding from people of ill will. Lukewarm acceptance is much more bewildering than outright rejection.

I had hoped that the white moderate would understand that law and order exist for the purpose of establishing justice, and that when they fail to do this they become the dangerously structured dams that block the flow of social progress. I had hoped that the white moderate would understand that the present tension in the South is merely a necessary phase of the transition from an obnoxious negative peace, where the Negro passively accepted his unjust plight, to a substance-filled positive peace, where all men will respect the dignity and worth of human personality. Actually, we who engage in nonviolent direct action are not the creators of tension. We merely bring to the surface the hidden tension that is already alive. We bring it out in the open where it can be seen and dealt with. Like a boil that can never be cured as long as it is covered up but must be opened with all its pus-flowing ugliness to the natural medicines of air and light, injustice must likewise be exposed, with all of the tension its exposing creates, to the light of human conscience and the air of national opinion before it can be cured.

In your statement you asserted that our actions, even though peaceful, must be condemned because they precipitate violence. But can this assertion be logically made? Isn't this like condemning the robbed man because his possession of money precipitated the evil act of robbery? Isn't this like condemning Socrates because his unswerving commitment to truth and his philosophical delvings precipitated the misguided popular mind to make him drink the hemlock? Isn't this like condemning Jesus because His unique God consciousness and never-ceasing devotion to His will precipitated the evil act of crucifixion? We must come to see, as federal courts have consistently affirmed, that it is immoral to urge an individual to withdraw his efforts to gain his basic constitutional rights because the quest precipitates violence. Society must protect the robbed and punish the robber.

I had also hoped that the white moderate would reject the myth of time. I received a letter this morning from a white brother in Texas which said: "All Christians know that the colored people will receive equal rights eventually, but is it possible that you are in too great of a religious hurry? It has taken Christianity almost 2000 years to accomplish what it has.The teachings of Christ take time to come to earth." All that is said here grows out of a tragic misconception of time. It is the strangely irrational notion that there is something in the very flow of time that will inevitably cure all ills. Actually time is neutral. It can be used either destructively or constructively. I am coming to feel that the people of ill will have used time much more effectively than the people of good will. We will have to repent in this generation not merely for the vitriolic words and actions of the bad people, but for the appalling silence of the good people. We must come to see that human progress never rolls in on wheels of inevitability. It comes through the tireless efforts and persistent work of men willing to be co-workers with God, and without this hard work time itself becomes an ally of the forces of social stagnation.

We must use time creatively, and forever realize that the time is always ripe to do right. Now is the time to make real the promise of democracy, and transform our pending national elegy into a creative psalm of brotherhood. Now is the time to lift our national policy from the quicksand of racial injustice to the solid rock of human dignity.

You spoke of our activity in Birmingham as extreme. At first I was rather disappointed that fellow clergymen would see my nonviolent efforts as those of the extremist. I started thinking about the fact that I stand in the middle of two opposing forces in the Negro community. One is a force of complacency made up of Negroes who, as a result of long years of oppression, have been so completely drained of self-respect and a sense of "somebodiness" that they have adjusted to segregation, and of a few Negroes in the middle class who, because of a degree of academic and economic security, and because at points they profit by segregation, have unconsciously become insensitive to the problems of the masses. The other force is one of bitterness and hatred and comes perilously close to advocating violence. It is expressed in the various black nationalist groups that are springing up over the nation, the largest and best known being Elijah Muhammad's Muslim movement. This movement is nourished by the contemporary frustration over the continued existence of racial discrimination. It is made up of people who have lost faith in America, who have absolutely repudiated Christianity, and who have concluded that the white man is an incurable "devil." I have tried to stand between these two forces saying that we need not follow the "do-nothingism" of the complacent or the hatred and despair of the black nationalist. There is the more excellent way of love and nonviolent protest. I'm grateful to God that, through the Negro church, the dimension of nonviolence entered our struggle. If this philosophy had not emerged I am convinced that by now many streets of the South would be flowing with floods of blood. And I am further convinced that if our white brothers dismiss us as "rabble rousers" and "outside agitators"— those of us who are working through the channels of nonviolent direct action—and refuse to support our nonviolent efforts, millions of Negroes, out of frustration and despair, will seek solace and security in black nationalist ideologies, a development that will lead inevitably to a frightening racial nightmare.

Oppressed people cannot remain oppressed forever. The urge for freedom will eventually come. This is what has happened to the American Negro. Something within has reminded him of his birthright of freedom; something without has reminded him that he can gain it. Consciously and unconsciously, he has been swept in by what the Germans call the *Zeitgeist*, and with his black brothers of Africa, and his brown and yellow brothers of Asia, South America, and the Caribbean, he is moving with a sense of cosmic urgency toward the promised land of racial justice. Recognizing this vital urge that has engulfed the Negro community, one should readily understand public demonstrations. The Negro has many pent-up resentments and latent frustrations. He has to get them out. So let him march sometime; let him have his prayer pilgrimages to the city hall; understand why he must have sit-ins and freedom rides. If his repressed emotions do not come out in these nonviolent ways, they will come out in ominous expressions of violence. This is not a threat; it is a fact of history. So I have not said to my people, "Get rid of your discontent." But I have tried to say that this normal and healthy discontent can be channeled through the creative outlet of nonviolent direct action. Now this approach is being dismissed as extremist. I must admit that I was initially disappointed in being so categorized.

But as I continued to think about the matter I gradually gained a bit of satisfaction from being considered an extremist. Was not Jesus an extremist in love? "Love your enemies, bless them that curse you, pray for them that despitefully use you." Was not Amos an extremist for justice—"Let justice roll down like waters and righteousness like a mighty stream." Was not Paul an extremist for the gospel of Jesus Christ—"I bear in my body the marks of the Lord Jesus." Was not Martin Luther an extremist—"Here I stand; I can do none other so help me God." Was not John Bunyan an extremist—"I will stay in jail to the end of my days before I make a butchery of my conscience." Was not Abraham Lincoln an extremist—"This nation cannot survive half slave and half free." Was not Thomas Jefferson an extremist—"We hold these truths to be self-evident that all men are created equal." So the question is not whether we will be extremist but what kind of extremist will we be. Will we be extremists for hate or will we be extremists for love? Will we be extremists for the preservation of injustice—or will we be extremists for the cause of justice? In that dramatic scene on Calvary's hill three men were crucified. We must never forget that all three were crucified for the same crime—the crime of extremism. Two were extremists for immorality, and thus fell below their environment. The other, Jesus Christ, was an extremist for love, truth, and goodness, and thereby rose above His environment. So, after all, maybe the South, the nation, and the world are in dire need of creative extremists.

I had hoped that the white moderate would see this. Maybe I was too optimistic. Maybe I expected too much. I guess I should have realized that few members of a race that has oppressed another race can understand or appreciate the deep groans and passionate yearnings of those that have been oppressed, and still fewer have the vision to see that injustice must be rooted out by strong, persistent, and determined action. I am thankful, however, that some of our white brothers have grasped the meaning of this social revolution and committed themselves to it. They are still all too small in quantity, but they are big in quality. Some like Ralph McGill, Lillian Smith, Harry Golden, and James Dabbs have written about our struggle in eloquent, prophetic, and understanding terms. Others have marched with us down nameless streets of the South. They have languished in filthy, roach-infested jails, suffering the abuse and brutality of angry policemen who look on them as "dirty nigger lovers." They, unlike so many of their moderate brothers and sisters, have recognized the urgency of the moment and sensed the need for powerful "action" antidotes to combat the disease of segregation.

Let me rush on to mention my other disappointment. I have been so greatly disappointed with the white Church and its leadership. Of course there are some notable exceptions. I am not unmindful of the fact that each of you has taken some significant stands on this issue. I commend you, Rev. Stallings, for your Christian stand on this past Sunday, in welcoming Negroes to your service on a non-segregated basis. I commend the Catholic leaders of this state for integrating Springhill College several years ago.

But despite these notable exceptions I must honestly reiterate that I have been disappointed with the Church. I do not say that as one of those negative critics who can always find something wrong with the Church. I say it as a minister of the gospel, who loves the Church; who was nurtured in its bosom; who has been sustained by its spiritual blessings and who will remain true to it as long as the cord of life shall lengthen.

I had the strange feeling when I was suddenly catapulted into the leadership of the bus protest in Montgomery several years ago that we would have the support of the white Church. I felt that the white ministers, priests, and rabbis of the South would be some of our strongest allies. Instead, some have been outright opponents, refusing to understand the freedom movement and misrepresenting its leaders; all too many others have been more cautious than courageous and have remained silent behind the anesthetizing security of stained glass windows.

In spite of my shattered dreams of the past, I came to Birmingham with the hope that the white religious leadership of this community would see the justice of our cause and, with deep moral concern, serve as the channel through which our just grievances could get to the power structure. I had hoped that each of you would understand. But again I have been disappointed.

I have heard numerous religious leaders of the South call upon their worshippers to comply with a desegregation decision because it is the law, but I have longed to hear white ministers say: "Follow this decree because integration is morally right and the Negro is your brother." In the midst of blatant injustices inflicted upon the Negro, I have watched white churches stand on the sideline and merely mouth pious irrelevancies and sanctimonious trivialities. In the midst of a mighty struggle to rid our nation of racial and economic injustice, I have heard so many ministers say, "Those are social issues with which the Gospel has no real concern." and I have watched so many churches commit themselves to a completely otherworldly religion which made a strange distinction between body and soul, the sacred and the secular.

So here we are moving toward the exit of the twentieth century with a religious community largely adjusted to the status quo, standing as a taillight behind other community agencies rather than a headlight leading men to higher levels of justice.

I have travelled the length and breadth of Alabama, Mississippi, and all the other Southern states. On sweltering summer days and crisp autumn mornings I have looked at her beautiful churches with their spires pointing heavenward. I have beheld the impressive outlay of her massive religious education buildings. Over and over again I have found myself asking: "Who worships here? Who is their God? Where were their voices when the lips of Governor Barnett dripped with words of interposition and nullification? Where were they when Governor Wallace gave the clarion call for defiance and hatred? Where were their voices of support when tired, bruised, and weary Negro men and women decided to rise from the dark dungeons of complacency to the bright hills of creative protest?"

Yes, these questions are still in my mind. In deep disappointment, I have wept over the laxity of the Church. But be assured that my tears have been tears of love. There can be no deep disappointment where there is not deep love. Yes, I love the Church; I love her sacred walls. How could I do otherwise? I am in the rather unique position of being the son, the grandson, and the great-grandson of preachers. Yes, I see the Church as the body of Christ. But, oh! How we have blemished and scarred that body through social neglect and fear of being nonconformist.

There was a time when the Church was very powerful. It was during that period when the early Christians rejoiced when they were deemed worthy to suffer for what they believed. In those days the Church was not merely a thermometer that recorded the ideas and principles of popular opinion; it was a thermostat that transformed the mores of society. Wherever the early Christians entered a town the power structure got disturbed and immediately sought to convict them for being "disturbers of the peace" and "outside agitators." But they went on with the conviction that they were a "colony of heaven" and had to obey God rather than man. They were small in number but big in commitment. They were too God-intoxicated to be "astronomically intimidated." They brought an end to such ancient evils as infanticide and gladiatorial contest.

Things are different now. The contemporary Church is so often a weak, ineffectual voice with an uncertain sound. It is so often the arch-supporter of the status quo. Far from being disturbed by the presence of the Church, the power structure of the average community is consoled by the Church's silent and often vocal sanction of things as they are.

But the judgment of God is upon the Church as never before. If the Church of today does not recapture the sacrificial spirit of the early Church, it will lose its authentic ring, forfeit the loyalty of millions, and be dismissed as an irrelevant social club with no meaning for the twentieth century. I am meeting young people every day whose disappointment with the Church has risen to outright disgust.

Maybe again I have been too optimistic. Is organized religion too inextricably bound to the status quo to save our nation and the world? Maybe I must turn my faith to the inner spiritual Church, the church within the Church, as the true *eccelesia* and the hope of the world. But again I am thankful to God that some noble souls from the ranks of organized religion have broken loose from the paralyzing chains of conformity and joined us as active partners in the struggle for freedom. They have left their secure congregations and walked the streets of Albany, Georgia, with us. They have gone through the highways of the South on torturous rides for freedom. Yes, they have gone to jail with us. Some have been kicked out of their churches and lost the support of their bishops and fellow ministers. But they have gone with the faith that right defeated is stronger than evil triumphant. These men have been the leaven in the lump of the race. Their witness has been the spiritual salt that has preserved the true meaning of the Gospel in these troubled times. They have carved a tunnel of hope through the dark mountain of disappointment.

I hope the Church as a whole will meet the challenge of this decisive hour. But even if the Church does not come to the aid of justice, I have no despair about the future. I have no fear about the outcome of our struggle in Birmingham, even if our motives are presently misunderstood. We will reach the goal of freedom in Birmingham and all over the nation, because the goal of America is freedom. Abused and scorned though we may be, our destiny is tied up with the destiny of America. Before the pilgrims landed at Plymouth, we were here. Before the pen of Jefferson etched across the pages of history the majestic words of the Declaration of Independence, we were here. For more than two centuries our foreparents labored in this country without wages; they made cotton "king"; and they built the homes of their masters in the midst of brutal injustice and shameful humiliation—and yet out of a bottomless vitality they continued to thrive and develop. If the inexpressible cruelties of slavery could not stop us, the opposition we now face will surely fail. We will win our freedom because the sacred heritage of our nation and the eternal will of God are surely embodied in our echoing demands.

I must close now. But before closing I am impelled to mention one other point in your statement that troubled me profoundly. You warmly commended the Birmingham police force for keeping "order" and "preventing violence." I don't believe you would have so warmly commended the police force if you had seen its angry violent dogs literally biting six unarmed, nonviolent Negroes. I don't believe you would so quickly commend the policemen if you would observe their ugly and inhuman treatment of Negroes here in the city jail; if you would watch them push and curse old Negro women and young Negro girls; if you would see them slap and kick old Negro men and young Negro boys; if you will observe them, as they have done on two occasions, refuse to give us food because we wanted to sing our grace together. I'm sorry that I can't join you in your praise for the police department.

It is true that they have been rather disciplined in their public handling of the demonstrators. In this sense they have been rather publicly "nonviolent." But for what purpose? To preserve the evil system of segregation. Over the last few years I have consistently preached that nonviolence demands that the means we use must be as pure as the ends we seek. So I have tried to make it clear that it is wrong to use immoral means to attain moral ends. But now I must affirm that it is just as wrong, or even more so, to use moral means to preserve immoral ends. Maybe Mr. Connor and his policemen have been publicly nonviolent, as Chief Prichett was in Albany, Georgia, but they have used the moral means of nonviolence to maintain the immoral end of flagrant racial injustice. T. S. Eliot has said that there is no greater treason than to do the right deed for the wrong reason.

I wish you had commended the Negro sit-inners and demonstrators of Birmingham for their sublime courage, their willingness to suffer, and their amazing discipline in the midst of the most inhuman provocation. One day the South will recognize its real heroes. They will be the James Merediths, courageously and with a majestic sense of purpose, facing jeering and hostile mobs and the agonizing loneliness that characterizes the life of the pioneer. They will be old, oppressed, battered Negro women, symbolized in a seventy-two year old woman of Montgomery, Alabama, who rose up with a sense of dignity and with her people decided not to ride the segregated buses, and responded to one who inquired about her tiredness with ungrammatical profundity: "My feets is tired, but my soul is rested." They will be young high school and college students, young ministers of the gospel and a host of the elders, courageously and nonviolently sitting in at lunch counters and willingly going to jail for conscience sake. One day the South will know that when these disinherited children of God sat down at lunch counters they were in reality standing up for the best in the American dream and the most sacred values in our Judeo-Christian heritage, and thus carrying our whole nation back to great wells of democracy which were dug deep by the founding fathers in the formulation of the Constitution and the Declaration of Independence.

Never before have I written a letter this long (or should I say a book?). I'm afraid that it is much too long to take your precious time. I can assure you that it would have been much shorter if I had been writing from a comfortable desk, but what else is there to do when you are alone for days in the dull monotony of a narrow jail cell other than write long letters, think strange thoughts, and pray long prayers?

If I have said anything in this letter that is an overstatement of the truth and is indicative of an unreasonable impatience, I beg you to forgive me. If I have said anything in this letter that is an understatement of the truth and is indicative of my having a patience that makes me patient with anything less than brotherhood, I beg God to forgive me.

I hope this letter finds you strong in the faith. I also hope that circumstances will soon make it possible for me to meet each of you, not as an integrationist or a civil rights leader, but as a fellow clergyman and a Christian brother. Let us all hope that the dark clouds of racial prejudice will soon pass away and the deep fog of misunderstanding will be lifted from our fear-drenched communities and in some not too distant tomorrow the radiant stars of love and brotherhood will shine over our great nation with all of their scintillating beauty.

Yours for the cause of Peace and Brotherhood

Martin Luther King Jr.

Russell B. Connors (1948–2011) was a beloved professor and chair of the theology department at St. Kate's until his death from cancer in 2011. He taught courses on a variety of topics related to Christian ethics, and published three books and a host of scholarly articles, many of them addressing Catholic Social Teachings (CST). In this article, Connors explains seven central convictions that are the basis of CST and then makes connections to three contemporary ethical issues. As you read, it may be helpful to analyze Connors's explanation of CST by the categories suggested in Heitzeg. What are the sources of these teachings? What moral standards do the CST suggest, and what is the scope of Catholic teaching about justice? To whom or what does it apply?

Catholic Social Teaching—Convictions and Connections[1]

Russell B. Connors Jr.

Introduction: Vignettes

As a state senator, Adam's positions on two issues have been clear and consistent: he has been strongly in favor of state-supported quality health care for all, and he has been opposed—just as strongly—to cutbacks in social services for the poor in recent years. In an interview in the local newspaper, the senator was quite forthright about the connections between his faith and his political life. "Some of my deepest convictions about justice," he explained, "have long been grounded in Catholic social teaching."

One of the students asked Sister MaryAnn how, given her feminist convictions, she remained part of a church that seems so riddled with sexism. Quickly and candidly she replied, "It's largely because of Catholic social teaching that I remain a Catholic, much less a sister. And besides," she went on, "it's my church too."

They were there every Saturday morning, the busiest time at the local grocery store. Their signs marked a protest of the store's continued policy of selling fruits and vegetables grown and picked by non-union farm workers. When asked why they were there each week, some of them referred to Catholic social teaching in their answer.

The pastor, Fr. Jordan, has "taken some heat" from some in the parish for the welcoming things he has been saying in recent Sunday homilies regarding gay and lesbian persons. And he has made church meeting rooms available for a prayer and study program sponsored by a group of gay and lesbian Catholics. As he said in the church bulletin, "There is a direct link between Catholic social teaching and our embrace of gay and lesbian persons."

"In the U.S.," Martina says, "we approach immigration from the point of view of the stresses on our own country. I understand that, but it is wrong. We must see this from the point of view of those who often suffer. The stresses on us are minor compared to the suffering of many who desire to come here." Martina has been called naïve by some of her colleagues at the University, but she does not flinch in her views. A convert to Catholicism, Martina says that one of the most attractive things about the Catholic Church to her was its social teaching, especially its notion of the "option for the poor."

Sheila has enough to do. But several weeks ago she found the time to distribute fliers about her nursing association's opposition to the state initiative to legalize physician-assisted suicide. A member of her church's "Peace and Justice Commission," next week she will be part of a panel discussion at the local public high school on capital punishment. She is similarly opposed to the death penalty. When asked to explain her convictions about these issues, Sheila refers to Catholic social teaching.

"I need to be clear with you, however, before I accept the position as principal of this school. The salaries of our teachers are simply unjust. I will not stop bringing this up until the situation improves dramatically." This is what John had said to the pastor and members of the finance commission as he accepted the position as principal of the Catholic elementary school. And it came to pass. For the past four years, at budget time, John has battled for more just wages for the teachers, grounding a strong and convincing argument in Catholic social teaching.

People make connections between Catholic social teaching and an amazing spectrum of issues, often doing so (as these vignettes make clear) in startlingly diverse ways, in ways that defy categorization as conservative or liberal, Republican or Democrat.

The phrase "Catholic social teaching," refers to the sum total of teachings provided by Catholic leaders—popes, bishops, and sometimes theologians—concerning the social issues of the day, especially over the last 100 years. Christian faith does not shield believers from difficult social issues, but rather, impels them to try to contribute to their solutions. In that spirit, the popes and bishops do not presume to offer simple answers to complex questions, but try to show what the relationship might be between Christian faith and social issues. Catholic teachings are put forth in various types of documents, as the Works Cited pages of this article illustrate. Invariably, those documents include both *convictions* and *connections*. By *convictions* I mean the fundamental presuppositions that ground Catholic involvement in social issues. And by *connections* I mean the way those convictions might be applied to specific questions and concerns. The purpose of this article is to uncover those key *convictions* and to examine how the *connections* get made.

It seems right to state four things very clearly at the start. The first is a bias: I am a Roman Catholic and I am proud of Catholic social teaching (henceforth, CST). As others have observed, it is sadly one of Catholicism's "best kept secrets" (Henriot). To say this is not to claim that it is a tradition that is perfect, completely consistent, or without blind spots. CST is a work-in-progress. Indeed, that is one of its virtues. Secondly, it is important not to reduce Catholicism to its teachings about justice. As important as those are, Catholicism also stands for other things, things like the phenomenon of sacramentality. This is the idea that the created universe is a medium through which we have contact with the divine. Catholic intellectual tradition emphasizes its confidence in humanity's pursuit of truth and wisdom wherever it is to be found. Catholic tradition also celebrates the sacredness and inviolability of conscience, the importance of community, etc. As we proceed I will look for ways to show the connections between CST and some of these other important features of Catholicism. Thirdly, extolling the virtues of CST is not my way of attempting to gloss over the faults and sins of the Catholic Church itself. As we will see, CST is not about what *everyone else* should do. The convictions of justice that are the heart of CST *apply to the church itself.* Indeed, there are some signs that the church is getting a bit better at acknowledging its own injustice and sinfulness and its ongoing need of reformation. The "papal apologies" of Pope John Paul II in 2000 for ". . . the past and present sins of her [the Church's] sons and daughters" may be the most dramatic example (John Paul II, 649; McDonough and Michaud, 103). Fourthly, this is an overview, an introduction. I will have accomplished my goal if, at the end, the reader feels she has tasted of some of the primary flavors of CST. The works cited or recommended at the end will point to a fuller menu.

The remainder of this article is in two unequal parts. After a brief historical introduction, Part One will present what I think are the key *convictions* that are the heart of CST. I will first state the convictions themselves and then elaborate on their sources and their significance. Part One will close with a word about the interpretation and application of the seven major convictions to concrete issues, and with a reflection on the purposes of CST. More briefly, Part Two will explore the *connections* between CST and specific issues. We will do this by focusing simply on two of the key convictions of CST—the dignity and rights of every human being and the option for the poor—seeing how those convictions *connect* to some contemporary questions and concerns.

Part One: Catholic Social Teaching—Convictions

History.[2] Modern CST is commonly thought to have begun with the encyclical letter "Rerum Novarum" ("The Condition of Labor") of Pope Leo XIII in 1891. In that letter the pope faced squarely the conditions of workers in what had become industrialized and urbanized Europe. In a word, conditions were miserable. Many workers (including children) worked long hours in sometimes horrific environments for shockingly small wages—nothing close to a wage that would support a family. Housing and living conditions in the large industrial cities of Europe were equally miserable. Poverty was rampant.

The approach of Leo XIII's letter of concern was new in that rather than simply call for a renewed effort at works of *charity* to assist those in need (although that was indeed part of his message), he called for *social justice.* He called for a change in the social structures and institutions of the day that were the causes of the poverty and misery of the workers. He called for a just and living wage, for working conditions that were safe, and for laws that would prevent the abuse of children in the workforce. Fundamental to all of this was his insistence on the dignity of all people as children of God. He insisted that human dignity must be recognized and respected in the workers of the world.

Since Leo XIII, the Church has taken it to be its responsibility to address the issues of the day that concern the human community—sometimes matters of hunger and poverty, sometimes matters of prejudice and discrimination, sometimes matters of war and peace. Christian faith, the pope and bishops have argued, should not lead us to try to escape these difficult problems, but to try to contribute to their solution in light of the Gospel of Christ. This has given rise over the last 100 years to Catholic social teaching.

Convictions. Many people who discuss CST do so by naming and analyzing some basic moral *principles*. I think it is more helpful to state *convictions*. The word *principles* may suggest to some that what we are dealing with here is theory, philosophically precise but abstract moral principles that await application in the real world. The word *convictions* is better, I think, because it suggests that CST is not only about ideas, but about *passions*, the emotions, attitudes, and dispositions that fuel action on behalf of justice. That is the goal. If there were time for it here (there is not), history would demonstrate that the convictions to follow are not the result of someone's doctoral dissertation; rather, they are the result of the church's reflection on what (in its better moments) it has been *doing*.

At the heart of CST we find seven important convictions:

- *Human Dignity*. The life and dignity of every human being is of incalculable worth and must be recognized, respected, and reverenced.

Human rights, "the minimum conditions for life in community," must be protected and promoted in order for human dignity to be respected and for human beings to flourish. (U.S. Catholic Bishops, "Economic Justice for All" par. 17)

- *Community.* Human beings, social by nature, flourish in association with others in community. Everyone has a need, a right, and a responsibility to participate in community life. "Society as a whole, acting through public and private institutions," is responsible for protecting and promoting not only the good of individual persons, but also the common good of the society as a whole. (U.S. Bishops, "Economic Justice for All," par. 18)
- *Equality.* All human beings are fundamentally equal, regardless of race, creed, gender, sexual orientation, and educational or economic status. Every "-ism" that alienates and oppresses people must be opposed and overcome.
- *Work.* Work is critically important for human flourishing. Accordingly, the dignity of work and the rights of workers are the foundation of economic justice.
- *Option for the Poor.* "All members of society have a special obligation to the poor and vulnerable"—not only in our own country, but also around the world. (U.S. Bishops, "Economic Justice for All," par. 16)
- *Peace.* As history sadly demonstrates, war and other forms of violence are the enemies of human well-being. There must be a presumption against war and every other use of force.
- *Care for the Earth.* With increasing conviction, CST calls for the care of the earth itself, for the protection and promotion of the wellbeing of the natural environment not only for the sake of human beings (including future generations), but also for the earth itself and *all* its inhabitants.

Elaboration. Let us explore the significance of these seven convictions, paying attention not only to their sources, but also to some of the issues to which they have been connected over the years.

Human Dignity. Authors who write about the central convictions of CST invariably enumerate and describe them differently. Whether there are seven or nine or nineteen convictions and how they should be stated and described are matters of some opinion. But virtually everyone familiar with this tradition agrees that however many convictions there are, the first and most basic one is about the dignity of human beings. In the introduction to their 1983 pastoral letter on war and peace, the U.S. Catholic Bishops explained the reason for their concern about war and peace by referring to a central conviction about human beings:

> At the center of the Church's teaching on peace and at the center of all Catholic social teaching are the transcendence of God and the dignity of the human person. The human person is the clearest reflection of God's presence in the world; all of the Church's work in pursuit of both justice and peace is designed to protect and promote the dignity of every person. For each person not only reflects God, but is the expression of God's creative work and the meaning of Christ's redemptive ministry. Christians approach the problem of war and peace with fear and reverence (U.S. Catholic Bishops, "The Challenge of Peace: God's Promise and Our Response," par. 15).

With this passage as a starting point, three comments concerning Catholicism's emphasis on human dignity are in order. First, as the statement from the bishops makes clear, the source of CST's emphasis on human dignity is religious in nature. That source is the Christian belief (found also in Judaism and Islam) that each human being is created by God and is a unique reflection of God's holy presence in the world. It is also part of Christian faith that the entire universe, as created by God, is somehow "charged with the grandeur of God," as Gerard Manley Hopkins once put it. CST affirms this, but without embarrassment emphasizes that in a preeminent way *human beings* reflect God's presence in the world. Surely one can be convinced about the dignity of human beings for many reasons. Human intelligence and freedom—our abilities to think and to choose (perhaps especially to love)—as well as some of the amazing accomplishments of humankind (scientific, artistic, altruistic) are certainly good enough reasons to respect human life. CST affirms those reasons. But its deepest convictions about human dignity are rooted in the Christian belief about humanity's relation to God. *In and through* our contact with God's creation—especially (but not exclusively) other human beings—we come into contact with God. Theologian Richard McBrien refers to this as the principle of *sacramentality.* He suggests that it is one of the distinguishing characteristics of Catholicism: the Creator is encountered through the creation (McBrien, pp. 9–11). If this is right, then so too are the bishops: human life is not simply to be respected, but reverenced.

Let us return to the quote above from the U.S. Bishops for a second observation about CST's emphasis on human dignity. As we have seen, the quote is from a pastoral letter on war and peace. But as a matter of fact, one could very easily take out the words *on war and peace* in the opening line and make a wide variety of substitutions. Thus, the sentence could read, "At the center of the Church's teaching [*on economic justice* or *on abortion and euthanasia,* or *on health care reform,* or *on capital punishment,* or *on domestic abuse,* or *on global poverty and hunger,* etc., etc., etc.] and at the center of all Catholic social teaching are the transcendence of God and the dignity of the human person." You get the idea. This emphasis on human dignity grounds CST's interest and involvement in *all* social issues. CST offers no recipe for simple answers to complex questions; it has no formula for ensuring universal agreement on social issues. (It is wise to be suspicious of anyone who does.) What CST does offer is a starting point and a central conviction. In the U.S. political system, for instance, whether one is a liberal democrat or a conservative republican, CST proposes a broad but exceedingly important criterion for moral discernment: the protection and promotion of the dignity of human beings.

Third, CST's conviction about human dignity calls for the recognition of and respect for fundamental *human rights*. Unlike some philosophical approaches to human rights, CST insists that human rights are not conferred upon an individual because they are citizens of a given society. No, the origin of human rights is found in the nature of the human person as such; they are neither given to persons nor (legitimately, at least) taken away from persons by society.

What exactly do we mean by "rights"? Theologian J. Milburn Thompson described human rights as *those basic human goods that are due to human beings so that they can develop themselves fully as persons living in community* (Thompson, pp. 92–102). Some like to think of human rights as the minimum that we have "coming to us" simply because we are human beings. Protection and promotion of human rights is important not simply so that we can survive or "get by" in life, but so that we can strive to flourish as human persons.

It is important to flesh out Catholicism's view of human rights with some examples. Let us consider Pope John XXIII's list of human rights in his 1963 encyclical letter "Pacem in Terris":

- The right to life and a worthy standard of living. These rights include the right to bodily integrity, to food, clothing, shelter, healthcare and necessary social services.
- Rights pertaining to moral and cultural values. These include the right to one's good reputation, the right to search for truth, the right to be informed about public matters of concern, etc.
- The right to worship God according to one's conscience.
- The right to choose one's state in life.
- Economic rights. These include a right to work, to work in a safe environment, and to receive a just wage. Economic rights include a right to private property (and other sources of wealth) as long as this does not interfere with more basic rights of others.
- The right to meet and associate with others.
- The right to emigrate and to immigrate. These rights are especially necessary given the injustices and oppression that exist in some places.
- Political rights. These involve one's ability to take an active part in the civil and political life of one's community.

Obviously a lot of detail is left for interpretation and application—such as what one means by "necessary social services," or what exactly a right to healthcare includes. In the U.S., for example, it would not be hard to imagine both Democrats and Republicans espousing this list of human rights, but disagreeing on how minimally or maximally the government should become involved in seeing to it that they are secured. Even so, by any standard this exposition of human rights sets an agenda for what every society should be concerned about. Flowing from human dignity, CST insists, human rights are important so that we can strive to develop ourselves fully as human beings, in keeping with our common vocation to live as creatures fashioned in the image of God.

Community. If an emphasis on the dignity and rights of every human being is the right hand of CST, emphasis on the importance of community is the left hand. It is only for the sake of simplicity that we discuss them separately here. If Richard McBrien is right, another distinguishing characteristic of Catholicism is its emphasis on the importance of community for human flourishing (McBrien, pp. 12–14). Far different from those aspects of our culture that display a particularly stubborn form of rugged, competitive, and isolating individualism (Bellah), CST insists that the good of the individual is essentially bound up with the good of the community. Following the lead of Catholic social ethicist Thomas Massaro, let us look briefly at three elements of CST's stress on community: *solidarity, common good, and participation* (Massaro, pp. 119–124).

Solidarity is a word that is easier to describe than it is to define. It refers both to an inner conviction and to an outer commitment. The inner conviction involves both the intellectual insight and the affective appreciation of the reality of interdependence: we are all connected; we need one another. CST invites us to believe that at our best moments, simply as human beings, we are able to recognize within ourselves a deep sense of care for one another. When we see the suffering of others (I am thinking especially of the suffering that results from oppression and injustice) it is our sense of solidarity that moves us to "feel for" them and, in some elusive but real way, to share in their suffering. Solidarity enables us to "feel for" others not only because "it could have been me," but because of the nearly mystical conviction that when one person is denied her rights, in some way we all are; when one group is enslaved, none of us is free; when one group suffers from violence and oppression, we are all diminished. Solidarity begins with this kind of conviction of the heart, but it does not end there. The test of genuine solidarity is that it moves to committed action. Action may vary greatly depending on one's closeness to the situation at hand, as well as one's resources (often more extensive than we think). But real solidarity manifests itself in action on behalf of others, caring, committed action—frequently in the social, political arena—that is aimed at dismantling oppression and building justice.

As is obvious, solidarity presumes an appreciation of the *common good*. Pope John Paul II has written about the connection between these two ideas as follows:

> This then [solidarity] is not a feeling of vague compassion or shallow distress at the misfortunes of so many people, both near and far. On the contrary, it is a *firm and persevering determination* to commit oneself to the *common good*, that is to say to the good of all and of each individual, for we are *all* really responsible for *all* (John Paul II, "On Social Concern," par. 38).

Those with a sense of solidarity, CST suggests, are convinced that one's own individual good is woven into the fabric of the good of others. The common good is "the good of all and of each individual." It presumes that one's individual good must not come at the expense of others: the good of management must not be at the expense of labor, the thriving of the wealthiest must not involve the suffering of the poorest, the well-being of men must not be built upon the oppression of women, the welfare of human beings must not involve the mistreatment of other creatures on the planet. When such inequities exist, CST suggests, we not only have a lack of the common good, but a caricature of individual good. Individual "good" that is the fruit of injustice bears within it the seed of its own destruction.

This understanding of the relationship between the individual good and the common good logically includes an emphasis on the importance of *participation* in social life. CST insists that we all have the right and the responsibility to participate in the life of community. Precisely because of our solidarity with one another, our interdependence, we are called to participate in community life, as much as our abilities enable us to do so. Not only because it is important for us to "speak up on our own behalf," but also because of the contributions we can make to other individuals and to society at large, every human being must be given the opportunity to participate fully in the social institutions and communities. When it is only a powerful few who exercise authority, when it is only the wealthy whose voice is heard, when it is only the men who hold positions of influence (whether in our halls of government or in our places of worship), something is terribly wrong with the picture. Calling the church itself to examine its own conscience, CST suggests that the ability of all to participate and contribute fully in the life of community is very simply a matter of justice.

Equality. The first two convictions of CST that we have just described are on virtually every list of the "basic principles" of Catholic social thought. Equality is not. Nevertheless, it is an important aspect of contemporary Catholic social thought. The following passage from the bishops at the Second Vatican Council (1962–1965) displays well, I think, the church's view on equality:

> Since all . . . possess a rational soul and are created in God's likeness, since they have the same nature and origin, have been redeemed by Christ, and

> enjoy the same divine calling and destiny, the basic equality of all must receive increasingly greater recognition. True, all . . . are not alike from the point of view of varying physical power and the diversity of intellectual and moral resources. Nevertheless, with respect to the fundamental rights of the person, every type of discrimination, whether social or cultural, whether based on sex, race, color, social condition, language, or religion, is to be overcome and eradicated as contrary to God's intent ("Pastoral Constitution on the Church in the Modern World," par. 29).

The phrase "must receive increasingly greater recognition" should be seen for what it really is: an acknowledgment that not only in society at large but within the church itself, recognition of the fundamental equality of all human beings as persons has been slow in coming. Historically, most of the major institutions of Western Civilization have not been democracies; they have not been grounded in a conviction about the fundamental equality of all people, and they have been slow to recognize those various "isms" that constitute sins against equality. For instance, as Marvin Mich has documented well in his recent book, until fairly recent times, the church (along with other institutions) did not see any great difficulty with slavery, at least not enough to lead the way in dismantling it: ". . . it was common for Catholic laity, bishops, priests, and religious orders to be slaveholders" (Mich, p. 135). In a similar vein, Catholicism's struggle to recognize the equal dignity of women and men and its resistance to allow that recognition to show itself in its own structures displays the fact that whatever equality might mean in Catholic thought, it has not meant (and does not now mean) equal access to all positions of leadership within the church itself. Bishop Ray Lucker from New Ulm, Minnesota, has called for the church to own up to its own sins of racism and sexism, insisting that equality must indeed receive "greater recognition" within the church itself (Lucker). Equality, as one of the key convictions of CST, is a work in progress.

Work. During the last hundred years, the theme of work has received important attention in CST. Catholic social thought looks at work not simply from the perspective of what workers do, but what work does to and for workers. Pope John Paul II has written much about this, especially in his 1981 encyclical letter "Laborem Exercens" ("On Human Work"). Obviously work is important both because many of us spend a high percentage of our lives at our work, and also because it is essential for our livelihood. But CST suggests something more. It is through work that we fulfill a part of our human nature. Work is one of the ways we develop ourselves as persons. It is through our work that we are able to express ourselves, to fulfill ourselves, and to contribute to the human community (Pope John Paul II, "On Human Work," par. 6). These ideas may strike some of us as unrealistic, as ideals that are a long way from reality. Sadly, for too many people that is the case. Work for many is routine, burdensome, and even oppressive. CST argues that that is not as it should be. Workers ought to be given an opportunity to take responsibility for what they do, to make their work their own. The more that happens, the more work can become an opportunity for self-expression, for personal fulfillment, and for the satisfaction that comes from making a genuine contribution, even if a small one, to the well-being of other people. Put differently, if work is for people, and not the other way around, then those responsible for the work that other people do should be looking for ways in which that work can both express and promote human dignity.

Lest all this seems to be too lofty a goal to have in mind regarding human work, the recent *Catechism of the Catholic Church* names several more concrete things that relate to justice for workers. Men and women, first of all, should have *access to employment* in ways that are fair. The professions and the workforce should be ". . . open to all without discrimination" (#2433). Secondly, workers are entitled to a *just wage* for the work that they do. This means a wage that allows one to provide a reasonable and dignified quality of life for oneself and one's family materially, socially, culturally, and spiritually (#2434). The *Catechism* notes that it is not morally sufficient that a contract has been reached between employers and workers. A just wage must meet more stringent criteria; it must take into account the quality of life it allows a person and his or her family to enjoy (#2434). Thirdly, workers should have *recourse to a strike* when it becomes morally legitimate (#2435). Reasons that might warrant strikes include not only unjust wages, but also unsafe or burdensome working conditions. The dignity and rights of persons call for safe working environments. Finally, workers have a right to *social security contributions,* which (in countries like our own) are required by legitimate authority (#2436). The *Catechism* does not include healthcare benefits with this, largely because in many countries healthcare is provided by the state and not linked to employment. In the U.S. access to healthcare (which Pope John XXIII listed as a human right) is linked to employment, an argument could surely be made from CST that employers should be required to see to it that their workers are provided with healthcare benefits. In exchange for all of this, workers indeed have serious obligations to fulfill their own responsibilities to their employers with honesty and integrity. Though it seems accurate to say that the emphasis in CST is clearly on the rights of workers, it is also true that rights and responsibilities go together.

"Option for the Poor." One of the most celebrated and controversial of the key convictions of CST is what has become known as "the option for the poor." Thomas Massaro is right in noting that there is something both new and old about this idea. It is new in that the phrase appears in no official church documents until the 1970s; it is old in that the idea seems evident in Christian tradition from the beginning. Just as in the Old Testament book of Exodus God seemed to intervene in human history to "take the side of" the enslaved Hebrews (Exodus, chapters 3–15), leading them (*in and through* Moses) from oppression to freedom, so too in our day, God is "taking the side of" the poor and oppressed *in and through* all those people (Christians and others) who commit themselves to the social struggle for justice and liberation. Commitment—that is the fundamental meaning of the word "option" in CST. And just as Jesus of Nazareth liberated all people from the bondage of sin and the sting of death, and called his followers to commit themselves, as he had, to "proclaiming glad tidings to the poor" and bringing "liberty to captives" (Luke 4: 18–19), so too, the followers of Jesus are true to their real mission to the extent that they commit themselves to the ongoing work of liberation, the work of helping to fashion God's reign of justice, love and peace (Gutierrez, Boff, Schubeck, *Liberation Ethics*).

The contemporary emphasis on an option for the poor emerges from a very specific historical, political situation: the situation of poverty and injustice in Latin America, poverty and injustice that was and remains essentially linked to social and political structures. Beginning in the 1960s and '70s, Christian theologians in those countries began to make connections between their social/political situation and the essential message of Christianity. What does God want, these theologians asked, in situations of structural poverty and injustice? God wants nothing less than the liberation of all people from any and all things that are the cause of oppression and injustice.

In a fresh and challenging way liberation theology has reminded the Christian community that even though it is true that God loves all people (rich and poor alike, and yes, not only the oppressed, but the oppressors as well), and even though we should try not to pit one group against another or to involve ourselves in violence, Christian faith does call us to make a special option for the poor. Not unlike a parent who loves all her children, but whose love is poured out regularly on behalf of the child most in need, so too "the heart of God" and the passionate care and commitment of Christian people needs to be directed regularly to those most in need, to those who suffer.

If there is something new and fresh about the theme of option for the poor, as it emerged from liberation theology, there is something ancient about the theme as well. Latin American liberation theologians helped the church across the world to recognize that God's option for the poor and our call to make a similar option is implicit in the scriptural stories about God's involvement with humankind, including God's involvement with us through Jesus Christ. By the mid-'70s the option for the poor began to be spoken about directly and forcefully by popes and bishops, enough that today virtually no one writing about CST would leave it off the list of key principles or convictions. (Pope John Paul II, "On the Hundredth Anniversary of 'Rerum Novarum,'" par. 11).

Although liberation theology—and its call for an option for the poor—originated in a specific social situation in Latin America, since the 1980s it has undergone a variety of transformations. The general theme of liberation and the specific call for an option for the poor have been taken up by Christian theologians around the world as they have considered a host of other instances of structural injustice and oppression in society and in the church itself. Drawing on these themes, African-American theologian James Cone has helped to pioneer "black theology," spelled out especially in his influential *A Black Theology of Liberation* (1970). And of course many (not all) feminist theologians have welcomed these same themes and have drawn out their implications for patriarchal cultures, including the Catholic Church. Anne E. Patrick's *Liberating Conscience* (1996) is a fine recent example of a Catholic feminist theology of liberation. The collection of articles called *Liberation Theology,* edited by Curt Cadorette, et. al., displays the wide variety of ways in which liberation theology and its option for the poor have made their mark not only on CST but on Christian theology around the world.

Peace. It should come as a shock to no one: CST is decidedly in favor of peace. Most people, of course, are. Hopefully Christians take it to be part of their responsibility, both as citizens of the earth and as followers of Christ, to do all in their power to eliminate (or at least to minimize) violence in the world and to work for peace.

But there are two things about CST's convictions regarding peace that are distinctive and that deserve attention here: its theology of peace and, for lack of a better phrase, its contributions to "the politics of peace."

Catholicism's theology of peace is captured briefly but clearly in the following two passages from the U.S. Catholic Bishops' pastoral letter on peace in 1983:

> Because peace, like the kingdom of God itself, is both a divine gift and a human work, the Church should continually pray for the gift and share in the work. We are called to be a Church at the service of peace, precisely because peace is one manifestation of God's word and work in our midst. ("The Challenge of Peace," par. 23).

> Let us have the courage to believe in the bright future and in a God who wills it for us—not a perfect world, but a better one. The perfect world, we Christians believe, is beyond the horizon, in an endless eternity where God will be all in all. But a better world is here for human hands and hearts and minds to make ("The Challenge of Peace," par. 337).

By the phrase "kingdom of God" or "reign of God" Christians believe that God is "up to something" in the world. Especially through the life, teaching, and dying and rising of Jesus Christ, God has inaugurated a victory of grace over sinfulness, justice over oppression, peace over violence and, most dramatically, life over death. In this way, Christian faith provides believers with a view of history, a very hopeful one. God has been and remains "up to" the transformation of the human race and all of creation. Christian faith daringly insists that God is fashioning a new heaven and a new earth, one which will be characterized by justice, love, and peace. This is what God wants; this is what God is doing.

But how? So far this theology of peace is all about what *God* is doing; it is God's gift, with only glimpses of it on the horizon of human existence. But part of Christian faith concerning the "reign of God" is that we are called to participate in what God is doing through the way in which we live our lives, through the ways in which we work for love and justice and peace. There is not only *discontinuity* between this real world and what lies "beyond the horizon," there is *continuity* as well. A "perfect" world, a *perfectly peaceful* world, Christian faith suggests, is beyond us. But a better world, a more peaceful world, is ours to fashion. *In and through* our peacemaking efforts the "reign of God" is being fashioned. This, I think, is the heart of CST's theology of peace.

But we must speak also (and less poetically) of "the politics of peace." I have two things in mind here: CST's convictions about non-violence and its espousal of just-war theory. These two seemingly conflicting traditions are two different threads woven into the one fabric of Catholicism's approach to peace.

History is important here. In the earliest centuries of Christianity the followers of Jesus were faced with questions concerning how deeply they should become involved in the social, political, and military structures of the culture in which they found themselves, the Roman Empire. Many scholars believe that in the earliest decades after Christ—the decades in which the writings of the New Testament were being formulated—Christians believed that the return of Christ and the end of the world as we know it was on the immediate horizon. In such a context, some of the "hard sayings" attributed to Jesus in the New Testament, particularly the radical call to non-violence (". . . I say to you, offer no resistance to one who is evil. When someone strikes you on your right cheek, turn the other one to him as well" [Matthew 5: 39]) seem to be more palatable. If the world is ending tomorrow, endurance may be an easier pill to swallow. In fact, many of the earliest Christians suffered persecution because of their faith, and so the "hard saying" about non-violence may well have reflected the actual experience of some of Jesus' first followers. All of this contributed to the fact that not only in the first few decades, but also for the first several centuries of the life of the church, non-violence was taken to be the way of Jesus and the way for his followers to live.

Lisa Sowle Cahill (whose book on this topic is a masterful analysis of this part of Catholic tradition) is among those who suggest that once Christianity became "mainstreamed" in the time of Constantine (fourth century), Christians' involvement in the military and justification of the use of force (including killing) on behalf of the state became more widely accepted (Cahill, p. 40). Although peace remained the ideal, justification of the use of force in this less-than-perfect world became widespread. Under the leadership of Augustine (354–430), criteria were developed for determining a just war, and as Massaro notes, "The just-war theory came to form the mainstream of Christian reflection on violence for many centuries" (Massaro, p. 152).

Over the centuries the criteria for determining a just war and for determining just actions within war have evolved. In a contemporary way the 1983 pastoral letter of the U.S. Bishops stated the criteria as follows:

- just cause (protecting innocent persons, securing human rights, etc.)
- competent authority (war must be declared by those with authority for the public order; leaving ambiguous the status of revolutions)
- comparative justice (a criteria that calls for an analysis of which side is sufficiently "right" in a dispute)
- right intention (only the reasons that provide the just cause can be intended, not revenge or violence for its own sake)
- last resort (all possibilities for non-violent resolutions have been tried and exhausted)
- probability of success (there should be some prospect that the use of force will accomplish the goals identified in the just cause)
- proportionality (the damage done to all parties must be proportionate to the good that is hoped for) (U.S. Bishops, "The Challenge of Peace," pars. 86–99).

In addition to these seven criteria for determining when it may be *just to go to war,* the Bishops also provided two criteria for determining what would and would not constitute *just actions within the war* itself:

- proportionality. There must be a proper proportion between the damage one's actions (e.g., bombing) cause to opposing forces, to civilian populations, and to the environment and the good that is likely to be achieved by such actions (103).
- discrimination. "The response to unjust aggression must be discriminate; it must be directed against unjust aggressors, not against innocent people caught up in a war not of their making" (104).

If taken seriously these two criteria are very stringent. Think for a moment of what was done in Hiroshima and Nagasaki at the end of World War II. In a world in which the weapons of war have become capable of ever more massive destruction, not only of opposing forces, but of civilian population centers and the natural environment itself, meeting the criteria of proportionality and discrimination in the conduct of war is very difficult, some think virtually impossible.

It should be obvious that these criteria are far from some simple checklist for determining a just war or for determining just actions within war. Each criterion calls for analysis, and relative to specific situations (e.g., the War in Iraq) each one is open to a variety of interpretations and opinions. As a result, in many circles there is an understandable degree of cynicism about the usefulness of the just war theory itself.

The two traditions of non-violence and just war theory have existed side by side as part of Catholic social thought for centuries. In truth, however, the just-war tradition came to overshadow the tradition of non-violence. Although there have always been challenging, prophetic voices within Catholicism that have attempted to remind the church of the universal call to peace and even the "hard sayings" about non-violence, mostly they have been individual, lonely voices. Today, however, there is a good deal of evidence that that may be changing (Mich, 275–312). CST has given increasing attention to non–violence in recent years. Perhaps as the flaws and the limits of the just war theory become more and more evident (especially in this nuclear age), the presumption against war and the promotion for peace have received greater and greater emphasis. CST still struggles with difficult political situations in which the human rights of innocent people are trampled upon; in such situations, in this sin-riddled world, is violence a regretful but necessary evil? Or does the use of force and violence simply breed more violence? There are no easy answers (Himes).

Care of the Earth. Twenty years ago it would have been unthinkable that someone would list "Care of the Earth" as one of the key convictions of CST. If any of the convictions being described here are evidence that CST is a work-in-progress, this one is. But with increasing strength in its voice, CST proclaims that that we are all charged to care for the earth. What exactly this means, however, and how precisely this conviction is related to most of those that have been described above, is less clear. To explore this, let us look at Catholicism's approach to "care of the Earth" in three ways (to some extent in historical fashion) by examining three concepts laid out well by Catholic "ecofeminist" theologian Elizabeth A. Johnson: *kingship, stewardship,* and *kinship* (Johnson, pp. 29–40).

KINGSHIP. The idea of kingship is based upon what Johnson describes as hierarchical dualism:

> It is based on hierarchical dualism that sees humanity separated from the earth and placed in a position of absolute dominion over all other creatures who are made for us. In this view, the creatures of the world are ranked . . . with greater value being assigned to those up on the great chain of being. At

> the lowest level is inorganic matter; next comes vegetative matter, followed by animals, human beings, and non-physical spirits or angels. In the progression from the pebble to the peach to the poodle to the person, with women somewhere between the latter two, the higher order of creatures has the right to use and control the lower . . . This is the patriarchal pyramid again, resulting in a top-down domination of nature by man (Johnson 29).

From the perspective of kingship, the world has been created for us and awaits our dominion and control. Related to this is a 1967 article published by Lynn White, a widely respected historian who taught at Princeton, Stanford and UCLA. It was entitled "The Historical Roots of Our Ecological Crisis," and it argued that the Judeo-Christian tradition—which claimed, with biblical authority (Genesis 1:28), that humans are to subdue the earth and have dominion over all things—is largely to blame for the ecological crisis in which we find ourselves. White's argument corresponds a great deal with Johnson's idea of kingship. At our worst, these thinkers claim (and I would agree), not only has "care of the Earth" not predominated in Catholic thought, but in the past Catholic teaching has contributed to an attitude of dominion that has been part of humanity's irresponsibility and recklessness in regard to the earth.

STEWARDSHIP. But Christian tradition has also espoused stewardship as a way of viewing humanity's relation to the earth. In Johnson's view, stewardship "... keeps the structure of hierarchical dualism but calls for human beings to be responsible caretakers or guardians of the earth and all its creatures... In this model humanity is still at the top of the pyramid of being but has the duty to protect and preserve what seems weaker and more vulnerable" (Johnson, p. 30). Stewardship is often found in the writings of the pope and bishops. In 1991, for example, the U.S. Catholic bishops wrote that we must be "faithful stewards" of the gift of God's creation. Stewardship, they suggested, means that ". . . we must both care for creation according to standards that are not of our own making and at the same time be resourceful in finding ways to make the earth flourish."(U.S. Catholic Bishops, "Renewing the Earth," 429).

When combined with several of the key convictions we have already discussed—especially convictions about human rights, equality, and the option for the poor—the idea of stewardship can generate and motivate very strong convictions and actions directed to care for the earth. The idea of stewardship, in combination with the human rights tradition, is compatible with the idea that all persons (including future generations of people) have a right to a safe and healthy environment. A commitment to stewardship, combined with CST's conviction that racism is a crime against human dignity and equality, would also lead one to be deeply concerned about "environmental racism"—the phenomenon that people of color are regularly and systematically exposed to a disproportionate degree of environmental harm and hazard (Bullard). To be sure, not all are satisfied with stewardship as the appropriate way to think about our charge to care for the earth. But it is a long way from kingship or dominion. As I see it, stewardship is the predominant way that CST currently calls for environmental responsibility.

KINSHIP. But for Johnson and others, stewardship does not go far enough. The idea of kinship, she argues, takes us where we must go: "If separation is not the ideal but connection is; if dualism is not the ideal but the relational embrace of diversity is; if hierarchy is not the ideal but mutuality is; then the kinship model more closely approximates reality. It sees human beings and the earth with all its creatures intrinsically related as companions in a community of life. . . This kinship attitude does not measure differences on a scale of higher or lower ontological dignity but appreciates them as integral elements in the robust thriving of a whole" (Johnson, p. 30).

Two comments about kinship are important. First, it is an attempt to recognize and celebrate the diversity of all creatures in a way that steadfastly avoids the pattern of "higher" and "lower," or what Johnson has called "hierarchical dualism." The idea of kinship is not that there are no "distinctions between human beings and other forms of life": a rock is not a tree, and a tree is not a person. Instead, the conviction of kinship is that it is both unnecessary and irresponsible to assign "greater" and "lesser" value to diverse creatures. The relation of humanity to the rest of creation should be marked not by superiority, but by the recognition of interconnectedness and mutuality.

The second thing that should be said about Johnson's idea of kinship is that the idea is not entirely new. Although some version of the stewardship model has usually been at the center of Catholic thinking, traces of the kinship model have been part of Catholic social thought all along. In "Creation and an Environmental Ethic," Michael and Kenneth Himes demonstrate how the idea of kinship (they prefer *companionship*) was part of the thinking of St. Augustine, St. Thomas Aquinas, and above all St. Francis of Assisi and is part of a "sacramental vision" that sees ". . . every creature, human and non-human, animate and inanimate" a sign of the love and presence of God (Himes, 112).

To espouse kinship as the right way to envision humanity's relation to the rest of the universe would be a stretch for CST. At first glance it might seem that the first six convictions of CST that we have discussed are so centered on the dignity of human beings that there is little room for the rest of creation in the energy of CST. Admittedly, Catholic social thought—to date at least—has focused on the well-being of human beings. But perhaps scholars like Elizabeth Johnson are helping the Christian community appreciate in fresh ways the intimate connections between the welfare of people and the welfare of the earth and all its inhabitants. It may well be that one of the contributions feminist, non-dualistic, and non-hierarchical thought patterns are starting to make for CST is the ability to emphasize the dignity and sacredness of humankind without compromising the dignity and sacredness of the earth and all its creatures. We are in this together. That conviction, I believe, is "going forward" in many places in our world today, including in CST.

CST: Justice and a Principle of Application. We have come to the end of this reflection on seven key convictions of CST. By way of conclusion, I would like to reflect briefly on two questions. First, what might the word ***justice*** mean in light of the seven key convictions of CST? Second, how might these seven convictions *connect* with some specific issues? This latter question will lead to two observations: the first regards some principles of application regarding the seven convictions, and the second concerns the purposes of Catholic moral teachings, including CST.

CST and Justice. Justice is hard to define; it involves many things. It is both a virtue of individual persons (so we might say "Nelson Mandela is a just man."); and at the same time it is "larger" than the virtue of individuals (and thus we might also say "South Africa has become a more just society in recent years.") In this latter case, the virtue of individuals is surely involved, but a country is said to be just to the degree that justice is embedded in the *social structures and practices* (the regular way of doing business) of the society itself. Put differently, there is of course a relationship between justice as a virtue and justice as a characteristic of a society: just persons, working together, strive to create just social structures and practices, that is, just communities.

Key to understanding justice is *relationship*. Justice means *right relationship*. Justice exists in a community, large or small, when (and to the extent that) the relationships of the members of the community can be characterized as right relationships. There is not a "one size fits all" formula for determining when right relationships exist. Context is important. But there are a number of criteria from Catholic Social Teaching that can be used to determine when communal or social relationships are "right," that is, when they are just.

Right relationship exists when, and to the extent that, the dignity and sacredness of every living being are recognized and respected. Right relationship exists when, and to the extent that, the well-being and rights of every living being *(especially those who are most vulnerable)* are recognized, protected and promoted. Rights are articulated in different ways in different contexts, but in every context they include a right to life and to the things that are necessary to live with dignity, for one to flourish: a right to food, clothing, shelter, and health care; a right to freedom of relationship, freedom in speech, religion, association and public gatherings; and a right to participate in the economic and political activities of the community, including a right to dignified, meaningful work for a living, just wage. Right relationships exist—justice exists—when, and to the extent that, peace is being promoted.

It must be understood that along with every right there exits a corresponding responsibility. Right relationship exits when, and to the extent that, rights and responsibilities are exercised in a mutual manner.

Right relationship exists when, and to the extent that, the good of individual beings and the common good of all are being protected and promoted. (Notice that "individual beings" includes human beings, persons, but it is not limited to humans. Right relationship has a good deal to do the way human beings treat one another, but it also encompasses human beings' ways of relating to and responding to the earth itself and to others with whom humans share the natural environment.)

None of these observations about justice translate into a formula for simple solutions to complex social and ethical questions. CST yields no such formulas. Nevertheless, the key convictions of CST and the account of justice that accompanies it name some important moral values that should command our attention as well as criteria that may help us think about how we should respond to pressing social and ethic issues.

A Principle of Application. In their 1986 pastoral letter on economic justice, the U.S. Bishops spoke first about general *principles* and then went on to make *applications* to specific issues of economic policy. I have followed this line of thought as I have named general *convictions* of CST and, shortly, will make *connections* to some concrete issues. CST recognizes important differences between principle and application (conviction and connection), acknowledging that the movement from one to the other is neither easy nor obvious. The bishops describe this movement as follows. It is important to quote at some length.

> In focusing on some of the central economic issues and choices in American life in the light of moral principles, we are aware that the movement from principle to policy is complex and difficult and although moral values are essential in determining public policies, they do not dictate specific solutions. They must interact with empirical data, with historical, social, and political realities, and with competing demands on limited resources. The soundness of our prudential judgments depends not only on the moral force of our principles, but also on the accuracy of our information and the validity of our assumptions. Our judgments and recommendations on specific economic issues, therefore, do not carry the same moral authority as our statements of universal moral principles and formal church teaching; the former are related to circumstances which can change or which can be interpreted differently by people of good will. We expect and welcome debate on our specific policy recommendations. Nevertheless, we want our statements on these matters to be given serious consideration by Catholics as they determine whether their own moral judgments are consistent with the Gospel and

> with Catholic social teaching. We believe that differences on complex economic questions should be expressed in a spirit of mutual respect and open dialogue (U.S. Bishops, "Economic Justice for All," pars. 134–135).

In a church with a reputation for its emphasis on authority, these words from the bishops have a refreshing humility about them, indeed realism (which, in the end, is what humility really is). Keenly aware of the complexity of the economic issues they were addressing, the bishops proceeded by naming some general, but admittedly somewhat abstract moral principles that should govern economic policy choices. Two examples suffice: "Every economic decision and institution must be judged in light of whether it protects or undermines the dignity of the human person" (par. 13); "All members of society have a special obligation to the poor and vulnerable" (par. 16). The bishops acknowledged that there is a difference between general principles and specific recommendation regarding economic policy. People of good will—Catholic or otherwise—may agree that we have special obligations to the poor, but disagree profoundly regarding which revisions in, say, a taxation plan would best meet the needs of the poor. And yes, (as much as it might pain me at times to admit this) both Democrats and Republicans can espouse the convictions of CST, but disagree about many matters of public policy. This doesn't mean that CST means nothing, only that it may mean more than one thing. CST provides critical criteria for assessing public policy. Does a proposed taxation plan help or hinder the quality of life of the poor and vulnerable? CST is convinced that that is the right question, even as it admits that the answer is far from obvious.

Purposes of CST. I think it can be said that the purposes of CST—and of all of the church's moral teachings—are twofold. First, they are intended to lift up the moral dimension of important issues of the day and in that way to contribute to public discussion of issues that effect the common good. Second, they exist to help form the consciences of Catholic people so that they might make judgments and choices that are not only wise, but which bear the mark of Christian faith convictions.

In the introduction to their pastoral letter on economic justice the bishops noted that they intended to speak both because they were Americans and also because they were pastors. As Americans, they strove to address public issues in ways that would make sense to all Americans. Groups as diverse as the National Organization for Women and the National Rifle Association do the same: they address public issues, attempting to persuade others concerning their values and convictions. So too, CST is often addressed to "the public," attempting to lift up the moral dimensions of important social issues.

As pastors, the bishops addressed members of the Catholic Church. As part of their teaching office, it is the responsibility of the pope and bishops to make connections between Catholic faith and important moral issues in order to guide the consciences of Catholics. In the pastoral letter quoted above, the bishops stated that they hoped both their general principles and their specific policy applications would be "given serious consideration by Catholics as they determine whether their own moral judgments are consistent with the Gospel and with Catholic social teaching" (par. 135). That captures well what Catholic teaching is concerning the responsibilities of Catholics regarding the moral teachings of the church. In the words of the bishops at Vatican II, in forming their consciences, Catholics are to "pay careful attention to" the moral teachings of the church ("Declaration on Religious Liberty," par. 14). Catholicism is not "in the business" of assuming moral responsibility for others; or at least it ought not be. But it is "in the business" of naming the moral aspects of important social issues and contributing to consciences that are wise and just.

Part Two: Catholic Social Teaching—Connections

In the concluding part of this article (much more brief than Part One) it is neither possible nor necessary to try to even touch on the wide array of social issues that have commanded the attention of CST in recent years. My purpose here is simply this: I would like to show how some of CST's key convictions—especially about human dignity and the option for the poor—*connect* to three specific issues: capital punishment, immigration, and the place of gay and lesbian persons in the church. What should emerge is the fact that CST is not simply a matter of general or vague convictions, but includes the drive to make connections with the important issues of the day.

Capital Punishment: Does Every Life Count? Catholic Social Teaching is opposed to the use of the death penalty as a legitimate means of punishment. That simple sentence captures the way CST's conviction about the dignity of every human being connects with this perennially difficult issue. Having said that, however, it is also true that there is nothing simple about Catholic teaching on capital punishment. As James Megivern's recent 600-page history on this issue illustrates, Catholic convictions have changed dramatically on this issue. In what follows let us simply take note of some of the historical features of this issue, examine the "why" of current Catholic opposition to capital punishment, and see how CST's contemporary stance on the death penalty connects with other issues in which human life is at stake.

Toward the end of his historical treatment of Catholicism's view of the death penalty, Megivern quotes from a 1960 article by Jesuit theologian Antonio Messineo as a way of summarizing the predominant stance of the church:

> The Church, from the Fathers to St. Thomas Aquinas down to our own day, with unswerving unanimity, taught the legitimacy of capital punishment, and that therefore it could confidently be affirmed that the death penalty was in perfect accord with Christian thought (Megivern, p. 460).

As Megivern chronicles, the *reasons* for the church's predominant approval (there were always "voices of dissent") of the legitimacy of the death penalty evolved over the centuries. In the fourth and fifth centuries, as Christianity became the "established" religion of the Roman Empire, it was virtually unthinkable that the state could not exercise lethal force, including the exercise of capital punishment (3). From the eleventh through the seventeenth centuries the church invoked various arguments to explain why the death penalty could be seen as a justifiable way of dealing with heresy, more precisely with heretics (3–4). This period saw the establishment of the Inquisition, which involved both the torture and death of heretics. And it was during this period that St. Thomas Aquinas invoked the image of a "diseased organ" to explain the justifiability of capital punishment: just as a surgeon removes a diseased organ for the welfare of the total body, so too the state may "remove" a "diseased member" for the overall good of the community (Megivern, pp. 115–116). In more recent centuries the argument tended to move toward just defense: the state may exercise capital punishment as a necessary way of defending itself against those prone to heinous crimes against the state and its citizens. As recently as 1952, Pope Pius XII, attempting to uphold both the inviolability of the right to life and the justifiability of the death penalty, argued that the state, in exercising capital punishment, does not/can not take away the right to life from an individual. Instead, through the death penalty the state deprives the criminal of the *good* of life "after he by his crime has already been dispossessed of his right to life" (Megivern, p. 459).

Given this history, why is it that the church *today* is opposed to the use of capital punishment? Pope John Paul II's words from "The Gospel of Life" (1995) are important here. After affirming the rightful place of punishment the pope argued as follows:

> . . . the nature and extent of the punishment must be carefully evaluated and decided upon, and ought not go to the extreme of executing the offender except in cases of absolute necessity: in other words, when it would not be possible otherwise to defend society. Today however, as a result of steady improvements in the organization of the penal system, such cases are very rare, if not practically non-existent ("The Gospel of Life," par. 56).

Noteworthy is the fact that the pope did not quibble with the state's theoretical right to capital punishment. Instead, his argument focused on the rightness of the *use* of capital punishment in ordinary circumstances today. Under normal circumstances, he argued, capital punishment is not right precisely because it is not necessary; the rightful purposes of punishment can be served otherwise. This argument, essentially that of the U.S. Bishops in a 1980 statement on the issue, expresses current CST on the matter.

For some, more important and more convincing than the pope's argument for the non-use of the death penalty, is the fact that the church's current teaching emphasizes the conviction that every human life is sacred, yes, even the life of those whose actions have violated life. For many, our call to recognize the dignity of every human being and the value of every human life is upheld in a powerful way through CST's stand against the death penalty. Perhaps no one has dramatized this conviction more effectively than Helen Prejean, CSJ, in her book (and later the film) *Dead Man Walking: An Eyewitness Account of the Death Penalty in the United States.* She and others like her argue that there are a host of things wrong with the death penalty: judicial errors *do* take place that result in the execution of innocent people; there is evidence of racial bias at work in the disproportionate way people of color are sent to their death; and the notion that capital punishment deters others from violent crime seems largely unsubstantiated. But beyond these arguments there is something more. Does not capital punishment simply continue a senseless circle of violence? Does it not make us killers ourselves? And do we not deaden a voice within us that calls us to mercy, even for those who have offended us so terribly? Prejean and others answer yes to these questions. They think that yes, part of the core of Christian faith, is also accessible to all people of good will. I believe they are right.

A final word about CST's current stance on capital punishment is this: it is part of what the late Cardinal Joseph Bernardin (Chicago) called "a consistent ethic of life." This is the idea that there is fundamental value that grounds Catholic teaching on all issues related to life: the dignity and inviolability of the life of every human being. Put differently, the fundamental value CST is attempting to protect and promote in its teachings on abortion, euthanasia, assisted-suicide and capital punishment is the value of every human life. Even more precisely, as the teaching on abortion makes explicit, we ought not discriminate or "cut corners" on the dignity of human life because of its stage of development (Congregation for the Doctrine of the Faith, "Declaration on Procured Abortion," par. 11). To be sure, CST recognizes the value of the life and well-being of a mother in an unplanned and unwanted pregnancy; it embraces the virtue of compassion that motivates those who propose assisted-suicide or euthanasia as a way to respond to the suffering of a loved one; and it stands in awe in the face of the rage and devastation of those who have lost a loved one through violent crime. But with all that, CST suggests that the taking of life through abortion, assisted-suicide or euthanasia, or through capital punishment pits values and even human lives against one another in ways that cause us not to flourish, but to diminish. On these issues CST constitutes "hard sayings." That is obvious. But the "consistent ethic of life" is not simply about what CST opposes; it is about a conviction it wishes to celebrate: every life counts.

Immigration: Who Is a Neighbor? Catholic Social Teaching, seeing immigration from the point of view of those whose social condition of poverty or oppression leads them to emigrate, argues that such persons have a right to emigrate and that countries that are able have a responsibility to provide residence, indeed welcome. This sentence captures the way CST makes a *connection* between its convictions about human dignity and the option for the poor and the issue of immigration.

There are religious roots for the concern about immigration in both Judaism and Christianity. Perhaps the most important of all the stories in the Hebrew Scriptures is the story of the Exodus (Exodus, chapters 3–15). In the story, God heard the cries of the Jews suffering from slavery and oppression in Egypt and God did something about it. In and through the leadership of Moses, the story goes, God enabled the Jews to flee from oppression and led them safely (eventually!) to their own land. The "moral lesson" is that God cares for those who suffer, God cares for migrants and refugees. God's people should do the same.

By almost anyone's standard, the story of the Good Samaritan in the New Testament is one of the classic texts in all of literature. I won't do justice to it here. But among other things, the story is about an encounter between two people who are "set up" to be enemies, to despise one another. The one who has been beaten, presumably a Jew, is ignored by his own religious leaders. And then a Samaritan (stereotypically a bitter enemy of the Jews) enters the scene. In a remarkably grace-filled moment, he is "moved with pity" and proceeds to go out of his way, to inconvenience himself, to take practical steps to tend to the man's needs. In Luke's Gospel, after Jesus' instructions to love our neighbor as ourselves, this story is told in response to the question "And who is my neighbor?" (Luke 10: 25–29). So among the "moral lessons" of the story there is this one: we should consider carefully what it means to be a neighbor. "Neighbor" is not simply about living close to someone else; and it is not simply about "feeling comfortable" with others. In the Good Samaritan story "neighbor" is more of a verb than a noun. The word "neighbor," the story suggests, describes the way we respond to the "the other," "the stranger," particularly the stranger who suffers.

What this faith tradition provides for CST is not a detailed set of proposals regarding immigration policies. Rather, it provides a perspective, a starting point. CST enters discussions about immigration from the perspective of those whose poverty or oppression causes them to leave their home, suggesting that when it is necessary the ability "to emigrate to other countries and to take up residence there" is a matter of human rights (Pope John XXIII, "Peace on Earth," par. 25). Motivated by a conviction about the dignity of *all* persons and, even more, by its option for the poor, CST argues that the right to emigrate calls for a corresponding responsibility for those who are able to provide a safe haven for those who need it, and indeed to provide the social services that may be necessary to secure a quality of life that befits human dignity. Put more simply, we are to be "neighbor" to those who suffer. And as in the New Testament story, "being neighbor" may involve overcoming racism and other forms of discrimination that are often at work in our personal attitudes toward refugees and migrants as well as in our institutional and national policies (Pope John Paul II, "On Human Work," par. 23).

None of this is to say, as Catholic theologians William O'Neill and William Spohn have noted, that there should not be a fair distribution of both the burdens (which countries should offer asylum) and benefits (which countries should benefit from immigration of skilled workers) of immigration policies internationally (O'Neill and Spohn, 100–101). Indeed, there may be reasons to limit immigration. However, CST suggests that such limitation has a condition: "Efforts to stem migration that do not effectively address its root causes are not only ineffectual, but permit the continuation of the political, social, and economic inequities that cause it" (U.S. Bishops Committee on Migration, "One Family Under God," 13).

It should be clear that CST does not offer a detailed proposal regarding immigration policies nationally or internationally. What it does offer is a perspective we might adopt regarding migrants and refugees. Who are these people? They are our brothers and sisters. Their ability to flee from poverty and oppression is a matter of human rights. Our call to provide welcome, to "be neighbor," is a matter of human responsibility. Many questions remain, but that is a start, a challenging one.

Gay and Lesbian Persons in the Church: Who Belongs at the Table? Catholic Social Teaching recognizes that gay and lesbian persons, created in the image and likeness of God and brothers and sisters to us all, unfortunately often suffer from discrimination and violence, even murder. Every form of prejudice or oppression directed against gay and lesbian persons—whether in society at large or within the Christian community itself—is an offense against human dignity and human rights and should be eradicated. Gay and lesbian persons should receive a particular welcome in the church—not only because of what the Christian community may offer them, but also because of the way their particular experiences can enrich the church.

I am well aware of the complexity and the controversy of the issue at hand. Had I asked, I know there are many who would have suggested that I conclude with something else. But the issue is important, very important. And as the opening paragraph above suggests (a paragraph that belongs well within the bounds of official Catholic teaching on the connections between homosexuality and justice), some of Catholicism's most important convictions relative to homosexuality are more about justice than they are about sex. Knowing that many questions will remain when I have finished, let me offer just two comments on the place of gay and lesbian persons within the church.

As we have seen, two of the most important convictions of CST are about human dignity/human rights and an option for the poor and vulnerable. The Christian community has special obligations to gay and lesbian persons. There is no need to document the ways in which gay and lesbian persons often suffer from discrimination (or something worse) precisely because of their sexual orientation. Gay and lesbian persons have experienced everything from raised eyebrows to laughter to ridicule to marginalization to the denial of human rights to violence to murder. Without question, their human dignity has often been defaced. And they remain "vulnerable" in a variety of ways. CST's convictions about the dignity of *all* persons and the desire to "take the side" of the poor and vulnerable are the reason the church should muster its best energies to help eradicate such discrimination both in society and in the Christian community. That should begin by providing a special degree of welcome in the church itself, as the U.S. Bishops put it, "a special degree of pastoral understanding and care" ("To Live in Christ Jesus," par. 4; Peddicord). To say this differently, gay and lesbian persons belong at *all* our tables. As the pastor in one of this article's opening vignettes seems to understand, the church must do much better extending hospitality toward gay and lesbian persons, especially at the nourishing table of the Eucharist.

But there is another, equally important reason for such hospitality. To put it simply, the Catholic Church has unfinished business regarding its own teaching on homosexuality. The unfinished business will not be attended to well without the voice of gay and lesbian persons themselves. Now there are many who think that the church's current teaching about homosexuality (briefly, that a homosexual orientation does not involve any moral fault, but that homosexual relations *do* precisely because *all* sexual relations, for *all* people, belong exclusively within the context of heterosexual marriage) is just right. But of course there are many who do not. Some think that the church's teaching on this needs to be expressed better, more cogently, more compassionately. Others think that the teaching is so riddled with "heterosexism" that we must "erase the board and start over." The tensions, indeed divisions, within the church on this issue are more pronounced than ever. In my view, the experience—especially the moral experience—of gay and lesbian persons must be "factored in" to Catholic theological reflection about homosexuality more than it ever has before. If, as I believe, Christian ethics is reflection on moral experience in the light of Christian faith, then Christian ethical reflection about homosexuality cannot help but be well served by paying particularly close attention to the experience and narratives of gay and lesbian persons themselves.

As I hope this article has made clear, CST—indeed Catholic teaching on all matters of morality—is an evolving reality. In my view, that is not a weakness of Catholic teaching, but one of its strengths. Good teaching requires good listening. So, as CST urges, let us make sure that gay and lesbian persons know they are welcome at our table. And let us not only speak, let us listen.

Works Cited and Recommended Sources

Bellah, Robert N., Madsen, Richard, Sullivan, William M., Swindler, Ann, Tipton, Steven M. *Habits of the Heart: Individualism and Commitment in American Life*. New York: Harper & Row, 1985.

Bernardin, Joseph Cardinal. *Consistent Ethic of Life*. Thomas G. Fuechtmann, Ed. Kansas City, MO: Sheed & Ward, 1988.

Boff, Leonardo. *Jesus Christ Liberator*. Maryknoll, NY: Orbis Books, 1978.

Bullard, Robert D., Ed. *Confronting Environmental Racism: Voices from the Grassroots*. Boston, MA: South End Press, 1993.

Cadorette, Curt, Giblin, Marie, Legge, Marilyn J., Snyder, Mary H. *Liberation Theology: An Introductory Reader*. Maryknoll, NY: Orbis Press, 1992.

Cahill, Lisa Sowle. *Love Your Enemies: Discipleship, Pacifism, and Just War Theory*. Minneapolis, MN: Fortress Press, 1994.

Catechism of the Catholic Church. English Ed., United States Catholic Conference, Inc.–Libreria Editrice Vaticana, 1994.

Congregation for the Doctrine of the Faith. "Declaration on Procured *Abortion" (1974)*. Excerpts. *Medical Ethics: Sources of Catholic Teachings*. Kevin D. O'Rourke, OP, and Philip Boyle, OP., Eds. St. Louis, MO: Catholic Health Association. 1989, 37–39.

Elsbernd, Mary, and Bieringer, Reimund. *When Love Is Not Enough*. Collegeville, MN: The Liturgical Press, 2002.

Gutierrez, Gustavo. *A Theology of Liberation*. London: SCM Press, LTD, 1974.

Henriot, Peter J., DeBerri, Edward P., Schultheis, Michael J. *Catholic Social Teaching: Our Best Kept Secret*. Maryknoll, NY: Orbis Books, 1992.

Himes, Kenneth R., OFM. "The Morality of Humanitarian Intervention." *Theological Studies*. March 1994 Vol. 55, No. 1. 82–105.

Himes, Michael J. and Himes, Kenneth R. , OFM. "Creation and an Environmental Ethic." *Fullness of Faith: The Public Significance of Theology*. Mahwah, NJ: Paulist Press, 1993 104–124.

Hopkins, Gerard Manley. "God's Grandeur." *The Norton Anthology of English Literature*, Revised, Vol. 2. New York: W. W. Norton & Co., 1968, 1433.

Johnson, Elizabeth A. *Women, Earth, and Creator Spirit*. Mahwah, NJ: Paulist Press, 1993.

Keenan, James F., SJ. "The Open Debate: Moral Theology and the Lives of Gay and Lesbian Persons." *Theological Studies*. V. 64, No. 1. March, 2003. 127–150.

Lucker, Raymond A. "Justice in the Church: The Church as Example." *One Hundred Years of Catholic Social Thought: Celebration and Challenge*. John A. Coleman, SJ, Ed. New York: Orbis Books, 1991, 88–100.

Massaro, Thomas, SJ. *Living Justice: Catholic Social Teaching in Action*. Franklin, Wisconsin: Sheed & Ward, 2000.

McBrien, Richard P. "What Is Catholicism?" *Catholicism*. Revised ed. New York: Harper, 1994, 3–17.

McCormick, Patrick T. *A Banqueter's Guide to the All-Night Soup Kitchen of the Kingdom of God*. Collegeville, MN: The Liturgical Press, 2004.

McDonough, William C., and Michaud, Catherine R., CSJ, "Papal Apologies Embody and Advance Vatican II on 'the Tradition Poured Out in the Church,'" Ch. 6 of *Revelation and the Church: Vatican II in the Twenty-first Century*. Maryknoll, NY: Orbis Books, 2003. 103–122.

Megivern, James J. *The Death Penalty: An Historical and Theological Survey*. Mahwah, NJ: Paulist Press 1997.

Mich, Marvin L. Krier. *Catholic Social Teaching and Movements*. Mystic, CT: Twenty-Third Publications 1998.

O'Neill, William R., SJ, and Spohn, William C. "Rights of Passage: The Ethics of Immigration and Refugee Policy." *Theological Studies*. March, 1998. Vol. 59, No. 1 84–106.

Patrick, Anne E. *Liberating Conscience: Feminist Explorations in Catholic Moral Theology*. New York: Continuum 1996.

Peddicord, Richard, OP. *Gay and Lesbian Rights—A Question: Sexual Ethics or Social Justice?* Kansas City, MO: Sheed & Ward, 1996.

Prejean, Helen, CSJ. *Dead Man Walking: An Eyewitness Account of the Death Penalty in the United States*. New York: Random House 1993.

Pope John XXIII. "Pacem in Terris" ("Peace on Earth") (1963). *Catholic Social Thought: The Documentary Heritage*. Ed. David J. O'Brien and Thomas A. Shannon. Maryknoll, NY: Orbis Books, 1997.

Pope John Paul II. "Centesimus Annus" ("On the Hundredth Anniversary of 'Rerum Novarum'") (1991). *Catholic Social Thought: The Documentary Heritage* 439–488.

Pope John Paul II. "Evangelium Vitae" ("The Gospel of Life") (1995). Vatican City: Libreria Editrice Vaticana 1995.

Pope John Paul II. "Jubilee Characteristic: The Purification of Memory." *Origins* 29/40. (March 23, 2000). 648–650.

Pope John Paul II. "Laborem Exercens" ("On Human Work") (1981). *Catholic Social Thought: The Documentary Heritage* 352–392.

Pope John Paul II. "Peace With All Creation" (January 1, 1990). *Origins,* Vol. 19 465–468.

Pope John Paul II. "Sollicitudo Rei Socialis" ("On Social Concern") (1987). *Catholic Social Thought: The Documentary Heritage* 395–436.

Pope Leo XIII. "Rerum Novarum" ("The Condition of Labor") (1891). *Catholic Social Thought: The Documentary Heritage* 14–39.

Schubeck, Thomas L., SJ. *Liberation Ethics: Sources, Models, and Norms.* Minneapolis, MN: Fortress Press 1993.

Thompson, J. Milburn. *Justice & Peace: A Christian Primer.* Maryknoll, NY: Orbis Books, 1997 179–205.

U.S. Catholic Bishops. "The Challenge of Peace: God's Promise and Our Response" (1983). *Catholic Social Thought: The Documentary Heritage* 489–571.

U.S. Catholic Bishops. "Economic Justice for All" (1986). Catholic Social Thought: The Documentary Heritage 572–680.

U.S. Catholic Bishops. "Renewing the Earth" (November 14, 1991). Origins, Vol. 21, 425–432.

U.S. Catholic Bishops. "Statement on Capital Punishment." Washington, DC: U.S.CC 1980.

U.S. Catholic Bishops. "To Live as Christ Jesus." Washington, DC: U.S.CC 1976.

U.S. Catholic Bishops. Committee on Migration. "One Family Under God." Washington, DC: U.S.CC, 1998.

Vatican II, Catholic Bishops. "Dignitatis Humanae" ("Declaration on Religious Liberty") (1965). *Documents of Vatican II.* Ed. Austin P. Flannery. Grand Rapids, MI: Eerdmans, 1975).

Vatican II, Catholic Bishops. "Gaudium et Spes" ("Pastoral Constitution on the Church in the Modern World") (1965). *Catholic Social Thought: The Documentary Heritage* 166–237.

White, Lynn. "The Historical Roots of our Ecological Crisis." Ch. 2 of *Environmental Ethics: Readings in Theory and Application,* Third Edition, Louis P. Pojman, editor. Belmont, CA: Wadsworth/Thomson Learning, 2001. 13–19.

Notes

[1] This is a modest revision of my article (with the same title) that appeared first in *The Global Search for Justice:* The College of St. Catherine. Acton, MA: Copley Custom Publishing Group, 2000.

[2] As is the case with several sections of this article, this history is drawn from my *In the Breath of God: Christian Morality,* Ch. 7 "Christian Morality and Social Responsibility" (Chicago: Loyola Press, 2000).

Audre Lorde (1934–1992) was an American poet, theorist, and activist born to West Indian immigrants in New York City. Once declared legally blind, she was employed as a factory worker, X-ray technician, social worker, and medical clerk until she completed her master's degree in library science from Columbia University and later became a successful writer. Lorde, a self-described "black feminist lesbian poet," criticized white feminists for ignoring difference, exhorting them to a stronger consciousness of race, class, and sexuality. After being diagnosed with breast cancer (from which she died in 1992), Lorde wrote the following essay, published in The Cancer Journals *(1980). What types of fear keep us from speaking out? What harm can silence do to our lives? What difference does our speaking make for the communities we live in?*

The Transformation of Silence into Language and Action

Audre Lorde

I have come to believe over and over again that what is most important to me must be spoken, made verbal and shared, even at the risk of having it bruised or misunderstood. That the speaking profits me, beyond any other effect. I am standing here as a Black lesbian poet, and the meaning of all that waits upon the fact that I am still alive, and might not have been. Less than two months ago I was told by two doctors, one female and one male, that I would have to have breast surgery, and that there was a 60 to 80 percent chance that the tumor was malignant. Between that telling and the actual surgery, there was a three-week period of the agony of an involuntary reorganization of my entire life. The surgery was completed, and the growth was benign.

But within those three weeks, I was forced to look upon myself and my living with a harsh and urgent clarity that has left me still shaken but much stronger. This is a situation faced by many women, by some of you here today. Some of what I experienced during that time has helped elucidate for me much of what I feel concerning the transformation of silence into language and action.

In becoming forcibly and essentially aware of my mortality and of what I wished and wanted for my life, however short it might be, priorities and omissions became strongly etched in a merciless light, and what I most regretted were my silences. Of what had I *ever* been afraid? To question or to speak as I believed could have meant pain, or death. But we all hurt in so many different ways, all the time, and pain will either change or end. Death, on the other hand, is the final silence. And that might be coming quickly, now, without regard for whether I had ever spoken what needed to be said, or had only betrayed myself into small silences, while I planned someday to speak, or waited for someone else's words. And I began to recognize a source of power within myself that comes from the knowledge that while it is most desirable not to be afraid, learning to put fear into a perspective gave me great strength.

I was going to die, if not sooner then later, whether or not I had ever spoken myself. My silences had not protected me. Your silence will not protect you. But for every real word spoken, for every attempt I had ever made to speak those truths for which I am still seeking, I had made contact with other women while we examined the words to fit a world in which we all believed, bridging our differences. And it was the concern and caring of all those women which gave me strength and enabled me to scrutinize the essentials of my living.

The women who sustained me through that period were Black and white, old and young, lesbian, bisexual, and heterosexual, and we all shared a war against the tyrannies of silence. They all gave me a strength and concern without which I could not have survived intact. Within those weeks of acute fear came the knowledge—within the war we are all waging with the forces of death, subtle and otherwise, conscious or not—I am not only a casualty, I am also a warrior.

What are the words you do not yet have? What do you need to say? What are the tyrannies you swallow day by day and attempt to make your own, until you will sicken and die of them, still in silence? Perhaps for some of you here today, I am the face of one of your fears. Because I am woman, because I am Black, because I am lesbian, because I am myself—a Black woman warrior poet doing my work—come to ask you, are you doing yours?

And of course I am afraid, because the transformation of silence into language and action is an act of self-revelation, and that always seems fraught with danger. But my daughter, when I told her of our topic and my difficulty with it, said, "Tell them about how you're never really a whole person if you remain silent, because there's always that one little piece inside you that wants to be spoken out, and if you keep ignoring it, it gets madder and madder and hotter and hotter, and if you don't speak it out one day it will just up and punch you in the mouth from the inside."

In the cause of silence, each of us draws the face of her own fear—fear of contempt, of censure, or some judgment, or recognition, of challenge, of annihilation. But most of all, I think, we fear the visibility without which we cannot truly live. Within this country where racial difference creates a constant, if unspoken, distortion of vision, Black women have on one hand always been highly visible, and so, on the other hand, have been rendered invisible through the depersonalization of racism. Even within the women's movement, we have had to fight, and still do, for that very visibility which also renders us most vulnerable, our Blackness. For to survive in the mouth of this dragon we call America, we have had to learn this first and most vital lesson—that we were never meant to survive. Not as human beings. And neither were most of you here today, Black or not. And that visibility which makes us most vulnerable is that which also is the source of our greatest strength. Because the machine will try to grind you into dust anyway, whether or not we speak. We can sit in our corners mute forever while our sisters and our selves are wasted, while our children are distorted and destroyed, while our earth is poisoned; we can sit in our safe corners mute as bottles, and we will still be no less afraid.

In my house this year we are celebrating the feast of Kwanza, the African-American festival of harvest which begins the day after Christmas and lasts for seven days. There are seven principles of Kwanza, one for each day. The first principle is Umoja, which means unity, the decision to strive for and maintain unity in self and community. The principle for yesterday, the second day, was Kujichagulia—self-determination—the decision to define ourselves, name ourselves, and speak for ourselves, instead of being defined and spoken for by others. Today is the third day of Kwanza, and the principle for today is Ujima—collective work and responsibility—the decision to build and maintain ourselves and our communities together and to recognize and solve our problems together.

Each of us is here now because in one way or another we share a commitment to language and to the power of language, and to the reclaiming of that language which has been made to work against us. In the transformation of silence into language and action, it is vitally necessary for each one of us to establish or examine her function in that transformation and to recognize her role as vital within that transformation.

For those of us who write, it is necessary to scrutinize not only the truth of what we speak, but the truth of that language by which we speak it. For others, it is to share and spread also those words that are meaningful to us. But primarily for us all, it is necessary to teach by living and speaking those truths which we believe and know beyond understanding. Because in this way alone we can survive, by taking part in a process of life that is creative and continuing, that is growth.

And it is never without fear—of visibility, of the harsh light of scrutiny and perhaps judgment, of pain, of death. But we have lived through all of those already, in silence, except death. And I remind myself all the time now that if I were to have been born mute, or had maintained an oath of silence my whole life long for safety, I would still have suffered, and I would still die. It is very good for establishing perspective.

And where the words of women are crying to be heard, we must each of us recognize our responsibility to seek those words out, to read them and share them and examine them in their pertinence to our lives. That we not hide behind the mockeries of separations that have been imposed upon us and which so often we accept as our own. For instance, "I can't possibly teach Black women's writing—their experience is so different from mine." Yet how many years have you spent teaching Plato and Shakespeare and Proust? Or another, "She's a white woman and what could she possibly have to say to me?" Or, "She's a lesbian, what would my husband say, or my chairman?" Or again, "This woman writes of her sons and I have no children." And all the other endless ways in which we rob ourselves of ourselves and each other.

We can learn to work and speak when we are afraid in the same way we have learned to work and speak when we are tired. For we have been socialized to respect fear more than our own needs for language and definition, and while we wait in silence for that final luxury of fearlessness, the weight of that silence will choke us.

The fact that we are here and that I speak these words is an attempt to break that silence and bridge some of those differences between us, for it is not difference which immobilizes us, but silence. And there are so many silences to be broken.

Cynthia Enloe is research professor in the department of International Development, Community, and Environment at Clark University, where she was formerly director of the women's studies program. A noted feminist scholar, she earned her PhD in political science from University of California, Berkeley in 1967 and has been an active and engaged scholar ever since, editing feminist scholarly journals and writing nine books. Bananas, Beaches, and Bases, *from which this essay was taken, exposes links between women across cultures—links that implicate Western women in systems of oppression. How does Enloe construct her argument from evidence? In what ways does she address this essay to an audience of educated Western women? Can reading an analysis like this one inspire Western women to act differently?*

Blue Jeans and Bankers

Cynthia Enloe

Polyester. The very word conjures up an entire era. Shopping malls. Drip-dry. Consciousness-raising groups. Ho, ho, ho, we won't go. Hard hats for Nixon.

Polyester caused a major shift in American fashion in the late 1960s that lasted until the mid-1970s. Although it was invented during World War II, polyester, a plastics-based cloth, didn't become a household word until twenty-five years later, when chemical companies, textile manufacturers, machinery producers, fashion designers and garment manufacturers got together to create polyester double-knit clothing for women. At about the same time British consumers were switching from fish and chips to Indian take-aways and from Indian cotton to chemical-based brushed nylon.

Paris Knitting Mills is a clothing company in Ozone Park, across the river from Manhattan in Queens, an industrial neighborhood and home of generations of new American immigrants. Paris joined other garment companies in targeting a particular class of women for the new textile. Polyester double-knit suits were to be a godsend for 'the working mother.' Joseph Lombardo, formerly a presser for Paris and now a union organizer lurking for Queens' steadily shrinking membership, was clear about this targeted consumer.

Paris did not sell to the designer group . . . Paris made double-knit suits for your mother or my mother—three-piece suits, with a blouse, a Chanel-type jacket, and a skirt or a pair of pants. They sold for thirty-five or forty dollars . . .

For a forty-year-old woman who was going back to work after raising her kids it was ideal, because she could have three suits for a hundred dollar investment. She could mix and match.

Polyester and the working mother. This was America in the early 1970s. Whereas in 1950 only 11.9 per cent of American married women with children under six had paid jobs, by 1970 the proportion had risen to 30.3 per cent. Two decades later it would reach 56 per cent.

The polyester formula was inspired by anxiety over global competition. While the peace movement and Henry Kissinger had their eyes on Vietnam, Al Paris of Knitting Mills fixed his attention on Hong Kong and Taiwan. In the US and Europe managers of textile and garment companies were beginning to worry about the rising tide of Asian-made goods that were attracting their customers. 'Buy American'. 'Buy British'. These were the calls made to post-empire women. When they shopped for clothes at Sears or Marks and Spencer women were to be patriotic. This was off-the-rack nationalism. Manufacturers hoped women in polyester and brushed-nylon suits would stave off foreign competition. They counted on the working-class working woman to be attracted to its wash-and-wear convenience, its low cost, its indestructibility. She could balance her family's check book and meet the demands of femininity by purchasing a locally produced, chemical-based wardrobe.

Polyester permitted Western manufacturers to play their strong cards: capital and technology. Their new Asian rivals had cheap female labor, but that wasn't the only asset in the international garments competition. Their new fabric and new knitting machines required large investments and engineering know-how that Taiwan and Hong Kong companies couldn't yet afford. Looking back at the polyester era, Art Ortenberg, one of the founders of Liz Claiborne clothing, saw a 'natural marriage between the international knitting-machinery manufacturers and the large chemical companies in the United States—mainly DuPont'.

At the same time, European and North American working mother's fashion sense was presumed to be unsophisticated. Thus the clothes marketed to them could be kept simple. Paris Knitting Mills could grow only if its women sewing-machinists didn't have to be paid a lot to acquire complicated new skills: 'The beauty of Paris was that the jackets were all so much alike that the girls could sew them with their eyes closed'.

But polyester turned shiney after several washings. And the colors that worked best were bland—pastel blue, pink, yellow, aqua. Chemical engineers may have liked polyester, but the designers didn't. Moreover, Asian manufacturers began to learn how to produce their own double-knit suits. By the mid-1970s Asian-produced polyester clothes were turning up in the ladies-wear department of J. C. Penney's in Ozone Park. The final straw was blue jeans. Women began to wear jeans—'designer jeans'—where before they would have felt they had to wear more formal double-knit suits to be publicly presentable: the dress code was shifting, if not crumbling. As feminine respectability was redefined, the international political economy lurched in a new direction.

Al Paris, who in his heyday had opened up plants in Montreal and Dublin, began to lay off workers. Pressers like Joseph Lombardo lost their jobs. But most of the laid-off workers were women, since they comprised the majority of the garment factories' workers. Unemployment soared in the working-class neighborhoods of Queens and in scattered rural towns where many American garment companies now had their plants. Between 1970 and 1986 the International Ladies Garment Workers Union, one of the two major unions in the US garment industry, lost more than 200,000 members. The cause was easy to spot: production of women's and children's clothes in the United States had dropped by more than 50 per cent. Still, the New York metropolitan area remained home for thousands of women and men working in garment factories. In 1986 the ILGWU, with its mainly male leadership and overwhelmingly female rank and file, had 75,400 New York members. 'Deindustrialization' has become a political catchword since industrial decline meant the lay-off of male factory workers in steel and automobile towns. Garment workers' earlier economic hardships and the international transformations they reflected had been easier to overlook because the workers were women, many of them immigrant or poor rural women.

The Benetton Model

Some Western manufacturers and design houses tried to beat the overseas competition by seeking out lower-paid workers in their own countries, British companies looked to Black and Asian British women, many of them recent arrivals and thus vulnerable to isolation in seasonal employment at low pay with minimum benefits and maximum health hazards. Large retailers such as Marks and Spencer, which sells one fifth of all garments bought in Britain, decided to become 'manufacturers without factories.' Their managers began farming out contracts to smaller producers, who hired workers or employed another layer of subcontractors. Today some 600 different suppliers feed Marks and Spencer alone. Each tries to cope with the constant adjustments as giant retailers refine their strategies to compete with Benetton, Next and other up-market entrepreneurs. Subcontractors prop up their profits yet satisfy their large clients by keeping costs low while offering garments with ever more fashionable stitching.

This has meant finding a way to pass on the costs and the work pressures. British contractors and subcontractors have passed them on to women, specifically Asian and Black British women. Some were hired to work in factories. Others were hired by subcontractors to work in their own homes. These arrangements often appealed to women with small children. Despite lower wages and the lack of benefits and health protection, many women, could look after their children while earning an income for their families, thus not having to choose between motherhood and paid work. Home work also appealed to many of the women's fathers or husbands. They believed that the women of their communities should be protected from the harsh realities—and perhaps immoral temptations—of white-dominated British society. The sexual and racial politics of migration were woven into blouses destined for Marks and Spencer

> When you live in Newham [the East End of London], you have little choice, sister. Burning down of an Asian home does not even make news any longer . . . How can I look for jobs outside my home in such a situation? I want to remain invisible, literally.
>
> Also, sister, I am a widow and I really do not know what my legal status is . . . At the moment, my uncle brings machining work to my home. It works out to be 50 pence per hour, not great! But I earn and I feed my children somehow. Most of all, I do not have to deal with the fear of racist abuse in this white world.

In the United States, manufacturers, encouraged by regional governors, moved their factories south in search of cheaper, non-unionized workers, who would enable them to compete with the Asian and Latin American imports. Black, Latina and rural white women became America's secret weapon against Mexican, Haitian and Korean goods. American companies also moved off the mainland to Puerto Rico, which fell under US customs protection and thus provided the best of all worlds: a Third World labor force inside the American trade sphere. At the same time, smaller firms in the US and Canada adopted the home-work strategy. As in Britain, the majority of home workers were women of color, again recent immigrants, often fearful of deportation. In Montreal, Toronto, Winnipeg, New York, Miami and Los Angeles, it was Filipino, Vietnamese, Chinese, Greek, Dominican, Cuban, Salvadorean, Haitian and Jamaican women who became essential to garment companies' global strategies.

Feminized patterns of racial and regional inequality—interwoven with ideas about motherhood and feminine respectability—helped those European and North American garment companies who felt threatened by the restructured world economy but who did not possess the resources necessary to move their factories overseas. Garment-company executives in alliance with local officials came up with a formula that has suited electronics companies, toy manufacturers and food processors as well: if you can't move to the Third World, create a feminized Third World in your own back yard.

The re-emergence of sweatshops and home working might seem to be a turning back of the modernist clock. But just as plantations are being fashioned to fit the 1990s, so sweatshops and home working are being given a contemporary look.

Benetton is the successful garment company based in northern Italy, a region of farms and small towns whose newly prosperous industrial companies have earned it the nickname of 'the Third Italy'. With its revolutionary knitting technology and its scores of computer-coordinated small shops, Benetton is being heralded by business-school professors and financial reporters as a model of the way to do business in the era of global competition.

> [Luciano] Benetton, whose leonine curling gray-brown hair and horn-rimmed glasses are familiar to millions of Italians from endless photographs in the press, was dressed in his usual assortment of casual clothes: voluminous khaki pants, brown L. L. Bean-style oxfords, a tweed jacket, and a shirt with a button-down collar . . . [He was on his way to do something that] excited him more than anything else in life: the opening of a Benetton store in a 'remote, almost unbelievable' part of the world. We were going that morning to attend a Benetton opening in Prague . . .

Benetton is admired for its stylish designs and its ability to change fashions as rapidly as consumers change their fickle tastes. This combination depends on *flexibility*. In practice, this means that Benetton has to be able to employ advanced computer technology to redesign patterns at a moment's notice. That is the high-tech side. Simultaneously, maximizing flexibility means Benetton's executives being able to call on small-scale local sewing workshops to change their products faster than most big companies can. However, prices must be low enough to enable Benetton to keep ahead of Marks and Spencer. The solution: Italian family-based subcontractors hiring women to work in their homes or in small non-unionized workshops. Although Benetton has eight plants of its own in northern Italy, these operations employ only 2,000 of its 8,000 garment workers. Most of the Italian women who depend on Benetton for their livelihood don't work directly for the company. This is one of the secrets of a corporate model that maximizes flexibility. When the company gives tours to visiting reporters it doesn't include the small, non-unionized shops clustered around Benetton's impressive new plants, even though those subcontractors perform about 40 per cent of Benetton's knitting and 60 per cent of the garment assembly.

Girls, now a prime consumer market, began to adopt the 'Benetton look' in the mid-1980s. With their 'colors of the world' advertising campaign, Benetton executives set out to create a style that could dissolve national borders. Benetton was preparing Europe's adolescents for 1992. Economic planners were taking notice. Benetton's flexibility formula, relying on subcontracting and using women workers in small workshops, has attracted foreign imitators as this advertisement by the government of the Republic of Cyprus makes clear.

The Benetton Approach: A Turning Point for Cyprus

> We are thinking in terms of the Italian model rather than the Korean and the Taiwanese. That means flexible" socialization where you create for a high quality market like Europe: the Benetton approach.

The cult of flexibility has also taken hold in Cyprus's competitor, Ireland, as well as in countries past their industrial prime. Government policy-makers and company officials both see new method of controlling women's work as ammunition in current international politics. But those methods require that women—in Italy, Cyprus, Ireland, Britain, Canada—find flexibility attractive for their own reasons, appeals which off-set the lack of promotion, training, benefits or bargaining power. 'Mother's hours' are being joined to communications satellites as international politics enter the twenty-first century.

The Banker and the Seamstress

Despite the 'Benetton model' and the attractions of employing low-paid women of color at home, during the 1980s American and European fashion designers and their clothing marketers increasingly contracted directly with garment firms abroad, especially in Asia, North Africa, Latin America and the Caribbean. American industry analysts predict that by the mid-1990s over half of all clothes sold in the United States will be manufactured in foreign factories. The US executives who are moving their orders overeas—either under contract with a foreign firm or investing in plants of their own—claim that the more American consumers demand styles with complicated stitching, the more they must search out the lowest-priced seamstresses: 'A polyester-wool blazer costs $65 to make domestically . . . We can produce the same garment with hand tailoring in the Orient for $47.50.'

Overseas imports may have been hurting garment factory owners like Al Paris, but they were proving very profitable for other American and European clothing companies. Liz Claiborne, Jean Pierre and The Gap, for instance, all contract with the same Hong Kong company, Fang Brothers. Thanks to their business, the Fang Brothers themselves have built up a multinational operation. By the late 1980s these Hong Kong entrepreneurs had factories employing women in Panama, Ireland, Thailand and San Francisco. Such is the current international political system that Hong Kong Chinese businessmen fill orders for American clothing companies by hiring Panamanian women; Panama is the Caribbean's largest Export Processing Zone and thrives despite the US government's efforts to bring down the Panamanian government.

A consumer in Boston, Rome or Osaka can trace the complexities of international garment-trade politics by reading the labels on her jeans, bras or sweaters. Just as Chiquita and Geest stickers are clues to the origins of bananas, so clothing labels tell where a garment was made. Two decades ago the labels were likely to read: USA, Britain, Canada, Ireland, Taiwan, Portugal, Hong Kong. Today, those labels are still on the racks, but they have been joined by labels that say: Panama, Indonesia, China, Bangladesh, Mexico, Jamaica, Morocco, the United Arab Emirates, Sri Lanka or Lesotho.

Garment factories have become part of the local landscape in countries which otherwise are radically different. White South African government officials have encouraged foreign companies to set up shop in bantustans, a scheme intended to bolster apartheid and the fiction of self-sustaining Black 'homelands'. Companies from Hong Kong, Taiwan and Israel have been among those to accept Pretoria's invitation. For their part, Vietnamese government officials have introduced policies to encourage garment factories to produce clothing for sale on the international market. In 1986 6,000 Vietnamese shirts were exported to Canada via Hungary. Under a joint-venture agreement with the Vietnamese government, a Hungarian firm sends cloth to Vietnam; Vietnamese workers sew the shirts; the shirts then are sent back to Hungary for sale or export to buyers in countries such as Canada. In Fiji the government has been nervously courting foreign garment manufacturers. The government has been trying to compensate for a long-term slump in world sugar prices and a more recent sharp fall in tourism revenues following Fiji's military coup in 1988. Its Trade and Investments Board has tried to entice Australian and New Zealand companies to set up factories with a special offer intended to undercut Fiji's Asian neighbors. In so doing, it is hoped, Fijian women's sewing will bandaid over the problems caused by a plantation economy, ethnic strife and militarization.

The international politics of garments stretches from the women at their sewing machines stitching polyester sleeves to the men in the board rooms and ministerial offices drafting memos on investments. It is impossible to make sense of the actions and beliefs of one without being curious about the actions and assumptions of the others. And, increasingly, the board rooms and ministerial offices have resonated with bankers voices. Bankers need to make loans. Bankers need to assess risks. Bankers need to collect on their loans. In the last two decades American, European and Japanese bankers have made high-risk, high-interest loans to Third World governments. For risk-taking has been at the core of the masculinized conception of banking. Just as travel to exotic regions was once imagined to be a risky and therefore peculiarly masculine form of adventure, so today risk-taking is thought by many financiers to be integral to doing competitive international business. The value assigned to risk-taking, furthermore, has become even greater since the 'Big Bang' in 1987—governments' deregulation of banking. 'Big Bang' reforms made a distinctly American, masculinized style of banking more popular in

Are My Hands Clean? (3:03)

I wear garments touched by hands from all over the
world
35% cotton, 65% polyester, the journey begins in
Central America
In the cotton fields of El Salvador
In a province soaked in blood, pesticide-sprayed
workers toil in a broiling sun
Pulling cotton for two dollars a day

Then we move on up to another rung—Cargill
A top forty trading conglomerate, takes the cotton
thru
the Panama Canal
Up the Eastern seaboard, coming to the U.S. of A.
for
the first time

In South Carolina
At the Burlington mills
Joins a shipment of polyester filament courtesy of the
New Jersey petro-chemical mills of Dupont

Dupont strands of filament begin in the South
American country of Venezuela
Where oil riggers bring up oil from the earth for six
dollars a day
Then Exxon, largest oil company in the world
Upgrades the product in the country of Trinidad and
Tobago
Then back into the Caribbean and Atlantic Seas
To the factories of Dupont
On the way to the Burlington mills

Britain, France, West Germany and Japan. This masculinized style has helped sustain cooperative relations between otherwise fiercely competitive male bankers. It has also helped keep women on the margins of the financial world, providing crucial support services but only occasionally gaining promotions that give them the chance to make policy decisions. By 1982, after a decade of rapid expansion and computer revolution in the finance industry, women comprised 57 per cent of all banking employees in Britain. Yet at the managerial level, 90 per cent of all posts were filled by men. Only 5 per cent of the thousands of British women working for local and multinational banks hold policy-making posts. Likewise, women are barely visible when the major banking countries, the Group of Ten, gather to resolve problems of trade imbalances and international debt.

In South Carolina
To meet the cotton from the blood-soaked fields of El
Salvadore

In South Carolina
Burlington factories hum with the business of weaving
oil and cotton into miles of fabric for Sears
Who takes this bounty back into the Caribbean Sea
Headed for Haiti this time
May she be one day soon free

Far from the Port-au-Prince palace
Third world women toil doing piece work to Sears
specifications
For three dollars a day my sisters make my blouse
It leaves the third world for the last time . . .
Coming back into the sea to be sealed in plastic for
me
This third world sister
And I go to the Sears department store where I buy
my
blouse
On sale for 20% discount

Are my hands clean?

Composed for Winterfest, Institute of Policy Studies.
The lyrics are based on an article by Institule fellow John Cavanagh, "The Journey of the Blouse: A Global Assembly."
Lyrics and music by Bernice Johnson Reagon. Songtalk Publishing Co. © 1985

This sort of masculinized international banking has been politically costly. It has destabilized more governmental regimes than all the world's terrorists combined. Most Third World countries scarcely have the currency to keep up with the astronomical interest payments due to their foreign creditors, much less to repay the principal. But Japanese, British, American and other large lenders and their governments fear that global default would topple the international political economy so carefully constructed in the years following World War II. So lenders and their allies, who include their own governments and the International Monetary Fund (in which the US and Japanese governments now wield the most votes), are trying to make the debtor countries make good their mammoth debts. The most popular formula pressed on debtor governments combines cuts in government expenditure on 'non-productive' public services with an expansion of exports.

The centerpiece of the bankers' export strategy has been the 'Export Processing Zone'. Indebted governments set aside territory specifically for factories producing goods for the international market. Governments lure overseas companies to move their plants to these EPZs by offering them sewers, electricity, ports, runways, tax holidays and police protection. Most attractive of all is the governments' offer of cheap labor. Women's labor has been the easiest to cheapen, so it shouldn't be surprising that in most Export Processing Zones at least 70 per cent of the workers are women, especially young women. The eighteen-year-old woman at the sewing machine—or electronics assembly line or food-processing plant—Panama's Colon Export Processing Zone has become the essential though unequal partner of the banker in his glass and chrome office in London or Chicago. The risk-taking banker needs the conscientious seamstress to hold his world together. The politician and his technocratic advisor need the seamstress to keep the banker and his home government pacified. If the seamstress rebels, if she rethinks what it means to be a woman who sews for a living, her country may turn up on the list of 'unstable regimes' now kept by politically sensitive bankers.

Making Women's Labor Cheap

It has become commonplace to speak of 'cheap women's labor'. The phrase is used in public discussions as if cheapness were somehow inherent in women's work. In reality women's work is only as unrewarded or as low-paid as it is made to be.

The international economy works the way it does, and has done for the last two centuries, in part because of the decisions which have cheapened the value of women's work. These decisions have first feminized certain home and workplace tasks—turning them into 'women's work'—and then rationalized the devaluation of that work. Without laws and cultural presumptions about sexuality, marriage and feminine respectability these transformations wouldn't have been possible.

Organizing factory jobs, designing machinery and factory rules to keep women productive and feminine—these were crucial strategies in Europe's industrial growth. Industrialized textile production and garment-making were central to Britain's global power. Both industries feminized labor in order to make it profitable and internationally competitive. Other countries learned the British lesson in order to compete in the emerging global political economy and to stave off foreign control. The making of the 'mill girl' proved crucial. American textile investors travelled from Boston to England to learn the formula in the early decades of the nineteenth century. Japanese entrepreneurs, backed by their government's Meiji reforms to resist Western colonization, also chose young rural women as their first industrial workers. In industrializing Tsarist Russia, owners of new textile factories steadily increased the proportion of women workers, with government approvals. In the pre-World War I period gendered formulas for factory-fueled capitalism seemed to be traded as energetically as railroad stocks. Neither war nor revolution has done much to transform the feminizing strategies used by both capitalist and socialist garment-factory managers. In the Soviet Union, which has undergone a radical reordering of its political system as well as Draconian industrialism, women in 1970 still compmrised 93 per cent of all sewing-machine operators.

Feminization, however, has never been as easy as later historians, through their own lack of curiosity, make it seem. Textile and garment workers frequently shrugged off, even laughed derisively at their employers' efforts to lecture to them on Victorian propriety. Sometimes women went on strike. It took threats, coercion and revised legal structures to bring them back into line. Occasionally the very technology factory owners installed to feminize labor threw feminine respectability into question.

In June 1853 an advertisement appeared in the American *Illustrated News* celebrating Singer's newly patented sewing machine:

> The sewing machine has within the last two years acquired a wide celebrity and established its character as one of the most efficient labour-saving instruments ever introduced to public notice . . .
>
> We must not forget to call attention to the fact that this instrument is peculiarly calculated for female operatives. They should never allow its use to be monopolized by men.

The sewing machine was praised by feminists. It drew crowds when it was demonstrated at the 1851 Exposition in London and at the 1855 Exposition in Paris. Thomas Cook's guided tourists were among the throngs who heard the sewing machine being heralded as woman's liberator. It symbolized progress: technology was a liberator of women and men. Countries whose women had access to sewing machines could congratulate themselves on their women's freedom from the sort of physical toil that characterized the benighted societies crowded at the bottom of the global ladder.

While women were encouraged to see the sewing machine as a home appliance, entrepreneurs were being urged to purchase the machines by the dozen for women who would work outside the home in factories. The sewing machine allowed company owners to break down the process of making a dress or a pair of pants into discrete operations and thus impose a rationalized factory system on the seamstresses: each woman would sew only a small part of the garment—a sleeve, a tuck, a back pocket, it also allowed owners to pay their employees by the piece, rather than by the hour or by an entire finished product. The piece-rates increased competitiveness between women workers as well as extending a factory manager's control over the entire production process.

None the less, the sewing machine had its detractors. In French towns large numbers of women were employed to work sewing machines by the 1860s and many complained of fatigue and ill health. Eugène Guibout, a Parisian physician, reported to the Société Médicale des Hospitaux in 1866 that he believed that

> the extended use of the machine produced extensive vaginal discharges, sometimes haemorrhages, and extreme genital excitement, due to rubbing of the thighs during operation of the double pedal mechanism that then powered the machines used in industrial production.

The debate spilled over to Germany and Italy. Some male scientists were less alarmed than Dr. Guibout, but they, too, raised their eyebrows at the potentially masturbatory effects of the bi-pedal sewing machine. There was palpable relief in international medical circles when a single-pedal machine was introduced. Still, it wasn't until the advent of the electrically powered sewing machine in the next century that the controversy over the sewing machine's sexual consequences was laid to rest.

Garment-company managers have drawn on various patriarchal assumptions to help keep wages and benefits, low in their factories. First, they have defined sewing as something that girls and women do 'naturally' or 'traditionally'. An operation that a person does 'naturally' is not a 'skill', for a skill is something one has to be trained to do, for which one should then be rewarded. Such thinking may be convenient and save money, but is it accurate? Many a schoolgirl has struggled through a home economics class trying to make the required skirt or apron without much success. One garment-factory manager explained that he preferred to hire young Filipino women who *didn't* know how to sew, so that 'we don't have to undo the bad habits they've learned'. But the myth of women as natural sewers persists and is used to deflate women garment workers' actual skills.

Second, a women's labor can be kept cheap if those jobs which even the factory managers acknowledge are 'skilled' can be reserved for men. Levis Jeans in Manila is remarkably like garment factories in New York, Manchester, Toronto, Moscow or Colombo: women are the sewing-machinists; men are the cutters and the pressers. Men also are selected to run specialized machines, like the zipper inserters. Cutting, pressing and zippering are all paid more than sewing. The managerial rationale for this sexual division of labor is that cutting, pressing and running specialized machinery require physical strength that only men have. This argument ignores the options available when technology is designed, the physical demands made on women by housework and farming, and the fact that some men are weaker than some women.

Third, managers justify paying women workers less by imagining that women are merely secondary wage earners in their families. They assume that men—as fathers and husbands—are the 'breadwinners'. This presumption prevails not just in popular thinking but in the statistical reports of bodies such as the national census bureau, the World Bank, and development agencies. Such reports are a boon to garment-factory managers. They make the practice of paying their women workers *as if* they were being supported at home by a man seem up-to-date and sophisticated. Thus the international garment industry, on which so many governments rely for foreign currency, is deeply dependent on ideas about the family and marriage.

Even those managers who prefer to hire single women—as many do—use the marriage factor to suppress wages. They can presume that the single woman is just earning 'pin money' for herself because she has a wage-earning father who supports her and her mother. Or they can claim that the single woman is not a 'serious' member of the laborforce because she intends to work until she finds a husband and 'settles down', supported by him. Therefore, she does not need to be paid as if she were a career worker; when she is sewing sleeves for the Fang Brothers or a back pocket for Levis she is just going through 'a phase'.

If their own parents, teachers and religious leaders encourage them to think of their 'real' vocation—what will bring them community respect, personal gratification and moral reward—as being a wife and a mother, then it is not surprising that the young women themselves find it difficult to question their employers' contention that they don't deserve better pay because they are 'only working until they marry'. Local community expectations thus combine with World Bank statistical practices to strengthen the garment-factory manager's cost-cutting hand. Take away or transform either and it might prove far more difficult for managers in garment manufacturing and other light industries to use 'cheap women's labor' to ensure international competitiveness.

At the turn of the century many Jewish and Italian women working in New York City's then thriving garment factories endured the low pay, lint dust, eye strain and six-day working week dreaming of marriage and of becoming housewives. It was a dream that made their parents and their employers comfortable.' It was a dream that frustrated their coworkers who wanted them to organize, to protest, to strike. Even today, marriage is not just about heterosexual conformity. It is an escape. A husband, many women workers hope, will be a way out of patriarchal factory toil.

> It's not easy to teach us union.
> Garment girls shift like sand, start
> too young in the trade, wait for
>
> Prince Charming to take em away . . .

Feminist researchers in Sri Lanka interviewed women working for garment and electronics companies in the government-supported Export Processing Zone outside Colombo. Workers told them that they saw their jobs as lasting only a few years; they hoped they would be 'phase jobs', 'not careers. They also realized that their employers preferred single women. Because so many women in the Export Processing Zone didn't see themselves as 'workers', but as daughters, prospective wives and members of their community, feminists trying to build support around work issues had to radically rethink what a 'work issue' was. They discovered that women working in the factories felt intimidated by men who harassed them as they traveled to and from the Export Processing Zone. This wasn't the sort of issue that an orthodox union would take seriously, but it was significant for these young women workers. Working together, the activists outside the factories and the women employees built a coalition of village elders, religious groups and the women themselves to reduce the harassment. Had they confined their organizing to the factory floor, they would have been subject to dismissal, failed to engage many of the women workers and lost the chance to mobilize the groups with whom the women workers still chiefly identified.

To make women's labor cheap garment-factory managers also find it useful to imagine marriage an inevitable and lasting state for adult women. If factory managers do have to hire married women, and if governments have to acknowledge that balance of trade depends on women over twenty being part of the laborforce, then both are most comfortable assuming that, as a wife, a woman will be economically dependent on a man and put her wifely and motherly roles before any other.

This hardly matches contemporary reality. Today one third of the world's households are headed by women. The single mother—the woman responsible for supporting herself and at least one child—is not simply a phenomenon of affluent societies. In Kenya as well as in Denmark over 30 per cent of households are headed by women. The same is true in Barbados, Vietnam, Zimbabwe, Nicaragua, Jamaica and Lesotho.

Finally, women's labor is made cheap by preventing women from organizing. This tactic rarely succeeds unless managers have assistance from government officials and women workers' male relatives. Fathers, brothers and husbands of women workers sometimes try to keep them from becoming politically involved because it might jeopardize the income they bring into the family. They also often object because political activity seems to violate codes of feminine respectability by involving women in public conflict, conflict with men of authority. Male workmates are not always supportive, seeing some of the women's demands (for protection against sexual harassment, for maternity leave) as irrelevant to 'serious' trade-union activity. Government officials have done their part to keep women's labor cheap by passing laws banning unions or authorizing only unions friendly to management. On occasion also they have called out their police to support managers. This can create a hostile confrontation that seriously jeopardizes a woman's reputation.

Thus keeping women's labor cheap requires vigilance and daily effort. That effort is an integral part of what is called 'international political economy'. Factory managers alone cannot keep women's labor cheap: it takes a combination of allies and ideas—about skills, marriage, feminine respectability, fashion. The politics of the international garment industry are sustained by relationships inside the home, in the community, in and between governments, as well as on the factory floor.

'The Light Industry Girls'

Those most eager to pay as little as possible for human labor are those who run firms that are most dependent on human labor to produce their product. The more a firm can design its production system to minimize that dependence, the less preoccupied its managers will be about cutting labor costs. Nowadays the kinds of industries that are most labor-intensive are 'light industries'. Light industries and heavy industries differ in the mix of capital equipment—furnaces, turbines, computers, robots, looms, sewing machines—and human labor each needs to turn out a saleable product.

Because light industries are more labor-intensive and less reliant on large infusions of capital, they are also less likely to be concentrated in the hands of a few owners. There are many more players in any light-industry market. This makes light industries more decentralized and more competitive.

This sounds reassuringly democratic and efficient. But for the workers—sewing polyester suits for Al Paris or Liz Claiborne jeans for the Fang Brothers—light industry's decentralized competitiveness may not be benign. For the very intensity of the competition only heightens the determination of owners and managers to keep labor costs as low as possible. Cutting labor costs is seen as one of the chief strategies for beating

Light Industries	Heavy Industries
Textiles	Steel
Garments	Automobiles (including tanks and armored vehicles)
pood processing	Chemicals and petrochemicals
Cigarettes	Aircraft and aerospace
Joys	Shipbuilding
Shoes	Machinery
Electronics	
Data entry (insurance data, airline reservations, etc.)	

one's rivals. And the industry's decentralization makes it hard for even a committed government to implement worker safety laws effectively. It is much easier to hide an illegal dress factory than to conceal an illegal automobile plant.

'Light industries' have been most feminized, while 'heavy industries' have been most masculinized. Thus how light and heavy industries relate to each other politically may depend in part on the relative influence possessed by women and men in a country. If women are seen mainly as mothers, part-time employees and unskilled workers, if they do not have control over the unions they are members of or have no unions at all, if they are not considered serious allies or opponents by men in government I ministries or political parties, then it will be especially difficult for light industry to hold its own in politics in a way that benefits not only the managers but also the workers. Put another way, the power that men working in mining, aerospace, automobile, steel or petrochemical industries can bring to bear on their country's political system not only privileges heavy industry, it serves to undercut women bunched together in light industry.

This sexual division of labor has had the effect of further masculinizing national and international politics. For government officials in most countries have come to think of 'heavy industries' as the very stuff of national power. Having its own steel industry is held as proof that a country has 'graduated', *arrived*.

While officials in South Korea, Brazil, and other countries that have developed masculinized heavy industries express pride in their elevated international status, their counterparts in 'mature' countries such as the United States, Britain and France feel as though they are losing their grip on world politics because of the decline of their steel and automobile companies. When political commentators accord the fortunes of their countries' steel, aircraft or automobile companies the seriousness reserved for issues of 'national security', they are further entrenching the masculinization of international politics.

First the Japanese and more recently the South Korean economies have 'graduated' from garments to steel. That is, they have moved up from feminized industries to masculinized industries. Hosting the Olympics has become the world's graduation present.

As South Korean government officials were bidding to have their country chosen as the site of the 1988 Olympics, some commentators were talking about the 'two Koreas'. They didn't mean North and South. They were referring to the South Korea of large, capitalized heavy industries and the South Korea of the back-alley garment workshop. In 1988 women made up an estimated two thirds of workers in South Korea's world-famous export-oriented factories. They were working more hours per week than their male counterparts and being paid on average one third less, producing clothes, electronics, shoes and data services—industries that enabled South Korean businessmen to accumulate enough capital to launch their own companies. Those Korean women factory workers who went on strike in the 1980s to bring down the authoritarian military government were protesting against both the myth of the successful South Korea and the price that South Korean factory women were expected to pay to sustain that myth.

> Past the rows of charred sewing machines, amid the smoke-blackened piles of timber and cinder, lie the keepsakes of the women who worked and died here. These were among the remains of the Green Hill Textile Company: a snapshot of a young girl smiling in a field of red flowers, a magazine clipping of a singer, a letter from a young man in the army.

In March 1988 a fire tore through the Green Hill Textile Company's small factory, squeezed between a billiard parlor, a restaurant and a church in a dormitory community outside Seoul. Lee Pung Won, the 44-year-old owner, was considered a good employer, who treated his workers 'more like a family'. Most of his employees were young single women who had come from the countryside to the city in hope of finding a waged job. They were paid approximately $1.75 per hour by Lee Pung Won, who expected them to work fifty-seven hours a week. In this, their lives were similar to those of other Korean women working in nearby factories producing shoes and televisions for export. When the factory received a big order, as often happened in the seasonal garment trade, their employer expected the women to work even longer hours:

> The fire broke out in late March as twenty-eight young textile workers lay sleeping in the factory that doubled as their dormitory in this suburb of Seoul. With the stairways locked and heaped with sweaters the women had knit that day, only a few escaped. Twenty-two workers died.

Making it as a 'world class' player has come with a gendered price tag.

An Earthquake Is Only the Beginning

At 7:19 on the morning of September 19 1985, Mexico City experienced one of North America's worst earthquakes. It left thousands of people homeless, modern office buildings cracked and useless and Mexico's ruling Institutionalized Revolutionary Party (the PRI) badly shaken. For the seamstresses who worked in the factories clustered in the neighborhood of San Antonio Abad, the earthquake marked a political and personal turning point. An estimated 800 small garment factories in Mexico City were destroyed that morning, killing over 1,000 garment workers and leaving another 40,000 without jobs.

Women who were just arriving at work as the quake shook Mexico City stood looking at the rubble that an hour before had been their source of livelihood. It was a Thursday, payday. Many of them were single mothers and their families depended on their wages. But their first thought was of those women, already at work at 7: a.m., who were trapped inside the flattened buildings. Managers usually kept windows closed and doors locked to stop women from taking work breaks or stealing materials, so few of their coworkers inside had had any chance of escaping. Some buildings held up to fifty different garment companies, several per floor. The floors and cement pillars on which they rested could hardly have been expected to hold the weight of industrial sewing machines and tons of fabric, though no government inspector had complained. Most companies were small subcontractors, usually backed by foreign money. Though not as well-known as the more visible 'maquiladoras' strung along the US—Mexican border, these firms were part of the Mexican government's policy of using tourism and light-industry exports to pay off its spiraling led and joint-venture factories such as those in San Antonio Abad had displaced tourism as the country's second largest source of foreign exchange.

Women outside the collapsed building tried to climb over the debris to rescue their coworkers trapped inside. Hastily mobilized government soldiers told them to get back and cordoned off the building. Within a day the company owners arrived, accompanied by the army. Equipped with cranes, soldiers began to pull away piles of fallen cement so that owners' could retrieve their machinery. Employees still standing in the sun on the other side of the ropes watched with mounting horror and indignation as their bosses and the soldiers chose to rescue sewing machines before women.

At this point something new began to happen. Mexican women who worked in garment factories had tried to organize and strike before. But each time they had been defeated. Employers fired the 'troublemakers', while adopting a fatherly attitude toward those women who accepted the terms of work. Many women needed their meager paychecks to support their children especially as the indebted Mexican government, which had counted on oil to solve the country's problems, was now cutting food subsidies and devaluing the peso to meet foreign bankers' demands. Even those women who were willing to risk being fired had to face male partners who resented their staying out after work to attend meetings. On top of these obstacles, left-wing opposition parties paid scant attention to women working in small sweatshops, preferring to court the more politically influential male oil workers. Small groups of Mexican feminists were active, but they were mostly middle-class and scarcely understood the needs of poor women with only primary-school education. Previously these obstacles had prevented independent women workers organizing. But the earthquake made blatantly clear what hesitant women workers had once been able to overlook: behind a façade of paternalism, employers and their government allied in valuing machines over the women who worked and voted for them.

Becoming more and more angry at what they saw, women at the scene of the disaster began to talk to each other about what this meant. Some women spontaneously moved to block the trucks that were about to carry off the owners' precious machines. Other women confronted the owners. They wanted their paychecks. They wanted to be compensated for the days of lost work. When the owners shrugged their shoulders and claimed they had no money, women began to shout: 'Compensation! Compensation.' Several dozen women decided that they would have to stay at the site over night in order to prevent the army trucks from moving and thus the owners from leaving the scene of death and destruction without fulfilling their legal responsibilities. Staying over night meant having to stay away from male partners and children who expected them at home.

At about this time, middle-class women from feminist groups in Mexico City—some affiliated with political parties and some independent—began to hear of the garment workers' distress and came to several building sites to offer assistance. It wasn't immediately clear to the seamstresses, however, just what their priorities should be. Looking back afterward, some remembered that the feminists seemed to be urging the women workers to organize a union; political concerns were at the top of their agenda. But should this be the seamstresses' most pressing demand? If they did immediately form a union, especially one not affiliated to the PRI federation, maybe they would risk government reprisal and so alienate their bosses that they would never receive the cash they so desperately needed. Women workers also had to figure out how to respond to the offers of support from suddenly attentive left-wing parties. And what about their compañeros, their male partners: would they feel threatened if women began to take their working conditions so seriously? How could they be persuaded that a woman who stayed out in the evening was being political not unfaithful?

In the months that followed the earthquake garment workers gradually made a number of decisions that matched their own needs and resources. They kept up their road-block and vigil outside the factories until the government pushed the owners to pay compensation for lost wages. They did this in part by embarrassing the president and then leader of the PRI by publicizing the army's role in removing the sewing machines before rescuing trapped women workers. In their public-relations campaign, middle-class feminists proved valuable allies; they had more contacts with the press and helped to raise funds to buy typewriters. Feminists also knew lawyers who could help the seamstresses find their way through the bureaucratic labyrinths of the Ministry of Labor. But women workers remained skeptical of the middle-class women. Too often in the past well-meaning feminists had tried to speak on their behalf, to run meetings and rallies. So they took steps to ensure that whatever organization grew out of the earthquake's aftermath was run by seamstresses on terms that seamstresses themselves found most comfortable and practical.

The union that they created in the autumn of 1985 is the September 19th Garment Workers Union. By 1987 it had gained workers' support and official recognition in twelve factories. It has been difficult, however, to give assistance to women in factories as far away as Juarez or the Yucatan. Bus fares are expensive. The union has remained independent of all political parties and of the PRI federation. Debate over exactly what this independence meant during Mexico's first ever competitive presidential election campaign in 1988 strained bonds of unity inside the union. But such unity was essential given the continuing pressures from outside. The union had managed to gain Ministry of Labor certification in its early days largely because the PRI was running to catch up with the grassroots organizing that spread like wildfire through the neighborhoods in the wake of the earthquake. But once the foreign reporters went home and public attention flagged, the government joined with the garment companies to withdraw official certification. Teenage male thugs were sent to the factories to throw stones at women activists. Some compañeros prohibited their wives and companions from taking part in activities that carried such physical risks.

In reaction to this danger women active in the September 19th Union have worked with middle-class feminists to create links with garment workers, union activists and feminists in the United States. If they could mount letter writing campaigns to the Mexican government, officials might stop their efforts to discredit them to avoid international embarrassment. Making a film and organizing speaking tours to Los Angeles, New York, Chicago and Boston helped the Mexican women trade experiences and lessons with Latina and Chinese-American women garment workers. These trips also enabled September 19th union activists to track down those who were making the decisions in their factories. For instance, the Roberts company, a maker of men's suits, had taken the lead among factory owners in Mexico City in trying to persuade the Ministry of Labor that the union was not operating legally. But who owned Roberts? It is difficult to sit at a machine on the shop floor in San Antonio Abad and figure out who your boss reports to across the border. Women in the United States were able to help union organizers locate the Roberts company's headquarters in Maine. American women were also able to put pressure on the company's U.S. outlets.

The September 19th women spent hours at their newly acquired headquarters in a cement-covered vacant lot across from the ruined factories. They discussed ways to lessen their partners' and their families' resistance to their spending so much time away from home. The union became an all-women organization precisely so that garment workers could bring these questions to their meetings without anyone charging them with being trivial or divisive. There are men in Mexico's garment factories—pressers and cutters—but from the start the seamstresses saw theirs as a women's organization addressing women's needs and remaining accessible to women. At first women felt as though they had to choose either to end their participation in the new union or to leave their male partners. A number of women now serving on the union's executive committee have left their compañeros. The need for such a choice had to be challenged, or it would have severely restricted the union's potential membership and made it hard to gain an audience in factories not yet organized. So members chose to try to make children and partners feel like participants in union activities. Setting up a child-care center at their headquarters was intended to relieve some of the tensions that were mounting between union work, factory work and family responsibilities. More recently, child care has fulfilled another purpose. Union women have invited women active in neighborhood organizations to use the child-care center too. Cooperation between Mexico City's unions and its neighborhood organizers—the majority of them women—is a new phenomenon in Mexican grassroots politics.

Conclusion

A leaner, more competitive world is what leading politicians are prescribing for the 1990s. The prescription goes by several names: restructuring, *perestroika,* the four modernizations. It is providing a new common language for George Bush, Margaret Thatcher, Mikhail Gorbachev, Brian Mulroney, Deng Xiaoping and Sosuke Uno. They and their aides discuss these restructuring policies in terms of high-technology research, managerial flexibility, decentralized productivity. Their discourse has a futuristic ring: traditional national boundaries will mean less data and capital goods are transferred electronically around the globe; teenagers in their Benetton sweaters will grow up with a global consciousness. But to turn this vision into reality government officials are relying on old-fashioned ideas about women.

This seductive 1990s formula needs women from Leningrad to Tokyo to continue to see themselves as mothers, wives and daughters. It is as mothers that Canadian or Italian women will be grateful for the introduction of more and more home-based jobs, jobs that allow managers and government planners to reduce costly overhead expenditures. It is as wives that American and Panamanian women will be willing to take the lower-paid assembly jobs in high- and low-tech light industry, permitting managers and government officials to compete with foreign rivals. It is as daughters that Soviet and Japanese women will accept the increasingly common part-time jobs which enable officials to fine-tune the economy.

Yet this Brave New Old-Fashioned World is being planned without taking account of many women's mounting ambivalence about the meaning of marriage, motherhood and familial responsibility. It ignores the significance of single mothers and women as family breadwinners throughout the world. It dismisses many women's sophisticated organizational skills. Its proponents are remarkably uncurious about the changing dynamics within households.

To say this is not to suggest that all women everywhere are willing to see other women as allies rather than as competitors or strangers. Nor is it to imply that many women's relationships to male supervisors, husbands and fathers are not problematic. But as we enter the next decade, women as consumers and producers are not simply modern versions of Victorian domestic angels and obedient mill girls. And even those mythologized pioneers of the Industrial Revolution were not as passive as they are often made out to be.

The Mexican garment workers' experience suggests several things. First, despite their striking similarities, garment and other light-industry factories use the women who make up the majority of their workers in different ways., There is no Universal Garment Factory. Some factories are in capital cities, while others are far from the seats of power. Being in the capital does not guarantee influence for the women workers, since they may be employed by the smallest, most marginalized subcontracting factories, neglected by political activists, academics and reporters. But the location did help the Mexico City seamstresses to gain the resources to challenge the government directly when other conditions were on their side. Working for a company in an Export Processing Zone also has mixed implications. Local governments courting investment have designed the EPZs so that workers can be easily controlled. But those conditions can give women a sense of their shared interests. And, as women in the Philippines and Sri Lanka have shown, once they begin to organize, the 'very intensity of the EPZ experience can generate activism. Then there are the thousands of women who don't do their industrial sewing in a factory at all. In the name of post-modern managerial flexibility, they are hired by subcontractors to work in their own homes. For home workers, recognizing unfair practices and organizing to challenge them may be especially difficult.

The September 19th Union's story also warns us not to collapse all 'women in Third World countries into a single homogeneous category. There is no such thing as '*the* Third World woman'. Third World peasant women may feel they have little in common with women working in foreign-owned urban factories. Middle-class women, even if they are feminists and want to support factory women in Third World societies, often speak a political language that is unfamiliar, even alienating to the very women they wish to help. And of course, as in industrialized countries, there are those Third World women, admittedly a minority, who are so comfortable with their class and racial privileges that they feel quite threatened when garment workers challenge established ideas about respectable feminine behavior *and* their government's scheme to pay off foreign bankers.

Feminization is being publicly rationalized in terms that appeal to a woman's desire to contribute to her nation, and that appear sympathetic to the double-burdened worker-mother. In the process, the politics of micro-chips and information are becoming as dependent on a particular politics of marriage and femininity as the politics of blouses and jeans were before them. For women assembling micro-chips for state-of-the-art computers and lethal weaponry or entering data for publishers and hospitals, the technology has changed, but. the ideology on which it rests has not. So, as the Mexican garment workers have demonstrated, success in altering managerial and political policies will require taking up sensitive questions about home life, issues that male union leaders and nationalist intellectuals have dismissed as divisive or trivial.

What if . . . What if women continue to change their ideas about husbands as breadwinners? What if increasing numbers of women change their ideas about what a good mother does with her evenings? What if women in more and more countries change their ideas about what constitutes a 'skill'? If any of these ideas could be changed permanently, men in their board rooms, government ministries and union halls would have to revise their own ways of confronting the challenges of the next decade.

Ursula K. Le Guin was a prolific American author of novels, poetry, children's books, essays, and short stories, mostly in fantasy and science fiction genres. She has received numerous awards, including the Library of Congress Living Legends Award for significant contributions to America's cultural heritage. A Phi Beta Kappa graduate of Radcliffe with a masters from Columbia University, Le Guin explores concepts from sociology, anthropology, and political science through Taoist, anarchist, and feminist perspectives. This selection, "The Ones Who Walk Away from Omelas," won a Hugo Award for best short story in 1974. Why would Le Guin explore social justice in this fable-like style? What does the child represent in her extended metaphor? Is there evidence that the characters in this story engage in reflection, analysis, and judgment before taking action? What do you think it means to walk away from Omelas?

The Ones Who Walk Away from Omelas

Ursula K. Le Guin

With a clamor of bells that set the swallows soaring, the Festival of Summer came to the City of Omelas, bright-towered by the sea. The rigging of the boats in harbor sparkled with flags. In the streets between houses and red roofs and painted walls, between old moss-grown gardens and under avenues of trees, past great parks and public buildings, processions moved. Some were decrous: old people in long stiff robes of mauve and grey, grave master workmen, quiet, merry women carrying their babies and chatting as they walked. In other streets the music beat faster, a shimmering of gong and tambourine, and the people went dancing, the procession was a dance. Children dodged in and out, their high calls rising like the swallows' crossing flights over the music and the singing. All the processions wound towards the north side of the city, where on the great water-meadow called the Green Fields boys and girls, naked in the bright air, with mud-stained feet and ankles and long, lithe arms, exercised their restive horses before the race. The horses wore no gear at all but a halter without bit. Their manes were braided with streamers of silver, gold, and green. They flared their nostrils and pranced and boasted to one another; they were vastly excited, the horse being the only animal who has adopted our ceremonies as his own. Far off to the north and west the mountains stood up half encircling Omelas on her bay. The air of morning was so clear that the snow still crowning the Eighteen Peaks burned with white-gold fire across the miles of sunlit air, under the dark blue of the sky. There was just enough wind to make the banners that marked the racecourse snap and flutter now and then. In the silence of the broad green meadows one could hear the music winding through the city streets, farther and nearer and ever approaching, a cheerful faint sweetness of the air that from time to time trembled and gathered together and broke out into the great joyous clanging of the bells.

Joyous! How is one to tell about joy? How describe the citizens of Omelas?

They were not simple folk, you see, though they were happy. But we do not say the words of cheer much any more. All smiles have become archaic. Given a description such as this one tends to make certain assumptions. Given a description such as this one tends to look next for the King, mounted on a splendid stallion and surrounded by his noble knights, or perhaps in a golden litter borne by great-muscled slaves. But there was no king. They did not use swords, or keep slaves. They were not barbarians. I do not know the rules and laws of their society, but I suspect that they were singularly few. As they did without monarchy and slavery, so they also got on without the stock exchange, the advertisement, the secret police, and the bomb. Yet I repeat that these were not simple folk, not dulcet shepherds, noble savages, bland utopians. They were not less complex than us. The trouble is that we have a bad habit, encouraged by pedants and sophisticates, of considering happiness as something rather stupid. Only pain is intellectual, only evil interesting. This is the treason of the artist: a refusal to admit the banality of evil and the terrible boredom of pain. If you can't lick 'em, join 'em. If it hurts, repeat it. But to praise despair is to condemn delight, to embrace violence is to lose hold of everything else. We have almost lost hold; we can no longer describe a happy man, nor make any celebration of joy. How can I tell you about the people of Omelas? They were not naïve and happy children—though their children were, in fact, happy. They were mature, intelligent, passionate adults whose lives were not wretched. O miracle! but I wish I could describe it better. I wish I could convince you. Omelas sounds in my words like a city in a fairy tale, long ago and far away, once upon a time. Perhaps it would be best if you imagined it as your own fancy bids, assuming it will rise to the occasion, for certainly I cannot suit you all. For instance, how about technology? I think that there would be no cars or helicopters in and above the streets; this follows from the fact that the people of Omelas are happy people. Happiness is based on a just discrimination of what is necessary, what is neither necessary nor destructive, and what is destructive. In the middle category, however—that of the unnecessary but undestructive, that of comfort, luxury, exuberance, etc.—they could perfectly well have central heating, subway trains, washing machines, and all kinds of marvelous devices not yet invented here, floating light-sources, fuelless power, a cure for the common cold. Or they could have none of that; it doesn't matter. As you like it. I incline to think that people from towns up and down the coast have been coming to Omelas during the last days before the Festival on very fast little trains and double-decked trams, and that the train station of Omelas is actually the handsomest building in town, though plainer than the magnificent Farmers' Market. But even granted trains, I fear that Omelas so far strikes some of you as goody-goody. Smiles, bells, parades, horses, bleh. If so,please add an orgy. If an orgy would help, don't hesitate. Let us not, however, have temples from which issue beautiful nude priests and priestesses already half in ecstasy and ready to copulate with any man or woman, lover or stranger, who desires union with the deep godhead of the blood, although that was my first idea. But really it would be better not to have any temples in Omelas—at least, not manned temples. Religion yes, clergy no. Surely the beautiful nudes can just wander about, offering themselves like divine soufflés to the hunger of the needy and the rapture of the flesh. Let them join the processions. Let tambourines be struck above the copulations, and the glory of desire be proclaimed upon the gongs, and (a not unimportant point) let the offspring of these delightful rituals be beloved and looked after by all. One thing I know there is none of in Omelas is guilt. But what else should there be? I thought at first there were no drugs, but that is puritanical. For those who like it, the faint insistent sweetness of *drooz* may perfume the ways of the city, *drooz* which first brings a great lightness and brilliance to the mind and limbs, and then after some hours a dreamy languor, and wonderful visions at last of the very arcana and inmost secrets of the Universe, as well as exciting the pleasure of sex beyond belief; and it is not habit-forming. For more modest tastes I think there ought to be beer. What else, what else belongs in the joyous city? The sense of victory, surely, the celebration of courage. But as we did without clergy, let us do without soldiers. The joy built upon successful slaughter is not the right kind of joy; it will not do; it is fearful and it is trivial. A boundless and generous contentment, a magnanimous triumph felt not against some outer enemy but in communion with the finest and fairest in the souls of all men everywhere and the splendor of the world's summer: this is what swells the hearts of the people of Omelas, and the victory they celebrate is that of life. I really don't think many of them need to take *drooz*.

Most of the processions have reached the Green Fields by now. A marvelous smell of cooking goes forth from the red and blue tents of the provisioners. The faces of small children are amiably sticky; in the benign gray beard of a man a couple of crumbs of rich pastry are entangled. The youths and girls have mounted their horses and are beginning to group around the starting line of the course. An old woman, small, fat, and laughing, is passing out flowers from a basket, and tall young men wear her flowers in their shining hair. A child of nine or ten sits at the edge of the crowd, alone, playing on a wooden flute. People pause to listen, and they smile, but they do not speak to him, for he never ceases playing and never sees them, his dark eyes wholly rapt in the sweet, thin magic of the tune.

He finishes, and slowly lowers his hands holding the wooden flute.

As if that little private silence were the signal, all at once a trumpet sounds from the pavilion near the starting line: imperious, melancholy, piercing. The horses rear on their slender legs, and some of them neigh in answer. Sober-faced, the young riders stroke the horses' necks and soothe them, whispering, "Quiet, quiet, there my beauty, my hope . . . ." They begin to form in rank along the starting line. The crowds along the racecourse are like a field of grass and flowers in the wind. The Festival of Summer has begun.

Do you believe? Do you accept the festival, the city, the joy? No? Then let me describe one more thing.

In a basement under one of the beautiful public buildings of Omelas, or perhaps in the cellar of one of its spacious private homes, there is a room. It has one locked door, and no window. A little light seeps in dustily between cracks in the boards, secondhand from a cobwebbed window somewhere across the cellar. In one corner of the little room a couple of mops, with stiff, clotted, foul-smelling heads, stand near a rusty bucket. The floor is dirt, a little damp to the touch, as cellar dirt usually is. The room is about three paces long and two wide: a mere broom closet or disused tool room. In the room a child is sitting. It could be a boy or a girl. It looks about six, but actually is nearly ten. It is feeble-minded. Perhaps it was born defective, or perhaps it has become imbecile through fear, malnutrition, and neglect. It picks its nose and occasionally fumbles vaguely with its toes or genitals, as it sits hunched in the corner farthest from the bucket and the two mops. It is afraid of the mops. It find them horrible. It shuts its eyes, but it knows the mops are still standing there; and the door is locked; and nobody will come. The door is always locked; and nobody ever comes, except that sometimes—the child has no understanding of time or interval—sometimes the door rattles terribly and opens, and a person, or several people, are there. One of them may come in and kick the child to make it stand up. The others never come close, but peer in at it with frightened, disgusted eyes. The food bowl and the water jug are hastily filled, the door is locked, the eyes disappear. The people at the door never say anything, but the child, who has not always lived in the tool room, and can remember sunlight and its mother's voice, sometimes speaks. "I will be good," it says. "Please let me out. I will be good!" They never answer. The child used to scream for help at night, and cry a good deal, but now it only makes a kind of whining "eh-haa, eh-haa" and it speaks less and less often. It is so thin there are no calves to its legs; its belly protrudes; it lives on a half-bowl of corn meal and grease a day. It is naked. Its buttocks and thighs are a mass of festered sores, as it sits in its own excrement continually.

They all know it is there, all the people of Omelas. Some of them have come to see it, others are content merely to know it is there. They all know that it has to be there. Some of them understand why, and some do not, but they all understand that their happiness, the beauty of their city, the tenderness of their friendships, the health of their children, the wisdom of their scholars, the skill of their makers, even the abundance of their harvest and the kindly weathers of their skies, depend wholly on this child's abominable misery.

This is usually explained to children when they are between eight and twelve, whenever they seem capable of understanding; and most of those who come to see the child are young people, though often enough an adult comes, or comes back, to see the child. No matter how well the matter has been explained to them, these young spectators are always shocked and sickened at the sight. They feel disgust, which they had thought themselves superior to. They feel anger, outrage, impotence, despite all the explanations. They would like to do something for the child. But there is nothing they can do. If the child were brought up into the sunlight out of that vile place, if it were cleaned and fed and comforted, that would be a good thing, indeed; but if it were done, in that day and hour all the prosperity and beauty and delight of Omelas would wither and be destroyed. Those are the terms. To exchange all the goodness and grace of every life in Omelas for that single, small improvement: to throw away the happiness of thousands for the chance of the happiness of one: that would be to let guilt within the walls indeed.

The terms are strict and absolute; there may not even be a kind word spoken to the child.

Often the young people go home in tears, or in a tearless rage, when they have seen the child and faced this terrible paradox. They may brood over it for weeks or years. But as time goes on they begin to realize that even if the child could be released, it would not get much good of its freedom: a little vague pleasure of warmth and food, no doubt, but little more. It is too degraded and imbecile to know any real joy. It has been afraid too long ever to be free of fear. Its habits are too uncouth for it to respond to humane treatment. Indeed, after so long it would probably be wretched without walls about it to protect it, and darkness for its eyes, and its own excrement to sit in. Their tears at the bitter injustice dry when they begin to perceive the terrible justice of reality, and to accept it. Yet it is their tears and anger, the trying of their generosity and the acceptance of their helplessness, which are perhaps the true source of the splendor of their lives. Theirs is no vapid, irresponsible happiness. They know that they, like the child, are not free. They know compassion. It is the existence of the child, and their knowledge of its existence, that makes possible the nobility of their architecture, the poignancy of their music, the profundity of their science. It is because of the child that they are so gentle with children. They know that if the wretched one were not there snivelling in the dark, the other one, the flute-player, could make no joyful music as the young riders line up in their beauty for the race in the sunlight of the first morning of summer.

Now do you believe in them? Are they not more credible? But there is one more thing to tell, and this is quite incredible.

At times one of the adolescent girls or boys who go to see the child does not go home to weep or rage, does not, in fact, go home at all. Sometimes also a man or woman much older falls silent for a day or two, and then leaves home. These people go out into the street, and walk down the street alone. They keep walking, and walk straight out of the city of Omelas, through the beautiful gates. They keep walking across the farmlands of Omelas. Each one goes alone, youth or girl, man or woman. Night falls; the traveler must pass down village streets, between the houses with yellow-lit windows, and on out into the darkness of the fields. Each alone, they go west or north, towards the mountains. They go on. They leave Omelas, they walk ahead into the darkness, and they do not come back. The place they go towards is a place even less imaginable to most of us than the city of happiness. I cannot describe it at all. It is possible that it does not exist. But they seem to know where they are going, the ones who walk away from Omelas.

Ruth Forman is an award-winning African-American poet and the author of We Are the Young Magicians *(1993) (the source of this poem) and* Renaissance *(1997). How does the imagery in this poem symbolize community? What significance do you think poetry plays in describing social injustices?*

Poetry Should Ride the Bus

Ruth Forman

poetry should hopscotch in a polka dot dress
wheel cartwheels
n hold your hand
when you walk past the yellow crackhouse

poetry should wear bright red lipstick
n practice kisses in the mirror
for all the fine young men with fades
shootin craps around the corner

poetry should dress in fine plum linen suits
n not be so educated that it don't stop in
every now n then to sit on the porch
and talk about the comins and goins of the world

poetry should ride the bus
in a fat woman's Safeway bag
between the greens n chicken wings
to be served with Tuesday's dinner

poetry should drop by a sweet potato pie
ask about the grandchildren
n sit through a whole photo album
on a orange plastic covered La-Z-Boy with no place to go

poetry should sing red revolution love songs
that massage your scalp
and bring hope to your blood
when you think you're too old to fight

yeah
poetry should whisper electric blue magic
all the years of your life
never forgettin to look you in the soul
every once in a while
n smile

Mohandas K. Gandhi (1869–1948) was an Indian political activist and spiritual leader who came to be called Mahatma, meaning "Great Soul." Trained as a lawyer in England, he worked in South Africa for civil rights for the Indian population there, and then in his homeland to end the British colonial system. He developed a powerful form of non-violent protest and civil disobedience which came to be called satyagraha. Gandhi explains that his movement initially used the phrase "passive resistance" to describe its methods, but he was uncomfortable with Europeans' understanding of this phrase as connoting weakness, hatred, and the possibility of violence. A newspaper reader suggested satyagraha, *an invented word combining* sat *(truth) and* agraha *(firmness) in the Gujarati language. In these selections Gandhi describes how satyagraha works in practice, a philosophical and spiritual standpoint that later was to influence Dr. Martin Luther King Jr. Gandhi, who was assassinated in 1948, is now called the "Father of India." As you read Gandhi's essay, think about how his movement might be a model for building community. Is a nonviolent approach truly an effective way to achieve social justice?*

from Non-Violent Resistance

Mohandas K. Gandhi

Satyagraha, Civil Disobedience, Passive Resistance, Non-Co-Operation

Satyagraha, then, is literally holding on to Truth and it means, therefore, Truth-force. Truth is soul or spirit. It is, therefore, known as soul-force. It excludes the use of violence because man is not capable of knowing the absolute truth and, therefore, not competent to punish. The word was coined in South Africa [in 1908] to distinguish the non-violent resistance of the Indians of South Africa from the contemporary "passive resistance" of the suffragettes and others. It is not conceived as a weapon of the weak.

Passive resistance is used in the orthodox English sense and covers the suffragette movement as well as the resistance of the nonconformists. Passive resistance has been conceived and is regarded as a weapon of the weak. Whilst it avoids violence, being not open to the weak, it does not exclude its use if, in the opinion of a passive resister, the occasion demands it. However, it has always been distinguished from armed resistance and its application was at one time confined to Christian martyrs.

Civil disobedience is civil breach of unmoral statutory enactments. The expression was, so far as I am aware, coined by Thoreau to signify his own resistance to the laws of a slave state. He has left a masterly treatise on the duty of civil disobedience. But Thoreau was not perhaps an out-and-out champion of non-violence. Probably, also, Thoreau limited his breach of statutory laws to the revenue law, i.e., payment of taxes, whereas the term "civil disobedience" as practiced in 1919 covered a breach of any statutory and unmoral law. It signified the resister's outlawry in a civil, i.e., nonviolent manner. He invoked the sanctions of the law and cheerfully suffered imprisonment. It is a branch of satyagraha.

Non-co-operation predominantly implies withdrawing of co-operation from the state that in the non-co-operator's view has become corrupt and excludes civil disobedience of the fierce type described above. By its very nature, non-co-operation is even open to children of understanding and can be safely practiced by the masses. Civil disobedience presupposes the habit of willing obedience to laws without fear of their sanctions. It can therefore be practiced only as a last resort and by a select few in the first instance at any rate. Non-co-operation, too, like civil disobedience is a branch of satyagraha which includes all non-violent resistance for the vindication of Truth.

Satyagraha—Not Passive Resistance

The force denoted by the term "passive resistance" and translated into Hindi as *nishkriya pratirodha* is not very accurately described either by the original English phrase or by its Hindi rendering. Its correct description is "satyagraha." Satyagraha was born in South Africa in 1908. There was no word in any Indian language denoting the power which our countrymen in South Africa invoked for the redress of their grievances. There was an English equivalent, namely, "passive resistance," and we carried on with it. However, the need for a word to describe this unique power came to be increasingly felt, and it was decided to award a prize to anyone who could think of an appropriate term. A Gujarati-speaking gentleman submitted the word "satyagraha," and it was adjudged the best.

"Passive resistance" conveyed the idea of the Suffragette Movement in England. Burning of houses by these women was called "passive resistance" and so also their fasting in prison. All such acts might very well be "passive resistance" but they were not "satyagraha." It is said of "passive resistance" that it is the weapon of the weak, but the power which is the subject of this article can be used only by the strong. This power is not "passive" resistance; indeed it calls for intense activity. The movement in South Africa was not passive but active. The Indians of South Africa believed that Truth was their object, that Truth ever triumphs, and with this definiteness of purpose they persistently held on to Truth. They put up with all the suffering that this persistence implied. With the conviction that Truth is not to be renounced even unto death, they shed the fear of death. In the cause of Truth, the prison was a palace to them and its doors the gateway to freedom.

Satyagraha is not physical force. A satyagrahi does not inflict pain on the adversary; he does not seek his destruction. A satyagrahi never resorts to firearms. In the use of satyagraha, there is no ill-will whatever.

Satyagraha is pure soul-force. Truth is the very substance of the soul. That is why this force is called satyagraha. The soul is informed with knowledge. In it burns the flame of love. If someone gives us pain through ignorance, we shall win him through love. "Non-violence is the supreme dharma" is the proof of this power of love. Non-violence is a dormant state. In the waking state, it is love. Ruled by love, the world goes on. In English there is a saying, "Might is Right." Then there is the doctrine of the survival of the fittest. Both of these ideas are contradictory to the above principle. Neither is wholly true. If ill-will were the chief motive-force, the world would have been destroyed long ago; and neither would I have had the opportunity to write this article nor would the hopes of the readers be fulfilled. We are alive solely because of love. We are ourselves the proof of this. Deluded by modern western civilization, we have forgotten our ancient civilization and worship the might of arms.

We forget the principle of non-violence, which is the essence of all religions. The doctrine of arms stands for irreligion. It is due to the sway of that doctrine that a sanguinary war is raging in Europe.

In India also we find worship of arms. We see it even in that great work of Tulsidas. But it is seen in all the books that soul-force is the supreme power. . . .

It brings good both to the satyagrahi and his adversary. It is ever victorious. For instance, Harishchandra was a satyagrahi, Prahlad was a satyagrahi, Mirabai was a satyagrahi. Daniel, Socrates and those Arabs who hurled themselves on the fire of the French artillery were all satyagrahis. We see from these examples that a satyagrahi does not fear for his body, he does not give up what he thinks is Truth; the word "defeat" is not to be found in his dictionary, he does not wish for the destruction of his antagonist, he does not vent anger on him; but has only compassion for him.

A satyagrahi does not wait for others, but throws himself into the fray, relying entirely on his own resources. He trusts that when the time comes, others will do likewise. His practice is his precept. Like air, satyagraha is all-pervading. It is infectious, which means that all people—big and small, men and women—can become satyagrahis. No one is kept out from the army of satyagrahis. A satyagrahi cannot perpetrate tyranny on anyone; he is not subdued through application of physical force; he does not strike at anyone. Just as anyone can resort to satyagraha, it can be resorted to in almost any situation.

People demand historical evidence in support of satyagraha. History is for the most part a record of armed activities. Natural activities find very little mention in it. Only uncommon activities strike us with wonder. Satyagraha has been used always and in all situations. The father and the son, the man and the wife are perpetually resorting to satyagraha, one towards the other. When a father gets angry and punishes the son, the son does not hit back with a weapon, he conquers his father's anger by submitting to him. The son refuses to be subdued by the unjust rule of his father but he puts up with the punishment that he may incur through disobeying the unjust father. We can similarly free ourselves of the unjust rule of the Government by defying the unjust rule and accepting the punishments that go with it. We do not bear malice towards the Government. When we set its fears at rest, when we do not desire to make armed assaults on the administrators, nor to unseat them from power, but only to get rid of their injustice, they will at once be subdued to our will.

The question is asked why we should call any rule unjust. In saying so, we ourselves assume the function of a judge. It is true. But in this world, we always have to act as judges for ourselves. That is why the satyagrahi does not strike his adversary with arms. If he has Truth on his side, he will win, and if his thought is faulty, he will suffer the consequences of his fault.

What is the good, they ask, of only one person opposing injustice; for he will be punished and destroyed, he will languish in prison or meet an untimely end through hanging. The objection is not valid. History shows that all reforms have begun with one person. Fruit is hard to come by without *tapasya* [self-sacrifice]. The suffering that has to be undergone in satyagraha is *tapasya* in its purest form. Only when the *tapasya* is capable of bearing fruit, do we have the fruit. This establishes the fact that when there is insufficient *tapasya,* the fruit is delayed. The *tapasya* of Jesus Christ, boundless though it was, was not sufficient for Europe's need. Europe has disapproved Christ. Through ignorance, it has disregarded Christ's pure way of life. Many Christs will have to offer themselves as sacrifice at the terrible altar of Europe, and only then will realization dawn on that continent. But Jesus will always be the first among these. He has been the sower of the seeds and his will therefore be the credit for raising the harvest.

It is said that it is a very difficult, if not an altogether impossible, task to educate ignorant peasants in satyagraha and that it is full of perils, for it is a very arduous business to transform unlettered ignorant people from one condition into another. Both the arguments are just silly. The people of India are perfectly fit to receive the training of satyagraha. India has knowledge of dharma [religious duty], and where there is knowledge of dharma, satyagraha is a very simple matter. The people of India have drunk of the nectar of devotion. This great people overflows with faith. It is no difficult matter to lead such a people on the right path of satyagraha. Some have a fear that once people get involved in satyagraha, they may at a later stage take to arms. This fear is illusory. From the path of satyagraha [clinging to Truth], a transition to the path of a-satyagraha [clinging to untruth] is impossible. It is possible of course that some people who believe in armed activity may mislead the satyagrahis by infiltrating into their ranks and later making them take to arms. This is possible in all enterprises. But as compared to other activities, it is less likely to happen in satyagraha, for their motives soon get exposed and when the people are not ready to take up arms, it becomes almost impossible to lead them on to that terrible path. The might of arms is directly opposed to the might of satyagraha. Just as darkness does not abide in light, soulless armed activity cannot enter the sunlike radiance of soul-force. Many Pathans took part in satyagraha in South Africa abiding by all the rules of satyagraha.

Then it is said that much suffering is involved in being a satyagrahi and that the entire people will not be willing to put up with this suffering. The objection is not valid. People in general always follow in the footsteps of the noble. There is no doubt that it is difficult to produce a satyagrahi leader. Our experience is that a satyagrahi needs many more virtues like self-control, fearlessness, etc., than are requisite for one who believes in armed action. The greatness of the man bearing arms does not lie in the superiority of the arms, nor does it lie in his physical prowess. It lies in his determination and fearlessness in face of death. . . . The strength of a warrior is not measured by reference to his weapons but by his firmness of mind. A satyagrahi needs millions of times more of such firmness than does a bearer of arms. The birth of such a man can bring about the salvation of India in no time. Not only India but the whole world awaits the advent of such a man. We may in the meanwhile prepare the ground as much as we can through satyagraha. . . .

For swaraj, satyagraha is the unfailing weapon. Satyagraha means that what we want is truth, that we deserve it and that we will work for it even unto death. . . .

Truth alone triumphs. There is no dharma [religion] higher than Truth. Truth always wins. We pray to God that in this sacred land we may bring about the reign of dharma by following satyagraha and that thus our country may become an example for all to follow.

There are two methods of attaining one's goal. Satyagraha and *duragraha*. In our scriptures, they have been described, respectively, as divine and devilish modes of action. In satyagraha, there is always unflinching adherence to truth. It is never to be forsaken on any account. Even for the sake of one's country, it does not permit resort to falsehood. It proceeds on the assumption of the ultimate triumph of truth. A satyagrahi does not abandon his path, even though at times it seems impenetrable and beset with difficulties and dangers, and a slight departure from that straight path may appear full of promise. Even in these circumstances, his faith shines resplendent like the midday sun and he does not despond. With truth for his sword, he needs neither a steel sword nor gunpowder. Even an inveterate enemy he conquers by the force of the soul, which is love. Love for a friend is not put to the test. There is nothing surprising in a friend loving a friend; there is no merit in it and it costs no effort. When love is bestowed on the so-called enemy, it is tested, it becomes a virtue and requires an effort, and hence it is an act of manliness and real bravery. We can cultivate such an attitude even towards the Government and, doing so, we shall be able to appreciate their beneficial activities and, as for their errors, rather than feel bitter on their account, point them out in love and so get them rectified. Love does not act through fear. Weakness there certainly cannot be. A coward is incapable of bearing love, it is the prerogative of the brave. Looking at everything with love, we shall not regard the Government with suspicion, nor believe that all their actions are inspired with bad motives. And our examination of their actions, being directed by love, will be unerring and is bound, therefore, to carry conviction with them.

Love can fight; often it is obliged to. In the intoxication of power, man fails to see his error. When that happens, a satyagrahi does not sit still. He suffers. He disobeys the ruler's orders and his laws in a civil manner, and willingly submits to the penalties of such disobedience, for instance, imprisonment and gallows. Thus is the soul disciplined. In this, one never finds that one's time has been wasted and, if it is subsequently realized that such respectful disobedience was an error, the consequences are suffered merely by the satyagrahi and his co-workers. In the event, no bitterness develops between the satyagrahi and those in power; the latter, on the contrary, willingly yield to him. *They discover that they cannot command the satyagrahi's obedience. They cannot make him do anything against his will. And this is the consummation of swaraj, because it means complete independence.* It need not be assumed that such resistance is possible only against civilized rulers. Even a heart of flint will melt in the fire kindled by the power of the soul. Even a Nero becomes a lamb when he faces love. This is no exaggeration. It is as true as an algebraic equation. This satyagraha is India's distinctive weapon. It has had others but satyagraha has been in greater use. It is an unfailing source of strength, and is capable of being used at all times and under all circumstances. It requires no stamp of approval from the Congress or any other body. He who knows its power cannot but use it. Even as the eyelashes automatically protect the eyes, so does satyagraha, when kindled, automatically protect the freedom of the soul.

But *duragraha* is a force with the opposite attributes. . . . The man who follows the path of *duragraha* becomes impatient and wants to kill the so-called enemy. There can be but one result of this. Hatred increases. The defeated party vows vengeance and simply bides its time. The spirit of revenge thus descends from father to son. It is much to be wished that India never give predominance to this spirit of *duragraha.* If the members of this assembly deliberately accept satyagraha and chalk out its program accordingly, they will reach their goal all the more easily for doing so. They may have to face disappointment in the initial stages. They may not see results for a time. But satyagraha will triumph in the end. The *duragrahi,* like the oilman's ox, moves in a circle. His movement is only motion but it is not progress. The satyagrahi is ever moving forward. . . .

The right thing to hope from India is that this great and holy Aryan land will ever give the predominant place to the divine force and employ the weapon of satyagraha, that it will never accept the supremacy of armed strength. India will never respect the principle of might being right. She will ever reserve her allegiance to the principle: "Truth alone triumphs."

On reflection, we find that we can employ satyagraha even for social reform. We can rid ourselves of the many defects of our caste system. We can resolve Hindu-Muslim differences and we can solve political problems. It is all right that, for the sake of convenience, we speak of these things as separate subjects. But it should never be forgotten that they are all closely inter-related. It is not true to say that neither religion nor social reform has anything to do with politics.

Duty, Democracy and Swaraj

You want democracy—the rule of the people, by the people, for the people. Surely, all the 75,000 people of Rajkot* cannot become rulers or administrators. Democracy must in essence, therefore, mean the art and science of mobilizing the entire physical, economic and spiritual resources of all the various sections of the people in the service of the common good of all.

Service of the family has been the motive behind all our activities hitherto. We must now learn to broaden our outlook so as to include in our ambit the service of the people as a whole.

We are familiar with several conceptions of village work. Hitherto it has mostly meant propaganda in the villages to inculcate upon the village masses a sense of their rights. Sometimes it has also meant conducting welfare activity among them to ameliorate their material condition. But the village work that I have now come to place before you consists in educating the villager in his duties.

Rights accrue automatically to him who duly performs his duties. In fact the right to perform one's duties is the only right that is worth living for and dying for. It covers all legitimate rights. All the rest is garb under one guise or another and contains in it seeds of *himsa.*

* City in the western state of Gujarat.

The swaraj of my conception will come only when all of us are firmly persuaded that our swaraj has got to be won, worked and maintained through truth and ahimsa alone. True democracy or the swaraj of the masses can never come through untruthful and violent means, for the simple reason that the natural corollary to their use would be to remove all opposition through the suppression or extermination of the antagonists. That does not make for individual freedom. Individual freedom can have the fullest play only under a regime of unadulterated ahimsa.

We cannot afford to have discord in our midst if we are to educate the people. We must all speak with one voice. If we want to weld the various sections into one people—and that is the *sine qua non* of democracy—we may not, in rendering service, make any distinction between those who took part in our struggle and those who did not.

We want to set up democracy in Rajkot. A born democrat is a born disciplinarian. Democracy comes naturally to him who is habituated normally to yield willing obedience to all laws, human or divine. I claim to be a democrat both by instinct and training. Let those who are ambitious to serve democracy qualify themselves by satisfying first this acid test of democracy. Moreover, a democrat must be utterly selfless. He must think and dream not in terms of self or party but only of democracy. Only then does he acquire the right of civil disobedience. I do not want anybody to give up his convictions or to suppress himself. I do not believe that a healthy and honest difference of opinion will injure our cause. But opportunism, camouflage or patched-up compromises certainly will. If you must dissent, you should take care that your opinions voice your innermost convictions and are not intended merely as a convenient party cry.

Today our democracy is choked by our internecine strife. We are torn by dissensions—dissensions between Hindus and Mussalmans, Brahmins and non-Brahmins, Congressmen and non-Congressmen. It is no easy task to evolve democracy out of this mobocracy. Let us not make confusion worse confounded by further introducing into it the virus of sectionalism and party spirit.

I value individual freedom but you must not forget that man is essentially a social being. He has risen to this present status by learning to adjust his individualism to the requirements of social progress. Unrestricted individualism is the law of the beast of the jungle. We have learnt to strike the mean between individual freedom and social restraint. Willing submission to social restraint for the sake of the well-being of the whole society enriches both the individual and the society of which one is a member.

Democracy disciplined and enlightened is the finest thing in the world. A democracy prejudiced, ignorant, superstitious will land itself in chaos and may be self-destroyed.

I hold that self-government is not an end, but only a means to good government. And true democracy is what promotes the welfare of the people. The test of a good government lies in the largest good of the people with the minimum of controls. The test of autocracy, socialism, capitalism, etc., is also people's welfare or good government. In themselves they are of no value. Any system of government can fail if people do not have honesty and a feeling of brotherhood. There may be work, there may be women to do the work and tools with which to do it, yet in my view a system that admits of poverty and unemployment is not fit to survive even for a day.

Democracy is where even the man in the street is heard. When we are out to establish a democratic order, the Viceroy's House, or even Jawaharlal's [Nehru] house, is not the seat of the Government. I have described Jawaharlal as the uncrowned king. And we are a poor nation. We are so poor that we shall walk rather than ride in a car. Even if somebody offers us a lift in his car, we shall decline his offer saying that he can keep his car, we would rather walk. If we are over-hungry, we shall eat a little more. Thus democracy means the rule of the man in the street.

Democracy is an impossible thing until the power is shared by all, but let not democracy degenerate into mobocracy. Even a pariah, a laborer, who makes it possible for you to earn your living, will have his share in self-government. But you will have to touch their lives. Go to them, see their hovels where they live packed like sardines. It is up to you to look after this part of humanity. It is possible for you to make their lives or mar their lives.

In this age of democracy it is essential that desired results are achieved by the collective effort of the people. It will no doubt be good to achieve an objective through the effort of a supremely powerful individual, but it can never make the community conscious of its corporate strength. An individual's success will be like a millionaire doling free food to millions of starving people. We should, therefore, bend our energies to a fulfillment of the thirteenfold constructive programme. It may or may not bring swaraj, but we shall surely have the satisfaction of having done our best.

All Hindus, Muslims, Sikhs, Parsis, Christians and Jews who people this country from Kanyakumari to Kashmir and from Karachi to Dibrugarh in Assam and who have lovingly and in a spirit of service adopted it as their dear motherland, have an equal right to it. No one can say that it has place only for the majority and the minority should be dishonored. Whoever serves it with the purest devotion must have the first right over it. Therefore, anyone who seeks to drive out the Muslims is Delhi's enemy number one and therefore India's enemy number one. We are heading towards that catastrophe. Every Indian must do his bit to ward it off.

What should we do then? If we would see Panchayat Raj, i.e., democracy established, we would regard the humblest and the lowliest Indian as being equally the ruler of India with the tallest in the land. For this everyone should be pure. If they are not they should become so. He who is pure will also be wise. He will observe no distinctions between caste and caste, between touchable and untouchable, but will consider everyone equal with himself. He will bind others to himself with love. To him no one would be an untouchable. He would treat the laborers the same as he would the capitalists. He will, like the millions of toilers, earn his living from service of others and will make no distinction between intellectual and manual work. To hasten this desirable consummation, we should voluntarily turn ourselves into scavengers. He who is wise will never touch opium, liquor or any intoxicants. He will observe the vow of swadeshi and regard every woman who is not his wife as his mother, sister or daughter according to her age, and never see anyone with eyes of lust. He will concede to woman the same rights he claims for himself. If need be he will sacrifice his own life but never kill another.

. . . I have suggested that you [a Hindu majority, in 1947, after independence] should adopt the ways followed by all democratic countries. In democracy, every individual has to abide by the wishes of the people, that is, the Government, and has to direct his own wishes in that light. If every man takes the law into his own hands the State cannot function. It would mean anarchy, which means end of social order. That is, the State would not exist. That is the way to lose our independence. I believe that if you would let the Government carry out its tasks, there is no doubt that every Hindu and Sikh refugee would return home with honor and respect. But you cannot expect these things to happen if you want your Muslim compatriots to be driven out of India. I find any such thing dreadful. You cannot secure justice by doing injustice to the Muslims.

The spirit of democracy, which is fast spreading throughout India and the rest of the world, will, without a shadow of doubt, purge the institution of the idea of predominance and subordination. The spirit of democracy is not a mechanical thing to be adjusted by abolition of forms. It requires change of the heart. If caste is a bar to the spread of that spirit, the existence of five religions in India—Hinduism, Islam, Christianity, Zoroastrianism, and Judaism—is equally a bar. The spirit of democracy requires the inculcation of the spirit of brotherhood, and I can find no difficulty in considering a Christian or a Mohammedan to be my brother in absolutely the same sense as a blood brother, and Hinduism that is responsible for the doctrine of caste is also responsible for the inculcation of the essential brotherhood, not merely of man but even of all that lives.

Thomas H. West is professor emeritus at St. Kate's, having taught in the theology department for more than thirty years. One of the founders of the St. Catherine Core Curriculum, he was also one of the first TRW teachers. Author of Ultimate Hope without God: The Atheistic Eschatology of Ernst Bloch *(1991),* Jesus and the Quest for Meaning *(2001) and other works, Professor West often linked theology with justice in his teaching. In this excerpt, he revisits the story of the "good Samaritan." In this essay, what is agapic love and how does it lead to social justice? With an expanding global perspective, how do we enact the Samaritan story and identify our neighbors?*

Love into Justice: The Good Samaritan Revisited

Thomas H. West

Most Christians would say that the foundation of social justice is love, especially love of neighbor, *agape*. But how do we get from agape to an active commitment to social justice? We do not answer this question well if we say simply that agapic love and social justice are the same thing. They are not. Yet I want to argue that work for social justice is a necessary expression of agapic love.

In the New Testament, the epitome of agapic love is the Good Samaritan. We do not ordinarily think of the Good Samaritan as practicing social justice. We see him as practicing compassion, performing an act of charity, carrying out a mission of mercy, not, surely, working for social justice. What the Good Samaritan did and what a social reformer like Martin Luther King, Jr. did are clearly very different things.

But is social justice so sharply different from agapic love? In this chapter I shall argue that there is indeed a distinction between agapic love and social justice, but it is a distinction within a unity.

Luke's Parable of the Good Samaritan

Here is the parable of the Good Samaritan as told in Luke's gospel:

> Just then a lawyer stood up to test Jesus. "Teacher," he said, "what must I do to inherit eternal life?" He said to him, "What is written in the law? What do you read there?" He answered, "You shall love the Lord your God with all your heart, and with all your soul, and with all your strength, and with all your mind; and your neighbor as yourself." And he said to him, "You have given the right answer; do this, and you will live."

> But wanting to justify himself, he asked Jesus, "And who is my neighbor?" Jesus replied, "A man was going down from Jerusalem to Jericho, and fell into the hands of robbers, who stripped him, beat him, and went away, leaving him half dead." Now by chance a priest was going down the road; and when he saw him, he passed by on the other side. So likewise a Levite, when he came to the place and saw him, passed by on the other side. But a Samaritan while traveling came near him; and when he saw him, he was moved with compassion. He went to him and bandaged his wounds, having poured oil and wine on them. Then he put him on his own animal, brought him to an inn, and took care of him. The next day he took out two denarii, gave them to the innkeeper, and said, "Take care of him; and when I come back, I will repay you whatever more you spend" (Luke 10:25–35).

Luke situates the parable of the Good Samaritan within the "travel narrative" (Luke 9: 51–19: 27) that follows Jesus' journey from Galilee to Jerusalem.[1]

During the journey Jesus frequently pauses to instruct his followers in the way of discipleship. One day he instructed them by telling the parable of the Good Samaritan.

The Good Samaritan parable is classified by Joachim Jeremias as a "parable of realized discipleship,"[2] though it is not a parable in the narrow or typical sense. Rather, it is an *example story*, not an extended metaphor or simile where the figures and events symbolize something else, as when the mustard seed symbolizes the reign of God (see Mt. 13: 31–32) or the generous vineyard owner (see Mt. 20: 1–16), God's unconditional love.[3] The Good Samaritan parable does not refer beyond itself in this way. Jesus is not saying that "God acts like the Good Samaritan," but rather, "You should act like the Good Samaritan."

The Good Samaritan story does, however, display other elements typical of a parable, most obviously the element of surprise. The surprise is not that the priest and the Levite (a Temple official subordinate to the priests) pass by an injured man. Out in the countryside, "anti-clericalism" was widespread among Jews. That Jesus would portray Temple officials as morally callous would evoke a knowing murmur from his Jewish audience. His audience would then expect Jesus to finish off his story by having an Israelite layperson like themselves stop and do the right thing.[4] Instead, the *Samaritan* stops, and, "moved with compassion," does the right thing. This is a major surprise to Jesus' Jewish audience. John Donahue reminds us: "Centuries of pious reflection have dulled our sensibilities to the hatred that existed between Jews and Samaritans." Jews regarded Samaritans not only as a mongrel people who had intermarried with pagan invaders, but as deserters of the Jewish religion.[5] That a Jew could love the Samaritan as a neighbor, and a Samaritan could love the Jew as a neighbor, well, it's a scandal, it's out of the question. When the lawyer asked Jesus, "Who is my neighbor?" he was being serious. There was genuine debate among Jews at this time about who was included under "neighbor." According to Jeremias, "It was generally agreed that the term connoted fellow countrymen, including full proselytes."[6] It did not include Samaritans. Jesus defines *neighbor* to include the hated Samaritan, depicting the Samaritan as one who is a neighbor precisely by treating the injured Jew as a neighbor. This is a surprise. This is a shock.

In the parable of the Good Samaritan, Jesus offers an example of agapic love in action. Such love imitates the love shown by Jesus, and Jesus' love is in turn an imitation of God's love. Such is the nature of Jesus' radical moral demand on those called to the mission of bringing people into the reign of God. In the parable, agapic love shows the following qualities:

- It is unconditional. The Samaritan does not demand that the person injured fulfill any conditions before the Samaritan is willing to give help.
- This love is universal. The Samaritan does not care to which gender, race, class, religion, or ethnic group the injured person belongs. A human being is hurt. This Samaritan would have reached out to any human being who was suffering.
- This love is unconcerned with merit or just deserts. The Samaritan does not say to himself, "This person in the ditch half dead does not deserve my help because he had it coming. He didn't take sufficient care to avoid the threat of robbery." The Samaritan does not say to himself, "There is probably some past sin in the victim's life. God through this violent assault and robbery is punishing him."
- It is love moved by compassion. The Samaritan is moved by feeling. Indeed, one can imagine him seized by feeling and impelled to the ditch beside the road.
- It is a love that is spontaneous and uncalculating. The Samaritan is moved to act, quickly. He is not shown pondering the pros and cons. He is not shown engaging in subtle calculations about precisely what he should do. He spends no time in rational analysis.
- It is a love that goes beyond the minimum one would expect of even the most decent person. That is, it is supererogatory; it goes beyond what is asked. He doesn't just bandage the injured man's wounds and get him to the next town, but stays with him, takes care of him, pays his lodging, and then—and here is the special touch—says to the innkeeper: "If it comes to more than this, I'll pay the difference on my way back." Here the Samaritan shows himself to be a virtuoso of the supererogatory.[7]

These qualities constitute agapic, that is, Christian, love in action, in the public sphere, among strangers, who through love become neighbors and friends.

Now if the Christian moral life were simply a matter of letting oneself be moved to uncalculating love towards any human being in special need, we would have no need for lengthy books on Christian morality and justice. But the Christian moral life often requires us to go beyond spontaneous acts of agapic love. Morality then becomes more complex, and when it does, it begins to move from agapic love pure and simple to agapic love that expresses itself in the work of justice.

2. Love into Interpersonal Justice

The great American theologian Reinhold Niebuhr said that Christian love becomes justice when there are three or more people in the room.[8] Expanding on the story of the Good Samaritan, let us imagine that the Samaritan, instead of discovering one robbery victim in the ditch, discovers three. The Samaritan is moved by compassion to go over to the three victims, but as soon as he arrives, he finds himself having to step back from the situation and from his feeling in order to engage in some rational analysis and calculation. He finds himself engaged in what we today call *triage*. Triage is a system of principles and rules by which one judges how one can best treat victims like these, given one's resources. Whenever my family calls our Health Maintenance Organization after hours, we talk first to the triage nurse; using a complex system of principles and rules she decides what the HMO can and should do for us given our ailments and given their resources.

Coming upon the three victims, the Good Samaritan must also practice triage. The principles and rules of triage he uses will be undoubtedly less explicit and formalized than those of the HMO triage nurse; nevertheless, if he is to do *justice* to these three victims he will have to turn his thoughtful attention to *some* principles and rules, however rudimentary they might be.

In practicing triage, the Samaritan does not completely turn from feeling to thought, but he does distance himself enough to allow a rational analysis of the situation. If he lets himself be ruled only by feeling, he might spontaneously attend first to the victim who is screaming and moaning the loudest, but to do so would be unjust. One of the first principles of triage is that one should attend first to the victim who is most seriously injured and then make a judgment about whether one has the resources to help him or her. The Samaritan coolheadedly turns his attention very self-consciously towards this principle and sets about putting it into practice. He first gathers empirical data about the condition of the victims. He discovers that the victim screaming the loudest is a teenage boy holding his ankle. A second victim is very quiet, is not bleeding, but he has a weak pulse. A third victim is bleeding profusely from the neck. He decides to help her first, and bandages her wounds, and stops the bleeding. On her he decides to concentrate his maximum effort. He has acted justly.

Yet it would be unfair, it would be unjust, if he were to cease thinking about the other two. They, after all, are human beings, with their inherent dignity and worth. He can*not* give them his *maximum* effort in this situation, but he feels bound to give them at least a minimum of attention. But what precisely is the minimum he owes them in this situation? The answer requires another calculation on his part. To the boy holding his ankle, he decides that the injury is not that serious, and he limits himself to wrapping the ankle and uttering words of comfort. And he double-checks the person with the weak pulse to make sure that he still is alive.

At this point the Samaritan is now expressing his love in the form of justice, and specifically, *interpersonal* justice. Interpersonal justice refers to the justice that is practiced by one individual to another in a situation where the person practicing the justice has to distance himself somewhat from his feelings, consult a set of principles and rules, gather data about this situation, and make a rational decision about what should be done. Interpersonal justice requires attention to the questions of what is equal treatment, what is fair treatment, what is the minimum one owes each individual who is present, and what is the maximum one can offer, given one's resources. This kind of analysis tells the Samaritan that it would be wrong, it would violate the principles of interpersonal justice, if he were to spend himself totally in selfless and supererogatory love on only one of the victims that now confront him. He must therefore carefully and rationally distribute his efforts in an equal yet fair manner, giving the most he can give to one without at the same time totally neglecting the others.

Interpersonal justice is not only practiced in the kind of extraordinary situation in which the Samaritan finds himself. It is in fact the stuff of ordinary daily life, in a way that heedless agapic love can never be. Every day we have many encounters with our fellow human beings. Not every encounter is, or should be, an occasion for agapic love in the pure form. Rather, we should treat those individuals we encounter every day with a simple, interpersonal justice, with a basic respect for their worth, dignity, and autonomy.[9] There is a minimum that we owe everyone. Some might require more than the minimum from us. We must weigh matters and decide what we can give. Knowing how this is done takes much training and learning. Some people take to this very well and show an acute ethical intelligence.

Let us return to our story. The Samaritan has bound the wounds of the woman bleeding, attended to the man with the weak pulse, and calmed the boy with the injured ankle. Somehow, after making a whole series of further decisions, all accompanied by considerable rational analysis, he gets them to the nearest town and arranges for their care, though this time a check of his financial resources precludes an offer to pay the innkeeper and the local physician. He has done justice to these people.

But the whole experience has left him angry. For the fourth time this month he has encountered victims of brutal robberies left to die in the ditch. What would have happened to these poor people had he not happened along? The Samaritan thinks on the many others who were passed by and left to suffer and die. This tragic situation is more than he as an individual can manage. He is moved to conclude that one-to-one agapic love and interpersonal justice are not enough. He decides to move into social justice.

3. Love into Social Justice

The Good Samaritan decides to involve the larger community and attempt a more systematic solution to this terrible problem of assault and robbery.[10] He decides thereby to make the move from *interpersonal* justice to the work of *social* justice. Social justice is justice practiced by a group or community towards individuals or other groups or communities. Social justice is a social endeavor, which involves the creation of *social structures.*

Social structures have two elements: the mental and the institutional. The *first* element is concerned with the consciousness, the mind, the attitude, the ethos, of the community. It is obvious to the Samaritan that many people are passing by these victims in the ditch and not doing anything to help. "There is a deeply faulty ethos in these parts," he says to himself. "People around here are indifferent to this kind of human misery."

The Good Samaritan resolves to change the ethos, to raise consciousness, to change the mentality. On his next trip down this road, he stops at each village and gives a little talk to the villagers, alerting them to the suffering of the victims of these robberies and urging them not to pass by the victims. He talks about the basic dignity and equality of all human beings. All human beings, he insists, have a claim on our love and justice, especially those who are suffering. He even includes in his talk a rudimentary introduction to triage. In his efforts to create a new social mentality, the Samaritan enjoys some success. People become more sensitized. More people than before are reaching out with agapic love and interpersonal justice.

In one village this new consciousness becomes so pervasive that helping robbery victims becomes what sociologists call an *institution,* that is, an *established pattern of behavior,* which is the *second* element of a social structure.[11] Helping victims is something that villagers practice without hesitation. The institution in this case is a *custom,* a pattern of behavior that establishes itself quite spontaneously and lacks formal organization.

Nevertheless, this proves to be not enough. There are still many victims and many people are passing them by. The ethos of reaching out to help is indeed deeper and more widespread, but it is far from pervasive. Human beings, after all, are free to defy ethos and custom and are especially prone to do so when they are asked to go outside themselves for someone else's sake. And so the Samaritan decides to move beyond custom and create a more formal institution.

He decides to create an institution in which groups of volunteers will patrol the road in shifts in search of victims.[12] To insure that these volunteers will be skilled in applying triage, he arranges for training sessions. He rents several buildings in the villages in which to hold these sessions. Since those who conduct the sessions will be engaged in virtually full-time work, he decides to pay them. Realizing that he does not have enough money for rent and salaries, he sets out to raise money, trusting that the ethos he created earlier is wide and deep enough to produce people willing to contribute. He organizes a fund drive, to occur on a regular basis. His institution comes thereby to depend on both the willingness of people to volunteer their time to work on the patrols and their willingness to contribute money on a regular basis. And since the contributions of time and money depend on the continued vitality of the ethos, the Samaritan must continue to give talks to raise ethical consciousness; that is, he must continue to be concerned with the element of mentality.

The Samaritan has thus created not only a new mentality, but also new institutions. And many robbery victims are helped.

Yet, many victims continue to die in the ditch, unhelped. The crime rate is up. Also, there are difficulties with the Samaritan's institutional structure. The patrols are staffed largely by unpaid volunteers, who are free to cease volunteering, and quite regularly one or more will suddenly and unpredictably pull out. On nights before holidays, the most dangerous nights, whole patrols have to be canceled for lack of volunteers.

Funding is a continuing problem. The regional economy fluctuates wildly and along with that, financial contributions fluctuate wildly. Sometimes the Samaritan has the funds to do the training, sometimes not. A fickleness and unpredictability pervade the institution making for a fickle and unpredictable service to the victims along the road. One of the principles of justice is universality of coverage: all persons will receive the minimum due them. This institution is failing to provide that coverage, which causes acute pangs of conscience in the Samaritan. The compassion that moved him to that first act of agapic love has now moved him towards the work of justice that aims to reach all those suffering, but he is *not* reaching them all in any consistent way.

For a while the Samaritan considers going to what we now call the free-market approach. In order to guarantee more predictable and reliable staff he could staff the patrols with paid professionals. To pay for them, he could market their services by charging the victims—with some provision for their ability to pay—or by selling their services to villages along the road or to groups of travelers. To raise the initial capital outlay for this service, he could sell shares to the enterprise and then pay the shareholders out of the profits.

But he decides against going into the market. He is not opposed to the market as such, for he is a businessperson and believes firmly that some goods and services are best delivered to people through the market. But he has come to believe that a robbery victim in the ditch has not just a *need* for help, but also a *right* to help. A right means that the victim has an absolute claim on the community for a consistent, predictable, and skilled response to his or her suffering. The free market approach introduces the profit motive and with that the inevitable tendency to provide the best service to those who have the most money to pay for it. But this is the kind of service that every human being has a right to, irrespective of wealth or social position.

So the Samaritan chooses another step, namely, he decides to go to the state, that is, to the institutions of government. This road is in a province under the jurisdiction of Rome. He decides to go to the Roman governor and ask that a new social structure be created. While talking with the governor and his aides, he learns that the problems occurring along this road are occurring on roads throughout the province. The governor is responsive. He petitions Rome for the permission to create a new structure and collect a tax to pay for it. The Roman senate passes a law, the emperor approves it, and the governor's bureaucrats work out detailed policies, that is, principles and rules, to guide the new institution in its service. Paid governmental patrols are put in place along the roads. They deliver medical help more quickly and predictably and thus provide coverage that approaches universal. Because the government owns the means of legalized violence, it equips the patrols with the physical means to pursue, subdue, and arrest the violent robbers who are causing so much human suffering.[13] And since the taxes are set and levied by law, funding is more predictable year-to-year.

The Good Samaritan is quite satisfied with his work. He has moved from agapic love to interpersonal justice, and finally, to social justice. To be sure, he has not ceased practicing agapic love—indeed, just the other night an opportunity again presented itself and he reached out to help a victim—but he has spent most of his time these past several years on the long march through social structures.

Despite his general satisfaction, the Samaritan has frequently found the work of social justice tedious and boring. Giving ethical pep talks, finding buildings to rent, training volunteers, writing up detailed policy suggestions for the governor—more than once during all this he has felt a slackening in his original agapic motivation. Indeed there have been moments when he becomes wistful for the spontaneous purity of that original act of agapic love. He recalls the deep joy and peace he felt after he had paid the innkeeper, knowing that he had done the right thing.

In addition, he is no naïve reformer. He has seen the negative side of this movement from agapic love to social justice. He worries, for example, about the impersonality of the new government structure. He has talked with some members of the patrols and found that quite a few are not motivated by the desire to help their neighbors but by the desire to advance their careers. Some government administrators appear less interested in providing a good service than in protecting their turf and increasing their budgets. He worries that with the movement to a government structure, the community ethos will decline. There is already much grumbling about the new taxes. Taxes, after all, are coercive. They are extracted by law and backed by the organized violence of the state. The other day he heard someone say, "They're confiscating my hard-earned money to pay for these patrols—I never even take those roads. It's not fair!" He fears that giving this work of social justice over to the state will diminish the motivating energy of agapic love to the point where individuals will pass by victims in the ditch with the excuse, "I don't need to stop, a patrol will be by soon." He has even heard rumors that some patrols are abusing their power and using their instruments of violence not to protect the victims but to blackmail them. Social justice, when it is carried out by the structures of government, has its dark side.

But all in all, despite these concerns, the Samaritan remains cautiously proud of his work. He is convinced that this new social structure has reduced the total amount of human suffering. Social justice has accomplished more than his individual acts of agapic love ever could.

As we watch the Samaritan move from agapic love to social justice from our perspective, we notice something missing from his vision and practice. At no time does the Samaritan engage in an in-depth social, political, and economic analysis of his society. He does not ask himself why there are so many robberies. He does not link the rise in the crime rate with the high concentration of wealth in the hands of a few large absentee landowners. He fails to bring into view the many tenant farmers who live in virtual slavery.[14] Many are so poor that they are drawn to lives of crime. As he journeys to see the governor, he does not wonder if perhaps his work of social justice wouldn't be more effective if this region were not under imperial rule and if Jews and Samaritans were independent peoples with grassroots, egalitarian political structures more immediately responsive to crime and its victims. This kind of analysis might very well have led the Samaritan to a vision of radical and sweeping change in the social, economic, and political structures of his day. But this kind of analysis, and the radical vision that often goes with it, is a relatively recent development in the history of ethical intelligence. Jesus did not undertake this kind of analysis.[15]

Nor did the early Church. And the Catholic Church was indifferent, sometimes even hostile, to this kind of analysis until late in the nineteenth century. In our day, however, virtually all Christians engaged in the work of social justice are aware of the need for complex social analysis.

I hope that my revisit of the Good Samaritan story has shown that the distinctions among agapic love, interpersonal justice, and social justice are real, but not hard and fast. Agapic love, Christian love, is not *replaced* by interpersonal and social justice, but continues to accompany both as their motivational fount, energizing both,[16] preventing each from becoming impersonal and bloodless. Justice has been described as the *public* expression of love, a definition that strikes me as particularly apt. The movement from agapic love to social justice is continuous and necessary. Any theology that draws too sharp a separation between love and justice, or which sees them as belonging to utterly different spheres, or which sees them in opposition, is a deeply flawed theology.

Just as there is a natural movement from agapic love to social justice, so too is there a natural move from social justice to agapic love. Even the most intense, one-to-one expression of agapic love does not occur in a social vacuum. Social structures—mentality, ethos, custom, laws, institutions—all pre-shape even the most private actions. The Good Samaritan, after all, is a member of a schismatic Jewish sect whose members followed the Torah, the Jewish law found in the first five books of the Hebrew Bible. The heart of this law is the two-fold commandment to love God and love your neighbor as yourself. This two-fold law was part of the Samaritan ethos and passed on to the Good Samaritan through the institutions of religious learning and instruction. The religious and ethical logic of the two-fold law led him to oppose a mentality that would forbid him to help an injured Jew. And therefore his spontaneous act of agapic love as told in Jesus' story did not arise solely out of his own spontaneity, it was not utterly his own, *sui generis*, but in part was the consequence of a social structure. Indeed the very spontaneity of his action is partly a sign of how thoroughly he was socialized by the redemptive elements of this structure.[17] And we must not forget, the parable of the Good Samaritan was told by Jesus, who was raised a Jew and was taught the same two-fold law of love.

We must, therefore, be wary of drawing overprecise distinctions among Christian love, interpersonal justice, and social justice. The distinctions are real, but within an unfolding unity. In his story of the Good Samaritan, Jesus beautifully captured the first and decisive moment of agapic love. Yet we can well imagine that the logic of love carried the Good Samaritan, as it should carry us, into the work of justice.

But with all this talk of social justice we dare not forget that the direction of agapic love is not only out into the public sphere of social structures.[18]

There is the other direction, towards the intimacy of full mutuality, towards friendship, romantic love, and family. What is the final purpose of just social structures if not a world where mutuality can flourish? Mutuality with God and mutuality with others. The full terror of a corrupt social structure is the way its destructive power makes even the intimacy of mutuality impossible. Agapic love achieves public expression in justice, but its fulfillment in mutual self-giving.[19]

Notes

[1] See John Donahue, *The Gospel in Parable: Metaphor, Narrative, and Theology in the Synoptic Gospels* (Philadelphia: Fortress Press, 1988), 126ff.

[2] Joachim Jeremias, *The Parables of Jesus* (New York: Charles Scribner's Sons, 2nd rev. ed., 1972), 198ff.

[3] Donahue, *The Gospel in Parable*, 12f.

[4] Jeremias, *The Parables of Jesus*, 204.

[5] Donahue, *The Gospel in Parable*, 130f., supplies a short history of the relations between Jews and Samaritans to show why they were such enemies.

[6] Jeremias, *The Parables of Jesus*, 202.

[7] Donahue, *The Gospel in Parable*, tells us that the Samaritan's extra help at the inn is more than just a sign of the supererogatory: "As a paradigm for compassionate entry into the world of an injured brother or sister, this final action is indispensable. According to the law at the time, a person with an unpaid debt could be enslaved until the debt was paid (see Matt. 18:23–35). Since the injured man was robbed and stripped—deprived of all resources—he could have been at the mercy of the innkeeper, a profession that had a bad reputation for dishonesty and violence. The parable assures the injured man's freedom and independence" (133).

[8] Actually, Niebuhr said it more abstractly than that: "An immediately felt obligation towards obvious need may be prompted by the emotion of pity. But a continued sense of obligation rests upon and expresses itself in rational calculations of the needs of others as compared with our own interests. A relation between the self and one other may be partly ecstatic; and in any case the calculation of relative interests may be reduced to a minimum. But as soon as a third person is introduced into the relation even the most perfect love requires a rational estimate of conflicting needs and interests." Reinhold Niebuhr, *The Nature and Destiny of Man: A Christian Interpretation. Volume II: Human Destiny*, (New York: Charles Scribner's Sons, 1943), 248.

[9] Following the rules of common courtesy can fulfill more than a small part of interpersonal justice on a day-to-day level. It is amazing how much of the advice that Ms. Manners gives in her syndicated newspaper column can be seen as the application of interpersonal justice. She shows an acute sense for the intersection of morality and manners. Though insofar as her rulings on courtesy precipitate a widespread pattern of behavior in society, she is creating a social structure; that is, she is doing the work of social justice.

[10] Another re-telling of the Good Samaritan story, which makes much the same move to social justice as I make here, is that of Stephen Mott. See his *Biblical Ethics and Social Change* (New York: Oxford University Press, 1982), 58f. I am

not indebted to Mott's re-telling, but the parallel is striking. For the Mott reference I am indebted to Garth L. Hallet, *Christian Neighbor Love: An Assessment of Six Rival Positions* (Washington, D.C.: Georgetown University Press, 1989), 118.

[11] On institutionalization, see Peter L. Berger and Thomas Luckmann, *The Social Construction of Reality: A Treatise on the Sociology of Knowledge* (New York: Doubleday Anchor Books, 1967), 54–61.

[12] A volunteer patrol is a good example of what Catholic social teaching calls a "mediating structure" or an "intermediate structure." Such structures carry out the "principle of subsidiarity," which could be summed up this way: before creating larger, governmental structures, first create smaller, local, nongovernmental structures. See Fred Kammer, *Doing Faithjustice: An Introduction to Catholic Social Thought* (New York: Paulist Press, 1991), 184.

[13] Here we have an example of the twin functions of government. On the one hand, it has the more positive function of extending medical help to all who need it. On the other hand, it has the more negative function of countering violence with violence, of enforcing order against the forces of anarchy and destruction. There are two traditions in Western political theory that tend to focus on one function at the expense of the other. Martin Luther (and before him Augustine and after him Hobbes) tends to reduce government to the "negative" function, that is, "to bear the secular sword and punish the wicked" (see "Secular Authority: To What Extent it Should be Obeyed," in John Dillenberger, ed., *Martin Luther Selections from his Writings* [New York: Doubleday Anchor Books, first published in 1523, this edition, 1961] 363–402, here 374). Government indeed is willed by God, but by God's "left hand." Its work is God's work, yet an "alien work" (377). If there had been no sin there would be no government. The scriptural source for this tradition can be found in Rom. 13:4 and 1 Pet. 1: 13. Another tradition, going back to Plato and Aristotle, stresses that government is a good, and natural to human life. Christian socialists and welfare state liberals add to this the agapic motivation and welcome government structures in their "positive" function of meeting a broad range of human needs. Reinhold Niebuhr keeps these two traditions in good balance: "All structures of justice do indeed presuppose the sinfulness of man, and are all partly systems of restraint which prevent the conflict of wills and interests from resulting in a consistent anarchy. But they are also all mechanisms by which men fulfill their obligations to their fellow men, beyond the possibilities offered in direct and personal relationships. The Kingdom of God and the demands of perfect love are therefore relevant to every political system and impinge upon every social situation in which the self seeks to come to terms with the claims of other life." See *The Nature and Destiny of Man: A Christian Interpretation. Volume II: Human Destiny*, 192.

[14] One of the effects of the widespread indebtedness among the peasants in Palestine was virtual slavery for those who could not pay their debts. Many took to banditry. See Richard A. Horsley, *Sociology and the Jesus Movement* (New York: Crossroad, 1989), 88–90.

[15] I am not denying that people in Jesus' time could not have visions of a new world where life would be radically different. Jesus had that vision, as did the many other "millenarian prophets" of his time. What I don't see is the combination of radical vision and social analysis, as epitomized, for example, in the work of Karl Marx.

[16] In the words of Fred Kammer: "Instead of a tension between love and justice, love as the soul of justice gives the Christian passion for building a more just order." See *Doing Faithjustice: An Introduction to Catholic Social Thought* (New York: Paulist Press, 1991), 181.

[17] An extraordinary example of agapic love practiced spontaneously more because of communal ethos than individual heroic virtue is the story of the French mountain village of Le Chambon, whose 5000 inhabitants sheltered 5000 Jews during World War II. The documentary, produced by Pierre Sauvage, that tells the story has many interviews with individuals who participated in this good work. What is remarkable is how self-effacing they are. Indeed, they appear somewhat baffled by the attention. What emerges out of the interviews is that these people performed individual acts of love because that is what one does if one is a member of that community. There appears to have been very little agonizing over the risks. It was the triumph of an ethos and thus of the work of social justice. See also Philip P. Hallie, *Lest Innocent Blood Be Shed: The Story of the Village of Le Chambon and How Goodness Happened There* (New York: Harper and Row, 1979). And yet reading Hallie's book reveals how mysteriously complex all this is. For the ethos of Le Chambon would not have attained its spontaneous strength without the inspired work of two individuals, the pastor and his wife, André and Magda Trocmé. For a very interesting philosophical examination of both the village ethos and the moral achievement of the Trocmés, see Lawrence A. Blum, *Moral Perception and Particularity* (New York: Cambridge University Press, 1994), 73–4, 85–9, 91–2, 151–2, 175–80.

[18] Within the public sphere of social justice there are several sub-spheres that correspond to different kinds of social justice. These sub-spheres are: 1) basic human rights and freedoms: freedom of speech, of worship, of movement, and so on; 2) economic justice: the duty of society to ensure that goods and services are fairly and equally distributed and the duty of individuals to contribute to the production of goods and services; 3) political justice: the duty of society to ensure that political power is fairly and equally distributed and the duty of individuals to contribute to political decision-making; 4) criminal justice: the duty of the society to fairly and equally enforce the law and the duty of individuals to obey the law; 5) environmental justice: the duty to protect the inorganic and organic world so that all being will flourish, not just human being; 6) intergenerational justice: duty of the present generation to pass on just social structures to the next generation and not overburden the next generation with debt and environmental degradation; 7) international justice: the duty of nations to live in comity with other nations and to create international social structures to solve social problems that are global in their effects. To all these duties are corresponding rights; indeed, one of the tasks of social justice is to find the proper balance of duties (responsibilities) and rights (entitlements), or to put it another way, the proper mix of what the larger society should distribute to sub-societies and individuals, and what individuals and sub-societies should contribute to the larger society.

[19] The works of two contemporary theorists of agapic love show these two tendencies. Gene Outka in his *Agape: an Ethical Analysis* (New Haven: Yale University Press, 1972), defines agapic love as "universal equal regard." Although he does accept mutuality as a proper fulfillment of agape, his understanding of agape leads his analysis more naturally towards justice. Stephen Post, in his *A Theory of*

Agape: On the Meaning of Christian Love (Lewisburg, PA: Bucknell University Press, 1990) shows agapic love as seeking out mutual response in "special relations." My own view is that both tendencies must be kept together in dialectical unity. I like the words of Gilbert Meilander: "We ought not give up the desire for mutual love and try to be stoics. Neither ought we permit our love to be limited to the small circle of those who return it." See *Friendship: A Study in Theological Ethics* (South Bend: University of Notre Dame Press, 1981), 50.

Eyes Open on a World *was written as part of the 150th anniversary of the arrival of the Sisters of St. Joseph in St. Paul. In it, the sisters reflect on the many changes that have taken place in the world over the past several decades and, hence, in their very own community. As you absorb this final reading, ponder how the CSJs have embodied the college's mission of seeking social justice and evoking hope for all. Has this effort influenced your education? Have you been inspired to continue to carry out this mission?*

Eyes Open on a World: Responding to Societal Needs

A Collaboration by the Sisters of St. Joseph of Carondelet St. Paul Province

The story of Sister Rita Steinhagen reflects the evolution of many sisters from institutionally based ministries to direct social services and then to social justice issues and political action. As Sister Rita explains, "One thing led to another." After illness demanded she leave her work as a medical technologist, Sister Rita opened a Free Store on the West Bank in Minneapolis, a place where people could "shop" for what they needed. She became acquainted with many people, including runaway youth who spent their days and nights on the streets. One day a youth asked her, "Why don't you get us a place to stay?" So Sister Rita founded the Bridge, a shelter for runaway youth, not far from the Free Store.

"I was learning about the oppressive and unjust systems—what it is like to be poor with a constant struggle just to survive," recalls Sister Rita. Because many of the people she met spoke Spanish, "I decided it was time to learn that language. So I went to a small language school in El Paso, Texas, and worked at a nearby shelter for refugees. It was there that I first learned about the School of the Americas." After hearing the refugees' stories, Sister Rita went to Central America as a Witness for Peace and lived in the war zones in northern Nicaragua.

When she returned home, Sister Rita worked for seven years at the Center for Victims of Torture. Haunted by her experience of seeing the results of torture and by her knowledge of U.S. complicity in training Latin American soldiers in methods of torture, she went to Fort Benning, Georgia, to participate in demonstrations opposing the School of the Americas. Because she "crossed the line a second time," a judge sentenced her to six months in federal prison, where "I got a crash course in our prison system and the unfairness of it all." Now, besides continuing to work to close the School of the Americas, she is involved with changing prison policies that are especially harsh on women with children.

Like Sister Rita, many sisters have become active in social justice movements. With the growing understanding in the 1960s that our religious vow of obedience meant much more than listening to the directives of our superiors and included being open to the Spirit by listening to the people and events of our times, we felt called to confront injustices wherever we saw them.

Like our first sisters in France we continue to give direct service to those in need and work for systemic change. Sister Florence Steichen uses the phrase "walking on the two feet of justice," a metaphor developed in the 1970s to describe this dual task. Our stories from the past fifty years show how leadership has emerged whenever sisters have seen needs and responded to them.

Sisters, of course, have been responding to needs all along. Sister Lillian Meyer went to political caucuses in the early 1950s, subscribed to the *Congressional Record,* and vigorously contributed her knowledge and opinions in Saturday classes on current affairs she took at the College of St. Catherine. In the 1940s and 1950s Sister Julienne Foley taught Mexican children and adults. Downtown St. Paul merchants and cab drivers recognized her resolute gait as she fearlessly approached them for food and clothing for "her people" or asked for free rides. Throughout the years sisters visited students and families in their homes and provided clothing and other necessities. They also visited those who were poor and elderly at the Ramsey County "poor farm," in hospitals, and in prisons, as our earliest members had done.

Some of our sisters worked at the Catholic Infant Home, a residence program for pregnant girls. The sisters provided child care and personal and spiritual enrichment classes for the girls, while other organizations provided health care services. As attitudes toward single pregnant women changed, so did the program. This ministry, now called Seton Center, is no longer a residence and offers a variety of services for single parents and married couples.

As social issues and reform movements surfaced in the 1960s, our community experienced transition from total separation to deep involvement in world affairs and ambivalence over our sisters being involved in public issues. By the end of the decade, however, we had a clear affirmation from our congregational leaders and from one another that social activism is part of our call. We welcomed the pastoral letter *Justice in the World,* issued by the U.S. bishops in 1971. One statement reinforced our conviction that working for justice is not an optional pursuit but is integral to the gospel: "Action on behalf of justice and participation in the transformation of the world appear to us as a constitutive dimension of the preaching of the gospel, or, in other words, of the church's mission for the redemption of the human race and its liberation from every oppressive situation." We celebrated this liberating statement as a landmark.

Sisters participated in political caucuses and demonstrations, including vigils for slain civil rights workers and protests against the Vietnam War and the Gulf War. Some also protested Honeywell's production of cluster bombs. Sisters Char Madigan and Rita Foster were among the early organizers of nonviolent protests there. In the early 1990s when Honeywell moved its weapons making to Alliant Technical Systems in Hopkins, the protesters moved there, too. Several sisters took part in antiwar demonstrations protesting the U.S. bombing of Iraq, the sanctions on Iraq, and intervention in Yugoslavia.

Societal conditions and movements provided impetus for political action. Some sisters became active in the Civil Rights movement, which in the beginning was primarily concerned with voting rights of African Americans. The notion of civil rights soon expanded to include the right to be born, to be housed adequately, and to be employed. Civil rights further evolved to encompass Native Americans and other ethnic minorities, sexual minorities, and women.

The *Roe v. Wade* Supreme Court decision in 1973 legalizing abortion in every state brought our deep convictions about the sacredness of life to the forefront. As a community we support all efforts to reverence and enhance the life of each person from beginning to end. Some of us are active in the prolife movement. Others focus their energy on abolishing the death penalty. After Sister Helen Prejean, a Sister of St. Joseph from the Medaille congregation and a well-known author and advocate for abolishing the death penalty, spoke at a gathering of the Federation of Sisters of St. Joseph in St. Louis in 2000, the 1,550 sisters present released a public statement on their stand against capital punishment. Also in the summer of 2000 Sister Mary Mark Mahoney, retired for many years, and Sister Carol Neuburger testified at a court appeal in Oklahoma and tried, unsuccessfully, to commute the death sentence of a prisoner with whom Sister Mary Mark had been corresponding for three years. She continues her special ministry by corresponding with other prison "pen pals."

As we moved from convents and from institutions into neighborhoods, many of us became more involved in public issues. When some of us moved from the College of St. Catherine into neighborhood housing in 1968, the college's student publication, *The Catherine Wheel* (May 10, 1968, p. 8) described the experience as not a departure from traditional religious living but rather as an opportunity to open up new possibilities of religious life in the spirit of renewal.

Moving into different living situations brought us into new ministries and political involvement. In the mid-1970s, Sisters Jean Campbell and

Jackie Slater moved into the Cedar-Riverside housing project in Minneapolis, a multiracial, multi-economic, integrated community. Sister Jackie's work there led her to run for the city council. She reported: "A few of the older and more traditional Catholics were upset about my candidacy for office. They were concerned that a nun would have a hard time in the nasty world of politics, or they were clinging to the notion that sisters should be either teachers or nurses. But there were also many who were very much in favor of it and they gave me their support and votes" (*Minneapolis Star Tribune*, December 24, 1977). Jackie won the election and became an influential as well as controversial council member. After her sudden death in 1984, the city of Minneapolis honored her by naming a renovated block of housing near downtown Minneapolis Slater Square.

Sister Jackie was not the first sister from the St. Paul Province to seek public office. Running on a prolife platform, Sister Elizabeth Regnier narrowly missed being elected to the North Dakota state legislature in 1972. Two years earlier in Jamestown, North Dakota, Sister Rose Alma Woychik lost the election to a ward precinct post by two votes.

While some sisters sought to influence public policy through elected office, Sister Mary Madonna Ashton received a state appointment from Minnesota Governor Rudy Perpich. During her tenure as Commissioner of Health from 1983 to 1991, Minnesota led the nation in addressing major health concerns by implementing tobacco control programs and HIV/AIDS prevention measures.

A number of us received our political initiation when Senator Eugene McCarthy from Minnesota sought the Democratic nomination for president in 1968. At the precinct caucus so many sisters showed up that we overwhelmed the proceedings. Some of us remember how upset the politician who chaired the meeting was when he saw all of us. Suspicious of the sisters' unaccustomed activism, he told us in no uncertain terms that he expected us to continue to come to the subsequent caucuses, and we did.

Some of us believed that protesting was part of our mission. In addition to her political involvement, Sister Rose Alma Woychik protested at missile bases in Jamestown, North Dakota, beginning in the mid-1960s. In a 1975 letter to Sister Frances Babb, she expressed the pivotal shift from suspicion of the world and withdrawal from it to wholehearted engagement with the world, which came to characterize the thinking of many sisters in the remaining decades of the twentieth century. She wrote: "I am not willing to admit that being interested in politics necessarily means that I am less interested in the love of God and my neighbor, or the spread of the gospel."

While some sisters protested against the Vietnam War and others demonstrated against legalized abortion, still others lobbied for fair housing, jobs, health care, education, and welfare legislation. Seeing government cuts in human services and increases in military spending, we insisted that enormous expenditures for weapons to protect the national security were creating havoc in our cities. As Sister Rita Steinhagen keeps saying, "One thing led to another." We did social analysis, asking who benefits and who suffers. We learned from our sisters in Peru that multinational success and security for developed countries meant tragic insecurity to the majority in developing countries.

When Sister Char Madigan began working in a downtown parish in the 1970s, she realized she was saying good night to people at 5:00 P.M. knowing they had no home to go to. Sisters Rita Steinhagen, Laura Geyer, and Char Madigan began offering shelter in their upper flat convent. That eventually led to the opening of St. Joseph's House, Ascension Place, and Incarnation House, all in Minneapolis, which were transitional housing shelters designed to empower women to live healthy, independent lives. In November 2000, Incarnation House began a new phase of service to women and children as it held an open house to celebrate its partnership with Wayside, a Minneapolis-based program designed to help women achieve their full potential and become productive members of the community.

Experience in these newly established shelters and runaway centers led Sister Marguerite Corcoran and three of the McDonald sisters, Rita, Brigid, and Jane, to question what was going on in the broader world community. A fourth McDonald sister, Kate, who along with others taught English to refugees and immigrants, had the same question. Her sister, Sister Brigid, while working at Incarnation House, connected us with Women Against Military Madness (WAMM) to pressure legislative bodies to direct government funds to welfare rights instead of to military spending. A growing interest in liberation theology, which focuses on the struggles of those who are poor and encourages religious people to champion nonviolent resistance, motivated many sisters to support WAMM's work.

Sisters have joined in solidarity with our Native American sisters and brothers seeking to preserve their cultural beliefs. At the invitation of Ojibwe elder woman Bea Swanson, Sister Jane McDonald helps staff an intergenerational and interracial prayer lodge at All Nations Church in Minneapolis. That experience led her to stand in solidarity with Native American struggles against land pollution—for example, the pollution of Prairie Island Indian land with the storing of nuclear waste. In the late 1990s Sisters Jane McDonald, Jan Dalsin, and Mary O'Brien and others joined the Native American protest against a highway reroute that sacrificed sacred sites, including trees and spring-fed waters, for the sake of a highway expansion. Other sisters helped Native Americans adjust to urban life by providing basic necessities and connecting them with social service agencies.

For twenty years our sisters have worked with the Resource Center of the Americas and other Sanctuary movements, both for indigenous peoples in other lands and with refugees fleeing those lands. While serving as director of a sanctuary house in Waco, Texas, Sister Marie Richard King worked to provide temporary safe haven for undocumented persons from Mexico. Sisters have been arrested, and some imprisoned, for such "illegal" activities as supporting the César Chavez United Farm Workers grape boycott in 1968, standing with Salvadoran refugees who sought sanctuary in the Cathedral of St. Paul, and demonstrating against the manufacture of nuclear weapons. After more than twenty years of involvement in human rights issues, Sister Betty McKenzie connected sisters to the St. Paul Ecumenical Alliance of Churches (SPEAC), an ecumenical effort to work locally for housing, fair wages, and environmental issues.

The plight of persons who are homeless continues to be of deep concern to us. In one instance, both serendipity and providence played a part in the opening of an overnight shelter. Sister Dolore Rochon, an administrator at St. Joseph's Hospital in downtown St. Paul, was having coffee with Sister Rita Steinhagen one blizzardy December day in 1981. Sister Rita, then working at the nearby Dorothy Day Center, expressed concern that so many homeless people were sleeping in downtown doorways and in caves near the river. Sister Dolore, aware there was an empty floor in Mary Hall, the nurses' residence at the hospital, persuaded hospital and province leaders to convert this space into overnight housing for homeless persons. A week later, on New Year's Eve, with a wind chill of seventy degrees below zero, the doors of Mary Hall opened. Sisters volunteered to spend nights with the guests until Catholic Charities assumed responsibility for the residence.

Another dream became reality when Sister Rose Tillemans established Peace House, a space where people gather during the day for sharing and prayer. To her, Peace House is "one answer to the seldom looked-at question of what do the poor and disadvantaged do after they have some food, clothing, and shelter." She set up a storefront in 1985 on Franklin Avenue in Minneapolis, and since then people have come each day for coffee, food, and meditation. Together, they form community in a safe atmosphere built on acceptance, a sense of belonging, friendship, dignity, and mutuality of service.

Our commitment to supporting people who experience poverty, abuse, torture, mental illness, or discrimination remains strong. In Minneapolis, sisters are involved in INSTEP, a child care program that helps low-income parents pursue work and/or educational opportunities to become more self-sufficient. When the Derham Convent building in St. Paul became available in the 1990s, the province opened Sarah's Oasis, a temporary home for women, including refugees, some of whom come from the Center for the Victims of Torture in Minneapolis. At Sarah's women live in a safe environment that fosters relationships, reflection, and self-empowerment.

As a psychologist, Sister Karen Hilgers worked with many adult women who had survived abuse. She dreamed of a peaceful residence—not a hospital—where women in crisis could spend a few days with a supportive staff to regain their equilibrium. In collaboration with a small group of other psychologists Sister Karen developed this new approach to treatment. In 1996, Cornelia Place opened its doors in Minneapolis, providing the care and support the women needed. Although the model Sister Karen and her colleagues created proved to be a successful crisis management model, the residential portion of the program closed because of lack of funding. Cornelia Place now operates as a mental health clinic specializing in the treatment of women with posttraumatic stress disorder.

Through our experiences in pastoral and social ministries, we realized that unjust economic systems are significant factors leading to the oppression of people. This insight led Sister Mary Ellen Foster to complete a master's degree at the New School for Social Research in New York City, a school that critiques economic systems with an eye towards social transformation. Following her studies, Sister Mary Ellen began to teach classes in economics stressing the impact of economic systems on the world and urging her students to engage in activities that lead to systemic change.

Clearly, our concerns for social justice extend beyond the U.S. boundaries. Recognizing needs around the globe, sisters have responded in various ways. While Sister Florence Steichen served as registrar at Bethlehem University in the occupied West Bank, the Israeli military governor closed the university for three years because of the *Intifada,* the struggle of Palestinian young people to gain independence. Sister Florence played a major role in arranging for off-campus classes to help Palestinian students continue their education. She and other sisters who taught at Bethlehem University returned home with a commitment to further Palestinian rights by speaking, writing, contacting legislators, and seeking funds for Bethlehem University from our Partners in Justice fund. Continuing her advocacy for peace in the Middle East, Sister Florence works with Minnesota Middle East Peace Now and the Middle East Committee of Women Against Military Madness.

Representing our province at the United Nations Fourth World Conference on Women in Beijing in 1995, Sister Susan Oeffling learned firsthand about the status and plight of women throughout the world. While she was in Beijing, at the invitation of Minnesota Public Radio, Sister Susan called in regularly to report on the conference and answer listeners' questions. Upon returning home, she gave numerous talks on her Beijing experience to parish, school, corporate, and religious groups and published an article entitled "Keep on Keeping On" in *Sisters Today*. She joined the nonviolence working group of the Justice Commission, which then changed its name to Beyond Beijing: Women and Violence to focus on implementation of the Beijing platform.

As we struggled to "walk on the two feet of justice" in these last fifty years, we realized that we needed education and support in our efforts. As coordinator of the Social Justice Secretariat from 1979 to 1982, Sister Kathy Roehl kept us informed about justice issues and actions we could take to address the issues. We then established the Social Justice Task Force in 1982, which evolved into the Justice Commission in 1984. Sister Carol Neuburger, the first chair of the commission, brought energy and initiative to the work of justice. With her guidance, the province developed a process for sisters in the province to take a "corporate stand," that is, to make a public statement in the name of the Sisters of St. Joseph of the St. Paul Province. The process ensured that a corporate stand would represent the will of a majority of sisters, not a small group within the province. We took our first corporate stand in 1986 as a strong symbolic action for peace: "To declare as nuclear-free zones properties owned by the Sisters of St. Joseph in the St. Paul Province."

The province hired Joänne Tromiczak-Neid, a former Sister of St. Joseph, in 1992 as the full-time justice coordinator to help us address issues of social justice discussed at the congregational chapter and written in our Acts of Chapter. In addition to networking with local and national justice groups, Joanne was instrumental in starting Women Religious for Justice, a collaborative effort of area religious communities. Among the founders of www.Sistersonline.org, a collaborative venture begun in 1996 with other communities of women religious in Minnesota, Joänne sees the website as facilitating outreach "to women and children who suffer from the multiple manifestations of injustice" (*Together*, November 1999, p. 13). As part of a global movement of women who care deeply about what is happening with the world, the earth, and its people, Sistersonline's 1999–2000 focus included debt relief and women in prison.

The role of women in the church is the concern of many of us. Sister Frances Babb, throughout her long life, was an ardent feminist. At the age of six in 1912, she handed out women's suffrage pamphlets with her mother. From the age of sixteen, she was certain that she had a vocation to the ordained priesthood, and throughout her life she was a persuasive spokeswoman for the ordination of women. In 1975 she spoke eloquently and painfully, with her commanding voice and strong Maine accent, of her desire to be a priest when she presented a petition to the official board for the Permanent Diaconate asking that the St. Paul and Minneapolis Archdiocese permit women to enter the Permanent Diaconate Training program. No action was taken on her petition.

Our first public efforts on behalf of gay, lesbian, bisexual, and transgendered (GLBT) persons were undertaken by Sister Sarah O'Neill, who dedicated much of her time and energy to seeking reconciliation and support between the Catholic Church and Catholic gays and lesbians. She worked tirelessly to assist with the founding of the Catholic Pastoral Committee on Sexual Minorities (CPCSM). In the years since Sister Sarah's death, some sisters have participated in demonstrations against repression of GLBT persons and sought to help families/friends both understand the church's position on GLBT persons and respect the individual's conscience. In June of 1999, twenty-two sisters and consociates marched in the Twin Cities Gay Pride Parade. They carried a large banner stating, "Sisters of St. Joseph of Carondelet, St. Paul, MN, Justice Commission, Standing for Human Rights and Justice." It was the first time we had walked in the parade so publicly.

As we look to the future, we recognize that the need to "walk on the two feet of justice" at times exceeds our ability to be involved personally and directly. In recent years we have found additional ways to support our quest for justice. After we sold St. John's Hospital in Fargo, North Dakota, we established the Giving Board in 1987, which allowed sisters to request grants for persons with immediate needs such as child care and living expenses. The sale of St. Mary's Hospital in Minneapolis presented us with a unique opportunity and challenged us to use the money generated to fulfill our mission. We developed a focus statement to guide our vision: "We, the community of the Sisters of St. Joseph [of the St. Paul Province], in keeping with our commitment to the gospel, choose, in dialogue with one another to use our spiritual, material, and personal resources in collaborative efforts to support those in need."

An Allocations Task Force recommended that the funding of ministries be spread across a range of categories representing a continuum of risk, from sponsored institutions and affiliated ministries to new, ongoing, or collaborative projects and individual radical responses to the gospel. As a result of the work of the task force, we established the Partners in Justice fund, which supports ministries that respond uniquely to unmet needs of the economically oppressed and to ministries that further our historical commitment to women and children.

Another vehicle for funding our ministries, the Partners in Ministry fund of our Ministries Foundation, "seeks to make a difference in the lives of those in need by generating and allocating funds to support present and future ministries of the Sisters of St. Joseph of Carondelet" (Ministries Foundation mission statement, 1995). Foundation board members, both sisters and laypeople, dedicate their time and efforts to ensuring that our mission and ministries continue into the future.

As we look back on the last fifty years we see how we have divided the city and sought to be attentive to the needs of our neighbors. Although, at times, tensions existed among us and we do not always agree on how to address the needs, we have grown in respect for one another as we realized that there are many ways to do the works of justice. Our Congregation of the Sisters of St. Joseph of Carondelet "encourages each sister [and consociate] to witness in areas of concern according to the dictates of an informed conscience and supports the rights of members to take a public stand on matters of justice" (Complementary Document 1984, p. 12). As needs continue to manifest themselves, we are confident that, like our foremothers, our sisters, consociates, and partners in ministry will divide the city and stand with the dear neighbor.

The Reflective Woman

Resources

Mission Statement

St. Catherine University educates students to lead and influence. Inspired by its visionary founding in 1905 by the Sisters of St. Joseph of Carondelet, more than a century later the University serves diverse students, with a baccalaureate college for women at its heart and graduate and associate programs for women and men.

At all degree levels, St. Catherine integrates liberal arts and professional education within the Catholic tradition, emphasizing intellectual inquiry and social teaching, and challenging students to transformational leadership. Committed to excellence and opportunity, St. Catherine University develops ethical, reflective and socially responsible leaders, informed by the philosophy of the women's college and the spirit of the founders.

Roman Catholic Identity Statement

Throughout the history of St. Catherine University, founded by the Sisters of St. Joseph of Carondelet, we have been dedicated as a University community to our Roman Catholic heritage and identity. In light of the rich and diverse history of the Church and the vision of Vatican II, we affirm aspects of that identity that are particularly appropriate to higher education.

From the Church's intellectual tradition, which has equated the search for truth with true liberation, we value an open atmosphere of critical inquiry, cross-cultural studies and interdisciplinary teaching.

From its social tradition, with its consistent commitment to the poor and outcast, we value and reach out to those marginalized by our society and churches, and in particular, we seek to promote women's leadership.

From its sacramental tradition, which has emphasized ritual, symbol and the use of material things as signs of grace, we value the integration of the material and spiritual, and the use of creative rituals for prayer and celebration.

From the tradition that has stressed both communal participation and the worth of the individual, we value dialogue, respect for diversity and the nurturing of personal conscience. From the call of Jesus himself, that all should be one (John 17:21), we value ecumenism and collaboration among all faiths.

Drawing upon those traditions, we seek to promote — through our student services, campus ministry, administration, faculty and staff —a common search for wisdom and the integration of our daily lives and work with our spirituality. Without being exclusive of other ecclesial and spiritual traditions, we will continue to ask ourselves how this Catholic heritage enhances the people we serve and the well-being of our planet.

March 26, 1996

Ellen Richter-Norgel is associate dean for students and retention and Joann Bangs is interim dean of the School of Business and Professional Studies. Together, they co-chair the St. Catherine Experience Task Force and are passionate about creating a holistic experience for students. As you read this essay, consider how you can take advantage of the best of what St. Catherine University offers to students. How can you become fully engaged in claiming your education?

The St. Catherine Experience

Owning Your Education: Fully Engaging in the St. Catherine Experience

Ellen Richter-Norgel and Joann Bangs

> *"When I first came to St. Kate's, all I cared about was getting my degree. I just wanted to get in and get out. Just do my schoolwork, and that was it. But, now I feel differently. As the year has gone by, I've invested in issues and relationships; I've encouraged and tutored younger students. I have grown to care about bearing good fruit at St. Kate's. I have grown to feel like I want to give everything I can to this community and get all that I am supposed to get out of being here at this school."*
>
> —Kathleen Woodbury, past TRW class

Welcome to St. Catherine University! We are excited about the amazing journey you are about to begin. We join you in your anticipation, and we are excited to provide you with some guidance and support to fully realize your academic and personal goals. At St. Catherine, we take seriously the idea of "claiming an education." We invite you to explore the meaning of Adrienne Rich's (1979) suggestion that "there is a more essential experience that you owe yourselves . . . which finally depends on you, in all your interactions with yourself and your world" (233). Rich is referring to taking responsibility for your own education, which means "refusing to let others do your thinking, talking, and naming for you; [responsibility] means learning to respect and use your own brains and instincts; hence, grappling with hard work" (233). You will want to examine critically the sources of ideas, explore different perspectives and struggle with difficult concepts. Owning your education also means recognizing that your learning extends outside the classroom to what is commonly referred to in academia as the co-curriculum. The co-curriculum includes a diverse offering of programs and services that support your learning as well as contribute to your development as a whole person. These programs and services, such as social justice trips, study abroad, service learning activities and internships, impact your development. These experiences will open your eyes to a different worldview. Through your work both inside and outside the classroom, you will build skills related to your professional and personal development.

> *The Reflective Woman really has given me a good sense of community . . . The most important thing I learned from The Reflective Woman is that everyone has a voice and everyone is truly unique in their own individual way. We all come from a different background and we each have our own collection of experiences. Every person has different contributions to offer; we each need to listen and grow in what we learn.*
>
> —Allyson Benz, Elementary Education, past TRW class

The Core Curriculum

You have begun your introduction to this community of learners in The Reflective Woman (TRW). This first Core course is organized around three key ideas: **Composing a Life** looks at what has constituted your life so far and what will inform your future. You will explore issues of identity, representation, privilege, vocation and values. In **Searching for Truths** you explore what comprises a strong argument, what makes a source credible, and from what perspective you critically evaluate sources. **Working Towards Community and Social Justice** asks you to locate yourself in relationship to others: How do you define community? How are justice and charity different? What is your responsibility and role in creating more just communities? Because we deeply value art and aesthetics, these concepts are woven through the course.

You will explore each of these ideas through the processes of reading, reflecting, researching, writing and discussing with others. Thus, your class becomes a small community of learners where you discuss the readings and explore ideas that have emerged as you individually interact with the readings and themes. There is a shared responsibility for learning, with your teacher serving mainly as facilitator rather than an expert. This exploration is happening in all the other sections as well as your own, thus making *connections* a central theme in The Reflective Woman.

After taking The Reflective Woman (TRW) you will continue with the Core curriculum engaging in the liberal arts requirements at the university. You will explore courses in literature, history, the arts, science and math, social sciences, philosophy, theology, language, and exercise science, building the foundation of a meaningful education. You will explore ideas, think critically and creatively, and communicate effectively.

Your Core experience culminates in The Global Search for Justice (GSJ), a focused seminar that again calls you to explore ideas within a community of learners. You will focus on social justice and be called to responsible action in the world. You will choose a GSJ section developed around one of six broad themes such as environmental justice, justice in Latin America, or social movements for change, which form a kind of case study for social justice. All sections share common readings, objectives and core knowledge but give you the opportunity to choose the topic of study that interests you or connects with your major. In some sections, you will have the chance to participate in volunteer work with communities on issues of injustice in local neighborhoods and abroad. These powerful learning experiences are designed to encourage you to see yourself and your life choices in much larger terms. This community work component also provides another occasion to link curricular and co-curricular activities. Campus Ministry can help you connect with the community work of the Sisters of St. Joseph locally and internationally. Additionally, you can work with the Office of Global Studies to combine an off-campus or international study experience with your Global Search for Justice course by enrolling in a focused section of GSJ offered in countries such as India, China, Mexico or Jamaica.

A Unique Community of Learners

As an Associate of Arts student in Minneapolis, or an incoming first year, transfer or Evening/Weekend/Online (E/W/O) student on the St. Paul campus, you are joining a unique community of learners, "[a] group of people engaged in intellectual interaction for the purpose of learning" (Cross, 1998, p.4). You will be engaging in a learning environment at St. Catherine that is

- Collaborative. It values shared learning among students, faculty, and staff.
- Flexible. It allows faculty and student roles to shift from expert to learner and learner to expert.
- Student-Centered. It encourages the development of your own voice and perspective.
- Challenging. It expects you to own your education.
- Diverse. It invites you to engage diversity and global perspectives with respect.
- Encompassing. It recognizes that learning takes place in and out of the classroom.
- Holistic. It places your growth as a whole person paramount—intellectually, spiritually, emotionally, socially and physically.
- Supportive. It establishes a network of support to meet your learning needs.
- Reflective. It offers opportunities for synthesizing your learning.

At St. Catherine University, we value that ways women learn. Relationships and the sequence of learning experiences are important aspects of how women learn, according to Belenky (1986) et. al, authors of *Women's Ways of Knowing*. Finding one's place is believed to be a requirement for critical reflection. "For women, confirmation and community are prerequisites rather than consequences of development" (194). Our community uses what we know about learning structures to best facilitate your intellectual development.

The St. Catherine Experience: An Intentional Structure That Supports Your Educational Path

—I wish I had 30 hours in a day to do all that is offered at St. Kate's.

—Senior, Spanish and Psychology

The St. Catherine Experience integrates the curriculum and co-curriculum, enabling you to experience the best of what St. Kate's offers. Intentional links help you identify and navigate important components, from matriculation to graduation to fully realize your education. Across all degree programs, associate, baccalaureate and graduate, the St. Catherine Experience is characterized by eight themes of engagement.

Eight Themes of Engagement

To find the best way to describe the St. Catherine Experience, a task force of faculty and staff conducted focus groups with over 100 students and asked them to describe what they believed to be the essential elements of their education at St. Kate's. In a separate group, faculty and staff were asked the same question. Without knowing what the other group said, both groups identified an identical set of eight themes. This consensus was a powerful affirmation of the St. Catherine Experience. The themes are as follows:

Scholarship and Excellence describes how your major is enhanced by engaging and challenging academic experiences. You may participate in the Antonian Honors Program; enroll in upper-division courses in Ireland, France or Ecuador through one of the many Global Studies opportunities; be mentored for one of the post-graduate national fellowships and scholarships including Rhodes, Fulbright or Truman Scholarship; serve as a Teaching or Research Assistant in the Assistant Mentorship Program; or become a member of Phi Beta Kappa, to name a few opportunities.

I served as a TA and Lab Instructor in the Psychology department. What was so mind-blowing for me is that the faculty actually asked my opinion about what changes to be made in the curriculum after my second semester of serving as a TA.

—Junior, Psychology

Lead and Influence describes your development as an ethical leader for our multicultural and global community. You will live out our stated vision to "lead and influence" by participating in the abundant development opportunities offered in academic departments, student government, clubs and organizations, through Student Employment, and through the many opportunities in the Abigail Quigley McCarthy Center for Women.

—Leadership opportunities are everywhere; if you want a leadership experience, you can have five! There are so many opportunities—everywhere you go. I've had leadership roles in Senate, in my RA job, working individually with professors. It seems the opportunities here are endless.

—Junior, International Business and
Economics and Marketing Management

Engagement describes the number of ways you find your niche within the University and the ways in which your passions are nurtured. You may compete as an athlete; become an actor, stage manager, or costume designer in one of the theater productions; conduct research with a faculty member abroad; compete in Model UN or MOCK Trial; present a paper at one of the ACTC, national or international conferences; work as summer scholar in the Undergraduate Collaborative Research Program; conduct an internship; or take a course with a community, work and learning component.

—There is so much to put on my resume that I can't keep it to one page, even after just two years here.

—Sophomore transfer student,
International Business and Economics

Liberal Arts and Your Program refers to becoming grounded in the core courses of humanities, arts and sciences that provide a springboard to your program of study. You can hear engaging speakers in the Core Convocations, delve deep into your major courses and see the connections between your liberal arts core courses and your major. Consider double majoring to deepen your learning, to make meaningful connections and, to apply multiple intellectual perspectives across your programs.

—Students here are referred to and treated as scholars; I like the use of this language; we are expected to wrestle with the material and concepts until we understand them.

—Junior, Biology

Social Justice and Spiritual Development refers to the ways in which you will experience the spirit and practices of the founding Sisters of St. Joseph of Carondelet as well as develop your sense of spiritual self. You will be introduced to the Principles of Catholic Social Teaching and Catholic Intellectual Traditions in your TRW course. You can continue your spiritual development by participating in one of the Justice Learning and Outreach trips, developing a practice of reflection and meditation, finding beauty and spaces in our grounds to find solace, and engaging in meaningful, courageous conversations with members of the community.

—[Social Justice and Spiritual Development] is the reason I came to St. Kate's . I got connected to the Music Ministry Alive. I was an active participant and knew from that experience that I was going to be able to develop my spirituality here. Now I'm an AMP student with Lori True in Campus Ministry."

—Senior, Foods and Nutrition Science

Meaningful Mentoring refers to the significant relationships you will develop with faculty and staff members. Your mentors will challenge and support you to become your best self and to take advantage of opportunities that the University offers. In the Assistant Mentor Program you will be mentored by a faculty or staff member in your role as Teaching Assistant, Research Assistant or Program Collaborator. You become a mentor to other students: serve as a Peer Mentor with MIPS, a Resident Assistant or a Writing or Math Tutor in the O'Neill Center. You will find that mentoring relationships take place in the daily interactions between you and your academic advisor, career counselor, financial aid counselor and club/organization advisor.

> *—The instructors make you think you are more than you think you are. They believe in us and what we are capable of doing.*
>
> —Sophomore, Evening/Weekend/
> On-line, Communications Studies

> *—I spent the summer with Professor Jill Welter in California conducting research; it was awesome.*
>
> —Senior, Biology

Diversity and Global Perspectives refers to the ways that St. Catherine University honors diversity in all its forms and responsibilities of global citizenship. You will discuss race, class and privilege in your courses. You can participate in the Cornbread and Chili discussions about various social justice topics offered by MIPS, and you can participate in the interfaith practices offered by Campus Ministry. Opportunities in Global Studies and Community, Work and Learning will take you out of your comfort zone as you experience communities different from your own.

> *—I love the diverse culture that I saw [when touring St. Kate's]. . . . I was thinking of attending another institution, but St. Kate's offered so much more diversity. . . . Diversity is more free-flowing[and]differences are obvious.*
>
> —Sophomore transfer student,
> International Business and Economics

Preparing for the Future includes activities inside and outside the classroom that will help you integrate and then implement your academic and career goals in a satisfying plan following graduation. You can meet with a career counselor to hone your job-search skills. You can complete internships that will help you develop confidence and skills that support your professional goals. You can also work with the pre-law, pre-med or another pre-professional advisor to take the steps necessary to become a competitive candidate for graduate or professional programs. Join a professional organization associated with your discipline to develop a strong network of alumnae, faculty, and professionals in the field.

The St. Catherine Advising Tool

To help you own your education, each major/program of study provides students with a St. Catherine Advising Tool that is tailored to that discipline.[1] Embedded in these advising tools are the eight themes of engagement as described above. The advising tools help you identify key links between co-curricular programs and academic programs of study including areas such as academic advising, career development, service learning, leadership development, internship opportunities, learning communities, social justice and volunteer experiences.

For example, using the St. Catherine Experience Advising Tool, a student majoring in American Sign Language (ASL) or Interpreting, will be encouraged to connect early with her advisor to identify courses that will be important to take during her first and second term. An ASL/Interpreting Transfer student can refer to the tool and identify any opportunities she has not yet been able to take advantage of due to attendance at a prior institution. ASL/Interpreting students will learn about the ASL Club, Silent Lunches, and Deaf community events hosted on campus. Students using the tool will be informed about the ASL Honor Society, Antonian Scholars Honors Program, and criteria required for invitation to Phi Beta Kappa so that they can build their GPA and prepare for consideration. As a sophomore, ASL students will be reminded that they can live in the ASL Residential Learning Community to further ASL skills, and to engage in programming and events that create connections with the Deaf Community.

The ASL/Interpreting Advising Tool identifies important deadlines to be considered for leadership and student employment positions within the department. It also identifies opportunities to make connections with the Minnesota Registry of Interpreters for the Deaf, a network that helps students establish professional relationships in the field. During the junior and senior year, the tool highlights leadership opportunities available including Research or Program Assistant, ASL Peer Tutor, and ASL Residential Learning Community Resident Assistant. The advising tool also reminds students of the importance of working with Career Development staff to develop solid job-search skills for a successful transition to professional work environments.

The SCE Advising Tools created for each program of study, will articulate specific events available to you within your major and co-curriculum, beginning with your first year through your graduating year. Copies of the St. Catherine Advising Tool are available from your academic advisor, in your department, in the offices of Academic Advising and Career Development. You can also download the SCE Advising Tools from the St. Catherine Experience website: www2/stkate.edu/sce/ home.

Summary

We are acutely aware that you may enter college with multiple demands that can compromise your focus on academics: full-time or part-time work, financial worries, parenting responsibilities or caring for extended family members. These pressures can easily distract from your ability to fully participate in what the St. Catherine Experience offers. Please know that St. Kate's offers an array of support systems that can help you address these pressures. The Learning Center and O'Neill Center staff members are ready to work closely with you to develop good time management skills and help create a schedule that that allows for study, work, and other demands. St. Kate's Money Management staff can help you develop a financial budget that addresses your financial concerns. Counseling staff members can provide you with strategies for stress management, dealing with homesickness, relationships and other personal issues. The Butler Center offers programs to help you learn mind/body/spirit practices that allow for balance in your life. *Use your St. Catherine Experience Advising Tool* to help you embrace and own your education by taking full advantage of the remarkable opportunities offered by St. Catherine University.

Note

The authors would like to acknowledge Suzanne Hendricks for her contributions in an earlier version of this article entitled, Engagement, Commitment, Connection: Owning Your St. Catherine Education.

[1] At the writing of this article, the St. Catherine Experience Advising Tools are not yet completed for all programs of study.

References

Belenky, M. F., B. M. Clinchy, N. R. Goldberger, and J. M. Tarule. *Women's Ways of Knowing: The Development of Self, Voice, and Mind.* New York: Basic Books, 1986. Print.

Cross, K. P. (1998). "Why Learning Communities? Why Now?" *About Campus*, 3(3), 4–11.

Rich, A. "Claiming an Education." *On Lies, Secrets, and Silence: Selected Prose* 1966–1978. (pp. 231–235) New York: Norton, 1979. Print.

Joanne Cavallaro, professor of English, has been chair of English and of women's studies, as well as director of the O'Neill Center and of writing programs at St. Kate's. A specialist in language studies and linguistics, she works and plays with words. In this essay, she emphasizes the importance of the writing process. In what ways is it "a process of discovery" for you?

How Writing Works

Joanne Cavallaro

Writing is a complex process. Indeed, it often seems mysterious or magical to people who don't write much. Often, people assume that a good writer is somehow born that way. Well, some people may be born with a talent for putting words together in interesting and evocative ways, but most good writers, whether published novelists or good student writers, have learned how to write through practice and feedback. Writing is a skill anyone can learn. We may not all end up published writers, but we can all learn enough to handle well any writing task we may encounter in college or on the job.

> How do I know what I think until I see what I say?—E. M. Forster

Writing is a process of discovery. Despite what you may have been told before, most writers, when they start a project, do not usually have a complete picture of what they will write. Generally, they discover what it is they want to say as they go through the process of writing. They gather ideas and facts, start writing, see where the writing leads them, get feedback, write some more, get more facts and ideas, write again, revise, rewrite, change, add, delete, edit.

This process may seem messy and meandering, but if you learn to trust it, it works. Writing helps us give form to thought. When we try to write something down, we soon discover whether we really understand it or not. When we write our ideas down, we can examine them from different angles; we can question them, see where they lead us. By writing, we not only discover what we have to say, we also learn to say it better.

Sometimes writing takes place far away from pen and paper, or computer and printer. As we drive to school, wait for the bus, stand in line for a sandwich at the Grill, we can continue to work on our writing by thinking about it. Many of the best introductions I have written have come to me as I've showered in the morning. They've just popped into my head, probably because I went to bed the night before thinking about what I was writing. I also constantly write down ideas for papers on napkins, receipts, anything I find handy when an idea appears. Good writers often continue to work at their writing even away from the desk.

Good writers also know that writing is hard work. Someone once said that writing a college essay is cognitively one of the hardest things most of us are ever asked to do. The hard work comes from thinking things out. And it's only when we've written down our ideas and tried to develop them that we can see if they make sense and are worth keeping.

> I suffer always from fear of putting down that first line. It is amazing the terrors, the magics, the prayers, the straightening shyness that assails one.
>
> —John Steinbeck

Sometimes the hardest part about writing is just getting started, so many writers use "tricks" to get started and keep themselves going to produce a first draft. The following section includes a list of some of these tricks that might be useful to you. Most writers know that they will be able to work things out if they just get started and keep going. They know they will revise their first drafts, so they don't need to worry about getting it all perfect the first time. In fact, they know that the quest for perfection early in the process will stymie their creativity and thinking. They write freely for the first draft, not worrying about spelling and punctuation for now. And they know that if they hit a stumbling block, they can mark it on the draft and come back to it later when they revise.

Planning what you want to write before you begin your draft helps make the writing easier, so most writers have some sort of plan before they sit down to write their draft. It may be an outline, or it may be a list of ideas on a sheet of scratch paper. They use the information they have gathered before they started to write the draft to help them create their plan. And for most writers, whatever plan they produce is tentative. Since we usually discover more about our topic as we write, any plan needs to be flexible, able to be refined and revised during the process of writing.

> I have never thought of myself as a good writer. Anyone who wants reassurance of that should read one of my first drafts. But I'm one of the world's great revisers.—James Michener

Writing is rewriting, as Donald Murray says. Good writing rarely appears full blown on a first draft. To produce strong writing, writers have to revise, often going through several drafts. Hemingway claimed he rewrote the ending to *A Farewell to Arms* 39 times. When asked why, he answered, "To get the words right." Revising is an opportunity to get the words right. It's also an opportunity to gain an entirely new perspective on your subject, an opportunity to delve more deeply into your ideas. It may mean adding lots of new material or cutting out lots of stuff you've already written (always a difficult thing to do!). It may mean moving things around or rewriting whole sections. It may mean starting all over. The following section contains some strategies that might be useful for you as you revise.

Well, it's a beautiful feeling, even if it's hard work.—Anne Sexton

Writing the Draft

As you write your first draft, it is best to focus on what you want to say first and worry about how it looks later. Remember, this is a draft, so you will have an opportunity to go back and change it later. If you find that you worry so much about spelling and mechanics that you sometimes forget what you were trying to say, it might be best to stop worrying about those things for now. Worry about spelling and punctuation and precise word choice and other sentence-level matters only after you're satisfied that you've said what you want to say. It's not very efficient to stop and carefully fix all the possible errors in a paragraph that you may well delete later when you revise. Leave the editing until later.

1. Focus on your ideas first. As you write your draft, keep rereading what you've written and ask yourself: What am I trying to tell my reader? What's my point, my story here? What else needs to be added? What's no longer necessary? If you're stuck for a word or a transition, leave a blank or a mark that will remind you to come back to that spot later.

2. Allow yourself time. If a paper is due next week, start it this week, even if you don't yet have all the data or ideas you want. Beginning to write, if only for 10 minutes, will start the incubation process in your own mind. You'll find that once you start it, you'll actually be working on the paper in your subconscious as you go through your day. Plan to do more than one draft; very few writers can create a good paper in their first draft.

3. Imagine a real audience as you write and revise. Think of your classmates or teacher as your audience unless you have a more specific audience you are writing to. Ask yourself what information they will need in order to follow what you're trying to say. You already know that information and probably take it for granted; does your audience know it? If not, put it in.

4. Play with titles, introductions, and conclusions. These are important, highly visible points in any paper. Provocative titles catch readers' attention; good introductions keep readers going; strong conclusions leave strong memories in readers' minds. But these same elements work on the writer as well as the reader, for a good title, introduction or conclusion can suggest changes for what follows or precedes. Sometimes these elements come early in the process, as controlling ideas. Sometimes they come later. In any case, they can capture the essence of your paper, telling you what to keep and what to cut.

5. Use a word processor. Some people write out their first draft by hand and then type it on a computer. Others compose directly onto the computer. Use

whatever way suits you best, but do use a computer. Computers make all the difference when it comes to making changes easy. You can move things around, add and delete easily. When writers go to revise their drafts, most find it more efficient to print the drafts out and read them on paper rather than on the screen. It is much easier to see the whole picture when you read it on paper. It's also easier on paper to find your mistakes when you come to the editing and proofreading stage.

Some General Strategies for Revision

Once you've written your draft, take some time away from it; let it rest for a few hours at least. If you can, leave it overnight or a few days before you look at it again. That way, you can approach it more objectively, the way your reader will, without already knowing exactly what it says.

You may already have some ideas about what you want to change in your draft. That's a good place to start. Even if you do know what you want to change, it's a good idea to sit down and reread the entire thing, making notes as you go along.

Re-Reading Your Draft

1. Read the whole thing first. Read it straight through to see what it says, to find its central point. You may be surprised to find that it doesn't say exactly what you thought you were saying. That's OK right now. At this point, it's helpful to first get an overall sense of what your draft actually says. One way to do this is to outline your draft. The outline needn't be too detailed, just one that summarizes the main point of each paragraph. In addition to an outline, try writing down what the purpose of your essay is, who the audience is, and what strategy you have used in each paragraph to achieve your purpose (in other words, what each paragraph does). Jot down problem areas or things to return to later. As you read, keep asking yourself, "What am I trying to say here?"

2. Try to read the draft as your reader would. Remember, your reader doesn't know everything that was in your head as you wrote the essay. As you read, you might know the background information necessary to fully understand your points, but will the reader know that information? Ask yourself what information the reader needs to know that you take for granted.

3. It's difficult to be objective about one's own writing, so getting someone else to read your draft is very helpful. Give it to a friend, or even better take it to the Writing Center. Either way, ask your reader or tutor to tell you if there are any parts that are difficult to understand, that need more elaboration, more support. Are there any connections that are not clear? Start by asking about the clarity and development of your ideas;

leave the grammar issues for later. Make notes on the paper as you listen to your readers' reactions. Most good writers ask others to read and react to their work before the final copy is due.

Revising Your Draft

When you sit down to revise, don't try to do it all at once. Break the process up into stages. Look at the whole first and then move on to parts.

1. Start with the big picture, the main points, your overall purpose. Think about what you want to say. Does the draft say what you want it to? Is your thesis clear? Can the reader tell easily what your main points are? Do you develop your ideas enough? Do you support your points rather than just state them? Do you need to add more information? Have you thought through your ideas thoroughly? What are you really trying to say? Have you said it? Have you said it all?

Writers often don't get to the point they really want to make until the end of the first draft. If that happens to you, if you find you've gotten to your main point at the end of the draft, then use that main point. Begin a new draft with that point as your thesis. Use ideas and information from your first draft if they're relevant, but don't be afraid to throw things out if they don't belong. Cutting our own words is often hard to do, but almost always necessary. If you find it difficult, create a file (on your computer or in a file folder) and put the sentences or phrases you cut into this file to be used in a later paper.

2. Check your writing for clarity and coherence. Can your reader easily follow what you are saying? Is the organization logical? Is it clear to the reader as well as to you? Are there transitions that show the connections among your ideas?

3. Move on to style only after you have made your major revisions. Look at your sentences. Do you like the way they sound? Is your tone appropriate to your content? Reading your essay out loud is helpful in really hearing what you have said. Try reading it aloud to a friend or to a tutor in the Writing Center; you'll be amazed at how much you notice about your own writing style.

4. Finally, proofread for grammatical errors. It's best to leave this stage until the end; after all, what's the use of correcting sentences that you may well change later? Also, too much attention to errors too early in the writing process can limit your ideas and creativity. As with revision, it's more effective if you leave some time after you've written the final draft to read it over for spelling, punctuation, mechanics, grammar.

Using Your Instructor's Comments

If you are lucky enough to have an instructor who will read and comment on your draft, use the comments wisely. They are an indication of what your instructor thinks is important. When you receive your draft back, read it and the comments over carefully. Start with the substantive comments, ones about your ideas, about how well you explain them, about how clearly you state them. If you do not understand any comment, ask your instructor for clarification. If you are still unsure or if you cannot ask your instructor, bring the draft to the Writing Center.

As with revision in general, work on the big things first, the content, organization and clarity. If there are questions in the comments, be sure you have answered them in your revision. This may mean adding more information, elaborating on the ideas you already have, or even doing more research.

Once you have revised your essay to your satisfaction and have addressed the comments of your instructor, go on to look at the errors corrected or comments about grammar and usage. You may well have changed the sentence the original correction was in, but look at the correction anyway and see if you understand why your instructor made it. What was the error? How can you correct it? How can you work to avoid that error next time you write?

Remember, you are not your draft. When other people comment on your work, especially when they criticize it, they are not attacking or criticizing you. They are merely commenting on a draft, on an unfinished product, not on you.

Brian Fogarty, professor of sociology, was the first director of core curriculum at St. Kate's. You may recognize his name from the essay earlier in this collection, "Art Matters." As he approached retirement, he gathered the wisdom from his years of teaching and put together some sound advice for students. How can you "learn more in less time?" Which of these bits of wisdom most apply to you?

Learn More in Less Time!

Brian E. Fogarty

I really struggled with learning and studying when I was a student, and it took me a long time to really figure things out (I was probably in my forties!). Here are some bits of wisdom that I hope will make learning **easier** and **more pleasant** for you—not harder and more tedious, which is what most advice from educators seems to do.

Don't study harder, study smarter.

Most of my college career (and a lot of my professional career) I drove myself crazy thinking I should spend more time studying. I berated myself for being so lazy, which was depressing, which only made me more lazy. Over time it finally dawned on me that it wasn't that I was studying too little, but that I didn't know how to learn.

The lesson is to find new and more efficient ways to learn, not to do the same old thing that may not be working all that well anyway. Your overall goal should be to study *less*, not more, by doing it better.

Avoid perfectionism.

I never suffered from this, but many of my students do—I think it may be a gender thing, or maybe a generation thing. You've grown up in a "Go for it!" culture, in which you're told "You can be the best if you just try hard enough!" So you've come to feel obliged to excel at everything.

But the truth is, none of us can be excellent at everything. Worse, if you try to achieve excellence at everything, you'll put too much energy into the wrong things, which is inefficient. I've seen lots of my majors' grades suffer in sociology because they wanted to get an A in something else. The key to success, I think, is: try to be "good enough" at everything, and excellent at a few things.

Look ahead, not back.

This isn't a philosophical position, but a practical one. If you get behind in a class due to illness or absence or some crisis, try to avoid "catching up" by completing past work. Instead, try to get a fresh start from where the class is now, and take your lumps on past assignments. I see many students trying to make up work they missed because they want those points so their grade won't suffer (see "avoid perfectionism," above). What happens almost every time is that they dig themselves into a deeper hole, because they're working on past work and not doing the current work, or not doing it well.

So if possible, forget the stuff you missed and start fresh. Note that this won't always work—for example, if you missed a big project, or if the course material builds on previous material, as in math or a foreign language.

Focus.

This is sort of a Zen thing, really, and applies to all of life. If you're doing the dishes, focus fully on that task, experience it completely, and get it done. If you're watching a movie, give it your complete attention and enjoy it completely. And if you're studying, then really study, without distractions or a million stray thoughts.

If you're reading an assignment, do it when you're able to shut off the phone, the TV, the iPod, the roommate, and give it your full attention. You'll finish sooner and you'll have gotten more out of it. People who say music or TV "relaxes" them while they study are kidding themselves. You shouldn't be relaxed when studying, anyway—you should be in a heightened state of awareness and attention. You don't want to spend all that time for nothing, do you?

Rest.

More and more research shows that sleep and rest are really important to effective living. Unfortunately, we live in a culture that rewards people who are *doing* all the time, being busy and active and generally driving themselves nuts. We're even expected to multitask, doing two or three things at once (see "Focus," above). But that's for suckers. Recreation ("re-creation") and sleep are important for the brain, body, and spirit. Staying up til 4:00AM to study for a test is a fool's economy—the return on studying when tired is very small, and you're draining your intellectual battery the whole time. The result is often that you don't have your wits about you the next day during the exam, you can't recall things that you really know, you make stupid errors, etc. Oh, and you feel like crap.

Albert Einstein said the best locations for thinking were "the bed, the bath, and the bus." Others have called the afternoon nap "the scholar's best friend." However you put it, rest and recreation are far, far more important to successful learning than you realize.

Discover what you're good at.

This is the principal reason for liberal-arts requirements—to force students to pursue areas they don't know much about, so they have maximum opportunities to find what they're good at. Your great talent may be in something you've never tried before. This happened to me—I never had heard of sociology or anthropology until I went to college. I had to take sociology as a liberal-arts requirement, and discovered I had a real knack for understanding its principles and ideas. The rest, as they say, is history.

When you discover what you're good at, or if you already know, pursue it with diligence even if it's not your major or not a likely career. It will make education more enjoyable, and it might someday, when you least expect it, pay off. But also, keep in mind that your only chance at real greatness will be to pursue what you're really talented at—you'll never be great at something that you pursued just because it was going to lead to a job or seemed like a good major to take up. Picasso might have made a nice living as an accountant, but he was really, really good at art. Give yourself at least a chance to become a Picasso, or Marie Curie, or Toni Morrison, even if it is a long shot.

Value the learning.

We have to be grade motivated, and we have to be credit-motivated—that's the system we're in. But you need to focus on your development, too, or else you'll become bitter and alienated from your own education. Try to pay attention to how much you're learning, how many things you can do that you couldn't before, or how much better you do them. Look at old papers and compare them to recent ones, for example. Remember when you couldn't speak a foreign language at all, or when you didn't know anything about calculus, or Asian history. You're making yourself into a better and better person every day you work at learning. *That's* the purpose of education, and if you keep that purpose in mind, you'll find it easier to study and learn.

The Catherine Core

The Catherine Portrait
Patricia Olson
oil on panel
2008 - 2011
16-inches square each

Introduction:
The Catherine Core

This section of the *Catherine Core Reader* includes essays, poetry, web links to music, a short play and a work of art—pieces selected by the faculty who teach the courses included in the liberal arts distribution requirements, the heart of the Catherine Core Curriculum. The funny thing is that the selections aren't what you might expect. The Theater and Mathematics faculty chose poems; the offering from English is a play; faculty in Critical Studies of Race and Ethnicity and Art/Art History opted for essays by contemporary novelists, while the Women's Studies and International Languages choices are literary criticism. What is going on?

The simple answer is that education is going on. Committed as the St. Kate's faculty is to rich and rigorous liberal arts learning for our students, we find ourselves practicing the values that we espouse. I'm an English professor, but some of the best-read people I know at the university are in Biology—they tell me about the latest literary sensations. My colleagues in art are serious feminist theorists, and some of the professors teaching your science classes are artists on the side. Your French professor could be a poet, your theology professor a memoirist, your literature professor a therapist, your sociology professor a dancer. What we enact here is what we hope for our students—a life abundant with art and ideas, characterized by the pursuit of excellence and the cultivation of curiosity.

It's a commitment we inherit from the Sisters of St. Joseph, our founders—and, for many of us, our mentors. You may recall from the introductory essays in this book that Mother Antonia McHugh was fierce in her defense of high-quality education for women—immigrant women, farmwomen, the poor and the privileged. They were all taken seriously as scholars at St. Catherine. Today, our core curriculum continues that tradition by requiring every student to study in the liberal arts and sciences. No matter what your major or what job you will have when you graduate, the faculty here promise to engage you in our disciplines, in these core classes, as earnestly as we do the students who major in our fields. And you promise, in return, to carry your St. Kate's education with you when you leave.

Recently, I have had the privilege of visiting with alumnae chapters all over the country to teach a one-day Reflective Woman course. As I tell them about today's students and the courses they take, I draw them back into their own undergraduate years and insist that they tell me stories. What sticks with you today, I ask them, from all that you learned at St. Kate's? And every time they tell me about a nun who demanded a lot from them, a course they had to study really hard for, a teacher who saw their potential and called it out. One woman in Denver, a 1955 graduate, told me about Sr. Mona Riley's required Humanities course and how it has stayed with her, though it had very little to do with her major or her career. After she retired she began working as a docent at an art museum; there, as she walked through the familiar galleries with confidence, she realized, "I could still hear her voice in my head," all those years later. Another alumna at that same meeting told me how her love for opera began in a required music appreciation class that she didn't even want to take—and that how love has continued unabated since, enriching her life.

A liberal arts education—a lot of people talk about it, but it's often hard to pin down what they mean by it. Here at St. Kate's, for our faculty, it means that our curriculum requires demanding study in the liberal arts and sciences disciplines. It means that we, too, hear those Sisters voices in our heads when we insist that you read a (really big) novel, practice (and practice) a mathematical proof, untangle a challenging philosophical question, deeply examine a moment in history, or conduct a scientific experiment in the lab. The liberal arts core is where you learn practices of the mind, where you find unexpected passions, where you write, think and create. It's where you claim a St. Catherine education.

Cecilia Konchar Farr
Sr. Mona Riley Endowed Chair in the Humanities
Professor of English and Women's Studies
March 2014

Literature

Representing the English Department's contribution to The Catherine Core is a one-act play by Susan Glaspell (1876–1948). Glaspell was one of the founders of the Provincetown Players, famous for their modernist sensibility and for the contributions of their most famous member, Eugene O'Neill, one of the pillars of American drama. Raised on the banks of the Mississippi River in Iowa, Glaspell, a farmer's daughter, became a prolific writer—a journalist, Pulitzer-Prize-winning playwright, novelist, short story writer and biographer—most famous today for "Trifles." As a feminist thinker and avant-garde artist, she headed the Works Progress Administration's Federal Theater Project, Midwest Bureau, during the Great Depression.

Reading this play in a literature class would be an exercise in reading about reading. First, we read the play itself: Who was the audience? What was the play's purpose? How does this short drama affect us today? What does it challenge us to notice, to consider? Then we would go more deeply into the play and read with the farmwomen as they assess what happened in their neighbor's house. The house itself becomes a text, as the men set out to check the windows and examine the barn, while the women probe a sewing basket and sigh over spilled jelly, piecing together truth from trifles that the men consider unimportant. Reading is like this. It is a foundational liberal arts skill, involving practices of careful observation and empathy, of close attention to details and thoughtful assessment of what you know and what you discover.

Trifles

Susan Glaspell

First performed by the Provincetown Players at the Wharf Theatre, Provincetown, Mass., August 8, 1916.

GEORGE HENDERSON (County Attorney)

HENRY PETERS (Sheriff)

LEWIS HALE, A neighboring farmer

MRS PETERS

MRS HALE

SCENE: The kitchen is the now abandoned farmhouse of JOHN WRIGHT, a gloomy kitchen, and left without having been put in order—unwashed pans under the sink, a loaf of bread outside the bread-box, a dish-towel on the table—other signs of incompleted work. At the rear the outer door opens and the SHERIFF comes in followed by the COUNTY

ATTORNEY and HALE. The SHERIFF and HALE are men in middle life, the COUNTY ATTORNEY is a young man; all are much bundled up and go at once to the stove. They are followed by the two women—the SHERIFF's wife first; she is a slight wiry woman, a thin nervous face. MRS HALE is larger and would ordinarily be called more comfortable looking, but she is disturbed now and looks fearfully about as she enters. The women have come in slowly, and stand close together near the door.

COUNTY ATTORNEY: (rubbing his hands) This feels good. Come up to the fire, ladies.

MRS PETERS: (after taking a step forward) I'm not—cold.

SHERIFF: (unbuttoning his overcoat and stepping away from the stove as if to mark the beginning of official business) Now, Mr Hale, before we move things about, you explain to Mr Henderson just what you saw when you came here yesterday morning.

COUNTY ATTORNEY: By the way, has anything been moved? Are things just as you left them yesterday?

SHERIFF: (looking about) It's just the same. When it dropped below zero last night I thought I'd better send Frank out this morning to make a fire for us—no use getting pneumonia with a big case on, but I told him not to touch anything except the stove—and you know Frank.

COUNTY ATTORNEY: Somebody should have been left here yesterday.

SHERIFF: Oh—yesterday. When I had to send Frank to Morris Center for that man who went crazy—I want you to know I had my hands full yesterday. I knew you could get back from Omaha by today and as long as I went over everything here myself—

COUNTY ATTORNEY: Well, Mr Hale, tell just what happened when you came here yesterday morning.

HALE: Harry and I had started to town with a load of potatoes. We came along the road from my place and as I got here I said, I'm going to see if I can't get John Wright to go in with me on a party telephone.' I spoke to Wright about it once before and he put me off, saying folks talked too much anyway, and all he asked was peace and quiet—I guess you know about how much he talked himself; but I thought maybe if I went to the house and talked about it before his wife, though I said to Harry that I didn't know as what his wife wanted made much difference to John—

COUNTY ATTORNEY: Let's talk about that later, Mr Hale. I do want to talk about that, but tell now just what happened when you got to the house.

HALE: I didn't hear or see anything; I knocked at the door, and still it was all quiet inside. I knew they must be up, it was past eight o'clock. So I knocked again, and I thought I heard somebody say, 'Come in.' I wasn't sure, I'm not sure yet, but I opened the door—this door (indicating the door by which the two women are still standing) and there in that rocker—(pointing to it) sat Mrs Wright.

(They all look at the rocker.)

COUNTY ATTORNEY: What—was she doing?

HALE: She was rockin' back and forth. She had her apron in her hand and was kind of—pleating it.

COUNTY ATTORNEY: And how did she—look?

HALE: Well, she looked queer.

COUNTY ATTORNEY: How do you mean—queer?

HALE: Well, as if she didn't know what she was going to do next. And kind of done up.

COUNTY ATTORNEY: How did she seem to feel about your coming?

HALE: Why, I don't think she minded—one way or other. She didn't pay much attention. I said, 'How do, Mrs Wright it's cold, ain't it?' And she said, 'Is it?'—and went on kind of pleating at her apron. Well, I was surprised; she didn't ask me to come up to the stove, or to set down, but just sat there, not even looking at me, so I said, 'I want to see John.' And then she—laughed. I guess you would call it a laugh. I thought of Harry and the team outside, so I said a little sharp: 'Can't I see John?' 'No', she says, kind o' dull like. 'Ain't he home?' says I. 'Yes', says she, 'he's home'. 'Then why can't I see him?' I asked her, out of patience. ''Cause he's dead', says she. 'Dead?' says I. She just nodded her head, not getting a bit excited, but rockin' back and forth. 'Why—where is he?' says I, not knowing what to say. She just pointed upstairs—like that (himself pointing to the room above) I got up, with the idea of going up there. I walked from there to here—then I says, 'Why, what did he die of?' 'He died of a rope round his neck', says she, and just went on pleatin' at her apron. Well, I went out and called Harry. I thought I might—need help. We went upstairs and there he was lyin'—

COUNTY ATTORNEY: I think I'd rather have you go into that upstairs, where you can point it all out. Just go on now with the rest of the story.

HALE: Well, my first thought was to get that rope off. It looked . . . (stops, his face twitches) . . . but Harry, he went up to him, and he said, 'No, he's dead all right, and we'd better not touch anything.' So we went back down stairs. She was still sitting that same way. 'Has anybody been notified?' I asked. 'No', says she unconcerned. 'Who did this, Mrs Wright?' said Harry. He said it business-like—and she stopped pleatin' of her apron. 'I don't know', she says. 'You don't know?' says Harry. 'No', says she. 'Weren't you sleepin' in the bed with him?' says Harry. 'Yes', says she, 'but I was on the inside'. 'Somebody slipped a rope round his neck and strangled him and you didn't wake up?' says Harry. 'I didn't wake up', she said after him. We must 'a looked as if we didn't see how that could be, for after a minute she said, 'I sleep sound'. Harry was going to ask her more questions but I said maybe we ought to let her tell her story first to the coroner, or the sheriff, so Harry went fast as he could to Rivers' place, where there's a telephone.

COUNTY ATTORNEY: And what did Mrs Wright do when she knew that you had gone for the coroner?

HALE: She moved from that chair to this one over here (pointing to a small chair in the corner) and just sat there with her hands held together and looking down. I got a feeling that I ought to make some conversation, so I said I had come in to see if John wanted to put in a telephone, and at that she started to laugh, and then she stopped and looked at me—scared, (the COUNTY ATTORNEY, who has had his notebook out, makes a note) I dunno, maybe it wasn't scared. I wouldn't like to say it was. Soon Harry got back, and then Dr Lloyd came, and you, Mr Peters, and so I guess that's all I know that you don't.

COUNTY ATTORNEY: (looking around) I guess we'll go upstairs first—and then out to the barn and around there, (to the SHERIFF) You're convinced that there was nothing important here—nothing that would point to any motive.

SHERIFF: Nothing here but kitchen things.

(The COUNTY ATTORNEY, after again looking around the kitchen, opens the door of a cupboard closet. He gets up on a chair and looks on a shelf. Pulls his hand away, sticky.)

COUNTY ATTORNEY: Here's a nice mess.

(The women draw nearer.)

MRS PETERS: (to the other woman) Oh, her fruit; it did freeze, (to the LAWYER) She worried about that when it turned so cold. She said the fire'd go out and her jars would break.

SHERIFF: Well, can you beat the women! Held for murder and worryin' about her preserves.

COUNTY ATTORNEY: I guess before we're through she may have something more serious than preserves to worry about.

HALE: Well, women are used to worrying over trifles.

(The two women move a little closer together.)

COUNTY ATTORNEY: (with the gallantry of a young politician) And yet, for all their worries, what would we do without the ladies? (the women do not unbend. He goes to the sink, takes a dipperful of water from the pail and pouring it into a basin, washes his hands. Starts to wipe them on the roller-towel, turns it for a cleaner place) Dirty towels! (kicks his foot against the pans under the sink) Not much of a housekeeper, would you say, ladies?

MRS HALE: (stiffly) There's a great deal of work to be done on a farm.

COUNTY ATTORNEY: To be sure. And yet (with a little bow to her) I know there are some Dickson county farmhouses which do not have such roller towels. (He gives it a pull to expose its length again.)

MRS HALE: Those towels get dirty awful quick. Men's hands aren't always as clean as they might be.

COUNTY ATTORNEY: Ah, loyal to your sex, I see. But you and Mrs Wright were neighbors. I suppose you were friends, too.

MRS HALE: (shaking her head) I've not seen much of her of late years. I've not been in this house—it's more than a year.

COUNTY ATTORNEY: And why was that? You didn't like her?

MRS HALE: I liked her all well enough. Farmers' wives have their hands full, Mr Henderson. And then—

COUNTY ATTORNEY: Yes—?

MRS HALE: (looking about) It never seemed a very cheerful place.

COUNTY ATTORNEY: No—it's not cheerful. I shouldn't say she had the homemaking instinct.

MRS HALE: Well, I don't know as Wright had, either.

COUNTY ATTORNEY: You mean that they didn't get on very well?

MRS HALE: No, I don't mean anything. But I don't think a place'd be any cheerfuller for John Wright's being in it.

COUNTY ATTORNEY: I'd like to talk more of that a little later. I want to get the lay of things upstairs now. (He goes to the left, where three steps lead to a stair door.)

SHERIFF: I suppose anything Mrs Peters does'll be all right. She was to take in some clothes for her, you know, and a few little things. We left in such a hurry yesterday.

COUNTY ATTORNEY: Yes, but I would like to see what you take, Mrs Peters, and keep an eye out for anything that might be of use to us.

MRS PETERS: Yes, Mr Henderson.

(The women listen to the men's steps on the stairs, then look about the kitchen.)

MRS HALE: I'd hate to have men coming into my kitchen, snooping around and criticising.

(She arranges the pans under sink which the LAWYER had shoved out of place.)

MRS PETERS: Of course it's no more than their duty.

MRS HALE: Duty's all right, but I guess that deputy sheriff that came out to make the fire might have got a little of this on. (gives the roller towel a pull) Wish I'd thought of that sooner. Seems mean to talk about her for not having things slicked up when she had to come away in such a hurry.

MRS PETERS: (who has gone to a small table in the left rear corner of the room, and lifted one end of a towel that covers a pan) She had bread set. (Stands still.)

MRS HALE: (eyes fixed on a loaf of bread beside the bread-box, which is on a low shelf at the other side of the room. Moves slowly toward it) She was going to put this in there, (picks up loaf, then abruptly drops it. In a manner of returning to familiar things) It's a shame about her fruit. I wonder if it's all gone. (gets up on the chair and looks) I think there's some here that's all right, Mrs Peters. Yes—here; (holding it toward the window) this is cherries, too. (looking again) I declare I believe that's the only one. (gets down, bottle in her hand. Goes to the sink and wipes it off on the outside) She'll feel awful bad after all her hard work in the hot weather. I remember the afternoon I put up my cherries last summer.

(She puts the bottle on the big kitchen table, center of the room. With a sigh, is about to sit down in the rocking-chair. Before she is seated realizes what chair it is; with a slow look at it, steps back. The chair which she has touched rocks back and forth.)

MRS PETERS: Well, I must get those things from the front room closet, (she goes to the door at the right, but after looking into the other room, steps back) You coming with me, Mrs Hale? You could help me carry them.

(They go in the other room; reappear, MRS PETERS carrying a dress and skirt, MRS HALE following with a pair of shoes.)

MRS PETERS: My, it's cold in there.

(She puts the clothes on the big table, and hurries to the stove.)

MRS HALE: (examining the skirt) Wright was close. I think maybe that's why she kept so much to herself. She didn't even belong to the Ladies Aid. I suppose she felt she couldn't do her part, and then you don't enjoy things when you feel shabby. She used to wear pretty clothes and be lively, when she was Minnie Foster, one of the town girls singing in the choir. But that—oh, that was thirty years ago. This all you was to take in?

MRS PETERS: She said she wanted an apron. Funny thing to want, for there isn't much to get you dirty in jail, goodness knows. But I suppose just to make her feel more natural. She said they was in the top drawer in this cupboard. Yes, here. And then her little shawl that always hung behind the door. (opens stair door and looks) Yes, here it is.

(Quickly shuts door leading upstairs.)

MRS HALE: (abruptly moving toward her) Mrs Peters?

MRS PETERS: Yes, Mrs Hale?

MRS HALE: Do you think she did it?

MRS PETERS: (in a frightened voice) Oh, I don't know.

MRS HALE: Well, I don't think she did. Asking for an apron and her little shawl. Worrying about her fruit.

MRS PETERS: (starts to speak, glances up, where footsteps are heard in the room above. In a low voice) Mr Peters says it looks bad for her. Mr Henderson is awful sarcastic in a speech and he'll make fun of her sayin' she didn't wake up.

MRS HALE: Well, I guess John Wright didn't wake when they was slipping that rope under his neck.

MRS PETERS: No, it's strange. It must have been done awful crafty and still. They say it was such a—funny way to kill a man, rigging it all up like that.

MRS HALE: That's just what Mr Hale said. There was a gun in the house. He says that's what he can't understand.

MRS PETERS: Mr Henderson said coming out that what was needed for the case was a motive; something to show anger, or—sudden feeling.

MRS HALE: (who is standing by the table) Well, I don't see any signs of anger around here, (she puts her hand on the dish towel which lies on the table, stands looking down at table, one half of which is clean, the other half messy) It's wiped to here, (makes a move as if to finish work, then turns and looks at loaf of bread outside the breadbox. Drops towel. In that voice of coming back to familiar things.) Wonder how they are finding things upstairs. I hope she had it a little more red-up up there. You know, it seems kind of sneaking. Locking her up in town and then coming out here and trying to get her own house to turn against her!

MRS PETERS: But Mrs Hale, the law is the law.

MRS HALE: I s'pose 'tis, (unbuttoning her coat) Better loosen up your things, Mrs Peters. You won't feel them when you go out.

(MRS PETERS takes off her fur tippet, goes to hang it on hook at back of room, stands looking at the under part of the small corner table.)

MRS PETERS: She was piecing a quilt. (She brings the large sewing basket and they look at the bright pieces.)

MRS HALE: It's log cabin pattern. Pretty, isn't it? I wonder if she was goin' to quilt it or just knot it?

(Footsteps have been heard coming down the stairs. The SHERIFF enters followed by HALE and the COUNTY ATTORNEY.)

SHERIFF: They wonder if she was going to quilt it or just knot it! (The men laugh, the women look abashed.)

COUNTY ATTORNEY: (rubbing his hands over the stove) Frank's fire didn't do much up there, did it? Well, let's go out to the barn and get that cleared up. (The men go outside.)

MRS HALE: (resentfully) I don't know as there's anything so strange, our takin' up our time with little things while we're waiting for them to get the evidence. (she sits down at the big table smoothing out a block with decision) I don't see as it's anything to laugh about.

MRS PETERS: (apologetically) Of course they've got awful important things on their minds.

(Pulls up a chair and joins MRS HALE at the table.)

MRS HALE: (examining another block) Mrs Peters, look at this one. Here, this is the one she was working on, and look at the sewing! All the rest of it has been so nice and even. And look at this! It's all over the place! Why, it looks as if she didn't know what she was about!

(After she has said this they look at each other, then start to glance back at the door. After an instant MRS HALE has pulled at a knot and ripped the sewing.)

MRS PETERS: Oh, what are you doing, Mrs Hale?

MRS HALE: (mildly) Just pulling out a stitch or two that's not sewed very good. (threading a needle) Bad sewing always made me fidgety.

MRS PETERS: (nervously) I don't think we ought to touch things.

MRS HALE: I'll just finish up this end. (suddenly stopping and leaning forward) Mrs Peters?

MRS PETERS: Yes, Mrs Hale?

MRS HALE: What do you suppose she was so nervous about?

MRS PETERS: Oh—I don't know. I don't know as she was nervous. I sometimes sew awful queer when I'm just tired. (MRS HALE starts to say something, looks at MRS PETERS, then goes on sewing) Well I must get these things wrapped up. They may be through sooner than we think, (putting apron and other things together) I wonder where I can find a piece of paper, and string.

MRS HALE: In that cupboard, maybe.

MRS PETERS: (looking in cupboard) Why, here's a bird-cage, (holds it up) Did she have a bird, Mrs Hale?

MRS HALE: Why, I don't know whether she did or not—I've not been here for so long. There was a man around last year selling canaries cheap, but I don't know as she took one; maybe she did. She used to sing real pretty herself.

MRS PETERS: (glancing around) Seems funny to think of a bird here. But she must have had one, or why would she have a cage? I wonder what happened to it.

MRS HALE: I s'pose maybe the cat got it.

MRS PETERS: No, she didn't have a cat. She's got that feeling some people have about cats—being afraid of them. My cat got in her room and she was real upset and asked me to take it out.

MRS HALE: My sister Bessie was like that. Queer, ain't it?

MRS PETERS: (examining the cage) Why, look at this door. It's broke. One hinge is pulled apart.

MRS HALE: (looking too) Looks as if someone must have been rough with it.

MRS PETERS: Why, yes.

(She brings the cage forward and puts it on the table.)

MRS HALE: I wish if they're going to find any evidence they'd be about it. I don't like this place.

MRS PETERS: But I'm awful glad you came with me, Mrs Hale. It would be lonesome for me sitting here alone.

MRS HALE: It would, wouldn't it? (dropping her sewing) But I tell you what I do wish, Mrs Peters. I wish I had come over sometimes when she was here. I—(looking around the room)—wish I had.

MRS PETERS: But of course you were awful busy, Mrs Hale—your house and your children.

MRS HALE: I could've come. I stayed away because it weren't cheerful—and that's why I ought to have come. I—I've never liked this place. Maybe because it's down in a hollow and you don't see the road. I dunno what it is, but it's a lonesome place and always was. I wish I had come over to see Minnie Foster sometimes. I can see now—(shakes her head)

MRS PETERS: Well, you mustn't reproach yourself, Mrs Hale. Somehow we just don't see how it is with other folks until—something comes up.

MRS HALE: Not having children makes less work—but it makes a quiet house, and Wright out to work all day, and no company when he did come in. Did you know John Wright, Mrs Peters?

MRS PETERS: Not to know him; I've seen him in town. They say he was a good man.

MRS HALE: Yes—good; he didn't drink, and kept his word as well as most, I guess, and paid his debts. But he was a hard man, Mrs Peters. Just to pass the time of day with him—(shivers) Like a raw wind that gets to the bone, (pauses, her eye falling on the cage) I should think she would 'a wanted a bird. But what do you suppose went with it?

MRS PETERS: I don't know, unless it got sick and died.

(She reaches over and swings the broken door, swings it again, both women watch it.)

MRS HALE: You weren't raised round here, were you? (MRS PETERS shakes her head) You didn't know—her?

MRS PETERS: Not till they brought her yesterday.

MRS HALE: She—come to think of it, she was kind of like a bird herself—real sweet and pretty, but kind of timid and—fluttery. How—she—did—change. (silence; then as if struck by a happy thought and relieved to get back to everyday things) Tell you what, Mrs Peters, why don't you take the quilt in with you? It might take up her mind.

MRS PETERS: Why, I think that's a real nice idea, Mrs Hale. There couldn't possibly be any objection to it, could there? Now, just what would I take? I wonder if her patches are in here—and her things.

(They look in the sewing basket.)

MRS HALE: Here's some red. I expect this has got sewing things in it. (brings out a fancy box) What a pretty box. Looks like something somebody would give you. Maybe her scissors are in here. (Opens box. Suddenly puts her hand to her nose) Why—(MRS PETERS bends nearer, then turns her face away) There's something wrapped up in this piece of silk.

MRS PETERS: Why, this isn't her scissors.

MRS HALE: (lifting the silk) Oh, Mrs Peters—it's—

(MRS PETERS bends closer.)

MRS PETERS: It's the bird.

MRS HALE: (jumping up) But, Mrs Peters—look at it! It's neck! Look at its neck!

It's all—other side to.

MRS PETERS: Somebody—wrung—its—neck.

(Their eyes meet. A look of growing comprehension, of horror. Steps are heard outside. MRS HALE slips box under quilt pieces, and sinks into her chair. Enter SHERIFF and COUNTY ATTORNEY. MRS PETERS rises.)

COUNTY ATTORNEY: (as one turning from serious things to little pleasantries) Well ladies, have you decided whether she was going to quilt it or knot it?

MRS PETERS: We think she was going to—knot it.

COUNTY ATTORNEY: Well, that's interesting, I'm sure. (seeing the birdcage) Has the bird flown?

MRS HALE: (putting more quilt pieces over the box) We think the—cat got it.

COUNTY ATTORNEY: (preoccupied) Is there a cat?

(MRS HALE glances in a quick covert way at MRS PETERS.)

MRS PETERS: Well, not now. They're superstitious, you know. They leave.

COUNTY ATTORNEY: (to SHERIFF PETERS, continuing an interrupted conversation) No sign at all of anyone having come from the outside. Their own rope. Now let's go up again and go over it piece by piece. (they start upstairs) It would have to have been someone who knew just the—

(MRS PETERS sits down. The two women sit there not looking at one another, but as if peering into something and at the same time holding back. When they talk now it is in the manner of feeling their way over strange ground, as if afraid of what they are saying, but as if they can not help saying it.)

MRS HALE: She liked the bird. She was going to bury it in that pretty box.

MRS PETERS: (in a whisper) When I was a girl—my kitten—there was a boy took a hatchet, and before my eyes—and before I could get there—

(covers her face an instant) If they hadn't held me back I would have—(catches herself, looks upstairs where steps are heard, falters weakly)—hurt him.

MRS HALE: (with a slow look around her) I wonder how it would seem never to have had any children around, (pause) No, Wright wouldn't like the bird—a thing that sang. She used to sing. He killed that, too.

MRS PETERS: (moving uneasily) We don't know who killed the bird.

MRS HALE: I knew John Wright.

MRS PETERS: It was an awful thing was done in this house that night, Mrs Hale. Killing a man while he slept, slipping a rope around his neck that choked the life out of him.

MRS HALE: His neck. Choked the life out of him.

(Her hand goes out and rests on the bird-cage.)

MRS PETERS: (with rising voice) We don't know who killed him. We don't know.

MRS HALE: (her own feeling not interrupted) If there'd been years and years of nothing, then a bird to sing to you, it would be awful—still, after the bird was still.

MRS PETERS: (something within her speaking) I know what stillness is. When we homesteaded in Dakota, and my first baby died—after he was two years old, and me with no other then—

MRS HALE: (moving) How soon do you suppose they'll be through, looking for the evidence?

MRS PETERS: I know what stillness is. (pulling herself back) The law has got to punish crime, Mrs Hale.

MRS HALE: (not as if answering that) I wish you'd seen Minnie Foster when she wore a white dress with blue ribbons and stood up there in the choir and sang. (a look around the room) Oh, I wish I'd come over here once in a while! That was a crime! That was a crime! Who's going to punish that?

MRS PETERS: (looking upstairs) We mustn't—take on.

MRS HALE: I might have known she needed help! I know how things can be—for women. I tell you, it's queer, Mrs Peters. We live close together and we live far apart. We all go through the same things—it's all just a different kind of the same thing, (brushes her eyes, noticing the bottle of fruit, reaches out for it) If I was you, I wouldn't tell her her fruit was gone. Tell her it ain't. Tell her it's all right. Take this in to prove it to her. She—she may never know whether it was broke or not.

MRS PETERS: (takes the bottle, looks about for something to wrap it in; takes petticoat from the clothes brought from the other room, very nervously begins winding this around the bottle. In a false voice) My, it's a good thing the men couldn't hear us. Wouldn't they just laugh! Getting all stirred up over a little thing like a—dead canary. As if that could have anything to do with—with—wouldn't they laugh!

(The men are heard coming down stairs.)

MRS HALE: (under her breath) Maybe they would—maybe they wouldn't.

COUNTY ATTORNEY: No, Peters, it's all perfectly clear except a reason for doing it. But you know juries when it comes to women. If there was some definite thing. Something to show—something to make a story about—a thing that would connect up with this strange way of doing it—

(The women's eyes meet for an instant. Enter HALE from outer door.)

HALE: Well, I've got the team around. Pretty cold out there.

COUNTY ATTORNEY: I'm going to stay here a while by myself, (to the SHERIFF) You can send Frank out for me, can't you? I want to go over everything. I'm not satisfied that we can't do better.

SHERIFF: Do you want to see what Mrs Peters is going to take in?

(The LAWYER goes to the table, picks up the apron, laughs.)

COUNTY ATTORNEY: Oh, I guess they're not very dangerous things the ladies have picked out. (Moves a few things about, disturbing the quilt pieces which cover the box. Steps back) No, Mrs Peters doesn't need supervising. For that matter, a sheriff's wife is married to the law. Ever think of it that way, Mrs Peters?

MRS PETERS: Not—just that way.

SHERIFF: (chuckling) Married to the law. (moves toward the other room) I just want you to come in here a minute, George. We ought to take a look at these windows.

COUNTY ATTORNEY: (scoffingly) Oh, windows!

SHERIFF: We'll be right out, Mr Hale.

(HALE goes outside. The SHERIFF follows the COUNTY ATTORNEY into the other room. Then MRS HALE rises, hands tight together, looking intensely at MRS PETERS, whose eyes make a slow turn, finally meeting MRS HALE's. A moment MRS HALE holds her, then her own eyes point the way to where the box is concealed. Suddenly MRS PETERS throws back quilt pieces and tries to put the box in the bag she is wearing. It is too big. She opens box, starts to take bird out, cannot touch it, goes to pieces, stands there helpless. Sound of a knob turning in the other room. MRS HALE snatches the box and puts it in the pocket of her big coat. Enter COUNTY ATTORNEY and SHERIFF.)

COUNTY ATTORNEY: (facetiously) Well, Henry, at least we found out that she was not going to quilt it. She was going to—what is it you call it, ladies?

MRS HALE: (her hand against her pocket) We call it—knot it, Mr Henderson.

(CURTAIN)

Philosophy

Peter Singer is the Ira W. DeCamp Professor of Bioethics at Princeton University. The following passages come from his book The Life You Can Save *(2010). Here Singer raises questions about our common conception of charity and of what we owe to others. His argument begins by drawing on our shared response to his example of the pond. He works to show what that shared response seems to entail about our ethical obligations to those who can be helped by foreign aid organizations. Along the way, he considers objections to his argument and attempts to justify our common understanding of the notion of charity. In this work we find practices common in philosophy—philosophers make use of careful reasoning as a way to lend support to their thinking and to critically assess their thinking and the thinking of others. But as we see in these passages, such an investigation may well call on us to respond in a way that extends beyond a mere revision in our concepts. It may call on us to act, to change how we live.*

from The Life You Can Save

Peter Singer

1. Saving a Child

> On your way to work, you pass a small pond. On hot days, children sometimes play in the pond, which is only about knee-deep. The weather's cool today, though, and the hour is early, so you are surprised to see a child splashing about in the pond. As you get closer, you see that it is a very young child, just a toddler, who is flailing about, unable to stay upright or walk out of the pond. You look for the parents or babysitter, but there is no one else around. The child is unable to keep his head above the water for more than a few seconds at a time. If you don't wade in and pull him out, he seems likely to drown. Wading in is easy and safe, but you will ruin the new shoes you bought only a few days ago, and get your suit wet and muddy. By the time you hand the child over to someone responsible for him, and change your clothes, you'll be late for work. What should you do?

I teach a course called Practical Ethics. When we start talking about global poverty, I ask my students what they think you should do in this situation. Predictably, they respond that you should save the child. "What about your shoes? And being late for work?' I ask them. They brush that aside. How could anyone consider a pair or shoes, or missing an hour or two at work, a good reason for not saving a child's life?

In 2007, something resembling this hypothetical situation actually occurred near Manchester, England. Jordon Lyon, a ten-year old boy, leaped into a pond after his stepsister Bethany slipped in. He struggled to support her but went under himself. Anglers managed to pull Bethany out but by then Jordon could no longer be seen. They raised the alarm, and two police community support officers soon arrived; they refused to enter the pound to find Jordon. He was later pulled out, but attempts at resuscitation failed. At the inquest on Jordon's death, the officers' inaction was defended on the grounds that they had not been trained to deal with such situations. The mother responded: "If you're walking down the street and you see a child drowning you automatically go in that water . . . You don't have to be trained to jump in after a drowning child."

I think its safe to assume that most people would agree with the mother's statement. But consider that, according to UNICEF, nearly 10 million children under five years old die each year from causes related to poverty. Here is just one case, described by a man in Ghana to a researcher from the World Bank:

> Take the death of this small boy this morning, for example. The boy died of measles. We all know he could have been cured at the hospital. But the parents had no money and so the boy died a slow and painful death, not of measles but out of poverty.

Think about something like that happening 27,000 times everyday. Some children die because they don't have enough to eat. More die, like that small boy in Ghana, from measles, malaria, and diarrhea, conditions that either don't exist in developed nations, or, if they do, are almost never fatal. The children are vulnerable to these diseases because they have no safe drinking water, or no sanitation, and because when they do fall ill, their parents can't afford any medical treatment. UNICEF, Oxfam, and many other organizations are working to reduce poverty and provide clean water and basic health care, and these efforts are reducing the toll. If the relief organizations had more money, they could do more, and more lives would be saved.

Now think about your own situation. By donating a relatively small amount of money, you could save a child's life. Maybe it takes more than the amount needed to buy a pair of shoes -but we all spend money on things we don't really need, whether on drinks, meals out, clothing, movies, concerts, vacations, new cars, or house renovation. Is it possible that by choosing to spend your money on such things rather than contributing to an aid agency, you are leaving a child to die, a child you could have saved?

Poverty Today

A few years ago, the World Bank asked researchers to listen to what the poor are saying. They were able to document the experiences of 60,000 women and men in seventy-three countries. Over and over, in different languages and on different continents, poor people said that poverty meant these things:

- You are short of food for all or part of the year, often eating only one meal per day, sometimes having to choose between stilling your child's hunger or your own, and sometimes being able to do neither.
- You can't save money. If a family member falls ill and you need money to see a doctor, or if the crop fails and you have nothing to eat, you have to borrow from a local moneylender and he will charge you so much interest as the debt continues to mount and you may never be free of it.
- You can't afford to send your children to school, or if they do start school, you have to take them out again if the harvest is poor.
- You live in an unstable house, made with mud or thatch that you need to rebuild every two or three years, or after severe weather.
- You have no nearby source of safe drinking water. You have to carry your water a long way, and even then, it can make you ill unless you boil it.

But extreme poverty is not only a condition of unsatisfied material needs. It is often accompanied by a degrading state of powerlessness. Even in countries that are democracies and are relatively well governed, respondents to the World Bank survey described a range of situations in which they had to accept humiliation without protest. It someone takes what little you have, and you complain to the police, they may not listen to you. Nor will the law necessarily protect you from rape or sexual harassment. You have a pervading sense of shame and failure because you cannot provide for your children. Your poverty traps you, and you lose hope of ever escaping from a life of hard work for which, at the end, you will have nothing to show beyond bare survival.

The World Bank defines extreme poverty as not having enough income to meet the most basic human needs for adequate food, water, shelter, clothing, sanitation, health care, and education. Many people are familiar with the statistic that 1 billion people are living on less than one dollar per day. That was the World Bank's poverty line until 2008, when better data on international price comparisons enabled it to make a more accurate calculation of the amount people need to meet their basic needs. On the basis of this calculation, the World Bank set the poverty line at $1.25 per day. The number of people whose income puts them under this line is not 1 billion but 1.4 billion. That there are more people living in extreme poverty than we thought is, of course, bad news, but the news is not all bad. On the same basis, in 1981 there were 1.9 billion people living in extreme poverty. That was about four in every ten people on the planet, whereas now fewer than one in four are extremely poor.

South Asia is still the region with the largest number of people living in extreme poverty, a total of 600 million, including 455 million in India. Economic growth has, however, reduced the proportion of South Asians living in extreme poverty from 60 percent in 1981 to 42 percent in 2005. There are another 380 million extremely poor people in sub-Saharan Africa, where half the population is extremely poor—and that is the same percentage as in 1981. The most dramatic reduction in poverty has been in East Asia, although there are still more than 200 million extremely poor Chinese, and smaller numbers elsewhere in the region. The remaining extremely poor people are distributed around the world, in Latin America and the Caribbean, the Pacific, the Middle East, North Africa, Eastern Europe, and Central Asia.

In response to the "$1.25 a day" figure, the thought may cross your mind that in many developing countries, it is possible to live much more cheaply than in the industrialized nations. Perhaps you have even done it yourself, backpacking around the world, living on less than you would have believed possible. So you may imagine that this level of poverty is less extreme than it would be if you had to live on that amount of money in the United States, or any industrialized nation. IF such thoughts did occur to you, you should banish them now, because the World Bank has already made the adjustment in purchasing power: Its figures refer to the number of people existing on a daily total consumption of goods and services— whether earned or home-grown—comparable to the amount of goods and services that can be bought in the United States for $1.25.

In wealthy societies, most poverty is relative. People feel poor because many of the good things they see advertised on television are beyond their budget—but they do have a television. In the United States, 97 percent of those classified by the Census Bureau as poor own a color TV. Three quarters of them own a car. Three quarters of them have air conditioning. Three quarters of them have a VCR or DVD player. All have access to health care. I am not quoting these figures in order to deny that the poor in the United States face genuine difficulties. Nevertheless, for most, these difficulties are of a different order than those of the world's poorest people. The 1.4 billion people living in extreme poverty are poor by an absolute standard tied to the most basic human needs. They are likely to be hungry for at least part of each year. Even if they can get enough food to fill their stomachs, they will probably be malnourished because their diet lacks essential nutrients. In children, malnutrition stunts growth, and can cause permanent brain damage. The poor may not be able to afford to send their children to school. Even minimal health care services are usually beyond their means.

This kind of poverty kills. Life expectancy in rich nations averages seventy-eight years; in the poorest nations, those officially classified as "least developed," it is below fifty. In rich countries, fewer than one in a hundred children die before the age of five; in the poorest countries, one in five does. And to the UNICEF figure of nearly 10 million young children dying every year from avoidable, poverty-related causes, we must add at least another 8 million older children and adults.

Affluence Today

Roughly matching the 1.4 billion people living in extreme poverty, there are about a billion living at a level of affluence never previously known except in the courts of kings and nobles. As king of France, Louis XIV, the '"Sun King," could afford to build the most magnificent palace Europe had ever seen, but he could not keep it cool in summer as effectively as most middle-class people in industrialized nations can keep their homes cool today. His gardeners, for all their skill, were unable to produce the variety of fresh fruits and vegetables that we can buy all year-round. If he developed a toothache or fell ill, the best his dentists and doctors could do for him would make us shudder.

But we're not just better off than a French king who lived centuries ago. We are also much better off than our own great-grandparents. For a start, we can expect to live about thirty years longer. A century ago, one child in ten died in infancy. Now, in most rich nations, that figure is less than one in two hundred. Another telling indicator of how wealthy we are today is the modest number of hours we must work in order to meet our basic dietary needs. Today Americans spend, on average, only 6 percent of their income on buying food. If they work a forty-hour week, it takes them barely two hours to earn enough to feed themselves for the week. That leaves far more to spend on consumer goods, entertainment, and vacations.

And then we have the superrich, people who spend their money on palatial homes, ridiculously large and luxurious boats, and private planes. Before the 2008 stock market crash trimmed the numbers, there were more than 1,100 billionaires in the world, with a combined net worth of $4.4 trillion. To cater to such people, Lufthansa Technik unveiled its plans for a private configuration of Boeing's new 787 Dreamliner. In commercial service, this plane will seat up to 330 passengers. The private version will carry 35, at a price of $150 million. Cost aside, there's nothing like owning a really big airplane carrying a small number of people to maximize your personal contribution to global warming. Apparently, there are already several billionaires who fly around in private commercial-sized airliners, from 747s down. Larry Page and Sergey Brin, the Google cofounders, reportedly bought a Boeing 767 and spent millions fitting it out for their private use. But for conspicuous waste of money and resources it is hard to beat Anousheh Ansari, an Iranian-American telecommunications entrepreneur who paid a reported $20 million for eleven days in space. Comedian Lewis Black said on Jon Stewart's *The*

Daily Show that Ansari did it because it was "the only way she could achieve her life's goal of flying over every single starving person on earth and yelling 'Hey, look what I'm spending my money on!'"

While I was working on this book, a special advertising supplement fell out of my Sunday edition of the *New York Times*: a sixty-eight-page glossy magazine filled with advertising for watches by Rolex, Patek Philippe, Breitling, and other luxury brands. The ads didn't carry price tags, but a puff piece about the revival of the mechanical watch gave guidance about the lower end of the range. After admitting that inexpensive quartz watches are extremely accurate and functional, the article opined that there is something engaging about a mechanical movement." Right, but how much will it cost you to have this engaging something on your wrist? "You might think that getting into mechanical watches is an expensive proposition, but there are plenty of choices in the $500–$5000 range." Admittedly, "these opening-price-point models are pretty simple: basic movement, basic time display, simple decoration and so on." From which we can gather that most of the watches advertised are priced upward of $5,000, or more than one hundred times what anyone needs to pay for a reliable, accurate quartz watch. That there is a market for such products—and one worth advertising at such expense to the wide readership of *The New York Times*—is another indication of the affluence of our society.

If you're shaking your head at the excesses of the superrich, though, don't shake too hard. Think again about some of the ways Americans with average incomes spend their money. In most places in the United States, you can get your recommended eight glasses of water a day out of the tap for less than a penny, while a bottle of water will set you back $1.50 or more. And in spite of the environmental concerns raised by the waste of energy that goes into producing and transporting it, Americans are still buying bottled water, to the tune of more than 31 billion liters in 2006. Think, too, of the way many of us get our caffeine fix: You can make coffee at home for pennies rather than spending three dollars or more on a latte. Or have you ever casually said yes to a waiter's prompt to order a second soda or glass of wine that you didn't even finish? When Dr. Timothy Jones, an archaeologist, led a U.S. government–funded study of food waste, he found that 14 percent of household garbage is perfectly good food that was in its original packaging and not out of date. More than half of this food was dry-packaged or canned goods that keep for a long time. According to Jones, $100 billion of food is wasted in the United States every year. Fashion designer Deborah Lindquist claims that the average woman owns more than $600 worth of clothing that she has not worn in the last year. Whatever the actual figure may be, it is fair to say that almost all of us, men and women alike, buy things we don't need, some of which we never even use.

Most of us are absolutely certain that we wouldn't hesitate to save a drowning child, and that we would do it at considerable cost to ourselves. Yet while thousands of children die each day, we spend money on things we take for granted and would hardly notice if they were not there. Is that wrong? If so, how far does our obligation to the poor go?

2. Is It Wrong Not to Help?

> Bob is close to retirement. He has invested most of his savings in a very rare and valuable old car, a Bugatti, which he has not been able to insure. The Bugatti is his pride and joy. Not only does Bob get pleasure from driving and caring for his car, he also knows that its rising market value means that he will be able to sell it and live comfortably after retirement. One day when Bob is out tor a drive, he parks the Bugatti near the end of a railway siding and goes for a walk up the track. As he does so, he sees that a runaway train, with no one aboard, is rolling down the railway track. Looking farther down the track, he sees the small figure of a child who appears to be absorbed in playing on the tracks. Oblivious to the runaway train, the child is in great danger. Bob can't stop the train, and the child is too far away to hear his warning shout, but Bob can throw a switch that will divert the train down the siding where his Bugatti is parked. If he does so, nobody will be killed, but the train will crash through the decaying barrier at the end of the siding and destroy his Bugatti. Thinking of his joy in owning the car and the financial security it represents, Bob decides not to throw the swatch.

The car or the child?

Philosopher Peter Unger developed this variation on the story of the drowning child to challenge us to think further about how much we believe we should sacrifice in order to save the life of a child. Unger's story adds a factor often crucial to our thinking about real-world poverty: uncertainty about the outcome of our sacrifice. Bob cannot be certain that the child will die if he does nothing and saves his car. Perhaps at the last moment the child will hear the train and leap to safety. In the same way, most of us can summon doubts about whether the money we give to a charity is really helping the people it's intended to help.

In my experience, people almost always respond that Bob acted badly when he did not throw the switch and destroy his most cherished and valuable possession, thereby sacrificing his hope of a financially secure retirement. We can't take a serious risk with a child's life, they say, merely to save a car, no matter how rare and valuable the car may be. By implication, we should also believe that with the simple act of saving money for retirement, we are acting as badly as Bob. For in saving money for retirement, we are effectively refusing to use that money to help save lives. This is a difficult implication to confront. How can it be wrong to save for a comfortable retirement? There is, at the very least, something puzzling here.

Another example devised by Unger tests the level of sacrifice we think people should make to alleviate suffering in cases when a life is not at stake:

> You are driving your vintage sedan down a country lane when you are stopped by a hiker who has seriously injured his leg. He asks you to rake him to the nearest hospital. If you refuse, there is a good chance that he will lose his leg. On the other hand, if you agree to take him to hospital, he is likely to bleed onto the seats, which you have recently, and expensively, restored in soft white leather.

Again, most people respond that you should drive the hiker to the hospital. This suggests that when prompted to think in concrete terms, about real individuals, most of us consider it obligatory to lessen the serious suffering of innocent others, even at some cost (even a high cost) to ourselves.

The Basic Argument

The above examples reveal our intuitive belief that we ought to help others in need, at least when we can see them and when we are the only person in a position to save them. But our moral intuitions are not always reliable, as we can see from variations in what people in different times and places find intuitively acceptable or objectionable. The case for helping those in extreme poverty will be stronger if it does not rest solely on our intuitions. Here is a logical argument from plausible premises to the same conclusion.

First premise: Suffering and death from lack of food, shelter, and medical care are bad.

Second premise: If it is in your power to prevent something bad from happening without sacrificing anything nearly as important, it is wrong not to do so.

Third premise: By donating to aid agencies, you can prevent suffering and death from lack of food, shelter, and medical care, without sacrificing anything nearly as important.

Conclusion: Therefore, if you do not donate to aid agencies, you are doing something wrong.

The drowning-child story is an application of this argument for aid, since running your shoes and being late for work aren't nearly as important as the life of a child. Similarly, re-upholstering a car is not nearly as big a deal as losing a leg. Even in the case of Bob and the Bugatti, it would be a big stretch to suggest that the loss of the Bugatti would come close to rivaling the significance of the death of an innocent person.

Ask yourself if you can deny the premises of the argument. How could suffering and death from lack of food, shelter, and medical care not be really, really bad? Think of that small boy in Ghana who died of measles.

How you would feel if you were his mother or father, watching helplessly as your son suffers and grows weaker? You know that children often die from this condition. You also know that it would be curable, if only you could afford to take your child to a hospital. In those circumstances you would give up almost anything for some way of ensuring your child's survival.

Putting yourself in the place of others, like the parents of that boy, or the child himself, is what thinking ethically is all about. It is encapsulated in the Golden Rule, "Do unto others as you would have them do unto you." Though the Golden Rule is best known to most westerners from the words of Jesus as reported by Matthew and Luke, it is remarkably universal, being found in Buddhism, Confucianism, Hinduism, Islam, and Jainism, and in Judaism, where it is found in Leviticus, and later emphasized by the sage Hillel. The Golden Rule requires us to accept that the desires of others ought to count as if they were our own. If the desires of the parents of the dying child were our own, we would have no doubt that their suffering and the death of their child are about as bad as anything can be. So if we think ethically, then those desires must count as if they were our own, and we cannot deny that the suffering and death are bad.

The second premise is also very difficult to reject, because it leaves us some wiggle room when it comes to situations in which, to prevent something bad, we would have to risk something nearly as important as the bad thing we are preventing. Consider, for example, a situation in which you can only prevent the deaths of other children by neglecting your own children. This standard does not require you to prevent the deaths of the other children.

"Nearly as important" is a vague term. That's deliberate, because I'm confident that you can do without plenty of things that are clearly and in arguably not as valuable as saving a child's life. I don't know what you might think is as important, or nearly as important, as saving a life. By leaving it up to you to decide what those things are, I can avoid the need to find out. I'll trust you to be honest with yourself about it.

Analogies and stories can be pushed too far. Rescuing a child drowning in front of you, and throwing a switch on a railroad track to save the life of a child you can see in the distance, where you are the only one who can save the child, are both different from giving aid to people who are far away. The argument I have just presented complements the drowning-child case, because instead of pulling at your heartstrings by focusing on a single child in need, it appeals to your reason and seeks your assent to an abstract but compelling moral principle. That means that to reject it, you need to find a flaw in the reasoning.

You might now be thinking to yourself that the basic argument—that we should donate to aid agencies when by doing so we can prevent suffering and death without giving up anything nearly as important—isn't all that controversial. Yet if we were to take it seriously, our lives would be changed dramatically, for while the cost of saving one child's life by a donation to an aid organization may not be great, after you have donated that sum, there remain more children in need of saving, each one of whom can be saved at a relatively small additional cost. Suppose you have just sent $200 to an agency that can, for that amount, save the life of a child in a developing country who would otherwise have died. You've done something really good, and all it has cost you is the price or some new clothes you didn't really need anyway. Congratulations! But don't celebrate your good deed by opening a bottle of champagne, or even going to a movie. The cost of that bottle or movie, added to what you could save by cutting down on a few other extravagances, would save the life of another child. After you forgo those items, and give another $200, though, is everything else you are spending on as important, or nearly as important, as the life of a child? Not likely! So you must keep cutting back on unnecessary spending, and donating what you save, until you have reduced yourself to the point where if you give any more, you will be sacrificing something nearly as important as a child's life—like giving so much that you can no longer afford to, give your children an adequate education.

We tend to assume that if people do not harm others, keep their promises, do not lie or cheat, support their children and their elderly parents, and perhaps contribute a little to needier members of their local community, they've done well. If we have money left over after meeting our needs and those of our dependents, we may spend it as we please. Giving to strangers, especially those beyond one's community, may be good, but we don't think of it as something we have to do. But if the basic argument presented above is right, then what many of us consider acceptable behavior must be viewed in a new, more ominous light. When we spend our surplus on concerts or fashionable shoes, on fine dining and good wines, or on holidays in faraway lands, we are doing something wrong.

Suddenly the three premises laid out above are much harder to swallow. You may now be questioning whether a moral argument that has such radically demanding implications can possibly be sound. And so it's worth stepping back a moment to look at how this argument fits into some of our most respected ethical traditions.

Traditional Views on Helping the Poor

In the Christian tradition, helping the poor is a requirement for salvation. Jesus told the rich man: "If you want to be perfect, go, sell your possessions and give to the poor." To make sure his message wasn't missed, he went on to say that it is easier for a camel to go through the eye of a needle than for a rich man to enter the kingdom of God. He praised the Good Samaritan who went out of his way to help a stranger. He urged those who give feasts to invite the poor, the maimed, the lame, and the blind. When he spoke of the last judgment, he said that God will save those who have fed the hungry, given drink to the thirsty, and clothed the naked. It is how we act toward "the least of these brothers of mine" that will determine, Jesus says, whether we inherit the kingdom of God or go into the eternal fire. He places far more emphasis on charity for the poor than on anything else.

Not surprisingly, early and medieval Christians took these teachings very seriously. Paul, in his second letter to the Corinthians, proposed that those with a surplus should share with the needy: "Your surplus at the present time should supply their needs, so that their surplus may also supply your needs, that there may be equality." The members of the early Christian community in Jerusalem, according to the account given in the Acts of the Apostles, sold all their possessions and divided them according to need. The Franciscans, the order of monks founded by Francis of Assisi, took a vow of poverty and renounced all private property. Thomas Aquinas, the great medieval scholar whose ideas became the semi-official philosophy of the Roman Catholic church, wrote that whatever we have in "superabundance"—that is, above and beyond what will reasonably satisfy our own needs and those of our family, for the present and the foreseeable future—"is owed, of natural right, to the poor for their sustenance." In support of this view, he quoted Ambrose, one of the four original "Great Doctors" or teachers of the Church. He also cited the Decretum Gratiani, a twelfth-century compilation of canon law that contains the powerful statement, "The bread which you withhold belongs to the hungry: the clothing you shut away, to the naked: and the money you bury in the earth is the redemption and freedom of the penniless."

Note that "owed" and "belongs." For these Christians, sharing our surplus wealth with the poor is not a matter of charity, but of our duty and their rights. Aquinas even went so far as to say: "It is not theft, properly speaking, to take secretly and use another's property in a case of extreme need: because that which he takes for the support of his life becomes his own property by reason of that need." This isn't just a Roman Catholic view. John Locke, the favorite philosopher of America's founding fathers, wrote that "charity gives every man a title to so much out of another's plenty, as will keep him from extreme want, where he has no means to subsist otherwise."

Today, some Christians are seeking a renewed focus on the message of the gospels. Jim Walks, founder and editor of the Christian magazine *Sojourners*, likes to point out that the Bible contains more than three thousand references to alleviating poverty—enough reason, he thinks, for making this a central moral issue for Christians. Rick Warren, author of *The Purpose Driven Life* and pastor of the Saddleback Church, visited South Africa in 2003 and came across a tiny church operating from a dilapidated tent and sheltering twenty-five children orphaned by AIDS.

This was, Warren says, "like a knife in the heart: I realized they were doing more for the poor than my entire megachurch." Since then, with his encouragement, more than 7,500 Saddleback Church members have paid their own way to developing countries to do volunteer work fighting poverty and disease. Once they have seen the situation for themselves, many want to keep helping. Warren himself now says, "I couldn't care less about politics, the culture wars. My only interest is to get people to care about Darfurs and Rwandas."

Helping the poor is also strongly emphasized in Judaism, the source of many of those three thousand biblical references to helping the poor. The Hebrew word for "charity," *tzedakah,* simply means "justice" and, as this suggests, for Jews, giving to the poor is no optional extra but an essential part of living a just life. In the Talmud (a record of discussions of Jewish law and ethics by ancient rabbis) it is said that charity is equal in importance to all the other commandments combined, and that Jews should give at least 10 percent of their income as *tzedakah.*

Islam, too, requires its adherents to help those in need. Each year, Muslims above a minimum level of wealth must give *zakat* in proportion to their assets (not income). For gold and silver—which today are understood to include cash and other liquid, assets—the requirement is to give 2.5 percent every year. In addition, one may give *sadaqa,* which may include both money and labor—for example, digging a well so that travelers will have water, or helping build a mosque. Unlike *zakat, sadaqa* is optional.

Judaism, Christianity, and Islam are related traditions with their roots in the same part of the world. The Chinese tradition is quite distinct and, it is sometimes said, more focused on how one acts to those with whom one is in some relationship, especially familial; yet here, too, it is possible to find a very strong statement of our obligations to the poor. Mencius, who lived about three hundred years before the Christian era, is regarded as the most authoritative interpreter of the Confucian tradition, and in terms of his influence on Chinese thought is second only to Confucius himself. One of the works that describes his teachings recounts a visit he paid to the court of King Hui of Liang. On arriving, he met the king and said to him:

> There are people dying from famine on the roads, and you do not issue the stores of your granaries for them. When people die, you say, "It is not owing to me; it is owing to the year." In what does this differ from stabbing a man and lulling him, and then saying "It was not I, it was the weapon?"

There is nothing new about the idea that we have a strong moral obligation to help those in need. In one-on-one situations where rescue is easy, our intuitions tell us that it would be wrong not to do it. We all see or read appeals to help those living in extreme poverty in the world's poorest countries. And yet most of us reject the call to "do unto others." I'll turn now to some of the reasons we give for our failure to act.

3. Common Objections to Giving

You may think of yourself as a charitable person. Most Americans do, and the $306 billion they donated to charities in 2007, three quarters of which came directly from individuals, lends support to that belief. In the United States, charitable giving is around 2.2 percent of gross national income. That's significantly more than in any other country, and about double the level of charitable giving in most other rich nations. About seven in every ten households in the United States made some form of gift to charity in 2007. Americans also give time: Nearly 30 percent do some kind of volunteer work, most with religious, educational, or community organizations, with the average amount given being about 50 hours a year. In contrast to financial donations, however, when it comes to volunteering, the United States lags behind several European nations, especially the Dutch, who give more than twice as much of their time. When financial donations and volunteering are combined, the United States ranks as the world's third most generous nation, behind the Netherlands and Sweden.

But beneath these encouraging numbers is a slightly less encouraging picture, at least as concerns those who live in extreme poverty. According to "Giving USA 2008," the most authoritative report on U.S. charity, the largest portion of the money Americans give, fully a third of it, goes to religious institutions, where it pays for the salaries of the clergy and for building and maintaining churches, synagogues, and mosques. Some of that—but by the most optimistic estimate, less than 10 percent—is passed on as aid for developing countries. The next biggest sector is education, including universities, colleges, and libraries. Again, a small percentage of that goes toward scholarships to students from developing countries, or to fund research that can help reduce poverty and disease. "Giving USA 2008" lumps donations to international aid organizations together with gifts to other organizations that do not give aid to the poor but, for example, run international exchange programs or work for international peace and security. This entire category received only 4.3 percent of all American charitable giving. According to statistics from the Organisation for Economic Co-operation and Development (OECD), U.S. private philanthropy for foreign aid amounts to only 0.07 percent of the nation's gross national income (that's just 7 cents for every $ 100 of income).

As someone who has chosen to read this book, you are probably among those who give to charity or who volunteer in their community; despite that, you may be less inclined to give a substantial portion of your income to save the lives of those living in extreme poverty in faraway places. Charity begins at home, the saying goes, and I've found that friends, colleagues, students, and lecture audiences express that resistance in various ways. I've seen it in columns, letters, and blogs too. Particularly interesting, because they reflect a line of thought prevalent in affluent America, were comments made by students taking an elective called Literature and Justice at Glennview High (that's not its real name), a school in a wealthy Boston suburb. As part of the reading for the course, teachers gave students an article that I wrote for the *New York Times* in 1999, laying out a version of the argument you have just read, and asked them to write papers in response. Scott Seider, then a graduate student at Harvard University researching how adolescents think about obligations to others, interviewed thirty-eight students in two sections of the course and read their papers.

Let's look at some of the objections raised by these varied sources. Perhaps the most fundamental objection comes from Kathryn, a Glennview student who believes we shouldn't judge people who refuse to give:

> There is no black and white universal code for everyone. It is better to accept that everyone has a different view on the issue, and all people are entitled to follow their own beliefs.

Kathryn leaves it to the individual to determine his or her moral obligation to the poor. But while circumstances do make a difference, and we should avoid being too black-and-white in our judgments, this doesn't mean we should accept that everyone is entitled to follow his or her own beliefs. That is moral relativism, a position that many find attractive only until they are faced with someone who is doing something really, really wrong. If we see a person holding a cat's paws on an electric grill that is gradually heating up, and when we vigorously object he says, "But it's fun, see how the cat squeals," we don't just say, "Oh, well, you are entitled to follow your own beliefs," and leave him alone. We can and do try to stop people who are cruel to animals, just as we stop rapists, racists, and terrorists. I'm not saying that failing to give is like committing these acts of violence, but if we reject moral relativism in some situations, then we should reject it everywhere.

After reading my essay, Douglas, another Glennview student, objected that I "should not have the right to tell people what to do." In one sense, he's correct about that. I've no right to tell you or anyone else what to do with your money, in the sense that that would imply that you have to do as I say. I've no authority over Douglas or over you. On the other hand, I do have the right of free speech, which I'm exercising right now by offering you some arguments you might consider before you decide what to do with your money. I hope that you will want to listen to a variety of views before making up your mind about such an important issue. If I'm wrong about that, though, you are free to shut the book now, and there's nothing I can do about it.

It's possible, of course, to think that morality is not relative, and that we should talk about it, but that the right view is that we aren't under any obligation to give anything at all. Lucy, another Glennview High student, wrote as follows:

> If someone wants to buy a new car, they should. If someone wants to redecorate their house, they should, and. if they need a suit, get it. They work for their money and. they have the right to spend it on themselves.

You've probably already had this thought: You've worked hard to get where you are now, so haven't you earned a right to enjoy it? This seems both fair and reflective of our basic economic values. Yet, when thinking about fairness, you might also consider that if you are a middle-class person in a developed country, you were fortunate to be born into social and economic circumstances that make it possible for you to live comfortably if you work hard and have the right abilities. In other places, you might have ended up poor, no matter how hard you worked. Warren Buffett, one of the world's richest people, acknowledged as much when he said: "If you stick me down in the middle of Bangladesh or Peru, you'll find out how much this talent is going to produce in the wrong kind of soil." Nobel Prize–winning economist and social scientist Herbert Simon estimated that "social capital" is responsible for at least 90 percent of what people earn in wealthy societies. Simon was talking about living in a society with good institutions, such as an efficient banking system, a police force that will protect you from criminals, and courts to which you can turn with reasonable hope of a just decision if someone breaches a contract with you. Infrastructure in the form of roads, communications, and a reliable power supply is also part of our social capital. Without these, you will struggle to escape poverty, no matter how hard you work. And most of the poor do work at least as hard as you. They have little choice even though most people in rich nations would never tolerate the working conditions in poor countries. Work in poor countries is more likely to involve hard physical labor, because there are fewer machines to do the job; office workers in poor countries in the tropics rarely have the luxury of air-conditioning. If poor people are not working it is likely because unemployment is higher in poor nations than in rich ones, and that is not the fault of the poor.

Lucy said that people have a right to spend the money they earn on themselves. Even if we agree with that, having a right to do something doesn't settle the question of what you should do. If you have a right to do something, I can't justifiably force you not to do it, but I can still tell you that you would be a fool to do it or that it would be a horrible thing to do or that you would be wrong to do it. You may have a right to spend your weekend surfing, but it can still be true that you ought to visit your sick mother. Similarly, we might say that the rich have a right to spend their money on lavish parties, Patek Philippe watches, private jets, luxury yachts, and space travel, or, for that matter, to flush wads of it down the toilet. Or that those of us with more modest means shouldn't be forced to forgo any of the less-expensive pleasures that offer us some relief from all the time we spend working. But we could still think that to choose to do these things rather than use the money to save human lives is wrong, shows a deplorable lack of empathy, and means that you are not a good person.

If we have the right to do as we wish with our money, that right would supply an objection to any attempt to force the rich to give their money away, or to attempts to take it from them, for example by taxation. I don't agree that we have such a right, but I am not arguing here for higher taxation or any other coercive means of increasing aid. I am talking about what we should choose to do with our money if we are to live ethically. At the same time, I'm not arguing against a governmental role in reducing global poverty. Whether governments should play such a role is simply a separate question from the argument I am making. My aim is to convince you, the individual reader, that you can and should be doing a lot more to help the poor.

Libertarians resist the idea that we have a duty to help others. Canadian philosopher Jan Narveson articulates that point of view:

> We are certainly responsible for evils we inflict on others, no matter where, and we owe those people compensation . . . Nevertheless, I have seen no plausible argument that we owe something, as a matter of general duty, to those to whom we have done nothing wrong.

There is, at first glance, something attractive about the political philosophy that says: '"You leave me alone, and I'll leave you alone, and we'll get along just fine." It appeals to the frontier mentality, to an ideal of life in the wide-open spaces where each of us can carve out our own territory and live undisturbed by the neighbors. At first glance, it seems perfectly reasonable. Yet there is a callous side to a philosophy that denies that we have any responsibilities to those who, through no fault of their own, are in need. Taking libertarianism seriously would require us to abolish all state-supported welfare schemes for those who can't get a job or are ill or disabled, and all state-funded health care for the aged and for those who are too poor to pay for their own health insurance, how people really support such extreme views. Most think that we do have obligations to those we can help with relatively little sacrifice—certainly to those living in our own country, and I would argue that we can't justifiably draw the boundary there. But if I have not persuaded you of that, there is another line of argument to consider: If we have, in fact, been at least in part a cause of the poverty of the world's poorest people—if we are harming the poor—then even libertarians like Narveson will have to agree that we ought to compensate them.

Some people imagine that the wealth of the world is a static quantity, like a pie that must be divided among a lot of people. In that model, the bigger the slice the rich get, the less there is for the poor. If that really were how the world works, then a relatively small elite would be inflicting a terrible injustice on everyone else, for just 2 percent of the world's people own half the world's wealth, and the richest 10 percent own 85 percent of the wealth. In contrast, half the world's people have barely 1 percent of the world's assets to split among them. But the world's wealth is not fixed in size. The world is vastly richer now than it was, say, a thousand years ago. By finding better ways to create what people want, entrepreneurs make themselves rich, but they don't necessarily make others poorer. This book is about absolute poverty, not about being poor relative to how wealthy your neighbors are; in absolute terms, entrepreneurs increase the world's wealth. So the unequal distribution of the world's wealth—startling though it is—is not sufficient to show that the rich have harmed the poor.

There are many ways in which it is clear, however, that the rich *have* harmed the poor. Ale Nodye knows about one of them. He grew up in a village by the sea, in Senegal, in West Africa. His father and grandfather were fishermen, and he tried to be one too. But after six years in which he barely caught enough fish to pay for the fuel for his boat, he set out by canoe for the Canary Islands, from where he hoped to become another of Europe's many illegal immigrants. Instead, he was arrested and deported. But he says he will try again, even though the voyage is dangerous and one of his cousins died on a similar trip. He has no choice, he says, because "there are no fish in the sea here anymore." A European Commission report shows that Nodye is right: The fish stocks from which Nodye's father and grandfather took their catch and fed their families have been destroyed by industrial fishing fleets that come from Europe, China, and Russia and sell their fish to well-fed Europeans who can afford to pay high prices. The industrial fleets drag vast nets across the seabed, damaging the coral reefs where fish breed. As a result, a major protein source for poor people has vanished, the boats are idle, and people who used to make a living fishing or building boats are unemployed. The story is repeated in many other coastal areas around the world.

Or consider how we citizens of rich countries obtain our oil and minerals. Teodoro Obiang, the dictator of tiny Equatorial Guinea, sells most of his country's oil to American corporations, among them Exxon Mobil, Marathon, and Hess. Although his official salary is a modest $60,000, this ruler of a country of 550,000 people is richer than Queen Elizabeth II. He owns six private jets and a $35 million house in Malibu, as well as other houses in Maryland and Cape Town and a fleet of Lamborghinis, Ferraris, and Bentleys. Most of the people over whom he rules live in extreme poverty, with a life expectancy of forty-nine and an infant mortality of eighty-seven per one thousand (this means that more than one child in twelve dies before its first birthday). Equatorial Guinea is an extreme case, but other examples are almost as bad. In 2005, the Democratic Republic of the Congo exported minerals worth $200 million. From this, its total tax revenues were $86,000. Someone was surely making money from these dealings, but not the people of the Congo. In 2006, Angola made more than $30 billion in oil revenue, about $2,500 for each of its 12 million citizens. Yet the majority of Angolans have no access to basic health care; life expectancy is forty-one years; and one child in four dies before reaching the age of five. On Transparency International's corruption perception index, Angola is currently ranked 147th among 180 countries.

In their dealings with corrupt dictators in developing countries, international corporations are akin to people who knowingly buy stolen goods, with the difference that the international legal and political order recognizes the corporations not as criminals in possession of stolen goods but as the legal owners of the goods they have bought. This situation is, of course, profitable for corporations that do deals with dictators, and for us, since we use the oil, minerals, and other raw materials we need to maintain our prosperity. But for resource-rich developing countries, it is a disaster. The problem is not only the loss of immense wealth that, used wisely, could build the prosperity of the nation. Paradoxically, developing nations with rich deposits of oil or minerals are often worse off than otherwise comparable nations without those resources. One reason is that the revenue from the sale of the resources provides a huge financial incentive for anyone tempted to overthrow the government and seize power. Successful rebels know that if they succeed, they will be rewarded with immense personal wealth, they can also reward those who backed their coup, and they can buy enough arms to keep themselves in power no matter how badly they rule. Unless, of course, some of those to whom they give the arms are themselves tempted by the prospect of controlling all that wealth . . . Thus the resources that should benefit developing nations instead become a curse that brings corruption, coups, and civil wars. If we use goods made from raw materials obtained by these unethical dealings from resource-rich but money-poor nations, we are harming those who live in these countries.

One other way in which we in the rich nations are harming the poor has become increasingly clear over the past decade or two. President Yoweri Museveni of Uganda put it plainly, addressing the developed world at a 2007 meeting of the African Union: "You are causing aggression to us by causing global warming. . . . Alaska will probably become good for agriculture, Siberia will probably become good for agriculture, but where does that leave Africa?"

Strong language, but the accusation is difficult to deny. Two-thirds of the greenhouse gases now in the atmosphere have come from the United States and Europe. Without those gases, there would be no human-induced global warming problem. Africa's contribution is, by comparison, extremely modest: less than 3 percent of the global emissions from burning fuel since 1900, somewhat more if land clearing and methane emissions from livestock production are included, but still a small fraction of what has been contributed by the industrialized nations. And while every nation will have some problems in adjusting to climate change, the hardship will, as Museveni suggests, fall disproportionately on the poor in the regions of the world closer to the equator. Some scientists believe that precipitation will decrease nearer the equator and increase nearer the poles. In any case, the rainfall upon which hundreds of millions rely to grow their food will become less reliable. Moreover, the poor nations depend on agriculture to a far greater degree than the rich. In the United States, agriculture represents only 4 percent of the economy; in Malawi it is 40 percent, and 90 percent of the population are subsistence fanners, virtually all of whom are dependent on rainfall. Nor will drought be the only problem climate change brings to the poor. Rising sea levels will inundate fertile, densely settled delta regions that are home to tens of millions of people in Egypt, Bangladesh, India, and Vietnam. Small Pacific Island nations that consist of low-lying coral atolls, like Kiribati and Tuvalu, are in similar danger, and it seems inevitable that in a few decades they will be submerged.

The evidence is overwhelming that the greenhouse gas emissions of the industrialized nations have harmed, and are continuing to harm, many of the world's poorest people—along with many richer ones, too. If we accept that those who harm others must compensate them, we cannot deny that the industrialized nations owe compensation to many of the world's poorest people. Giving them adequate aid to mitigate the consequences of climate change would be one way of paying that compensation. In a world that has no more capacity to absorb greenhouse gases without the consequence of damaging climate change, the philosophy of "You leave me alone, and I'll leave you alone" has become almost impossible to live by, for it requires ceasing to put any more greenhouse gases into the atmosphere. Otherwise, we simply are not leaving others alone.

> America, is a generous nation. As Americans, we are already giving more than our share of foreign aid through our taxes. Isn't that sufficient?

Asked whether the United States gives more, less, or about the same amount of aid, as a percentage of its income, as other wealthy countries, only one in twenty Americans gave the correct answer. When my students suggest that America is generous in this regard, I show them figures from the website of the OECD, on the amounts given by all the organization's donor members. They are astonished to find that the United States has, for many years, been at or near the bottom of the list of industrialized countries in terms of the proportion of national income given as foreign aid. In 2006, the United States fell behind Portugal and Italy, leaving Greece as the only industrialized country to give a smaller percentage of its national income in foreign aid. The average nation's

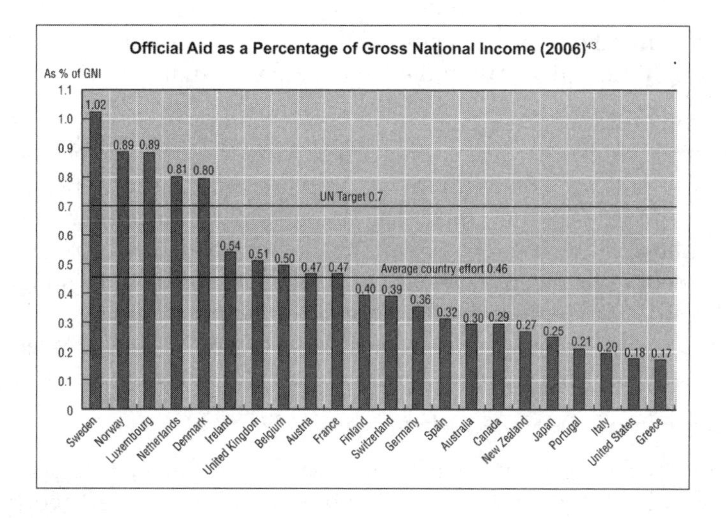

effort in that year came to 46 cents of every $100 of gross national income, while the United States gave only 18 cents of every $100 it earned.

In four different surveys that asked Americans what portion of government spending (not national income) goes to foreign aid, the median answers ranged from 15 percent to 20 percent. The correct answer is less than 1 percent.

Asked what share of America's national income the United States gives in foreign aid, 42 percent of respondents believed chat rhe nation gives more than four times as much as it actually gave, while 8 percent of Americans thought that the United States gives more than 100 times the actual amount!

A majority of people in these surveys also said that America gives too much aid—but when they were asked how much America should give, the median answers ranged from 5 percent to 10 percent of government

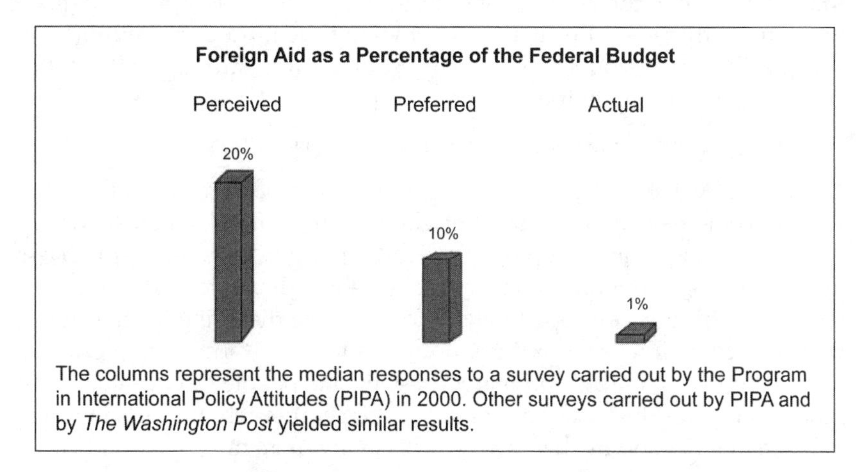

The columns represent the median responses to a survey carried out by the Program in International Policy Attitudes (PIPA) in 2000. Other surveys carried out by PIPA and by *The Washington Post* yielded similar results.

spending. In other words, people wanted foreign aid "cut" to an amount five to ten times greater than the United States actually gives!

Some contend that these figures for official aid are misleading because America gives much more than other countries in private aid. But although the United States gives more private aid than most rich nations, even its private giving trails that of Australia, Canada, Ireland, and Switzerland as a percentage of national income, and is on a par with giving by people in Belgium and New Zealand. Adding U.S. nongovernmental aid, of 7 cents per $100 earned, to U.S. government aid leaves America's total aid contribution at no more than 25 cents of every $100 earned, still near the bottom of the international aid league.

Philanthropic responses undermine real political change.

If those on the right fear that I am encouraging the state to seize their money and give it to the world's poor, some on the left worry that encouraging the rich to donate to aid organizations enables them to salve their consciences while they continue to benefit from a global economic system that makes them rich and keeps billions poor. Philanthropy, philosopher Paul Gomberg believes, promotes "political quietism," deflecting attention from the institutional causes of poverty—essentially, in his view, capitalism—and from the need to find radical alternatives to these institutions.

Although I believe we ought to give a larger portion of our income to organizations combating poverty, I am open-minded about the best way to combat poverty. Some aid agencies, Oxfam for example, are engaged in emergency relief, development aid, and advocacy work for a fairer global economic order. If, after investigating the causes of global poverty and considering what approach is most likely to reduce it, you really believe that a more revolutionary change is needed, then it would make sense to put your time, energy, and money into organizations promoting that revolution in the global economic system. But this is a practical question, and if there is little chance of achieving the kind of revolution you are seeking, then you need to look around for a strategy with better prospects of actually helping some poor people.

Giving people money or food breeds dependency.

I agree that we should not be giving money or food directly to the poor, except in emergencies like a drought, earthquake, or flood, where food may need to be brought in to stop people from starving in the short term. In less dire situations, providing food can make people dependent. If the food is shipped in from a developed nation, for example the United States, it can destroy local markets and reduce incentives for local farmers to produce a surplus to sell. We need to make it possible for people to earn their own money, or to produce their own food and meet their other needs in a sustainable manner and by their own work. Giving them money or food won't achieve that. Finding a form of aid that will really help people is crucial, and not a simple task, but as we'll see, it can be done.

Cash is the seed corn of capitalism. Giving it away will reduce future growth.

Gaetano Cipriano contacted me after reading one of my articles because he thought that as an entrepreneurial capitalist, he could offer a helpful perspective. The grandson of immigrants to America, he owns and runs EI Associates, an engineering and construction firm based in Cedar Knolls, New Jersey, that has assets of around $80 million. "Cash is the seed corn of capitalism" is his phrase. Gaetano told me that he deploys his capital to the best of his ability to promote profits and enduring growth, and that giving more of it away would be "cutting my own throat." But he does not spend extravagantly. "I do not live in a splendid house," he told me. "I have no second home. I drive a 2001 Ford Explorer with 73,000 miles. I belong to a nice squash club, and have four suits and two pairs of black shoes. When I take vacations they are short and local. I do not own a boat or a plane." While he does give to charity, he does it "at a level which is prudent and balanced with sustainable growth." If he were to give much more money away, it would have to come out of sums that he now reinvests in his business. That, in turn, would reduce his future earnings and perhaps the number of people he is able to employ, or how well he can pay them. It would also leave him with less to give if, later in life, he decides that he wants to give more.

For similar reasons, we can agree that it's a good thing Warren Buffett did not give away the first million dollars he earned. Had he done so, he would not have had the investment capital he needed to develop his business, and would never have been able to give away the $31 billion that he has now pledged to give. If you are as skilled as Buffett in investing your money, I urge you to keep it until late in life, too, and then give away most of it, as he has done. But people with less-spectacular investment abilities might do better to give it away sooner.

Claude Rosenberg, who died in 2008, was founder and chairman of RCM Capital Management, an institutional money management firm, so he knew something about investing, but he also knew a lot about philanthropy. He founded a group called New Tithing and wrote *Wealthy and Wise: How You and America Can Get the Most Out of Your Giving*. He argued that giving now is often a better value than investing your money and giving later, because the longer social problems are left unchecked, the worse they get. In other words, just as capital grows when invested, so the costs of fixing social problems are likely to grow. And, in Rosenberg's view, the rate at which the cost of fixing social problems grows is "exponentially greater" than the rate of return on capital. In support of this belief Rosenberg pointed to the cascading impact of poverty and other social problems, not just on one person but on future venerations and society at large. The claim is a broad one, difficult to prove or disprove; but, if it is true for poverty in the United States, then it is even more likely to hold for poverty in developing countries, in part because it is easier to get a high percentage return when starting from a low base. Of course, that assumes that there are things we can do in developing countries that will be effective in reducing poverty.

> What if you took every penny you ever had and gave it to the poor of Africa . . . ? What we would have is no economy, no ability to generate new wealth or help anybody.

This objection comes from Colin McGinn, a professor of philosophy at the University of Miami. It isn't clear whether McGinn's "you" is you, the individual reader, or the group an American Southerner might refer to as "y'all." If you [insert your name], took every penny you ever had and gave it to the poor of Africa, our national economy would not notice. Even if every reader of this book did that, the economy would barely hiccup (unless the book's sales exceed my wildest dreams). If everyone in America did it, the national economy would be ruined. But, at the moment, there is no cause for worry about the last possibility: there is no sign of it happening, and I am not advocating it.

Because so few people give significant amounts, the need for more to be given is great, and the more each one of us gives, the more lives we can save. If everyone gave significantly more than they now give, however, we would be in a totally different situation. The huge gulf between rich and poor means that if everyone were giving, there would be no need for them to take every penny they ever had and give it all to Africa. As you'll see before the end of this book, quite a modest contribution from everyone who has enough to live comfortably, eat out occasionally, and buy bottled water, would suffice to achieve the goal of lifting most of the world's extremely poor people above the poverty line of $ 1.25 per day. If that modest contribution were given, we would no longer be in a situation in which 10 million children were dying from poverty every year. So whether a small number of people give a lot, or a large number of people give a little, ending large-scale extreme poverty wouldn't cripple out national economy. It leaves plenty of scope for entrepreneurial activity and individual wealth. In the long run, the global economy would be enhanced, rather than diminished, by bringing into it the 1.4 billion people now outside it, creating new markets and new opportunities for trade and investment.

> People do have special relationships with their families, their communities, and their countries. This is the standard equipment of humanity, and most people, in all of human history, have seen nothing wrong with it.
>
> —Alan Ryan, philosopher and warden of New College, Oxford

It is true that most of us care more about our family and friends than we do about strangers. That's natural, and there is nothing wrong with it. But how far should preference for family and friends go? Brendan, a Glennview High student, thought that instead of going to aid for the poor, money "can be better spent helping your family and friends who need the money as well." If family and friends really *need* the money, in anything remotely like the way those living in extreme poverty need it, it would be going too much against the grain of human nature to object to giving to them before giving to strangers. Fortunately, most middle-class people in rich nations don't have to make this choice. They can take care of their families in an entirely sufficient way on much less than they are now spending, and thus have money left over that can be used to help those in extreme poverty. Admittedly, saying just where the balance should be struck is difficult. I'll return to that question later in the book.

Kiernan, another Glennview High School student, made a point similar to Alan Ryan's:

> [Giving what we don't need to the poor] would make the world, a better, more equal place. But it is like a little kid buying a pack of candy, keeping one piece, and giving the rest away. It just doesn't happen.

The issue raised by all these remarks is the link between what we humans are (mostly) like, and what we *ought* to do. When Brendan O'Grady, a philosophy student at Queen's University in Ontario, posted a blog about this issue, he got the following response from another Canadian philosophy student Thomas Simmons:

> Of course I do not want people to die, but I just feel generally unattached to them. I have no doubt that if I were to take a trip to places where people are starving then I might think differently, but as it stands now they are just too far removed. In not making these donations, I am implicitly valuing the affluence of my own life over the basic sustenance of many others. And, well, I guess I do. Am I immoral for doing so? Maybe.

When O'Grady queried this, Simmons clarified his position: "I don't intend to make a moral defense, but rather just reveal my personal feelings—that is, just to explain how I feel." The distinction between describing how things are and saying how they ought to be is also relevant to what Kiernan and Alan Ryan are saying. The fact that we tend to favor our families, communities, and countries may explain our failure to save the lives of the poor beyond those boundaries, but it does not justify that failure from an ethical perspective, no matter how many generations of our ancestors have seen nothing wrong with it. Still, a good explanation of why we behave as we do is an important first step toward understanding to what extent change is possible.

Theology

Most people assume that studying theology means studying what we know or what we claim to know about God. Often people think that this entails studying material that is obscure, irrelevant, and unchanging—as if, at the beginning of time, God dropped these materials down from heaven once and for all. Luckily for us, however, theology is not in fact about heaven-sent answers, but about very human, and very relevant, questions.

This is true because theologians study not just God, but human beings and the world we live in. Who are we, really, as human beings? Are we basically good, or sort of broken, or flatly a mess? Is the world a good place, or a dangerous one, or both, and what would any of those mean for how we are supposed to live? In the end, what theologians want to know is: what is really going on? Do we really live in a world where power is the measure of all things? Which is stronger, a tank or a single person standing in its way? Is human evolution a winner-take-all story of cut-throat competition, or is it the story of communities that care for their sick and elderly and tend one another so that the many survive where the individual could not? What is really going on?

In this essay, Colleen Mary Carpenter, associate professor of theology at St. Catherine, is attempting an answer to the question, "What is really going on when women suffer in childbirth?" Some Christian theologians would say that they are being punished for the sin of Eve, but that answer seems inadequate at best, and flatly cruel at worst. Is there a richer way to think theologically about this question—perhaps one that supports the flourishing of women rather than proclaiming their condemnation? The author of this piece answers that question with a resounding "Yes!" and shows us how we might practice that kind of theology.

Note: In order to follow the author's argument, there are a few theological terms that you need to know. First, incarnation: to incarnate is to become flesh. When Christians speak of the Incarnation, they are talking about God becoming human (taking on human flesh) in the life of Jesus. Next, a theodicy is an attempt to justify God's goodness despite suffering or tragedy: when we claim that someone "deserved it," or if we say that "we're just too small to understand the complexity of God's plan," we are working in the realm of theodicy. Finally, divinization refers to the idea that God loves human beings so much that their ultimate end is union with God, which would mean in some sense becoming divine, or divinized.

In Pain and Sorrow: Childbirth, Incarnation, and the Suffering of Women

Colleen Mary Carpenter

Almost ten years ago, I gave birth to a ten-pound, two-ounce baby boy after a long day and an even longer night of labor. The labor was obstructed: not only was he huge, he was turned sideways and had absolutely no intention of entering the world in the way of most babies. The midwife spent hours instructing me in various techniques and positions that were supposed to help shift the baby's position and get him moving, but nothing worked. In the end, the obstetrician was called and Thomas was safely delivered via C-section. Aside from a relatively small scar, I emerged from the experience physically unscathed.

Yet it was weeks—perhaps months—before I could talk about Thomas's birth without sobbing uncontrollably: the experience of being in such pain for so long, and the lingering terror that it would have gone on and on and on—perhaps until my death—if I did not live in a time and a place where surgical intervention was possible, had left a part of me completely undone. But as it happened, of course, I was fine, and Thomas was fine, and that was the end of it.

Until, that is, I read about what really happens in obstructed labor when surgery is unavailable. I had always assumed, of course, that the mother dies—that I would have died. In fact, the reality of obstructed labor and its aftermath is far worse than that. Such labors can go on for days, even up to week (which is, to put it mildly, an absolutely terrifying amount of time). The baby usually dies after the first few days, but is only born much later, when the mother's body has been so injured by the unrelenting pressure of the child's body pushing against hers—resulting in a good bit of her living skin and muscle and tissue dying from lack of blood flow—that her body rips apart and frees the dead child at long last. In the best case scenario, the tear opens her bladder and she is left incontinent, unable to contain a constant flow of urine. In the worst case, the tear opens not only her bladder but her rectum, and both feces and urine spill forth from her body in a relentless, unstoppable flow that—without surgical repair—will last for the rest of her life. Some women also have nerve damage and find themselves unable to move their legs properly, or at all. So: a child born dead, grievous untended internal injuries, filth, stench, perhaps even paralysis. Of course, this is only the beginning: who would live with such a creature? She smells, she cannot keep herself clean or dry, she is not fit for society and barely fit for work. Her husband leaves her. The other women of the village shun her. Her child is dead. She is, in the words of Dr. Catherine Hamlin, a surgeon who has dedicated her life to the repair of obstetric fistulae in Ethiopia, "abandoned to her shame . . . [and] spends the rest of her life in misery" (Hamlin x).

This is the fate of some 100,000 women a year—or girls, really, since it is usually young mothers, perhaps fourteen, fifteen years old, bearing their first child, who suffer fistula. The United Nations estimates that up to two million women in the developing world are living with fistula—a nearly unimaginable living death. Clearly this is a public health disaster of the highest order: it is a medical problem, a problem of poverty and access to health care. It is also a political problem, having to do with government priorities, distribution of scarce resources, and unintended consequences of supposedly unrelated policies, like agricultural subsidies in the First World that destroy the farming economies of the Third World. Surely it is also a problem rooted in sexism, in the patriarchy that marks so many societies and makes women and women's health of such small value.

But it is also a theological problem, one with roots deep within our understanding of both incarnation and salvation—indeed, deep within the fundamental story Christians tell about the history of God's relationship to humanity. The destruction of women's bodies and their lives through obstetric fistula and its social consequences is deeply colored by our Christian assessment of the value of women's bodies and the importance (even, perhaps, the necessity) of women's suffering. The Christian understanding of human bodies is of course deeply linked to our understanding of the Incarnation, the event in which God took on a human body in Jesus; it is also true that how Christians understand physical suffering is driven by our understanding of sin and redemption, especially with respect to the suffering of Christ during his Passion. Finally, how we think about women and suffering (especially in childbirth) carries us straight back to Eve, and the idea that the Incarnation was necessary only because of her sin—and that she and all her descendants will be punished for her crime by bearing children in great pain.

Is fistula, then, simply an extreme version of the punishment of Eve? Do we see in the faces of these suffering girls and women the face of evil, of pride, of the destruction of Paradise? "Because of you, even the son of God had to die," Tertullian once said of women. In such a worldview, fistula is simply part of the just punishment handed out by God to sinful women. Surely not many would dare say that today to a young girl whose life has been devastated by fistula . . . but our current theology of incarnation does in fact still point us in that direction—and in the 21st century we can no longer claim ignorance or innocence if we choose to continue to live within a destructive and sexist formulation of a central doctrine of Christian faith. Fortunately, our tradition contains within it an alternative understanding of incarnation that emphasizes not women's sin but God's original and ongoing love for humanity. Accordingly, I believe that we are called today to jettison our long-standing but destructive understanding of incarnation as a response to sin, especially women's sin, and return to the other ancient tradition of seeing incarnation as part of God's ongoing plan of revelation. It is only by making this choice—and it is a dramatic one, one that fundamentally reshapes our understanding of the relationship between humanity and God—that our theology will be able to respond in justice and with the Good News of Christ for the women whose lives have been devastated by fistula.

Childbirth in Christian Tradition

Before specifically addressing incarnation, I want to discuss the traditional Christian understanding of the pains of childbirth. These two things are linked of course by the story of Eve: both pain in childbirth and the Incarnation are said to be a direct result of her sin, the first as punishment and the second as the first step in God's forgiveness and redemption of the whole human race.

The pain of childbirth has been seen to require some sort of explanation since ancient times. It is a puzzle, of course—why should the necessary human activity of giving birth be such a painful and harmful and sometimes even deadly experience? Eating doesn't hurt; breathing doesn't hurt; most human activities necessary to life only hurt if something is terribly wrong. Animals give birth far more easily than human beings, and that fact would surely have been noted as soon as domesticated animals became a part of human communities. Why do women suffer so? Clearly the pain of childbirth is a mystery—and like all mysteries, especially those having to do with life and death, the best explanation available to our earliest thinkers was that this must have something to do with God. Given the ancient assumptions that God actively controls our fate, and that good things happen to good people and bad things only happen to those who invite punishment by some sort of crime against God, it makes a sad sort of sense that our earliest understanding of the pain of childbirth is that women must have somehow deserved it. A just God could not possibly inflict such suffering on the innocent—and so women's guilt, as a class, as an entire sex, is proven by their suffering.

Theodicies of this type, which defend God's justice by blaming victims for their fate, are remarkably persistent even today (there are those who, for example, think that New Orleans was destroyed by Hurricane Katrina because of its sinfulness). However, the theological struggle against this type of thinking goes back at least to the book of Job. Christian theology has long recognized that the suffering of the innocent does in fact exist, and must be accounted for, or at least given meaning (hence the idea that our suffering participates in Christ's, or that it can be "offered up" on behalf of others). Yet in the case of childbirth, the possibility of innocent suffering was never seriously considered. Scripture was absolutely clear on this point: the pains of childbirth are punishment for sin, period. Moreover, since Scripture so explicitly connects the pains of childbirth to the crime of Eve—which allowed sin to enter the world, destroyed the perfection of humanity, and forced God to allow the brutal murder of his only Son in order to offer us forgiveness—given all this, it is not surprising that there was not much room theologically for sympathy for a woman in labor.

Further, the deep theological connection between women's pain in childbirth and the whole narrative of Christian salvation meant that there was a sacred dimension to this pain: it was decreed by God from the beginning of time, and marked out women forever as the guilty ones, the broken ones, the ones who caused the whole mess in which we live. It is no wonder that many Christian clergy in the 19th century opposed the newfound medical ability to offer women pain relief during childbirth; it is no wonder that in 17th-century France, women were taught prayers like this:

> In my confinement, strengthen my heart to endure the pains that come therewith, and let me accept them as the consequence of your judgment upon our sex, for the sin of the first woman. In view of that curse, and of my own offenses in marriage, may I suffer the cruelest pangs with joy, and may I join them with the sufferings of your Son upon the cross, in the midst of which He engendered me into eternal life. Never can they be as harsh as I deserve, for although holy matrimony has made my conception legitimate, I confess that concupiscence mingled its venom therewith and that it has urged me to commit faults which displease you. If it be your will that I die in my confinement, may I adore it, bless it, and submit to it (Frymer-Kensky 183).

Such prayers have no place in the delivery rooms of Christian mothers today; indeed, the sentiments expressed in the prayer would shock most Western Christian women. In childbirth classes today, women are often taught that the pain of labor is "good pain": it is an indication of how hard their bodies are working to do something incredibly difficult. On the other hand, evolutionary biologists tell us that most mammals give birth without nearly as much difficulty and pain as human beings, who suffer as a result of the mismatch between our large brains and the pelvic design required to enable us to walk upright. The pain is merely the consequence of an evolutionary compromise, and carries with it no inherent valuation, neither good nor bad. Both of these explanations stand in stark contrast to traditional Christian teaching: it would appear that acceptance of either would mean, in the end, rejection of the entire Christian narrative of salvation.

Yet clearly that is not what is going on: it is not only secular mothers who ask for epidurals during labor, but pious Christian women as well. Christian women as a class do not refuse pain relief in labor on religious grounds[1] (although some refuse out of concern about the effects of the drugs on the child)—and this is not a sign of their ignorance of tradition nor of their sinful rejection of the just teachings of the Church. Instead, I will argue that it is perfectly possible to reject the mythological understanding of the origins of painful childbirth *and its accompanying understanding of sin as the reason for the Incarnation* and still celebrate the Good News of the Incarnation, life, death, and resurrection of Christ Jesus.

Incarnation

The traditional Western narrative of God's relationship to humanity goes something like this: out of nothing, God created a perfect world, a world in which humanity was deeply connected to God and did not suffer the separation and alienation from God or from each other that we do today. Then, tragically, this perfection was broken: the first woman committed the first sin, and urged her husband to follow her. In punishment for their crime, creation itself changed dramatically: the Earth was no longer a garden, but yielded food only with sweat and labor; God no longer walked in the midst of creation; and women were condemned to pain in childbirth and to subjection to their husbands. Pain, hierarchy, difficult physical labor, and the loss of God's felt presence among us were all results of sin. The worst punishment, in the end, was the loss of God—the banishment from Eden—and the knowledge that nothing we ever did could bring us back into God's presence, or bring God back to walk among us again. We were banished; we were lost. In the early Church's understanding, the coming of Jesus was a direct response to this terrible situation: in the Christus Victor understanding of atonement, which dominated the church for centuries, Jesus came to free us from our bondage to sin and the Devil; the death of Jesus was both payment of the debt of sin and a ruse that forced the Devil to free humanity forever. A thousand years ago, Anselm proposed a different understanding of "Cur Deus Homo," or why God became human: he argued that Jesus' death did not pay off the Devil, but was instead payment, or satisfaction, owed to God from sinful humanity. That understanding, with some modifications, still undergirds most thought on redemption today, especially popular thought.

There is, of course, another long-standing Christian understanding of why the Incarnation happened—and how to describe the fundamental relationship between God and humanity. In the early church, the Greek Fathers "dared to speak of humanity's 'deification' . . . [the idea that humanity is] called to become by grace what God is by nature" (Ware 21). In order for human beings to share in God's glory, the Eastern Fathers argued, a bridge must exist between the divine and the human, and that bridge is Jesus Christ, fully human and fully divine (Ware 21). The Incarnation was not merely a response to sin—although certainly it did respond to humanity's sin—but instead had been decreed from the beginning of creation, as it was necessary to fully bind human creatures to their divine Maker. St. Athanasius boldly claimed that "God became human that we might be made God," (*On the Incarnation*, 54); here the Incarnation is rooted in God's eternal love for humanity, not in a complex scheme concocted only in response to humanity's failings. Indeed, medieval Franciscan scholar John Duns Scotus argued that it is flatly inconceivable that "God's supreme work"—the Incarnation—was an afterthought in creation, or that it might never have happened at all if we had behaved ourselves.

Instead, arguing from Scripture (especially the Prologue to John's Gospel) as well as drawing on the work of the Eastern Fathers, Duns Scotus claimed boldly that "the Incarnate Word is the foundation of the creative plan of God, the very reason for the existence of all creation" (Overberg 3). The reason for the incarnation then, has nothing to do with Eve: human sin is not the beginning of the story of Jesus. Instead, human sin is always embraced by and subject to the grace and love of God which preceded it. The Christian narrative of God's engagement with humanity has thus been profoundly reconfigured: *sin is no longer the pivot around which the entire story turns*; rather, the centerpiece of the story is (as it should be) the love and self-communication of God.

In our own time, Karl Rahner's christology forwarded this understanding of the incarnation as rooted primarily in God's original and ongoing love for humanity, and God's original and ongoing plan for human transformation and divinization. In addition, Rahner made the intriguing (and appropriate) move of setting this understanding of incarnation within the context of an evolving universe and evolving humanity, both of which are realities completely unknown to all but the most recent of Christian theologians. Up until now, the alternative understanding of incarnation presented here merely sidestepped the importance of Eve to the Christian story—but the acceptance of evolution as part of the Christian story means that the entire framework of an original perfection destroyed by sin falls away. There was no original perfection: trace humanity back far enough and you do not find Adam and Eve, fully and consciously human but innocent; instead, you find a continuum of creatures developing towards consciousness and modern human intellectual ability—creatures who most likely (as our closest relatives, the apes, do) lived in hierarchical social arrangements, struggled to find food, and *in their pre-rational innocence* already suffered all the "punishments" human beings supposedly earned only through Eve's sin.

Evolution, then, requires us to rethink the Christian story and the traditional understanding of why Incarnation happened. Interestingly, the minority tradition of incarnation as the route to divinization gives us the theological tools we need to incorporate the new science into our religious understanding of the history of the world and of humanity. Incarnation as divinization always implied some sort of evolution of humanity: to find the details of this evolution not only in human beings but in the very structure of the universe is a powerful confirmation of the theological suspicion that Incarnation was meant to call us forward to something new, not repair an unexpected flaw in what should have been a static perfection.

There is still, however, the matter of suffering (and not just suffering in childbirth). The amount of suffering, over billions of years, required in the scientific story of the evolution of the universe is a profound challenge to those who would believe in a loving God. Darwin and many other scientists were driven to atheism when they began to grasp that evolution functions in large part through destruction, and that the lion and lamb are not predator and prey because of sin (and so without sin they could lie down together), but they are who they are because the mechanism of God's creation led them to be that way. In other words, violence, death, and suffering are an inescapable part of our world. How can this be? Is it even possible that a good and loving God—a God who Christians name as the incarnation of Love and Compassion—would create such a universe, and design it so that life must feed on suffering and death? Why wouldn't a good and loving God create a perfect universe, one in which life did not depend on death, or at least in which suffering was not so staggeringly prominent? Theologian John Haught offers an explanation that challenges our basic conception of God: he argues that only when we understand God not as Coercive, Kingly Power, or as Infinitely Powerful Clockmaker, but instead as suffering, humble love will we understand why the universe has unfolded in such a slow and stumbling manner:

> If ultimate reality is conceived of . . . as self-emptying, suffering love, we should already anticipate that nature will give every appearance of being in some sense autonomously creative . . . *Since it is the nature of love, even at the human level, to refrain from coercive manipulation of others, we should not expect the world that a generous God calls into being to be instantaneously ordered to perfection.* Instead, in the presence of the self-restraint befitting an absolutely self-giving love, the world would unfold by responding to the divine allurement at its own pace and in its own particular way. The universe then would be spontaneously self-creative and self-ordering. (Haught 53; italics added).

Indeed, Haught goes on to claim that the suffering, humble love revealed in the processes that brought the universe into being are definitively on display in the incarnation, life, death and resurrection of Jesus: the suffering, self-giving love embodied here is the truth of the universe, the ultimate truth of our lives: self-giving love will always entail suffering, but it also births new life.

And here we come to a startling consequence of our investigation: we began with the ancient idea that the suffering of women proved their sinfulness. In this new configuration of how suffering, incarnation, and the love of God come together, the idea that women suffer in giving birth can in fact be understood through the lens of God's suffering to give birth to humanity through the Incarnation. In other words, the image of a woman in labor, struggling to give birth to a child, can be placed alongside the image of Jesus on the cross, suffering to give birth to graced, divinized humanity. Intriguingly, this connection was made long ago, centuries before evolution reconfigured the Christian story, and is perhaps best expressed in the words of a woman, Julian of Norwich:

> But our true Mother—Jesus, All love—alone bears us for joy and for endless living . . . he sustains us within himself in love and hard labor, until the fulness of time. Then he willed to suffer the sharpest thorns and most grievous pains that ever were or ever will be, and at the last he died. And when he had finished, and had borne us so for bliss, still all this could not satisfy his wonderful love (*Revelations of Divine Love* 60).

And even more dramatic are the words of Margaret Hammer, a contemporary pastoral theologian, who offers this prayer to be said by a laboring woman: "Lord Jesus Christ, who gave birth on the cross, bless us as we labor" (Frymer-Kensky 187).

Women with Fistula in an Evolutionary Christianity

When the Incarnation is not a response to sin but a gift of love given from eternity; when Eve is not a focal point of the relationship between human and divine; when suffering exists in God's evolving creation but is not a judgment upon its creatures: when all this is true, how do we as Christians understand and respond to women suffering in childbirth—and in the extreme case, a woman injured by fistula?

First, I would suggest, we should respond to women injured in childbirth in the same way Jesus' tender women friends responded to his body after it had been taken down from the cross. As soon as their Sabbath rest had ended, they made haste to care for him tenderly, bringing spices and ointments and clean linen cloths. His body mattered to them. Even so, the bodies of women in labor should matter to us, and we should rush to attend to them with honor, ceremony, and dignity. Further, moving from the realm of story and image to the more strict demands of theological reflection, we know that as human beings called to self-transcendence towards God, we act in discipleship to the One who was entirely open to the radical presence of God in the world. And that openness, that "yes," had a lot to do with healing, with priorities that put the poor and the suffering first, with a critique of social and religious structures that burdened and oppressed the people of God, and with joy. Christians, then, would do well to respond to women with fistula with Drs. Catherine and Reg Hamlin as their models. The Hamlins moved to Ethiopia in 1959, and have since performed over 25,000 successful fistula surgeries. They founded a hospital completely dedicated to the care of women with fistula, and have trained surgeons from all over the developing world in the repair of fistulae. Obviously the vast majority of us are not surgeons and cannot join the work of physically curing women with fistula. But most of us could support the work of fistula repair: the UN has begun raising money for fistula repair and preventive obstetric care, and the Hamlin's hospital, the Addis Abbaba Fistula Hospital, has a foundation which is continually in need of funding. Perhaps even more important than supporting the work of fistula repair is supporting the eradication of the problem: it does not, after all, exist in the

West. It would be possible to live in a world without fistula. According to Dr. Catherine Hamlin, however, this would require far more than the extension of good obstetric care and adequate transportation services to the remotest of poor villages around the world: it would also—and more importantly, require:

> a whole new attitude to marriage and childbirth . . . Parents have to change their minds about the worth of their daughters. Teachers and religious heads have to show a lead, and the girls themselves must somehow learn that they do not have to marry when they are still children . . . Grass-roots community education programs are [beginning] . . . The [educators] know that they need to involve the men of the village, as unless they co-operate and are convinced that women often need help during labor, there is nothing the women can do on their own. All the decisions in the family are made by men (Hamlin 259-60, 300).

Parents must change their minds about the worth of their daughters; the daughters themselves must learn their own worth; the husbands must learn the value of their wives. Fistula will exist, in other words, until the fundamental, God-given dignity of women is recognized and respected. Fistula will exist until people look at—and smell—a woman with fistula and do not see "damaged goods" or a burden for the community or a punished sinner . . . but a neighbor in need of compassion and care, and a human being who was injured in the service of self-giving love. Theology has a role here, as Dr. Hamlin speaks of "teachers and religious heads" who can and should be teaching Christian theology, especially incarnational theology, in a way that does not devalue women. Certainly not all of these leaders are Christian (though many are): some are Muslim, some are traditional tribal religious leaders. This means that our work is not limited to educating Christian pastors and teachers in a contemporary understanding of incarnation and women's dignity before God, but should also extend to interfaith dialogue about the value of all people, the structures of marriage, and the relationship between a community and its sick or injured.

We have, in the end, much theological work to do; we have even more practical work to do in teaching and preaching what we have studied and researched. God was enfleshed in the human being Jesus of Nazareth, and because of that we recognize God's presence in all human flesh—even or perhaps especially in flesh that is broken and bleeding, even or perhaps especially in the bodies of women broken by fistula.

Works Cited

Frymer-Kensky, Tikva. *Motherprayer: The Pregnant Woman's Spiritual Companion*. New York: Riverhead Books, 1995.

Hamlin, Catherine, with John Little. *The Hospital By the River: A Story of Hope.* Oxford, UK and Grand Rapids, MI: Monarch Books, 2001.

Haught, John. *God After Darwin: A Theology of Evolution*. Boulder, Colorado: Westview Press, 2000.

Julian of Norwich. *Revelations of Divine Love*. Translated and with an introduction by M. L. del Mastro. New York: Image Books, 1977.

Overberg, Kenneth R., S.J. "The Incarnation: Why God Wanted to Become Human," *Catholic Update* (December 2002), St. Anthony Messenger Press.

Rahner, Karl. *Foundations of Christian Faith: An Introduction to the Idea of Christianity*. Translated by William V. Dych. New York: Crossroad, 1987.

Ware, Timothy (Bishop Kallistos). *The Orthodox Church: new edition.* New York: Penguin, 1997. Originally published 1963.

Note

[1] In fact, however, some Christian women today do refuse pain relief because they believe that their suffering is mandated by God. A friend recently asked me if it was true that she couldn't accept any drugs during childbirth because it would be sinful. The idea that women "must" suffer, not because of their own faults or sins, but simply because they are women, is still very much alive.

History

Historians use all kinds of documents and evidence from the past to develop their interpretations of what life was like in previous eras for various groups of people or individuals. Until about forty years ago, men wrote most of the history written in Western Society (Europe and its colonies, and the United States), and they ignored the lives and contributions of women because they assumed the female experience was insignificant. Since the social movements of the 1960s, including the women's movement, historiography *(the literature of history) has expanded dramatically to include research and writing on the history of women, as well as other groups and subjects previously neglected by historians.* Primary sources *(written evidence created in a past era) created by or about women are of central importance to historians who want to tell the story of the female experience in earlier times. Here are three examples of primary sources created by women in the past. The first is comprised of excerpts from a woman's diary, circa 202 CE; the second is Olympe des Gouges' declaration demanding equal rights for women during the French Revolution; and the last is a document written by American feminist leader Elizabeth Cady Stanton calling for women's equality in 1848.*

Each primary source provides one picture of human experience in the past, but, by itself, one source never tells the entire story. Analyzing a primary source requires reading with a critical and questioning eye. As you consider these three sources consider the following questions: What was happening in the world when each source was being written? What common themes are evident in the three works? In what ways are these works different in content and style? What does each reveal about women's roles and status in their respective eras? What does the existence of such documents reveal about the importance of female literacy in the past? How can we know whether these works were representative of the broader female population? How and why is the theme of motherhood raised in each document?

from The Martyrdom of Saints Perpetua and Felicitas

This is the prison diary of a young woman martyered in Carthage in 202 or 203 CE. The beginning and ending are related by an editor/narrator; the central text contains the words of Perpetua herself. We read about Perpetua's newborn child in the text, but it gives no mention of her husband; it is assumed that he left her when it became clear she was not willing to renounce her Christianity.

From the Editor:

A number of young catechumens were arrested, Revocatus and his fellow slave Felicitas, Saturninus and Secundulus, and with them Vibia Perpetua, a newly married woman of good family and upbringing. Her mother and father were still alive and one of her two brothers was a catechumen like herself. She was about twenty-two years old and had an infant son at the breast. From this point on the entire account of her ordeal is her own, according to her own ideas and in the way that she herself wrote it down.

• • •

While we were still under arrest, my father out of love for me was trying to persuade me and shake my resolution. 'Father,' said I, 'do you see this vase here, for example, or waterpot or whatever?'

'Yes, I do', said he.

And I told him: 'Could it be called by any other name than what it is?'

And he said: 'No.'

'Well, so too I cannot be called anything other than what I am, a Christian.'

At this my father was so angered by the word 'Christian' that he moved towards me as though he would pluck my eyes out. But he left it at that and departed, vanquished along with his diabolical arguments.

For a few days afterwards I gave thanks to the Lord that I was separated from my father, and I was comforted by his absence. During these few days I was baptized, and I was inspired by the Spirit not to ask for any other favor after the water but simply the perseverance of the flesh. A few days later we were lodged in the prison; and I was terrified, as I had never before been in such a dark hole. What a difficult time it was! With the crowd the heat was stifling; then there was the extortion of the soldiers; and to crown all, I was tortured with worry for my baby[1] while I was there.

Then Tertius and Pomponius, those blessed deacons who tried to take care of us, bribed the soldiers to allow us to go to a better part of the prison to refresh ourselves for a few hours. Everyone then left that dungeon and shifted for himself. I nursed my baby, who was faint from hunger. In my anxiety I spoke to my mother about the child, I tried to comfort my brother, and I gave the child in their charge. I was in pain because I saw them suffering out of pity for me. These were the trials I had to endure for many days. Then I got permission for my baby to stay with me in prison. At once I recovered my health, relieved as I was of my worry and anxiety over the child. My prison had suddenly become a palace, so that I wanted to be there rather than anywhere else.

Then my brother[2] said to me: 'Dear sister, you are greatly privileged; surely you might ask for a vision to discover whether you are to be condemned or freed.'

Faithfully I promised that I would, for I knew that I could speak with the Lord, whose great blessings I had come to experience. And so I said: 'I shall tell you tomorrow.' Then I made my request and this was the vision I had.

I saw a ladder of tremendous height made of bronze, reaching all the way to the heavens, but it was so narrow that only one person could climb up at a time. To the sides of the ladder were attached all sorts of metal weapons: there were swords, spears, hooks, daggers, and spikes; so that if anyone tried to climb up carelessly or without paying attention, he would be mangled and his flesh would adhere to the weapons.

At the foot of the ladder lay a dragon of enormous size, and it would attack those who tried to climb up and try to terrify them from doing so. And Saturus was the first to go up, he who was later to give himself up of his own accord. He had been the builder of our strength, although he was not present when we were arrested. And he arrived at the top of the staircase and he looked back and said to me: 'Perpetua, I am waiting for you. But take care; do not let the dragon bite you.'

'He will not harm me,' I said, 'in the name of Christ Jesus.'

Slowly, as though he were afraid of me, the dragon stuck his head out from underneath the ladder. Then, using it as my first step, I trod on his head and went up.

Then I saw an immense garden, and in it a gray-haired man sat in shepherd's garb; tall he was, and milking sheep. And standing around him were many thousands of people clad in white garments. He raised his head, looked at me, and said: 'I am glad you have come, my child.'

He called me over to him and gave me, as it were, a mouthful of the milk he was drawing; and I took it into my cupped hands and consumed it. And all those who stood around said: 'Amen!' At the sound of this word I came to, with the taste of something sweet still in my mouth. I at once told this to my brother, and we realized that we would have to suffer, and that from now on we would no longer have any hope in this life.

A few days later there was a rumor that we were going to be given a hearing. My father also arrived from the city, worn with worry, and he came to see me with the idea of persuading me.

'Daughter,' he said, 'have pity on my grey head—have pity on me your father, if I deserve to be called your father, if I have favored you above all your brothers, if I have raised you to reach this prime of your life. Do not abandon me to be the reproach of men. Think of your brothers, think of your mother and your aunt, think of your child, who will not be able to live once you are gone. Give up your pride! You will destroy all of us! None of us will ever be able to speak freely again if anything happens to you.'

This was the way my father spoke out of love for me, kissing my hands and throwing himself down before me. With tears in his eyes he no longer addressed me as his daughter but as a woman. I was sorry for my father's sake, because he alone of all my kin would be unhappy to see me suffer.

I tried to comfort him saying: 'It will all happen in the prisoner's dock as God wills; for you may be sure that we are not left to ourselves but are all in his power.'

And he left me in great sorrow.

One day while we were eating breakfast we were suddenly hurried off for a hearing. We arrived at the forum, and straight away the story went about the neighborhood near the forum and a huge crowd gathered. We walked up to the prisoner's dock. All the others when questioned admitted their guilt. Then, when it came my turn, my father appeared with my son, dragged me from the step, and said: 'Perform the sacrifice—have pity on your baby!'

Hilarianus the governor, who had received his judicial powers as the successor of the late proconsul Minucius Timinianus, said to me: 'Have pity on your father's grey head; have pity on your infant son. Offer the sacrifice for the welfare of the emperors.'

'I will not', I retorted.

'Are you a Christian?' said Hilarianus.

And I said: 'Yes, I am.'

When my father persisted in trying to dissuade me, Hilarianus ordered him to be thrown to the ground and beaten with a rod. I felt sorry for father, just as if I myself had been beaten. I felt sorry for his pathetic old age.

Then Hilarianus passed sentence on all of us: we were condemned to the beasts, and we returned to prison in high spirits. But my baby had got used to being nursed at the breast and to staying with me in prison. So I sent the deacon Pomponius straight away to my father to ask for the baby. But father refused to give him over. But as God willed, the baby had no further desire for the breast, nor did I suffer any inflammation; and so I was relieved of any anxiety for my child and of any discomfort in my breasts.

A few days after, while we were all praying, suddenly in the midst of the prayer I uttered a word and named Dinocrates[3] and I was amazed because he had never come into my mind save then; and I sorrowed, remembering his fate. And straightway I knew that I was worthy, and that I ought to ask for him. And I began to pray for him long, and to groan unto the Lord. Immediately the same night, this was shown me.

I beheld Dinocrates coming forth from a dark place, where were many others also; being both hot and thirsty, his clothes foul, his color pale; and the wound on his face which he had when he died. This Dinocrates had been my brother in the flesh, seven years old, who being diseased with ulcers of the face had come to a horrible death, so that his death was abominated of all men. For him therefore I had made my prayer; and between him and me was a great gulf, so that either might not go to the other. There was moreover, in the same place where Dinocrates was, a fountain full of water, having its edge higher than he was able to reach; and Dinocrates stretched up as though to drink. I was sorry that the fountain had water in it, and yet because of the height of the edge he might not drink.

And I awoke, and I knew that my brother was suffering. Yet I was confident I should ease his pain; and I prayed for him every day till we passed over into the camp prison. (For it was in the camp games that we were to fight; and the time was the feast of the Emperor Geta's birthday.) And I prayed for him day and night with groans and tears, that he might be saved by me.

On the day when we were held in the stocks, this was shown me.

I saw that place which I had before seen, and Dinocrates was there, but now clean of body, finely clothed, and in comfort; and the fountain I had seen before, but now the edge of it was only at the boy's navel; and he drew water from it which flowed without ceasing. And on the edge was a golden cup full of water; and Dinocrates came up and began to drink from it; and the cup never went dry. And being satisfied he departed away from the water and began to play as children will, joyfully.

And I awoke. Then I understood that he was translated from his pains.

Some days later, an adjutant named Pudens, who was in charge of the prison, began to show us great honor, realizing that we possessed some great power within us. And he began to allow many visitors to see us for our mutual comfort.

Now the day of the contest was approaching, and my father came to see me overwhelmed with sorrow. He started tearing the hairs from his beard and threw them on the ground; he then threw himself on the ground and began to curse his old age and to say such words as would move all creation. I felt sorry for his unhappy old age.

The day before we were to fight with the beasts I saw the following vision:

Pomponius the deacon came to the prison gates and began to knock violently. I went out and opened the gate for him. He was dressed in an unbelted white tunic, wearing elaborate sandals. And he said to me: 'Perpetua, come; we are waiting for you.'

Then he took my hand and we began to walk through rough and broken country. At last we came to the amphitheater out of breath, and he led me into the center of the arena.

Then he told me: 'Do not be afraid. I am here, struggling with you.' Then he left.

I looked at the enormous crowd who watched in astonishment. I was surprised that no beasts were let loose on me; for I knew that I was condemned to die by the beasts. Then out came an Egyptian against me, of vicious appearance, together with his seconds, to fight with me. There also came up to me some handsome young men to be my seconds and assistants.

My clothes were stripped off, and suddenly I was a man. My seconds began to rub me down with oil (as they are wont to do before a contest). Then I saw the Egyptian on the other side rolling in the dust. Next there came forth a man of marvelous stature, such that he rose above the top of the amphitheater. He was clad in a beltless purple tunic with two stripes (one on either side) running down the middle of his chest. He wore sandals that were wondrously made of gold and silver, and he carried a wand like an athletic trainer and a green branch on which there were golden apples.

And he asked for silence and said: 'If this Egyptian defeats her he will slay her with the sword. But if she defeats him, she will receive this branch.' Then he withdrew.

We drew close to one another and began to let our fists fly. My opponent tried to get hold of my feet, but I kept striking him in the face with the heels of my feet. Then I was raised up into the air and I began to pummel him without as it were touching the ground. Then when I noticed there was a lull, I put my two hands together linking the fingers of one hand with those of the other and thus I got hold of his head. He fell flat on his face and I stepped on his head.

The crowd began to shout and my assistants started to sing psalms. Then I walked up to the trainer and took the branch. He kissed me and said to me: 'Peace be with you, my daughter!' I began to walk in triumph towards the Gate of Life. Then I awoke. I realized that it was not with wild animals that I would fight but with the Devil, but I knew that I would win the victory. So much for what I did up until the eve of the contest. About what happened at the contest itself, let him write of it who will.

The Editor resumes:

As for Felicitas, she too enjoyed the Lord's favor in this way. She had been pregnant when she was arrested, and was now in her eighth month. As the day of the spectacle drew near she was very distressed that her martyrdom would be postponed because of her pregnancy; for it is against the law for women with child to be executed. Thus she might have to shed her holy, innocent blood afterwards along with others who were common criminals. Her comrades in martyrdom were also saddened; for they were afraid that they would have to leave behind so fine a companion to travel alone on the same road to hope. And so, two days before the contest, they poured forth a prayer to the Lord in one torrent of common grief. And immediately after their prayer the birth pains came upon her. She suffered a good deal in her labor because of the natural difficulty of an eight months' delivery.

Hence one of the assistants of the prison guards said to her: 'You suffer so much now—what will you do when you are tossed to the beasts? Little did you think of them when you refused to sacrifice.'

'What I am suffering now', she replied, 'I suffer by myself. But then another will be inside me who will suffer for me, just as I shall be suffering for him.'

And she gave birth to a girl; and one of the sisters brought her up as her own daughter.

Therefore, since the Holy Spirit has permitted the story of this contest to be written down and by so permitting has willed it, we shall carry out the command or, indeed, the commission of the most saintly Perpetua, however unworthy I might be to add anything to this glorious story. At the same time I shall add one example of her perseverance and nobility of soul.

The military tribune had treated them with extraordinary severity because on the information of certain very foolish people he became afraid that they would be spirited out of the prison by magical spells.

Perpetua spoke to him directly. 'Why can you not even allow us to refresh ourselves properly? For we are the most distinguished of the condemned prisoners, seeing that we belong to the emperor; we are to fight on his very birthday. Would it not be to your credit if we were brought forth on the day in a healthier condition?'

The officer became disturbed and grew red. So it was that he gave the order that they were to be more humanely treated; and he allowed her brothers and other persons to visit, so that the prisoners could dine in their company. By this time the adjutant who was head of the gaol was himself a Christian.

On the day before, when they had their last meal, which is called the free banquet, they celebrated not a banquet but rather a love feast. They spoke to the mob with the same steadfastness, warned them of God's judgment, stressing the joy they would have in their suffering, and ridiculing the curiosity of those that came to see them. Saturus said: 'Will not tomorrow be enough for you? Why are you so eager to see something that you dislike? Our friends today will be our enemies on the morrow. But take careful note of what we look like so that you will recognize us on the day.' Thus everyone would depart from the prison in amazement, and many of them began to believe.

The day of their victory dawned, and they marched from the prison to the amphitheater joyfully as though they were going to heaven, with calm faces, trembling, if at all, with joy rather than fear. Perpetua went along with shining countenance and calm step, as the beloved of God, as a wife of Christ, putting down everyone's stare by her own intense gaze. With them also was Felicitas, glad that she had safely given birth so that now she could fight the beasts, going from one blood bath to another, from the midwife to the gladiator, ready to wash after childbirth in a second baptism.

They were then led up to the gates and the men were forced to put on the robes of priests of Saturn, the women the dress of the priestesses of Ceres. But the noble Perpetua strenuously resisted this to the end.

'We came to this of our own free will, that our freedom should not be violated. We agreed to pledge our lives provided that we would do no such thing. You agreed with us to do this.'

Even injustice recognized justice. The military tribune agreed. They were to be brought into the arena just as they were. Perpetua then began to sing a psalm: she was already treading on the head of the Egyptian. Revocatus, Saturninus, and Saturus began to warn the on looking mob. Then when they came within sight of Hilarianus, they suggested by their motions and gestures: 'You have condemned us, but God will condemn you' was what they were saying.

At this the crowds became enraged and demanded that they be scourged before a line of gladiators. And they rejoiced at this that they had obtained a share in the Lord's sufferings.

But he who said, Ask and you shall receive, answered their prayer by giving each one the death he had asked for. For whenever they would discuss among themselves their desire for martyrdom, Saturninus indeed insisted that he wanted to be exposed to all the different beasts, that his crown might be all the more glorious. And so at the outset of the contest he and Revocatus were matched with a leopard, and then while in the stocks they were attacked by a bear. As for Saturus, he dreaded nothing more than a bear, and he counted on being killed by one bite of a leopard. Then he was matched with a wild boar; but the gladiator who had tied him to the animal was gored by the boar and died a few days after the contest, whereas Saturus was only dragged along. Then when he was bound in the stocks awaiting the bear, the animal refused to come out of the cages, so that Saturus was called back once more unhurt.

For the young women, however, the Devil had prepared a mad cow. This was an unusual animal, but it was chosen that their sex might be matched with that of the beast. So they were stripped naked, placed in nets and thus brought out into the arena. Even the crowd was horrified when they saw that one was a delicate young girl and the other was a woman fresh from childbirth with the milk still dripping from her breasts. And so they were brought back again and dressed in unbelted tunics.

First the cow tossed Perpetua and she fell on her back. Then sitting up she pulled down the tunic that was ripped along the side so that it covered her thighs, thinking more of her modesty than of her pain. Next she asked for a pin to fasten her untidy hair: for it was not right that a martyr should die with her hair in disorder, lest she might seem to be mourning in her hour of triumph.

Then she got up. And seeing that Felicitas had been crushed to the ground, she went over to her, gave her hand, and lifted her up. Then the two stood side by side. But the cruelty of the mob was by now appeased, and so they were called back through the Gate of Life.

There Perpetua was held up by a man named Rusticus who was at the time a catechumen and kept close to her. She awoke from a kind of sleep (so absorbed had she been in ecstasy in the Spirit) and she began to look about her. Then to the amazement of all she said: 'When are we going to be thrown to that heifer or whatever it is?'

When told that this had already happened, she refused to believe it until she noticed the marks of her rough experience on her person and her dress. Then she called for her brother and spoke to him together with the catechumens and said: 'You must all stand fast in the faith and love one another, and do not be weakened by what we have gone through.'

At another gate Saturus was earnestly addressing the soldier Pudens. 'It is exactly', he said, 'as I foretold and predicted. So far not one animal has touched me. So now you may believe me with all your heart: I am going in there and I shall be finished off with one bite of the leopard.' And immediately as the contest was coming to a close a leopard was let loose, and after one bite Saturus was so drenched with blood that as he came away the mob roared in witness to his second baptism: 'Well washed! Well washed!' For well washed indeed was one who had been bathed in this manner.

Then he said to the soldier Pudens: 'Good-bye. Remember me, and remember the faith. These things should not disturb you but rather strengthen you.'

And with this he asked Pudens for a ring from his finger, and dipping it into his wound he gave it back to him again as a pledge and as a record of his bloodshed.

Shortly after he was thrown unconscious with the rest in the usual spot to have his throat cut. But the mob asked that their bodies be brought out into the open that their eyes might be the guilty witnesses of the sword that pierced their flesh. And so the martyrs got up and went to the spot of their own accord as the people wanted them to, and kissing one another they sealed their martyrdom with the ritual kiss of peace. The others took the sword in silence and without moving, especially Saturus, who being the first to climb the stairway was the first to die. For once again he was waiting for Perpetual Perpetua, however, had yet to taste more pain. She screamed as she was struck on the bone; then she took the trembling hand of the young gladiator and guided it to her throat. It was as though so great a woman, feared as she was by the unclean spirit, could not be dispatched unless she herself were willing.

Ah, most valiant and blessed martyrs! Truly are you called and chosen for the glory of Christ Jesus our Lord! And any man who exalts, honours, and worships his glory should read for the consolation of the Church these new deeds of heroism which are no less significant than the tales of old. For these new manifestations of virtue will bear witness to one and the same Spirit who still operates, and to God the Father almighty, to his Son Jesus Christ our Lord, to whom is splendour and immeasurable power for all the ages. Amen.

Notes

[1] Her baby is being cared for by her family at home. He has not yet been weaned at this point, so she both misses him and fears for his health.

[2] It was common for Christians to address or describe one another in familial terms.

[3] Perpetua's brother who died at age 7, whose tragic illness is described below.

The Rights of Woman

Olympe de Gouges

Man, are you capable of being just? It is a woman who poses this question; you will not deprive her of this right at least. Tell me, what gives you the sovereign power to oppress my sex? Your strength? Your talents? Observe the creator in his wisdom; survey in all her grandeur that very nature with whom you seem to wish to be in harmony, and give me, if you dare, just one example of this tyrannical empire. Go back to the animals, consult the elements, study the plants, and finally cast a glance at all the modifications of organic matter, and surrender to the evidence when I offer you the means to do so; search, probe deeper, and try to distinguish, if you can, the sexes in the administration of nature. Everywhere you will find them mingled; every where they cooperate in harmonious togetherness in this immortal masterpiece.

Man alone has raised his exceptional circumstances to a principle. Bizarre, blind, bloated with science and degenerated—in a century of enlightenment and wisdom—into the crassest of ignorance, he wants to command as a despot, a sex which is endowed with all intellectual faculties; he pretends to enjoy the Revolution and reclaim his rights to equality, in order to say nothing more about it.

Declaration of the Rights of Woman and of the Woman-Citizen

To be declared by the National Assembly in its last sessions or in those of the next legislature.

Preamble

Mothers, daughters, sisters [and, the] representatives of the nation demand to be constituted into a national assembly. Considering that ignorance, omission, or scorn for the rights of the woman are the only causes of public misfortunes and of the corruption of governments, they have resolved to set forth in a solemn declaration the natural, inalienable, and sacred rights of the woman, in order that this declaration, being constantly exposed before all the members of the society, may ceaselessly remind them of their rights and duties; in order that the authoritative acts of women and the authoritative acts of men may be at each moment compared with and, be respectful of the purpose of all political institutions; and in order that the Woman-citizens' demands, henceforth based on simple and incontestable principles, may always support the constitution, good mores, and the happiness of all.

In consequence, the sex that is as superior in beauty as it is in courage during the suffering of maternity recognizes and declares, in the presence and under the auspices of the supreme being, the following Rights of Woman and of the Woman-Citizen.

Article 1

Woman is born free and remains equal to man in her rights. Social distinctions can be based only upon the common utility.

Article 2

The purpose of any political association is the conservation of the natural and unwritten rights of woman and of man: these rights are liberty, prosperity, security, and especially resistance to oppression.

Article 3

The principle of all sovereignty resides essentially in the nation, which is nothing but the union of woman and man: no body and no individual can exercise any authority that does not come expressly from it.

Article 4

Liberty and justice consist of restoring all that belongs to others; hence, the only limits on the exercise of the natural rights of woman are those that emanate from perpetual male tyranny; these limits are to be reformed according to the laws of nature and reason.

Article 5

Laws of nature and reason prohibit all acts harmful to society: all that is not forbidden by these wise and divine laws, can not he prohibited, and no one can be constrained to do that which these laws do not command.

Article 6

The laws must be the expression of the general will; all female and male citizens must take part either personally or through their representatives in its formation; it must be the same for all: male and female citizens, being equal in the eyes of the law, must be equally eligible for all honors, positions, and public offices according to their capacity and without other distinctions besides those of their virtues and talents.

Article 7

No woman is an exception: she is accused, arrested, and detained according to cases determined by law. Women, like men, obey this rigorous law.

Article 8

The law must establish only those penalties that are strictly and obviously necessary, and no woman can be punished except by virtue of a law established and promulgated prior to the offence and legally applicable to women.

Article 9

Any woman being declared guilty, all severity is exercised by the law.

Article 10

No one is to be harmed even for his very basic opinions. Woman has the right to mount the scaffold; she must equally have the right to take the rostrum, provided that her demonstrations do not disturb the legally established public order.

Article 11

The free communication of thoughts and opinions is one of the most precious rights of woman, since this liberty assures the recognition of children by their fathers. Any Woman-Citizen thus may say freely, I am the mother of this child which belongs to you, without being forced by a barbarous prejudice to conceal the truth; save to respond to the abuse of this liberty in cases determined by the law.

Article 12

The guarantee of the rights of woman and of the Woman-citizen implies a major benefit; this guarantee must be instituted for the advantage of all, and not for the specific use of those to whom it is entrusted.

Article 13

For the support of the public force and the expenses of administration, the contributions of women and men are equal. Woman has a share in all the duties and in all the painful tasks; therefore, she must have the same share in the distribution of posts, employments, offices, honors and jobs.

Article 14

Female and male citizens have the right to verify, either by themselves or through their representatives, the necessity of the public fund. This can apply to women only if they are granted an equal share, not only in wealth, but also in public administration, and in the determination of the quota, the tax base, the collection, and the duration of the tax.

Article 15

The collectivity of women, along with men contributing to the public fund, has the right to demand an accounting of its administration, from any public agent.

Article 16

No society has a constitution without the guarantee of the rights and the separation of powers: the constitution is null if the majority of individuals comprising the nation have not cooperated in drafting it.

Article 17

Property belongs to both sexes whether united or separate; for each it is an inviolable and sacred right; no one can be deprived of it, since it is the true heritage of nature, unless the legally determined public need obviously dictates it, and then only under the condition of a just and prior indemnity.

Postambule

Woman, wake up! The tocsin of reason is being heard throughout the universe; recognize your rights. The powerful empire of nature is no longer surrounded by prejudice, fanaticism, superstition, and lies. The flaming torch of truth has dispersed all the clouds of folly and usurpation. Enslaved man has multiplied his strength and, needs recourse to yours to break his chains. Having become free, he has become unjust to his companion. O women! Women, when will you cease to be blind? What advantages have you received from the Revolution? A more pronounced scorn, a more marked disdain. In the centuries of corruption you have ruled only over the weakness of men. Your empire is destroyed, what then are you left with? The conviction of man's injustices and, the reclamation of your patrimony, based on the wise decrees of nature—what have you to dread from such a fine undertaking? The *bon mot* of the legislator of the marriage of Cana?[1] Do you fear that our French legislators, correctors of morality, long ensnared by political practices and, hanging from the branches of politics now out of date, will only say again to you: women, what is there in common between you and us? Everything, you will have to answer. If they stubbornly persist in their weakness in putting this *non sequitur* in contradiction to their principles, oppose courageously with the force of reason the empty pretensions of superiority; unite yourselves beneath the standards of philosophy; deploy all the energy of your character, and you will soon see that these haughty men, will not be groveling at your feet as servile adorers, but will be proud to share with you the treasures of the supreme being. Regardless of what barriers confront you, it is in your power to free yourselves; you have only to wish it. Let us pass now to the shocking tableau of what you have been in the past; and since national education is in the air at this moment, let us see whether our wise legislators will think judiciously about the education of women.

Women have done more harm than good. Constraint and dissimulation have been their lot. What force has robbed them of, guile has returned to them; they had recourse to all the resources of their charms, and the most irreproachable person could not resist them. Poison, the chains and the sword were all subject to them; they commanded crime, fortune and virtue. The French government especially depended throughout the centuries on the nocturnal administrations of women, the cabinet kept no secret from their indiscretion; embassies, military commands, ministry, presidency, pontificate, college of cardinals; in short, anything which characterizes the folly of men, profane and sacred, all have been subject to the cupidity and ambition of this sex, formerly contemptible and respected, and since the revolution, respectable and disdained.

In this sort of contradictory situation, what remarks could I not make! I have but a moment to make them, but this moment will arrest the attention of the remotest posterity. Under the Ancien Regime, all was perverted, all guilty; but could not the amelioration of conditions be perceived even in the very substance of vices? A woman only had to be beautiful or pleasant; when she possessed these two advantages, she saw a hundred fortunes at her feet. If she did not profit from them, then she was a bizarre character or had a rare philosophy which made her scorn wealth; then she was deemed to be considered a crazy, headstrong woman; the most indecent woman made herself respected with gold; and, commerce in women was a kind of industry in the upper classes, which, henceforth, will have no more credit. If it still had it, the revolution would be lost, and under the new relationships we would still be corrupt. However, can reason conceal the fact that any other path to fortune is closed to the woman bought by a man like the slave on the African coasts? The difference is great; that is known. The slave is commanded by the master; but if the master gives her liberty without recompense, and at an age when the slave has lost all her charms, what will become of this unfortunate woman? She will be the toy of scorn, even the doors of charity are closed to her; she is poor and old, and they say: why did she not know how to make her fortune? Reason finds other examples that are even more touching. A young, inexperienced woman, seduced by a man whom she loves, will abandon her parents to follow him; the ingrate will leave her after a few years, and the older she has become with him, the more inhuman is his inconstancy; if she has children, he will abandon her all the same. If he is rich, he will consider himself excused from sharing his fortune with his noble victims. If some involvement binds him to his duties, he will deny them, trusting that the laws will support him. If he is married, any other obligation loses its rights. Then what laws remain to extirpate this vice all the way to its roots? The law of dividing wealth between men and women and public administration. It can easily be seen that one who is born into a rich family gains very much from such equal sharing; but the one born into a poor family with merit and virtue : what is her lot? Poverty and opprobrium. If she does not excel precisely in music or painting, she cannot be admitted to any public function even when she has all the capacity for it. I will go more deeply into this in the new edition of all my political writings, with notes, which I propose to give to the public in a few days.[2]

Now, again on the subject of mores. Marriage is the tomb of trust and love. The married women can with impunity give bastards to her husband, and also give them the wealth which does not belong to them. The woman who is unmarried has only one feeble right; ancient and inhuman laws refuse to her and to her children the right to the name and the wealth of their father; and no new laws have been made in this matter. If it is considered a paradox and impossibility on my part to try to give my sex an honorable and just place, then I leave it to future people to attain glory for dealing with this matter; but while we wait, the way can be prepared through national education, by restoring customs and conjugal conventions.

Notes

1 It is written in the Bible that Jesus performed his first miracle in a festival in the town of Cana, in ancient Palestine. Here the author compared the parliamentary sessions of post-revolutionary France with that festival.

2 The French civilization took more than two hundred years to cover these "few days" of Olympe de Gouges. A critical edition of her political writings was published in 1993.

Declaration of Sentiments

Elizabeth Cady Stanton

When, in the course of human events, it becomes necessary for one portion of the family of man to assume among the people of the earth a position different from that which they have hitherto occupied, but one to which the laws of nature and of nature's God entitle them, a decent respect to the opinions of mankind requires that they should declare the causes that impel them to such a course.

We hold these truths to be self-evident; that all men and women are created equal; that they are endowed by their Creator with certain inalienable rights; that among these are life, liberty, and the pursuit of happiness; that to secure these rights governments are instituted, deriving their just powers from the consent of the governed. Whenever any form of Government becomes destructive of these ends, it is the right of those who suffer from it to refuse allegiance to it, and to insist upon the institution of a new government, laying its foundation on such principles, and organizing its powers in such form as to them shall seem most likely to effect their safety and happiness. Prudence, indeed, will dictate that governments long established should not be changed for light and transient causes; and accordingly, all experience hath shown that mankind are more disposed to suffer, while evils are sufferable, than to right themselves, by abolishing the forms to which they are accustomed. But when a long train of abuses and usurpations, pursuing invariably the fame object, evinces a design to reduce them under absolute despotism, it is their duty to throw off such government, and to provide new guards for their future security. Such has been the patient sufferance of the women under this government, and such is now the necessity which constraint them to demand the equal station to which they are entitled.

The history of mankind is a history of repeated injures and usurpations on the part of man toward woman, having in direct object the establishment of an absolute tyranny over her. To prove this, let facts be submitted to a candid world.

He has never permitted her to exercise her inalienable right to the elective franchise.

He has compelled her to submit to laws, in the formation of which she had no voice.

He has withheld from her rights which are given to the most ignorant and degraded men—both natives and foreigners.

Having deprived her of this first right of a citizen, the elective franchise, thereby leaving her without representation in the halls of legislation, he has oppressed her on all sides.

He has made her, if married, in the eye of the law, civilly dead.

He has taken from her all right in property, even to the wages she earns.

He has made her, morally, an irresponsible being, as she can commit many crimes with impunity, provided they be done in the presence of her husband. In the covenant of marriage, she is compelled to promise obedience to her husband, he becoming, to all intents and purposes, her master—the law giving him power to deprive her of her liberty, and to administer chastisement.

He has so framed the laws of divorce, as to what shall be the proper causes of divorce; in case of separation, to whom the guardianship of the children shall be given, as to be wholly regardless of the happiness of women—the law, in all cases, going upon the false supposition of the supremacy of man, and giving all power into his hands.

After depriving her of all rights as a married woman, if single and the owner of property, he has taxed her to support a government which recognizes her only when her property can be made profitable to it.

He has monopolized nearly all the profitable employments, and from those she is permitted to follow, she receives but a scanty remuneration.

He closes against her all the avenues to wealth and distinction, which he considers most honorable to himself. As a teacher of theology, medicine, or law, she it not known.

He has denied her the facilities for obtaining a thorough education—all colleges being closed against her.

He allows her in Church as well as State, but a subordinate position, claiming Apostolic authority for her exclusion from the ministry, and, with some exceptions, from any public participation in the affairs of the Church. He has created a false public sentiment, by giving to the world a different code of morals for men and women, by which moral delinquencies which exclude women from society, are not only tolerated but deemed of little account in man.

He has usurped the prerogative of Jehovah himself, claiming it as his right to assign for her a sphere of action, when that belongs to her conscience and her God.

He has endeavored, in every way that he could to destroy her confidence in her own powers, to lessen her self-respect, and to make her willing to lead a dependent and abject life.

Now, in view of this entire disfranchisement of one-half the people of this country, their social and religious degradation,—in view of the unjust laws above mentioned, and because women do feel themselves aggrieved, oppressed, and fraudulently deprived of their most sacred rights, we insist that they have immediate admission to all the rights and privileges which belong to them as citizens of these United States.

In entering upon the great work before us, we anticipate no small amount of misconception, misrepresentation, and ridicule; but we shall use every instrumentality within our power to effect our object. We shall employ agents, circulate tracts, petition the State and national Legislatures, and endeavor to enlist the pulpit and the press in our behalf. We hope this Convention will be followed by a series of Conventions, embracing every part of the country.

Firmly relying upon the final triumph of the Right and the True, we do this day affix our signatures to this declaration.

Signers of the Declaration of Sentiments, Seneca Falls, New York, July 19–20, 1848

Barker, Caroline
Barker, Eunice
Barker, William G.
Bonnel, Rachel D. (Mischell)
Bunker, Joel D.
Burroughs, William
Capron, E.W.
Chamberlain, Jacob P.
Conklin, Elizabeth
Conklin, Mary
Culvert, P. A.
Davis, Cynthia
Dell, Thomas
Dell, William S.
Doty, Elias J.
Doty, Susan R.
Douglass, Frederick
Drake, Julia Ann
Eaton, Harriet Cady
Foote, Elisha
Foote, Eunice Newton
Frink, Mary Ann
Fuller, Cynthia
Gibbs, Experience
Gilbert, Mary
Gild, Lydia
Hallowell, Sarah
Hallowell, Mary H.
Hatley, Henry
Hoffman, Sarah
Hoskins, Charles L.
Hunt, Jane C.
Hunt, Richard P.
Jenkins, Margaret
Jones, John
Jones, Lucy
King, Phebe
Lantham, Hannah J.
Lantham, Lovina
Leslie, Elisabeth
Martin, Elisa
Martin, Mary
Mathews, Delia
Mathews, Dorothy
Mathews, Jacob
M'Clintock, Elizabeth W.
M'Clintock, Mary
M'Clintock, Mary Ann
M'Clintock, Thomas
Metcalf, Jonathan

Milliken, Nathan J.
Mirror, Mary S.
Mosher, Pheobe
Mosher, Sarah A.
Mott, James
Mott, Lucretia
Mount, Lydia
Paine, Catharine C.
Palmer, Rhoda
Phillips, Saron
Pitcher, Sally
Plant, Hannah
Porter, Ann
Post, Amy
Pryor, George W.
Pryor, Margaret
Quinn, Susan
Race, Rebecca
Ridley, Martha
Schooley, Azaliah
Schooley, Margaret
Scott, Deborah
Segur, Antoinette E.
Seymour, Henry
Seymour, Henry W.
Seymour, Malvina
Shaw, Catherine
Shear, Stephen
Sisson, Sarah
Smallbridge, Robert
Smith, Elizabeth D.
Smith, Sarah
Spalding, David
Spalding, Lucy
Stanton, Elizabeth Cady
Stebbins, Catherine F.
Taylor, Sophronia
Tewksbury, Betsey
Tillman, Samuel D.
Underhill, Edward F.
Underhill, Martha
Vail, Mary E.
Van Tassel, Isaac
Whitney, Sarah
Wilbur, Maria E.
Williams, Justin
Woods, Sarah R.
Woodward, Charlotte
Woodworth, S.E.
Wright, Martha C.

International Languages

The essay below, by Felicia Cruz, Associate Professor of Spanish at St. Kate's, introduces readers to the cross-cultural, interdisciplinary critical and worldly textual analyses that scholars in the languages dabble in when they are modeling for their students, in dramatic fashion, idioms and verb conjugations in French, Spanish and, yes, even Spanglish.

Professor Cruz majored in Spanish at Carleton College, earned her PhD in Hispanic Studies at Northwestern University and has taught at SCU since 2002. She also taught in diverse settings and places—Carthage College, Emory University, Alfred University and the University of Pittsburgh-Greensburg—before she wended her way back home to the Twin Cities (incidentally, a place she hadn't fully appreciated until she left). What has remained constant, however, is the passion of her discipline for reading of all sorts, from ingesting and pondering world literature, to perusing cookbooks for prospective ingredients and sumptuous side dishes in hopes of one day concocting the proverbial perfect meal. Incidentally, the cookbooks give pause for pointing out polyglot aspects of English (the language) and Anglophone culture—the cross-lingual, cross-cultural pollination that increasingly characterizes the U.S.A.

On the "Simplicity" of Sandra Cisneros' *The House on Mango Street*

Felicia Cruz

Cisneros' Meteoric Rise to the Top[1]

Within seven years of its publication in 1984 by Arte Público,[2] a small, now defunct Hispanic publishing house, Sandra Cisneros' *The House on Mango Street* was taken on by mainstream publisher, Vintage Books (a division of Random House). Nicolás Kanellos, the founding publisher of Arte Público, included Cisneros in a "new" generation of college-educated Chicano writers whose works were endorsed by prestigious foundations and published by mainstream houses. This generation of writers "inscribed themselves on the published page precisely at the time when literary publishing was [in particular] opening up to women as writers and intellectuals" (Kanellos, xix). At the same time, these writers, especially Chicanas, were keenly "aware of the business of writing": knowing "the industry's networks" and "norms of language, metaphor, and craft protected by the academy," they broke "into commercial and intellectual circles and cause[d] a stir" (Kanellos, xix). Consequently, two prestigious foundations, the National Endowment of the Arts (NEA) and the Macarthur Foundation, later awarded fellowships to Cisneros.

The Novel as *Vox Populi* (Voice of the People)

On the heels of *Mango Street*'s nearly instantaneous conversion into "It-book" within Chicano literary circles in the mid-1980s, was the expansion of its readership beyond Chicano and Latino communities. According to critic María Elena de Valdés, an essay on Chicano criticism, from1988, marked "a turning point in Cisneros' criticism," which then branched out into "the richer context of North American literature and out of the limited area of ethnic writing" (290). "In 1989 and 1990," notes Valdés, "criticism no longer [had] to explain the barrio or the author's relation to it or what it means to be a Chicana writer" (290). A significant portion of early enthusiasts of *Mango Street* were teachers, who introduced and discussed with their students the story of its protagonist, Esperanza, a working-class Chicana whose tale about growing up in a Chicago barrio resonated with them; in turn, parents of various students would take their copy of *Mango Street* to book signings, eager to forge a real-life connection to the now very famous writer. Remarks Cisneros: "I've witnessed families buying my book for themselves and for family members, families for whom spending money on a book can be a sacrifice" (Introduction xix). Cisneros also alludes to copious, grateful feedback she has received in writing: "[T]here are letters from readers of all ages and colors who write to say that I have written their stories" (Introduction xix). These comments, in addition to others that Cisneros has made, underline the universal appeal and popularity of *Mango Street*, and attest to the strong, personal and emotional impact it has had on members of the general public, across ethnic, gender, and generational lines. It is thus not surprising that it has been translated worldwide, long ago having acquired the status of "classical" work in the canon of coming-of-age tales.

Beyond the ongoing critical and popular acclaim of Cisneros' (to date) magnum opus, *Mango Street* remains a mainstay in educational curricula nationwide and throughout the world—from elementary, middle and high schools, to colleges, universities and graduate programs. Compulsory reading in numerous Latino(a) and/or Chicano(a) literature courses at the undergraduate and graduate levels, Cisneros' book, according to critic Delia Poey, also appears in courses on American, multicultural, and women's literatures (216). Concerning feminist approaches to *Mango Street*, critic Andrea O'Reilly Herrera remarks that it "raises disturbing questions regarding both female nature and the realities and fictions of development for women in general, and Chicanas in particular" (199).

O'Reilly Herrera's comments about the complex questions the book invites, in fact, differ markedly from the general consensus among my students in 1994 and 2000. Initially taught to undergraduate students at a small private college in Kenosha, Wisconsin, and subsequently to undergraduate students at a small private university in Upstate New York, the general consensus among both groups was that *Mango Street* is eminently readable (i.e., simple).

Herstory: Some Day My House Will Come . . .

For various readers, Cisneros' book chronicles the straightforward story of Esperanza, a young Chicana girl who lives in a barrio in Chicago, and subsequently resolves to leave behind the Mango Street community, in order to pursue and hopefully attain the American dream. If, however, her name, on one hand, means "hope" (in Spanish), on the other hand, Esperanza's name and reality connote and underline the degree to which Esperanza-from-the-hood must wait (and toil) prior to beginning to pursue, and bringing into existence, her interpretation and version of "I-Have-a-Dream."

However, well before the Cordero family manages to procure a "real" house—if not the Parade-of-Homes "house-of-their-own," so coveted by Esperanza's parents—their oldest daughter, Esperanza, is haunted by poignantly traumatic moments, such as her encounter with a nun from school. In the passage that follows, Esperanza, not unlike Cisneros herself in graduate school, is made painfully aware of her essential difference, and exclusion, from "the Others," or mainstream society:

> Once when we were living on Loomis, a nun from my school passed by and saw me playing out front. [. . .]
>
> Where do you live? she asked.
>
> There, I said pointing up to the third floor.
>
> You live *there*?
>
> *There*. I had to look to where she pointed—the third floor, the paint peeling, wooden bars Papa had nailed on the windows so we wouldn't fall out. You live *there*? The way she said it made me feel like nothing. *There*. I lived *there*. I nodded. I knew then I had to have a house. A real house.
>
> One I could point to. (5)

Esperanza, as critics Rosaura Sánchez and Alvina Quintana point out, actually experiences concurrent inclusion in *and* exclusion from mainstream society. "On an ideological level, [she] dreams the American dream; [but] on a material level, like all in her community she remains systematically excluded from it" (Quintana 57). Critic Reuben Sánchez furthermore calls attention to the importance, for the Chicano community as a whole, of the gender of *Mango Street*'s protagonist: "The Chicana's concern with 'place'—a house, or room of one's own is a reaction against the patriarchal myth that denies the Chicana a place of her own. . . .The reality the Chicana addresses, . . . is the reality of her restriction to the urban setting—particularly the house or the room. That setting is Esperanza's past and her present in [the novel]; she [thus] recognizes . . . it might very well be her future as well" (229).

On Reading: Do You See What I Wee?

Whereas Esperanza's resolve to distance herself from her family and community has struck and strikes readers in some communities as puzzling, if not reprehensible, for other individuals, solitude, striking it out on one's own, and breaking away from one's family, constitute the very steps needed for growing up, and by extension, becoming part of the "real world." My undergraduate seminar students (in 1994 and 2000), for example, by and large viewed Esperanza's desire to acquire a house and her vow to become independent and self-sufficient as universal ideals and or goals that correspond to a *natural* right which—in the liberal democratic spirit of the Founding Fathers—is, or should be available to *all* American citizens. My students, who seemed to have uncritically identified with mainstream views, inscribed Esperanza's dream in a foundational democratic rhetoric and declaration: that the pursuit of freedom, liberty, and happiness *is* the right of all American citizens. They did so reflexively, in the naïve, albeit earnest belief that an iron will and hard work (i.e., the Protestant work ethic) *would* eventually lead Esperanza to the materialization of her dream. What, then, might we make of the diametrically opposed perceptions of some working-class Chicanos and those of my middle-class, mostly Caucasian students, regarding the textual focus on and portrayal of Esperanza's desire and quest for autonomy, self-sufficiency and the pursuit and achievement of individual goals?

If, on the one hand, the uncritical transcription of Esperanza as the "voice" of Cisneros is carried out by numerous readers—including students, scholars and critics—then, on the other hand, there may be a marked difference between (and among) each group's perception of what the novel's prevalent themes or issues are. As a case in point, the majority of my college students (both times *Mango Street* was taught) overlooked the regional specificity of the novel, foregoing what for me and the handful of Latino students in each class seemed to be a deliberate focus on the relation among issues of ethnicity, race and class; they overlooked the novelistic representation of ideologies of exclusion related to Esperanza's background, her working-class roots, and her view of the clash between "Them," mainstream society, and "Us"—the haves and have-nots.[3]

Overall, my students generally focused on malaise in *Mango Street*, connecting with Esperanza's feelings of alienation, discomfiture, and solitude, which they too had experienced as children, tween-agers and adolescents.[4] Critic Jody Norton notes: "Because most of us have our own memories of a moment when our preadolescent reality seemed suddenly to have shifted to one side without telling us . . . it is easy to engage Cisneros's poignant (because simple and frank) account, and to make literary experience through the intertextual relation of Cisneros's fiction and our emotional past" (595).

Penultimate Thoughts on *Mango Street* as Autobiographical (?) Mirror Onto Life

Beyond the power Esperanza's story has to evoke childhood memories—from all stages of life, but in particular (according to Norton), those related to adolescence—*Mango Street* appears to have a "performative" ability or power to prompt readers, of all ages, from all walks of life, to react and relate to Esperanza's story in mimetic fashion, as a direct reflection of reality or: mirror of life.[5] This tendency is in great part due to Cisneros' skillful use of first-person narrative (i.e., Esperanza as "I"), which has presumably played no small part in forging a connection between readers and the teller of the tales.

Yet, however gratifying and/or poignant such moments of *I-felt-as-if-I-were-there* can be, and indeed, at times are, chances of a spoiler alert remain moderate, if not altogether high. (In other words, there will always be some willing passer-by—usually a critic or [gasp] "an academic"—who, if even unwittingly, pops the bubble). To critic Terry Eagleton's way of thinking, for example, reflexive ingestion, or relating to stories as if they were real, may encourage the "naïve notion that a literary text *is a kind of transcript of the living voice* of a real man or woman addressing us" (120, my emphasis). Hence, the understandable knee-jerk reaction that has caused and still prompts numerous readers to view *Mango Street*'s Esperanza *as* Cisneros.

In fact Cisneros herself confirms the would-be autobiographical nature of her book. Responding to the question of whether or not *Mango Street* is "about her," she explains: "When I began [it, in 1977, as a graduate student in Iowa City], I thought I was writing a memoir. By the time I finished it [in 1982, however, it] was no longer a memoir, no longer autobiographical" (Introduction xi–xii). At the same time, Cisneros remains coy about the very matter that her readers *really* want to know: *is* she Esperanza? For reasons as yet unbeknownst to this reader, the response of the now not-so-young girl's creator is at once evasive and coy: "Yes. And no. And then again, perhaps maybe" (Introduction xix). Whatever else Cisneros' answer might mean, it certainly portends, in performative fashion, the possibility of giving the novel another go.

Notes

[1] This essay was adapted from my article, "On the 'Simplicity' of Sandra Cisneros's *House on Mango Street*, published in *Modern Fiction Studies*, 2001. MFS: 47.4, Winter 2001: 910–46.

[2] Arte Público Press published the novel in 1984, 1985, and 1986. In 1989, Arte Público published a slightly altered edition of Mango Street. Subsequently, in 1991 Vintage Books published the revised 1989 edition of the book. Knopf followed suit in 1994. Unless otherwise noted, all quotes from the novel are taken from the Vintage Books edition, 1991.

[3] In his essay, "Race under Representation," David Lloyd identifies "exclusion" as one of the predominant terms that has been commonly deployed in anti-racist cultural politics and discourse in recent years. Among the other terms cited by Lloyd are "euro-" and "ethnocentrism," "marginalization," and the critical categories "orientalism" and the "West," expressions which, in his view, share the common trait of being "spatial" terms (62).

[4] My students' sensitivity to and/or sympathy for gender- and family-related issues addressed in *Mango Street* might be related to the fact that the class consisted primarily of white, middle-class women, several of whom had identified themselves as liberal and feminist and/or had taken classes that had incorporated feminist approaches to literature. All students, including the lone male, expressed sympathy for the plight of Esperanza, primarily on the basis that they, as children, had experienced or encountered similar situations.

[5] For a more detailed account of the "performative" nature of language, see J. L. Austin, *How to Do Things with Words.*

Works Cited

Austin, J. L. *How to Do Things with Words.* Ed. J. O. Urmson. New York: Oxford UP, 1962.

Cisneros, Sandra. *The House on Mango Street.* New York:Vintage, 1991.

———. Introduction. *The House on Mango Street.* New York: Knopf, 1994. xi–xx.

———. "Return to One's House:An Interview with Sandra Cisneros." Interview with Martha Satz. *Southwest Review* 82.2 (1997): 166–85

Eagleton, Terry. *Literary Theory: An Introduction.* Minneapolis: U of Minnesota P, 1983.

Kanellos, Nicolás. Introduction. *The Hispanic Literary Companion.* Ed. Nicolás Kanellos. Detroit: Visible Ink, 1997.

Lloyd, David."Race Under Representation." *Oxford Literary Review* 13.1–2 (1991): 62–94.

Norton, Jody. "History, Rememory, and Transformation: Actualizing Literary Value." *The Centennial Review* 38.3 (1994): 589–602.

O'Reilly Herrera, Andrea. "'Chambers of Consciousness': Sandra Cisneros and the Development of the Self and the Development of the Self and the BIG *House on Mango Street.*" *Bucknell Review* 39.1 (1995): 191–204.

Poey, Delia. "Coming of Age in the Curriculum: *The House on Mango Street* and *Bless Me, Ultima* as Representative Texts." *Americas Review* 24.3–4 (1996): 201–17.

Quintana, Alvina. *Home Girls: Chicana Literary Voices*. Philadelphia: Temple UP, 1996.

Sánchez, Reuben. "Remembering to Always Come Back:The Child's Wished-For Escape and the Adult's Self-Empowered Return in Sandra Cisneros's *House on Mango Street*." *Children's Literature* 23 (1995): 221–41.

Sánchez, Rosaura. "Ethnicity, Ideology, and Academia." *Americas Review* 15.1 (1987): 80–88.

Valdés, María Elena de. "The Critical Reception of Sandra Cisneros's *The House on Mango Street*." *Gender, Self, and Society*. Ed. Renate von Bardeleben. Frankfurt: Peter Lang, 1993. 287–300.

Mathematical Sciences

Mathematics is often thought of as a stiff and dry subject. After all, most of what we all learned in grade and high school is what the Ancient Greeks, Romans, and Arabians developed. Mathematics is so much more than these ancient operations. While they are important, the learning of them often clouds the thinking and relationships that they are all about. Mathematicians play with ideas and patterns; they consider relationships, and rearrange parts to see what happens to the whole; they experiment with ideas, playfully putting restrictions on aspects of their ideas to see what happens or how these constraints influence new relations and connections. In the excerpts below, Paul Lockhart explores this aspect of a mathematician's work and Eveline Pye shows the mathematics in an art form.

from A Mathematician's Lament

Paul Lockhart

Mathematics and Culture

The first thing to understand is that mathematics is an art. The difference between math and the other arts, such as music and painting, is that our culture does not recognize it as such. Everyone understands that poets, painters, and musicians create works of art, and are expressing themselves in word, image, and sound. In fact, our society is rather generous when it comes to creative expression; architects, chefs, and even television directors are considered to be working artists. So why not mathematicians?

Part of the problem is that nobody has the faintest idea what it is that mathematicians do.The common perception seems to be that mathematicians are somehow connected with science—perhaps they help the scientists with their formulas, or feed big numbers into computers for some reason or other. There is no question that if the world had to be divided into the "poetic dreamers" and the "rational thinkers" most people would place mathematicians in the latter category.

Nevertheless, the fact is that there is nothing as dreamy and poetic, nothing as radical, subversive, and psychedelic, as mathematics. It is every bit as mind blowing as cosmology or physics (mathematicians *conceived* of black holes long before astronomers actually found any), and allows more freedom of expression than poetry, art, or music (which depend heavily on properties of the physical universe). Mathematics is the purest of the arts, as well as the most misunderstood.

So let me try to explain what mathematics is, and what mathematicians do. I can hardly do better than to begin with G. H. Hardy's excellent description:

> A mathematician, like a painter or poet, is a maker of patterns. If his patterns are more permanent than theirs, it is because they are made with *ideas*.

So mathematicians sit around making patterns of ideas. What sort of patterns? What sort of ideas? Ideas about the rhinoceros? No, those we leave to the biologists. Ideas about language and culture? No, not usually. These things are all far too complicated for most mathematicians' taste. If there is anything like a unifying aesthetic principle in mathematics, it is this: *simple is beautiful*. Mathematicians enjoy thinking about the simplest possible things, and the simplest possible things are *imaginary*.

For example, if I'm in the mood to think about shapes—and I often am—I might imagine a triangle inside a rectangular box:

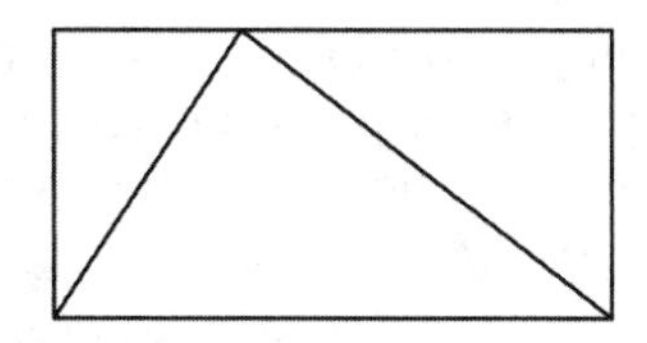

I wonder how much of the box the triangle takes up? Two-thirds maybe? The important thing to understand is that I'm not talking about this *drawing* of a triangle in a box. Nor am I talking about some metal triangle forming part of a girder system for a bridge. There's no ulterior practical purpose here. I'm just *playing*. That's what math is—wondering, playing, amusing yourself with your imagination. For one thing, the question of how much of the box the triangle takes up doesn't even make any *sense* for real, physical objects. Even the most carefully made physical triangle is still a hopelessly complicated collection of jiggling atoms; it changes its size from one minute to the next. That is, unless you want to talk about some sort of *approximate* measurements. Well, that's where the aesthetic comes in. That's just not simple, and consequently it is an ugly question which depends on all sorts of real-world details. Let's leave that to the scientists. The *mathematical* question is about an imaginary triangle inside an imaginary box. The edges are perfect because I want them to be—that is the sort of object I prefer to think about. This is a major theme in mathematics: things are what you want them to be. You have endless choices; there is no reality to get in your way.

On the other hand, once you have made your choices (for example I might choose to make my triangle symmetrical, or not) then your new creations do what they do, whether you like it or not. This is the amazing thing about making imaginary patterns: they talk back! The triangle takes up a certain amount of its box, and I don't have any control over what that amount is.There is a number out there, maybe it's two-thirds, maybe it isn't, but I don't get to say what it is. I have to *find out* what it is.

So we get to play and imagine whatever we want and make patterns and ask questions about them. But how do we answer these questions? It's not at all like science. There's no experiment I can do with test tubes and equipment and whatnot that will tell me the truth about afigment of my imagination. The only way to get at the truth about our imaginations is to use ourimaginations, and that is hard work.

In the case of the triangle in its box, I do see something simple and pretty:

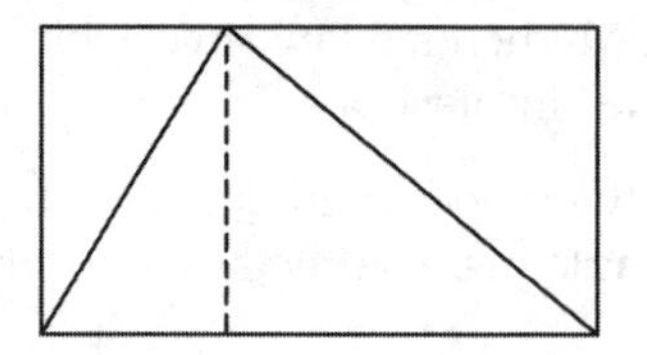

If I chop the rectangle into two pieces like this, I can see that each piece is cut diagonally in half by the sides of the triangle. So there is just as much space inside the triangle as outside. That means that the triangle must take up exactly half the box!

This is what a piece of mathematics looks and feels like. That little narrative is an example of the mathematician's art: asking simple and elegant questions about our imaginary creations, and crafting satisfying and beautiful explanations. There is really nothing else quite like this realm of pure idea; it's fascinating, it's fun, and it's free!

Now where did this idea of mine come from? How did I know to draw that line? How does a painter know where to put his brush? Inspiration, experience, trial and error, dumb luck. That's the art of it, creating these beautiful little poems of thought, these sonnets of pure reason. There is something so wonderfully transformational about this art form. The relationship between the triangle and the rectangle was a mystery, and then that one little line made it obvious. I couldn't see, and then all of a sudden I could. Somehow, I was able to create aprofound simple beauty out of nothing, and change myself in the process. Isn't that what art is all about?

Numerical Landscape

Evelyn Pye

Like a tracker, I smell the earth
on my fingers, listen for the slightest
echo as I stare out at a world
where bell-shaped curves loom

as mountains and negative exponentials
foretell dangerous descents, imminent
disaster. All around, cliff edges crash
down to restless seas while a solitary

outlier shines in the southern sky: a freak
of random sampling or a guiding light?
Are others buried deep, confounded
by experimental design? On my path,

a decision tree, so many branches spring
from its trunk, so many choices. Statistics
feels like poetry—endless searching,
never-ending uncertainty.

Why can't numbers be beautiful too?

Evelyn Pye

We all talk of beautiful words, art, buildings
and they're not part of the natural world, either.
An *x* in Algebra is no more abstract than
an idea in philosophy, just more useful.

But it can't be use that makes the difference.
Keats found beauty in a Grecian urn,
surely practical at some time
and no one is blind to the beauty of symmetry.

We all get Blake's awe of the tiger's stripes.
Why not awe at Gaussian curves? Of course,
I know there is no great beauty in a single number,
in a four or a seven or an eight, but it is the same

with the alphabet. Where is the wonder in a *b*
or a *k* or a *t*? It is only the combinations,
the meanings, the relationships between
the letters that make the words and sounds we love.

—And so, why can't my numbers be beautiful to me?
Why the scorn, the doubt in your face? Do you think
I am brittle and dusty as old paper?
Look again. See the numbers shine in my eyes.

Theater

Theater has long existed as a site of diversity, multiple perspectives, and transformation. It crosses boundaries, for through theater, we walk in others' shoes. While communal, theater is also highly personal; it means different things to different people and inspires a vast array of experiences. At its core, good theater sparks dialogue. *To continue fostering such dialogue, St. Catherine University's theater faculty offers a missive written by one of the world's most significant, passionate, and lauded female directors: Ariane Mnouchkine. As the founder and artistic director of the renowned Theatre du Soleil, a company that collectively creates conceptually bold and socially relevant stage works, Mnouchkine delivered the key World Theatre Day message to the international theater community. In her address, she expresses and explores the transformative power of theater.*

Help!

Ariane Mnouchkine

Theatre, come to my rescue!
I am asleep, Awake me
I am lost in the dark, guide me, at least toward a candle
I am lazy, shame me
I am tired, raise me up
I am indifferent, strike me
I remain indifferent, beat me up
I am afraid, encourage me
I am ignorant, teach me
I am monstrous, make me human
I am pretentious, make me die of laughter
I am cynical, take me down a peg
I am foolish, transform me
I am wicked, punish me
I am dominating and cruel, fight against me
I am pedantic, make fun of me
I am vulgar, elevate me
I am mute, untie my tongue
I no longer dream, call me a coward or a fool
I have forgotten, throw Memory in my face
I feel old and stale, make the Child in me leap up
I am heavy, give me Music
I am sad, bring me Joy
I am deaf, make Pain shriek like a storm

I am agitated, let Wisdom rise within me
I am weak, kindle Friendship
I am blind, summon all the Lights
I am dominated by Ugliness, bring in conquering Beauty
I have been recruited by Hatred, unleash all the forces of Love.

Music

Everyone experiences music in her/his life. Everyone forms opinions about what kinds of music they like, what moves them, perhaps what differentiates "art music" from "commercial music." For consideration in the Catherine Core Reader, *the music faculty offers interviews by two internationally known American composers of the twentieth and twenty-first centuries, as well as samplings of their music. The two interviews—one reproduced here in print and the other an audio/visual link—provide viewpoints on the nature of music and afford glimpses into the life of the composer/artist. We hope that both will spark interesting discussions. Each interview is paired with a performance of the composer's music, found on the Core Curriculum D2L site.*

The two composers are John Cage (1912–1992) and Libby Larsen (b. 1950). The former, and more famous, is described in the introduction to his interview. The latter lives in the Twin Cities and sat on The Distinguished Women's Advisory Council for St. Kate's. She has collaborated with St. Catherine musicians in performances of her music, including a piece that sets a poem by Professor Emerita of English, Sister Mary Virginia Micka, CSJ, to music. Enjoy!

Boulevard Blazer

Anne Hamre

Libby Larsen is a rarity in the music world—a living, woman composer. A graduate of the University of Minnesota (undergraduate, master's and Ph.D. programs), Larsen has created more than 500 compositions, from individual vocal pieces to chamber music to full orchestral works, plus more than 15 operas. She co-founded the Minnesota Composers Forum, now known as the American Composer's Forum, in 1973. She is the first woman to serve as a resident composer with a major orchestra (the Minnesota Orchestra), and is a professional composer as well as an advocate for music and musicians.

Larsen spoke with the Minnesota Women's Press about storytelling through composition, advocating for women in music and the importance of music.

Minnesota Women's Press: You were the first woman to serve as a resident composer with a major orchestra. What was the significance of that to you?

Libby Larsen: That Meet the Composer orchestral residency program mu designed to place composers in orchestras, major orchestras, so that composers who actually are alive can become part of the orchestral world, the orchestral repertoire. When that program was launched, I felt that it was really important, really essential, that this program include women.

This was in the early 1980s. The question in my mind was, if there's a national program that's being launched and all of the composers who are part of the first round of composers in residence are male, white male, then we've missed an opportunity to learn and change. So it wasn't really so important that I was the composer in residence; it was important that a female be part of that first round. Otherwise, we would run the risk of maintaining a heavily gender-biased art form for another 50 years.

MWF: Who has inspired you?

LL: I tend to like the free spirits. In the classical world, I really like Hector Berlioz, who was writing in the early 1800s; he was writing music that nobody else was writing. In our century, Lou Harrison . . . John Cage . . . James Brown . . . Big Mama Thornton . . . Rufus Thomas, who is extraordinarily important in American music . . . Chuck Berry. Musicians who had something to say, were really alive and just blazed their own path.

MWP: You've also been described as a leader, a change-maker for women's careers in music and a champion of the music and musicians of our time. Do you agree?

LL: In retrospect, I do agree with it, and it makes me feel very proud—because I am not setting out to change the world. And I'm saying that in the present tense, because with every piece I write I'm setting out what it's like to be alive right now. I was about 20 years into my professional life when I began to understand that one way to make a change for women—and this was a conscious thought—was just to consistently put out at a professional level whatever that is . . . just be consistently public. At a college I was visiting around that time, someone asked, "Are you a path blazer?" and I was fumbling around trying to answer, and a young woman in the audience said, "No, no, it's not a path, it's a boulevard." And I thought, wow . . . that's fabulous.

MWP: How do you think the world of music is changing?

LL: The definition of a composer is changing, away from the European dead white guy who's a marble bust on your piano to the fact that each one of us, each person, has the capacity for expressing themselves through making music that is their own music. You now can compose on your iPhone. You don't have to learn to play a cello for 20 years and pass through all kinds of rigorous tests to be considered an expert and therefore a composer. We have the capacity to put our material out in public and receive feedback for it in ways that haven't been possible. That changes the whole discussion of what is good, what is terrible, what is better—and does it matter?

MWP: What kinds of stories are you telling in your compositions?

LL: It's not really stories, per se; it's more like essays or memoirs of energy and emotion and tempo.

For instance, I'm really interested in the whole idea of ridge running. If you look it up, it says it's a hillbilly term and it's used for moonshiners. But the way I interpret it is that there are a lot of us alive today who, in an abstract way, are ridge runners. In other words, we're trying to survive; our survival depends on our wit. If you've been laid off [from] your job for five years and you can't find a job, you become a ridge runner, meaning that you have to make your life up . . . in order to put food on the table or whatever. You have to make up your life in a way that is much more improvisational than it would be if you had a steady job.

So the story I'm telling is not of an Appalachian moonshiner. The stories I tell in my music are stories of energy and emotion as I observe it culturally. Kind of cultural anthropology.

MWP: Why does music matter?

LL: There isn't a culture ever discovered that hasn't expressed itself, in some way, musically. Music is an essential part of the human condition. So why does it matter? It matters as much as breathing matters. Or drinking water matters. It is an essential mode of communication—internal communication and external communication.

MWP: What would you like your musical legacy to be?

LL: I hope that the music I've created in this short span has given whoever has come in contact with it a heightened sense of who they are. If they hate the music, that's fine; if they love the music, that's fine. If they perform the music, that's fine. But [I'd like to give people] a heightened sense of their own time here on earth.

Art and Art History

Art does many things. It offers an opportunity for aesthetic enjoyment and a chance to contemplate beauty. It presents us with evidence of the richness of human creativity and creates breathing room in our increasingly chaotic lives. It even enlivens the book you are reading. But we also need to allow it to be more. At its best, art is difficult. It confronts well-worn beliefs and asks us to cede territory to the uncomfortable. It asks us to see past the familiarity of our own limited experience and to come to terms with what we cannot neatly file away. Art pushes back. It lingers and it nags. If we are willing to give it the time that it requires, art also restores hope by showing us that we still have a lot to learn. It reminds us that, in spite of ready access to more information than at any point in human history, we still have not seen (or know) all there is to see. In Art Objects, *Jeanette Winterson reminds us that looking, really looking at a work of art, changes us.*

Art Objects

Jeanette Winterson

I was in Amsterdam one snowy Christmas—when the weather had turned the canals into oblongs of ice. I was wandering happy, alone, playing the *flâneur,* when I passed a little gallery and in the moment of passing saw a painting that had more power to stop me than I had power to walk on.

The quality of the draughtsmanship, the brush strokes in thin oils, had a Renaissance beauty, but the fearful and compelling thing about the picture was its modernity. Here was a figure without a context, in its own context, a haunted woman in blue robes pulling a huge moon face through a subterranean waterway.

What was I to do, standing hesitant, my heart flooded away?

I fled across the road and into a bookshop. There I would be safe, surrounded by things I understood, unchallenged, except by my own discipline. Books I know, endlessly, intimately. Their power over me is profound, but I do know them. I confess that until that day I had not much interest in the visual arts, although I realise now, that my lack the kind of interest was the result of the kind of ignorance I despair of in others. I knew nothing about painting and so I got very little from it. I had never given a picture my full attention even for one hour.

What was I to do?

I had intended to leave Amsterdam the next day. I changed my plans, and sleeping fitfully, rising early, queued to get into the Rijksmuseum, into the Van Gogh Museum, spending every afternoon at any private galleries I could find, and every evening, reading, reading, reading. My turmoil of mind was such that I could only find a kind of peace by attempting to determine the size of the problem. My problem. The paintings were perfectly at ease. I had fallen in love and I had no language. I was dog-dumb. The usual response of 'This painting has nothing to say to me' had become 'I have nothing to say to this painting'. And I desperately wanted to speak.

Long looking at paintings is equivalent to being dropped into a foreign city, where gradually, out of desire and despair, a few key words, then a little syntax make a clearing in the silence. Art, all art, not just painting, is a foreign city, and we deceive ourselves when we think it familiar. No-one is surprised to find that a foreign city follows its own customs and speaks its own language. Only a boor would ignore both and blame his defaulting on the place. Every day this happens to the artist and the art.

We have to recognise that the language of art: all art, is not our mother-tongue.

I read Ruskin's *Modern Painters.* I read Pater's *Studies of the History of the Renaissance.* Joshua Reynolds' *Discourses,* Bernard Berenson, Kenneth Clark, Sickert's *A Free House!,* Whistler's *Ten O'Clock Lecture,* Vasari, Michael Levey, William Morris. I knew my Dante, and I was looking for a guide, for someone astute and erudite with whom I had something in common, a way of thinking. A person dead or alive with whom I could talk things over. I needed someone I could trust, who would negotiate with me the sublimities and cesspits of regions hitherto closed. Someone fluent in this strange language and its dialects, who had spent many years in that foreign city and who might introduce me to the locals and their rather odd habits. Art is odd, and the common method of trying to fit it into the scheme of things, either by taming it or baiting it, cannot succeed. Who at the zoo has any sense of the lion?

At last, back home, and ransacking the shelves of secondhand bookshops, I found Roger Fry.

It may seem hopelessly old-fashioned to have returned to Bloomsbury, but I do not care about fashion, only about permanencies, and if books, music and pictures are happy enough to be indifferent to time, then so am I.

Fry was the one I wanted. For me, at least, a perfect guide, close enough in spirit to Walter Pater, but necessarily firmer. I had better come clean now and say that I do not believe that art (all art) and beauty are ever separate, nor do I believe that either art or beauty are optional in a sane society. That puts me on the side of what Harold Bloom calls 'the ecstasy of the privileged moment'. Art, all art, as insight, as rapture, as transformation, as joy. Unlike Harold Bloom, I really believe that human beings can be taught to love what they do not love already and that the privileged moment exists for all of us, if we let it. Letting art is the paradox of active surrender. I have to work for art if I want art to work on me.

I knew about Roger Fry because I had read Virginia Woolf's biography of him, and because it is impossible to be interested in Modernism without finding reference to him. It was he who gave us the term 'Post-Impressionist', without realising that the late twentieth century would soon be entirely fenced in with posts.

A Quaker, trained as a scientist, passionate about painting, Roger Fry did more than anyone else in Britain to promote and protect new work during the first thirty years of the century. The key quality in Fry's writing is enthusiasm. Nothing to him is dull. Such a life-delighting, art-delighting approach, unashamed of emotion, unashamed of beauty, was what I needed.

I decided that my self-imposed studentship would perform a fight of eight. I would concentrate my reading on priests and prophets of the past, while focusing my looking on modern painters. This saved me from the Old Master syndrome and it allowed me to approach a painting without unfelt reverence or unfit complacency. At the same time it allowed me to test out the theories and assumptions of the art writers whose company I kept. For me, this lemniscate of back and forth has proved the right method. I still know far far less about pictures than I do about books and this will not change. What has changed is my way of seeing. I am learning how to look at pictures. What has changed is my capacity of feeling. Art opens the heart.

Art takes time. To spend an hour looking at a painting is difficult. The public gallery experience is one that encourages art at a trot. There are the paintings, the marvellous speaking works, definite, independent, each with a Self it would be impossible to ignore, if . . . if . . . , it were possible to see it. I do not only mean the crowds and the guards and the low lights and the ropes, which make me think of freak shows, I mean the thick curtain of irrelevancies that screens the painting from the viewer. Increasingly, galleries have a habit of saying when they acquired a painting and how much it cost . . .

Millions! The viewer does not see the colours on the canvas, he sees the colour of the money.

Is the painting famous? Yes! Think of all the people who have carefully spared one minute of their lives to stand in front of it.

Is the painting Authority? Does the guide-book tell us that it is part of The Canon? If Yes, then half of the viewers will admire it on principle, while the other half will dismiss it on principle.

Who painted it? What do we know about his/her sexual practices and have we seen anything about them on the television? If not, the museum will likely have a video full of schoolboy facts and tabloid gossip.

Where is the tea-room / toilet / gift shop?

Where is the painting in any of this?

Experiencing paintings as moving pictures, out of context, disconnected, jostled, over-literary, with their endless accompanying explanations, overcrowded, one against the other, room on room, does not make it easy to fall in love. Love takes time. It may be that if you have as much difficulty with museums as I do, that the only way into the strange life of pictures is to expose yourself to as much contemporary art as you can until you find something, anything, that you will go back and back to see again, and even make great sacrifices to buy. Inevitably, if you start to love pictures, you will start to buy pictures. The time, like the money, can be found, and those who call the whole business elitist, might be fair enough to reckon up the time they spend in front of the television, at the DIY store, and how much the latest satellite equipment and new PC has cost.

For myself, now that paintings matter, public galleries are much less dispiriting. I have learned to ignore everything about them, except for the one or two pieces with whom I have come to spend the afternoon.

Supposing we made a pact with a painting and agreed to sit down and look at it, on our own, with no distractions, for one hour. The painting should be an original, not a reproduction, and we should start with the advantage of liking it, even if only a little. What would we find?

Increasing discomfort. When was the last time you looked at anything, solely, and concentratedly, and for its own sake? Ordinary life passes in a near blur. If we go to the theatre or the cinema, the images before us change constantly, and there is the distraction of language. Our loved ones are so well known to us that there is no need to look at them, and one of the gentle jokes of married life is that we do not. Nevertheless, here is a painting and we have agreed to look at it for one hour. We find we are not very good at looking.

Increasing distraction. Is my mind wandering to the day's work, to the football match, to what's for dinner, to sex, to whatever it is that will give me something to do other than to look at the painting?

Increasing invention. After some time spent daydreaming, the guilty or the dutiful might wrench back their attention to the picture.

What is it about? Is it a landscape? Is it figurative? More promisingly, is it a nude? If the picture seems to offer an escape route then this is the moment to take it. I can make up stories about the characters on the canvas much as art-historians like to identify the people in Rembrandt's *The Night Watch*. Now I am beginning to feel much more confident because I am truly engaging with the picture. A picture is its subject matter isn't it? Oh dear, mine's an abstract. Never mind, would that pink suit me?

Increasing irritation. Why doesn't the picture *do* something? Why is it hanging there staring at me? What is this picture for? Pictures should give pleasure but this picture is making me very cross. Why should I admire it? Quite clearly it doesn't admire me . . .

Admire me is the sub-text of so much of our looking; the demand put on art that it should reflect the reality of the viewer. The true painting, in its stubborn independence, cannot do this, except coincidentally. Its reality is imaginative not mundane.

When the thick curtain of protection is taken away; protection of prejudice, protection of authority, protection of trivia, even the most familiar of paintings can begin to work its power. There are very few people who could manage an hour alone with the *Mona Lisa*.

But our poor art-lover in his aesthetic laboratory has not succeeded in freeing himself from the protection of assumption. What he has found is that the painting objects to his lack of concentration; his failure to meet intensity with intensity. He still has not discovered anything about the painting but the painting has discovered a lot about him. He is inadequate and the painting has told him so.

It is not as hopeless as it seems. If l can be persuaded to make the experiment again (and again and again), something very different might occur after the first shock of finding out that I do not know how to look at pictures, let alone how to like them.

A favourite writer of mine, an American, an animal trainer, a Yale philosopher, Vicki Hearne, has written of the acute awkwardness and embarrassment of those who work with magnificent animals, and find themselves at a moment of reckoning, summed up in those deep and difficult eyes. Art has deep and difficult eyes and for many the gaze is too insistent. Better to pretend that art is dumb, or at least has nothing to say that makes sense to us. If art, all art, is concerned with truth, then a society in denial will not find much use for it.

In the West, we avoid painful encounters with art by trivialising it, or by familiarising it. Our present obsession with the past has the double advantage of making new work seem raw and rough compared to the cosy patina of tradition, whilst refusing tradition its vital connection to what is happening now. By making islands of separation out of the unbreakable chain of human creativity, we are able to set up false comparisons, false expectations, all the while lamenting that the music, poetry, painting, prose, performance art of Now, fails to live up to the art of Then, which is why, we say, it does not affect us. In fact, we are no more moved by a past we are busy inventing, than by a present we are busy denying. If you love a Cézanne, you can love a Hockney, can love a Boyd, can love a Rao. *If* you love a Cézanne rather than lip-service it.

We are an odd people: We make it as difficult as possible for our artists to work honestly while they are alive; either we refuse them money or we ruin them with money; either we flatter them with unhelpful praise or wound them with unhelpful blame, and when they are too old, or too dead, or too beyond dispute to hinder any more, we canonise them, so that what was wild is tamed, what was objecting, becomes Authority. Canonising pictures is one way of killing them. When the sense of familiarity becomes too great, history, popularity, association, all crowd in between the viewer and the picture and block it out. Not only pictures suffer like this, all the arts suffer like this.

That is one reason why the calling of the artist, in any medium, is to make it new. I do not mean that in new work the past is repudiated; quite the opposite, the past is reclaimed. It is not lost to authority, it is not absorbed at a level of familiarity. It is re-stated and re-instated in its original vigour. Leonardo is present in Cézanne, Michelangelo flows through Picasso and on into Hockney. This is not ancestor worship, it is the lineage of art. It is not so much influence as it is connection.

I do not want to argue here about great artists, I want to concentrate on true artists, major or minor, who are connected to the past and who themselves make a connection to the future. The true artist is connected. The true artist studies the past, not as a copyist or a pasticheur will study the past, those people are interested only in the final product, the art object, signed sealed and delivered to a public drugged on reproduction. The true artist is interested in the art object as an art process, the thing in being, the being of the thing, the struggle, the excitement, the energy, that have found expression in a particular way. The true artist is after the problem. The false artist wants it solved (by somebody else).

If the true artist is connected, then he or she has much to give us because it is connection that we seek. Connection to the past, to one another, to the physical world, still compelling, in spite of the ravages of technology. A picture, a book, a piece of music, can remind me of feelings, thinkings, I did not even know I had forgot. Whether art tunnels deep under consciousness or whether it causes out of its own invention, reciprocal inventions that we then call memory, I do not know. I do know that the process of art is a series of jolts, or perhaps I mean volts, for art is an extraordinarily faithful transmitter. Our job is to keep our receiving equipment in good working order.

How?

It is impossible to legislate taste, and if it were possible, it would be repugnant. There are no Commandments in art and no easy axioms for art appreciation. 'Do I like this?' is the question anyone should ask themselves at the moment of confrontation with the picture. But if 'yes', why 'yes'? and if 'no', why 'no'? The obvious direct emotional response is never simple, and ninety-nine times out of a hundred, the 'yes' or 'no' has nothing at all to do with the picture in its own right.

'I don't understand this poem'

'I never listen to classical music'

'I don't like this picture'

are common enough statements but not ones that tell us anything about books, painting, or music. They are statements that tell us something about the speaker. That should be obvious, but in fact, such statements are offered as criticisms of art, as evidence against, not least because the ignorant, the lazy, or the plain confused are not likely to want to admit themselves as such. We hear a lot about the arrogance of the artist but nothing about the arrogance of the audience. The audience, who have not done the work, who have not taken any risks, whose life and livelihood are not bound up at every moment with what they are making, who have given no thought to the medium or the method, will glance up, flick through, chatter over the opening chords, then snap their fingers and walk away like some monstrous Roman tyrant. This is not arrogance; of course they can absorb in a few moments, and without any effort, the sum of the artist and the art.

If the obvious direct emotional response is to have any meaning, the question 'Do I like this?' will have to be the opening question and not the final judgement. An examination of our own feelings will have to give way to an examination of the piece of work. This is fair to the work and it will help to clarify the nature of our own feelings; to reveal prejudice, opinion, anxiety, even the mood of the day. It is right to trust our feelings but right to test them too. If they are what we say they are, they will stand the test, if not, we will at least be less insincere. But here we come back to the first hurdle of art, and it is a high one; it shows us up.

When you say 'This work has nothing to do with me'. When you say 'This work is boring/pointless/silly/ obscure/ élitist etc.', you might be right, because you are looking at a fad, or you might be wrong because the work falls so outside of the safety of your own experience that in order to keep your own world intact, you must deny the other world of the painting. This denial of imaginative experience happens at a deeper level than our affirmation of our daily world. Every day, in countless ways, you and I convince ourselves about ourselves. True art, when it happens to us, challenges the 'I' that we are.

A love-parallel would be just; falling in love challenges the reality to which we lay claim, part of the pleasure of love and part of its terror, is the world turned upside down. We want and we don't want, the cutting edge, the upset, the new views. Mostly we work hard at taming our emotional environment just as we work hard at taming our aesthetic environment. We already have tamed our physical environment. And are we happy with all this tameness? Are you?

Art cannot be tamed, although our responses to it can be, and in relation to The Canon, our responses are conditioned from the moment we start school. The freshness which the everyday regular man or woman pride themselves upon; the untaught 'I know what I like' approach, now encouraged by the media, is neither fresh nor untaught. It is the half-baked sterility of the classroom washed down with liberal doses of popular culture.

The media ransacks the arts, in its images, in its adverts, in its copy, in its jingles, in its little tunes and journalist's jargon, it continually offers up faint shadows of the form and invention of real music, real paintings, real words. All of us are subject to this bombardment, which both deadens our sensibilities and makes us fear what is not instant, approachable, consumable. The solid presence of art demands from us significant effort, an effort anathema to popular culture. Effort of time, effort of money, effort of study, effort of humility, effort of imagination have each been packed by the artist into the art. Is it so unreasonable to expect a percentage of that from us in return? I worry that to ask for effort is to imply élitism, and the charge against art, that it is élitist, is too often the accuser's defence against his or her own bafflement. It is quite close to the remark 'Why can't they all speak English?', which may be why élitist is the favourite insult of the British and the Americans.

But, you may say, how can I know what is good and what is not good? I may wince at the cheap seascape over the mantelpiece but does that necessarily mean I should go to the Tate Gallery and worship a floor full of dyed rice?

Years ago, when I was living very briefly with a stockbroker who had a good cellar, I asked him how I couid learn about wine.

'Drink it' he said.

It is true. The only way to develop a palate is to develop a palate. That is why, when I wanted to know about paintings, I set out to look at as many as I could, using always, tested standards, but continuing to test them. You can like a thing out of ignorance, and it is perhaps a blessing that such naiveté stays with us until we die. Even now, we are not as closed and muffled as art-pessimists think we are, we do still fall in love at first sight. All well and good, but the fashion for dismissing a thing out of ignorance is vicious. In fact, it is not essential to like a thing in order to recognise its worth, but to reach that point of self-awareness and sophistication takes years of perseverance.

For most of us the question 'Do I like this?' will always be the formative question. Vital then, that we widen the I that we are as much as we can. Vital then, we recognise that the question 'Do I like this?' involves an independent object, as well as our own subjectivity.

I am sure that if as a society we took art seriously, not as mere decoration or entertainment, but as a living spirit, we should very soon learn what is art and what is not art. The American poet Muriel Rukeyser has said:

> There is art and there is non-art; they are two universes (in the algebraic sense) which are exclusive . . . It seems to me that to call an achieved work 'good art' and an unachieved work 'bad art', is like calling one colour 'good red' and another 'bad red' when the second one is green.

If we accept this, it does not follow that we should found an Academy of Good Taste or throw out all our pet water-colours, student posters or family portraits. Let them be but know what they are, and perhaps more importantly, what they are not. If we sharpened our sensibilities, it is not that we would all agree on everything, or that we would suddenly feel the same things in front of the same pictures (or when reading the same book), but rather that our debates and deliberations would come out of genuine aesthetic considerations and not politics, prejudice and fashion .... And our hearts? Art is aerobic.

It is shocking too. The most conservative and least interested person will probably tell you that he or she likes Constable. But would our stalwart have liked Constable in 1824 when he exhibited at the Paris Salon and caused a riot? We forget that every true shock in art, whether books, paintings or music, eventually becomes a commonplace, even a standard, to later generations. It is not that those works are tired out and have nothing more to offer, it is that their discoveries are gradually diluted by lesser artists who can only copy but do know how to make a thing accessible and desirable. At last, what was new becomes so well known that we cannot separate it from its cultural associations and time-honoured values. To the average eye, now, Constable is a pretty landscape painter, not a revolutionary who daubed bright colour against bright colour ungraded by· chiaroscuro. We have had a hundred and fifty years to get used to the man who turned his back on the studio picture, took his easel outdoors and painted in a rapture of light. It is easy to copy Constable. It was not easy to be Constable.

I cannot afford a Constable, or a Picasso, or a Leonardo, but to profess a love of painting and not to have anything original is as peculiar as a booklover with nothing on her shelves. I do not know why the crowds and crowds of visitors to public galleries do not go out and support new work. Are we talking love-affair or peep-show?

I move gingerly around the paintings I own because I know they are looking at me as closely as I am looking at them. There is a constant exchange of emotion between us, between the three of us; the artist I need never meet, the painting in its own right, and me, the one who loves it and can no longer live independent of it. The triangle of exchange alters, is fluid, is subtle, is profound and is one of those unverifiable facts that anyone who cares for painting soon discovers. The picture on my wall, art object and art process, is a living line of movement, a wave of colour that repercusses in my body, colouring it, colouring the new present, the future, and even the past, which cannot now be considered outside of the light of the painting. I think of something I did, the picture catches me, adds to the thought, changes the meaning of thought and past. The totality of the picture comments on the totality of what I am. The greater the picture the more complete this process is.

Process, the energy in being, the refusal of finality, which is not the same thing as the refusal of completeness, sets art, all art, apart from the endstop world that is always calling 'Time Please!'.

We know that the universe is infinite, expanding and strangely complete, that it lacks nothing we need, but in spite of that knowledge, the tragic paradigm of human life is lack, loss, finality, a primitive doomsaying that has not been repealed by technology or medical science. The arts stand in the way of this doomsaying. Art objects. The nouns become an active force not a collector's item. Art objects.

The cave wall paintings at Lascaux, the Sistine Chapel ceiling, the huge truth of a Picasso, the quieter truth of Vanessa Bell, are part of the art that objects to the lie against life, against the spirit, that it is pointless and mean. The message coloured through time is not lack, but abundance. Not silence but many voices. Art, all art, is the communication cord that cannot be snapped by indifference or disaster. Against the daily death it does not die.

All painting is cave painting; painting on the low dark walls of you and me, intimations of grandeur. The painted church is the tattooed body of Christ, not bound into religion, but unbound out of love. Love, the eloquent shorthand that volumes out those necessary invisibles of faith and optimism, humour and generosity, sublimity of mankind made visible through art.

Naked I came into the world, but brush strokes cover me, language raises me, music rhythms me. Art is my rod and staff, my resting place and shield, and not mine only; for art leaves nobody out. Even those from whom art has been stolen away by tyranny, by poverty, begin to make it again. If the arts did not exist, at every moment, someone would begin to create them, in song, out of dust and mud, and although the artifacts might be destroyed, the energy that creates them is not destroyed. If, in the comfortable West, we have chosen to treat such energies with scepticism and contempt, then so much the worse for us. Art is not a little bit of 'evolution that late-twentieth-century city dwellers can safely do without. Strictly, art does not belong to our evolutionary pattern at all. It has no biological necessity. Time taken up with it was time lost to hunting, gathering, mating, exploring, building, surviving, thriving. Odd then, that when routine physical threats to ourselves and our kind are no longer a reality, we say we have no time for art.

If we say that art, all art is no longer relevant to our lives, then we might at least risk the question 'What has happened to our lives?' The usual question, 'What has happened to art?' is too easy an escape route.

I did not escape. At an Amsterdam gallery I sat down and wept.

When I sold a book I bought a Massimo Rao. Since that day I have been filling my walls with new light.

Sciences

How do we know what we know? This is a question that any critical thinker should ask, especially with the incredible amount of information now available to us. Science is both a body of knowledge and a way of knowing. An informed citizen should understand how scientific inquiry increases our understanding of the natural world; she should be exposed to fundamental knowledge and concepts in a variety of scientific fields. If we don't understand the process of science—how the scientific method is applied to achieve understanding of natural phenomena—and the nature of scientific knowledge as true without 100 percent certainty, then we will be vulnerable to misconceptions and misconstruing of scientific knowledge.

The essay below is from a book by Eugenie Scott, PhD, a physical anthropologist who has been a university professor and executive director of the National Center for Science Education, 1987–2014. Her career has focused on defending the integrity of science education. In "Truth without Certainty" Scott explores various ways of knowing about the natural world—authority, revelation, logic, and science. While statements are often accepted as truth when they come from a source of authority or as the result of logical reasoning, scientific truth is the product of testing and evaluation. The strength in the scientific method lies in the willingness of scientists to modify or adapt their theories through observation and experimentation. What makes Scott claim, "If one wished to know about the natural world and how it works, science is superior to other ways of knowing"? How can a scientist be certain about something, when science can never "prove" things? Can there be truth without certainty?

Science: Truth without Certainty

Eugenie C. Scott

We live in a universe made up of matter and energy, a material universe. To understand and explain this material universe is the goal of science, which is a methodology as well as a body of knowledge obtained through that methodology. Science is limited to matter and energy, but as will become clear when we discuss religion, most individuals believe that reality includes something other than matter and energy. The methodology of science is a topic on which any college library has dozens of feet of shelves of books and journals, so obviously just one chapter won't go much beyond sketching out the bare essentials. Still, I will try to show how science differs from many other ways of knowing and how it is particularly well suited to explaining our material universe.

Ways of Knowing

Science requires the testing of explanations of the natural world against nature itself and the discarding of those explanations that do not work. What distinguishes science from other ways of knowing is its reliance upon the natural world as the arbiter of truth. There are many things that people are interested in, are concerned about, or want to know about that science does not address. Whether the music of Madonna or Mozart is superior may be of interest (especially to parents of teenagers), but it is not something that science addresses. Aesthetics is clearly something outside of science. Similarly, literature or music might generate or help to understand or cope with emotions and feelings in a way that science is not equipped to do. But if one wishes to know about the natural world and how it works, science is superior to other ways of knowing. Let's consider some other ways of knowing about the natural world.

Authority

Dr. Jones says, "Male lions taking over a pride will kill young cubs." Should you believe her? You might know that Dr. Jones is a famous specialist in lion behavior who has studied lions for twenty years in the field. Authority leads one to believe that Dr. Jones's statement is true. In a public bathroom, I once saw a little girl of perhaps four or five years old marvel at faucets that automatically turned on when hands were placed below the spigot. She asked her mother, "Why does the water come out, Mommy?" Her mother answered brightly, if unhelpfully, "It's magic, dear!" When we are small, we rely on the authority of our parents and other older people, but authority clearly can mislead us, as in the case of the magic spigots. And Dr. Jones might be wrong about lion infanticide, even if in the past she has made statements about animal behavior that have been reliable. Yet it is not "wrong" to take some things on authority. In northern California, a popular bumper sticker reads Question Authority. Whenever I see one of these, I am tempted to pencil in "but stop at stop signs." We all accept some things on authority, but we should do so critically.

Revelation

Sometimes people believe a statement because they are told it comes from a source that is unquestionable: from God, or the gods, or some other supernatural power. Seekers of advice from the Greek oracle at Delphi believed what they were told because they believed that the oracle received information directly from Apollo; similarly, Muslims believe the contents of the Koran were revealed to Muhammad by God; and Christians believe the New Testament is true because the authors were directly inspired by God. A problem with revealed truth, however, is that one must accept the worldview of the speaker in order to accept the statement; there is no outside referent. If you don't believe in Apollo, you're not going to trust the Delphic oracle's pronouncements; if you're not a Mormon or a Catholic, you are not likely to believe that God speaks directly to the Mormon president or the pope. Information obtained through revelation is difficult to verify because there is not an outside referent that all parties are likely to agree upon.

Logic

A way of knowing that is highly reliable is logic, which is the foundation for mathematics. Among other things, logic presents rules for how to tell whether something is true or false, and it is extremely useful. However, logic in and of itself, with no reference to the real world, is not complete. It is logically correct to say, "All cows are brown. Bossy is not brown. Therefore Bossy is not a cow." The problem with the statement is the truth of the premise that all cows are brown, when many are not. To know that the proposition about cows is empirically wrong even if logically true requires reference to the real world outside the logical structure of the three sentences. To say, "All wood has carbon atoms. My computer chip has no carbon atoms. Therefore my computer chip is not made of wood" is both logically and empirically true.

Science

Science does include logic—statements that are not logically true cannot be scientifically true—but what distinguishes the scientific way of knowing is the requirement of going to nature to verify claims. Statements about the natural world are tested against the natural world, which is the final arbiter. Of course, this approach is not perfect: one's information about the natural world comes from experiencing the natural world through the senses (touch, smell, taste, vision, hearing) and instrumental extensions of these senses (e.g., microscopes, telescopes, telemetry, chemical analysis), any of which can be faulty or incomplete. As a result, science, more than any of the other ways of knowing described here, is more tentative in its claims. Ironically, the tentativeness of science ultimately leads to more confidence in scientific understanding: the willingness to change one's explanation with more or better data, or a different way of looking at the same data, is one of the great strengths of the scientific method. The anthropologist Ashley Montagu summarized science rather nicely when he wrote, "The scientist believes in proof without certainty, the bigot in certainty without proof" (Montagu 1984: 9).

Thus science requires deciding among alternative explanations of the natural world by going to the natural world itself to test them. There are many ways of testing an explanation, but virtually all of them involve the idea of holding constant some factors that might influence the explanation so that some alternative explanations can be eliminated. The most familiar kind of test is the direct experiment, which is so familiar that it is even used to sell us products on television.

Direct Experimentation

Does RealClean detergent make your clothes cleaner? The smiling company representative in the television commercial takes two identical shirts, pours something messy on each one, and drops them into identical washing machines. RealClean brand detergent goes into one machine and the recommended amount of a rival brand into the other. Each washing machine is set to the same cycle, for the same period of time, and the ad fast-forwards to show the continuously smiling representative taking the two shirts out. Guess which one is cleaner.

Now, it would be very easy to rig the demonstration so that RealClean does a better job: the representative could use less of the other detergent, use an inferior-performing washing machine, put the RealClean shirt on a soak cycle forty-five minutes longer than for the other brand, employ different temperatures, wash the competitor's shirt on the delicate rather than regular cycle—I'm sure you can think of a lot of ways that RealClean's manufacturer could ensure that its product comes out ahead. It would be a bad sales technique, however, because we're familiar with the direct experimental type of test, and someone would very quickly call, "Foul!" To convince you that they have a better product, the makers of the commercial have to remove every factor that might possibly explain why the shirt came out cleaner when washed in their product. They have to hold constant or control all these other factors—type of machine, length of cycle, temperature of the water, and so on—so that the only reasonable explanation for the cleaner shirt is that RealClean is a better product. The experimental method—performed fairly—is a very good way to persuade people that your explanation is correct. In science, too, someone will call, "Foul!" (or at least, "You blew it!") if a test doesn't consider other relevant factors.

Direct experimentation is a very powerful—as well as familiar—research design. As a result, some people think that this is the only way that science works. Actually, what matters in science is that explanations be tested, and direct experimentation is only one kind of testing. The key element to testing an explanation is to hold variables constant, and one can hold variables constant in many ways other than being able to directly manipulate them (as one can manipulate water temperature in a washing machine). In fact, the more complicated the science, the less likely an experimenter is to use direct experimentation.

In some tests, variables are controlled statistically; in others, especially in biological field research or in social sciences, one can find circumstances in which important variables are controlled by the nature of the experimental situation itself. These observational research designs are another type of direct experimentation. Noticing that male guppies are brightly colored and smaller than the drab females, you might wonder whether having bright colors makes male guppies easier prey. How would you test this idea? If conditions allowed, you might be able to perform a direct experiment by moving brightly colored guppies to a high-predation environment and monitoring them over several generations to see how they do. If not, though, you could still perform an observational experiment by looking for natural populations of the same or related species of guppies in environments where predation was high and in other environments where predation was low. You would also want to pick environments where the amount of food was roughly the same—can you explain why? What other environmental factors would you want to hold constant at both sites?

When you find guppy habitats that naturally vary only in the amount of predation and not in other ways, then you're ready to compare the brightness of color in the males. Does the color of male guppies differ in the two environments? If males were less brightly colored in environments with high predation, this would support the idea that brighter guppy color makes males easier prey. (What if in the two kinds of environments, male guppy color is the same?)

Indirect experimentation is used for scientific problems where the phenomena being studied—unlike color in guppies—cannot be directly observed.

Indirect Experimentation

In some fields, not only is it impossible to directly control variables but also the phenomena themselves may not be directly observable. A research design known as indirect experimentation is often used in such fields. Explanations can be tested even if the phenomena being studied are too far away, too small, or too far back in time to be observed directly. For example, giant planets recently have been discovered orbiting distant stars—though we cannot directly observe them. Their presence is indicated by the gravitational effects they have on the suns around which they revolve: because of what we know about how the theory of gravitation works, we can infer that the passage of a big planet around a sun will make the sun wobble. Through the application of principles and laws in which we have confidence, it is possible to infer that these planetary giants do exist and to make estimates of their size and speed of revolution.

Similarly, the subatomic particles that physicists study are too small to be observed directly, but particle physicists certainly are able to test their explanations. By applying knowledge about how particles behave, they are able to create indirect experiments to test claims about the nature of particles. Let's say that a physicist wants to ascertain properties of a particle—its mass, charge, or speed. On the basis of observations of similar particles, he makes an informed estimate of the speed. To test the estimate, he might bombard it with another particle of known mass, because if the unknown particle has a mass of m, it will cause the known particle to ricochet at velocity v. If the known particle does ricochet as predicted, this would support the hypothesis about the mass of the unknown particle. Thus, theory is built piece by piece, through inference based on accepted principles.

In truth, most scientific problems are of this if-then type, whether or not the phenomena investigated are directly observable. If male guppy color is related to predation, then we should see duller males in high-predation environments. If a new drug stimulates the immune system, then individuals taking it should have fewer colds than the controls do. If human hunters were involved in the destruction of large Australian land mammals, we should see extinction events that correlate with the appearance of the first Aborigines. We test by consequence in science all the time. Of course—because scientific problems are never solved so simply—if we get the consequence we predict, this does not mean we have proved our explanation. If you found that guppy color does vary in environments where predation differs, this does not mean you've proved yourself right about the relationship between color and predation. To understand why, we need to consider what we mean by proof and disproof in science.

Proof and Disproof

Proof

Scientists don't usually talk about proving themselves right, because **proof** suggests certainty (remember Ashley Montagu's truth without certainty!). The testing of explanations is in reality a lot messier than the simplistic descriptions given previously. One can rarely be sure that all the possible factors that might explain why a test produced a positive result have been considered. In the guppy case, for example, let's say that you found two habitats that differed in the number of predators but were the same in terms of amount of food, water temperature, and number and type of hiding places—you tried to hold constant as many factors as you could think of. If you find that guppies are less colorful in the high-predation environment, you might think you have made the link, but some other scientist may come along and discover that your two environments differ in water turbidity. If turbidity affects predation—or the ability of female guppies to select the more colorful males—this scientist can claim that you were premature to conclude that color is associated with predation. In science we rarely claim to prove a theory—but positive results allow us to claim that we are likely to be on the right track. And then you or some other scientist can go out and test some more. Eventually we may achieve a consensus about guppy color being related to predation, but we wouldn't conclude this after one or a few tests. This back-and-forth testing of explanations provides a reliable understanding of nature, but the procedure is neither formulaic nor especially tidy over the short run. Sometimes it's a matter of two steps forward, a step to the side (maybe down a blind alley), half a step back—but gradually the procedure, and with it human knowledge, lurches forward, leaving us with a clearer knowledge of the natural world and how it works.

In addition, most tests of anything other than the most trivial of scientific claims result not in slam-dunk, now-I've-nailed-it, put-it-on-the-T-shirt conclusions, but rather in more or less tentative statements: a statement is weakly, moderately, or strongly supported, depending on the quality and completeness of the test. Scientific claims become accepted or rejected depending on how confident the scientific community is about whether the experimental results could have occurred that way just by chance—which is why statistical analysis is such an important part of most scientific tests. Animal behaviorists note that some social species share care of their offspring. Does this make a difference in the survival of the young? Some female African silverbacked jackals, for example, don't breed in a given season but help to feed and guard the offspring of a breeding adult. If the helper phenomenon is directly related to pup survival, then more pups should survive in families with a helper.

One study tested this claim by comparing the reproductive success of jackal packs with and without helpers, and found that for every extra helper a mother jackal had, she successfully raised one extra pup per litter over the average survival rate (Hrdy 2001). These results might encourage you to accept the claim that helpers contribute to the survival of young, but only one test on one population is not going to be convincing. Other tests on other groups of jackals would have to be conducted to confirm the results, and to be able to generalize to other species the principle that reproductive success is improved by having a helper would require conducting tests on other social species. Such studies in fact have been performed across a wide range of birds and mammals, and a consensus is emerging about the basic idea of helpers increasing survivability of the young. But there are many remaining questions, such as whether a genetic relationship always exists between the helper and either the offspring or the helped mother.

Science is quintessentially an open-ended procedure in which ideas are constantly tested and rejected or modified. Dogma—an idea held by belief or faith—is anathema to science. A friend of mine once was asked to explain how he ended up a scientist. His tongue-in-cheek answer illustrates rather nicely the nondogmatic nature of science: "As an adolescent I aspired to lasting fame, I craved factual certainty, and I thirsted for a meaningful vision of human life—so I became a scientist. This is like becoming an archbishop so you can meet girls" (Cartmill 1988: 452).

In principle, all scientific ideas may change, though in reality there are some scientific claims that are held with confidence, even if details may

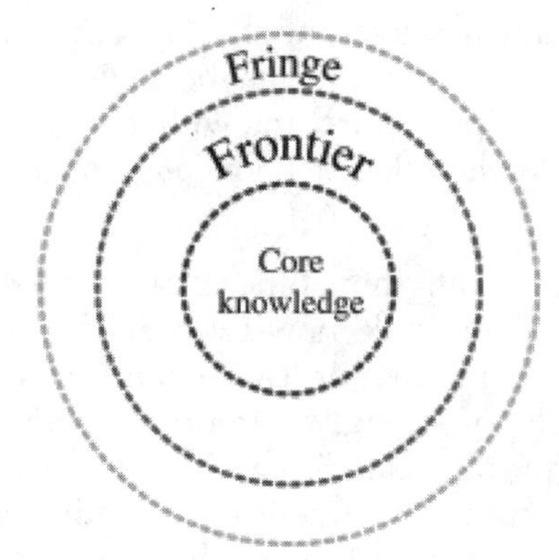

Figure 1.1

Scientific concepts and theories can be arranged as a set of nested categories with core ideas at the center, frontier ideas surrounding them, and fringe ideas at the edge (after Trefil 1978). Courtesy of Alan Gishlick.

be modified. The physicist James Trefil (1978) suggested that scientific claims can be conceived of as arranged in a series of three concentric circles (see Figure 1.1). In the center circle are the core ideas of science: the theories and facts in which we have great confidence because they work so well to explain nature. Heliocentrism, gravitation, atomic theory, and evolution are examples. The next concentric circle outward is the frontier area of science, where research and debate are actively taking place on new theories or modifications and additions to core theories. Clearly no one is arguing with the basic principle of heliocentrism, but on the frontier, planetary astronomers still are learning things and testing ideas about the solar system. That matter is composed of atoms is not being challenged, but the discoveries of quantum physics are adding to and modifying atomic theory.

The outermost circle is the fringe, a breeding ground for ideas that very few professional scientists are spending time on: unidentified flying objects, telepathy and the like, perpetual motion machines, and so on. Generally the fringe is not a source of new ideas for the frontier, but occasionally (very occasionally!) ideas on the fringe will muster enough support to warrant a closer look and will move into the frontier. They may well be rejected and end up back in the fringe or be discarded completely, but occasionally they may become accepted and perhaps eventually become core ideas of science. That the continents move began as a fringe idea, then it moved to the frontier as data began to accumulate in its favor, and finally it became a core idea of geology when seafloor spreading was discovered and the theory of plate tectonics was developed.

Indeed, we must be prepared to realize that even core ideas may be wrong, and that somewhere, sometime, there may be a set of circumstances that could refute even our most confidently held theory. But for practical purposes, one needn't fall into a slough of despond over the relative tentativeness of scientific explanation. That the theory of gravitation may be modified or supplemented sometime in the future is no reason to give up riding elevators (or, even less advisedly, to jump off the roof). Science gives us reliable, dependable, and workable explanations of the natural world—even if it is good philosophy of science to keep in mind that in principle anything can change.

On the other hand, even if it is usually not possible absolutely to prove a scientific explanation correct—there might always be some set of circumstances or observations somewhere in the universe that would show your explanation wrong—to disprove a scientific explanation is possible. If you hypothesize that it is raining outside, and walk out the door to find the sun is shining and the ground is dry, you have indeed disproved your hypothesis (assuming you are not hallucinating). So disproving an explanation is easier than proving one true, and, in fact, progress in scientific explanation has largely come by rejecting alternative explanations. The ones that haven't been disconfirmed yet are the ones we work with—and some of those we feel very confident about.

Disproof

Now, if you are a scientist, obviously you will collect observations that support your explanation, but others are not likely to be persuaded just by a list of confirmations. Like proving RealClean detergent washes clothes best, it's easy to find—or concoct— circumstances that favor your view, which is why you have to bend over backward in setting up your test so that it is fair. So you set the temperature on both washing machines to be the same, you use the same volume of water, you use the recommended amount of detergent, and so forth. In the guppy case, you want to hold constant the amount of food in high-predation environments and low-predation environments, and so on. If you are wrong about the ability of RealClean to get the stains out, there won't be any difference between the two loads of clothes, because you have controlled or held constant all the other factors that might explain why one load of clothes emerged with fewer stains. You will have disproved your hypothesis about the allegedly superior stain-cleaning qualities of RealClean. You are conducting a fair test of your hypothesis if you set up the test so that everything that might give your hypothesis an advantage has been excluded. If you don't, another scientist will very quickly point out your error, so it's better to do it yourself and save yourself the embarrassment!

What makes science challenging—and sometimes the most difficult part of a scientific investigation—is coming up with a testable statement. Is the African AIDS epidemic the result of tainted oral polio vaccine (OPV) administered to Congolese in the 1950s? Chimpanzees carry simian immunodeficiency virus, which researchers believe is the source of the AIDS-causing virus HIV (human immunodeficiency virus). Poliovirus is grown on chimp kidney culture or monkey kidney culture. Was a batch of OPV grown on kidneys from chimps infected with simian immunodeficiency virus the source of African AIDS? If chimpanzee DNA could be found in the fifty-year-old vaccine, that would strongly support the hypothesis. If careful analysis did not find chimpanzee DNA, that would fail to support the hypothesis, and you would have less confidence in it. Such a test was conducted, and after very careful analysis, no chimp DNA was found in samples of the old vaccine. Instead, macaque monkey DNA was found (Poinar, Kuch, and Pääbo 2001).

The study by Poinar and colleagues did not disprove the hypothesis that African AIDS was caused by tainted OPV (perhaps some unknown batch of OPV is the culprit), but it is strong evidence against it. Again, as in most science, we are dealing with probabilities: if all four batches of OPV sent to Africa in the 1950s were prepared in the same manner, at the same time, and in the same laboratory, what is the probability that one would be completely free of chimp DNA and one or more other samples would be tainted? Low, presumably, but because the probability is not 0 percent, we cannot say for certain that the OPV-AIDS link is out of the question. However, we have research from other laboratories on other samples, and they also were unable to find any chimpanzee genes in the vaccine (Weiss 2001). Part of science is to repeat tests of the hypothesis, and when such repeated tests confirm the conclusions of early tests, it greatly increases confidence in the answers. Because the positive evidence for this hypothesis for the origin of AIDS was thin to begin with, few people now are taking the hypothesis seriously. Both disproof of hypotheses and failure to confirm are critical means by which we eliminate explanations and therefore increase our understanding of the natural world.

Now, you might notice that although I have not defined them, I already have used two scientific terms in this discussion: theory and hypothesis. You may already know what these terms mean—probably everyone has heard that evolution is "just a theory," and many times you have probably said to someone with whom you disagree, "Well, that's just a hypothesis." You might be surprised to hear that scientists don't use these terms in these ways.

Facts, Hypotheses, Laws, and Theories

How do you think scientists would rank the terms fact, hypothesis, law, and theory? How would you list these four from most important to least? Most people list facts on top, as the most important, followed by laws, then theories, and then hypotheses as least important at the bottom:

Most important
Facts
Laws
Theories
Hypotheses
Least important

You may be surprised that scientists rearrange this list, as follows:

Most important
Theories
Laws
Hypotheses
Facts
Least important

Why is there this difference? Clearly, scientists must have different definitions of these terms compared to how we use them on the street. Let's start with facts.

Facts

If someone said to you, "List five scientific facts," you could probably do so with little difficulty. Living things are composed of cells. Gravity causes things to fall. The speed of light is about 186,000 miles/second. Continents move across the surface of Earth. Earth revolves around the sun—and so on. Scientific facts, most people think, are claims that are rock solid, about which scientists will never change their minds. Most people think that facts are just about the most important part of science, and that the job of the scientist is to collect more and more facts.

Actually, facts are useful and important, but they are far from being the most important elements of a scientific explanation. In science, facts are confirmed observations. When the same result is obtained after numerous observations, scientists will accept something as a fact and no longer continue to test it. If you hold up a pencil between your thumb and forefinger, and then stop supporting it, it will fall to the floor. All of us have experienced unsupported objects falling; we've leaped to catch the table lamp as a toddler accidentally pulls the lamp cord. We consider it a fact that unsupported objects fall. It is always possible, however, that some circumstance may arise when a fact is shown not to be correct. If you were holding that pencil while orbiting Earth on the space shuttle and then let it go, it would not fall (it would float). It also would not fall if you were on an elevator with a broken cable that was hurtling at 9.8 meters/second^2 toward the bottom of a skyscraper—but let's not dwell on that scenario. So technically, unsupported objects don't always fall, but the rule holds well enough for ordinary use. One is not frequently on either the space shuttle or a runaway elevator, or in other circumstances in which the confirmed observation of unsupported items falling will not hold. It would in fact be perverse for one to reject the conclusion that unsupported objects fall just because of the existence of helium balloons.

Other scientific facts (i.e., confirmed observations) have been shown not to be true. Before better cell-staining techniques revealed that humans have twenty-three pairs of chromosomes, it was thought that we had twenty-four pairs. A fact has changed, in this case with more accurate means of measurement. At one point, we had confirmed observations of twenty-four chromosome pairs, but now there are more confirmations of twenty-three pairs, so we accept the latter—although at different times, both were considered facts. Another example of something considered a fact—an observation— was that the continents of Earth were stationary, which anyone can see! With better measurement techniques, including using observations from satellites, it is clear that continents do move, albeit very slowly (only a few inches each year).

So facts are important but not immutable; they can change. An observation, though, doesn't tell you very much about how something works. It's a first step toward knowledge, but by itself it doesn't get you very far, which is why scientists put it at the bottom of the hierarchy of explanation.

Hypotheses

Hypotheses are statements of the relationships among things, often taking the form of if-then statements. If brightly colored male guppies are more likely to attract predators, then in environments with high predation, guppies will be less brightly colored. If levels of lead in the bloodstream of children is inversely associated with IQ scores, then children in environments with greater amounts of lead should have lower IQ scores. Elephant groups are led by matriarchs, the eldest females. If the age (and thus experience) of the matriarch is important for the survival of the group, then groups with younger matriarchs will have higher infant mortality than those led by older ones. Each of these hypotheses is directly testable and can be either disconfirmed or confirmed (note that hypotheses are not proved "right"—any more than any scientific explanation is proved). Hypotheses are very important in the development of scientific explanations. Whether rejected or confirmed, tested hypotheses help to build explanations by removing incorrect approaches and encouraging the further testing of fruitful ones. Much hypothesis testing in science depends on demonstrating that a result found in a comparison occurs more or less frequently than would be the case if only chance were operating; statistics and probability are important components of scientific hypothesis testing.

Laws

There are many laws in science (e.g., the laws of thermodynamics, Mendel's laws of heredity, Newton's inverse square law, the Hardy-Weinberg law). Laws are extremely useful empirical generalizations: they state what will happen under certain conditions. During cell division, under Mendel's law of independent assortment, we expect genes to act like particles and separate independently of one another. Under conditions found in most places on Earth's surface, masses will attract one another in inverse proportion to the square of the distance between them, following the inverse square law. If a population of organisms is larger than a certain size, is not undergoing natural selection, and has random mating, the frequency of genotypes of a two-gene system will be in the proportion $p2 + 2pq + q2$. This relationship is called the Hardy-Weinberg law.

Outside of science, we also use the term **law**. It is the law that everyone must stop for a stoplight. Laws are uniform and, in that they apply to everyone in the society, universal. We don't usually think of laws changing, but of course they do: the legal system has a history, and we can see that the legal code used in the United States has evolved over several centuries primarily from legal codes in England. Still, laws must be relatively stable or people would not be able to conduct business or know which practices or behaviors will get them in trouble. One will not anticipate that if today everyone drives on the right side of the street, tomorrow everyone will begin driving on the left. Perhaps because of the stability of societal laws, we tend to think of scientific laws as also stable and unchanging.

However, scientific laws can change or not hold under some conditions. Mendel's law of independent assortment tells us that the hereditary particles will behave independently as they are passed down from generation to generation. For example, the color of a pea flower is passed on independently from the trait for stem length. But after more study, geneticists found that the law of independent assortment can be "broken" if the genes are very closely associated on the same chromosome. So minimally, this law had to be modified in terms of new information—which is standard behavior in science. Some laws will not hold if certain conditions are changed. Laws, then, can change just as facts can.

Laws are important, but as descriptive generalizations, they rarely explain natural phenomena. That is the role of the final stage in the hierarchy of explanation: theory. Theories explain laws and facts. Theories therefore are more important than laws and facts, and thus scientists place them at the top of the hierarchy of explanation.

Theories

The word theory is perhaps the most misunderstood word in science. In everyday usage, the synonym of theory is guess or hunch. Yet according to the National Academy of Sciences (2008: 11), "The formal scientific definition of theory is quite different from the everyday meaning of the word. It refers to a comprehensive explanation of some aspect of nature that is supported by a vast body of evidence." A theory, then, is an explanation rather than a guess. Many high school (and even, unfortunately, some college) textbooks describe theories as tested hypotheses, as if a hypothesis that is confirmed is somehow promoted to a theory, and a really, really good theory gets crowned as a law. But rather than being inferior to facts and laws, a scientific theory incorporates "facts, laws, inferences, and tested hypotheses" (National Academy of Sciences 1998: 7). Theories explain laws! To explain something scientifically requires an interconnected combination of laws, tested hypotheses, and other theories.

Evolution and Testing

What about the theory of evolution? Is it scientific? Some have claimed that because no one was present millions of years ago to see evolution occur, evolution is not a scientific field. Yet we can study evolution in a laboratory even if no one was present to see zebras and horses emerge from a common ancestor. A theory can be scientific even if its phenomena are not directly observable. Evolutionary theory is built in the same way that theory is built in particle physics or any other field that uses indirect testing—and some aspects of evolutionary theory can be directly tested. I will devote chapter 2 to discussing evolution in detail, but let me concentrate here on the question of whether it is testable—and especially whether evolution is falsifiable.

The big idea of biological evolution (as will be discussed more fully in the next chapter) is descent with modification. Evolution is a statement about history and refers to something that happened, to the branching of species through time from common ancestors. The pattern that this branching takes and the mechanisms that bring it about are other components of evolution. We can therefore look at the testing of evolution in three senses: Can the big idea of evolution (descent with modification, common ancestry) be tested? Can the pattern of evolution be tested? Can the mechanisms of evolution be tested?

Testing the Big Idea

Hypotheses about evolutionary phenomena are tested just like hypotheses about other scientific topics: the trick (as in most science!) is to figure out how to formulate your question so it can be tested. The big idea of evolution, that living things have shared common ancestors, can be tested using the if-then approach—testing by consequences—that all scientists use. The biologist John A. Moore suggested a number of these if-then statements that could be used to test whether evolution occurred:

1. If living things descended with modification from common ancestors, then we would expect that "species that lived in the remote past must be different from the species alive today" (Moore 1984: 486). When we look at the geological record, this is indeed what we see. There are a few standout species that seem to have changed very little over hundreds of millions of years, but the rule is that the farther back in time one looks, the more creatures differ from present forms.

2. If evolution occurred, we "would expect to find only the simplest organisms in the very oldest fossiliferous [fossil-containing] strata and the more complex ones to appear in more recent strata" (Moore 1984: 486). Again going to the fossil record, we find that this is true. In the oldest strata, we find single-celled organisms, then simple multicelled organisms, and then simple versions of more complex invertebrate multicelled organisms (during the early Cambrian period). In later strata, we see the invasion of the land by simple plants, and then the evolution of complex seed-bearing plants, and then the development of the land vertebrates.

3. If evolution occurred, then "there should have been connecting forms between the major groups (phyla, classes, orders)" (Moore 1984: 489). To test this requires going again to the fossil record, but matters are complicated by the fact that not all connecting forms have the same probability of being preserved. For example, connecting forms between the very earliest invertebrate groups are less likely to be found because of their soft bodies, which do not preserve as well as hard body parts such as shells and bones, which can be fossilized. These early invertebrates also lived in shallow marine environments, where the probability of a creature's preservation is different depending on whether it lived under or on the surface of the seafloor: surface-living forms have a better record of fossilization due to surface sediments being glued together by bacteria. Fossilized burrowing forms haven't been found—although their burrows have. It might be expected to find connections between vertebrate groups because vertebrates are large animals with large calcium-rich bones and teeth that have a higher probability of fossilization than do the soft body parts of the earliest invertebrates. There are, in fact, good transitions that have been found between fish and amphibians, and there are especially good transitions between reptiles and mammals. More and more fossils are being found that show structural transitions between reptiles (dinosaurs) and birds. Within a vertebrate lineage, there are often fossils showing good transitional structures. We have good evidence of transitional structures showing the evolution of whales from land mammals, and modern, large, single-hoofed horses from small, three-toed ancestors. Other examples can be found in reference books on vertebrate evolution such as those by Carroll (1998) or Prothero (2007).

In addition to the if-then statements predicting what one would find if evolution occurred, one can also make predictions about what one would not find. If evolution occurred and living things have branched off the tree of life as lineages split from common ancestors, one would not find a major branch of the tree totally out of place. That is, if evolution occurred, paleontologists would not find mammals in the Devonian age of fishes or seed-bearing plants back in the Cambrian. Geologists are daily examining strata around the world as they search for minerals, or oil, or other resources, and at no time has a major branch of the tree of life been found seriously out of place. Reports of "man tracks" being found with dinosaur footprints have been shown to be carvings, or eroded dinosaur tracks, or natural erosional features. If indeed there had not been an evolutionary, gradual emergence of branches of the tree of life, then there is no scientific reason why all strata would not show remains of living things all jumbled together.

In fact, one of the strongest sources of evidence for evolution is the consistency of the fossil record around the world. Another piece of evidence is the fact that when we look at the relationships among living things we see that it is possible to group organisms in gradually broader classifications. There is a naturally occurring hierarchy of organisms that has been recognized since the seventeenth century: species can be grouped into genera, genera can be grouped into families, and on and on into higher categories. The branching process of evolution generates hierarchy; the fact that animals and plants can be arranged in a tree of life is predicted and explained by the inference of common descent.

We can test not only the big idea of evolution but also more specific claims within that big idea. Such claims concern pattern and process, which require explanations of their own.

Pattern and Process

Pattern. Consider that if evolution is fundamentally an aspect of history, then certain things happened and other things didn't. It is the job of evolutionary biologists and geologists to reconstruct the past as best they can and to try to ascertain what actually happened as the tree of life developed and branched. This is the pattern of evolution, and indeed, along with the general agreement about the gradual appearance of modern forms over the past 3.8 billion years, the scientific literature is replete with disputes among scientists about specific details of the tree of life, about which structures represent transitions between groups and how different groups are related. Morphologically, most Neanderthal physical traits can be placed within the range of variation of living humans, but there are tests on fossil mitochondrial DNA that suggest that modern humans and Neanderthals shared a common ancestor very, very long ago—no more recently than 300,000 years ago (Ovchinnikov et al. 2000). So are Neanderthals ancestral to modern humans or not? There is plenty of room for argument about exactly what happened in evolution. But how do you test such statements?

Tests of hypotheses of relationships commonly use the fossil record. Unfortunately, sometimes one has to wait a long time before hypotheses can be tested. The fossil evidence has to exist (i.e., be capable of being preserved and actually be preserved), be discovered, and be painstakingly (and expensively) extracted. Only then can the analysis begin. Fortunately, we can test hypotheses about the pattern of evolution— and the idea of descent with modification itself—by using types of data other than the fossil record: anatomical, embryological, or biochemical evidence from living groups. One reason why evolution—the inference of common descent—is such a robust scientific idea is that so many different sources of information lead to the same conclusions.

We can use different sources of information to test a hypothesis about the evolution of the first primitive amphibians that colonized land. There are two main types of bony fish: the very large group of familiar ray-finned fish (e.g., trout, salmon, sunfish) and the lobe-finned fish, represented today by only three species of lungfish and one species of coelacanth. In the Devonian, though, there were nineteen families of lungfish and three families of coelacanths. Because of their many anatomical specializations, we know that ray-finned fish are not part of tetrapod (four-legged land vertebrate) ancestry; we and all other land vertebrates are descended from the lobe-fin line. Early tetrapods and lobe-fins both had teeth with wrinkly enamel and shared characteristics of the shoulder girdle and jaws, plus a sac off the gut used for breathing (Prothero 1998: 358). But are we tetrapods more closely related to lungfish or to coelacanths? Is the relationship among these three groups more like Figure 1.2A or Figure 1.2B? We can treat the two diagrams as hypotheses and examine data from comparative anatomy, the fossil record, biochemistry, and embryology to confirm or disconfirm A or B.

Anatomical and fossil data support hypothesis B (Thomson 1994). Studies on the embryological development of tetrapod and fish limbs also support hypothesis B. Now, when contemplating Figure 1.2, remember that these two diagrams omit the many known fossil forms and show only living groups. It isn't that tetrapods evolved from lungfish, of course, but that lungfish and tetrapods shared a common ancestor, and they shared that common ancestor with each other more recently than they shared a common ancestor with coelacanths. There is a large series of fossils filling the morphological gaps between ancestors of lungfish and tetrapods (Carroll 1998) and more are being discovered (Shubin, Daeschler, and Jenkins 2006).

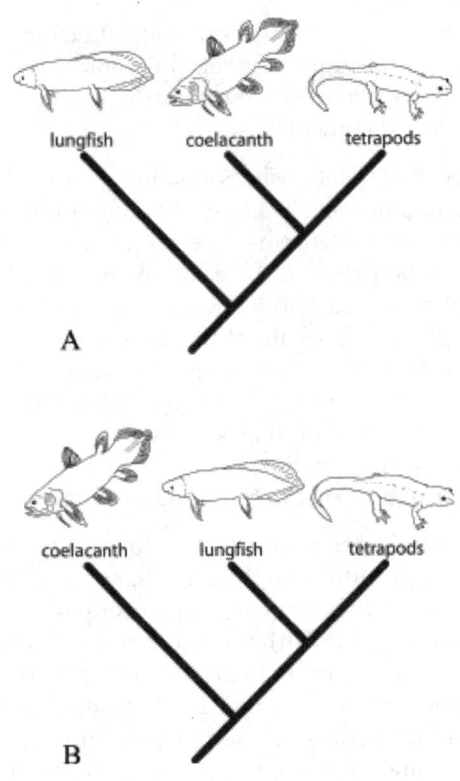

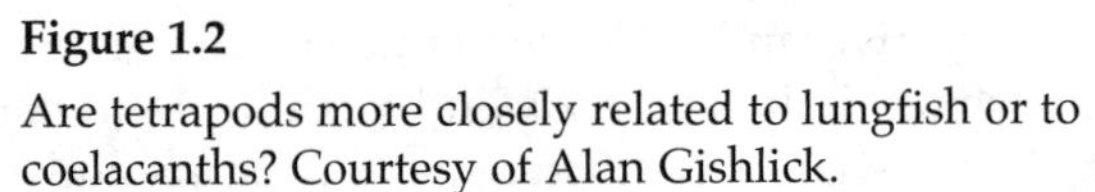

Figure 1.2

Are tetrapods more closely related to lungfish or to coelacanths? Courtesy of Alan Gishlick.

Another interesting puzzle about the pattern of evolution is ascertaining the relationships among the phyla, which are very large groupings of kinds of animals. All the many kinds of fish, amphibians, reptiles, birds, and mammals are lumped together in one phylum (Chordata) with some invertebrate animals such as sea squirts and the wormlike lancelet (amphioxus). Another phylum (Arthropoda) consists of a very diverse group of invertebrates that includes insects, crustaceans, spiders, millipedes, horseshoe crabs, and the extinct trilobites. So you can see that phyla contain a lot of diversity. Figuring out how such large groups might be related to one another is a challenging undertaking.

Phyla are diagnosed on the basis of basic anatomical body plans—the presence of such features as segmentation, possession of shells, possession of jointed appendages, and so forth. Fossil evidence for most of these transitions is not presently available, so scientists have looked for other ways to ascertain relationships among these large groups. The recent explosions of knowledge in molecular biology and of developmental biology are opening up new avenues to test hypotheses of relationships—including those generated from anatomical and fossil data. Chordates for a long time have been thought to be related to echinoderms on the basis of anatomical comparisons (larvae of some echinoderms are very similar to primitive chordates) and this relationship is being confirmed through biochemical comparisons (e.g., ribosomal RNA) (Runnegar 1992). Ideas about the pattern of evolution can be and are being tested.

Process. Scientists studying evolution want to know not only the pattern of evolution but also the processes behind it: the mechanisms that cause cumulative biological change through time. The most important is natural selection (discussed in chapter 2), but there are other mechanisms (mostly operating in small populations, like genetic drift) that also are thought to bring about change. One interesting current debate, for example, is over the role of genetic factors operating early in embryological development. How important are they in determining differences among—and the evolution of—the basic body plans of living things? Are the similarities of early-acting developmental genes in annelid worms and in primitive chordates like amphioxus indicative of common ancestry? Another debate has to do with the rate and pace of evolution: do changes in most lineages proceed slowly and gradually, or do most lineages remain much the same for long periods that once in a while are punctuated with periods of rapid evolution? We know that individuals in a population compete with one another, and that populations of a species may outbreed one another, but can there be natural selection between lineages of species through time? Are there rules that govern the branching of a lineage through time? Members of many vertebrate lineages have tended to increase in size through time; is there a general rule governing size or other trends? All of these issues and many more constitute the processes or mechanisms of evolution. Researchers are attempting to understand these processes by testing hypotheses against the fossil and geological records as well as other sources of information from molecular biology and developmental biology (embryology).

Natural selection and other genetically based mechanisms are regularly tested and are regularly shown to work. By now there are copious examples of natural selection operating in our modern world, and it is not unreasonable to extend its operation into the past. Farmers and agricultural experts are very aware of natural selection as insects, fungi, and other crop pests become resistant to chemical controls. Physicians similarly are very aware of natural selection as they try to counter antibiotic-resistant microbes. The operation of natural selection is not disputed in the creationism/evolution controversy: both supporters and detractors of evolution accept that natural selection works. Creationists, however, claim that natural selection cannot bring about differences from one "kind" to another.

Pattern and process are both of interest in evolutionary biology, and each can be evaluated independently. Disputes about the pattern of evolutionary change are largely independent of disputes about the process. That is, arguments among specialists about how fast evolution can operate, or whether it is gradual or punctuated, are irrelevant to arguments over whether Neanderthals are ancestral to modern Europeans and vice versa. Similarly, arguments about either process or pattern are irrelevant to whether evolution took place (i.e., the big idea of descent with modification). This is relevant to the creationism/evolution controversy because some of the arguments about pattern or process are erroneously used to support the claim that descent with modification did not occur. Such arguments confuse different levels of understanding.

Creationism and Testing

The topic of religion constitutes chapter 3, and creationism is a religious concept. Religion will be defined as a set of ideas concerning a nonmaterial reality; thus, it would appear that—given science's concern for material explanations—science and creationism have little in common. Yet the creationism/evolution controversy includes the claim made by some that creationism is scientific, or can be made scientific, or has scientific elements. The question naturally arises, then, Is creationism testable?

As discussed, science operates by testing explanations of natural phenomena against the natural world. Explanations that are disproved are rejected; explanations that are not disproved—that are corroborated—are provisionally accepted (though at a later time they may be rejected or modified with new information). An important element of testing is being able to hold constant some of the conditions of the test, so that a causative effect can be correctly assigned.

The ultimate statement of creationism—that the present universe came about as the result of the action or actions of a divine creator—is thus outside the abilities of science to test. If there is an omnipotent force in the universe, it would by definition be impossible to hold constant (to control) its effects. A scientist could control for the effects of temperature, light, humidity, or predators—but it would be impossible to control for the actions of God!

The question of whether God created cannot be evaluated by science. Most believers conceive of God as omnipotent, so God could have created everything just as we see it today, a theological position known as special creationism, or God could have created through a natural process such as evolution, a theological position known as theistic evolution. An omnipotent being could create the universe to appear as if it had evolved but actually have created everything five minutes ago. The reason that the ultimate statement of creationism cannot be tested is simple: the actions of an omnipotent creator are compatible with any and all observations of the natural world. The methods of science cannot choose among the possible actions of an omnipotent creator because by definition God is unconstrained.

Science is thus powerless to test the ultimate claim of creationism and must be agnostic about whether God did or did not create the material world. However, some types of creationism go beyond the basic statement "God created" to make claims of fact about the natural world. Many times these fact claims, such as those concerning the age of Earth, are greatly at variance with observations of science, and creationists sometimes invoke scientific support to support these fact claims. One creationist claim, for example, is that the Grand Canyon was laid down by the receding waters of Noah's flood. In cases like this, scientific methods can be used to test creationist claims, because the claims are claims of fact. Of course, it is always possible to claim that the creator performed miracles (that the layers of rocks in Grand Canyon were specially created by an omnipotent creator), but at this point one passes from science to some other way of knowing. If fact claims are made—assuming the claimer argues scientific support for such claims—then such claims can be tested by the methods of science; some scientific views are better supported than others, and some will be rejected as a result of comparing data and methodology. But if miracles are invoked, such occasions leave the realm of science for that of religion.

Conclusion

First, a caveat: the presentation of the nature of science and even the definitions of facts, hypotheses, laws, and theories I presented is very, very simplified and unnuanced, for which I apologize to philosophers of science. I encourage readers to consult some of the literature in philosophy of science; I think you'll find it a very interesting topic.

Science is an especially good way of knowing about the natural world. It involves testing explanations against the natural world, discarding the ones that don't work, and provisionally accepting the ones that do.

Theory building is the goal of science. Theories explain natural phenomena and are logically constructed of facts, laws, and confirmed hypotheses. Knowledge in science, whether expressed in theories, laws, tested hypotheses, or facts, is provisional, though reliable. Although any scientific explanation may be modified, there are core ideas of science that have been tested so many times that we are very confident about them and believe that there is an extremely low probability of their being discarded. The willingness of scientists to modify their explanations (theories) is one of the strengths of the method of science, and it is the major reason that knowledge of the natural world has increased exponentially over the past couple of hundred years.

Evolution, like other sciences, requires that natural explanations be tested against the natural world. Indirect observation and experimentation, involving if-then structuring of questions and testing by consequence, are the normal mode of testing in sciences such as particle physics and evolution, where phenomena cannot be directly observed.

The three elements of biological evolution—descent with modification, the pattern of evolution, and the process or mechanisms of evolution—can all be tested through the methods of science. The heart of creationism—that an omnipotent being created—is not testable by science, but fact claims about the natural world made by creationists can be.

References

Carroll, Robert L. 1998. *Vertebrate paleontology and evolution*. New York: W. H. Freeman.

Cartmill, Matt. 1988. Seventy-five reasons to become a scientist: *American Scientist* celebrates its seventy-fifth anniversary. *American Scientist* 76: 450–463.

Hrdy, Sarah Blaffer. 2001. Mothers and others. *Natural History* (May): 50–62.

Montagu, M. F. Ashley. 1984. *Science and creationism*. New York: Oxford University Press.

Moore, John A. 1984. Science as a way of knowing—Evolutionary biology. *American Zoologist* 24 (2): 467–534.

National Academy of Sciences. 1998. *Teaching about evolution and the nature of science*. Washington, DC: National Academies Press.

National Academy of Sciences and Institute of Medicine. 2008. *Science, Evolution, and Creationism*. Washington, DC: National Academies Press.

Ovchinnikov, I. V., A. Gotherstrom, G. P. Romanova, V. M. Kharitonov, K. Liden, and W. Goodwin. 2000. Molecular analysis of Neanderthal DNA from the northern Caucasus. *Nature* 404: 490–493.

Poinar, Hendrik, Melanie Kuch, and Svante Pääbo. 2001. Molecular analysis of oral polio vaccine samples. *Science* 292 (5517): 743–744.

Prothero, Donald R. 1998. Bringing fossils to life: An introduction to paleontology. Boston: WCB.

Prothero, Donald R. 2007. *Evolution: What the fossils say and why it matters.* New York: Columbia University Press.

Runnegar, Bruce. 1992. Evolution of the earliest animals. In *Major events in the history of life,* ed. J. W. Schopf. Boston: Jones and Bartlett. pp. 64–93.

Shubin, Neil H., Edward B. Daeschler, and Farish A. Jenkins Jr. 2006.A Devonian tetrapod-like fish and the evolution of the tetrapod body plan. *Nature* 440: 757–763.

Thomson, Keith Stewart. 1994. The origin of the tetrapods. In *Major features of vertebrate evolution,* ed. D. R. Prothero and R. M. Schoch. Pittsburgh, PA: Paleontological Society. pp. 85–107.

Trefil, James. 1978. A consumer's guide to pseudoscience. *Saturday Review,* April 29, 16–21.

Weiss, Robin A. 2001. Polio vaccines exonerated. *Nature* 410: 1035–1036.

Social Sciences

We all have difficulties in our lives: troubles in our relationships with our parents or spouses or kids, troubles at our jobs, troubles with money, with illness, and maybe with our very sense or who we are. Most of us, most of the time, tend to view these troubles as personal matters, caused either by our own personal failings or by someone else's, or simply by unknowable fate. In the essay below, C. Wright Mills offers a more thoughtful perspective. He suggests we try to cultivate what he calls the "sociological imagination," an ability to see our own lives, with their troubles as well as their triumphs, as part of a larger system of social forces. Some might recoil from this sort of thinking, viewing it as a fatalistic sense that we have no control, that the individual is but a leaf floating down a stream at the mercy of random eddies and currents. But Mills suggests a more empowering view: that acquiring a sociological imagination actually enables us to face our troubles with greater confidence and clarity, and, most important, to understand that by joining with others we can have a part in shaping the forces that cause them.

If "the unexamined life is not worth living" as Socrates said, then acquiring a sociological imagination is one way of making our lives a little more worth living. And this, after all, is the point of a liberal arts education. For social scientists, examining one's life is largely a matter of examining its interactions with the external context—ideas, communities, and geography—in which it is lived. Or, as Mills puts it, "Neither the life of the individual nor the history of a society can be understood without understanding both."

[By the way, notice how Mills's description of the fast pace of technological and social change reads like an article in today's newspaper—yet this piece was written in 1959!]

from The Sociological Imagination

C. Wright Mills

Nowadays people often feel that their private lives are a series of traps. They sense that within their everyday worlds, they cannot overcome their troubles, and in this feeling, they are often quite correct. What ordinary people are directly aware of and what they try to do are bounded by the private orbits in which they live; their visions and their powers are limited to the close-up scenes of job, family, neighborhood; in other milieux, they move vicariously and remain spectators. And the more aware they become, however vaguely, of ambitions and of threats which transcend their immediate locales, the more trapped they seem to feel.

Underlying this sense of being trapped are seemingly impersonal changes in the very structure of continent-wide societies. The facts of contemporary history are also facts about the success and the failure of individual men and women. When a society is industrialized, a peasant becomes a worker; a feudal lord is liquidated or becomes a businessman. When classes rise or fall, a person is employed or unemployed; when the rate of investment goes up or down, a person takes new heart or goes broke. When wars happen, an insurance salesperson becomes a rocket launcher; a store clerk, a radar operator; a wife or husband lives alone; a child grows up without a parent. Neither the life of an individual nor the history of a society can be understood without understanding both.

Yet people do not usually define the troubles they endure in terms of historical change and institutional contradiction. The well-being they enjoy, they do not usually impute to the big ups and downs of the societies in which they live. Seldom aware of the intricate connection between the patterns of their own lives and the course of world history, ordinary people do not usually know what this connection means for the kinds of people they are becoming and for the kinds of history-making in which they might take part. They do not possess the quality of mind essential to grasp the interplay of individuals and society, of biography and history, of self and world. They cannot cope with their personal troubles in such ways as to control the structural transformations that usually lie behind them.

Surely it is no wonder. In what period have so many people been so totally exposed at so fast a pace to such earthquakes of change? That Americans have not known such catastrophic changes as have the men and women of other societies is due to historical facts that are now quickly becoming 'merely history.' The history that now affects every individual is world history. Within this scene and this period, in the course of a single generation, one sixth of humankind is transformed from all that is feudal and backward into all that is modern, advanced, and fearful. Political colonies are freed; new and less visible forms of imperialism installed. Revolutions occur; people feel the intimate grip of new kinds of authority. Totalitarian societies rise, and are smashed to bits—or succeed fabulously. After two centuries of ascendancy, capitalism is shown up as only one way to make society into an industrial apparatus. After two centuries of hope, even formal democracy is restricted to a quite small portion of mankind. Everywhere in the underdeveloped world, ancient ways of life are broken up and vague expectations become urgent demands. Everywhere in the overdeveloped world, the means of authority and of violence become total in scope and bureaucratic in form. Humanity itself now lies before us, the super-nation at either pole concentrating its most coordinated and massive efforts upon the preparation of World War Three.

The very shaping of history now outpaces the ability of people to orient themselves in accordance with cherished values. And which values? Even when they do not panic, people often sense that older ways of feeling and thinking have collapsed and that newer beginnings are ambiguous to the point of moral stasis. Is it any wonder that ordinary people feel they cannot cope with the larger worlds with which they are so suddenly confronted? That they cannot understand the meaning of their epoch for their own lives? That—in defense of selfhood—they become morally insensible, trying to remain altogether private individuals? Is it any wonder that they come to be possessed by a sense of the trap?

It is not only information that they need—in this Age of Fact, information often dominates their attention and overwhelms their capacities to assimilate it. It is not only the skills of reason that they need—although their struggles to acquire these often exhaust their limited moral energy.

What they need, and what they feel they need, is a quality of mind that will help them to use information and to develop reason in order to achieve lucid summations of what is going on in the world and of what may be happening within themselves. It is this quality, I am going to contend, that journalists and scholars, artists and publics, scientists and editors are coming to expect of what may be called the sociological imagination.

The sociological imagination enables its possessor to understand the larger historical scene in terms of its meaning for the inner life and the external career of a variety of individuals. It enables him to take into account how individuals, in the welter of their daily experience, often become falsely conscious of their social positions. Within that welter, the framework of modern society is sought, and within that framework the psychologies of a variety of men and women are formulated. By such means the personal uneasiness of individuals is focused upon explicit troubles and the indifference of publics is transformed into involvement with public issues.

The first fruit of this imagination—and the first lesson of the social science that embodies it—is the idea that the individual can understand her own experience and gauge her own fate only by locating herself within her period, that she can know her own chances in life only by becoming aware of those of all individuals in her circumstances. In many ways it is a terrible lesson; in many ways a magnificent one. We do not know the limits of humans capacities for supreme effort or willing degradation, for agony or glee, for pleasurable brutality or the sweetness of reason. But in our time we have come to know that the limits of 'human nature' are frighteningly broad. We have come to know that every individual lives, from one generation to the next, in some society; that he lives out a biography, and lives it out within some historical sequence. By the fact of this living, he contributes, however minutely, to the shaping of this society and to the course of its history, even as he is made by society and by its historical push and shove.

The sociological imagination enables us to grasp history and biography and the relations between the two within society. That is its task and its promise. To recognize this task and this promise is the mark of the classic social analyst. It is characteristic of Herbert Spencer—turgid, polysyllabic, comprehensive; of E. A. Ross—graceful, muckraking, upright; of Auguste Comte and Emile Durkheim; of the intricate and subtle Karl Mannheim. It is the quality of all that is intellectually excellent in Karl Marx; it is the clue to Thorstein Veblen's brilliant and ironic insight, to Joseph Schumpeter's many-sided constructions of reality; it is the basis of the psychological sweep of W. E. H. Lecky no less than of the profundity and clarity of Max Weber. And it is the signal of what is best in contemporary studies of people and society.

No social study that does not come back to the problems of biography, of history and of their intersections within a society has completed its intellectual journey. Whatever the specific problems of the classic social analysts, however limited or however broad the features of social reality they have examined, those who have been imaginatively aware of the promise of their work have consistently asked three sorts of questions:

(1) What is the structure of this particular society as a whole? What are its essential components, and how are they related to one another? How does it differ from other varieties of social order? Within it, what is the meaning of any particular feature for its continuance and for its change?
(2) Where does this society stand in human history? What are the mechanics by which it is changing? What is its place within and its meaning for the development of humanity as a whole? How does any particular feature we are examining affect, and how is it affected by, the historical period in which it moves? And this period—what are its essential features? How does it differ from other periods? What are its characteristic ways of history-making?
(3) What varieties of men and women now prevail in this society and in this period? And what varieties are coming to prevail? In what ways are they selected and formed, liberated and repressed, made sensitive and blunted? What kinds of 'human nature' are revealed in the conduct and character we observe in this society in this period? And what is the meaning for 'human nature' of each and every feature of the society we are examining?

Whether the point of interest is a great power state or a minor literary mood, a family, a prison, a creed—these are the kinds of questions the best social analysts have asked. They are the intellectual pivots of classic studies of individuals in society—and they are the questions inevitably raised by any mind possessing the sociological imagination. For that imagination is the capacity to shift from one perspective to another—from the political to the psychological; from examination of a single family to comparative assessment of the national budgets of the world; from the theological school to the military establishment; from considerations of an oil industry to studies of contemporary poetry. It is the capacity to range from the most impersonal and remote transformations to the most intimate features of the human self—and to see the relations between the two. Back of its use there is always the urge to know the social and historical meaning of the individual in the society and in the period in which she has her quality and her being.

That, in brief, is why it is by means of the sociological imagination that men and women now hope to grasp what is going on in the world, and to understand what is happening in themselves as minute points of the intersections of biography and history within society. In large part, contemporary humanity's self-conscious view of itself as at least an outsider, if not a permanent stranger, rests upon an absorbed realization of social relativity and of the transformative power of history. The sociological imagination is the most fruitful form of this self-consciousness. By its use people whose mentalities have swept only a series of limited orbits often come to feel as if suddenly awakened in a house with which they had only supposed themselves to be familiar. Correctly or incorrectly, they often come to feel that they can now provide themselves with adequate summations, cohesive assessments, comprehensive orientations. Older decisions that once appeared sound now seem to them products of a mind unaccountably dense. Their capacity for astonishment is made lively again. They acquire a new way of thinking, they experience a transvaluation of values: in a word, by their reflection and by their sensibility, they realize the cultural meaning of the social sciences.

Perhaps the most fruitful distinction with which the sociological imagination works is between 'the personal troubles of milieu' and 'the public issues of social structure.' This distinction is an essential tool of the sociological imagination and a feature of all classic work in social science.

Troubles occur within the character of the individual and within the range of his or her immediate relations with others; they have to do with one's self and with those limited areas of social life of which one is directly and personally aware. Accordingly, the statement and the resolution of troubles properly lie within the individual as a biographical entity and within the scope of one's immediate milieu—the social setting that is directly open to her personal experience and to some extent her willful activity. A trouble is a private matter: values cherished by an individual are felt by her to be threatened.

Issues have to do with matters that transcend these local environments of the individual and the range of her inner life. They have to do with the organization of many such milieu into the institutions of an historical society as a whole, with the ways in which various milieux overlap and interpenetrate to form the larger structure of social and historical life. An issue is a public matter: some value cherished by publics is felt to be threatened. Often there is a debate about what that value really is and about what it is that really threatens it. This debate is often without focus if only because it is the very nature of an issue, unlike even widespread trouble, that it cannot very well be defined in terms of the immediate and everyday environments of ordinary people. An issue, in fact, often involves a crisis in institutional arrangements, and often too it involves what Marxists call 'contradictions' or 'antagonisms.'

In these terms, consider unemployment. When, in a city of 100,000, only one is unemployed, that is his personal trouble, and for its relief we properly look to the character of the individual, his skills and his immediate opportunities. But when in a nation of 50 million employees, 15 million people are unemployed, that is an issue, and we may not hope to find its solution within the range of opportunities open to any one individual. The very structure of opportunities has collapsed. Both the correct statement of the problem and the range of possible solutions require us to consider the economic and political institutions of the society, and not merely the personal situation and character of a scatter of individuals.

Consider war. The personal problem of war, when it occurs, may be how to survive it or how to die in it with honor; how to make money out of it; how to climb into the higher safety of the military apparatus; or how to contribute to the war's termination. In short, according to one's values, to find a set of milieux and within it to survive the war or make one's death in it meaningful. But the structural issues of war have to do with its causes; with what types of people it throws up into command; with its effects upon economic and political, family and religious institutions, with the unorganized irresponsibility of a world of nation-states.

Consider marriage. Inside a marriage a man and a woman may experience personal troubles, but when the divorce rate during the first four years of marriage is 250 out of every 1,000 attempts, this is an indication of a structural issue having to do with the institutions of marriage and the family and other institutions that bear upon them.

Or consider the metropolis—the horrible, beautiful, ugly, magnificent sprawl of the great city. For many members of the upperclass the personal solution to 'the problem of the city' is to have an apartment with private garage under it in the heart of the city and forty miles out, a house by Henry Hill, garden by Garrett Eckbo, on a hundred acres of private land. In these two controlled environments—with a small staff at each end and a private helicopter connection—most people could solve many of the problems of personal milieux caused by the facts of the city. But all this, however splendid, does not solve the public issues that the structural fact of the city poses. What should be done with this wonderful monstrosity? Break it all up into scattered units, combining residence and work? Refurbish it as it stands? Or, after evacuation, dynamite it and build new cities according to new plans in new places? What should those plans be? And who is to decide and to accomplish whatever choice is made? These are structural issues; to confront them and to solve them requires us to consider political and economic issues that affect innumerable milieux.

In so far as an economy is so arranged that slumps occur, the problem of unemployment becomes incapable of personal solution. In so far as war is inherent in the nation-state system and in the uneven industrialization of the world, the ordinary individual in her restricted milieu will be powerless—with or without psychiatric aid—to solve the troubles this system or lack of system imposes upon him. In so far as the family as an institution turns women into darling little slaves and men into their chief providers and unweaned dependents, the problem of a satisfactory marriage remains incapable of purely private solution. In so far as the overdeveloped megalopolis and the overdeveloped automobile are built-in features of the overdeveloped society, the issues of urban living will not be solved by personal ingenuity and private wealth.

What we experience in various and specific milieux, I have noted, is often caused by structural changes. Accordingly, to understand the changes of many personal milieux we are required to look beyond them. And the number and variety of such structural changes increase as the institutions within which we live become more embracing and more intricately connected with one another. To be aware of the idea of social structure and to use it with sensibility is to be capable of tracing such linkages among a great variety of milieux. To be able to do that is to possess the sociological imagination.

Critical Studies of Race and Ethnicity

Critical Studies of Race and Ethnicity (CRST) at St. Kate's is an interdisciplinary program derived from racial/ethnic studies programs (African American Studies, Asian American Studies, Chicano/Chicana Studies, and Native American Studies). These programs emerged out of the activism of the 1960s, with African American Studies paving the way. The scholarship of CRST engages the social issues, history, experiences, and contributions of people of color, and it aims to advance inclusion and social equality across the curriculum and co-curriculum.

To grasp Toni Morrison's short but complex essay, included below, some basic assumptions of CRST are important background—including the fact that current racial issues in the U.S. have historical roots. Morrison discusses how immigrants from Europe, in order to assimilate in the U.S., had to "become white"; the immigrants quickly learned that they had to separate themselves from "the interloper, the scorned black," in the American social order. Morrison has written elsewhere about how the shadow of slavery, and, here, the presence of a young black man, lingers in the white imagination as a signpost that signifies his group's status at the bottom rung of the social ladder. This racial signpost guides the way Americans perceive themselves as free—as not slaves—and as white—as not black. And the signpost is evident in the "race talk" that shows up in "popular culture shaped by film, theatre, advertising, the press, television, and literature." As Morrison posits, "It doesn't matter any more what shade the newcomer's skin is. A hostile posture must be struck at the Americanizing door before it will open." Whether one is an immigrant of color or a white "wannabe seeking social status," one knows to keep one's distance from the interloper unless, of course, one is standing "on the backs of Blacks" to climb that rickety racial ladder.

On the Backs of Blacks

Toni Morrison

Fresh from Ellis Island, Stavros gets a job shining shoes at Grand Central Terminal. It is the last scene of Elia Kazan's film *America, America,* the story of a young Greek's fierce determination to immigrate to America. Quickly, but as casually as an afterthought, a young black man, also a shoe shiner, enters and tries to solicit a customer. He is run off the screen—"Get out of here! We're doing business here!"—and silently disappears.

This interloper into Stavros' workplace is crucial in the mix of signs that make up the movie's happy-ending immigrant story: a job, a straw hat an infectious smile—and a scorned black. It is the act of racial contempt that transforms this charming Greek into an entitled white. Without it, Stavros' future as an American is not at all assured.

This is race talk, the explicit insertion into everyday life of racial signs and symbols that have no meaning other than pressing African Americans to the lowest level of the racial hierarchy. Popular culture, shaped by film, theater, advertising, the press, television and literature, is heavily engaged in race talk. It participates freely in this most enduring and efficient rite of passage into American culture: negative appraisals of the native-born black population. Only when the lesson of racial estrangement is learned is assimilation complete. Whatever the lived experience of immigrants with African Americans,—pleasant, beneficial or bruising—the rhetorical experience renders blacks as noncitizens, already discredited outlaws.

All immigrants fight for jobs and space, and who is there to fight but those who have both? As in the fishing ground struggle between Texas and Vietnamese shrimpers, they displace what and whom they can. Although U.S. history is awash in labor battles, political fights and property wars among all religious and ethnic groups, their struggles are persistently framed as struggles between recent arrivals and blacks. In race talk the move into mainstream America always means buying into the notion of American blacks as the real aliens. Whatever the ethnicity or nationality of the immigrant, his nemesis is understood to be African American.

Current attention to immigration has reached levels of panic not seen since the turn of the century. To whip up this panic, modern race talk must be revised downward into obscurity and nonsense if antiblack hostility is to remain the drug of choice, giving headlines their kick. PATTERNS OF IMMIGRATION FOLLOWED BY WHITE FLIGHT, screams the Star-Ledger in Newark. The message we are meant to get is that disorderly newcomers are dangerous to stable (white) residents. Stability is white. Disorder is black. Nowhere do we learn what stable middle-class blacks think or do to cope with the "breaking waves of immigration." The overwhelming majority of African Americans, hardworking and stable, are out of the loop, disappeared except in their less than covert function of defining whites as the "true" Americans.

So addictive is this ploy that the fact of blackness has been abandoned for the theory of blackness. It doesn't matter anymore what shade the newcomer's skin is. A hostile posture toward resident blacks must be struck at the Americanizing door before it will open The public is asked to accept American blacks as the common denominator in each conflict between an immigrant and a job or between a wannabe and status. It hardly matters what complexities, contexts and misinformation accompany these conflicts. They can all be subsumed as the equation of brand X vs. blacks.

But more than a job is at stake in this surrender to whiteness, more even than what the black intellectual W.E.B. Du Bois called the "psychological wage"—the bonus of whiteness. Racist strategies unify. Savvy politicians always include in the opening salvos of their campaigns a quick clarification of their position on race. It is a mistake to think that Bush's Willie Horton or Clinton's Sister Soul-jah was anything but a candidate's obligatory response to the demands of a contentious electorate unable to understand itself in any terms other than race. Warring interests, nationalities and classes can be merged with the greatest economy under that racial banner.

Race talk as bonding mechanism is powerfully on display in American literature. When Nick in F. Scott Fitzgerald's *The Great Gatsby* leaves West Egg to dine in fashionable East Egg, his host conducts a kind of class audition into WASP-dom by soliciting Nick's support for the "science" of racism. "If we don't lookout the white race will be . . . utterly submerged," he says. "It's all scientific stuff; it's been proved." It makes Nick uneasy, but he does not question or refute his host's convictions.

The best clue to what the country might be like without race as the nail upon which American identity is hung comes from Pap, in Mark Twain's *Huckleberry Finn,* who upon learning a Negro could vote in Ohio, "drawed out. I says I'll never vote ag'in." Without his glowing white mask he is not American; he is Faulkner's character Wash, in *Absalom, Absalom*!, who, stripped of the mask and treated like a "nigger" drives a scythe into the heart of the rich white man he has loved and served so completely.

For Pap, for Wash, the possibility that race talk might signify nothing was frightening. Which may be why the harder it is to speak race talk convincingly, the more people seem to need it. As American blacks occupy more and more groups no longer formed along racial lines, the pressure accelerates to figure out what white interests really are. The enlisted military is almost one-quarter black; police forces are blackening in large urban areas. But welfare is nearly two-thirds white; affirmative-action beneficiaries are overwhelmingly white women; dysfunctional white families jam the talk shows and court TV.

The old stereotypes fail to connote, and race talk is forced to invent new, increasingly mindless ones. There is virtually no movement up—for blacks or whites, established classes or arrivistes—that is not accompanied by race talk. Refusing, negotiating or fulfilling this demand is the real stuff, the organizing principle of becoming an American. Star spangled. Race strangled.

Women's Studies

AnaLouise Keating's article about Gloria Anzaldúa (1942–2004) offers a taste of the ideas Women's Studies is concerned with as an academic field committed to challenging individuals and changing the world. At St. Kate's, Women's Studies is integrated across the curriculum, especially in the arts and sciences. You will find our courses within the disciplines focusing on themes such as Women and Globalization, Feminist Philosophy, and Women in Art. Even in this Reader, you will find many essays from the perspectives of women artists and thinkers.

Women's Studies is also, and distinctively, interdisciplinary. Keating's essay exemplifies this, drawing on scholars from a range of fields to explore ideas that cannot be contained within one disciplinary perspective. Gloria Anzaldúa herself earned a B.A. in English, Art, and Secondary Education and a master's degree in English and Education. Like many early leaders of Women's Studies, she did not have a Women's Studies degree; the field was just getting started when Anzaldúa graduated from college in 1969. In fact, Anzaldúa was one of the people who created Women's Studies. Especially through her book Borderlands/La Frontera, *she shaped feminist theorizing and set a standard for integrating the analysis of gender and sexuality with race/ethnicity and colonial legacies. If you are the first generation in your family to go to college, if you are Chicana, if you grew up speaking Spanish, if you are a lesbian, if your family needs you to work quite a few hours a week while you attend college, if you live on a borderland between cultures, you have something in common with Anzaldúa.*

Interdisciplinary Women's Studies has made important contributions to theorizing about identity—who a person is in the context of where she is socially located in her society and in the world. As Keating explains, Anzaldúa connected identity, spirituality, and working for social justice. Through her concept of spiritual activism, Anzaldúa presented an expansive approach to identity that challenges individualism and focuses on who we are in relation to each other.

"I'm a citizen of the universe": Gloria Anzaldúa's Spiritual Activism as Catalyst for Social Change

AnaLouise Keating

> *With awe and wonder you look around, recognizing the preciousness of the earth, the sanctity of every human being on the planet, the ultimate unity and interdependence of all beings—somos todosun país. Love swells in your chest and shoots out of your heart chakra, linking you to everyone/everything . . . . You share a category of identity wider than any social position or racial label. This conocimiento motivates you*

> *to work actively to see that no harm comes to people, animals, ocean—to take up spiritual activism and the work of healing.*
>
> —Gloria E. Anzaldúa
>
> *now let us shift . . . the path of conocimiento . . .inner work, public acts*

In this passage, drawn from one of her final essays, Gloria Evangelina Anzaldúa describes a radically inclusionary politics, or what she calls "spiritual activism." . . . Anzaldúa's spiritual activism offers a visionary yet experientially based epistemology and ethics. Spiritual activism is spirituality for social change, spirituality that posits a relational worldview and uses this holistic worldview to transform one's self and one's worlds.[1] Throughout her career, from her earliest publications to her last writings, Anzaldúa worked to develop, refine, and enact her own unique version of spiritual activism.

• • •

As I will explain in the following pages, Anzaldúa's theory of spiritual activism is designed to meet twenty-first century needs; it offers valuable lessons for feminists and other social justice activists. Her politics of spirit demonstrates that holistic, spirit-inflected perspectives—when applied to racism, sexism, homophobia, and other contemporary issues—can sustain and assist us as we work to transform social injustice. First, though, I describe Anzaldúa's theory of spiritual activism in more detail.

> I struggle to "talk" from the wound's gash, make sense of the deaths and destruction, and pull the pieces of my life back together. I yearn to pass on to the next generation the spiritual activism I've inherited from my cultures.
>
> —Gloria E. Anzaldúa
> "let us be the healing of the wounds"

Anzaldúa's spiritual activism enabled her to make meaning out of the apparently meaningless events of her life, especially those situations—"the deaths and destruction"—that caused her the most pain. Significantly, this meaning-making endeavor was a difficult, often torturous, struggle. Although sometimes tempted to become immersed in despair or to give up in defeat, Anzaldúa drew on her holistic worldview and insisted on her personal agency, her ability to learn from even the most negative life events.

Anzaldúa offers the most extensive discussion to date[2] of her theory and praxis of spiritual activism in "now let us shift . . . the path of conocimiento . . . inner work, public acts." As the title implies, in this essay Anzaldúa urges herself and her readers to enact transformation (or "shift") by focusing simultaneously on self-change ("inner acts") and outwardly directed social activism ("public acts"). . . . Anzaldúa's spiritual activism intertwines "inner works" with "public acts," private concerns with social issues. Indeed, this simultaneous attention to personal and collective issues/concerns is a vital component in spiritual activism.

It is crucial, then, to distinguish Anzaldúa's spiritual activism both from the mainstream "New-Age" movement and from conventional organized religions. Unlike the former, which focuses almost, if not entirely, on the personal and thus leaves the existing oppressive social structures in place, spiritual activism's holistic approach encompasses both the personal and the systemic. Spiritual activism begins within the individual but moves outward as these individuals (or what Anzaldúa calls "spiritual activists") expose, challenge, and work to transform unjust social structures. And unlike the latter, which often impose authority on individuals through external teachings, texts, standards, and leaders, spiritual activism locates authority within each individual. As Anzaldúa explains in an early discussion of the ways U.S. women of colors have used spirituality to develop new forms of resistance: "Our spirituality does not come from outside ourselves. It emerges when we listen to the 'small still voice' within us which can empower us to create actual change in the world."[3] By reclaiming and nurturing this inner spiritual power, the women Anzaldúa describes become agents of change. More specifically, they acquire increased self-esteem and develop holistic epistemologies enabling them to expose social injustice. In this way, spiritual activists can work simultaneously for individual and collective change. Ana Castillo illustrates one form that this increased self-esteem can take in *Massacre of the Dreamers*. As she explains,

> acknowledgment of the energy that exists throughout the universe subatomically generating itself and interconnecting, fusing, and changing . . . offer[s] a personal response to the divided state of the individual who desires wholeness. An individual who does not sense herself as helpless to circumstances is more apt to contribute positively to her environment than one who resigns with apathy to it because of her sense of individual insignificance.[4]

Although spiritual activism begins at the level of the personal, it is not solipsistic; nor does it result in egocentrism, self-glorification, or other types of possessive individualism. Rather, spiritual activism combines self-reflection and self-growth with outward-directed, compassionate acts designed to bring about material change. Look for instance at the way Anzaldúa describes the closely entwined dynamics of self-awareness, oppression, resistance, and transformation in *Borderlands/La Frontera*:

> The struggle is inner: Chicano, indio, American Indian, mojado, mexicano, immigrant Latino, Anglo in power, working class Anglo, Black, Asian—our psyches resemble the bordertowns and are populated by the same people. The struggle has always been inner, and is played out in outer terrains. Awareness of our situation must come before inner changes, which in turn come before changes in society. Nothing happens in the "real" world unless it first happens in the images in our heads.[5]

In this passage, "inner" and "outer" are so intimately interrelated and interwoven as to occur simultaneously; each depends on, influences, and shapes the other.

For Anzaldúa and other spiritual activists, self-change and social transformation are mutually interdependent. In one of her earliest published writings, "La Prieta," Anzaldúa describes this intricate reciprocal process linking self-change with social justice actions:

> I believe that by changing ourselves we change the world, that traveling El Mundo Zurdo path is the path of a two-way movement—a going deep into the self and an expanding out into the world, a simultaneous recreation of the self and a reconstruction of society. And yet, I am confused as to how to accomplish this. I can't discount the fact that thousands go to bed hungry every night. The thousands that do numbing shitwork eight hours a day each day of their lives. The thousands that get beaten and killed every day. The millions of women who have been burned at the stake, the millions who have been raped. Where is the justice to this?[6]

I have quoted this passage at length because it so effectively illustrates three important dimensions of Anzaldúa's spiritual activism. First, Anzaldúa insists that self-change should not be an end in itself; instead, this "recreation of the self" must be part of a larger process requiring both intense self-reflection and back-and-forth action on individual and communal levels. Second, as Anzaldúa's frank question ("Where is the justice to this?") indicates, spiritual activism's transformative process is a difficult, complicated endeavor, filled with uncertainty and unanswered questions. Third, and closely related to this second point, Anzaldúa does not deny the violence, pain, and other forms of suffering that so often occur in this world. She addresses the injustice without downplaying or in any other way denying its significance. By so doing, she confronts the paradox of personal agency and structural determinacy. Rather than ignore, diminish, or attempt to resolve this paradoxical situation, she chooses the more difficult pathway and decided to inhabit the contradiction:

> I can't reconcile the sight of a battered child with the belief that we choose what happens to us, that we create our own world. *I cannot resolve* this in myself. I don't know. I can only speculate, try to integrate the experiences that I've had or have been witness to and try to make some sense of why we do violence to each other. In short, I'm trying to create a religion not out there somewhere, but in my gut. I am trying to make peace between what has happened to me, what the world is, and what it should be.[7]

Fully acknowledging the suffering, as well as the ambiguities, paradoxes, and unanswered questions, Anzaldúa confidently insists on the political effectiveness of her relational worldview. As I have argued elsewhere, she bases this confidence on her metaphysics of interconnectedness. Drawing on indigenous philosophies, Eastern thought, psychic literature, and her own experiences, she maintained her belief in a fluid, cosmic spirit/energy/force that embodies itself throughout—and *as*—all existence.[8] Thus in a 1982 interview she explained that "Spirit exists in everything; therefore God, the divine, is in everything . . . it's in the tree, the swamp, the sea. . . . Some people call it 'God'; some call it the 'creative force,' whatever. It's in everything." Twenty years later Anzaldúa made a similar claim: "Spirit infuses all that exists—organic and inorganic—transcending the categories and concepts that govern your perception of material reality."[9] I point out the time span between these two assertions in order to underscore the duration of Anzaldúa's belief. Despite the relentless racism, sexism, and other forms of oppression and despite the many communal and personal setbacks, private losses, and health-related difficulties she experienced throughout the years, Anzaldúa retained her relational worldview.

This belief in the interrelatedness of all life forms is a crucial component in Anzaldúa's theory of spiritual activism and facilitates the development of new tactics for survival, resistance, and transformation on all levels. In what follows, I build on this radical interconnectivity to explore one of spiritual activism's most important—yet difficult—theoretical implications: the invitation to move beyond the binary-oppositional frameworks we generally use in identity formation and social change.

> But I'm sure that with the Chicana dykes I've met, I'm odd, an outcast. Because a lot of them are nationalists and I don't believe in nationalism; I'm a citizen of the universe. I think it's good to claim your ethnic identity and your racial identity. But it's also the source of all the wars and all the violence, all these borders and walls people erect. I'm tired of borders and I'm tired of walls. . . . I don't believe that we're better than people in India or that we're different from people in Ethiopia. One billion people go to bed hungry every night. . . . There are droughts in Ethiopia, Kenya, and Eastern Africa. . . . People are dying every day. And then people talk about being proud to be American, Mexican, or Indian. We have grown beyond that. We are specks from this cosmic ocean, the soul, or whatever. We're not better than people from Africa or people from Russia. If something happens to the people in India or Africa—and they're starving to death and dying—then that's happening to us, too.
>
> —Gloria E. Anzaldúa, *Interviews/Entrevistas*

Anzaldúa's self-positioning in the above epigraph represents a startling contrast to conventional models of identity. Usually, self-identification functions through exclusion and binary opposition: we define who and what we are by defining who and what we are not. These exclusionary identities occur within a restrictive framework that marks, divides, and segregates human beings based on narrow, dualistic models of difference. As Patricia Hill Collins explains, "In either/or dichotomous thinking, difference is defined in oppositional terms. One part is not simply different from its counterpart; it is inherently opposed to its 'other.' Whites and Blacks, males and females, thought and feeling, are not complementary counterparts—they are fundamentally different entities related only through their definitions as opposites."[10] This oppositional logic reduces our interactional possibilities to-two mutually exclusive options: Either we are entirely the same or we are entirely different: In this either/or system, difference becomes rigidly divisive. When we view ourselves and others through this binary lens, we assume that our differences are too different—too *other*, as it were—to have *anything* of importance in common with those whom we have defined as our others. Such stark either/or assumptions leave no room for the messy complexities of compromise and exchange so vital to coalition work and community-building.

Anzaldúa's spiritual activism offers a different approach, one bypassing this exclusionary logic. As she explains in her introduction to *this bridge we call home: radical visions for transformation*, "Many of us identify with groups and social positions not limited to our ethnic, racial, religious, class, gender, or national classifications. Though most people self-define by what they exclude, we define who we are by what we include—what I call the new tribalism."[11] Significantly, Anzaldúa does not discount the importance of gender, ethnicity/'race,' sexuality, ability, and other identity-related components. However, she maintains that these conventional categories are too restrictive and cannot adequately define us. Indeed, she suggests that these identity-based categories have been and still are used to disempower and oppress us: 'the changeability of racial, gender, sexual, and other categories render[s] the conventional labelings obsolete. Though these markings are outworn and inaccurate, those in power continue using them to single out and negate those who are 'different' because of color, language, notions of reality, or other diversity."[12] When we base our assessments of others entirely—or even primarily—on their physical appearances and social locations, we make biased, inaccurate assumptions about their politics, worldviews, and so forth. When we act on these assumptions (as we too often do), we unnecessarily close ourselves off from potential allies. Or as Anzaldúa so eloquently asserts, "For the politically correct stance we let color, class, and gender separate us from those who would be kindred spirits. So the walls grow higher, the gulfs between us wider, the silences more profound."[13]

Positing radical interconnectedness, Anzaldúa dismantles these walls by building bridges. She adopts flexible, context-specific perspectives enabling her simultaneously to see and see through exclusionary identity classifications. She does not ignore the importance of color, class, gender, and other identity markers; however, she puts these classifications into a more holistic perspective. As in my epigraph to this section, she defines each person as a part of a larger whole—a "cosmic ocean, the soul, or whatever." By so doing, Anzaldúa can insist on a commonality shared by all human beings, a commonality we share despite the very real differences among us. For Anzaldúa, this "common factor" goes beyond—but does not ignore—identities based on gender, 'race,' or other systems of difference; it is "wider than any social position or racial label." Indeed, Anzaldúa locates this identity factor within nonhuman life as well. As she explains, "Your identity has roots you share with all people and other beings—spirit, feeling, and body comprise a greater identity category. The body is rooted in the earth, la tierra itself. You meet ensoulment in trees, in woods, in streams."[14] It's important to note that for Anzaldúa this shared identity factor does not make us identical. As I use the term, "commonality" and "sameness" are not synonymous. Anzaldúa's commonalities are heterogeneous and multifaceted.

Anzaldúa's practice and theory of El Mundo Zurdo, or "The Left-Handed World;" indicates one form her complex commonalities can take. As the phrase "left-handed world" might suggest, for Anzaldúa El Mundo Zurdo represents a highly creative fluid, and open-minded perspective and space. Thus she asserts that 'The left hand is not a fist pero una mano abierta [but an open hand] raised with others in struggle, celebration, and song."Anzaldúa's concept of El Mundo Zurdo is quite possibly her oldest concept. She began using the term "El Mundo Surdo"[15] in the late 1970s, when she organized a series of poetry readings with that title in San Francisco. She invited a variety of people, including feminists of all colors, U.S. "Third World" writers, lesbians, and gay men, to read in El Mundo Surdo Reading Series. Despite the many differences among them, participants shared several commonalities, including their so-called deviation from the dominant culture, their personal experiences of alienation/discrimination/oppression, their interest in issues of social justice, their shared rejection of the status quo, and their work as creative writers and artists. Several years later, in her introduction to the final section of *This Bridge Called My Back: Writings by Radical Women of Color* and in "La Prieta," Anzaldúa developed a theoretical description of El Mundo Zurdo. She explains that El Mundo Zurdo represents alliances among people from a variety of different social locations. Although inhabitanta of El Mundo Zurdo are very different from each other, they forge commonalities and develop alliances enabling them to work together to bring about revolutionary change: "We are the queer groups, the people that don't belong anywhere, not in the dominant world nor completely within our own respective cultures. Combined we cover so many oppressions. But the overwhelming oppression is the collective fact that we do not fit, and because we do not fit, *we are a threat*." Significantly, El Mundo Zurdo people are not all alike; their specific oppressions, solutions, and beliefs are different. Anzaldúa accepts these differences and uses them to forge commonalities, asserting that "these different affinities are not opposed to each other. In El Mundo Zurdo I with my affinities and my people with theirs can live together and transform the planet."[16]

I want to emphasize the innovative possibilities opened up by Anzaldúa's inclusionary models of identity formation. Typically, feminists and other social justice activists develop politics and actions around identity-related issues. As Leela Fernandes explains, "identity continues to serve as the ground from which to work for change and to which to retreat for a sense of safety and belonging." Although this approach can be useful, it limits us in at least two ways. First, because identity-based politics rely on already-existing categories that originated in oppressive histories, they inadvertently support the unjust socio-political framework under which we currently live. These tainted categories restrict our imaginations and thus limit our visions of social change. Fernandes makes a similar point, noting that,

> whole identity-based movements are effective in mobilizing short term political action, in the long run they cannot produce an alternative future that is free from the very identity-based divisions and inequalities that they oppose. While oppositional movements based on identity have been necessary to address the blindness to various forms of injustice, such movements cannot in the long run provide a viable alternative because they inevitably must rest on a form of identification that explicitly or implicitly is based on an oppositional distinction from another group.[17]

Second, identity-based politics' exclusionary categories can limit our ability to make useful alliances. Like the oppositional identities from which they emerge, identity-based politics rely on and reinforce an us-against-them worldview. When we ground identities and alliances in dualistically defined categories, we establish and police boundaries—boundaries that shut us in with those whom we have defined as "like" "us" and boundaries that close us off from those whom we define as different. These boundaries prevent us from recognizing our complex commonalities and developing broad-based projects for social change. In such instances, identities become ends in themselves, rather than useful tools as we move toward larger goals like transformation, liberation, and social justice.

My point here is not that we should dismiss all identity categories and declare ourselves from this day forward "color-blind," gender-blind, and so forth. Instead, I am concerned by the lack of self-reflection that so often accompanies identity-based politics. When we automatically label people by color, gender, sexuality, religion, or any other politically charged characteristics, we assume both a false homogeneity within and radical differences between various groups of people—and, by extension, the theoretical perspectives designed to represent them—become rigid, inflexible, and restrictive. These monolithic categories distort our perceptions, creating arbitrary divisions among us and a combative mentality that inhibits social change. When we use identity-based categories in such automatic, unthinking ways, the labels function as impenetrable, unsurmountable obstacles. We trap ourselves within narrow worldviews and cannot perceive our interconnectedness with others.

This binary-oppositional framework leads to frozen, dogmatic positions; intragroup battles; and judgmental, dismissive attitudes—or what Alexander appropriately describes as "mono-thinking."[18] When we structure our teaching, our politics, or, more generally, our lives according to this dualistic sameness/difference framework, we assume that there is only one right way to think, act, theorize, or self-define. These oppositional energies become poisonous when we direct them toward each other, as we too often do. In such instances, we engage in what Timothy Powell describes as "corrosive exchanges" and embark on "[a] downward spiral of ever more hostile counteraccusations."[19] Although Powell focuses specifically on debates within academic multiculturalism, I have seen (both in person and in print) this dynamic happen in a variety of situations, when people or groups oppressed in similar (not identical) ways attempt to develop alliances that fragment from within and often over fairly minor issues. The us-against-them stance we have employed in oppositional forms of consciousness seeps into all areas of our lives, infecting the way we perceive ourselves and each other. When we turn this lens against each other—as we so often do—we implode. Rather than work together to enact progressive social change, we battle each other, thus reproaching the status quo.[20]

Anzaldúa's spiritual activism compels me to question whether the binary-oppositional energies so crucial to many social justice theories are as useful today as they were in the past. Like Alexander, I believe that "[o]ur oppositional politic has been necessary, but it will never sustain us; while it may give us some temporary gains . . . it can never ultimately feed that deep place within us: that space of the erotic, the space of the soul, that space of the Divine."[21]

In her writings, Anzaldúa speaks from and to this "deep place within us." By so doing, she enacts a transformative politics of spirit seen in many of her theories, including (but not limited to) her theories of El Mundo Zurdo, conocimiento, mestizo consciousness, the Borderlands, nepantleras, nos/ostras, new tribalism, and spiritual acivism.[22] Positing our radical interconnectedness—or what she describes in "now let us shift" as "the deep common ground and interwoven kinship among all things and people."[23]—Anzaldúa challenges us to move beyond mono-thinking, binary-oppositional politics, and other forms of self-destructive thought and action. Her theories, and her willingness to risk ostracism by insisting on spiritual activitism, offer innovative tools we can build on as we create new theoretical perspectives, pedagogies, and social justice actions like "nepantlera activism," "healing sueños," and "listening with raw openness."[24]

Notes

[1] I have been thinking, talking, and trying to write about spiritual activism since I first encountered the term when I was editing Anzaldúa's interviews in the 1990s. This essay is only my most recent attempt to explore (and enact!) this complex theory. Thanks to the many people who have explored these ideas with me: Suzanne Bost, Renae Bredin, Irene Lara, Eddy Lynton, Carrie McMaster, Harry McMaster, Nery Morales, the students in my 2003 and 2004 Gloria Anzaldúa graduate seminar, and the audience at the 2002 NWSA panel on Anzaldúa. Special thanks to Gloria Anzaldúa for giving me the term "spiritual activism," for our many discussions on this topic, and for always taking those extreme risks. I dedicate this essay to her spirit.

[2] I say that Anzaldúa offers the most extensive discussion to date because she has several unpublished manuscripts that explore spiritual activism and related issues. See, for example, *The Gloria Anzaldúa Reader*, ed. AnaLouise Keating (forthcoming, Duke University Press, 2009).

[3] Gloria Anzaldúa, "El Mundo Zurdo," in *This Bridge Called My Back: Writings by Radical Women of Color*, 2d ed., ed. Cherrie Moraga and Gloria Anzaldúa (New York: Kitchen Table/Women of Color Press, 1983), 195. Anzaldúa cites Luisah Teish, "OK Momma. Who the Hell Am I? An Interview with Luisah Teish," also in *This Bridge Called My Back*.

[4] Ana Castillo, *Massacre of the Dreamers: Essays on Xicanisma* (Albuquerque: University of New Mexico Press, 1994), 159.

[5] Gloria Anzaldúa, *Borderlands/La Frontera: The New Mexico* (San Francisco: Aunt Lute, 1999), 87.

[6] Gloria Anzaldúa, "La Prieta," in *This Bridge Called My Back*, 208.

[7] Ibid., her italics.

[8] I discuss this metaphysics of interconnectedness in more detail in "Risking the Personal: An Introduction," in Anzaldúa's *Interviews/Entrevistas*, 11–12. Anzaldúa was especially influenced by Aztec and Toltec indigenous philosophies and by the writings of Sri Aurobindo, The Mother, and Jane Roberts.

[9] Anzaldúa, *Interviews/Entrevistas*, 100, twenty years later: Anzaldúa, "now let us shift, in *this bridge we call home*, 558. Alma Levine provides a detailed analysis of Anzaldúa's spiritualized epistemology in "Champion of the Spirit: Anzaldúa's Critique of Rationalist Epistemology," in *EntreMundos/Among Worlds*, 171–84.

[10] Patricia Hill Collins, *Black Feminist Thought: Knowledge, Consciousness, and the Politics of Empowerment* (New York: Routledge, 2000), 70.

[11] Anzaldúa, "(Un)natural bridges, (Un)safe spaces," in *this bridge we call home*, 3.

[12] Anzaldúa, "now let us shift," in *this bridge we call home*, 541.

[13] Anzaldúa, La Prieta," in *This Bridge Called My Back*, 206.

[14] Anzaldúa, "now let us shift," in *this bridge we call home*, 558.

[15] Note the change in spelling from "El Mundo Surdo" to "El Mundo Zurdo." This shift from "s" to "z" in the word "Zurdo" occurred during the copyediting of *This Bridge Called My Back*. Although Anzaldúa was not pleased with this alteration, eventually she accepted and adopted it. For more on this issue see

her archives, located at the Nettie Lee Benson Latin American Collection of the University of Texas, Austin.

[16] Anzaldúa, "La Prieta, in *This Bridge Called My Back*, 209, her italics.

[17] Leela Fernandes, *Transforming Feminist Practice: Non-Violence, Social Justice, and the Possibilities of a Spiritualized Feminism* (San Francisco: Aunt Lute, 2003), 28, 26–27, my emphasis.

[18] M. Jacqui Alexander, "Remembering This Bridge, Remembering Ourselves: Yearning, Memory, and Desire," in *this bridge we call home*, 98.

[19] Timothy B. Powell, "All Colors Flow into Rainbows and Nooses: The Struggle to Define Academic Multiculturalism," *Cultural Critique* 55 (Fall 2003): 168, 175.

[20] Alexander explores this dynamic in the final chapter of her *Pedagogies of Crossing*.

[21] Alexander, "Remembering *This Bridge*," in *this bridge we call home*, 99.

[22] Anzaldúa mentions many of these theories in the interviews collected in her *Interviews/Entrevistas*, and I explore them in more detail in my "Shifting Worlds, un entrada," in *EntreMundos/Among Worlds*, 1–12.

[23] Anzaldúa, "now let us shift," in *this bridge we call home*, 566.

[24] The term "nepantlera activism," is Kavitha Koshy's: she coins this term in her "Nepantlera-Activism in the Transnational Moment: In Dialogue with Gloria Anzaldúa's Theorizing of Nepantla," *Human Architecture: Journal of the Sociology of Self-knowledge* 4 (summer 2003): 147–62. The term "healing sueños" is Irene Lara's; she coins it in her "Healing Sueños for Academia," in *this bridge we call home*, 433–38. The term "listening with raw openness" is mine; I use it in my *Teaching Transformation: Transcultural Classroom Dialogues* (New York: Palgrave MacMillan, 2007).

The Catherine Core Resources

Goals of a Liberal Arts Education at St. Catherine University

St. Catherine University has identified seven themes of a St. Catherine's education encompassing the knowledge, skills, and attitudes that it seeks to develop in its graduates. Based on our commitment to women, the liberal arts, and the Catholic traditions of intellectual inquiry and social teaching, an education at St. Catherine's emphasizes:

Leadership and Collaboration

The ability to lead and influence for ethical and responsible action and for systemic change; the ability to work well with others, especially in joint intellectual effort.

Students will demonstrate leadership and collaboration by their ability to:

a) act from a strong self-concept;

b) transform information into knowledge and knowledge into judgment and action;

c) make timely and relevant decisions based on sound reasoning;

d) discern consequences, including ethical consequences, of decisions and actions;

e) articulate a positive sense of direction and evoke hope;

f) work well in teams and work groups of diverse composition, building consensus and integrating conflict resolution strategies.

Ethics and Social Justice

The ability to apply ethical standards to judge individual and collective actions; the development of attitudes and behaviors that reflect integrity, honesty, compassion, and justice in one's personal and professional life.

Students will demonstrate a commitment to ethics and social justice by their ability to:

a) understand principles of ethics and social justice from multiple perspectives;

b) understand Catholic Social Teaching and the Catholic commitment to social justice;

c) apply ethical and justice frameworks to contemporary issues;

d) exhibit personal and academic integrity;

e) practice social responsibility through community engagement, citizenship, and advocacy.

Diversity and Global Perspectives

The ability to understand and analyze the impact of diversity and systems of power and privilege on the individual and society; the ability to decipher and honor multiple and global perspectives in creating mutual understanding; the ability to imagine and take action toward justice.

Students will demonstrate a commitment to diversity and global perspectives by their ability to

a) understand the experiences and contributions of women across history and cultures;

b) recognize the historic and current relationships within and among cultural communities, locally, nationally, and globally;

c) identify and critically analyze the impact of race/ethnicity, gender, social class, religion, sexual orientation, age, ability, and other differences on identity, experience, and systems of power and privilege;

d) understand how economic, social, religious, and political systems interact and how those systems vary across societies;

e) understand the interrelationships between nature and humans and develop eco-centric perspectives;

f) increase critical cultural competencies and responsiveness through engaging with multiple communities;

g) take action to dismantle systems of oppression and build a more just world.

Critical and Creative Inquiry

The ability to gather, analyze, and critically evaluate information to develop reasonable arguments, sound judgments, and effective solutions. This ability is founded on a broad knowledge of the achievements of human creativity and of the variety of disciplinary approaches for exploring truths.

Students will demonstrate critical and creative inquiry by their ability to:

a) locate appropriate information from a variety of sources and evaluate its relevance and reliability;

b) organize, describe, interpret, and integrate both qualitative and quantitative information;

c) shape ideas and discern meaning from experience, observation, imagination, and passion;

d) analyze complex issues and arguments in various intellectual contexts (scientific, aesthetic, philosophical, etc.) and evaluate the validity and soundness of such arguments;

e) develop and evaluate action plans for solving significant social and intellectual problems;

f) demonstrate breadth of knowledge of the major accomplishments of human endeavors and of the distinct methods of exploring truths (in the natural sciences, social sciences, and the arts and humanities);*

g) identify and interpret similarities and differences among various disciplinary approaches and examine the relationships among them.

**Breadth of knowledge applies to all degrees except the graduate degrees, where the focus is on in-depth development of disciplinary skills.*

Discipline-Based Competence**

The ability to demonstrate in-depth knowledge, values, and skills in at least one major field of study and to relate disciplinary approaches to those of other fields.

Students will demonstrate discipline-based competence by their ability to:

a) use in-depth knowledge and engage key ideas in at least one field of study;

b) exercise disciplinary methods and skills, and carry out research or learn independently in that field;

c) develop disciplinary perspective and identity, including an understanding of the route to acquiring knowledge in that discipline;

d) identify and analyze similarities and differences between the student's major field and other disciplinary approaches.

***Discipline-Based Competence applies to all degree programs except the Associate of Arts Degree Program*

Effective Communication in a Variety of Modes

The ability to read, write, speak, view, and listen effectively; the ability to present information in a clear and engaging manner.

Students will demonstrate effective communication by the ability to:

a) read, view, and listen with understanding and critical discernment;

b) organize, evaluate, and communicate ideas effectively through writing and public speaking to various audiences;

c) prepare and present information visually and through the use of technology;

d) find expression in fine, literary, and performing arts;

e) develop and put into practice interpersonal, group, and cross-cultural communication skills and listening skills;

f) show competency in a second language (applies only to bachelor's degree).

Purposeful Life-long Learning

The ability to continue personal and professional development based on ongoing self-assessment, feedback from others, and new learning.

Students will demonstrate a commitment to purposeful life-long learning by:

a) assuming responsibility for their own learning;

b) engaging in and reflecting on opportunities that prepare for life after college;

c) practicing a variety of methods of learning, including reading and research, observing and listening, self assessment and feedback, work and life experience;

d) developing knowledge and strategies for maintaining a balance of body, mind, and spirit;

e) reflecting on and developing a meaningful, purposeful, and spiritual life.

The Global Search for Justice

Dreamed

Ka Thao
photography, drawing
and digital illustration
2013, 5 x 8-inches

Introduction:
The Global Search for Justice

We don't have to engage in grand, heroic actions to participate in the process of change. Small acts, when multiplied by millions of people, can transform the world . . .

—Howard Zinn

The Global Search for Justice is the capstone of your liberal arts education at St. Catherine University, the other "bookend" to your baccalaureate education. While *The Reflective Woman* introduces you to St. Catherine University, the goals of a liberal arts education, and, in many ways, to yourselves, *The Global Search for Justice* asks you to look outward, towards your career, the larger world and your role in it. And in that sense, this course is a stunning tribute to the vision of our founders, the Sisters of St. Joseph of Carondelet, and the mission of St. Kates. We are asking you to carry the spirit of love and justice with you out into the world. We are asking to you find your way, every day, towards the transformation of silence into language and action.

Global. No longer a concept about "over there," the meaning of *global* in this course focuses on the relationships that weave through each of our lives. Change and complexity in these relationships are reflected in new faces in our communities, by different languages in the air, and through stories and images we encounter that both enrich and shock us. Even simple questions—"What coffee should the campus sell?" or "Where will my discarded laptop end up?" challenge us to think more broadly about our responsibilities. This course is designed to expand that understanding of global relationships. In these readings, we join Robert Grunst and students puzzling about roses as they lunch on fava beans. We will ask, with Pamela Fletcher, what we can do to transform a now global rape culture. And we will meet a fourteen-year-old girl on the streets of Bangkok, who will reveal the surprising connections.

Search. As this search for justice takes us from the known and familiar to the unknown and uncomfortable, we must ask ourselves what kind of travelers we choose to be. Will we just take snapshots of some exotic images and pass them around as two-dimensional tokens of how much poorer, how much more violent, how very different and depressing we found those *other* lives? But, maybe instead, we will take the bravest journey, one that starts from knowing our own positions in the world, that examines what privileges and assumptions we are packing. In this kind of traveling, every step taken is revealed to be part of a common, global journey. We can ask, with Cecilia Konchar Farr four feminist questions for discipline-traveling. We can look to the five faces of oppression that Iris Marion Young analyzes to discuss the intersections dividing and uniting us. We can unpack, with Deep Shikha and Sharon Doherty, six seemingly simple sentences that hold a deep story of solidarity and strength.

Justice. By this point in your education, you most likely have already discussed justice in many different contexts and through many disciplinary lenses. Connors and Cadorette offer us insight into what justice requires from the theological grounding of Catholic Social Teaching. In philosophy, social science, nursing, social work, or business classes too, you may have discovered that justice is an expansive country. Sr. Amata Miller reveals the open space possible when a community embraces a wide array of justice perspectives. We will never find the borders in this global search, since justice may be sought on a personal level, between two people, in small groups and communities, and in large political and economic systems. Grasping at it will inevitably stretch our spirits and minds. Nancy Heitzeg describes this as a spiraling process of self-reflection, social analysis, moral judgment, and action. Understanding justice is understanding that something just must be done; there is no justice without action.

In an earlier edition of this Reader, former Associate Dean Marla Martin Hanley described liberal arts education as "a life-long pursuit to liberate ourselves to know who we are, not just who we are told we are; to seek truths, not passively accept what others would lead us to believe; and to claim our own visions and voices for creating the world we live in and leave for others." The word "action" appears in some form at least nine times in the Goals of a Liberal Arts Education at St. Catherine University, signifying that while students learn to discern, understand, analyze, articulate, interpret, and evaluate, a liberal arts education prepares us to have agency in our lives. The Global Search for Justice asks you to recognize opportunities and responsibilities beyond your assigned job description, to search for ways, large or small, to live out the mission of St. Catherine University, and, ultimately, to act.

> *And if we do act, in however small a way, we don't have to wait for some grand utopian future. The future is an infinite succession of presents, and to live now as we think human beings should live, in defiance of all that is bad around us, is itself a marvelous victory.*
>
> —Howard Zinn

Nancy A. Heitzeg
Professor of Sociology and GSJ Coordinator
March 2014

Sister Amata Miller, IHM, is a professor of economics and director of the Myser Initiative in Catholic Identity at St. Catherine University. With a doctorate from the University of California, Berkeley, Sister Amata views economics as a tool for social justice and this passion has guided five decades of teaching, scholarship, and leadership. She has worked as education coordinator and economic analyst for NETWORK, a national Catholic social justice lobby in Washington, D.C., as chief financial officer of Marygrove College, as financial vice president of the IHM congregation, and as a member of numerous corporate, healthcare, and higher education boards. This article is adapted from the Sister Ann Joachim Moore lecture at St. Catherine on January 27, 2009, in which Sister Amata explored how multiple perspectives enhance a community's understanding of—and commitment to—social justice. If our university embraces multiple perspectives of social justice, what complications and opportunities would that present? Which perspective seems most valuable for your major and the work you intend to pursue?

The Many Faces of Social Justice

Amata Miller, IHM

Introduction

This paper is part of the series in honor of Sister Ann Joachim Moore, who played such an important part in developing the particular student-oriented ethos of the Minneapolis Campus. It is a work in progress since I have much more to learn about social justice and how it is perceived from various perspectives.

As an economist, I have grappled for many years with questions about the ways the current economy systems have generated abundance and freedom for some while leaving many others in situations deleterious to their human dignity. How does this happen? Why have the structures of society that have benefitted so many, left so many others behind? How have these social injustices come to be?

Work on this paper has confirmed my sense that, in the particular culture of St. Kate's, there is an as-yet-fully untapped opportunity for a new synergy among those from various disciplines and departments. This would be a synergy of intentionality, which would enrich the education of our students as we work to prepare our graduates to lead and influence in an ethic grounded in social responsibility. This would also be a synergy that could enhance the societal contribution of St. Kate's.

This paper will posit that there are many different faces of social justice and there are many different kinds of action in working towards the vision of a more socially just society in our country and the world. This "both-and" approach reflects the sense of collaboration and community we endeavor to model at St. Kate's. It also challenges us to transcend our predisposition to cling to the perspective of our own discipline within which we have each learned so much and within which we find our comfort zone. Respecting multidisciplinary insights and sharing them in an integrated way is both a challenge and an opportunity for faculty, staff, and students.

Our Mission and Its Social Context

Our mission is what drew us here and keeps us here. The mission is, organizational theorists say, the glue that keeps institutions like this one together and focuses us as a community on our purpose. Our mission statement tells us and others who we are, and *why* we are. We are known as a mission-centered institution. So let us begin there.

As we all know, our mission statement characterizes the kind of education we provide at St. Kate's—an education in a learning environment shaped by the philosophy and spirit of the college for women, an education of excellence and opportunity for students from diverse backgrounds, integrating liberal arts and professional education within the Catholic traditions of intellectual inquiry and social teaching. We profess to offer an education that prepares graduates to lead and influence, to demonstrate ethical leadership grounded in social responsibility.

As we think about the meaning of social justice and social responsibility, we have to begin by looking at the social context of our lives. Harvard Professor Bryan Hehir makes the point that institutions have to reweave their identity—maintaining continuity and dynamism—in response to the questions that society puts to them. Our social context today is one that especially calls for an ethic of social responsibility—habits of heart and mind that are other-centered, focused on the common good.

First, excessive individualism pervades our national history, especially today's culture. Considering the long waves of human history, scholars have seen continuous tension between the one and the many, between individual freedom and the goals of groups. The philosophers and historians among us can document the ways that tension expressed itself over time—especially in the West. By way of exception, though, anthropologists point out that some land-based societies have united individual freedom and community in the way they have organized their social lives.

This tension has shown itself in alternating waves of individualism—and of collectivism. In some periods, like the one we call the Middle Ages, the interests of the group dominated. As those periods aged, people grew aware of the costs to individual freedom and creativity and a wave of the ascendancy of the individual replaced it. And so the Middle Ages gave way to the Renaissance and Enlightenment eras.

Observers point out that we, especially in the U.S.A., are at the cusp now of a long era of individualism—aware of the costs to the society of excessive emphasis on the individual to the neglect of the group—of its common good.

For example, in the early nineteenth century, Alexis de Tocqueville visited the United States and remarked (in the sexist language of the day) on the degree of individualism that he found here. "Individualism is a calm and considered feeling which disposes each citizen to isolate himself from the mass of his fellows and withdraw into the circle of his family and friends; with this little society formed to his taste, he gladly leaves the greater society to look after itself." And over a century later we find that "What does it mean for me" has become the accepted norm for decision making. Emphasis on rights without recognition of the corresponding duties to help guarantee the rights of others now holds sway. The common good, with its benefits and, also, its claims upon us, has been given much less priority in our choices than individual freedom.

Another example comes from financier George Soros (1999) who presciently wrote about what we have seen all too clearly in the current economic crisis. "Laissez-faire capitalism holds that the common good is best served by the uninhibited pursuit of self-interest. Unless it is tempered by the recognition of a common interest that ought to take precedence over particular interests, our present system is liable to break down."

Also, Canadian theologian Gregory Baum (1990) wrote that Western middle class ideology has turned us into a society of individualists who believe that each person must look after herself or himself, who are competitors, each responsible for our own personal advancement.

Sociologists, anthropologists, and social psychologists lament the fragmentation of communities as job locations split families, as we retreat into gated communities, and as businesses provide all manner of things to foster our urge toward "cocooning" in our individual cars and dwellings.

But there are signs of change and these provide special opportunity for us. First, our language is changing. Words like "altruism" instead of pure self-interest have been appearing in the media in recent years. Along with national governments, the U.N. now formally recognizes "civil society" as a group of NGOs and others speaking for the people. We are hearing again about "citizenship" and responsibility to the common good. The words "social justice" are showing up in a positive light in op-ed pieces.

Social entrepreneurship is being talked about in business schools. Scholars and others are telling us that we now have the knowledge to resolve some key social issues, *if* we would muster the political will to do so. Here at St. Kate's we are already doing much, but a greater synergy among us about education for social responsibility could enhance our ability to foster development of that political will within everyone in our educational community.

President Obama, in his inaugural address (2009), pointed out that new U.S. leadership holds promise and opportunity. He called for a new commitment to a positive societal transformation and emphasized that this is everyone's responsibility.

> . . . America has carried on not simply because of the skill or vision of those in high office, but because We the People have remained faithful to the ideals of our forbearers, and true to our founding documents.
>
> . . . The time has come to reaffirm our enduring spirit: to choose our better history; to carry forward that precious gift, the noble ideal passed on from generation to generation: the God-given promise that all are equal, all are free, and all deserve a chance to pursue their full measure of happiness.

Some years ago, Isabel Sawhill (1988), then from the Urban Institute, pointed out that the U.S. is a nation at a crossroads, facing a fundamental question: *What kind of nation do we want to be?* What kind of a country do we want to live in, to pass on to our children and grandchildren? She then wrote that the defining issues for us in the years ahead boil down to four key questions about the nature of our society. Clearly, they are calls for change.

- What will our role in the world be?
- What does one generation owe to the next and to the preceding one?
- What are the responsibilities of the "haves" to the "have-nots"?
- To what extent are we willing to limit individual freedom for the sake of the common good?

Dramatic changes in the form of new international interdependence have been led by technical and communications innovations that have made the world smaller and our interrelationships more and more apparent. We have seen this in global climate change, international terrorism, pandemics like HIV/AIDS, interconnected financial crises. Kofi Annan, previous General Secretary of the U.N., has deplored the lack of political institutions to deal with this growing interdependence. Developing these new institutions is the challenge before those being educated today.

Another dramatic change is the shifting of power dynamics in the world. Previously unheard peoples all over the world have been organizing for change and making their voices heard in the public square at key international meetings and in the halls of national governments and international bodies. "Another World is Possible" has become a mantra of those previously poor and powerless.

In another sign of change, the Universal Declaration of Human Rights, developed under the leadership of Eleanor Roosevelt, was adopted by the United Nations in 1948—not to be a legal document, but to be a standard of achievement that would stand as a norm for the human rights of people from every nation. It embodies the articulation of social and economic rights as well as political and civil rights and has become the basis of the human rights tradition. It envisioned "A World Made New!" It is important to note that, in the process of drafting the Declaration, a group of pre-eminent philosophers from all over the world was convened and formally recognized that they all held the same principles of human rights, but they agreed to disagree on what the **sources** of the principles were, whatever these differences (Glendon, 2001).

The principles of the Universal Declaration of Human Rights were concretized in the eight Millennium Development goals adopted by the nations of the world in 2000—each one with measurable targets. A financial plan was developed and progress is systematically monitored annually. The goals of a more socially just world are being pursued and progress and shortfalls are being documented. Nations—including the U.S.—are being called to account for doing their part.

So the educational task at St. Kate's has profound implications for our society and our world. Developing more fully the synergy that would come from interdisciplinary, interdepartmental collaboration is an exciting possibility for us—a new expression of our mission to prepare graduates grounded in an ethic of social responsibility. We are already doing much here. *But, could a greater intentionality and collaboration among us—across our disciplines—about educating for social responsibility—enhance the ways we foster development of the essential political will within our graduates and those they will influence?*

The Many Faces of Social Justice

As previously indicated, this time is fraught with new challenges and opportunities, especially for an institution of higher education whose mission clearly speaks of preparing graduates to lead and influence in a spirit of social responsibility. We have a unique capacity to recognize that there are things to be learned about social justice from the perspectives and scholarship of those in many different disciplines. Instead of holding out one face of social justice as the one correct one, there is so much we can learn from one another—and together. We have a unique opportunity in an educational institution to do what one member of our faculty calls "contextualized theorizing."

We can develop the best of the theory and practice around social justice. We can help foster development of the necessary political will for social transformation. And we can utilize the multicultural and multidisciplinary richness of our faculty, staff and student body to foster the global understandings essential for peace, social justice and sustainability.

In preparing this paper, I interviewed thirteen people from various disciplines and departments in order to learn more about views of social justice here. In person, by phone, and through e-mail, they responded to three questions:

- When you talk about social justice, what do you mean? How do you define it?
- What do you think it means to CSC faculty? Staff? Students?
- If you had a chance to speak to faculty and staff about it, as I do, what would you want to say?

Needless to say, I got a very thoughtful and rich panoply of answers to my questions, and I am very grateful to (in alphabetical order): Tone' Blechert, Mary Ann Brenden, Russ Connors, Sharon Doherty, Marla Martin Hanley, Nancy Heitzeg, Amy Hilden, Robin Lukes, Bill McDonough, Sr. Joan Mitchell CSJ, Cynthia Norton, Sr. Ann Redmond CSJ, and Sr. Catherine Steffens, CSJ. The synthesis in this paper is my own, built from the input from the interviewees and from learnings from many people and experiences over years of working for social justice in various venues.

There are classical ethical definitions, biblical justice definitions, Catholic Social Teaching definitions, those from other religious traditions, and from various social service and advocacy agencies. All of them come from a concern for the other, and for the common good. Each of the several faces of social justice has something to teach us and our students.

But first, let us remember that the term "social justice" is one of those "red flags" to some people. Each of us can probably think of some people whom we have encountered who think like that. For these people social justice is a code word for "do-goodism" and lack of personal freedom. It connotes anarchism and violence. It is a label which, once affixed, needs no further explanation. And it is an unexamined perspective, discussion of which usually generates more heat than light.

But for us at St. Kate's there are many positive faces of social justice, and there are several commonalities among them. All of them complement one another, each adding important nuances. All are founded on the equal dignity and moral value of each person. All recognize that individual flourishing requires the common good that involves a complex set of interrelationships and social institutions. And all of the faces of social justice have something to say about what achieving that common good requires. Here, seven faces of social justice will be mentioned.

First, social justice is a heritage from the Sisters of St. Joseph, our foundresses. They are women committed to expressing their love of God through love of the "dear neighbor without distinction" as they say it. They are women who, from their beginnings in the late 1700s, both served the needy and also founded workshops and schools to empower them to escape their poverty and realize their human dignity. The Sisters of St. Joseph here in Minnesota pioneered, staffed, and supported many works of social justice over the years. They are women who have taught generations of young people about social justice, who have made social responsibility a hallmark of education at all levels.

Second, social justice is a virtue. This comes from the classical ethical tradition. Social justice is a habit of thought and heart. It is born out of love, of care for the "dear neighbor," and for the common good that makes individual good possible. Social justice connotes other-centeredness, that transcendence of self which is the fullness of being human. It flows out of the widely accepted Golden Rule—for we are social beings. Without this motivation, the work of social justice is unlikely to continue for the long haul. Social justice has to be a virtue, a habit of mind and heart that gives priority to love of neighbor and concern for the common good that makes individual flourishing possible.

Third, social justice is a vision of a state of society. It is a vision of what could/should be. A socially just society is one in which the human rights of all are recognized in the social structures—health, education, nourishment, shelter and the rest. In a socially just society "right relationships," however defined by the culture, prevail. In a socially just society there is peace, economic justice, freedom and sustainability. This is Martin Luther King's "Beloved Community," what he learned from the theology of the social gospel, Walter Rauschenbusch's sense of the Kingdom of God (Smith & Zepp, 1998). The vision of the socially just society is also described in words attributed to Judy Chicago: "And then compassion will be wedded to power. . . . And then the greed of some will give way to the needs of many. . . . And then all will live in harmony with each other and the Earth. . . ." The socially just society is what political scientist Richard Falk has called "rooted utopianism" (1998), since it is a current aspiration for a better future that permits a new kind of order to emerge and is supported by some recent developments. The philosopher Albert Camus reminded those who tend to be cynical about the importance of imagining what this kind of world would look like: "Justice—we must make it imaginable again!"

Fourth, social justice is one of three dimensions of justice in Catholic social teaching and other Christian ethical traditions.

Most people in our individualistic culture think of justice only in its first dimension—*commutative justice*—which calls for fairness in all agreements and exchanges between individuals or private social groups, based on the equal dignity of all persons (National Conference of Catholic Bishops [NCCB], 1986, par. 69). This dimension of justice is represented by a blind figure holding a scale, but the other two dimensions of justice are not blind (Curran, 2002); the other two dimensions concern the rights and duties of persons and the societies within which they live.

Distributive justice makes specific the claim that every person has to share in the goods that are fundamentally public or social. It establishes the equal right of each person to share in those goods and opportunities that are necessary for genuine participation in the human community, and it specifies the duty of society as a whole to guarantee those rights (Hollenbach, 1977, 219–20). This dimension of justice makes specific the requirements of love and interdependence in society. It "requires that the allocation of income, wealth, and power in society be evaluated in light of its effect on persons whose basic material needs are unmet" (NCCB, 1986, par. 70). If people are to be recognized as members of the human community, then the community is obliged to help fulfill these basic needs unless it is not possible because of an absolute scarcity of resources. This dimension of justice focuses on the obligations of the community to the individuals within it.

Social justice focuses on the responsibilities of the members of the society "to help create the goods, services, and other nonmaterial or spiritual values necessary for the welfare of the whole community" (NCCB, 1986, par. 71). This dimension of justice can be called "contributive" justice (or legal justice). Social justice reminds citizens that each of us has a personal obligation to do what is needed to create a society of concern (in love/charity) for the concrete needs of all persons. In this sense, social justice is a political virtue; it refers to our political obligations of citizenship (Hollenbach, 1977, 220). It is focused on the responsibility of each to contribute to the common good.

Without a citizenry acting in a spirit of social justice, neither commutative nor distributive justice will be done. This is another way of saying that the lack of political will (of the virtue of social justice in the citizens) is what is preventing the eradication of poverty and lack of freedom.

Social justice requires social structures that make the other two forms of justice realizable. At St. Kate's we often use the description of social justice coined by Peter Henriot, S.J., who summarized the link between love for others and just social structures when he said: "Social justice means that I love others so much that I work to change structures that violate their dignity."

And when we ask: 'What am I to *do* about injustice, we see other faces of social justice—faces about which the social scientists and practitioners of the helping professions among us have learned. Taking the theory into practice means learning from what these disciplines have to teach us.

Fifth, social justice is a call to action for social transformation. Social justice is a call to action. It is not enough just to talk about it. It calls us to work in some collaborative way to eliminate the systemic/structural causes of injustice, the oppressions of racism, sexism, poverty and all the others. We are talking about the kind of action that requires specific knowledge, rational analysis, deliberation, and moral judgment in each case. A famous journalist, Ben Bagdikian, once reminded us: "The most dangerous kind of person is the uninformed activist." Responding to this call to action means building into one's life some ways of contributing to the common good according to one's talents and responsibilities—in one's own spheres of influence. It means leading and influencing in an ethic of social responsibility, participating in making the vision of a just society more real.

Sixth, social justice can be specified in a set of norms of human social behavior, a set of what ethicist Phillip Boyle calls "ethical guidelines" for individual and social decision-making. These guidelines give us a common language to concretize what a state of social justice would look like. They name *injustice*. These norms need the other faces of social justice to give them full meaning. The norms are specified in various religious traditions such as Catholic Social Teaching, the social documents of various faiths and the Global Ethic of the Parliament of World Religions. They are laid out in non-religious language in the thirty principles of the Universal Declaration of Human Rights and in the constitutions of various countries as well as in the codes of ethics of the professions.

Seventh, social justice is a responsibility of every person. Social responsibility for the shape of the society in which one lives is a part of human wholeness as we learn through literature, psychology, and the arts. Building into one's moral conscience the virtue of social justice is critical. That is what will call one to respond to societal structures that cause human suffering. Persons will exercise this responsibility differently at various times in their lives, according to their passions, talents, and other responsibilities, and within the spheres of influence of their own lives. Participation in social benefits requires participation in helping to create a society that generates those benefits for everyone. Individual good and the common good are not in competition with one another. Individuals cannot fulfill their own goals when the good of society is neglected.

Development of one or more of these seven faces of social justice can provide us all with the opportunity to learn from every discipline what concern for the other means—in practice. We might ask ourselves some questions in this regard: *Could we attend more fully to the social component of our major field? If we have a code of ethics could we identify the social ethical aspects of the code and its congruence with various sets of norms? Social work, physical therapy, occupational therapy, and nursing have done this here at St. Kate's. Could we deliberate about social concerns related to the subject matter of our classes and policies as some of the science classes are doing today? Can we contribute through our research and writing to the building of the common good and the political will to achieve it?*

Some Key Understandings in Action for Justice

Before we deal with the many different kinds of action necessary to move toward social justice, it will be useful to reflect briefly on three important understandings that have proved beneficial.

First, it is important to remember that there are two feet of social concern. Social service, one-on-one compassion, concern for the poor and vulnerable—feeding the hungry, sheltering the homeless, visiting the sick and imprisoned—these are absolutely essential works of care for the other. As long as there is social injustice these will be needed. This kind of service often leads to asking "Why?" What are the causes of this suffering? Immersion experiences open eyes to human needs and to the need for societal, structural, transformation.

So the other foot of social concern is social action for change (a face of social justice). It means addressing the causes of injustice through working to change sinful social structures. If this work is not motivated by love/charity it will not last.

It is not a case of movement from charity (the virtue) to justice. It is a movement from service to work to change causative structures. It is not a movement from a good to a better but to a different form of response to injustice. Mutual understanding of the importance of both is essential. The codes of ethics of the helping professions include both service to individuals and work for justice, but in our individualistic society the work for justice has often been neglected.

Second, the nature of social structures and of structural/systemic change is often talked about but seems to be mostly misunderstood. People say: "That's just the way it is. I can't do anything about it." We live our lives as unique persons, but within interpersonal networks of association. From these networks we learn who we are; within them we are nurtured and socialized. Most people's concern stops at the edge of these interpersonal relationships, the data shows.

But we are also living our personal and interpersonal lives within sets of social structures, social systems. These are the result of the values, goals, and history of our culture. These are human institutions, created by human beings, and so they can be changed by human beings also—taking various amounts of time and through various kinds of actions. Rational analysis of how social structures support or work against the common good requires knowledge. And here the expertise of social scientists, social workers, social psychologists, and others in the helping professions is essential.

For our purposes here, let us remind ourselves about what social structures actually include. For example, we can name the following: acceptable attitudes, customary social behavior, legally enforced policies, governmental and other programs, voluntary groups, media emphases, religious values, and cultural traditions. These structures express social values of the past and present. Insofar as they violate the norms of social justice, do not foster the values of a socially just society, social transformation is necessary.

Social structures are essential for life in society, but some social structures/systems are called "sinful" because they embody evil in the way that sinful deeds of individuals do. They originated in individual greed and thirst for power, and now we are socialized to them. Sinful social structures include those which destroy life (abortion, capital punishment, war); violate human dignity (poverty, torture); facilitate selfishness and greed (patterns of compensation, status symbols); perpetuate inequality and inequity (racist and sexist hiring practices, laws which discriminate against the mentally ill); fragment human community (patterns of domination, segregation); and hinder ecological sustainability (materialism, pollution) (Kammer, 2004). These social structures, then, need to be changed, and that is the business of social justice.

Third, if we are to help develop the habit of ethical decision-making for social responsibility, a method is useful. Building this kind of method regularly into our pedagogy and ways of operating could strengthen our preparation of graduates, who though they have been socialized to individualism, will be prepared to lead and influence ethically, not only personally, but in an ethic of social responsibility.

A model that is used in the development of Catholic social teaching, often called the "pastoral circle," is based on the pedagogy of Paolo Freire (1974) and is a model for individual and group discernment, for empowerment of people to take effective actions in response to injustices, given their own circumstances. It is also a method for individual discernment of how to integrate values and action, of how to act with personal integrity. The model/method has four moments (Hofbauer, Kinsella, and Miller, 1983):

- Reflection on Experience of injustice of some kind comes first. This can be my own experience or that of others, experienced through literature, art, or drama as well as through immersion of some kind. The aim is to arouse compassion, engage the habits of the heart, to direct the virtue of love for others into action for justice.

- Social Analysis of the situation of injustice involves engaging in rational analysis of the causes of the situation and of alternative solutions. It utilizes the world of scholars from various perspectives who have investigated the reality and the potential alternatives. It enables one to understand, with the people involved, the reality being experienced and the assets they have to bring to its solution.
- Moral Judgment involves an application of social ethical guidelines to the situation as experienced and analyzed. It formally brings the moral values into the decision-making process.
- Action Planning brings the individual or group to a realistic, rational, and principled decision. It calls for putting the previous three sets of elements together in order to come to a decision about a course of action that is likely to produce the desired change. It calls for a realistic assessment of the available resources and assignments for action.

This method will lead to a habit of thought and a practice of virtue that integrates compassion/love, rational analysis of the situation and alternatives, moral judgment in accord with one's values, and an action plan that has the probability of being effective in moving toward greater societal justice. All elements are needed for social justice.

As we reflect on action for social justice we might ask: *Could we use this model more widely as a way to teach habits of the heart and mind which prepare ourselves to lead and influence in an ethic grounded in social responsibility?*

Many Action Roles for Social Justice

Turning now to the question of the different ways to work for justice, we confront the fact that when people think about "social justice" they usually think of demonstrating, marching, or political action of some kind. That kind of thinking lets them off the hook, because they can say "that is not my thing!" So thinking about social change as a long-term process, involving many kinds of action is empowering to people, enabling them to think of ways in which they can be part of developing the political will for change, given their own passions, responsibilities, and talents and given their own sphere of influence.

There are different theories about social change and how it happens. Social change theorists (historians, social psychologists, sociologists, political scientists), have pointed out that it can happen linearly, according to plans; cyclically, in some kind of regular fashion; violently, through escalating the conflict. Physicist Fritjof Capra (1982) says we should apply the understandings of quantum physics to social change and recognize that social change takes place when there are enough pockets of energy in various places to create real social change, a "Big Bang."

British economist James Robertson applied this theory to social systems (1979). He pointed out the way to what he called a "SHE" future, a sane, humane, and ecological future, a vision of a socially just future that would square with the kind of social transformation that many would advocate. Robertson argued out that, if enough people in small groups in enough places have a *new intentionality* (a vision of a socially just world) and act accordingly, this will generate systemic change in the direction of social justice. He described a group of *action roles* to be carried out in light of the *new intentionality* (charity / virtue of social justice / vision of a better world). All of these roles are necessary. No one of them is sufficient by itself, but together they will bring change when enough groups of people act out of them. By thinking about all of these action roles one can get a glimpse of a community on the move. And this generates motivation to act for social justice.

As the often-quoted words of anthropologist Margaret Mead put it: "Never doubt that a small group of thoughtful, committed citizens can change the world. Indeed it's the only thing that ever has."

Robertson posits eight necessary and all-together sufficient *actions*. With the *new intentionality*, a social justice focus, someone must be involved in each of them. Consider some examples for student life and beyond.

- Study and teaching—Everyone needs a habit of life-long learning about the world around them, and some will be involved in research and teaching with a worldview motivated by love and concern for the whole human family—especially the poor and powerless in society. Can we further develop action research projects that focus on making local communities more socially just? Can we include consideration of social structures in more of our work for classes and events? Can we continue deeper conversations to probe into the many faces of social justice?
- Building a new value system—This means developing a set of priorities in which social justice values have become more attractive than individualistic ones. For example: People are more important than things. What I have is a gift and it must be shared with others. Conflicts can't be resolved by violence. This requires creative thinking and acting by parents, pastors, artists, poets, educators—all those whose work influences value formation, especially in the young. Can we more regularly model community in the way we act together, towards one another? Can we find ways to help ourselves and young children learn new ways of living unselfishly? Can we learn habits of sharing our various resources in light of the difficult choices to be made among competing priorities?
- Making life-style choices consonant with what a socially just world requires—This means recognizing that we in the U.S.A. have an

overabundant life-style, that some redistribution is necessary (as well as empowerment of the poor to help themselves). It means recognizing that the ecology of our earth requires us to live in less resource-using, less environmentally damaging ways. Can we model this in our own use of resources—recycling, reusing, restoring? Can we adopt less resource-using ways of celebrating? What about wasted food at our parties and other events?

- Fostering alternatives to current systems—Some of us have to be about creating new alternatives. (For example, the Sisters of St. Joseph created a system of free clinics to better meet the health needs of the underserved.) And some of us have to do the advertising, telling others about them and carrying them on when the founders move on to other works. Can we develop habits of always learning about solutions as well as problems, encouraging creative thinking and acting for social transformation? Can we use all the means at our disposal to share stories of people who have contributed to the common good? Can we use our own talents to learn how to be innovators?

- Transforming existing institutions from within—Some of us have to be about introducing social justice questions and patterns of behavior within existing institutions—schools, parishes, agencies, businesses, then these changes will ripple out beyond into other settings. For example, laws mandating working with people of color, reduced negative attitudes, increased familiarity. Can we be attentive to the implications among groups when considering practices and policies? Can we ensure that those who will be affected by decisions participate in some way in the making of them? Can we model community more fully in the way we act with others, eliminating unnecessary hierarchies and antagonisms?

- Participating in speaking truth to power—Some of us (most of us?) have to be active in groups that specifically work on actions for social change in political and corporate power. Memberships in Pax Christi, Green America, Bread for the World, Church World Service, Corporate Accountability, and/or NETWORK: National Catholic Social Justice Lobby are all important ways that we can be aware of petitions to be signed, letters to be written, lobbying to be done in support of social justice. These groups have newsletters to keep members informed and aware of effective ways to collaborate in effective action for change. Through exercising our citizenship by voting, communication with elected officials about issues, and holding them accountable, we also speak the truth to power. Can we incorporate into our own life active membership in some group organized for social change, contributing our insights and experience? Can we share our experience in our own spheres of influence in order to swell the numbers of persons aware and active? Can we find new ways to revitalize the sense of citizenship in our circles of influence?

- Stand in opposition to all that goes in the wrong direction—Some of us need to take part in prayer vigils and demonstrations that say "No" to injustice. Participating in boycotts, writing letters to the editor, op-ed pieces for newspapers, calling radio talk shows to express opposition, all these work to build political will for justice. Can we learn more and practice non-violent ways of settling conflict? Can we learn to model the art of disagreeing without being disagreeable in our dealings with one another? Can we learn to respect those who hold different points of view, while we rationally oppose their position?
- Live out of a justice-oriented spirituality—More and more writers are dealing with spirituality of all kinds, and the interest in spirituality is growing. Religious writers are showing how medieval and current mystics united their spirituality with their work for justice. Examples are Thomas Merton and Dorothy Day as well as medieval saints like Catherine of Siena (Rakoczy, 2006). Contemplation, a reflective spirit, and action for justice are inherently linked. The work for justice is never finished and the spirit must be continually nourished. The help of God, however we name the transcendent power, is critical. And the work for justice has to become an integral part of one's identity. Can we embody a reflective spirit within our lives, making room for development of the virtue of social justice, rooted in love for "the dear neighbor without distinction"? Can we develop the spiritual sources of patience and a sense of the common good that action for justice requires? Whatever our spirituality, can we collaborate, with a new intentionality, to overcome extreme individualism in order to lead and influence in a spirit of social responsibility?

Thinking about the many faces of social justice and the many action roles to bring it about, no one can say there is nothing she or he can do. And considering the eight action roles (all necessary and none sufficient in itself) gives us a glimpse of the power of a community on the move and adds to our understanding of Margaret Mead's statement about social change from the bottom up.

In summary, I have aimed to show: the power of the potential synergy for social transformation among a group of people committed to developing an ethic of social responsibility; the importance of developing that synergy at this point in human history; and the rich panoply of perspectives, expertise, and experience available to us. May we all be emboldened by these convictions to continue the conversation and the work for social justice, taking heart from Margaret Wheatley's words (2009, p. 26):

I have seen that there is not a more powerful way to initiate significant change than to convene a conversation. When a community of people discover that they share a concern, change begins. There is no power equal to a community discovering what it cares about.

References

Baum, Gregory. *Compassion and Solidarity: The Church for Others.* New York: Paulist Press, 1990.

Capra, Fritjof. *The Turning Point.* New York: Bantam Books, 1982.

Curran, Charles E. *Catholic Social Teaching 1891–Present: A Historical, Theological, and Ethical Analysis.* Washington, D.C.: Georgetown University Press, 2002, 188–198.

De Tocqueville, Alexis. *Democracy in America.* Trans. and eds., Harvey C. Mansfield, Delba Winthrop. Chicago: University of Chicago Press, 2000.

Falk, Richard. *Predatory Globalization: A Critique.* Ardsley, NY: Transnational Publishers, 1998.

Freire, Paulo. *Pedagogy of the Oppressed.* New York: Continuum. Seabury Press, 1974.

Glendon, Mary Ann. *A World Made New: Eleanor Roosevelt and the Universal Declaration of Human Rights.* New York: Random House, 2001.

Hofbauer, Rita, Dorothy Kinsella, and Amata Miller. *Making Social Analysis Useful.* Washington, D.C.: Leadership Conference of Women Religious, 1983.

Hollenbach, David. "Modern Catholic Teachings Concerning Justice." *The Faith That Does Justice: Examining the Christian Sources for Social Change.* John Haughey, Ed. New York: Paulist Press, 1977, 207–231.

Kammer, Fred, S. J. *Doing Faithjustice: An Introduction to Catholic Social Thought.* (Revised Edition). New York: Paulist Press, 2004, 205.

Massaro, Thomas, S. J. *Living Justice: Catholic Social Teaching in Action.* Franklin, WI: Sheed & Ward, 2000, 104–07,

National Conference of Catholic Bishops. *Economic Justice for All: Pastoral Letter on Catholic Social Teaching and the U.S. Economy.* Washington, D.C.: United States Catholic Conference, 1986, par. 68–76.

Obama, Barack. "Transcript: Barack Obama's Inaugural Address." The *New York Times.* (January 20, 2009).

Polish, Daniel, and Eugene Fisher (eds). *Liturgical Foundations of Social Policy in the Catholic and Jewish Traditions.* Notre Dame, IN: University of Notre Dame Press, 1983.

Rakoczy, Susan. *Great Mystics and Social Justice: Walking in the Two Feet of Love.* New York: Paulist Press, 2006.

Roberston, James. *The Sane Alternative.* St. Paul, MN: River Basin Press, 1979.

Sawhill, Isabel (ed). "Overview." *Challenge to Leadership: Economic and Social Issues for the Next Decade.* Washington, D.C.: Urban Institute, 1988, 3–4.

Schubeck, Thomas L. *Love That Does Justice.* Maryknoll, NY: Orbis Press, 2007.

Smith, Kenneth L., Ira G. Zepp Jr. *Search for the Beloved Community: The Thinking of Martin Luther King Jr.* Valley Forge, PA: Judson Press, 1998, 29–41.

Soros, George. "The Capitalist Threat." *Atlantic Monthly* (Feb. 1977), 45–58.

Walzer, Michael. *Spheres of Justice: A Defense of Pluralism and Equality.* New York: Basic Books, 1983.

Wheatley, Margaret J. *Turning to One Another: Simple Conversations to Restore Hope to the Future.* (2nd ed.) San Francisco, CA: Berrett-Koehler Publishers, 2009.

Iris Marion Young (1949–2006) held a PhD in philosophy and was professor of political science at the University of Chicago, affiliated with that institution's Center for Gender Studies and its Human Rights program. Author of six books, Young's scholarship in contemporary theories of justice, democracy and difference, feminist political theory, ethics and international affairs, gender, race, and public policy has been translated into several languages. She lectured widely around the world and held fellowships at universities in Germany, Austria, South Africa, and Australia. This selection, from a recent anthology of diversity and social justice readings, traces five different facets of oppression. Is the systemic nature of oppression visible in each face? What happens when individuals or groups experience multiple faces of oppression? Do Young's categories contribute to our understanding of multiple types of privilege as well?

Five Faces of Oppression

Iris Marion Young

Many people in the United States would not choose the term *oppression* to name injustice in our society. For contemporary emancipatory social movements, on the other hand—socialists, radical feminists, American Indian activists, black activists, gay and lesbian activists—oppression is a central category of political discourse. Entering the political discourse in which oppression is a central category involves adopting a general mode of analyzing and evaluating social structures and practices which is incommensurate with the language of liberal individualism that dominates political discourse in the United States.

A major political project for those of us who identify with at least one of these movements must thus be to persuade people that the discourse of oppression makes sense of much of our social experience. We are ill prepared for this task, however, because we have no clear account of the meaning of oppression.

In this chapter I offer some explanation of the concept of oppression as I understand its use by new social movements in the United States since the 1960s. My starting point is reflection on the conditions of the groups said by these movements to be oppressed: among others women, Blacks, Chicanos, Puerto Ricans and other Spanish-speaking Americans, American Indians, Jews, lesbians and gay men, Arabs, Asians, old people, working-class people, and the physically and mentally disabled. I aim to systematize the meaning of the concept of oppression as used by these diverse political movements, and to provide normative argument to clarify the wrongs the term names.

Obviously the above-named groups are not oppressed to the same extent or in the same ways. In the most general sense, all oppressed people suffer some inhibition of their ability to develop and exercise their capacities and express their needs, thoughts, and feelings. In that abstract sense all oppressed people face a common condition. Beyond that, in any more specific sense, it is not possible to define a single set of criteria that describe the condition of oppression of the above groups. Consequently, attempts by theorists and activists to discover a common description or the essential causes of the oppression of all these groups have frequently led to fruitless disputes about whose oppression is more fundamental or more grave. The contexts in which members of these groups use the term *oppression* to describe the injustices of their situation suggest that oppression names in fact a family of concepts and conditions, which I divide into five categories: exploitation, marginalization, powerlessness, cultural imperialism, and violence.

In this chapter I explicate each of these forms of oppression. . . .

Oppression as a Structural Concept

One reason that many people would not use the term *oppression* to describe injustice in our society is that they do not understand the term in the same way as do new social movements. In its traditional usage, oppression means the exercise of tyranny by a ruling group.

Oppression also traditionally carries a strong connotation of conquest and colonial domination. The Hebrews were oppressed in Egypt, and many uses of the term oppression in the West invoke this paradigm. . . . New left social movements of the 1960s and 1970s, however, shifted the meaning of the concept of oppression. In its new usage, oppression designates the disadvantage and injustice some people suffer not because a tyrannical power coerces them, but because of the everyday practices of a well-intentioned liberal society. . . .

Oppression refers to systemic constraints on groups that are not necessarily the result of the intentions of a tyrant. Oppression in this sense is structural, rather than the result of a few people's choices or policies. Its causes are embedded in unquestioned norms, habits, and symbols, in the assumptions underlying institutional rules and the collective consequences of following those rules. It names, as Marilyn Frye puts it, "an enclosing structure of forces and barriers which tends to the immobilization and reduction of a group or category of people" (1983, 11). In this extended structural sense, oppression refers to the vast and deep injustices some groups suffer as a consequence of often unconscious assumptions and reactions of well meaning people in ordinary interactions, media and cultural stereotypes, and structural features of bureaucratic hierarchies and market mechanisms—in short, the normal processes of everyday life. We cannot eliminate this structural oppression by getting rid of the rulers or making some new laws, because oppressions are systematically reproduced in major economic, political, and cultural institutions. . . .

I do not mean to suggest that within a system of oppression individual persons do not intentionally harm others in oppressed groups. The raped woman, the beaten Black youth, the locked-out worker, the gay man harassed on the street, are victims of intentional actions by identifiable agents. I also do not mean to deny that specific groups are beneficiaries of the oppression of other groups, and thus have an interest in their continued oppression. Indeed, for every oppressed group there is a group that is privileged in relation to that group. . . .

Racism, sexism, ageism, homophobia, some social movements asserted, are distinct forms of oppression with their own dynamics apart from those of class, even though they may interact with class oppression. From often heated discussions among socialists, feminists, and antiracism activists in the last ten years, a consensus is emerging that many different groups must be said to be oppressed in our society, and that no single form of oppression can be assigned causal or moral primacy (see Gottlieb 1987). The same discussion has also led to the recognition that group differences cut across individual lines in a multiplicity of ways that can entail privilege and oppression for the same person in different respects. Only a plural explication of the concept of oppression can adequately capture these insights.

Accordingly, I offer below an explication of five faces of oppression as a useful set of categories and distinctions which I believe is comprehensive in the sense that it covers all the groups said by new left social movements to be oppressed, and all the ways they are oppressed. I derive the five faces of oppression from reflection on the condition of these groups. Because different factors, or combinations of factors, constitute the oppression of different groups, making their oppression irreducible, I believe it is not possible to give one essential definition of oppression. The five categories articulated in this chapter, however, are adequate to describe the oppression of any group, as well as its similarities with and differences from the oppression of other groups. But first we must ask what a "group" is.

The Concept of a Social Group

. . . A social group is a collective of persons differentiated from at least one other group by cultural forms, practices, or way of life. Members of a group have a specific affinity with one another because of their similar experience (or way of life), which prompts them to associate with one another more than with those not identified with the group. Groups are an expression of social relations; a group exists only in relation to at least one other group. Group identification arises, that is, in the encounter and interaction between social collectivities that experience some differences in their way of life and forms of association, even if they also regard themselves as belonging to the same society.

As long as they associated solely among themselves, for example, an American Indian group thought of themselves only as "the people." The encounter with other American Indians created an awareness of difference; the others were named as a group, and the first group came to see themselves as a group. But social groups do not arise only from an encounter between different societies. Social processes also differentiate groups within a single society. The sexual division of labor, for example, has created social groups of women and men in all known societies. Members of each gender have a certain affinity with others in their group because of what they do or experience, and differentiate themselves from the other gender, even when members of each gender consider that they have much in common with members of the other, and consider that they belong to the same society. . . .

A social group is defined not primarily by a set of shared attributes, but by a sense of identity. What defines Black Americans as a social group is not primarily their skin color; some persons whose skin color is fairly light, for example, identify themselves as black. Though sometimes objective attributes are a necessary condition for classifying oneself or others as belonging to a certain social group, it is identification with a certain social status, the common history that social status produces, and self-identification that define the group as a group. . . .

Groups constitute individuals. A person's particular sense of history, affinity, and separateness—even the person's mode of reasoning, evaluating, and expressing feeling—are constituted partly by her or his group affinities. This does not mean that persons have no individual styles, or are unable to transcend or reject a group identity. Nor does it preclude persons from having many aspects that are independent of these group identities. . . .

A person joins an association, and even if membership in it fundamentally affects one's life, one does not take that membership to define one's very identity, in the way, for example, being Navaho might. Group affinity, on the other hand, has the character of what Martin Heidegger (1962) calls "throwness": one *finds oneself* as a member of a group, which one experiences as always already having been. For our identities are defined in relation to how others identify us, and they do so in terms of groups which are always already associated with specific attributes, stereotypes, and norms.

From the throwness of group affinity it does not follow that one cannot leave groups and enter new ones. Many women become lesbian after first identifying as heterosexual. Anyone who lives long enough becomes old.

These cases exemplify throwness precisely because such changes in group affinity are experienced as transformations in one's identity. Nor does it follow from the throwness of group affinity that one cannot define the meaning of group identity for oneself; those who identify with a group can redefine the meaning and norms of group identity. . . . While groups may come into being, they are never founded.

Groups, I have said, exist only in relation to other groups. A group may be identified by outsiders without those so identified having any specific consciousness of themselves as a group. Sometimes a group comes to exist only because one group excludes and labels a category of persons, and those labeled come to understand themselves as group members only slowly, on the basis of their shared oppression. In Vichy France, for example, Jews who had been so assimilated that they had no specifically Jewish identity were marked as Jews by others and given a specific social status by them. These people "discovered" themselves as Jews, and then formed a group identity and affinity with one another (see Sartre 1948). A person's group identities may be for the most part only a background or horizon to his or her life, becoming salient only in specific interactive contexts.

Some people think that social groups are invidious fictions, essentializing arbitrary attributes. From this point of view problems of prejudice, stereotyping, discrimination, and exclusion exist because some people mistakenly believe that group identification makes a difference to the capacities, temperament, or virtues of group members. This individualist conception of persons and their relation to one another tends to identify oppression with group identification. Oppression, on this view, is something that happens to people when they are classified in groups. Because others identify them as a group, they are excluded and despised. Eliminating oppression thus requires eliminating groups. People should be treated as individuals, not as members of groups, and allowed to form their lives freely with stereotypes or group norms.

This chapter takes issue with that position. While I agree that individuals should be free to pursue life plans in their own ways, it is foolish to deny the reality of groups. Despite the modern myth of a decline of parochial attachments and ascribed identities, in modern society group differentiation remains endemic. As both markets and social administration increase the web of social interdependency on a world scale, and as more people encounter one another as strangers in cities and states, people retain and renew ethnic, locale, age, sex, and occupational group identifications, and form new ones in the processes of encounter (cf. Ross 1980, 19; Rothschild 1981, 130). Even when they belong to oppressed groups, people's group identifications are often important to them, and they often feel a special affinity for others in their group. I believe that group differentiation is both an inevitable and a desirable aspect of modern social processes. Social justice requires not the melting away of differences, but institutions that promote reproduction of and respect for group differences without oppression.

Though some groups have come to be formed out of oppression, and relations of privilege and oppression structure the interactions between many groups, group differentiation is not in itself oppressive. Not all groups are oppressed. In the United States Roman Catholics are a specific social group, with distinct practices and affinities with one another, but they are no longer an oppressed group. Whether a group is oppressed depends on whether it is subject to one or more of the five conditions I shall discuss below. . . .

The Faces of Oppression

Exploitation

The central insight expressed in the concept of exploitation is that this oppression occurs through a steady process of the transfer of the results of the labor of one social group to benefit another. The injustice of class division does not consist only in the distributive fact that some people have great wealth while most people have little (cf. Buchanan 1982, 44–49; Holmstrom 1977). Exploitation enacts a structural relation between social groups. Social rules about what work is, who does what for whom, how work is compensated, and the social processes by which the results of work are appropriated operate to enact relations of power and inequality. These relations are produced and reproduced through a systematic process in which the energies of the have-nots are continuously expended to maintain and augment the power, status, and wealth of the haves. . . .

Feminists have had little difficulty showing that women's oppression consists partly in a systematic and unreciprocated transfer of powers from women to men. Women's oppression consists not merely in an inequality of status, power, and wealth resulting from men's excluding them from privileged activities. The freedom, power, status, and self-realization of men is possible precisely because women work for them. Gender exploitation has two aspects: transfer of the fruits of material labor to men, and the transfer of nurturing and sexual energies to men.

Christine Delphy (1984), for example, describes marriage as a class relation in which women's labor benefits men without comparable remuneration. She makes it clear that the exploitation consists not in the sort of work that women do in the home, for this might include various kinds of tasks, but in the fact that they perform tasks for someone on whom they are dependent. Thus, for example, in most systems of agriculture production in the world, men take to market the goods women have produced, and more often than not men receive the status and often the entire income from this labor.

With the concept of sex-affective production, Ann Ferguson (1984; 1989, chap. 4) identifies another form of the transference of women's energies to men. Women provide men and children with emotional care and provide men with sexual satisfaction, and as a group receive relatively little of either from men (cf. Brittan and Maynard 1984, 142–48). The gender socialization of women makes us tend to be more attentive to interactive dynamics than men, and makes women good at providing empathy and support for people's feelings and at smoothing over interactive tensions. Both men and women look to women as nurturers of their personal lives, and women frequently complain that when they look to men for emotional support they do not receive it (Easton, 1978). The norms of heterosexuality, moreover, are oriented around male pleasure, and consequently, many women receive little satisfaction from their sexual interactions with men (Gottlieb, 1984).

Most feminist theories of gender exploitation have concentrated on the institutional structure of the patriarchal family. Recently, however, feminists have begun to explore relations of gender exploitation enacted in the contemporary workplace and through the state. Carol Brown argues that as men have removed themselves from responsibility for children, many women have become dependent on the state for subsistence as they continue to bear nearly total responsibility of child rearing (Brown 1981; cf. Boris and Bardaglio 1983; and A. Ferguson 1984). This creates a new system of the exploitation of women's domestic labor mediated by state institutions, which Brown calls public patriarchy.

In twentieth-century capitalist economies the workplaces that women have been entering in increasing numbers serve as another important site of gender exploitation. David Alexander (1987) argues that typically feminine jobs involve gender-based tasks requiring sexual labor, nurturing, caring for others' bodies, or smoothing over workplace tensions. In these ways women's energies are expended in jobs that enhance the status of, please, or comfort others, usually men; and these gender-based labors of waitresses, clerical workers, nurses, and other caretakers often go unnoticed and undercompensated.

To summarize, women are exploited in the Marxist sense to the degree that they are wage workers. Some have argued that women's domestic labor also represents a form of capitalist class exploitation insofar as it is labor covered by the wages a family receives. As a group, however, women undergo specific forms of gender exploitation in which their energies and power are expended, often unnoticed and unacknowledged, usually to benefit men by releasing them for more important and creative work, enhancing their status or the environment around them, or providing them with sexual or emotional service. . . .

Is it possible to conceptualize a form of exploitation that is racially specific on analogy with the gender-specific forms just discussed? I suggest that the category of *menial* labor might supply a means for such conceptualization. In its derivation, "menial" designates the labor of servants. Wherever there is racism, there is the assumption, more or less enforced, that members of the oppressed racial groups are or ought to be servants of those, or some of those, in the privileged group. In most white racist societies this means that many white people have dark- or yellow-skinned domestic servants, and in the United States today there remains significant racial structuring of private household service. But in the United States today much service labor has gone public: anyone who goes to a good hotel or a good restaurant can have servants. Servants often attend the daily—and nightly—activities of business executives, government officials, and other high-status professionals. In our society there remains strong cultural pressure to fill servant jobs—bellhop, porter, chambermaid, busboy, and so on—with Black and Latino workers. These jobs entail a transfer of energies whereby the servers enhance the status of the served.

Menial labor usually refers not only to service, however, but also to any servile, unskilled, low-paying work lacking in autonomy, in which a person is subject to taking orders from many people. Menial work tends to be auxiliary work, instrumental to the work of others, where those others receive primary recognition for doing the job. Laborers on a construction site, for example, are at the beck and call of welders, electricians, carpenters, and other skilled workers, who receive recognition for the job done. In the United States explicit racial discrimination once reserved menial work for Blacks, Chicanos, American Indians, and Chinese, and menial work still tends to be linked to Black and Latino workers (Symanski 1985). I offer this category of menial labor as a form of racially specific exploitation, as a provisional category in need of exploration. . . .

The injustice of exploitation consists in social processes that bring about a transfer of energies from one group to another to produce unequal distributions, and in the way in which social institutions enable a few to accumulate while they constrain many more. The injustices of exploitation cannot be eliminated by the redistribution of goods, for as long as institutionalized practices and structural relations remain unaltered, the process of transfer will re-create an unequal distribution of benefits. Bringing about justice where there is exploitation requires reorganization of institutions and practices of decisionmaking, alteration of the division of labor, and similar measures of institutional, structural, and cultural change.

Marginalization

Increasingly in the United States, racial oppression occurs in the form of marginalization rather than exploitation. *Marginals* are people the system of labor cannot or will not use. Not only in Third World capitalist countries, but also in most Western capitalist societies, there is a growing underclass of people permanently confined to lives of social marginality, most of whom are racially marked—Blacks or Indians in Latin America, and Blacks, East Indians, Eastern Europeans, or North Africans in Europe.

Marginalization is by no means the fate only of racially marked groups, however. In the United States a shamefully large proportion of the population is marginal: old people, and increasingly people who are not very old but get laid off from their jobs and cannot find new work; young people, especially Black or Latino, who cannot find first or second jobs; many single mothers and their children; other people involuntarily unemployed; many mentally and physically disabled people; American Indians (especially those on reservations).

Marginalization is perhaps the most dangerous form of oppression. A whole category of people is expelled from useful participation in social life and thus potentially subjected to severe material deprivation and even extermination. The material deprivation marginalization often causes is certainly unjust, especially in a society where others have plenty. Contemporary advanced capitalist societies have in principle acknowledged the injustice of material deprivation caused by marginalization, and have taken some steps to address it by providing welfare payments and services. The continuance of this welfare state is by no means assured, and in most welfare state societies, especially the United States, welfare redistributions do not eliminate large-scale suffering and deprivation.

Material deprivation, which can be addressed by redistributive social policies, is not, however, the extent of the harm caused by marginalization. Two categories of injustice beyond distribution are associated with marginality in advanced capitalist societies. First, the provision of welfare itself produces new injustice by depriving those dependent on it of rights and freedoms that others have. Second, even when material deprivation is somewhat mitigated by the welfare state, marginalization is unjust because it blocks the opportunity to exercise capacities in socially defined and recognized ways. I shall explicate each of these in turn.

Liberalism has traditionally asserted the right of all rational autonomous agents to equal citizenship. Early bourgeois liberalism explicitly excluded from citizenship all those whose reason was questionable or not fully developed, and all those not independent (Pateman 1988, chap. 3; cf. Bowles and Gintis 1986, chap. 2). Thus, poor people, women, the mad and the feebleminded, and children were explicitly excluded from citizenship, and many of these were housed in institutions modeled on the modern prison: poorhouses, insane asylums, schools.

Today the exclusion of dependent persons from equal citizenship rights is only barely hidden beneath the surface. Because they depend on bureaucratic institutions for support or services, the old, the poor, and the mentally or physically disabled are subject to patronizing, punitive, demeaning, and arbitrary treatment by the policies and people associated with welfare bureaucracies. Being a "dependent" in our society implies being legitimately subject to the often arbitrary and invasive authority of social service providers and other public and private administrators who enforce rules with which the marginal must comply, and otherwise exercise power over the conditions of their lives. In meeting the needs of the marginalized, often with the aid of social scientific disciplines, welfare agencies also construct the needs themselves. Medical and social service professionals know what is good for those they serve, and the marginals and dependents themselves do not have the right to claim to know what is good for them (Fraser 1987a; K. Ferguson 1984, chap. 4). Dependency in our society thus implies, as it has in all liberal societies, a sufficient warrant to suspend basic rights to privacy, respect, and individual choice.

Although dependency produces conditions of injustice in our society, dependency in itself need not be oppressive. One cannot imagine a society in which some people would not need to be dependent on others at least some of the time: children, sick people, women recovering from childbirth, old people who have become frail, depressed or otherwise emotionally needy persons have the moral right to depend on others for subsistence and support.

An important contribution of feminist moral theory has been to question the deeply held assumption that moral agency and full citizenship require that a person be autonomous and independent. Feminists have exposed this assumption as inappropriately individualistic and derived from a specifically male experience of social relations, which values competition and solitary achievement (see Gilligan 1982; Friedman 1985). Female experience of social relations, arising both from women's typical domestic care responsibilities and from the kinds of paid work that many women do, tends to recognize dependence as a basic human condition (cf. Hartsock, 1983, chap. 10). Whereas on the autonomy model a just society would, as much as possible, give people the opportunity to be independent, the feminist model envisions justice as according respect and participation in decision making to those who are dependent as well as to those who are independent (Held 1987b). Dependency should not be a reason to be deprived of choice and respect, and much of the oppression many marginals experience would be lessened if a less individualistic model of rights prevailed.

Marginalization does not cease to be oppressive when one has shelter and food. Many old people, for example, have sufficient means to live comfortably but remain oppressed in their marginal status. Even if marginals were provided a comfortable material life within institutions that respected their freedom and dignity, injustices of marginality would remain in the form of uselessness, boredom, and lack of self-respect. Most of our society's productive and recognized activities take place in contexts of organized social cooperation, and social structures and processes that close persons out of such social cooperation are unjust. Thus, while marginalization definitely entails serious issues of distributive justice, it also involves the deprivation of cultural, practical, and institutionalized conditions for exercising capacities in a context of recognition and interaction.

The fact of marginalization raises basic structural issues of justice, in particular concerning the appropriateness of a connection between participation in production activities of social cooperation on the one hand, and access to the means of consumption on the other. As marginalization is increasing with no sign of abatement, some social policy analysts have introduced the idea of *social wage* as a guaranteed socially provided income not tied to the wage system. Restructuring of productive activity to address a right of participation, however, implies organizing some socially productive activity outside of the wage system (see Offe 1985, 95–100), through public works of self-employed collectives.

Powerlessness

As I have indicated, the Marxist idea of class is important because it helps reveal the structure of exploitation: that some people have their power and wealth because they profit from the labor of others. For this reason I reject the claim some make that a traditional class exploitation model fails to capture the structure of contemporary society. It remains the case that the labor of most people in the society augments the power of relatively few. Despite their differences from nonprofessional workers, most professional workers are still not members of the capitalist class. Professional labor either involves exploitative transfers to capitalists or supplies important conditions for such transfers. Professional workers are in an ambiguous class position, it is true, because they also benefit from the exploitation of nonprofessional workers.

While it is false to claim that a division between capitalist and working classes no longer describes our society, it is also false to say that class relations have remained unaltered since the nineteenth century. An adequate conception of oppression cannot ignore the experience of social division reflected in the colloquial distinction between the "middle class" and the "working class," a division structured by the social division of labor between professionals and nonprofessionals. Professionals are privileged in relation to nonprofessionals by virtue of their position in the division of labor and the status it carries. Nonprofessionals suffer a form of oppression in addition to exploitation, which I call *powerlessness*.

In the United States, as in other advanced capitalist countries, most workplaces are not organized democratically, direct participation in public policy decisions is rare, and policy implementation is for the most part hierarchical, imposing rules on bureaucrat and citizens. Thus, most people in these societies do not regularly participate in making decisions that affect the conditions of their lives and actions, and in this sense most people lack significant power. At the same time, domination in modern society is enacted through the widely dispersed powers of many agents mediating the decisions of others. To that extent many people have some power in relation to others, even though they lack the power to decide policies or results. The powerless are those who lack authority or power even in this mediated sense, those over whom power is exercised without their exercising it; the powerless are situated so that they must take orders and rarely have the right to give them. Powerlessness also designates a position in the division of labor and the concomitant social position that allows persons little opportunity to develop and exercise skills. The powerless have little or no work autonomy; exercise little creativity or judgment in their work; have no technical expertise or authority; express themselves awkwardly, especially in public or bureaucratic settings; and do not command respect. Powerlessness names the oppressive situations Sennett and Cobb (1972) describe in their famous study of working-class men.

This powerless status is perhaps best described negatively: the powerless lack the authority, status, and sense of self that professionals tend to have. The status privilege of professionals has three aspects, the lack of which produces oppression for nonprofessionals.

First, acquiring and practicing a profession has an expansive, progressive character. Being professional usually requires a college education and the acquisition of a specialized knowledge that entails working with symbols and concepts. Professionals experience progress first in acquiring the expertise, and then in the course of professional advancement and rise in status. The life of the nonprofessional by comparison is powerless in the sense that it lacks this orientation toward the progressive development of capacities and avenues for recognition.

Second, while many professionals have supervisors and cannot directly influence many decisions or the actions of many people, most nevertheless have considerable day-to-day work autonomy. Professionals usually have some authority over others, moreover—either over workers they supervise, or over auxiliaries or clients. Nonprofessionals, on the other hand, lack autonomy, and in both their working and their consumer/client lives often stand under the authority of professionals.

Though based on a division of labor between "mental" and "manual" work, the distinction between "middle class" and "working class" designates a division not only in working life, but also in nearly all aspects of social life. Professionals and nonprofessionals belong to different cultures in the United States. The two groups tend to live in segregated neighborhoods or even different towns, a process itself mediated by planners, zoning officials, and real estate people. The groups tend to have different tastes in food, decor, clothes, music, and vacations, and often different health and educational needs. Members of each group socialize for the most part with others in the same status group. While there is some intergroup mobility between generations, for the most part the children of professionals become professionals and the children of nonprofessionals do not.

Thus, the privileges of the professional extend beyond the workplace to a whole way of life. I call this way of life *respectability*. To treat people with respect is to be prepared to listen to what they have to say or to do what they request because they have some authority, expertise, or influence. The norms of respectability in our society are associated specifically with professional culture. Professional dress, speech, tastes, demeanor all connote respectability. Generally professionals expect and receive respect from others. In restaurants, banks, hotels, real estate offices, and many other such public places, as well as in the media, professionals typically receive more respectful treatment than nonprofessionals. For this reason nonprofessionals seeking a loan or a job, or to buy a house or a car, will often try to look "professional" and "respectable" in those settings.

The privilege of this professional respectability appears starkly in the dynamics of racism and sexism. In daily interchange, women and men of color must prove their respectability. At first they are often not treated by strangers with respectful distance or deference. Once people discover that this woman or that Puerto Rican man is a college teacher or a business executive, however, they often behave more respectfully toward her or him. Working-class white men, on the other hand, are often treated with respect until their working-class status is revealed.

I have discussed several injustices associated with powerlessness: inhibition in the development of one's capacities, lack of decisionmaking power in one's working life, and exposure to disrespectful treatment because of the status one occupies. These injustices have distributional consequences, but are more fundamentally matters of the division of labor. The oppression of powerlessness brings into question the division of labor basic to all industrial societies: the social division between those who plan and those who execute.

Cultural Imperialism

Exploitation, marginalization, and powerlessness all refer to relations of power and oppression that occur by virtue of the social division of labor—who works for whom, who does not work, and how the content of work defines one institutional position relative to others. These three categories refer to structural and institutional relations that delimit people's material lives, including but not restricted to the resources they have access to and the concrete opportunities they have or do not have to develop and exercise their capacities. These kinds of oppression are a matter of concrete power in relation to others—of who benefits from whom, and who is dispensable.

Recent theorists of movements of group liberation, notably feminist and Black liberation theorists, have also given prominence to a rather different form of oppression, which following Lugones and Spelman (1983) I shall call *cultural imperialism*. To experience cultural imperialism means to experience how the dominant meanings of a society render the particular perspective of one's own group invisible at the same time as they stereotype one's group and mark it as the Other.

Cultural imperialism involves the universalization of a dominant group's experience and culture, and its establishment as the norm.... Often without noticing they do so, dominant groups project their own experience as representative of humanity as such. Cultural products also express the dominant group's perspective on and interpretation of events and elements in the society, including other groups in the society, insofar as they attain cultural status at all.

An encounter with other groups, however, can challenge the dominant group's claim to universality; The dominant group reinforces its position by bringing the other groups under the measure of its dominant norms. Consequently, the difference of women from men, American Indians or Africans from Europeans, Jews from Christians, homosexuals from heterosexuals, workers from professionals becomes reconstructed largely as deviance and inferiority. Since only the dominant group's cultural expressions receive wide dissemination, their cultural expressions become the normal, or the universal, and thereby the unremarkable. Given the normality of its own cultural expressions and identity, the dominant group constructs the differences which some groups exhibit as lack and negation. These groups become marked as Other.

The culturally dominated undergo a paradoxical oppression in that they are both marked out by stereotypes and at the same time rendered invisible. As remarkable, deviant beings, the culturally imperialized are stamped with an essence. The stereotypes confine them to a nature which is often attached in some way to their bodies, and which thus cannot easily be denied. These stereotypes so permeate the society that they are not noticed as contestable. Just as everyone knows that the earth goes around the sun, so everyone knows that gay people are promiscuous, that American Indians are alcoholics, and that women are good with children. White males, on the other hand, insofar as they escape group marking, can be individuals.

Those living under cultural imperialism find themselves defined from the outside, positioned, placed, by a network of dominant meanings they experience as arising from elsewhere, from those with whom they do not identify and who do not identify with them. Consequently, the dominant culture's stereotyped and inferiorized images of the group must be internalized by group members at least to the extent that they are forced to react to the behavior of others influenced by those images. This creates for the culturally oppressed the experience that W E. B. Du Bois called "double consciousness"—"this sense of always looking at one's self through the eyes of others, of measuring one's soul by the tape of a world that looks on in amused contempt and pity" (Du Bois 1969, 45). Double consciousness arises when the oppressed subject refuses to coincide with these devalued, objectified, stereotyped visions of herself or himself. While the subject desires recognition as human—capable of activity, full of hope and possibility—she receives from the dominant culture only the judgment that she is different, marked, or inferior.

The group defined by the dominant culture as deviant, as a stereotyped Other, is culturally different from the dominant group, because the status of Otherness creates specific experiences not shared by the dominant group, and because culturally oppressed groups also are often socially segregated and occupy specific positions in the social division of labor. Members of such groups express their specific group experiences and interpretations of the world to one another, developing and perpetuating their own culture. Double consciousness, then, occurs because one finds one's being defined by two cultures: a dominant and a subordinate culture. Because they can affirm and recognize one another as sharing similar experiences and perspectives on social life, people in culturally imperialized groups can often maintain a sense of positive subjectivity.

Cultural imperialism involves the paradox of experiencing oneself as invisible at the same time that one is marked out as different. The invisibility comes about when dominant groups fail to recognize the perspective embodied in their cultural expressions as a perspective. These dominant cultural expressions often simply have little place for the experience of other groups, at most only mentioning or referring to them in stereotyped or marginalized ways. This, then, is the injustice of cultural imperialism: that the oppressed group's own experience and interpretation of social life finds little expression that touches the dominant culture, while that same culture imposes on the oppressed group its experience and interpretation of social life. . . .

Violence

Finally, many groups suffer the oppression of systematic violence. Members of some groups live with the knowledge that they must fear random, on oneself or family or friends deprives the oppressed of freedom and dignity; and needlessly expends their energy.

Violence is a social practice. It is a social given that everyone knows happens and will happen again. It is always at the horizon of social imagination, even for those who do not perpetrate it. According to the prevailing social logic, some circumstances make such violence more "called for" than others. The idea of rape will occur to many men who pick up a hitch-hiking woman; the idea of hounding or teasing a gay man on their dorm floor will occur to many straight male college students. Often several persons inflict the violence together, especially in all-male groupings. Sometimes violators set out looking for people to beat up, rape, or taunt. This rule-bound, social, and often premeditated character makes violence against groups a social practice.

Group violence approaches legitimacy, moreover, in the sense that it is tolerated. Often, third parties find it unsurprising because it happens frequently and lies as a constant possibility at the horizon of the social imagination. Even when they are caught, those who perpetrate acts of group-directed violence or harassment often receive light or no punishment. To that extent society renders their acts acceptable.

An important aspect of random, systemic violence is its irrationality. Xenophobic violence differs from the violence of states or ruling-class repression. Repressive violence has a rational, albeit evil, motive: rulers use it as a coercive tool to maintain their power. Many accounts of racist, sexist, or homophobic violence attempt to explain its motivation as a desire to maintain group privilege or domination. I do not doubt that fear of violence often functions to keep oppressed groups subordinate.

On the contrary, the violation of rape, beating, killing, and harassment of women, people of color, gays, and other marked groups is motivated by fear or hatred of those groups. Sometimes the motive may be a simple will to power, to victimize those marked as vulnerable by the very social fact that they are subject to violence. If so, this motive is secondary in the sense that it depends on a social practice of group violence. Violence-causing fear or hatred of the other at least partly involves insecurities on the part of the violators; its irrationality suggests that unconscious processes are at work.

Cultural imperialism, moreover, itself intersects with violence. The culturally imperialized may reject the dominant meanings and attempt to assert their own subjectivity, or the fact of the cultural difference may put the lie to the dominant culture's implicit claim to universality. The dissonance generated by such a challenge to the hegemonic cultural meanings can also be a source of irrational violence.

Violence is a form of injustice that a distributive understanding of justice seems ill equipped to capture. This may be why contemporary discussions unprovoked attacks on their persons or property, which have no motive but to damage, humiliate, or destroy the person. In American society women, Blacks, Asians, Arabs, gay men, and lesbians live under such threats of violence, and in at least some regions Jews, Puerto Ricans, Chicanos, and other Spanish-speaking Americans must fear such violence as well. Physical violence against these groups is shockingly frequent. Rape crisis center networks estimate that more than one-third of all American women experience an attempted or successful sexual assault in their lifetimes. Manning Marable (1984, 238–41) catalogs a large number of incidents of racist violence and terror against blacks in the United States between 1980 and 1982. He cites dozens of incidents of the severe beating, killing, or rape of Blacks by police officers on duty, in which the police involved were acquitted of any wrongdoing. In 1981, moreover, there were at least five hundred documented cases of random white teenage violence against Blacks. Violence against gay men and lesbians is not only common, but has been increasing in the last five years. While the frequency of physical attack on members of these and other racially or sexually marked groups is very disturbing, I also include in this category less severe incidents of harassment, intimidation, or ridicule simply for the purpose of degrading, humiliating, or stigmatizing group members.

Given the frequency of such violence in our society, why are theories of justice usually silent about it? I think the reason is that theorists do not typically take such incidents of violence and harassment as matters of social injustice. No moral theorist would deny that such acts are very wrong. But unless all immoralities are injustices, they might wonder, why should such acts be interpreted as symptoms of social injustice? Acts of violence or petty harassment are committed by particular individuals, often extremists, deviants, or the mentally unsound. How then can they be said to involve the sorts of institutional issues I have said are properly the subject of justice?

What makes violence a face of oppression is less the particular acts themselves—though these are often utterly horrible—than the social context surrounding them, which makes them possible and even acceptable. What makes violence a phenomenon of social injustice, and not merely an individual moral wrong, is its systemic character, its existence as a social practice.

Violence is systemic because it is directed at members of a group simply because they are members of that group. Any woman, for example, has a reason to fear rape. Regardless of what a Black man has done to escape the oppressions of marginality or powerlessness, he lives knowing he is subject to attack or harassment. The oppression of violence consists not only in direct victimization, but in the daily knowledge shared by all members of oppressed groups that they are *liable* to violation, solely on account of their group identity. Just living under such a threat of attack of justice rarely mention it. I have argued that group-directed violence is institutionalized and systemic. To the degree that institutions and social practices encourage, tolerate, or enable the perpetration of violence against members of specific groups, those institutions and practices are unjust and should be reformed. Such reform may require the redistribution of resources or positions, but in large part can come only through a change in cultural images, stereotypes, and the mundane reproduction of relations of dominance and aversion in the gestures of everyday life.

Applying the Criteria

Social theories that construct oppression as a unified phenomenon usually either leave out groups that even the theorists think are oppressed, or leave out important ways in which groups are oppressed. Black liberation theorists and feminist theorists have argued persuasively, for example, that Marxism's reduction of all oppressions to class oppression leaves out much about the specific oppression of Blacks and women. By pluralizing the category of oppression in the way explained in this chapter, social theory can avoid the exclusive and oversimplifying effects of such reductionism.

I have avoided pluralizing the category in the way some others have done by constructing an account of separate systems of oppression for each oppressed group: racism, sexism, classism, heterosexism, ageism, and so on. There is a double problem with considering each group's oppression a unified and distinct structure or system. On the one hand, this way of conceiving oppression fails to accommodate the similarities and overlaps in the oppressions of different groups. On the other hand, it falsely represents the situation of all group members at the same.

I have arrived at the five faces of oppression—exploitation, marginalization, powerlessness, cultural imperialism, and violence—as the best way to avoid such exclusions and reductions. They function as criteria for determining whether individuals and groups are oppressed, rather than as a full theory of oppression. I believe that these criteria are objective. They provide a means of refuting some people's beliefs that their group is oppressed when it is not, as well as a means of persuading others that a group is oppressed when they doubt it. Each criterion can be operationalized; each can be applied through the assessment of observable behavior, status relationships, distributions, texts, and other cultural artifacts. I have no illusions that such assessments can be value-neutral. But these criteria can nevertheless serve as means of evaluating claims that a group is oppressed, or adjudicating disputes about whether or how a group is oppressed.

The presence of any of these five conditions is sufficient for calling a group oppressed. But different group oppressions exhibit different combinations of these forms, as do different individuals in the groups. Nearly all, if not all, groups said by contemporary social movements to be oppressed suffer cultural imperialism. The other oppressions they experience vary. Working-class people are exploited and powerless, for example, but if employed and white do not experience marginalization and violence. Gay men, on the other hand, are not qua gay exploited or powerless, but they experience severe cultural imperialism and violence. Similarly, Jews and Arabs as groups are victims of cultural imperialism and violence, though many members of these groups also suffer exploitation or powerlessness. Old people are oppressed by marginalization and cultural imperialism, and this is also true of physically and mentally disabled people. As a group, women are subject to gender-based exploitation, powerlessness, cultural imperialism, and violence. Racism in the United States condemns many Blacks and Latinos to marginalization, and puts many more at risk, even though many members of these groups escape that condition; members of these groups often suffer all five forms of oppression.

Applying these five criteria to the situation of groups makes it possible to compare the oppressions without reducing them to a common essence or claiming that one is more fundamental than another. One can compare the ways in which a particular form of oppression appears in different groups. For example, while the operations of cultural imperialism are often experienced in similar fashion by different groups, there are also important differences. One can compare the combinations of oppressions groups experience, or the intensity of those oppressions. Thus, with these criteria one can plausibly claim that one group is more oppressed than another without reducing all oppressions to a single scale. . . .

References

Alexander, David. 1987. "Gendered Job Traits and Women's Occupations." Ph.D. dissertation, University of Massachusetts.

Boris, Ellen and Peter Bardaglio. 1983. "The Transformation of Patriarchy: The Historic Role of the State." In Irene Diamond, ed., *Families, Politics and Public Policy.* New York: Longman.

Bowles, Samuel and Herbert Gintis. 1986. *Democracy and Capitalism.* New York: Basic Books.

Brittan, Arthur and Mary Maynard. 1984. *Sexism, Racism and Oppression.* Oxford: Blackwell.

Brown, Carol. 1981. "Mothers, Fathers and Children: From Private to Public Patriarchy." In Lydia Sargent, ed., *Women and Revolution.* Boston: South End Press.

Buchanan, Allen. 1982. *Marx and Justice.* Totowa, N.J.: Rowman and Allanheld.

Delphy, Christine. 1984. *Close to Home: A Materialist Analysis of Women's Oppression*. Amherst: University of Massachusetts Press.

Du Bois, W. E. B. 1969 [1903]. *The Souls of Black Folk*. New York: New American Library.

Easton, Barbara. 1978. "Feminism and the Contemporary Family." *Socialist Review* 39 (May/June), 11–36.

Ferguson, Ann. 1984. "On Conceiving Motherhood and Sexuality: A Feminist Materialist Approach." In Joyce Trebilcot, ed., *Mothering: Essays in Feminist Theory*. Totowa, N.J.: Rowman and Allanheld.

_____. 1989. *Blood at the Root*. London: Pandora.

Ferguson, Kathy. 1984. *The Feminist Case against Bureaucracy*. Philadelphia: Temple University Press.

Fraser, Nancy. 1987. "Women, Welfare, and the Politics of Need Interpretation." *Hypatia: A Journal of Feminist Philosophy* 2 (Winter), 103–22.

Friedman, Marilyn. 1985. "Care and Context in Moral Reasoning." In Carol Harding, ed., *Moral Dilemmas: Philosophical and Psychological Issues in the Development of Moral Reasoning*. Chicago: Precedent.

Frye, Marilyn. 1983. "Oppression." In *The Politics of Reality*. Trumansburg, N.Y.: Crossing Press.

Gilligan, Carol. 1982. *In a Different Voice*. Cambridge, Mass.: Harvard University Press.

Gottlieb, Rhonda. 1984. "The Political Economy of Sexuality." *Review of Radical Political Economy* 16 (Spring), 143–65.

Gottlieb, Roger. 1987. *History and Subjectivity*. Philadelphia: Temple University Press.

Hartsock, Nancy. 1983. *Money, Sex and Power*. New York: Longman.

Heidegger, Martin. 1962. *Being and Time*. New York: Harper and Row.

Held, Virginia. 1987. "A Non-Contractual Society." In Marsha Hanen and Kai Nielsen, eds., *Science, Morality and Feminist Theory*. Calgary: University of Calgary Press.

Holmstrom, Nancy. 1977. "Exploitation." *Canadian Journal of Philosophy* 7 (June): 353–69.

Lugones, Maria C. and Elizabeth V. Spelman. 1983. "Have We Got a Theory for You! Feminist Theory, Cultural Imperialism and the Demand for 'the Woman's Voice.'" *Women's Studies International Forum* 6, 573–81.

Marable, Manning. 1984. *Race, Reform and Rebellion: The Second Reconstruction in Black America,* 1945–82. Jackson: University Press of Mississippi.

Offe, Claus. 1985. *Disorganized Capitalism*. Cambridge: MIT Press.

Pateman, Carole. 1988. *The Sexual Contract*. Stanford: Stanford University Press.

Ross, Jeffrey. 1980. Introduction to Jeffrey Ross and Ann Baker Cottrell, eds., *The Mobilization of Collective Identity*. Lanham, Md.: University Press of America.

Rothschild, Joseph. 1981. *Ethnopolitics*. New York: Columbia University Press.

Sartre, Jean-Paul. 1948. *Anti-Semite and Jew*. New York: Schocken.

Sennett, Richard and Jonathan Cobb. 1972. *The Hidden Injuries of Class*. New York: Vintage.

Symanski, Al. 1985. "The Structure of Race." *Review of Radical Political Economy* 17 (Winter), 106–20.

Robert Grunst is a professor of English at St. Catherine University. He has led several groups of St. Catherine students to Ecuador to focus on environmental justice issues, including controversies surrounding Ecuador's flower export industry. His experiences working as a commercial fisherman on Lake Michigan and Lake Superior have sharpened his interests in freshwater use and conservation. He has written many essays focusing on the material culture and storytelling traditions associated with Great Lakes fishing communities. A widely published poet, he is the author of a collection entitled The Smallest Bird in North America. *What are the various dilemmas presented to these students as they encounter lives and conditions in Ecuador?*

On the Legume Fava and Study Abroad, Cayambe, Ecuador

Robert Grunst

The Co-Operative Director and secretary have explained to us their credit union program aids in the launching of women-run businesses, small farming operations founded in the cultivation of the magical grain, *quinoa,* in the propagation of guinea pigs, in small goat and cow-milking enterprises where the end-product is Cayambe-labeled cheeses. We have visited a guinea pig "show house," a eucalyptus battened and raftered mud-walled structure with concrete floor and tile roof, all tilting with the landscape precisely in interest of sanitation. In the Andes the pragmatics of gravity are, perhaps, better understood than in Minnesota. People live nearer to the earth.

One of the co-op spokespersons has answered a student question in a pessimistic—disheartening way, or perhaps, in a realistic way, partly through the translator, Adrianna, partly through her own perfectly English English, English being elected, it seems, to bear the harshest news.

> There's nothing you can do. If all of you should refuse to buy the roses and everyone along with everyone everyone knows, then, yes, the rose-growers, perhaps, they would collapse and then the women and the children and the men who work for the growers and many who are sick already—and they probably will grow more sick in time—they will have no work and their problems will be greater because to have no work, you understand. You see them walking to the plantations, they hold themselves as people who labor because they do and others who do not, please, understand, you see, they do not hold themselves that way because they do not, which is a thing perhaps I do not know that you can understand or if I make it wrong.

The rose growing operations have transformed the environment around Cayambe, loading streams with fungicides, insecticides, and chemicals to alleviate the effects of other chemicals. There are lesions the like of which have never been known. There is asthma. There are troubles with the head, aches and piercing pains of unabating intensity. There are troubles with hearts. There are visions, doublings and triplings. There are miscarriages. There are abnormalities, secrets that are not secrets.

If a woman with a co-op loan can buy a small plot of land and can grow quinoa, potatoes, corn: But the rose plantations might pay as high as $140.00 for a month. If her husband works, or does not work . . . If her children have good health . . . If she herself. . . If her mother. . . If her aunt. . . If the doctor, who is on the payroll of the plantation, says. . .

We are citizens of the United States. We study and we teach at St. Catherine University in St. Paul, Minnesota. Our headaches cannot be attributed solely to the altitude. Study abroad is the same as study of enormities, or, say, of great sins if one must, and the same as study too of belongings then, of souvenirs in both our sense and in the French, of inventories, items in a closet, a cupboard, a garage, not to contemplate the omissions of *reality tv*.

You must imagine now, after the talk, we are sitting down at long benches at long tables in the co-op dining room. We are sitting down as children of the co-op school are filing out wide-eyed and whispering with astonishment. Some of the brave—loquacious ones are giggling. One is wiggling her ears with much encouragement from her admirers. Kitchen workers are setting out our lunch in ample bowls. They are setting out smaller bowls of salsa and pitchers of juice. Many of the children's parents, you must assume, are at work with the roses. In our bowls are potatoes cut into big fractions. Each bowl too bears an ear of corn unlike any corn known in these Midwestern states, corn with out-sized kernels—yellow and white, off-purple and off-red—kernels arranged strictly in defiance of Euclidean principles. There are fava beans too, thick-jacketed favas. Imagine, then, that we are surveying our bowls: All of us are searching our hearts—and not for the name of the beans.

Nancy A. Heitzeg is professor of sociology and co-director of the interdisciplinary program in critical studies of race and ethnicity at St. Catherine University. As a sociologist, Heitzeg has written and published widely on issues of inequality, their intersections, and corresponding actions toward social change. In this essay, she argues that systemic oppression is at the heart of justice issues, and that these must be addressed through a process of reflection, social analysis, moral evaluation, and action. Issues of criminal injustice in the Trayvon Martin case and the death penalty abolition work of Sister Helen Prejean, CSJ, illustrate this on-going process. How have Prejean's actions toward justice been informed by her own reflection, analysis, and evaluation? Which of the four parts of this process utilize your own strengths, and which parts are more challenging for you?

There Is No Justice without Action

Nancy A. Heitzeg

Justice and Action: A Theory

There can be no justice without peace and there can be no peace without justice.

—Martin Luther King Jr, 1968

"No Justice/No Peace." On February 26, 2012, 17 year old Trayvon Martin headed to a convenience store in Sanford, Florida to pick up ice tea and Skittles. He never made it back home. Self-appointed neighborhood watchman George Zimmerman profiled the hooded sweatshirt-wearing Trayvon as a potential "criminal," called 911, and then in defiance of the dispatcher's request to remain in his vehicle, followed Trayvon. An altercation occurred, ending with the unarmed Trayvon Martin being shot and killed by Zimmerman, who claimed self-defense under Florida's controversial Stand Your Ground law. Sanford Police failed to arrest Zimmerman that night, accepting without question his version of events (Nzegwu 2014).

Forty two days after Martin's death, Zimmerman was finally arrested and charged with the murder, only after mounting public pressure on the police and prosecutor. A Change.org petition created by Trayvon's parents, Tracy Martin and Sybrina Fulton, garnered over 2 million signatures, and both local and national protests kept the spot-light on the case. The profiling and killing of a young Black male for walking home was an eerily familiar story that recalled both slave patrols and the Jim Crow era policing of space and place that many had hoped was over. As Nzegwu (2014, p. 1–2) notes in the introduction to *Remembering Trayvon Martin, Special Edition of ProudFlesh*:

> The senseless and tragic murder of Trayvon Martin, an African-American teenager was troubling. In the aftermath of the killing and the national protests that ensued, a series of historical grievances against African-Americans were front and center. The litany of grievances includes racism, race relations, racial profiling, inequality, and vigilante killing, that are reminiscent of the Fugitive Slave Law period. The unmasking of these tensions ignited a national debate on race and racism, focusing attention on the embedded racism in the American legal system and the profiling of Black and Latino youths and men by law enforcement agencies.
>
> Fifty-eight years earlier, the brutal murder of fourteen year-old, Emmett Till, had occurred. Till was tortured, beaten, with his eyes gouged out, and shot in the head. Till's crime, at that time in 1955, was that he said "Bye baby" to a white woman, the wife of a shopkeeper, Carolyn Bryant, now Carolyn Donham. His mutilated body was dumped in the Tallahatchie River by Roy Bryant, the husband of Carolyn, and his brother, J. W. Milam. It was weighed down by a cotton gin until it surfaced three days later. Although Emmett's case is not a direct parallel to Trayvon Martin's, who was killed while walking in the gated community where his father and his fiancée lived, it shed light on the pattern of racism that pervades the country then and now.

The case of *State of Florida v George Zimmerman* went to trial on June 10, 2013. The prosecution presented what some felt was a lack-luster effort, while the defense succeeded in putting Trayvon Martin on trial as the aggressor who put George Zimmerman in fear for his life. The jury—5 white women and one Latina—agreed and, on July 13, 2013, found Zimmerman not guilty of Second Degree Murder and Manslaughter. The verdict again sent thousands in more than 100 cities back into the streets with hoodies up, chanting again, "Am I Next?", "I am Trayvon Martin", and yes, "No Justice/No Peace" (Heitzeg 2014).

"No Justice No Peace." On the face of it, many felt that this was an accurate assessment of the particular result in the Trayvon Martin case. Clearly, there was no legal justice for the dead Trayvon Martin, whose killer was very belatedly arrested, and then found not guilty. No Peace either, for his memory, now tainted by a legal verdict that in fact held him culpable for his own death, for Walking While Black with Skittles and ice tea. No Peace for his parents who continue their efforts to repeal Stand Your Ground laws in Florida and the other 30 states that allow for claims of self-defense without a requirement of retreat (Heitzeg 2013).

But "No Justice No Peace" meant something more. It was too about what Trayvon Martin represented; his case offered a glimpse into the long historical legacy of systemic racism in the criminal justice system. The story was old and familiar to scholars and those who have lived it. That's story is this: Prison in the United States is a direct outgrowth of slavery, a system designed and re-designed to exploit a largely black captive labor force—first with prison as plantations and convict lease labor all supported by legal segregation, Slave Codes transformed into Black Codes, and extra-legal lynching, and then later as the prison industrial complex and the death penalty (Davis 2003; Alexander 2010).

The War on Drugs, referred to by Alexander (2010) as "The New Jim Crow", has both escalated the incarceration rate and increased its' racial dynamic. The United States is the world's leader in incarceration with nearly 2.3 million people currently in prison or jail—a 500% increase over the past thirty years (Jones & Mauer 2013). Despite no statistical differences in rates of offending, this trend towards mass incarceration is marred by racial disparity. Policies such as intensive "stop and frisk" police practices, mandatory minimum prison sentences, and three-strike legislation all disproportionately affect people of color. While 1 in 35 adults is under correctional supervision and 1 in every 100 adults is in prison, 1 in every 36 Latino adults , one in every 15 black men, 1 in every 100 black women, and 1 in 9 black men ages 20 to 34 are incarcerated (Pew 2008).

A recent report issued by the Malcolm X Grassroots Movement, *Operation Ghetto Storm: 2012 Annual Report on the extrajudicial killing of 313 Black people by police, security guards and vigilantes* (2013), highlights the extent to which young Black males in particular are at risk for the sort of profiling that killed Trayvon Martin. The report further notes this:

> Every 28 hours in 2012 someone employed or protected by the US government killed a Black man, woman, or child. These killings—every 28 hours in 2012 someone employed or protected by the US government killed a Black man, woman, or child—come on top of other forms of oppression black people face. Mass incarceration of nonwhites is one of them. While African-Americans constitute 13.1% of the nation's population, they make up nearly 40% of the prison population. Even though African-Americans use or sell drugs about the same rate as whites, they are 2.8 to 5.5 times more likely to be arrested for drugs than whites. Black offenders also receive longer sentences compared to whites. Most offenders are in prison for nonviolent drug offenses.

"No Justice No Peace" is not just an immediate response to the case of Trayvon Martin; it is an indictment of the entire system of injustice. It is the grassroots articulation of a theory and a call to on-going action. Theory emerges from the lived experience of people as well as from scholarly works, and embedded in these words, is the everyday expression of a theory of justice and action, a theory where one cannot be imagined without the other.

"No Justice/No Peace" is a call to solidarity, a call to organize, a call to resistance in the face of systemic oppression. At the root, issues of justice are issues of oppression. Oppression is a collective, not just individual, concern; oppression involves the systematic domination and exclusion of groups via exploitation, marginalization, powerless, cultural domination and violence (Young 1990, p. 42). Oppression names some groups as "Other," and systematically disadvantages them while privileging the groups that they are not.

> Oppression refers to systemic constraints on groups that are not necessarily the intentions of a tyrant. Oppression in this sense is structural, rather than the result of a few people's choices or policies. Its causes are embedded in unquestioned norms, habits, and symbols, in the assumptions underlying institutional rules and the collective consequences of following these rules (Young 1990 p. 43).

Justice issues are systemic issues; they reflect larger structural patterns of inequality and disparity. Nationally and globally, systemic and institutionalized classism, racism, sexism, heterosexism, ageism, ableism, speciesism, anthropocentrism are pervasive and persistent systems of oppression. While each operates as a particular system of oppression, each also intersects with other systems to create what Hill- Collins terms a "matrix of domination." (Hill-Collins 2002), that is, oppressions are systemically connected. And, these oppressions, each and all, are perpetuated—not necessarily by the intentions of individuals—but by the reproduction of structures of power, privilege and domination.

> Oppression refers to the vast and deep injustices that some groups suffer as a consequence of often unconscious assumptions and reactions of well-meaning people in ordinary interactions, media and cultural stereotypes, and structural features of bureaucratic hierarchies and market mechanisms—in short, the normal processes of everyday life (Young 1990 p. 43).

Finally, perhaps most importantly, justice issues require action—"No Justice No Peace." There is, in fact, no justice without action; the two are inextricably linked. Oppression must be responded to both individually and collectively, and it must be responded to in a way that addresses the root structural issues. Charity—love, direct care and service to the immediate needs of the oppressed—while laudable and necessary in the short term, is not enough.

> We cannot eliminate this structural oppression by getting rid of rulers or making some new laws, because oppressions are systematically reproduced in major economic political and cultural institutions (Young 1990, p 43).

Since oppression is systemic, it requires an organized response. Taking action against injustice, against oppression may seem a daunting task. Social structures seem untouchable and immune to efforts at change. But social structures are created by social processes, and so by social action they can be undone. As Dinn (2008, p. 8) observes, "Even the most flawed social structure is an extension of ourselves." We of course can personally change, and so too, can we reorder structural arrangements to reflect justice—not oppression.

Taking action against injustice is an on-going process; social systems are rarely changed in just one day. Scholars from all disciplines of the Liberals Arts, spiritual leaders, and activists have outlined a process to guide action towards justice. It is a process rooted in the notion that knowledge is never neutral; knowledge reveals injustices, calls out for evaluation, and carries with it an obligation to act. Variously termed praxis (theory + action) or critical pedagogy by secular scholars (Marx, 1844, Gramsci 1971; Freire 1970; Horton and Freire 1991)) and "The Pastoral Circle" by religious traditions such as Catholic Social Teaching (Holland and Henroit 1990; Wilsen, Henroit and Mejia 2005), this process allows for continued engagement with personal experience, social analysis, moral judgment, and action plans. The process is not necessarily linear or always orderly; we may enter and re-enter at any stage. The open-ended diagram represents the key stages, which are clarified in the discussion below.

Figure 1. Moving from Making Social Analysis Useful by Rita Hofbauer, GNSH, Amata Miller IHM, and Dorothy Kinsella OSF, Leadership Conference of Women Religious (1983)

Reflection on Experience

We have all experienced injustice. Perhaps we are part of an oppressed group; perhaps we are allies; perhaps we have benefited—intentionally or not—from the oppression of others. Reflection on experience allows us to make the connections between our lives and the larger structural reality, or as the women's movement put it, to see that "the personal is political" (Hanish 1969). This may be done by recalling direct personal experience or via the vicarious experience offered by the arts—music, literature, art, theater and film. We must name our locations, our privileges and our oppressions, as well as the knowledge and talents we may translate into action.

Social Analysis

If we are to transform social structures, we must understand the difference between "personal troubles and social issues" (Mills 1959, p. 11). This stage of the process requires us to draw upon the best available information from a range of scholars and activists. We must analyze the scope of the justice issue, understand the social, economic, political, and cultural contributors, identify the groups who benefit and who are harmed, and examine both existing policies and potential solutions. We must know what we are up against. As Alinsky (1971, p. xix) observes, "It is necessary to begin with where the world is if we are going to change it to what we want it to be."

Moral Judgment

"We must always take sides. Neutrality helps the oppressor, never the victim. Silence encourages the tormentor, never the tormented." (Wiesel 1999) In the face of experience and evidence, we must evaluate. Our values guide our understanding of our experiences, the larger social analysis and our actions. Even if the origins of our values differ, we can agree on a common set of principles such as those expressed in the United Nations' Universal Declaration of Human Rights (1948). Various spiritual and philosophical traditions offer deeper insight into the justice issue, and prepare us to align our values with analysis and action.

Action Plan

We must engage in informed action—"The struggle may be a moral one, or it may be a physical one, or it may be both. But it must be a struggle. Power concedes nothing without a demand," (Douglass 1857). The range of potential actions against structural injustice is inexhaustible. We can speak out and we can write—poems, songs. novels, drama, letters, essays, journal articles and books. We can make art, protest, lobby, educate, vote, legislate, organize, mobilize, march, stand up, sit–in, jail-in, boycott, and still more. Some will resist in the courts; some will resist in the halls of Congress; some will resist in the streets. No Justice/No Peace.

The process of moving towards social justice, the process of challenging oppression, is better illustrated than explained. Scholars and activists have described the theory and process, but it is best understood by examining the practice. What follows is the example of Sister Helen Prejean, CSJ, and her journ[illegible]olish the death penalty. Sister Helen's story, like that of T[illegible], focuses specifically on the injustices associated [illegible] system and state-sponsored killings, but her activi[illegible]rates how this process may be applied to a partic[illegible]n. Her life and work evidence the on-going movem[illegible]nalysis to evaluation to action and back again, m[illegible]stice.

Moving Towards Social Justice: Sister Helen Prejean, CSJ

Comfort the afflicted and afflict the comfortable

—Dorothy Day 1952

It began—as it often does—with a seemingly simple question. Such seemingly simple questions often begin our longest, our most arduous and most transformative journeys. So it was for Sister Helen Prejean;

> When Chava Colon from the Prison Coalition asks me one January day in 1982 to become a pen pal for a death row inmate, I say, sure. The invitation seems to fit with my work at St. Thomas, a New Orleans housing project of poor black residents. Not exactly death row, but close . . . I've come to St Thomas to serve the poor, and I assume that someone occupying a cell on Louisiana's death row fits that category (Prejean 1993, p. 4).

Sister Helen (b.1939), a Sister of St. Joseph of Medaille since 1957, was well acquainted with issues of injustice. Leaving first, a privileged life in Baton Rouge and later an "ethereal faith" focused on inner peace, acts of charity, and the world beyond, Sister Helen had already chosen the path of justice, although "it would take me a long time to understand how systems inflict pain and hardship in people's live and to learn that being kind in an unjust system is not enough" (Ibid, p. 7). Originally a teacher, she had come to St. Thomas in 1981 as part of her Order's commitment to stand with the poor. Through her interactions with the residents—many whom had a relative in prison—and The Prison Coalition, she was already aware of the race and class disparities in police-citizen encounters, incarceration rates, and the application of the death penalty. And she was opposed to the death penalty, both her Christian faith—"Jesus Christ, whose way of life I try to follow refused to meet hate with hate and violence with violence" (Ibid, p. 21)—and the philosophy of Albert Camus (1957, p. 199)—"resist, do not collaborate in any with a deed you believe is evil"—guided her opposition.

Still, no one, certainly not Sister Helen, could anticipate that the response to the letter-writing request would mark the beginning of a long journey—"I don't know yet that the name on this tiny slip of white paper will be my transport into an eerie land that so far I have read only about in books." (Prejean 1993, p. 3–4)—a journey that would lead from the St Thomas Housing Projects of New Orleans to the death chamber at Louisiana State Penitentiary to international fame as a tireless advocate for the abolition of capital punishment.

Elmo Patrick Sonnier #95281 was the name on that slip of paper. Sonnier, a troubled youth with a past ridden with criminal activity, was convicted, along with his brother Eddie, for the November 5, 1977 rape and murder of Loretta Ann Bourque, 18, and the murder of David LeBlanc, 17. While both brothers were initially sentenced to death in Louisiana's electric chair aka "Gruesome Gertie", Eddie was sentenced to life in prison upon re-trial. In spite of her horror at Sonnier's crimes, Sister Helen wrote.

> The image in my mind was that if people were in prison they must be really bad and the people on death row . . . they've done the worst possible crimes. I think there is a kind of notion that people on death row are people who have killed and will kill again . . . they are just violent killer people. When I looked into Patrick Sonnier's face the first time I visited—I knew there was goodness in him from his letters, but when I visited him, I was so nervous and I was amazed when I looked into his face and saw how human he was and that we could talk to one another, just two human beings. It was such an amazing experience that has been confirmed in so many ways since (Andersen 1998).

Sister Helen's correspondence with Sonnier inevitably led to visits with him at the Death House at Louisiana State Penitentiary. It is here that she is transformed from pen-pal to spiritual advisor, a metamorphosis that was not without considerable pain and doubt. She becomes more convinced than ever that the State of Louisiana is involved with legitimated murder, murder which is tacitly supported by the Warden, the guards, the chaplains, the priests, the Governor, murder which is explicitly supported by the public at large and many of the families of the victims. She struggles with guilt and grief for the LeBlancs and the Bourques—families of the murdered teens—the vengeance they feel towards Sonnier and the anger they feel towards her. Has she betrayed, abandoned them, as she consoled their children's killer? And what of the family of the offender—are they not victims too?

Beyond the moral dilemmas presented by the particular case of Patrick Sonnier, the structural injustices of incarceration and capital punishment are further revealed to Prejean. The race, class gender disparities that mark the entire criminal justice system are magnified in death penalty cases. As she sees firsthand the composition of the inmate population at Angola, the racial dynamics of incarceration become clearer. LSP Angola is the largest prison (the only one to boast its' own Zip Code) in the United States—over 5000 inmates on over 18,000 acres. 90% of them are African American—the majority from New Orleans and Jefferson parishes—and 90% will die there. Angola is the site of the old Angola Plantation, which following the Civil War immediately became a prison, where inmates continue to labor for free due to the loophole that negates the liberatory promise of the 13th Amendment—"Slavery and involuntary servitude—except as a punishment for crime—shall be abolished" (Brewer and Heitzeg 2008, p. 67).

Prejean similarly becomes increasingly aware of the role of race in the death penalty and the prevalence of its use in the South; race of victim and race of offender remain the best predictors of prosecutorial decisions to pursue the death penalty who will be executed. African Americans are over-represented on death row relative to both their percentage of the population and their participation in the crime of murder. And cases involving white victims are most likely to be prosecuted as capital cases; nearly 80% of all murder victims in case involving an execution were white, even though whites represented only 50% of murder victims (Death Penalty Information Center, 2014). Prejean comes to agree with the assessment of scholars who argue that the death penalty is yet another mechanism for controlling blacks, especially in the South, where some have argued that the lynch mob has merely been replaced by the "killing state" (Ogletree and Sarat 2006). And yes, even though Sonnier is white, he is poor as are 99% of the more than 3100 death row inmates, whose reliance on public defenders in essence provides no defense at all. Sonnier and the other indigent inhabitants on death row illustrate the saying Prejean has heard often in the housing projects of St Thomas, "Capital punishment means those without the capital get the punishment." Inadequate defenses, an appeals process that is fraught with roadblocks for the accused, and endless personal trauma for both offenders and victims mark the way from trial to death.

On April 5 1984, Sister Helen is a witness to the execution of Sonnier, the first of 4 death row inmates that Sister Helen would eventually accompany to execution. Shortly after Sonnier's sentence was carried out, she began to organize, first with trainings for spiritual advisors, the creation of a legal aid office, a public awareness march from New Orleans to Baton Rouge, the founding of Survive—an organization designed to support families of victims of violence, and finally the decision to devote herself completely to the abolition of the death penalty.

> I realize that I cannot stand by silently as my government executes its citizens. If I do not speak out and resist, I am an accomplice. . . . No one in the entire State of Louisiana is working full-time to talk to the public about the death penalty. I will do this. The decision unfolds like a rose (Prejean 1993, p. 115–117).

Prejean later served as spiritual advisor to Robert Lee Willie. Willie was executed by electrocution on December 28 1984 for the kidnap, rape, and murder of 18 year old Faith Hathaway. His case, like that of Sonnier's, is filled with similar anguish, legal challenges and losses, and great struggles with the issue of vengeance felt by the victim's family. In 1993, Sister Helen chronicled her experience with both men in *Dead Man Walking: An Eyewitness Account of the Death Penalty in the United States*. In the introduction (Ibid p xi), she writes

> I stepped quite unsuspectingly from a protected middle-class environment into one of the most explosive and complex moral issues of our day, the question of capital punishment . . . I began naively. It took time—and mistakes—for me to sound out the moral perspective, which is the subject of this book. There is much pain in these pages. There are, to begin with, crimes that

> defy description. Then there is the ensuing rage, horror, grief, and fierce ambivalence. But also, courage and incredible human spirit. I have been changed forever by the experiences that I describe here.

The book becomes an international best seller translated into twelve languages, an opera, and an Academy Award nominated film in 1995 (Susan Sarandon won Best Actress for her portrayal of Prejean). Always searching for new ways to increase public dialogue about the death penalty, Sister Helen continued to write, speak, and organize. She founded the Death Penalty Discourse Center and the Moratorium Project as ways of promoting the national discourse on the death penalty and as a resource for abolitionists. And, she urged director/producer Tim Robbins to create a version of *Dead Man Walking* for the stage:

> Through the film, then the opera, I was convinced of the power of the arts to stir reflection and deepen public discourse . . . early in 2002 Tim wrote the play. He called me up to New York for a reading, and he and I and everyone in the room were blown away by its power, even though it was simply read. (http://www.dmwplay.org/playproject.html)

Prejean along with Tim Robbins, founded The *Dead Man Walking* School Theater Project. Directed by Sister Maureen Felton, OP, The Play Project allows high school and college students' easy access to performance rights for *Dead Man Walking*. The play has been performed by nearly 200 high schools and colleges—including the College of St Catherine in 2006.

Continuing as a spiritual advisor to death row inmates, Prejean tells the stories of Dobie Gillis Williams (executed by Louisiana in 1999) and Joseph O'Dell (executed by Virginia in 1997) in her 2005 book, *The Death of Innocents: An Eyewitness Account of Wrongful Executions*: She writes in the introduction, (ibid, p. 2)

> As in *Dead Man Walking*, this is my eyewitness account of accompanying two men to execution—but with one huge difference: I believe that the two men I tell about here—Dobie Gillis Williams and Joseph Roger O'Dell—were innocent. The courts of appeal didn't see it that way. Once the guilty verdicts were pronounced and the death sentences imposed every court in the land put their stamp of approval on the death sentences of these two men without once calling form a thorough review of their constitutional claims. The tragic truth is that you as a reader of this book have access to truths about forensic evidence, eyewitnesses, and prosecutorial maneuvers that Dobie's and Joseph's jurors never heard.

Through the cases of Williams and O'Dell, Prejean expands upon her previous moral and social analysis of the death penalty. In addition to the pervasive issues of race and class bias, *Death of Innocents* raises questions about the execution of those who are actually innocent, an issue that was coming to public attention at the time this book was written. Since 1973, work by Innocence Projects, mostly lead by college students, had lead to the exoneration of 143 death row inmates in 26 states (Death Penalty Information Center, 2014).

Death of Innocents contains a detailed history of the Catholic Church's position on the death penalty, which for 1600 years—from Augustine to Aquinas to the mid 20th century—supported the state's right, in self-defense, to kill those who had committed grave crimes. Prejean chronicles the slight but significant shift in position post Vatican II and her on-going dialogue with church officials, many who remained vocal supporters of the death penalty. It is the late Pope John Paul, responding to a growing global abolition movement, who signals the change in course. In *Evangelium Vitae* (1995), he urges church leaders to become more courageous in opposing the use of capital punishment. The pope also speaks out on behalf of Joseph O'Dell in 1997, and Prejean writes to him calling for a shift in the church's official position "I pray for the day when Catholic opposition to government executions will be unequivocal" (Prejean 2005 p. 127). Less than a week later the Vatican announces an official change to the Catechism; all language referring to the death penalty as an option is removed. It is not Prejean's letter alone but the combined efforts of over Catholics worldwide who had continuously and consistently expressed their opposition for decades. In the end, Prejean (2005, p 130) notes this about her interpretation[3] of the shift in the language of the Catechism:

> The omission changes everything, because Catholic teaching now says that no matter how grave, terrible, outrageous, heinous, cruel the crime, the death penalty is not to be imposed. . . . Whom then might governments kill?? No one.

To argue that the death penalty is morally wrong is one matter; it is another to document the blatant racism, classism, legal error, and sheer ineptitude play in the application of the death penalty in the United States. Prejean does that in *Death of Innocents* as well, detailing the recent history of Supreme Court rulings from the famed 1972 *Furman v Georgia* ruling to the present. Between 1967 and 1977, there were no executions in the United States as the Supreme Court heard a series of legal challenges to the constitutionality of the death penalty. All cases came from Southern states, including the landmark cases of *Furman v Georgia* (1972), *Gregg v Georgia* (1976), and *Coker v Georgia* (1977). All cases involved black men and raised legal questions with regard to the 8th Amendment prohibition against "cruel and unusual punishment' and the 14th Amendment clauses of "due process" and "equal protection of the laws," in essence, issues of racial discrimination. In sum, the Court ruled in Furman that capital punishment was cruel and unusual if it was applied in an "arbitrary and capricious manner" (*Furman v Georgia*, 1972) The result was a revision of state statues, affirmed by Gregg, as that allowed for the death penalty if (1) there were guidelines outlining capital offenses and allowing for consideration of aggravating and mitigating circumstances and (2) there was a two-part trial where the imposition of sentence as separated from the finding of guilt.(*Gregg v Georgia* 1976) These cases form the framework for the current application of the death penalty which is currently available in 32 states and at the federal level, with the United States remaining as the only so-called First World nation where the death penalty has not been abolished.[4]

Prejean decries these decisions as well as the ensuing cases, which ignore statistical evidence of institutionalized racism (*McKleskey v Kemp* 1987), split hairs over whether 15 or 16 or 17 year olds are mature enough to be executed (*Thompson v Oklahoma* 1986, *Stanford v Kentucky* 1989), allows for the execution of the mentally ill and the intellectually disabled (*Penry v Lynaugh* 1989, *Murray v Giarrano* 1989), permits court-appointed attorneys to be defined as "competent" even though they may be unqualified, asleep or even drunk at trial (*Herrea v Collins* 1993), and increasingly limits the avenues of appeal for death row inmates (*Strickland v Washington* 1984), even in cases like that of Dobie Gillis Williams or Joseph O'Dell where procedural error and evidence of actual innocence hang like a dark pall over the cases. She quotes 18th century philosopher and prison reformer Cesear Beccaria; she argues with elected Supreme Court justice ad death penalty advocate Antonin Scalia in the New Orleans airport; regrets that elected officials cannot be moved to compassion even in the face of inmate redemption, and in the end, urges the court to stand with the late Justice Harry Blackmun, who after 20 years of wrangling with the with the legal minutia of death penalty cases, finally and firmly declares, "I will no longer tinker with the machinery of death" (*Callins v Collins* 1994).

In the 30 years since she responded to Chava Colon's request to write Sonnier a letter, much has changed. Over 122 countries have abolished the death penalty in the law of practice (Amnesty International 2013). Every year since 1997, the UN annually passes a resolution calling for a moratorium on the death penalty, and the International Criminal Court has banned its use in any crime. The U.S. Supreme Court has deemed the execution of juveniles (*Roper v Simmons* 2005), the mentally retarded (*Atkins v Virginia,* 2002) and non-murderers (*Kennedy v Louisiana* 2009) unconstitutional. Legal challenges to the use of lethal injection continue and Nebraska has banned the use of the electric chair as cruel and unusual punishment. 6 additional states have abandoned capital punishment since 2009, leaving 32 states that retain this as a sentencing option. Public support for the death penalty is at a 40 year low, and U.S. executions and death sentences continue to decline with only 2% of counties accounting for more than 50% of all executions (Death Penalty Information Center, 2014). Religious and secular organizations from the U.S. Bishops to Amnesty International to the innocence Project continue to call for abolition.

And Sister Helen carries on. In an early interview, she was asked about the course her life had taken. Referring to her first intentions when she entered religious life, Prejean said that her life actually has not taken that different a course.

> 'I still feel like I am a teacher,' she said. 'My classroom's bigger now, it includes the United States and Europe and the United Nations and a lot of media interviews, but basically it's living the Gospel message the best that I can and sharing what I learn along the way' (Andersen 1998).

And so it is. Yes, Sister Helen carries on. Speaking, writing—now her spiritual memoir, *River of Fire*—, expanding the Play Project, collaborating with a wide range of abolitionist organizations, engaging the death penalty discourse in any and all ways possible, always moving towards social justice, always in that on-going process of reflection on experience, social analysis, moral judgment and action.

Another World Is Possible

We make the road by walking…

—Horton and Freire, 1991

The injustice of oppressive social structures must be named and must be challenged. In matters of justice, there is no neutral ground; we all stand—by design or default, by action or inaction—with the either oppressors or the oppressed. Those who wish to stand on the side of justice are compelled to act, for there can be no justice without action. The story of Sister Helen Prejean—and the stories of countless activists, some well-known and many not—illustrates this: moving towards social justice, moving towards an end to structural oppression, is an ever-emerging, always evolving process where new insights are continually gained, and new actions imagined and undertaken.

Moving towards social justice requires the recognition that each day, each setting, each circumstance provides new opportunities for action in any number of arenas. It requires the recognition that each of us can contribute in ways small or large. Lorde reminds us in *Transformation of Silence into Language and Action* (1984, p. 44) that simply speaking out is one of the most important actions towards justice that one can take: "it is not difference which immobilizes us but silence. And there are many silences to be broken."

And most of all, moving towards social justice requires patience, commitment, hope, and the "optimism of uncertainty" (Zinn, 2004). We must know—with Prejean and Trayvon's parents, supporters and the all rest—that we ourselves may not see the full realization of our efforts, but someone someday will. For yes, "the moral arc of the universe is long, but it does bend towards justice" (King 1968). And yes, that famed Margaret

Mead (1977) quote—*"Never doubt that a small group of thoughtful committed citizens can change the world. Indeed, it is the only thing that ever has"*—appears endlessly on t-shirts and bumper stickers and posters and buttons, only because it is so precisely true.

In the very last lines of the introduction to *The Death of Innocents* (2005 p. xvi), Sister Helen closes with these words, which bear repeating here—". . . May you be impassioned to devote your life to soul-size work. I hope what you learn here sets you on fire."

No Justice / No Peace.

Notes

[1] For centuries, the so-called "Castle Doctrine" has held that a homeowner may use deadly force against intruders and legally claim self-defense. Until recently, The Castle Doctrine (as expressed in various state laws) also required key elements in order for a successful claim of self-defense to be made. Generally, the person must be in their home, there be an unlawful intrusion (as opposed to standing on your lawn), the use of deadly force must be "reasonable," and in many cases, there is duty to retreat i.e. deadly force must be a last, rather than first, resort. Stand Your Ground legislation removes many of the limits imposed on shooters by the Castle Doctrine—the self-defense claim extends to public places, there is no requirement of "retreat," and the burden is now on the prosecution to determine "reasonableness." The first such legislation was passed in Florida in 2005. Pushed by the National Rifle Association and American Legislative Exchange Council, these laws spread quickly; 24 additional states now have comparable legislation. Stand Your Ground legislation has been associated with increased homicide rates, heightened risk for teenagers, and racial disparity in the application of the Self-defense claims. See Heitzeg, N. A. (2013, November 13), "Perceived Threat and Stand Your Ground", Criminal InJustice at Critical Mass Progress, Retrieved March 1, 2014 from http://criticalmassprogress.com/2013/11/13/ci-black-life-perceived-threat-and-stand-your-ground/

[2] The prison industrial complex is defined as follows: **"The prison industrial complex is a self-perpetuating machine where the vast profits** (e.g. cheap labor, private and public supply and construction contracts, job creation, continued media profits from exaggerated crime reporting and crime/punishment as entertainment) **and perceived political benefits** (e.g. reduced unemployment rates, "get tough on crime" and public safety rhetoric, funding increases for police, and criminal justice system agencies and professionals) **lead to policies that are additionally designed to insure an endless supply of "clients" for the criminal justice system** (e.g. enhanced police presence in poor neighborhoods and communities of color; racial profiling; decreased funding for public education combined with zero-tolerance policies and increased rates of expulsion for students of color; increased rates of adult certification for juvenile offenders; mandatory minimum and "three-strikes" sentencing; draconian conditions of incarceration and a reduction of prison services that contribute to the likelihood of "recidivism"; "collateral consequences"—such as felony disenfranchisement, prohibitions on welfare receipt, public housing, gun ownership,

voting and political participation, employment—that nearly guarantee continued participation in "crime" and return to the prison industrial complex following initial release) (Brewer and Heitzeg 2008, p. 620).

[3] The position of the Catholic Church is complicated. The Church has long held that governments have the right to use capital punishment in order to protect society. The current position reflected in the Catechism, The U.S. Bishops' statements and Pope John II's *Evangelium Vita* does not deny the right of governments to impose the death penalty, but increasingly argues against its' use; "If bloodless means are sufficient to defend human lives against an aggressor and to protect public order and the safety of persons, public authority must limit itself to such means, because they better correspond to the concrete conditions of the common good and are more in conformity to the dignity of the human person" (*Evangelium Vitae* par. 56).

[4] The use of capital punishment in the U.S. and around the world has a lengthy and complex social, legal and political history. For an overview and additional resources see Death Penalty Information Center http://www.deathpenaltyinfo.org/and Amnesty International http://www.amnesty.org/en/death-penalty

References

Alinsky, S. (1971) *Rules for Radicals: A Pragmatic Primer for Realistic Radicals* NY: Vintage.

Atkins v Virginia 536 US 304 (2002).

Alexander, M. (2010). *The new jim crow: Mass incarceration in the era of color-blindness*. New York: The Free Press.

Amnesty International. (2013). *Amnesty Report 2013*. NY: Amnesty International.

Anderson, T. (1998, November 20) Interview with Sister Helen, *Georgia Bulletin* Retrieved January 14, 2014 from: http://www. georgiabulletin.org/local/1998/07/16/b/).

Brewer, Rose M and Nancy A Heitzeg (2008) "The Racialization of Crime and Punishment: Criminal Justice, Color-Blind Racism and the Political Economy of the Prison Industrial Complex" *American Behavioral Scientist*. 51:5 65.

Callins v Collins 510 US 1141 (1994).

Coker v Georgia 433 US 584 (1977).

Collins, P. H. (2000). *Black feminist thought: Knowledge, consciousness, and the politics of empowerment* (2nd Ed.). NY: Routledge.

Davis, A. (2003). *Are prisons obsolete?* NY: Seven Stories Press.

Day, D. (1952) *The Long Loneliness: The Autobiography of Dorothy Day*. NY: HarperCollins.

Dead Man Walking School Theater Project http://www.dpdiscourse.org/play.htm .

Death Penalty Discourse Center http://www.dpdiscourse.org/.

Death Penalty Information Center (2014) *Death Penalty Fact Sheet* Washington DC: DPIC Retrieved January 20, 2014 from http://www. deathpenaltyinfo.org/documents/FactSheet.pdf.

Dinn, J. (2000) Justice and Charity. http://www.osjspm.org/charity_and_justice_chart.aspx.

Douglass, Frederick. [1857] (1985). "The Significance of Emancipation in the West Indies." Speech, Canandaigua, New York, August 3, 1857; collected in pamphlet by author. In *The Frederick Douglass Papers.* Series One: Speeches, Debates, and Interviews. Volume 3: 1855–63. Edited by John W. Blassingame. New Haven: Yale University Press, p. 204.

Freire, P. (1970) *Pedagogy of the Oppressed.* NY: Continuum.

Freire, P. (1994) *Pedagogy of Hope.* NY: Continuum.

Furman v Georgia 409 US 238 (1972).

Gramsci, A. (1971) *Selections from the Prison Notebook.* NY: International Publishers.

Gregg v Georgia 428 US 153 (1976).

Hanish, Carol. "The Personal Is Political" in Redstockings (1970) *Feminist Revolution: Notes from the Second Year* (p. 204–205). NY: Random House.

Heitzeg, N. A. (2013, November 13), "Perceived Threat and Stand Your Ground", *Criminal Injustice at Critical Mass Progress.* Retrieved January 14, 2014 from: http://criticalmassprogress.com/2013/11/13/ci-black-life-perceived-threat-and-stand-your-ground/

Heitzeg, N.A. (2013, July 17).Of the verdict, "whiteness", and abolition. In Remembering Trayvon Martin, Special Issue, *ProudFlesh: New Afrikan Journal of Culture, Politics, and Consciousness* edited by A. Nzegwu (1543–1855). Retrieved from: http://www.africaknowledge project.org/index.php/proudflesh/article/view/1755

Heitzeg, Nancy A. (2004) "Justice and Action: Frameworks and Foundations for Social Change", *Global Search for Justice Reader,* 3rd Edition, CSC, Copley Custom Publishing.

Herrea V Collins 506 US 390 (1993).

Holland, J. and P. Henroit. (1990) *Social Analysis: Linking Faith and Justice* Maryknoll NY: Orbis.

Hofbauer, Rita GNSH, Amata Miller IHM, and Dorothy Kinsella OSF. (1983) *Making Social Analysis Useful* Leadership Conference of Women Religious.

Hopcke, R. (2004) *Catholics and the Death Penalty* Cincinnati OH: St Anthony Messenger Press.

Horton, M., P. Freire et al. (1991) editors *We Make the Road by Walking: Conversations on Education and Social Change* Philadelphia. Temple University Press.

Jones, S. and M. Mauer. (2013). *Race to incarcerate: A graphic retelling.* New York: The Free Press.

King, M. L. Jr. (1968, March 31) "Remaining Awake through a Great Revolution." Retrieved January 15, 2008 from http://www.african americans.com/MLKRemainingAwakeThroughGreatRevolution.htm.

Lorde, A. (1984). *Sister outsider: essays and speeches.* Freedom, CA: Crossing Press.

Marx, K. and Engels, F. (1948) *The Communist Manifesto.* London: International Publishers.

McClesky v. Kemp 482 U.S.279 (1987).

Mead, M. (1977) *Letters from the Field 1925–1975* NY: Harper and Row.

Murray v Giarrano 492 US 1 (1989).

Nzegwu, A. (Ed.) (2013) Remembering Trayvon Martin, Special Issue, *ProudFlesh: New Afrikan Journal of Culture, Politics, and Consciousness, 7,* ISSN: 1543-1855, Retrieved January 14, 2014 from: http://www.africa knowledgeproject.org/index.php/proudflesh/ issue/view/147/showToc.

Ogletree C. Jr. and A. Sarat (2006) editors. *From Lynch Mobs to the Killing State: Race and Death Penalty in the United States.* NY: New York University Press.

PEW Center on the States. (2008). *One in 100: Behind bars in America 2008.* Washington DC.

Penry v Lynaugh 492 US 302 (1989).

Pope John Paul II. 1995. *Evangelicum Vitae.* Rome: The Vatican. Retrieved January 2 2009 from http://www.vatican.va/holy_father/john_ paul_ii/encyclicals/documents/hf_jp-ii_enc_25031995 _evangelium-vitae_en.html .

Prejean, Sister Helen. (1993) *Dead Man Walking: An Eyewitness Account of the Death penalty in the United States.* NY: Vintage.

Prejean, Sister Helen. (2005) *The Death of Innocents: An Eyewitness Account of Wrongful Executions*. NY: Random House.

Roper v Simmons 543 U.S. 551 (2005).

Stanford v Kentucky 492 US 361 (1989).

Strickland v Washington 466 US 668 (1984).

Thompson v Oklahoma 487 US 813 (1989).

Tucker, R. (1972). *The Marx–Engels Reader*. NY: W.W. Norton.

United Nations. (1948). *Universal Declaration of Human Rights*. NY: United Nations Retrieved January 2 2009 from http://un.org/Overview/rights.html

U.S. Conference of Catholic Bishops (2005) *Culture of Life and the Death Penalty*. Washington DC: U.S. Conference of Catholic Bishops.

Wiesel, E. (12 April 1999) "The Millennium Lecture: The Perils of Indifference." Retrieved January 2 2009 from http://www.historyplace.com/speeches/wiesel.htm

Wilsen, F., P. Henroit, and R. Mejia (2005) editors. *The Pastoral Circle Revisited: A Critical Quest for Truth and Transformation*. Maryknoll NY: Orbis.

Young, I. M. (1990) *Justice and the Politics of Oppression*. Princeton NJ: Princeton University Press.

Zinn, H. (2004) "The optimism of uncertainty". In *The impossible will take a little while: a citizen's guide to hope in a time of fear*. New York: Basic Books, pp. 63–72.

Curt Cadorette spent nearly twenty years as a missionary priest among the Aymara and Quechuan, the indigenous people of Peru and Bolivia. He still considers Lima home because of his great love for the Andean world, but left Peru in 1992 as political violence intensified. He is now endowed professor of Catholic studies at Rochester University in New York, and specializes in Latin American religion and culture and in issues of peace and justice. While living in Latin America, Cadorette witnessed the emergence of a particular understanding of the Christian message labeled "liberation theology." In the selection that follows, from the introduction to Liberation Theology: An Introductory Reader *(1992), he maintains that Christian theology works to "find the meaning of life in the world, not outside of it," and he traces the development of liberation theology in the context of historical and cultural factors that have shaped Christianity in the Western World. As Latin American Christians searched for meaning in their experiences of dehumanization, they found more in common with Africa and Asia than with European-rooted theology, and urged a shift of focus to the relevancy of Christianity for the poor and oppressed. Cadorette provides background for the next reading, by Luz Beatrice Arellano, that describes the powerful transformation experienced by Nicaraguan women in this liberation movement. What surprises you about the liberation theology in Cadorette's overview? What "faces" of oppression outlined by Young are revealed in his description of Christian experiences in Latin America?*

from Liberation Theology: Context and Method

Introduction

Curt Cadorette

Theology and the Search for Meaning

As we come to the end of the twentieth century, most people in the developed world lead lives that are far more secure and comfortable than those of their grandparents. At first sight, it might seem that we have solved most of our problems as human beings. Despite our sophistication and wealth, however, there are large numbers of people who find a meaningful life elusive. Unfortunately, none of our material possessions can really tell us who we are or how to live our lives. Even more disturbing is the large number of people in the developing world who die unnecessarily from hunger, disease, and oppression. We have taken immense scientific strides forward but only faltering steps in achieving a just and authentic human community.

We cannot expect science and technology to solve our problems and answer our questions about the meaning of life. They are marvelous tools for understanding and dealing with the material world, but tell us little or nothing about why it exists and how we should live in it. To answer those questions we need a vision, a transcendent understanding of ourselves that goes beyond the present moment and material world. The majority of people reach a transcendent understanding of themselves through the medium of religion. Over the centuries human beings have developed insightful religious traditions. All share a concern with the question of transcendence, but each understands and articulates it in different ways. What makes Christianity unique is its belief that Jesus of Nazareth, a first-century Palestinian Jew, articulated a transcendent vision of life of unparalleled incisiveness. He was able to do so because he embodied or incarnated the divine itself. He was a revelation of God in human form. Twenty centuries of reflection on God's presence in Jesus by his followers has produced a rich body of wisdom that we call Christian theology.

Christian theology is much more than a collection of texts. It is actually an on-going attempt to understand and respond to God's presence in history. There are serious presuppositions behind this statement. The most obvious is that Christians understand revelation as something that takes place in history. In other words, we find the meaning of life in the world, not outside of it. We also find it in relationship to our fellow men and women. For this reason, our particular historical context and the material conditions of our lives assume special importance in shaping our self-understanding and approach to God. The fact of being male or female, rich or poor, is not some insignificant biographical detail, but a matter of great consequence. Another result of Christianity's concern with history is that revelation is understood as an on-going event, not a static, once-and-for-all phenomenon. The Christian tradition perceives Jesus as an all-important revelation of God's presence in history. Christians, however, live in a changing world. This means that their belief in Jesus as God's incarnation must be expressed in ways that make sense in a given historical situation.

In the late twentieth century, Christians face a unique theological challenge. By the use of science and technology we have achieved remarkable material progress. We have also produced sprawling slums, the specter of nuclear war, and possible ecological catastrophe caused by global warming. What does it mean to believe in God in a world where the rich oppress the poor, men denigrate women, and human beings with white skin consider themselves superior to people of color? What do Christians have to say about these injustices? What is the relationship between their beliefs, their daily lives, and the suffering that afflicts millions of human beings? These are serious questions that go to the heart of the Christian message.

One of the tasks of the theologian is to make a correlation between revelation and history, always keeping in mind that while they are related, they are not the same thing. To confuse one with the other is to risk turning a particular historical moment into an idol. Thus, we end up worshipping ourselves, with terrible consequences. Christians must relate to their world dialectically, neither condemning nor accepting it too quickly. Achieving this balance is a perennial task that is crucial to the credibility and survival of the Christian community. It requires systematic analysis and study. In other words, it requires theology and theologians, the thinking members of the Christian community charged with articulating their faith in an intelligible way.

Christianity and the Western World: A Thumbnail Sketch

For more than a thousand years Catholic Christianity shaped the self-understanding of people in the West. From the reign of Constantine until the decline of the medieval world, most Europeans thought that there was one legitimate way of understanding life and God—theirs. This monolithic perspective began to break apart in the sixteenth century when Luther and other reformers challenged the power of institutional Catholicism the theological presuppositions behind it. Suddenly there were many ways of understanding and living the Christian faith. Tragically, however, Christians began to kill each other in large numbers because of theological differences. This led to an inevitable reaction against the churches, Protestant and Catholic, on the part of many educated Europeans. This anti-church sentiment is best exemplified by the thinkers of the Enlightenment, an eighteenth-century intellectual movement that produced many of the values that underpin our social and political world today.

The leaders of the Enlightenment saw reason, not religion, as the best way to answer people's questions about the meaning of life. They were convinced that human rationality, working with the sciences, could eventually create an ideal world. They tolerated religion as a social convention, but rejected any role for the institutional church in the new social order they advocated. There is much to admire in the Enlightenment. The notion of the individual as a person with inherent rights that the state must uphold and protect took shape during this period. Pluralism and tolerance of social difference became legal principles. At the same time, some Enlightenment figures put such stress on individual autonomy that they underemphasized the collective nature of society. They also suffered from an exaggerated confidence in the ability of scientific rationality to solve human problems.

From the eighteenth until the twentieth century a futile battle was waged in the West between religion and rationality. Caught between two hostile parties, people were often forced to choose between belief and non-belief, religion and modern social freedoms, as if there were no middle ground. This intense dualism began to diminish in the late nineteenth and early twentieth centuries. Protestant theologians were the first to stick their heads out of the trenches and come to the conclusion that many modern values could be reconciled with Christian belief. In certain theological faculties in northern Europe and North America a tradition known as liberalism developed. Its proponents accepted the validity of the Enlightenment and the modern state it helped develop. They also stressed the legitimacy of theology as an academic discipline and the reasonableness of Christianity as a religious system. They were intent on making Christianity a moral force again in Western culture, especially among the educated and affluent members of society, many of whom had lost contact with the institutional church or were non-believers. In Catholic circles it would take more time to declare a truce between the church and modernity. Still reeling from the Reformation and the attack on its power by Enlightenment thinkers, the Catholic church would remain a defensive bastion until the 1960s.

Protestant liberalism suffered major setbacks as the twentieth century moved forward. The mindless slaughter of the First World War, and the horror of Nazi death camps a generation later, pointed to basic flaws in modern values. Gruesome historical events called into question the liberal assumption that Europe and North America were Christian parts of the world. By the mid-point of the twentieth century self-doubt replaced self-confidence as the dominant mood of many people in the West. Both Christianity and rationality seemed to have failed when they were most needed. In response to this pervasive crisis of faith, theologians began to rethink the role of Christianity in society. Although they recognized that much of modernity was good, they also realized that certain of its presuppositions demanded criticism. The exaggerated individualism and materialism of the twentieth century were clearly related to the fragmentation and violence of the times.

Finally shaking off its defensiveness, the Catholic church addressed the crisis and challenge of modernity during the Second Vatican Council, held from 1962 until 1965. During this meeting an international body of bishops and theologians, from many cultures and every continent, tried to refashion their church as a prophetic force capable of satisfying people's thirst for a life-giving vision. After decades of negativity toward modernity, the bishops tried to understand it in a more balanced way, assessing both its positive and negative qualities. In documents like *Lumen Gentium* and *Gaudium et Spes*, the bishops called on Catholic Christians to live the gospel more seriously and carry its message to secular society in a more productive way. They looked for a resurgence of Christian faith that would replace the self-doubt and skepticism that afflicted so many people in the developed world.

When the Council ended a massive effort was undertaken to implement its insights in the Catholic community. In few parts of the world did this campaign achieve greater success than in Latin America. The people of this largely Catholic continent had experienced profound social and economic changes in the 1960s that prompted serious questions about the relationship between their faith and the societies in which they lived. The Council's call to take the world seriously and forge a more just social order was welcome news for Latin American Catholics. Long associated with social and political conservatism, members of the church moved to the vanguard of intellectual and social activism. The Council's mandate would be carried out by a new generation of energetic theologians. They would create a theology faithful to the letter and spirit of Vatican II while going beyond its sometimes limited, European perspective.

The Birth of Liberation Theology

In the late 1950s a number of gifted Latin American priests were sent to Europe for training. When they arrived they found the theological scene in a state of transition. Despite some opposition from conservative elements in the hierarchy, theologians like Teilhard de Chardin and Karl Rahner were exploring the relationship between modernity and Christian belief. Gradually their views gained wide acceptance in the church and influenced the discussion and documents of the Council itself.

Priests like Gustavo Gutiérrez from Peru and Juan Luis Segundo from Uruguay found themselves caught up in a rare moment of theological excitement. A lively dialogue going on in Europe between theologians and social theorists also fired their imaginations. Pitted at each other's throats for decades, certain social scientists had begun to discover the more progressive side of Christianity while theologians had come to appreciate better the social scientists' analysis of modernity. Latin American theologians began to study Marx and Freud as well as Augustine and Aquinas. They returned to their countries with new theological ideas and a solid grasp of sociology, psychology, economics, and political theory. They were well equipped to respond to Vatican II's call for a renewed, socially committed Christian community.

When this new generation of theologians returned from Europe they realized that much of what they learned had to be translated to fit their context. In the 1960s Europeans had achieved a high level of economic affluence and political stability. Many Latin American countries, however, had sunk into unprecedented levels of poverty and political violence. As much as they were committed to the theology and vision of Vatican II, the young theologians realized that its message was directed to an audience different from their own. Vatican II tried to address the question of the church's role in developed societies afflicted by a crisis of meaning. Latin America's problems, however, had little to do with belief or the pros and cons of the Enlightenment. The vast majority of Latin Americans were Christians and few even knew about the Enlightenment. The problem in Latin America, as well as in Africa and Asia, was dehumanization. How could anyone talk about God when millions of human beings had been turned into "non-persons" by economic exploitation and political repression?

In 1968 the bishops of Latin America assembled in Medellín, Colombia to develop a pastoral strategy for implementing Vatican II in their continent. The document they issued, shaped by theologians like Gutiérrez and Segundo, called for a radical transformation of the Latin American church, along with the sociopolitical structures of the continent. Soon after Medellín Gustavo Gutiérrez published *A Theology of Liberation* in which he insisted that Christians commit themselves to the liberation of the poor and oppressed. The title of this book would soon be applied to a larger theological and pastoral movement in the global church that began to take shape in the late 1960s.

For Gutiérrez the poverty and injustice inflicted on millions of women and men in the developing world was a scandal that demanded redress. But for Gutiérrez liberation entailed more than economic and political justice. He acknowledged also a transcendent or spiritual dimension to the struggle for liberation. Social systems that deprived people of bread and freedom also deprived them of their God-given dignity. It numbed them to their own worth and beauty. If Christians believed in an incarnate God revealed in history they had to do something about the impoverished human beings around them. If they did not their talk about God would be meaningless.

For the first time in Christian theological history the question of the poor, the "non-persons" in the developing world, became the focal point of discussion. Traditional European debates between conservatives and liberals about modernity were not the real issue in Latin America. The question was how impoverished and oppressed people in the developing world fit into the Christian community. What did the institutional church, its social teachings, and the Bible have to say to them? Was the Christian community in the developed world willing to listen and respond to these people?

Gutiérrez's ideas and writings quickly gained a readership in other parts of the world, particularly in developing nations afflicted with problems similar to Latin America's. He is sometimes known as "the father of liberation theology," but the title is not entirely accurate. At the same time that he was writing James Cone, an African-American theologian, was spelling out a powerful theology of Black liberation in the United States. Cone's ideas were published slightly before Gutiérrez's and were remarkable for their vigor and intellectual incisiveness. Cone provided the Christian community with a powerful service by pointing to the suffering and oppression of minority people in developed countries and the dismal record of the Christian churches in confronting the racism in their midst. Cone's ideas would be useful in turn to African theologians, especially those in South Africa who were confronting the evils of *apartheid*.

Liberation Theology: Its Concerns and Characteristics

As liberation theology emerged as a coherent movement it became clear that its proponents, despite geographic and cultural differences, faced a common oppressive reality that challenged their Christian beliefs. As liberation theologians looked over their social and economic environments they saw that the affluence and freedoms of the industrial world were confined to a small percentage of people in the northern hemisphere. They began to charge that this disparity was actually a result of the way modern economic and political systems worked. It was symptomatic of an economic and political order that exploited a majority for the sake of a privileged minority.

The first phase of liberation theology, roughly until the 1970s, focused heavily on the relationship between faith and socioeconomic issues. To overcome the suffering around them, liberation theologians first had to understand its causes. Since capitalism was the dominant mode of production throughout the world, linking developed and developing countries, it was important to understand its economic and political characteristics. Because a great deal of analysis of the capitalist system had been done by social theorists, liberation theologians selectively employed their insights. Few liberation theologians, however, were naive about the limitations of Marxism, or any particular method of social analysis. Economics and sociology were helpful in explaining how societies worked, but could not entirely explain the poverty and oppression of the developing world. A more fundamental explanation, and one familiar in theological language, was the reality of sin. Simply put, much of the developing world's suffering was the result of sinful behavior on the part of powerful, developed nations. Many people in developed countries considered the developing world simply as a source of cheap raw materials and labor.

It was obvious that a solution to this pervasive injustice would require more than economic or political action. It demanded a change of heart. The solution liberation theologians offered for the poverty and oppression around them was Christianity lived in a radical way. Without rejecting modernity, they pointed to the individualism and materialism of people in the developed world as manifestations of sin, of a disordered worldview that caused others to suffer. At the same time, they called on the victims of exploitation in the developing world, particularly members of the Christian community, to overcome their passivity and act as the "voice of the voiceless" in the struggle for justice. The concern of liberation theologians was to formulate an explanation of Christian faith that took into consideration the experience and hopes of the poor and oppressed.

. . . (T)he reader will come across a term that is dear to most liberation theologians—*praxis*. Its precise meaning varies from one author to another, but essentially praxis implies action informed by reflection. Liberation theologians see praxis, especially what they call liberative praxis, as the principal task of the Christian community in the world today. The believing community cannot counsel patience when children die of malnutrition or people are murdered because they merely ask for a just wage. In such situations the Christian community must act. Liberative praxis, however, is more than a knee-jerk reaction to injustice. It flows from the community's understanding of itself as a gathering of Jesus' disciples called to embody his vision of God. The community does not exist for its own sake, but for the sake of all women and men, whether Christian or not. It serves them by working for justice and freedom. It also serves them by providing a setting in which human beings can enjoy each other, worship God, and achieve spiritual depth. The life of the community is itself a type of liberative praxis. It is an example of living freedom and just relationships made possible by faith.

Praxis is ultimately an expression of the Christian community's commitment to the world and faith in the gospel's power to transform life in a positive way. These factors make the praxis of the Christian community different from the activities of a political party or social movement. Political and social actions are indispensable components in the process of liberation. For the Christian, however, the ultimate purpose of liberation is the material *and* spiritual redemption of human beings from suffering and sin. Liberation theologians constantly stress that the poor are not powerless. As Gustavo Gutiérrez has pointed out, the developing world is made up of "poor but believing" people. To the extent that they believe in each other and the God who gave them life, they have enormous strength.

Liberation theologians have occasionally been accused by some of their critics of treating the poor and history romantically. Liberation theologians, however, see a side to history academics in developed countries rarely discover. They see innumerable instances in history when poor but believing people have maintained their self-respect, solidarity, and hope for the future. The fact that many contemporary Christians are committed to the liberation of their societies, despite all sorts of repression, speaks of an enigmatic power that Gutiérrez has called "the power of the poor in history." This power is a thread that liberation theologians see running through the complex fiber of history, giving it coherence and a transcendent purpose visible to people of faith.

. . . (T)his anthology contain(s) quotations from scripture, both Hebrew and Christian. It will be clear that liberation theologians, both Catholic and Protestant, rely heavily on the Bible. They see it as a source of revelation that provides insight into the meaning of life and the significance of contemporary events. The Hebrews' escape from slavery in Egypt and

Jesus' preaching of the Beatitudes are paradigmatic stories and sayings that reveal the true purpose of human existence. For liberation theologians, the Bible has a unifying theme and purpose, despite its historical and literary complexity. It narrates how human beings come to perceive God in their midst. The God of the Bible is made manifest on Sinai and in the person of Jesus. But this same God is also present in the poor and oppressed, and in all people of good will. In a world characterized by exploitation and violence, the person who believes in the God of the Bible will inevitably be involved in the struggle for justice, much like the great figures of the Hebrew and Christian scriptures.

Liberation theologians approach the Bible as a source of continuing revelation rather than as a collection of ancient writings. In some ways, the Exodus is still going on and the Beatitudes are still being preached. In almost every base Christian community, the Bible is the central book used to help its members understand their faith and task in the world. By reading and discussing the texts they come to realize that their struggle for justice is part of God's plan for creation. They see a correlation between the Hebrews in bondage, Jesus' preaching, and themselves. This awareness gives them a sense of dignity and confidence they often have never had. The Bible, then, is a key tool in raising people's consciousness and helping them chart an effective course of action in society.

Apart from the Bible, liberation theologians are also sensitive to the importance of Christian tradition. It makes us aware of the pains and joys, failures and successes of the Christian community throughout its complex and varied history. It links the Christian people together with symbols and stories that are the heritage of every member of the church. Liberation theologians have come to appreciate tradition as a life-giving force whose power is often manifest in cultural and artistic activity. In the slums of South Africa and Indian villages of Guatemala they have heard songs and seen dances that celebrate the pains and joys of ordinary human beings. In base Christian communities, the poor and oppressed celebrate what has been called the "underside of history." They remember and act out the lives of their predecessors in faith, simple but courageous people whose names are not mentioned in history books. They celebrate what the German theologian Johann Metz has called the "dangerous memories" of the Christian people. Liberation theologians point to the subversive nature of these memories. The history of the poor and oppressed is marked by victimization, but not total acquiescence to injustice. Of course, many people are overwhelmed by situations beyond their control and become fatalistic or passive. Nonetheless, there is also a tradition of resistance that speaks of a vibrant vision of life that negates the effects of injustice. Workers organize unions and women in slums muster their meager resources to create soup kitchens because they have faith and hope.

What liberation theologians have attempted to do in their varied ways is to insure Christianity's continued vitality and significance in today's world. Living among the poor and oppressed, they have seen just how powerful and positive their faith can be. Their writings try to capture the promise of this faith for the sake of the entire Christian community, and a world that desperately needs liberation from injustice and sin. What is liberating and revolutionary about Christianity is that it recognizes every human being as a child of God, something we too often forget in our modern, materialistic world. Many of the poor and oppressed, however, have not forgotten. It is they, and their tenacious faith, that call us to conversion and the affirmation of our own transcendence. If liberation theologians are correct, it may be the poor and oppressed who help save modernity from its own destructive impulses. In their struggle for justice many of them have achieved a profound understanding of life that liberation theologians see as an integral part of God's redemptive plan.

Robert Hass (b. 1941) is an American poet and winner of the 2007 National Book Award and the 2008 Pulitzer Prize for Time and Materials, *from which this poem is taken. Born in California, Hass was highly influenced by the 1950s Beat poets Allen Ginsberg, Lew Welch, and Gary Snyder. He received a PhD in English from Stanford University and currently teaches at the University of California, Berkeley. His scholarship includes translating works of the Lithuanian-Polish poet Czeslaw Milosz, Chilean poet Pablo Neruda, and the classic haiku of the Japanese masters, Basho, Buson, and Issa. Hass served as poet laureate of the United States during 1995–1997, promoting literacy, poetry, and ecological awareness to corporate boards and civic groups. He serves on the board of the International Rivers Network that advocates for human rights for the millions of people around the world whose homes and ways of life are destroyed by giant dam construction projects. How is his global perspective on justice revealed in this poem?*

Ezra Pound's Proposition

Robert Hass

Beauty is sexual, and sexuality
Is the fertility of the earth and the fertility
Of the earth is economics. Though he is no recommendation
For poets on the subject of finance,
I thought of him in the thick heat
Of the Bangkok night. Not more than fourteen, she saunters up to
    you
Outside the Shangri-la Hotel
And says, in plausible English,
"How about a party, big guy?"

Here is more or less how it works:
The World Bank arranges the credit and the dam
Floods three hundred villages, and the villagers find their way
To the city where their daughters melt into the teeming streets,
And the dam's great turbines, beautifully tooled
In Lund or Dresden or Detroit, financed
By Lazeres Freres in Paris or the Morgan Bank in New York,
Enabled by judicious gifts from Bechtel of San Francisco
Or Halliburton of Houston to the local political elite,
Spun by the force of rushing water,
Have become hives of shimmering silver
And, down river, they throw that bluish throb of light
Across her cheekbones and her lovely skin.

Cecilia Konchar Farr is professor of English and women's studies at St. Catherine University. A literary theorist, she teaches and writes about contemporary culture and twentieth-century American literature, including two books about Oprah's Book Club: Reading Oprah *(SUNY 2004) and* The Oprah Affect *(SUNY 2008). In this article, first presented at a conference on "Inclusive Science" at CSC in 2008, she condenses the complexities of feminist theory into four justice-centered questions in order to explain how the same concepts have worked for literary theorists and scientists as well as other feminist questioners. How can a multidisciplinary perspective assist in analyzing social justice issues? Can analysis of a social justice issue be complete if Konchar Farr's four questions are not asked?*

The Feminist Critique: Four Questions for Theorizing across Disciplines

Cecilia Konchar Farr

Women's Studies scholars spend a lot of time discipline-traveling—that is, moving among ideas, roaming to the edges of our fields of research where our work intersects with the work of feminists in other academic areas. As with the main character in a popular 2003 novel *The Time Traveler's Wife,* who never knew when he would pop out of the present moment and into another decade, discipline-travel just happens to us. *Pop.* I'm in my feminist writing group trying to figure out the intricate biological (im)balances of menopause or the mechanics of mating in sex-role-changing snails as I read my colleagues' research. *Pop.* I'm in a St. Kate's literature class explaining why Wendy Wasserstein's challenge from *The Heidi Chronicles,* "You either shave your legs or you don't," though astute and funny, can't *really* encompass the complexities of feminist politics in the early seventies. *Pop.* I'm in my favorite coffee shop just down the street from the college where my daughter and her politically engaged friends are challenging me, in the midst of the 2008 presidential primaries, to explain why some early feminist activists (now in their sixties and older) seem determinedly blind to the interconnections of race and class, why they seem to see gender as the only significant form of oppression.

I am a humanities scholar, a feminist theorist, and a professor of literature—this is my disciplinary identity, my place in the academic world. But I also teach Women's Studies, and Women's Studies is arguably the most successful of recent *inter*-disciplinary innovations in higher education. Most Women's Studies scholars are, like me, both rooted in their disciplines and sensitive to the flowering of feminist scholarship wherever it grows. For example, I will happily talk your ear off about novels, literary aesthetics, women's social reading practices, or Oprah's Book Club (just ask my students). Then, as in the instances above, when I need to turn to basic biology, political science, or sociology to sort out feminist concepts, my interdisciplinary training prepares me to do that, too.

Interdisciplinary scholarship, grounded in shared principles and assumptions, allows scholars a meeting place at the intersections of our traditional academic disciplines. At St. Kate's we value interdisciplinary skills as foundational to a good liberal arts education. In fact, they are central to your Global Search for Justice course, where we aim to examine justice across many fields and practices, and where your perspective—from nursing or nutrition, English or economics—is essential to the conversations.

So when several of my Women's Studies colleagues put together a national conference on "Inclusive Science" at St. Kate's in the summer of 2008, they, not surprisingly, invited arts and humanities, professional, social science and health care faculty and students to help out. Along with Amy Hilden, my colleague in philosophy, my task was to present the basics of feminist theorizing, to lay out some shared assumptions on day one of the conference. As I prepared for that presentation, however, I found myself suffering a strange discipline-traveling dislocation, trying to track a clear path through what had suddenly become a dense forest of feminist thinking. I talked with, wrote with, studied with, even ran with, my Women's Studies colleagues nearly every day, but confronted with an audience full of feminist scientists, I lost my footing. What, specifically, *were* the basics, the shared assumptions, the methods or principles that connected such diverse disciplines as ours? What language would allow a philosopher and a literary theorist to open a fruitful discussion with a bunch of scientists? Good conversation and exhilarating brainstorming followed, as Professor Hilden and I turned our attention toward the task of explaining the practices of interdisciplinary feminist thinking and came up with a simple map—"The Four Questions."

These four questions are meant to serve as a general overview of interdisciplinary feminist thinking, not to be a comprehensive guide to its complexities. They are justice-centered, reflecting both the origin of Women's Studies in the Women's Movement and our continued commitment to placing activism side-by-side with intellectual inquiry. In short, they are a place to begin asking feminist questions, exploring where such questions have led us, and imagining where they may lead us in the future when others pick them up and set off discipline-traveling with us.

Question #1: Where Are the Women?

If we begin historically, this is an early question in nearly every academic discipline and the one that inspired feminist political action in the midst of the Civil Rights and Anti-war Movements of the nineteen-sixties. Think about the faces of U.S. Presidents in a history book, the cover of the *Norton Anthology of Literature,* the gallery cards on the paintings in the famous museums of Europe, the list of Nobel-Prize-winning scientists, or even the faces of the leading sixties activists, and the question emerges quite naturally: Where are the women? Since we're more than fifty percent of the population, why are we not represented in equal proportion in the Senate or in the Forbes 500? Where are the women's voices on the radio and in our lecture halls?

From the middle of the Twentieth Century, this question spurred an astounding social transformation that continues today. Women serve on juries now; we are doctors, professors, electricians, and engineers; the legislative action Title IX opened doors for women in sports. In literature, feminist thinkers in the early seventies produced piercing critiques exploring lost women writers and neglected texts. These critiques gave us back Zora Neale Hurston and Harriet Jacobs, Kate Chopin and Harriet Beecher Stowe, all of whom were nearly lost to literary history but now claim a prominent place in American literature courses. Art historians famously rediscovered Artemisia Gentileschi and Mary Cassatt, and feminist historians established the centrality of pioneer and native women to a previously masculine version of frontier history. And these are just a few examples.

It's a simple question, but its echoes still resound across American culture. It comes up every year at the Oscars. Even NASCAR wants to know. And scientists now routinely look at their research, especially medical studies, and ask the question. At the Inclusive Science conference, one of the keynote speakers, Sue Rosser, a zoologist and leading expert on women in science and technology, presented an elegant critique of the system to earn patents in the U.S., a critique that began with one question as she studied the list of scientists and engineers who applied for patents: Where are the women?

Question #2: Where Is the Power?

Soon, however, it wasn't enough to notice that women were missing from art and science, history and culture. Feminist theorists wanted to know why. Whose interest did this omission serve? Who benefits and who suffers when women are excluded? Feminists from the Women's Movement of the nineteen-sixties and -seventies (who we generally call "second-wave" feminists to distinguish them from the "first-wave" suffragists of the nineteenth century) leaned on the concept of "patriarchy" to explain a system of oppression based on gender. Many psychological, literary, linguistic, scientific, theological, philosophical, sociological, and political studies began to ground their analyses in this concept of patriarchy, and to meticulously examine systems of oppression to foreground their power structures.

For example, in analyzing domestic violence, feminist theorists looked not just at the individual behavior of violent aggressors, but at the social systems that permitted these behaviors. They studied sex trafficking and pornography and how their values spilled over into more normalized heterosexual relationships; they looked at how some successful businesses used war metaphors and celebrated dominance; they examined the practices of a justice system that considered domestic issues personal and would not intervene in them; they tried to sort out the many ways that our culture rewarded women for being passive and child-like objects of admiration rather than fully realized human beings; they even looked for similar violent behaviors in simian communities. All of these are examples of how feminist scholars from many fields of study identified and explored patriarchy, the system of oppression based on gender.

Adrienne Rich's 1980 essay "Compulsory Heterosexuality and Lesbian Existence" is a good example of what results from this line of questioning. This foundational essay of early feminist theory (by a creative writer, a poet and essayist) notes that relationships between women are seldom the focus of our stories. Instead, she writes, women are punished for loyalties that stray from the proscribed boundaries of heterosexual relationships, and then Rich lists the many ways this occurs in our culture. "What purpose does this serve?", she asks, then concludes that "what surely impresses itself is the fact that we are confronting not simple maintenance of inequality and property possession" in this system of oppression, "but a pervasive cluster of forces, ranging from physical brutality to control of consciousness, which suggests that an enormous potential counterforce is having to be restrained" (349). This counterforce, she argues, is women's love for other women—women's friendships, sisterhood, mothering, and other bonds on a continuum of woman-to-woman connection. Compulsory heterosexuality is an oppressive system that works to curtail this counterforce.

It's quite a breathtaking analysis of power that, if nothing else, gives a new spin on Disney movies that have their motherless heroines married off as teenagers to beasts and strangers and call this a happy ending, while their heroes light off for the territories, love their dogs, have adventures and seldom marry. Why do girls (and boys) need to be taught these very different goals from such a young age? Rich's essay has an answer. She also casts a new light on a marriage industry that insists that every girl see her wedding day as the most important day of her life. Why? Whose interest does this unrelenting PR campaign for heterosexual coupling serve, and why is it necessary to direct it toward women?

Inspired by Marxist theory, these analyses of power added gender considerations to class and race hierarchies. "Where is the power?" turned out to be no idle question. Its roots went deep. As Biologist Maureen Zuk explained in her keynote address at the Inclusive Science conference, many early Victorian scholars asserted a scientific hierarchy of biological diversity that placed white men on top, the most developed, the most evolved. They were, simply, superior by nature and destined to rule. This was the foundation of colonialism and imperialism. Who benefits and who suffers?

But these questions also provide a challenge for feminist thinkers. These systems of oppression which include gender are also fierce in the policing of racial and class hierarchies. Given this understanding, it follows that upper and middle-class white women can be complicit in the oppression of others, even while they are discriminated against for their gender. In asking "Where is the power," white women met the enemy, and she was us.

Question #3: Where Am I Standing?

It would be inaccurate to place the question "Where am I standing?" in chronological sequence with the analyses of power we have followed so far in the development of feminist thinking, though it might seem a logical move. The chronology is, actually, more complex. Women working in justice movements, especially women of color, began challenging white women to ask this question from the earliest days of second-wave feminism, and they asked it of themselves, insistently, urgently, until white feminists finally caught up: How am I complicit in the oppression of others?

Lesbian and heterosexual women tussled over the same question for the first decade of the Women's Movement, with some influential separatist theorists arguing that the only way to ensure that you weren't colluding with patriarchy was to leave it. And leave it they did, sometimes forming all-woman utopian communes and collectives that attempted to avoid hierarchies of any sort. The radical group Redstockings, in their 1969 Manifesto, for example, repudiated "all economic, racial, educational, or status privileges that divide us from other women." They sought to "identify with all women."

Aims such as these, well-intentioned as they certainly were, had hidden hazards. If activists weren't aware of their own assumptions, of where they were standing in hierarchies of power (even when they were alone in the deserts of New Mexico), they unconsciously reproduced the oppressions they sought to fight. Maria Lugones memorably highlights white women's unwitting reproduction of these power structures in her 1987 essay "Playfulness, 'World'-Travelling, and Loving Perception." She describes how "white/Anglo women" treated women of color who were their compatriots in the feminist movement: "[T]hey ignore us, ostracize us, render us invisible; stereotype us, leave us completely alone, interpret us as crazy," she writes. "All of this *while we are in their midst*. The more independent I am, the more independent I am left to be. Their world and their integrity do not require me at all" (423).

Such writings shocked many feminist thinkers into examining their perspective and asking "Where am I standing?" Theorists, especially in the nineteen-eighties, began routinely to "locate" themselves in their writing. Phrases like "as a white, lesbian feminist . . ." or "as a woman of color in the academy . . ." (or "I am a humanities scholar, a feminist theorist, and a professor of literature") were omnipresent in scholarship. The essay we call "Unpacking the Invisible Knapsack" in *The Reflective Woman* reader is exemplary of this turn in feminist thinking. It compares patriarchal and racist oppression and insists that white readers acknowledge their unearned privilege—everything from flesh-colored bandages to violence-free neighborhoods. In this essay Peggy McIntosh makes the invisible visible, calling white feminists' attention to where we are standing in the racial hierarchies of power and obliging us to take responsibility for our advantages.

For the many feminist thinkers who connect their ideas to activism, sometimes standing itself becomes the problem. We often use the metaphor of the moving sidewalk at the airport to explain how to respond to our location in, as bell hooks calls it, "white supremacist capitalist patriarchy."[1] If this culture is our context/concourse and the moving sidewalk pushes us through it, it is not enough for the well-intentioned just to stop walking with it and stand still. The sidewalk will keep us moving in the same direction. Active resistance is required. We need to turn around and walk quickly (or run!) in the opposite direction, more quickly than the sidewalk is moving, if change is to come. Most Women's Studies scholars would add to this metaphor another possibility—a solution based on collective rather than individual action. In this version, we learn to work together across our differences; we build coalitions of diverse activists to block the machinery or to climb underneath, figure out how the sidewalk works, and dismantle it.

At times, recognizing where we were standing leads feminists not to turn away from patriarchal organizations and communities or to dismantle them but to devote themselves to rethinking, reforming, reclaiming, or restructuring them. It was exactly this clear-eyed insistence on recognizing their location and owning it responsibly that impressed me about Sister Joan Mitchell and other Catholic feminists when I arrived at St. Kate's over a decade ago. You may remember this passage from Sr. Joan's essay "All Women Can Be: The Spirit of the Sisters of St. Joseph" in *The Reflective Woman* reader: "Withdrawing from the church is the easiest answer. It's the answer of preference among Catholics in their twenties. It's not mine. It's not a lot of people's. As a Sister of St. Joseph I am a publicly committed woman of the church. I say, 'We are the Church. This is our home. We won't be put out'"(8).

The tricky thing about "Where am I standing" is that it generally begins as a personal question, even when the responses it engenders are collective or social. Each person must recognize her place in the structures of power and take responsibility for what she perceives, and what she can do, from that location. When I was a graduate student at Michigan State University, for example, Linda-Susan Beard, a Black feminist scholar (then teaching at MSU, now a monk in the Emmaus Community in nearby Vestaburg and Associate Professor of English at Bryn Mawr), challenged my research on the literary canon with one question: Where are the Black women writers in your thesis? While I thought I had been asking about women writers generally, I had actually been studying white women. Her one simple question (in what may have been the only conversation we ever had) permanently rearranged my research paradigms, my activism and my self-perception. She vividly highlighted where, in that privileged white world of graduate study, I had been standing—and I knew immediately that I didn't want to stand there. Feminist scholar Sandra Shullman explains how responsible feminist scholarship requires such self-awareness: "I don't think you can just think about feminism for periods of time without the fundamental process of recognizing that you are part of what you are studying."[2]

In a similar way, the concept of "being part of what you are studying" undergirds some innovative feminist research in the sciences, such as the research on maize by the geneticist Barbara McClintock. McClintock conceptualized herself in relationship to corn, not apart from it, looking at it objectively from above. She realized that where we stand affects what we see. She tried, as a result, to "let the corn speak to her," as Evelyn Fox Keller writes, rather than observing it through her own assumptions. As with Dian Fossey's study of gorillas or Jane Goodall's work with chimpanzees, McClintock situated herself in relationship with what she studied, not, as in more conventional scientific method, as a detached observer; she saw where she was standing and reconceived her work in response to that awareness.

Question #4: Where Are the Connections?

This question feels like the over-the-rainbow question to me—where the black and white world of theorizing suddenly goes Technicolor. A 1977 statement from the Combahee River Collective, a consciousness-raising group of black feminists, captures its promise:

> The most general statement of our politics at the present time would be that we are actively committed to struggling against racial, sexual, heterosexual, and class oppression and see as our particular task the development of an integrated analysis and practice based upon the fact that *the major systems of oppression are interlocking*. The synthesis of these oppressions creates the conditions of our lives [emphasis mine].

In other words, "Where am I standing?" was a much more complicated question for these feminists who stood at the nexus of "interlocking systems of oppression." In their statement, the Combahee River Collective writers reconceived feminist thinking as an integrated analysis of multiple oppressions that couldn't and shouldn't be separate.

And that's where things go Technicolor. Asking "Where are the connections?" leads to intricate and fascinating studies, across disciplines, across oppressions, across continents. Being a part of what we are studying and working together across differences requires responsible feminist theorists to be more aware of the various ties we have with each other and the myriad implications of our work. Just between 1985 and 1995, for example, Donna Haraway produced the challenging "Cyborg Manifesto," imagining where feminism meets science and technology; Gloria Anzaldúa memorably charted the "Borderlands" of mestiza feminism at the intersections of race, gender, sexuality, culture, and geography; Judith Butler ruptured paradigms with her theories of gender performance, theories that didn't even begin with women but with male drag performers; and Winona La Duke linked the issues of indigenous people inexorably with a call for environmental responsibility. "One hundred years ago one of our great leaders, Chief Seattle, stated, 'What befalls the Earth, befalls the people of the Earth,'" she reminded her audience at an international conference in China in 1995. "And that is the reality today, and the situation of the status of women, and the status of indigenous women and indigenous peoples" (525).[3]

Integrated analyses such as these continue, with interrogations of gender and sexuality, race, ability, class, and global political efforts. And women of color often take the lead in this work, their intellectual perception drawing not just on rigorous research and scholarship but also on lived experience of multiple oppressions. At the Inclusive Science conference, in fact, the last keynote address was from Beverly Tatum, a clinical psychologist, President of Spelman College, and African-American woman, who has for years studied students of color and their identity development. She coached her audience on how to be more inclusive teachers, especially as we encourage women of color into the sciences.

Patricia Hill Collins, in *Black Feminist Thought*, explains how aiming for this more integrated, more sophisticated feminist analysis through accessing multiple perspectives brings us closer to truth than any attempts at detached objectivity could. Her process for conducting this analysis, called "standpoint theory," is also quite unlike the ways scholars have worked traditionally: "Each group speaks from its own standpoint and shares its own partial, situated knowledge. But because each group perceives its own truth as partial, its knowledge is unfinished. Each group becomes better able to consider other groups' standpoints without relinquishing the uniqueness of its own standpoint or suppressing other groups' partial perspectives" (270). In order to construct a basis of shared knowledge, however, the dominant group has to be "de-centered," to take its place as one voice among many. Similarly, Chandra

Talpade Mohanty reminds us that global feminist work must carefully maintain the "historical heterogeneities of the lives of women in the third world" or risk representing "a composite, singular 'third world woman,'" which finds its roots in the damaging discourse of colonialism (373).

Because "Where are the connections?" multiplies the possibilities of feminist analysis, it also discomfits some scholars who want a neater arrangement of ideas, a more carefully delineated border for our work. Let's face it: interdisciplinarity is messy and chaotic. It's not easy maintaining historic heterogeneities, attuning your ear to many voices, or being de-centered. Attention to this final question even transforms the three questions that preceded it. "Where are the women?" can't be what it often was in early feminist thinking (and what it was still for those Hillary supporters who irked my daughter during the 2008 presidential contest), i.e., "Where are the white women?" Likewise, "Where is the power?" And "Where am I standing?" can no longer occupy a metaphorical three-dimensional plane, a sidewalk, a ladder, or a hierarchy. They are alive with expanding dimensions and subatomic motion. But as American Civil Rights leader Septima Clark wrote, "I have great belief in the fact that whenever there is chaos, it creates wonderful thinking. I consider chaos a gift" (Lanker 164). The chaos of multiple connections has been a great gift to feminist thinking, enlivening scholarship, enhancing learning, and inspiring activism.

The discomfort of multiplicity is also characteristic of discipline-traveling, as any seasoned traveler will attest. We're always on the edges of our expertise, pushing ourselves to understand connections with ideas beyond our proficiencies. What's more, we're writing the guidebooks as we go. As Adrienne Rich notes in Poem XIII of her "Twenty-One Poems" (and Nancy Wanderer quotes in the "Frontline" documentary *Hillary's Class* that many of you watched in TRW), "Whatever we do together is pure invention/the maps they gave us were out of date by years."

I offer you "The Four Questions," then, as a starting place, a travel bug, maybe, that will stoke your own feminist inquiry. You can ask these questions of texts and histories, situations and studies, data and evidence. Feminist inquiry like this has already generated lively interdisciplinarity, productive multiplicity, unusual connections, and collective action. My hope is that more attention to this path-breaking feminist scholarship will open all of our fields to more, and more responsible, discipline-traveling.

My thanks to Amy Hilden and the conversations with her that inspired this paper, to Cindy Norton who included it in "Inclusive Science," to Sharon Doherty who demanded (as nicely as a Minnesotan can) that it be written, and to the other scholars in my Women's Studies writing group, discipline-travelers all.

Notes

[1] Beverly Tatum is likely the originator of this metaphor, though it is used often, in various ways, in activist work. She writes about the moving sidewalk in an essay on racism, "Defining Racism: Can We Talk," excerpted in *The Reflective Woman* reader from her book *Why Are All the Black Kids Sitting Together in the Cafeteria?*

[2] I have used this quote from Sandra Shullman for years. I found it, somewhere, during graduate school in the late eighties. When I tried to track down its source, I kept coming up empty. So about ten years ago, I located Professor Sandra Shullman, Ph.D., Professor of Counseling Psychology, and phoned her at Ohio State University, where she was on the faculty (and served in administration). She owned that it certainly sounded like something she says, but she wasn't sure of its origin, either. Probably the transcript of a speech, she decided. The point is I use it here with her permission. Dr. Shullman is currently Managing Partner of the Columbus office of the Executive Development Group, an international leadership development and consulting firm in Ohio.

[3] These examples (Harraway, Anzaldúa, Butler, and LaDuke) of innovations in feminist "intersectionality," as we call it, are selected from *Feminist Theory: A Reader*, 2nd edition (Wendy Kolmer and Frances Bartkowski, eds. Boston: McGraw-Hill, 2005).

Works Cited

Cambahee River Collective. "A Black Feminist Statement" in *Feminist Theory: A Reader* (2nd edition). Wendy Kolmer and Frances Bartkowski, eds. Boston: McGraw-Hill, 2005. 311–316.

Collins, Patricia Hill. *Black Feminist Thought: Knowledge, Consciousness, and the Politics of Empowerment* (2nd Edition). New York: Routledge, 2000.

Hillary's Class. "Frontline," 15 November 1994. Ofra Bikel and Rachel Dretzin, producers. WGBH Educational Foundation.

hooks, bell. *Feminist Theory from Margin to Center* (2nd edition). Cambridge MA: South End P, 2000.

Keller, Evelyn Fox. *A Feeling for the Organism: The Life and Work of Barbara McClintock* (10th Anniversary edition). New York: Times Books, 1984.

LaDuke, Winona. "Mothers of Our Nations: Indigenous Women Address the World" in *Feminist Theory: A Reader* (2nd edition). Wendy Kolmer and Frances Bartkowski, eds. Boston: McGraw-Hill, 2005. 525–528.

Lanker, Brian. *I Dream a World: Portraits of Black Women Who Changed America.* New York: Stewart, Tobori and Chang, 1989.

Lugones, Maria. "Playfulness, 'World'-Travelling, and Loving Perception" in *Women, Knowledge, and Reality*. Ann Garry and Marilyn

Pearsall, eds. New York: Routledge, 1996. 419-433. http//sc.temple.edu/shea/lugones.pdf (8 January 2009).

Mitchell, Joan, CSJ. "All Women Can Be: The Spirit of the Sisters of St. Joseph" in *The Reflective Woman* reader (7th edition). College of St. Catherine, 2008. 3–10.

McIntosh, Peggy. "White Privilege and Male Privilege" in *The Reflective Woman* reader (7th edition). College of St. Catherine, 2008. 91–103. From "Working Paper #189 of the Wellesley College Center for Research on Women," 1988.

Mohanty, Chandra Talpade. "Under Western Eyes: Feminist Scholarship and Colonial Discourses" from *Third World Women and the Politics of Feminism* excerpted in *Feminist Theory: A Reader* (2nd edition). Wendy Kolmer and Frances Bartkowski, eds. Boston: McGraw-Hill, 2005. 372–380.

Niffenegger, Audrey. *The Time Traveler's Wife*. San Francisco: McAdam/Cage, 2003.

"Redstockings Manifesto" in *Feminist Theory: A Reader* (2nd edition). Wendy Kolmer and Frances Bartkowski, eds. Boston: McGraw-Hill, 2005. 220–22.

Rich, Adrienne. "Compulsory Heterosexuality and Lesbian Existence" in *Blood, Bread and Poetry: Selected Prose 1979–1985*. New York: Norton, 1994.

_____. "Poem XIII" in *Dream of Common Language, Poems 1974–1977*. New York: Norton, 1993.

Shullman, Sandra. Origin unknown. Used with permission of author. *See note above.*

Tatum, Beverly Daniel. "Defining Race: Can We Talk" in *The Reflective Woman* reader (7th edition). College of St. Catherine, 2008. 320–332. Excerpted from *Why Are All the Black Kids Sitting together in the Cafeteria?: A Psychologist Explains the Development of Racial Identity* (Fifth Anniversary Revised Edition). New York: Basic Books (2003).

Wasserstein, Wendy. *The Heidi Chronicles, Uncommon Women and Others and Isn't it Romantic*. New York: Vintage, 1991.

Pamela R. Fletcher is associate professor of English, co-director of the interdisciplinary program in critical studies of race and ethnicity, and director of writing programs at St. Catherine University. She is co-editor (with Buchwald and Roth) of Transforming A Rape Culture *(1993, 1995, and 2005). In "Dismantling Rape Culture around the World: A Social Justice Imperative," Fletcher challenges us to see rape culture as an urgent social justice issue. What is rape culture? What are its global dimensions? How might Catholic Social Teaching and International Human Rights frameworks help us respond? What can we do in our daily lives to disrupt rape culture?*

Dismantling Rape Culture around the World: A Social Justice Imperative

Pamela R. Fletcher

Abstract

Many object to the term *rape culture*, deeming it an overstatement. Some even consider it an oxymoron, for how does rape and culture really connect? In speaking of culture, we editors of *Transforming A Rape Culture* (Buchwald, Fletcher and Roth 1993, 1995 and 2005) refer to the way in which a society operates formally and informally, based on attitudes, beliefs, customs, and rituals that its members sanction as acceptable and normal. Based on our research and analysis of the high incidence of sexual violence perpetrated around the world, we contend that the term encompasses widespread anti-female attitudes and values, and the resultant oppressive conditions women and children encounter in the global institution of patriarchy. Misogyny and sexism are the cornerstones of patriarchy that enable a rape culture to flourish.

In *Transforming A Rape Culture*, we define a rape culture as "a complex of beliefs that encourage male sexual aggression and supports violence against women [and girls], a society where violence is seen as sexy and sexuality as violent, and a continuum of threatened violence that ranges from sexual remarks to sexual touching to rape itself. A rape culture condones physical and emotional terrorism against women [and girls] and presents it as the norm" (Buchwald, Fletcher, and Roth 2005, XI). The physical and emotional terror that stems from sexual violence, while often deemed as terrible, is usually dismissed as individual misfortune rather than understood as a cultural phenomenon.

Introduction

In this internationally-focused paper, rape culture means, based on the Rome Statue, Article 7, of the International Criminal Court's definition of crimes against humanity, the violation of the mind, body, and spirit, whether in public or private life, including battery, molestation, sexual harassment, "rape, sexual slavery, enforced prostitution, forced pregnancy, enforced sterilization, and any other form of sexual violence of comparable gravity" (http://untreaty.un.org/cod/icc/statute/romefra.htm). In 1992, editors of *Transforming A Rape Culture* (1993, 1995, and 2005), held several focus groups in the Twin Cities of Minneapolis/St. Paul, Minnesota, and found among the diversity of the group members—male and female, white and of color—that nearly each of them has been affected somehow by rape culture (Buchwald, Fletcher, and Roth 2005, XI).

Although rape is underreported to the police, U.S. Department of Justice studies show that when rape survivors do report, more than 50% of them state that they knew the rapist (Ibid). World Health Organization (WHO) statistics report that in most countries, 30 percent to 60 percent of women encountered physical or sexual assault by an intimate partner (Kristof and WuDunn 2009, 61).

Given such a global trend, women and men accept sexual violence as normal and interminable. In their acceptance, they tacitly sanction the notion that women and children's bodies belong to men to treat according to their will. As a result, the unjust institution of patriarchy that condones and upholds a rape culture, which dehumanizes women and girls, tends to go unexamined and unchallenged. Rape culture will persist until societal values and attitudes change to create and institute gender parity, yielding social justice.

Looking at Rape Culture Through the Lens of Catholic Social Teaching

According to Theologian Russell B. Connors, Jr.,

> The phrase 'Catholic Social Teaching' refers to the sum total of teachings provided by Catholic leaders—popes, bishops, and sometimes theologians—concerning the social issues of the day, especially over the past 100 years. Christian faith does not shield believers from difficult social issues, but rather impels them to try to contribute to their solutions. In that spirit, the popes and bishops do not presume to offer simple answers to complex questions, but try to show what the relationship might be between Christian faith and social issues (Connors 2009, 124–125).

Of course, there are multiple and multifaceted perspectives of social justice, so why choose Catholic Social Teaching (CST) to address the issue of rape culture? CST challenges the *social structures* that underlie a rape culture.

In 1891, Pope Leo XIII led the way for confronting the social injustice of the day when he wrote his encyclical letter, "Rerum Novarum" ("The Condition of Labor") (Ibid, 126). In this letter, the pope confronted the terrible working conditions laborers encountered in the new industries of European cities: "He called for a change in the social structures and institutions . . . that were the causes of the poverty and misery of the workers. He called for a just and living wage, for working conditions that were safe, and for laws that would prevent the abuse of children in the workforce. . . . He insisted that human dignity must be recognized and respected in the workers of the world" (Ibid). Fundamental to CST are convictions of justice, like human dignity and equality, that challenge structural frameworks upholding injustice of *any* nature.

> *Humanity dignity* is one of the seven convictions of CST: The life and dignity of every human being is of incalculable worth and must be recognized, respected, and reverenced. Human rights, 'the minimum conditions of life for community,' (U.S. Catholic Bishops, 'Economic Justice for All,' par. 17) must be protected and promoted in order for human dignity to be respected and human beings to flourish (Ibid, 127).

Human dignity and human rights go hand in hand, according to CST, and both must be recognized and respected.

Theologian J. Milburn Thompson defines "rights" as "those basic human goods that are due to human beings so that they can develop themselves fully as persons living in community" (Ibid, 129). In his 1963 encyclical letter, "Pacem in Terris,"Pope John XXIII listed eight human rights. One of the rights directly applicable to self-development is "the right to choose one's state in life" (Ibid). Any human being subjected steadily to the will and abuse of another learns to live in fear and fails to live according to her own will, unable to thrive.

The 30 Articles of the United Nations' 1948 Universal Declaration of Human Rights establish secular perspectives of social justice; and, Article 1 reflects the CST conviction, *human dignity*. Article 1 states: "All human beings are born free and equal in dignity and rights. They are endowed with reason and conscience and should act towards each other in the spirit of [community] (Hanley et al 2009, 231)." (Here community replaces brotherhood). Article 1 also coincides with the CST conviction, equality: "Equality. All human beings are fundamentally equal, regardless of race, creed, gender, sexual orientation, and educational or economic status. Every '-ism' that alienates and oppresses people must be opposed and overcome" (Connors 2009, 127). Sexism and misogyny that alienates and oppresses women and children can be opposed and overcome through incremental structural, systemic change. The convictions of Catholic Social Teaching and the Articles of the U.N.'s 1948 Universal Declaration of Human Rights set the stage for such change globally.

Making Sexual Violence a Human Rights Issue

Following the creation of the United Nations' 1948 Declaration of Human Rights, the Fourth 1949 Geneva Convention, established international humanitarian law "relative to the Protection of Civilian Persons in Time of War." Article 27 proclaimed: "Protected persons are entitled, in all circumstances, to respect for their persons, their honour, their family rights, their religious convictions and practices, and their manners and customs. They shall at all times be humanely treated, and shall be protected especially against all acts of violence or threats thereof and against insults and public curiosity. Women shall be especially protected against any attack on their honour, in particular against rape, enforced prostitution, or any form of indecent assault" (http://www.icrc.org/ihl.nsf/full/380?opendocument). Vesna Kesic (2005, 280) points out, though, that a closer reading of this government document reveals that sexual violence against women during war is considered "an assault on honor or . . . a crime against morality and not . . . an act of violence against a human being." While the document calls for the protection of women, it doesn't include any repercussions for committing violence against women. In fact, the document offers no clear consequences for the violation of any of the 159 articles. Instead, it sets out to influence public policy. It acts as a standard of conduct, propelled by Henry Dunant and Gustave Moynier, co-founders of the Red Cross, who decided that their voluntary humanitarian organization would serve as a non-governmental organization in monitoring the treatment of prisoners of war and civilians during wartime.

According to Kesic (Ibid, 273), "Although sexual violence of women in wartime has been known throughout human history, rape had not been recognized specifically as a war crime. Wartime rapes had not been investigated, prosecuted, or punished because no laws covered them. Like peacetime sexual assaults against women, they remained crimes without a name." Notable incidents of such crimes are: The Rape of Nanjing in 1937, the exploitation of Japanese "comfort women" used as sexual slaves throughout Asia during WWII, the mass rape of German women at the end of WWII, and the widespread rapes of women during the Bangldesh-Pakistan war in the early 1970s (Ibid, 272). In the 1990s, however, the extensive media coverage and the general outrage about the mass rapes that had occurred in Bosnia and Rwanda caused an attitudinal shift.

Notably, in 1995, the U.N.'s Fourth World Conference on Women: Action for Equality, Development, and Peace took place in Beijing, China during September 4–15. The attendees addressed three critical issues: women and armed conflict, violence against women, and women's human rights. The conference's central concern was to address the inequality and discrimination occurring in women's private and public lives. There was a call to remove obstacles to women's public and private lives through a full and equal share in economic, social, cultural, and political decision-making (accessed July 8, 2010).

At this conference, during the time when she served as First Lady, Hilary Rodham Clinton delivered her famous speech, "Women's Rights are Human Rights." In this speech, she stated, "As long as discrimination and inequities remain so commonplace around the world—as long as girls and women are valued less, fed less, fed last, overworked, underpaid, not schooled and subjected to violence in and out of their homes—the potential of the human family to create a peaceful, prosperous world will not be realized. Let this Conference be our—and the world's call to action" (http://www.famousquotes.me.uk/speeches/Hillary-Clinton/). Clearly, Clinton and women worldwide were coalescing to raise consciousness about the injustice plaguing women and girls' lives and taking concrete action to make change.

In 1993, two years prior to the U.N.'s Fourth World Conference on Women, The Vienna Declaration and Program of Action, adopted by the U.N. World Conference on Human Rights, had paved the way for the recognition of women's rights as human rights. Although it specifically focused on women's rights *during wartime*, this document was the first to acknowledge women's status as human: "Violations of the human rights of women in situations of armed conflict are violations of the fundamental principles of international human rights and humanitarian law" (accessed on July 8, 2010).

The 1990s were a pivotal time, for also in 1993 and 1995, the International War Crimes Tribunal for the Former Yugoslavia (ICTY) and the Tribunal for Rwanda (ICTR) were established respectively. As Vesic (2005, 274–275) observes:

> The statue of the ICTY is the first international legal document that singles out rape as a crime against humanity. . . . The mass rapes that took place during the wars in the former Yugoslavia, particularly in Bosnia and Herzegovina, were the first in history to be brought before an international court, and these crimes, together with the mass rapes that occurred in Rwanda, contributed to groundbreaking changes in international humanitarian law.

Forty-five years later, since the various humanitarian stances of the United Nations, the 1949 Fourth Geneva Conference, and the Vienna Declaration and Program of Action, the 1993 ICTY statute finally authorizes the world court to institute and try rape as a crime against humanity.

From a feminist legal perspective, however, Kesic (2005, 286) explains that women lawyers and activists argue that the 1993 ICTY statue doesn't consider rape a *gender-specific* crime against women, but a crime against women as members of an ethnic or a national group: " It was not the atrocity as such (mass rape of women, harm done to the single woman), but the purpose of that atrocity, in these cases ethnic cleansing or genocide, that decided the character of the crime." The emphasis on gender-specific crimes occurred five yeas later with the creation of the International Criminal Court (ICC). Established in 1998 as a sort of watchdog, it investigates and prosecutes war crimes, crimes of genocide, and crimes against humanity when the national authorities shirk their responsibilities. Because the ICC recognizes the role gender plays in the perpetration of crimes against women, the Rome Statue includes the following:

1. Gender-specific crimes are now included under two of the three core crimes that are provided: crimes against humanity and war crimes.
2. The listing of the crimes cover a much broader spectrum than before (ICTY, ICTR). Rape, sexual slavery, enforced prostitution, forced pregnancy, enforced sterilization, and any other form of sexual violence of comparable gravity are defined as crimes against humanity (Ibid).

Through the persistence of women and their male allies, it took 50 years for women to gain status as human beings, particularly in the arena of international law. Yet, the struggle for women's rights as human rights still persists, in times of both war and peace.

The Continuum of Violence Against Women

Kesic (Ibid, 271) asks the following important question: "To what extent does gendered war violence differ from everyday peacetime violence against women, such as rape, battery, and sexual harassment? Do these different forms of violence all belong to the same continuum of violence against women?" A related question is also as important: Should the violence perpetrated against women and children in developing countries (rape and genocide in wartime, and sexual abuse and exploitation in peacetime) be ranked above the violence women and children suffer in wealthy countries? Clearly, the institution of patriarchy becomes distended during war, when men exaggerate their allegiance to the traditional notions of masculinity, exercising might over others who are deemed weak. The power that men assume by dominating, abusing, and exploiting women and children, male supremacy, becomes heightened during war. Nevertheless, this power to subjugate women and children, this male supremacy, still operates, mostly covertly, during peacetime and in wealthy countries.

Living in a wealthy country may lead some to feel a false sense of security or to trivialize pervasive sexual violence that may be concealed. Statistics, though, challenging to collect, indicate that much of the violence perpetrated against many women goes unnoticed and unreported to police. As Kristof and WuDunn (2009, 61) state, "A major study by the

World Health Organization [WHO] found that in most countries, between 30 percent and 60 percent of women had experienced physical or sexual assault by a husband or boyfriend. 'Violence against women by an intimate partner is the major contributor to the ill health of women,' said former director of WHO, Lee Jong-wook." Regarding the occurrence of intimate partner violence in the United States, the National Violence Against Women Survey (Buchwald, Fletcher and Roth 2005, 8) report,

> Violence against women is primarily intimate partner violence: 64 percent of the women who reported being raped, physically assaulted, or stalked since age eighteen were victimized by a current or former husband, cohabitating partner, boyfriend, or date. . . . The report concludes with the statement that violence against women, particularly intimate partner violence, should be classified as a major public health and criminal justice concern in the United States.

Despite the WHO statistics Kristof and WuDunn (2009, 61) cite in their work pertaining to intimate partner violence, they (Ibid, xv) contend, "Discrimination in western countries is often a matter of unequal pay or underfunded sports teams or unwanted touching from a boss. In contrast, in much of the world, discrimination is lethal." *There is no doubt*: in developing countries, poor women and girls suffer horrific, public treatment or death at the hands of men and boys. No one can argue against the degree or nature of violence that occurs. Yet, in western countries, the terrible and often secret treatment or death that women and girls endure is serious and noteworthy. For instance, one can find similarity in the incidence of rape that females encounter globally, as noted in the following statistics:

1. Women in the U.S. reported that they were raped at an early age: 17.6% said they had been victims of an attempted or a completed rape, 21.6% were younger than age 12, and 32.4% were between the ages 12 and 17 (Buchwald, Fletcher and Roth 2005, 7).

2. Twenty-one percent of young women surveyed in Ghana reported that their sexual initiation was by rape (Kristof and WuDunn 2009, 62).

3. Seventeen percent of Nigerian women said they had endured rape or attempted rape by the age of nineteen (Ibid).

4. Twenty-one percent of South African women reported that they had been raped by the age of fifteen (Ibid).

The statistics have a common thread: a significant percentage of *girls* were assaulted. All women and girls, no matter where they are in the world, experience some kind of gender discrimination, abuse, and violence, though the experience definitely varies in form and scale. The experience is especially insidious in the West because it is often veiled. Therefore, it is crucial to recognize the extent and the varied facets of patriarchy.

Without an understanding of how the institution of patriarchy functions, women cannot resist and struggle to overcome the structural, systemic force. It is *a way of life* around the world. It cannot be dismantled until the differential power of men fundamental to the institution of patriarchy—a structure that institutes, promotes, and perpetuates gender inequality, misogyny, and violence—is acknowledged as unjust by both men and women. Underlying a rape culture are vicious anti-female attitudes that even women harbor. Women's complicity, given its vast complexity, with the institution of patriarchy must also be acknowledged as part of the problem. In their attempt to persuade their reader to join the movement in "emancipating" poor women and girls in developing countries, Kristof and WuDunn (2009, 67–69) remark that men are not villains and tyrants. Yes, they admit: "Men are brutal to women." But, they argue, "Women themselves transmit misogynistic values just as men do. This is not a tidy world of tyrannical men and victimized women, but a messier realm of oppressive social customs adhered to by men and women. . . . These attitudes are *embedded in culture* and will change only with education and leadership" (Italics mine). On some level, they are right about women's complicity. They are right about the problem being structural and systemic, an institution of patriarchy upheld by everyone.

But their analysis is shortsighted because they don't acknowledge male supremacy that is foundational to patriarchy. The social injustice of rape culture will not cease without a true societal commitment to examining and addressing the social, political, and economic power men possess over women and children. This differential power infiltrates every aspect of the world, through every patriarchal structure of society, particularly the family and gender relations, accompanied by the resultant attitudes and beliefs about female inferiority.

The Challenge of Dismantling Rape Culture

Attitudes and values must continue to change. Change happens incrementally, slowly, as demonstrated over the 50 years it took to get international law to recognize and protect women's humanity and rights. It took even longer for American women to gain the right to vote through the 19th amendment—nearly 100 years. After the 19th amendment was passed in 1920, suffragist Alice Paul wrote the Equal Rights Amendment in 1921. It took 49 years for Congress to finally pass the amendment, but it fell short of the necessary three votes required for ratification by the July 1982 deadline. Given such national history, it's not ironic that the U.S.A., the number one super power in world politics, is less progressive in its views and values regarding women than, say, Rwanda, a worn-torn and violent country, where women hold 55 percent of the seats in the lower house of Parliament, or Liberia, another worn-torn and violent country, where a woman, Ellen Johnson Sirleaf, is the head of state. While the U.S.A. has a nice, shiny veneer, underneath lies a marred relationship to its female citizenry. This is what patriarchy looks like in the States. But, it's this nice, shiny veneer that lulls many American women into a false sense of security.

In the summer of 2009, Diplomatic Correspondent Mark Landler interviewed Secretary of State Hilary Rodham Clinton about a new international gender agenda before she left the U.S. for an 11-day trip to Africa. In noting that gender equality is not universally accepted, even in the U.S. A., he asked Clinton the following question:

"I've been at more than a few women's events with you overseas where the men in the audience drift off to their Blackberrys or into a snooze after a few minutes. How do you change the mind-set, not just over seas but at home and in this building, that tends to view women's issues as a pink ghetto?" (Landler 2009, 43). Clinton replied, "By making the arguments that I am making here—that the so-called women's issues are stability issues, security issues, equity issues (Ibid). Later in the interview, Landler mentioned the question that a young Indian woman in New Delhi asked Clinton: "How would you view the progress of women in both India and United States [where a female president is yet to be elected while India elected a woman prime minister within three decades of independence]?" (Ibid). Secretary of State Clinton stated, "My campaign for many millions of reasons gave a lot of heart to many young women . . . 'I went back to school because of your campaign.' So, it's unfinished business, and young women know it is unfinished business" (Ibid). Clinton is speaking about the comments of young women living around the world, including those living in the U.S.A. They expressed to her a common feeling that they have about the inequity women still face and the necessity to overcome that inequity.

Unlike some who think that one specific program, like education, would be the panacea, Clinton asserts, with insight,

> We are having as a signature issue the fact that women and girls are a core factor in our foreign policy. If you look at what has to be done, in some societies, it is a different problem than in others. In some of the societies where women are deprived of political and economic rights, they have access to education and health care. In some societies, they may have been given the right to vote, but girl babies are still being put out to die. So, it's not one specific program, so much as a policy.

In their book, *Half the Sky*, Kristof and WuDunn (2009, 238) insist that two of the best ways to affect change is through education and economic empowerment of women in developing countries: "We've argued that one way to soothe some conflict-ridden societies is to bring women and girls into schools, the workplace, government, and business, partly to boost the economy and partly to ease testosterone-laden values of these countries. We would never argue that the [economic] empowerment of women is a silver bullet, but it is an approach that offers a range of rewards that go far beyond simple justice." It is unclear what they mean by "simple justice," but their point is well taken when one considers the time it takes to shift or create public policy. And, one knows that legislation cannot change the hearts and minds of people, though it can regulate their conduct along the way.

Yet, the authors seem to have a blind spot regarding the role of patriarchy in the oppression of women and girls. For example, their use of language, like the phrase "testosterone-laden," is highly problematic, for it appears to trivialize the impact of male dominance. As journalists, Nicholas D. Kristof and Sheryl WuDunn (2009, 33) admit that before they began reporting on the violation of women's human rights for the New York Times around 1990, they didn't perceive the importance of doing such coverage: "Traditionally, the status of women was seen as a 'soft' issue—worthy but marginal. . . . We preferred to focus instead on the 'serious' international issues, like trade disputes or arms proliferation." Their initial consideration of women and girls' status as "marginal" merely reflects how the world at large has always devalued female lives.

If one peels back the proverbial onion, one would notice the stark connection between the lives of women/girls and war, and their lives and the global economy. For instance, in speaking to the importance of educating girls in developing countries, a 2008 Goldman Sachs research report stated, "Gender inequality hurts economic growth" (Kristof and WuDunn 2009, xx). The Goldman Sachs' report influenced the corporation to invest $100 million in the business education of 10,000 women (Ibid). Moreover, Kristof and WuDunn (2009, 28) assert,

> There's a growing recognition among everyone from the World Bank to the U.S. military's Joint Chiefs of Staff to aid organizations like CARE that focusing on women and girls is the most effective way to fight global poverty and extremism. That's why foreign aid is increasingly directed to women. The world is awakening to a powerful truth: Women and girls aren't the problem; they're the solution.

While the journalists, economists, and politicians identify the solution, they avoid naming the problem directly. Kristof and WuDunn point out women who became successful entrepreneurs in their communities, creating employment opportunities and working to build wealth. Yet, the majority of female workers will not become entrepreneurs but will work in factories. In viewing the big picture, can world poverty be solved when women are exploited in sweatshops?

Kristof and WuDunn (Ibid, 28–29) further declare, "The oppression of women worldwide is the human rights cause of our time. And their liberation could help solve many of the world's problems." However, in their analysis of the problems and the oppression women and girls endure, the writers often use passive language, omitting the agent of any action taken against the women and girls they mention. For instance, in the following statement, Kristof and WuDunn (Ibid, 33–34) state:

> The global statistics on the abuse of girls are numbing. It appears that more girls and women are now missing from the planet, precisely because they are female, than men were killed on the battlefield in all the wars of the 20th century. The number of victims of this routine 'gendercide' far exceeds the number of people who were slaughtered in all the genocides of the 20th century.

How can one make such an observation without addressing the underpinnings of "gendercide"? Who and what is behind the women and girls disappearing "precisely because they are female?" Their use of the word "numbing" to describe their response to the global statistics is telling: apparently, it's business as usual for the power brokers of the world to feel nothing about this grim reality.

When Kristof and WuDunn (Ibid, 36) do recognize sexism and misogyny, they appear to disregard the effects of these factors:

> It has long been known that a risk factor for turbulence and violence is the share of a country's population made up of young people. Now it is emerging that male domination of a society is also a risk factor; the reasons are not fully understood, but it may that when women are marginalized the nation takes on the testosterone-laden culture of a military camp or a high-school boys' locker room.

It is difficult to fathom how such a statement can be made in the context of an article that speaks of a Rwandan woman being held hostage in a "rape house" during the genocide. Moreover, it is incomprehensible that the journalists perceive male domination of a society as just a risk factor, "reasons not fully understood," for turbulence and violence.

In regards to "testosterone-laden" high school boys, Equalitynow.org (2010) reported, "At a boarding school in Kenya, 300 boys attacked the girls' dormitory. Seventy-one of the girls were raped. Nineteen were trampled to death in the stampede to escape. The school's vice principal remarked, 'The boys never meant any harm against the girls. They just wanted to rape.' The vice principal's nonchalance speaks to a prevailing attitude that the act of rape is amusing rather than violent, upholding and conveying the notion that females are objects and prey, dispensable in a patriarchal structure. Just as the principal lets the boys off the hook, it appears that Kristof and WuDunn let patriarchy off the hook by denying its central role in perpetuating rape culture.

Furthermore, in their enthusiasm about empowering women to contribute to the gross national product (GNP) of their countries, the authors overlook the oppressive conditions the women probably encounter in factories. For instance, the authors reveal: "The economic explosion in

Asia was, in large part, an outgrowth of the economic empowerment of women. 'They have smaller fingers, so they are better at stitching,' the manager of a purse factory explained. 'They're obedient and work harder than men,' said the head of a toy factory. 'And we can pay them less'" (Kristof and WuDunn 2009, xiv). The managers of the factories essentially admit that they are operating a sweatshop in which they expect the women to work harder than the men for less pay. One can imagine the conditions of the work environment. Can the women take breaks? How many hours do they work per day and how much do they earn each day? Do they have the option to buy health insurance and, if so, can they afford to buy it? Do Kristof and WuDunn ask such questions? Are they concerned with making structural, systemic change or writing and selling stories?

In *Half the Sky*, the authors feature some heart-breaking yet inspirational stories, rather Cinderella-like, to persuade their readers to take action in helping to solve the problems of poor women in developing countries. The book's huge influence is leading many to do good—and Oprah's endorsement doesn't hurt! But, how much can Western readers' actions deracinate the root of global rape culture if they don't comprehend patriarchy and don't understand that it is operating at home and aboard?

Uprooting Rape Culture, A Conclusion

Scholars (Gordon & Riger 1989; Estrich 1987; Brownmiller 1975) theorize about the problem and prevalence of sexual violence in the U.S.A. while journalists (Jones, 2010; Kristof and WuDunn 2009) recount the horror of rape culture in developing countries. Kristof and WuDunn also propose economic solutions to poverty. The other writers raise the following questions: "Where does [male] rage come from?" (Jones 2010, 6). "What was the overall impact of fear of rape on the quality of women's lives?" (Gordon & Riger 1989, xv). "Is it real rape?" (Estrich 1987, 8). "Who are victims of rape?" (Brownmiller 1975, 9). They pose important questions, but none of them ask this crucial question, "Why don't we end sexual violence?" In her essay, "I Want A Twenty-Four Hour Truce During Which There Is No Rape," Andrea Dworkin (2005, 19) asserts, "It is astonishing that in all our worlds of feminism and anti-sexism we never talk seriously about ending rape. Ending it. Stopping it. No more. No more rape." Instead of such call to action, each decade brings books that are more sensational than those of the past. How many more books must be written to explicate this persistent dilemma?

A dilemma involves two choices: Do we continue to live in a rape culture or do we struggle together to transform our world into a humane, safe place for everyone?

In *Transforming A Rape Culture* (Buchwald, Fletcher and Roth 2005), we made a clear-eyed decision to focus less on what we entitled, "Living in a Rape Culture" and more on "Strategies and Activism," and "Visions and Possibilities": "At one of our several focus groups in our community before the creation of the original edition, women responded enthusiastically to our emphasis on transformation. More than one person told us, 'We don't want to live in this culture as it is anymore. We've got to change it'" (Buchwald, Fletcher and Roth 2005, XIV). Offering concrete models and solutions for structural, systemic change is fundamental to the book's purpose.

Since the publication of the 1993 hardcover edition of *Transforming A Rape Culture,* we have spoken to many audiences in the U.S., Canada, and Ghana, West Africa, and their responses have conveyed to us that there is an urgent need for the cultural transformation we call for in the book. Many readers have written to say that the book has increased their understanding that the causes of sexual violence are structural, systemic, and interrelated. They see that once the causes are understood, the culture can change for the better.

Regarding upholding and protecting the rights of women and girls as "human rights," both men and women must continue the work of building a world that recognizes and respects the humanity of everyone. As Haki R. Madhubuti (2005, 182–183) declares in the following call to action:

> A growing part of the answer is that men, as difficult as it may seem, must view all women (no matter who they are—race, culture, religion, or nationality aside) as extended family. The question is, and I know that I am stretching, would we rape our mothers, grandmothers, sisters, or other female relatives? Would we even give such acts a thought? Can we extend this attitude to all women? Therefore, we must:

1. Teach our sons that it is their responsibility to be antiraptist; that is, they must be counterrapist in their thoughts, conversations, raps, organizations, and actions.
2. Teach our daughters how to defend themselves and maintain an uncompromising stance toward men and boys.
3. Understand that being a counterrapist is honorable, manly, and necessary for a just society.
4. Be glowing examples of men who are fighting to treat women as equals and to be fair and just in associations with women. This means at the core that we must continually reassess the family as now defined and constructed. In today's economy, most women, married and unmarried, must work. We men must be intimately involved in rearing children and doing housework.

5. Be bold and strong enough to stop other men (friends or strangers) from raping and to intervene in a rape in process with the fury and destruction of a hurricane against the rapist.

Madhubuti writes 12 action steps in all, and they each articulate how men must challenge their anti-female thinking, rid themselves of their male supremacist notions, and work responsibly with women to create a life-affirming and just society.

In Step #4, Madhubuti addresses the need for men to be involved in childrearing and Myriam Miedzian concurs that this involvement is essential to dismantling a rape culture. Based on her research regarding the development of masculine identity, Myriam Miedzian (2005, 162), believes: "In order to significantly decrease violence, including rape, we must begin to protect boys from violent entertainment and to teach them, from the youngest age, to view themselves as future nurturing, nonviolent, responsible fathers." Miedzian finds that programs in child rearing deter violence in three ways: "They encourage nurturing, caring, informed fathering; they make boys feel that empathy, sensitivity, and caring are acceptable—even desirable—male qualities; and they strongly discourage child battering." Miedzian encourages Americans to pressure their legislators and school boards to appropriate funds and develop child rearing classes. Such teaching is necessary, for it prevents the early indoctrination of misogynistic attitudes that often originate in the home.

In speaking to the need to reconstruct thinking around the development of masculinity and male sexuality, especially among male athletes, Michael Kimmel (2005, 156) asserts,

> Part of transforming a rape culture means transforming masculinity, encouraging and enabling men to make choices about what we do with our bodies, insisting that men utilize their own agency to make difficult sorts of choices. To ignore men, to believe that women alone will transform a rape culture, freezes men in a posture of defensiveness, defiance, and immobility. [Involving men makes a big difference]. Nowhere is this better expressed than on a splash guard that a colleague devised for Rape Awareness Week at his university and that I have been bringing with me to campuses around the country. For those who don't know, a splash guard is the plastic grate placed in public urinals to prevent splatter. These simple devices are placed in urinals all over campus. This one comes with a helpful slogan: "You hold the power to stop rape in your hand."

As Kimmel, Miedzian, and Madhubuti point out in various ways, a notion of masculinity considered antithetical and superior to femininity must be eradicated. In doing so, it is crucial for men to acknowledge the role they play in perpetuating a rape culture, whether passively or actively. Furthermore, it is necessary for men to examine, challenge, and abolish the idea of manhood that feeds on fear and relies on the subordination and violation of women and girls. It will demand a great deal of imagination accompanied with mental and spiritual strength to fashion a different idea of manhood, for it will require the letting go of the differential power that sustains male supremacy. What do adult male persons look like, think like, talk like, act like when they assume no power over females? The courageous, thoughtful male leadership that Madhubuti calls forth is vital in constructing masculine identity that accepts and values female equality in both private and public life.

How can women examine, challenge, and abolish sexist and misogynistic notions of masculinity and femininity that they have internalized? In "Seduced by Violence No More," bell hooks (2005, 298) writes,

> Women who engage in sexual acts with male partners must not only interrogate the nature of the masculinity we desire, we must actively construct radically new ways to think and feel as desiring subjects. By shaping our eroticism in ways that repudiate phallocentrism, we oppose rape culture. . . . By refusing to function within the heterosexist framework, which condones male erotic domination of women, females would be actively disempowering patriarchy.

bell hooks' thoughts on constructing and possessing one's sexuality is important because women, especially young women, grapple with understanding and defining their sexuality in a rape culture that continually spews out abject stereotypes and negative imagery of women in U.S. popular media that gets broadcast around the globe. No matter where a woman or girl lives, she is subject to viewing herself according to some Hollywood fantasy of femininity. The media seize control of female thinking and imagination to the point that it is nearly impossible to view oneself as anything other than an object or a victim. When interacting with media, women and girls must learn to reject anti-female messages in what they read, view and hear. Even imagery created, directed, and produced by women must be scrutinized.

Ten Things You Can Do to Transform a Rape Culture

This list was complied from the essays in *Transforming A Rape Culture* (Buchwald, Fletcher, and Roth 1993).

1. Remember that even though rape culture harms everyone, many of us get pleasure from it. **We are all responsible for perpetuating a rape culture.**

2. Teach your children to respect children of the opposite sex. Show them you believe that each sex has an immeasurable value and that neither is better, more powerful, or smarter, than the other.

3. Support your daughters, nieces, and neighbors. Encourage them to relish their physical strength and the strength of their minds.

4. Support and promote women who are positive role models. Celebrate the accomplishments of women with your children, partners, and friends. Teach others that the best women to look up to are the ones who are making a difference, not the ones who are the most famous, beautiful, or wealthy.
5. Do not listen quietly to sexist jokes or comments. Speak up when people make jokes or comments that you think are sexist. Tell your friends and family that you are uncomfortable with how they talk about women and girls. You have more personal power than you realize.
6. Do not be silent when you see a T-shirt, sign, movie, or anything you find offensive to women. Say something.
7. Have conversations of consent with a potential sexual partner. Verbally explore each others' comfort level with the activities taking place.
8. Learn to say "no." It's okay to be assertive, and it's possible to be nice while saying what you want and exerting your feelings.
9. Encourage the men you know to explore what it means to be anti-rapists.
10. Dare to dream of a culture free of sexual violence . . . a rape culture transformed into a culture of mutuality.

Coda

Resisting, opposing, and dismantling a rape culture that is embedded in our very being is an endless struggle, not one for the easily disheartened. bell hooks urges us, though, to have courage and to enjoy the struggle, for it's not going away—if history is any clear indication of what's in store. In struggling for worldwide change, it is important to remember that *striking at the foundation* of the unjust institution of patriarchy is necessary for true transformation. Misogynistic and sexist attitudes must change among everyone. We women must do our own work to be part of the solution. We must educate ourselves and ground ourselves in the reality of global female oppression, in the west and abroad, so we thoroughly understand the extent of the problem. Even though, we may become fearful of what we discover, we cannot allow fear to keep us from struggling to do our part to end the injustice. It is also important to remember that we may not live to see the change we struggle to achieve. But, living to see it is not the point. Striving for the vision of the change is the reward.

References

Buchwald, Emilie, Pamela R. Fletcher, and Martha Roth. *Transforming A Rape Culture.* Minneapolis: Milkweed Editions, 1993, 1995, 2005.

Brownmiller, Susan. *Against Our Will: Men, Women, and Rape.* New York: Fawcett Books, 1975.

Clinton, Hillary Rodham. "Women's Rights Are Human Rights." http://www.famousquotes.me.uk/speeches/Hillary-Clinton/.

Connors, Jr. , Russell B. "Catholic Social Teaching—Convictions and Connections." In *Global Search for Justice,* edited by Marla Hanly, Nancy Heitzeg, Sharon Doherty, RobertGrunst, and Russell B. Connors, Jr., 123152. St. Paul: St. Catherine University, 2009.

"Convention (IV) Relative to the Protection of Civilian Persons in Time of War, Article 27. Geneva, 12 August 1949. http://www.icrc.org/ihl.nsf/full/380?opendocument.

Dworkin, Andrea. "I Want a Twenty-Four-Hour Truce During Which There Is No Rape." In *Transforming A Rape Culture,* edited by Emilie Buchwald, Pamela R. Fletcher, and Martha Roth, 12-22 . Minneapolis: Milkweed, 2005.

Estrich, Susan. *Real Rape: How the Legal System Victimizes Women Who Say No.* Cambridge, Massachusetts: Harvard University Press, 1987.

Gordon, Margaret T., and Stephanie Riger. *The Female Fear: The Social Cost of Rape.* New York: Free Press, 1989.

hooks, bell. "Silenced By Violence No More." In *Transforming A Rape Culture,* edited by Emilie Buchwald, Pamela R. Fletcher, and Martha Roth, 294–299 . Minneapolis: Milkweed, 2005.

Jones, Ann. *War Is Not Over When It's Over: Women Speak Out From the Ruins of War.*New York: Metropolitan Books, 2010.

Kesic, Vesna. "Establishing Rape As A War Crime." In *Transforming A Rape Culture,* edited by Emilie Buchwald, Pamela R. Fletcher, and Martha Roth, 269–289. Minneapolis: Milkweed, 2005.

Kimmel, Michael. "Men, Masculinity, and the Rape Culture." In *Transforming A Rape Culture,* edited by Emilie Buchwald, Pamela R. Fletcher, and Martha Roth, 140–157. Minneapolis: Milkweed, 2005.

Kristof, Nicholas D., and Sheryl WuDunn. "The Women's Crusade." *The New York Times Magazine,* August 23, 2009: 28–39.

———. *Half the Sky: Turning Oppression into Opportunity for Women Worldwide.* New York: Knopf, 2009.

Landler, Mark. "A New Agenda." *The New York Times Magazine*, August 23, 2009: 41–43.

Madhubuti, Haki. "On Being Anti-Rapist." In *Transforming A Rape Culture*, edited by Emilie Buchwald, Pamela

R. Fletcher, and Martha Roth, 173-187. Minneapolis: Milkweed, 2005.

Miedzian, Myriam. "How Rape Is Encouraged in American Boys and What We Can Do to Stop It." In *Transforming A Rape Culture*, edited by Emilie Buchwald, Pamela R. Fletcher, and Martha Roth, 159–172. Minneapolis: Milkweed, 2005.

Rome Statue of the International Criminal Court. (UN. Doc. A/Conf. 183/9*), Article 7, *Crimes Against Humanity*. http://untreaty.un.org/cod/icc/statute/romefra.htm.

The Geneva Conventions. http://www.newworldencyclopedia.org/entry/Geneva Conventions. "The Noise-Maker Awards." *More*, December 2009/January 2010: 120–125.

The United Nations' Fourth World Conference on Women. Beijing, China, 1995. http://www.un.or.womenwatch/daw/beijing/platform/ armed.htm (accessed July 8, 2010)

United Nations. "Universal Declaration of Human Rights." In *Global Search for Justice*, edited by Marla Hanly, Nancy Heitzeg, Sharon Doherty, Robert Grunst, and Russell B. Connors, Jr., 231-236. St. Paul: St. Catherine University, 2009.

United Nations' World Conference on Human Rights. "Vienna Declaration and Program of Actions." http://www.un.or.womenwatch/daw/beijing/platform/armed.htm(accessed on July 8, 2010).

www.EqualityNow.org

www.karamah.org

Deep Shikha is professor of economics at St. Catherine University, where she chairs the economics department and is co-coordinator of the Center for Women, Economic Justice, and Public Policy. She grew up in Delhi, India and taught at the University of Delhi before moving with her family to the United States. Her research interests include micro-economic development and women's empowerment, global economic issues, and women's issues in developing and developed economies. Sharon Doherty is associate professor and chair of women's studies at St. Catherine University. She also teaches in the critical studies of race and ethnicity program and directs the Abigail Quigley McCarthy Center for Women. Doherty grew up on a small farm in western Minnesota, and got her start in thinking about community and equality from her large extended family. An anthropologist, Doherty has developed research interests in race/class/gender and community, feminist transformation of higher education, and the societal influences of foragers.

In this article, Shikha and Doherty unpack six sentences from their conversation with a feminist leader in India in order to explore ideas and strategies in women's movements. How could their reflections help us move forward with a more global approach to feminism and social justice?

Six Sentences: Toward Global Women's Movements

Deep Shikha and Sharon Doherty

"Look at these bangles," she said. "One of the women at Nupikeitel gave them to me. She put them on me. I have worn them ever since. . . . This was really a gift of love. . . . 'If you are going to fight for us, you must carry our symbol.'"

Dr. Vina Mazumdar was wearing these bangles in 2006, when we visited her in her office in Delhi, India. When she talked about the bangles and the woman who gave them to her, we realized that we did not know enough to fully comprehend what Dr. Mazumdar was telling us. To understand what was at stake, we followed her leads with some research of our own. In this article, we offer you what we know so far about the six sentences repeated above. In unpacking the six sentences, we engage some of the ideas and debates in global feminism today.

"Look at these bangles," she said.

The bangles are two thin bracelets, made of brass, intended to be worn together. These were forged by hand, by women crafters. Historically in India, bangles were worn by married women to claim their married status;

today almost all women—regardless of economic, social or religious affiliation—wear them. Women generally wear from two to twelve bangles on each wrist. The varied designs and materials reflect different meanings and aesthetic tastes, and range in price from expensive gold to low-cost glass. Bangles made from metals can be plain or etched with geometric designs and enhanced with precious or semi-precious stones. While upper class women often wear bangles made of gold, most of the women in rural and tribal areas of India wear brass bangles like Dr. Mazumdar's.[1]

"One of the women at Nupikeitel gave them to me."

We do not know the name of the woman who gave the bangles to Dr. Mazumdar, but we know that she was a market woman in Imphal City, Manipur, a state in northeast India. "Nupikeitel" translates to English as "women's market." She gave Dr. Mazumdar the bangles because Dr. Mazumdar was trying to help the local activists save their market from demolition. The bangles were given as a sign of solidarity. Dr. Mazumdar was told that by accepting these bangles she would become one of them. Since she was fighting with them for their rights, she was given the honor of wearing the bangles, claiming her adopted status as an indigenous woman from that area.

Those are the basic facts, but to understand them we needed to break the story down further, to find out more.

"One of the women at Nupikeitel"

In our research we found that in Manipur, "market woman" has a meaning beyond what the term means to people in many other parts of the world, or even in India. For centuries, market women have been powerful forces in shaping the Manipur economy and in standing up for the rights of their families and communities (Devi 2008).

The Nupikeitel in Imphal City is more than 300 years old (Chaki-Sircar 1984, p. 17) and is the second largest women's market in Asia (Laishram 2008). Unlike most markets throughout the world, this market is run entirely by women. The market is a round structure with a low circular wall all around. Within this each woman has a small stall (approximately two by six feet). Merchandise is displayed on wooden tables, with storage room under the table for extra goods. Each stall has a tin roof on it to protect it from rain and sun. The government makes these structures available to vendors and charges a small fee for them. No walls exist between shops, giving an aura of an open air market. Women who sell their merchandise in these stalls know each other and form a community. Most of the women in the Nupikeitel are from the Meitei, an indigenous[2] group in Manipur.

The Manipur region has a substantial tribal population, and many of the tribal groups are known for the relatively high status women hold. If you are surprised by this, you are not alone. Across the world, few people are aware of the fact that women have had quite a bit of power in many land-based societies. For many generations, Meitei women and men both have fulfilled important roles in the economy and have created "a complementary and a considerable egalitarian relationship . . . in the socioreligious sphere" (Chaki-Sircar 1984, p. 8).

One reason for the high status is women's central role in economic exchange. The "Keithel," which translates as market but again means more than we might associate with the word, historically was a central force for the region's finance and commerce. In the Keithel, each clan specialized in a type of product, such as rice and rice products, textiles, or fresh produce. Women elders represented their families, trading on the family's behalf and influencing the state's economic policies. This system was in place before the British colonized the region, and actually expanded during the early colonial period. But the colonizers saw this indigenous economic system as a threat, and put in place laws and structures to break the Keithel. The system lost power but did not die (Barua and Devi 2006).

"gave them to me."

"Me" is Vina Mazumdar, the pioneer of women's studies in India and a leading figure in India's feminist movement. *Deep: I grew up in Delhi and for years have considered Dr. Mazumdar a heroic person I would love to meet some day.* On our trip in 2006 we were making connections with some of India's current leaders in women's studies, including those at the Center for Women's Development Studies in Delhi. We met Dr. Mazumdar because we got mixed up about what floor we were on and walked into the wrong office. We sat down and began chatting with the woman sitting at the desk, as we were waiting for the person whose office we thought we were in. Not knowing who we were or why we were in her office, Dr. Mazumdar nevertheless welcomed us, offered tea, and began to talk about her work. *Sharon: This was my first trip to India. So many things already had happened on the trip where I didn't know what was going on that this situation did not seem unusual.* Dr. Shikha and Dr. Mazumdar got into an intense conversation about women's activism in India and eventually Dr. Shikha said, "And who are you?" When Dr. Mazumdar replied, Dr. Shikha sat stunned for a minute, and then began the conversation again.

Here is some information about the famous feminist who was so kind to us: Vina was born in 1927 to a middle class family from Calcutta, when India was still under British rule. Her family's status as high caste Hindus and educated professionals gave her educational opportunities available to very few women in British India. Her father's encouragement played a key role in Vina's decision to pursue an education beyond that of even most women from wealthy, high caste families. She was educated at Calcutta, Banaras, and Oxford, earning a D.Phil. from Oxford University. Vina's formative years corresponded with the heady years of India's independence movement. She started her career as an academic, teaching Political Science. Like so many other women, as a professional and a housewife Mazumdar felt torn between her responsibilities as a young mother and wife and her career as a teacher. Again with her father's encouragement, Vina continued her career while doing double duty as a wife and a mother for the next two decades.

The turning point in her career came in the 1970s, when the United Nations asked India to submit a report on the Status of Women. A commission was established in 1971 to write this report, and its members invited two social scientists, a social anthropologist and a political scientist (Dr. Mazumdar) to get academic perspective and input. Dr. Mazumdar, with a four-member drafting committee, was charged with writing the report. This work necessitated the group's interaction with women all over India with diverse economic, social, and cultural backgrounds. Commission members spoke to women who were the engine of economic activity in many farming communities, women who were common wives, women who operated under family systems ranging from matrilineal to polyandry. The writing group articulated and catalogued cases of extensive invisibility and marginalization of women's work and resulting poverty and deprivation—economic, social, and cultural—especially women who operated in the informal sector, 'women of the soil.' The report, submitted in January 1975, asked some essential questions about the decline in the status of women in India as evidenced by the declining sex ratio, increasing dowry practice, and policies that did not address women's concerns. Dr. Mazumdar and her coauthors concluded that the system failed to recognize women's contributions, from those of educated urban middle class women to rural women, the backbone of India's agrarian society.

The Indian Council of Social Science Research (ICSSR) Programme of Women's Studies undertook the challenge of studying and understanding these issues, using an interdisciplinary approach under Dr. Mazumdar's leadership. However, the research and prescribed policies failed to garner support from politicians and government officials in charge of making and implementing policies. This led to the development of an independent research institute, the Center for Women's Development Studies (CWDS), with Dr. Mazumdar as the founder-director of the Centre from 1980 to 1991. This Center was designed to be an autonomous institute to build on the work started by ICSSR. The CWDS broadened its agenda to include research that would lead to concrete actions and policies. Dr. Mazumdar's role as an activist in the women's movement and in academic women's studies was formalized through the work of CWDS.

(Mazumdar 2001) Since 1980 she has been regarded as an expert, activist, and a resource person on Women in Development.

She put them on me. I have worn them ever since. . . . This was really a gift of love. . . . 'If you are going to fight for us, you must carry our symbol.'"

Dr. Mazumdar told us about the bangles when we asked her how she thinks things have changed during the time of the women's movement in India. As we look back on the conversation, we believe she chose this particular story as a lesson in paying attention to old sources of women's well-being and activism, as well as newer ideas and movements for change. The market women had power long before the organized women's movement took shape, in India or in other places. While Dr. Mazumdar has been a leader of the feminist movement for over thirty years, she does not see activism that is named feminism as the only route to women's well-being in her country or anywhere.

We also have been thinking about the bangles as a gift of love and solidarity:

"'If you are going to fight for us, you must carry our symbol.'"

While the market women have indeed had power for centuries, their power eventually diminished under the colonial system, as the British imposed new laws and forms of commerce that rewarded outsiders and a few elites within the local community. The new system pushed the market women out of their central economic role in Manipur, but their trade and political organizing continued. After India gained independence from Great Britain in 1947, the Indian government carried on many of the practices that marginalized the local women's markets, but still the women continued to trade and to lead activist movements on behalf of their local communities. The world today—with an intensifying global economy and a modern Indian nation-state—threatens the market women's remaining power. The particular threat Dr. Mazumdar described was literal—the Manipur government was planning to demolish the women's market space to make way for economic development controlled by outsiders and driven by the concerns of multinational corporations. The developers intended to replace Nupikeital with a multi-story commercial building.

The market women said no. To block the demolition, the group devised an active resistance strategy with a 24-hour-a-day presence in the market. They were afraid that if they went home at the end of the day the market would be destroyed while it was unoccupied, so they decided to keep a vigil at this place throughout the day and night. During the day time, market went on as usual. During the night time, about twenty women would stay behind. Each of the women would secure mosquito netting over her stall and sleep right on it. They brought portable mud stoves and set them in between stalls; two or three women would share the food cooked on each stove. Outsiders who wanted to support the women began to visit the market, to sit with the activists. When Dr. Mazumdar went with others to be part of that support, the woman she did not know gave her the bangles.

This kind of solidarity often involves women who call themselves feminists working with women activists who do not identify as feminists. As they work and act together, they connect new ideas about women's rights with old ideas from tribal traditions unknown to many. This can be complicated, as university-educated women like Dr. Mazumdar work in solidarity with the market women, some of whom do not read and write. Respect grows through talking together and especially through working together. Humility, open-mindedness, and eagerness to learn new ways are prerequisites to building meaningful relationships and finding common ground.

Unpacking the Six Sentences

The story behind the six sentences offers a glimpse of the complexities regarding women's movements for justice across the world today. Feminist theorists and activists from the "Two-Thirds World"[3] argue that beginning with historical specificity is crucial to moving forward for justice (Anzaldua 1987, Chaudhuri 2003 and 2004a, Jordan 1985, Maathai 2006, Mohanty 2003, Sinha 2000). Without historical specificity, people—including theorists—can be tempted to jump to false universals. Well-meaning people from dominant societies are at risk of thinking that their ideas and values can be applied unilaterally across borders of nation and culture. This often fails because of misunderstanding combined with the dynamics of domination. We are not abandoning the idea of universal truths (as some postmodern theorists have done). Instead, we join those who challenge Eurocentric assumptions of universal truth, and in fact, any assumption of universal truth that is caught within a particular tradition of thought.

Related to this is the question of how ideas are presented. Indian feminist scholar Maitrayee Chaudhuri argues that theoretical work in India has sometimes not been recognized by feminists in the West because of "a misplaced but persistent belief in a disjuncture between theoretical and empirical work, as well as a failure to read theory when presented in a form and style different from accepted western academic protocol" (Chaudhuri 2004a, p. xiii). Chaudhuri offers a contextualized approach to theorizing; as she studied feminism in India she "found it almost *impossible to separate the history of action from the history of ideas*" (ibid., p. xii, emphasis in original). Like scholars in the U.S. whose work is connected to community priorities (Hill Collins 2000, Lugones and Spelman 1983), Chaudhuri questions the validity of abstract theorizing in a social vacuum.

To avoid the trap of imposing ideas from one group onto another, we need to find more effective ways to think together and work together for justice. This thinking and working is dangerous and difficult, because of the potential misunderstandings and the dynamics of domination. We believe that unpacking the six sentences demonstrates an approach to moving forward for justice. In unpacking the sentences, we begin to know more, by engaging with specific circumstances. This requires curiosity, work, time, a contextual approach to theorizing, and perhaps most importantly, respect for the ideas and actions of women from groups we don't know.

Learning across Borders; Resisting Relations of Domination

For those of us in the One-Third World to respect people's ideas and actions, to want to learn from them, to think they have something to teach us, requires more than merely to care about their suffering. A troubling reality is that sometimes when people from more affluent societies or groups express interest, *interest* comes across as domination. If you come from a poor or working class community, or a U.S. community of color, or a religious minority in any society, you probably know what we mean. You may have experienced the condescending caring of people who think they understand your life, have diagnosed your suffering, and have a plan to fix it/fix you. The fixing is sometimes accompanied by denial of difference, through such statements as "I don't even notice that she is Asian," a statement likely to be received more as a self-congratulatory short-cut than as an authentic witnessing of understanding and humility.

That approach connects to what Indian American feminist scholar Chandra Talpade Mohanty calls a "tourist" approach to activism. Speaking to feminists in particular, Mohanty presents three different models for how people from affluent countries or classes engage with women in the Two-Thirds World. Her goal is for those seeking justice to foster "democratization rather than colonization" (Mohanty 2003, p. 238).

If Dr. Mazumdar had been working within a Feminist-as-Tourist model, she would have looked for "particular cultural sexist practices" (ibid, p. 239) affecting the women at Nupikeitel. In the tourist model, the more affluent outsider may think *look at those unfortunate women,* without considering the fact that she (the outsider) might not understand what she is seeing or that the women may not consider themselves powerless or unfortunate.

The Feminist-as-Explorer model upends the tourist approach: *look at those wonderful women and learn from them.* As explorer, Dr. Mazumdar would have honored the strengths of the women at Nupikeitel, and potentially engaged in a complex cultural analysis. Missing from such an approach, however, is consideration of national and global relationships of domination (ibid., p. 241).

In our view, Dr. Mazumdar was working within a Feminist Solidarity model. This in part resembles the Explorer model (look at those wonderful women and learn from them), but requires the outsider activist to *(1) understand the global system and her part in it and (2) be in dialogue with the local women to learn their ideas about justice, and then develop strategies together to work for change.*

The solidarity model calls for those who seek justice to examine how our lives are connected to the lives of women, men, and children across the globe through economic and political systems. It also calls us to understand that our comprehension of alternative cultural practices, social norms, and strategies for justice is limited by our experiences and our own social and economic locations. We should be careful not to discount ideas because of our inability to understand the ideas or the paradigm in which they are expressed.

Building Global Feminism: Contexts, Theories, Actions, and Coalitions

Paying attention to ideas and actions developed around the world can help to build a global approach to feminism. Different models of women's activism emerge in different contexts, and the approaches do not break down neatly by national identity. In India, as in the United States, feminism has multiple sources and priorities. Dr. Mazumdar's six sentences help us to see two of the many distinct perspectives on women's activism within India: the middle and upper class feminist movement, led by Dr. Mazumdar and other university-educated feminists; and the activism of Meitei women, grounded in powerful roles in their history, traditions, and local communities. Both perspectives differ from U.S. feminism, which itself has a complex history with many different groups of women, sometimes with their male allies, pursing a range of goals from voting rights to equal pay, child care support to reproductive rights to battered women's shelters. Furthermore, as Mrinalini Sinha argues, "a model that merely contrasts Western and non-Western feminisms" does not adequately respond to how societies influence each other. It is necessary, she says to "revis[e] feminism as a whole from a 'global' perspective" (Sinha 2000, p. 170).

A global perspective on feminism calls us to explore similarities as well as differences in the two perspectives from India we are studying in this article. India's national identity creates an important framework. With a population of over 1.1 billion, India is the world's largest democracy. The nation includes more than 2000 ethnic groups, with different histories and complex relationships to each other. More than 70% of India's people "base their livelihoods on agriculture" (Shiva 2005, p. 66).

In her introduction to an anthology on feminism in India, Chaudhuri notes that "the personal is political" has been an important idea in many feminisms; though even that simple phrase has different meanings in different cultural contexts. Chaudhuri makes a distinction between what "personal" means in the U.S., which is greatly influenced by individualism (Miller 2009, this volume), and what it means in many nonwestern contexts: "In the African or Indian contexts, this distinction emanates from the largely communitarian and extended family complex of relations" (Chaudhuri 2004a, p. xxxiv).

Related to this, several of the authors in *Feminism in India* argue that movements for women's well being in their country have been less polarized from men than have many of the dominant feminisms in the United States. Suma Chitnis explains that the concept of equality is relatively new to Indian society, introduced through western liberalism in the early 1800s.

> But [equality] did not become an operational principle of Indian life until the country achieved independence and adopted a democratic system of government. At that point the constitution granted women political status fully equal to that of men. Thus Indian women did not have to bear the kind of injustices that women in the West had to suffer because of the continuing gap between political ideals and realities. Nor did they have to suffer the indignities European and American women have had to experience in the course of their efforts to bridge this gap (Chitnis 2004, p. 11).

In tracing the history of the Indian women's movement from the early 1900s to the present, Chaudhuri demonstrates that male allies played central roles in the movement from the beginning. Feminism was connected to the Indian independence movement, and the two were seen as related components of justice for the nation (Chaudhuri 2004a, p. xxxiii; 2004b, p. 117).

The Nupikeitel market women's activism has been even more connected to the well being of their entire community. Women's central role in Meitei society was in place long before western ideas of equality were introduced. As anthropologist Manjusri Chaki-Sircar found in her ethnographic research among the Meitei in the 1970s,

> Meitei ideology does not undermine the female role. There is no polarity of the sexes. Women's collective power has a recognized status in different cultural areas. . . . The sex role ideology of Meitei society is very different from that of Hindu society, which promotes the patriarchal model of male supremacy. . . .

> Here feminism . . . exists as . . . an integral part of the social system. Thus . . . there is a pervasive and distinctive role for women in the public sphere, viz political, economic, social and religious, found perhaps nowhere else in India (Chaki-Sircar 1984, pp. 8–10).

Meitei religion has played a central role in shaping women's status and influence. The religion, which has literature dating to the third century A.D. (ibid., p. 17), has survived in the face of pressures from both Hindus and Christians. Among the Meitei, women and men both have important positions in ritual life. It is a patrilineal society, but women counterbalance patrilineal forces with their collective power, religious centrality, and economic autonomy. These elements together create a situation in which women had power many generations before the feminist movements of either India or the U.S. Now, however, women in those movements can be helpful to Meitei women, can support their activism and work in solidarity, while learning from them about tested strategies for peaceful resistance. One role Dr. Mazumdar could play was as a bridge to the Indian government, using her networks, with the market women's permission, to advocate on their behalf.

The market women's activism over the years has been directed toward community survival, as an ethnic and religious minority attempting to protect their community from outside forces. This is reminiscent of the Chipko movement, a more well-known movement of rural women in India.

The *Chipko* (to embrace) movement originated in Garwahl and Kumaun districts in the Himalayan region in India. Subsistence agriculture is practiced by women in this region. Agricultural production, in addition to animal husbandry, takes care of the family's basic needs. This existence necessitates a heightened awareness of the natural connection between the environment and humans. For example, women rely on forests to get the firewood (dead tree branches) and fodder for their animals. They understand that a healthy forest will stop soil erosion and act as a barrier against destructive floods. The Government of India continued the logging practices initiated by British India in order to achieve a high rate of economic growth and earn foreign exchange through exports. These policies of the Government led to widespread discontent among the population of these areas, fueled by a major flood in 1970 that was caused in part by deforestation and soil erosion.

In 1974, in one incident village women found themselves facing the employees of the logging company with a contract to cut the trees. The head of the village Mahila Mandal (Women's Club) (Guha, p. 159), with other women in the village confronted the tree-cutters, hugged the trees, refused to move and forced the men to stop the operation. This event brought women to the forefront of this movement. They had a key role in the movement due to their roles in the subsistence economic system and their dependence on natural resources for survival. After this, Chipko movement spread like a fast burning forest fire to other parts of India and gave voice to marginalized communities in different rural and tribal regions. Chipko movement was rural in its inception and execution. It had both male and female leaders. While women worked at the local level, men leaders such as Sunderlal Bahuguna made this movement popular all over the country by using the Gandhian method of "Satyagraha, fasting and civil disobedience."

In societies across the world we can find many examples of both middle class and local community-based women's movements. University-educated women, in relatively elite positions, often are collaborating on justice work with local women in communal settings. From biologist Wangari Matthai (2006) leading the Green Belt Movement in Kenya, to attorney Shirin Ebadi (2006) seeking legal rights for women and men in Iranian struggles for justice, to Harvard graduate Winona LaDuke (2005) returning to her Anishinaabeg community near Detroit Lakes, Minnesota to direct the White Earth Land Recovery Project, we can learn about theorizing and action through a solidarity model.

For One-Third World women, the challenge is to leave our comfort zone, to step into a different context to think and work across differences. When we are able to recognize the differences in women's activism due to regional, economic, religious, and social locations, we will have begun the work of the feminist solidarity model. In dialogue, then, we can critically examine existing power structures—some in place due to the colonial world history—and acknowledge our own roles in those structures. We can move beyond personal defensiveness regarding our roles to understanding the actions of the groups and nations to which we belong. With a foundation of trust, common goals, and integrated complementary strategies, we can develop a global network of movements that are respectful and acceptable to all groups involved in activism for women, and women's activism for communities.

Notes

[1] In South Asia, bangles have been worn since ancient times. Archeologists in the region have found bangles made of shells dating back to at least 6,000 B.C.E. (Ray, p. 33). Today bangles often are made of metals such as gold, silver, brass, and copper. Thickness, ornamentation, and weight of these bangles will be reflected in the price. Cheaper bangles are made of glass in multiple colors, designs, and decorative themes. Glass bangles are a required accessory for married Hindu women, and a much-appreciated cosmetic accessory for unmarried girls and other women. Bangles of different materials, colors, and designs may cover half the forearm (four to six inches) of a newly married bride.

[2] Maitrayee Chaudhuri cautions scholars and activists to be careful with the word indigenous, because of the "contentious nature of defining what constitutes the ancient and indigenous in a plural and hierarchical societ." (Chaudhuri 2004a, p. xxvii). She notes that some authors are using the term "local" rather than

"indigenous" or "ethnic" to describe movements and sources of knowledge (ibid, p. xxix).

[3] Alfred Sauvy, a French demographer, coined the term "Third World" in 1952. "[T]he term was first used to suggest parallels between the *tiers monde* (the world of the poor countries) and the *tiers etat* (the third estate or common people of the French revolutionary era). The First World was the North American/European 'Western bloc' while the Soviet-led 'Eastern bloc' was the Second World" (Ellwood 2006, p. 23). Some authors substitute "non-Western" for "Third World."

A more recent pairing of terms is "One-Third World" versus "Two-Thirds World," with the accompanying concepts of social minorities and social majorities (Esteva and Prakash 1998, p. 16). The one-third world includes people in both Western and Third World countries who have a relatively affluent lifestyle, and the two-thirds world includes those who are less affluent. Each set of terms has its strengths and weaknesses, as Chandra Mohanty explains:

> By focusing on quality of life . . . , "One-Third/Two-Thirds World" draws attention to the continuities as well as the discontinuities between the haves and have-nots within the boundaries of nations and between nations and indigenous communities. This designation also highlights the fluidity and power of global forces that situate communities of people as social majorities/minorities in disparate form. "One-Third/Two-Thirds" is a non-essentialist categorization, but it incorporates an analysis of power and agency that is crucial. Yet what it misses is a history of colonization that the terms Western/Third World draw attention to (Mohanty 2003, p. 227).

References

Anzaldua, Gloria. (1987). *La Frontera/Borderlands*. San Francisco: Spinsters/Aunt Lute.

Barua, Indira and Anita Devi. (2006). Women Market of Manipur: An Anthropo-Historical Perspective. Retrieved December 18, 2008 from

http://www.manipuronline.com/Manipur/May2006/womenmarket15_1.ht

Chaki-Sircar, Manjusri. (1984). *Feminism in a Traditional Society: Women of the Manipur Valley*. Delhi, India: Central Electric Press.

Chaudhuri, Maitrayee. (2003). *The Practice of Sociology*. New Delhi: Orient Blackswan.

Chaudhuri, Maitrayee. (2004a). Introduction. *Feminism in India (Issues in Contemporary Indian Feminism)*, ed. Maitrayee Chaudhuri, xi-xlvi. London, New York: Zed Books.

Chaudhuri, Maitrayee. (2004b). The Indian Women's Movement. *Feminism in India (Issues in Contemporary Indian Feminism)*, ed. Maitrayee Chaudhuri, 117–133. London, New York: Zed Books.

Chitnis, Suma. (2004) Feminism: Indian Ethos and Indian Convictions. *Feminism in India (Issues in Contemporary Indian Feminism)*, ed. Maitrayee Chaudhuri, 8–25. London, New York: Zed Books.

Devi, L. K. (2008). Social Empowerment of Manipur Woman. Retrieved December 18, 2008 from http://manipurcomments.wordpress.com/2008/04/08/social-empowerment-of-manipuri-women/

Ebadi, Shirin and Azadeh Moaveni. (2006). *Iran Awakening: A Memoir of Revolution and Hope*. New York: Random House.

Ellwood, Wayne. (2006). *The No-Nonsense Guide to Globalization*. Oxford: New Internationalist Publications, Limited.

Esteva, Gustavo and Madhu Suri Prakash. (1998). *Grassroots Post-Modernism: Remaking the Soil of Cultures*. London: Zed Press.

Guha, Ramachandra. (1989). *The Unquiet Woods: Ecological Change and Peasant Resistance in the Himalaya*. Berkeley, CA: University of California Press.

Hill Collins, Patricia. (2000). *Black Feminist Thought: Knowledge, Consciousness, and the Politics of Empowerment*, 2nd edition. New York: Routledge.

Jordan, June (1985). Report from the Bahamas. Reprinted in *Identity Politics in the Women's Movement*, ed. by Barbara Ryan, 2001. New York: New York University Press, 120–126.

LaDuke, Winona. (2005). *Recovering the Sacred: The Power of Naming and Claiming*. Cambridge, MA: South End Press.

Laishram, Bedavati. (2008). Nupi Keithel: Colours of Manipur. Retrieved February 23, 2009 from http://manipurcomments.wordpress.com/2008/04/28/nupi-keithel-colours-of-manipur/.

Lugones, Maria C. and Elizabeth V. Spelman. (1983). Have we got a theory for you! Feminist theory, cultural imperialism and the demand for 'the woman's voice.' *Women's Studies International Forum*: Volume 6, Issue 6, 573–581.

Maathai, Wangari. (2006). *Unbowed*. New York: Alfred A. Knopf.

Mazumdar, Vina. (2001). Whose Past, Whose History, Whose Tradition?: Indigenizing Women's Studies in India. *Asian Journal of Women's Studies*, 7(1), 133–153.

Miller, Amata, IHM. (2009). The Many Faces of Social Justice. A. J. Moore lecture at the College of St. Catherine, delivered January 27, 2009.

Mohanty, Chandra Talpade. (2003). *Feminism without Borders: Decolonizing Theory, Practicing Solidarity.* Durham and London: Duke University Press.

Ray, Himanshu Prabha. (2003). *The Archaeology of Seafaring in Ancient South Asia.* New York: Cambridge University Press.

Shiva, Vandana. (2005). *Earth Democracy: Justice, Sustainability, and Peace.* Cambridge, MA: South End Press.

Sinha, Mrinalini. (2000). How History Matters: Complicating the Categories of "Western" and "Non-Western" Feminisms. (ed.). *Is Academic Feminism Dead? Theory in Practice,* ed. The Social Justice Group at the Center for Advanced Feminist Studies, 168–186. New York: New York University Press.

Marge Piercy (b. 1936) was born in Detroit in the midst of the Great Depression and was the first of her family to attend college. She has written seventeen volumes of poetry and seventeen novels, and has played a key role in the women's and antiwar movements. Through her art she explores complex social justice issues; for example, Piercy's acclaimed speculative/science fiction novel, Woman on the Edge of Time *(1976), mixes time travel with issues of feminism and the treatment of the mentally ill. This poem is from her collection,* The Moon Is Always Female, *which is considered a feminist poetry classic. In the poem, Piercy presents a central theme from Jewish mysticism that she often explores in her writing: "tikkun olum," or the "repair of the world." How many different strategies for repairing injustice does this poem describe?*

The Low Road

Marge Piercy

What can they do
to you? Whatever they want.
They can set you up, they can
bust you, they can break
your fingers, they can
burn your brain with electricity,
blur you with drugs till you
can't walk, can't remember, they can
take your child, wall up
your lover. They can do anything
you can't stop them
from doing. How can you stop
them? Alone, you can fight,
you can refuse, you can
take what revenge you can
but they roll over you.

But two people fighting
back to back can cut through
a mob, a snake-dancing file
can break a cordon, an army
can meet an army.

Two people can keep each other
sane, can give support, conviction,
love, massage, hope, sex.

Three people are a delegation,
a committee, a wedge. With four
you can play bridge and start
an organization. With six
you can rent a whole house,
eat pie for dinner with no
seconds, and hold a fund raising party.
A dozen make a demonstration.
A hundred fill a hall.
A thousand have solidarity and your own newsletter;
ten thousand, power and your own paper;
a hundred thousand, your own media;
ten million, your own country.

It goes on one at a time,
it starts when you care
to act, it starts when you do
it again after they said no,
it starts when you say *We*
and know who you mean, and each
day you mean one more.

Howard Zinn (b. 1922) is a first-generation American born in Brooklyn, New York. His parents were Jewish factory workers with little education and Zinn first worked as a shipyard worker and labor organizer. His experiences during World War II as a bombardier in the U.S. Army Air Corps, and his research on military bombing of civilian targets, led him to oppose war. With a PhD in history from Columbia University, Zinn was chair of the department of history and social sciences at Spelman, a premier African-American college in Atlanta. He was active in the Civil Rights movement and mentor to many of its student leaders during the 1950s and 1960s. Moving to Boston University, Zinn continued teaching, scholarship, and activism focused on issues of civil liberties, U.S. foreign policy, war and peace, and political dissent. He has authored over forty books, including A People's History of the United States, *which depicts the struggles of American Indians, African Americans, workers, immigrants, and women. The following essay, anthologized widely, explores why Zinn believes activists have reasons to be optimistic. In sharing examples from the long history of dissent in the U.S., how does Zinn make his case that change is possible?*

The Optimism of Uncertainty

Howard Zinn

In this awful world where the efforts of caring people often pale in comparison to what is done by those who have power, how do I manage to stay involved and seemingly happy?

Some quick lessons: Don't let "those who have power" intimidate you. No matter how much power they have, they cannot prevent you from living your life, thinking independently, speaking your mind.

Find people to be with who share your values and commitments, and who also have a sense of humor.

Understand that the major media will not tell you of all the acts of resistance taking place every day in the society—the strikes, protests, individual acts of courage in the face of authority. Look around (and you will certainly find it) for the evidence of these unreported acts. And for the little you find, extrapolate from that and assume there must be a thousand times as much as you've found.

Note that throughout history people have felt powerless before authority, but that at certain times these powerless people, by organizing, acting, risking, persisting, have created enough power to change the world around them, even if a little. That is the history of the labor movement, the women's movement, the anti–Vietnam War movement, the disabled persons' movement, the gay and lesbian movement, the movement of black people in the South.

Remember that those who have power and seem invulnerable are in fact quite vulnerable. Their power depends on the obedience of others, and when those others begin withholding that obedience, begin defying authority, that power at the top turns out to be very fragile. Generals become powerless when their soldiers refuse to fight, industrialists become powerless when their workers leave their jobs or occupy the factories.

When we forget the fragility of that power at the top we become astounded when it crumbles in the face of rebellion. We have had many such surprises in our time, both in the United States and in other countries.

Don't look for a moment of total triumph. See engagement as an ongoing struggle, with victories and defeats, but in the long run slow progress. So you need patience and persistence. Understand that even when you don't "win," there is fun and fulfillment in the fact that you have been involved, with other good people, in something worthwhile. You need hope.

Is an optimist necessarily a blithe, slightly sappy whistler in the dark of our time? I am totally confident not that the world will get better, but that only confidence can prevent people from giving up the game before all the cards have been played. The metaphor is deliberate; life is a gamble. Not to play is to foreclose any chance of winning. To play, to act, is to create at least a possibility of changing the world.

What leaps out from the history of the past hundred years is its utter unpredictability. This confounds us, because we are talking about exactly the period when human beings became so ingenious technologically that they could plan and predict the exact time of someone landing on the moon, or walk down the street talking to someone halfway around the Earth.

Who foresaw that, on that day in Montgomery, Alabama, in 1955, when Rosa Parks refused to move from the front of the bus, this would lead to a mass protest of black working people, and a chain of events that would shake the nation, startle the world, and transform the South?

Let's go back to the turn of the century. A revolution to overthrow the tsar of Russia, in that most sluggish of semi-feudal empires, not only startled the most advanced imperial powers, but took Lenin himself by surprise and sent him rushing by train to Petrograd. Given the Russian Revolution, who could have predicted Stalin's deformation of it, or Khrushchev's astounding exposure of Stalin, or Gorbachev's succession of surprises?

Who would have predicted the bizarre shifts of World War II—the Nazi–Soviet pact (those embarrassing photos of von Ribbentrop and Molotov shaking hands), and the German army rolling through Russia, apparently invincible, causing colossal casualties, being turned back at the gates of Leningrad, on the western edge of Moscow, in the streets of Stalingrad, followed by the defeat of the German army, with Hitler huddled in his Berlin bunker, waiting to die?

And then the post-war world, taking a shape no one could have drawn in advance: the Chinese Communist revolution, which Stalin himself had given little chance. And then the break with the Soviet Union, the tumultuous and violent Cultural Revolution, and then another turnabout, with post-Mao China renouncing its most fervently held ideas and institutions, making overtures to the West, cuddling up to capitalist enterprise, perplexing everyone.

No one foresaw the disintegration of the old Western empires happening so quickly after the war, or the odd array of societies that would be created in the newly independent nations, from the benign village socialism of Nyerere's Tanzania to the madness of Idi Amin's adjacent Uganda.

Spain became an astonishment. A million died in the civil war, which ended in victory for the Fascist Franco, backed by Hitler and Mussolini. I recall a veteran of the Abraham Lincoln Brigade telling me that he could not imagine Spanish Fascism being overthrown without another bloody war. But after Franco was gone, a parliamentary democracy came into being, open to Socialists, Communists, anarchists, everyone.

In other places too, deeply entrenched dictatorships seemed suddenly to disintegrate—in Portugal, Argentina, the Philippines, Iran.

The end of World War II left two superpowers with their respective spheres of influence and control, vying for military and political power. The United States and the Soviet Union soon each had enough thermonuclear bombs to devastate the Earth several times over. The international scene was dominated by their rivalry, and it was supposed that all affairs, in every nation, were affected by their looming presence.

Yet the most striking fact about these superpowers was that, despite their size, their wealth, their overwhelming accumulation of nuclear weapons, they were unable to control events, even in those parts of the world considered to be their respective spheres of influence.

The failure of the Soviet Union to have its way in Afghanistan, its decision to withdraw after almost a decade of ugly intervention, was the most striking evidence that even the possession of thermonuclear weapons does not guarantee domination over a determined population.

The United States has faced the same reality. It could send an army into Korea but could not win, and was forced to sign a compromise peace. It waged a full-scale war in Indochina, conducted the most brutal bombardment of a tiny peninsula in world history, and yet was forced to withdraw. And in Latin America, after a long history of U.S. military intervention having its way again and again, this superpower, with all its wealth and weapons, found itself frustrated. It was unable to prevent a revolution in Cuba, and the Latin American dictatorships that the United States supported from Chile to Argentina to El Salvador have fallen. In the headlines every day we see other instances of the failure of the presumably powerful over the presumably powerless, as in Brazil, where a grassroots movement of workers and the poor elected a new president pledged to fight destructive corporate power.

Looking at this catalog of huge surprises, it's clear that the struggle for justice should never be abandoned because of the apparent overwhelming power of those who have the guns and the money and who seem invincible in their determination to hold on to it. That apparent power has, again and again, proved vulnerable to human qualities less measurable than bombs and dollars: moral fervor, determination, unity, organization, sacrifice, wit, ingenuity, courage, patience—whether by blacks in Alabama and South Africa, peasants in El Salvador, Nicaragua, and Vietnam, or workers and intellectuals in Poland, Hungary, and the Soviet Union itself. No cold calculation of the balance of power need deter people who are persuaded that their cause is just.

I have tried hard to match my friends in their pessimism about the world (is it just my friends?), but I keep encountering people who, in spite of all the evidence of terrible things happening everywhere, give me hope. Especially young people, in whom the future rests. I think of my students. Not just the women of Spelman College, who leapt over a hundred years of national disgrace to become part of the civil rights movement. . . .

I think also of my students at Boston University and people all over the country who, anguished about the war in Vietnam, resisted in some way, facing police clubs and arrests. And brave high school students like Mary Beth Tinker and her classmates in Des Moines, Iowa, who insisted on wearing black armbands to protest the war and when suspended from school, took their case to the Supreme Court and won.

Of course, some would say, that was the Sixties. But throughout the period since, despite widespread head-shaking over the "apathy" of successive student generations, an impressive number of students continued to act.

I think of the determined little group at Boston University who, emulating groups at a hundred other schools, set up a "shantytown" on campus to represent apartheid in South Africa. The police tore it down, but the students refused to move and were arrested.

In South Africa, shortly before, I had visited Crossroads, a real shantytown outside of Cape Town, where thousands of blacks occupied places that looked like chicken coops, or were jammed together in huge tents, sleeping in shifts, six hundred of them sharing one faucet of running water. I was impressed that young Americans who had not seen that with their own eyes, had only read or seen photos, would be so moved to step out of their comfortable lives and act.

We have recently seen students all over the country campaigning for a living wage for campus employees, and against global sweatshops and pre-emptive wars. Beyond those activists, there is a much larger population of students who have no contact with any movement, yet have deep feelings about injustice.

Since I've stopped teaching, I've spent much of my time responding to invitations to speak. What I've discovered is heartening. In whatever town, large or small, in whatever state of the Union, there is always a cluster of men and women who care about the sick, the hungry, the victims of racism, the casualties of war, and who are doing something, however small, in the hope that the world will change.

Wherever I go—whether San Diego, Philadelphia, or Dallas; Ada, Oklahoma, or Shreveport, Louisiana; Presque Isle, Maine, or Manhattan, Kansas—I find such people. And beyond the handful of activists there seem to be hundreds, thousands more who are open to unorthodox ideas.

But they tend not to know of each other's existence, and so, while they persist, they do so with the desperate patience of Sisyphus endlessly pushing that boulder up the mountain. I try to tell each group that it is not alone, and that the very people who are disheartened by the absence of a national movement are themselves proof of the potential for such a movement. I suppose I'm trying to persuade myself as well as them.

Arriving at Morehead State University in rural eastern Kentucky, in the midst of the 2003 Iraq War, I found the lecture room crowded with fifteen hundred students (out of a total enrollment of six thousand). I spoke against the war and received an overwhelming reception. Earlier, when I'd been picked up at the airport by a group of faculty peace activists, one of them had brought their fourteen-year-old daughter, who'd defied her high school principal by wearing an anti-war T-shirt to school. I have found such people in all parts of the country, more and more, as evidence that the truth makes its way slowly but surely.

It is this change in consciousness that encourages me. Granted, racial hatred and sex discrimination are still with us, war and violence still poison our culture, we have a large underclass of poor, desperate people, and there is a hard core of the population content with the way things are, afraid of change.

But if we see only that, we have lost historical perspective, and then it is as if we were born yesterday and we know only the depressing stories in this morning's newspapers, this evening's television reports.

Consider the remarkable transformation, in just a few decades, in people's consciousness of racism, in the bold presence of women demanding their rightful place, in a growing public awareness that gays are not curiosities but sensate human beings, in the long-term growing skepticism about military intervention despite brief surges of military madness.

It is that long-term change that I think we must see if we are not to lose hope. Pessimism becomes a self-fulfilling prophecy; it reproduces itself by crippling our willingness to act.

There is a tendency to think that what we see in the present moment will continue. We forget how often in this century we have been astonished by the sudden crumbling of institutions, by extraordinary changes in people's thoughts, by unexpected eruptions of rebellion against tyrannies, by the quick collapse of systems of power that seemed invincible.

The bad things that happen are repetitions of bad things that have always happened—war, racism, maltreatment of women, religious and nationalist fanaticism, starvation. The good things that happen are unexpected. Unexpected, and yet explainable by certain truths that spring at us from time to time, but which we tend to forget.

Political power, however formidable, is more fragile than we think. (Note how nervous are those who hold it.)

Ordinary people can be intimidated for a time, can be fooled for a time, but they have a down-deep common sense, and sooner or later they find a way to challenge the power that oppresses them.

People are not naturally violent or cruel or greedy, although they can be made so. Human beings everywhere want the same things: They are moved by the sight of abandoned children, homeless families, the casualties of war; they long for peace, for friendship and affection across lines of race and nationality.

One semester, when I was teaching, I learned that there were several classical musicians signed up in my course. For the last class of the semester I stood aside while they sat in chairs up front and played a Mozart quartet. Not a customary finale to a class in political theory, but I wanted the class to understand that politics is pointless if it does nothing to enhance the beauty of our lives. Political discussion can sour you. We needed some music.

Revolutionary change does not come as one cataclysmic moment (beware of such moments!) but as an endless succession of surprises, moving zigzag toward a more decent society.

We don't have to engage in grand, heroic actions to participate in the process of change. Small acts, when multiplied by millions of people, can transform the world.

To be hopeful in bad times is not just foolishly romantic. It is based on the fact that human history is a history not only of cruelty, but also of compassion, sacrifice, courage, kindness. What we choose to emphasize in this complex history will determine our lives. If we see only the worst, it destroys our capacity to do something. If we remember those times and places—and there are so many—where people have behaved magnificently, this gives us the energy to act, and at least the possibility of sending this spinning top of a world in a different direction. And if we do act, in however small a way, we don't have to wait for some grand utopian future. The future is an infinite succession of presents, and to live now as we think human beings should live, in defiance of all that is bad around us, is itself a marvelous victory.

The Global Search for Justice

Resources

Universal Declaration of Human Rights

United Nations

Adopted and proclaimed by General Assembly Resolution 217 A (III) of 10 December 1948

On December 10, 1948, the General Assembly of the United Nations adopted and proclaimed the Universal Declaration of Human Rights the full text of which appears in the following pages. Following this historic act the Assembly called upon all Member countries to publicize the text of the Declaration and "to cause it to be disseminated, displayed, read, and expounded principally in schools and other educational institutions, without distinction based on the political status of countries or territories."

Article 1.

All human beings are born free and equal in dignity and rights. They are endowed with reason and conscience and should act towards one another in a spirit of brotherhood.

Article 2.

Everyone is entitled to all the rights and freedoms set forth in this Declaration, without distinction of any kind, such as race, colour, sex, language, religion, political or other opinion, national or social origin, property, birth, or other status. Furthermore, no distinction shall be made on the basis of the political, jurisdictional or international status of the country or territory to which a person belongs, whether it be independent, trust, non-self-governing or under any other limitation of sovereignty.

Article 3.

Everyone has the right to life, liberty and security of person.

Article 4.

No one shall be held in slavery or servitude; slavery and the slave trade shall be prohibited in all their forms.

Article 5.

No one shall be subjected to torture or to cruel, inhuman or degrading treatment or punishment.

Article 6.

Everyone has the right to recognition everywhere as a person before the law.

Article 7.

All are equal before the law and are entitled without any discrimination to equal protection of the law. All are entitled to equal protection against any discrimination in violation of this Declaration and against any incitement to such discrimination.

Article 8.

Everyone has the right to an effective remedy by the competent national tribunals for acts violating the fundamental rights granted him by the constitution or by law.

Article 9.

No one shall be subjected to arbitrary arrest, detention or exile.

Article 10.

Everyone is entitled in full equality to a fair and public hearing by an independent and impartial tribunal, in the determination of his rights and obligations and of any criminal charge against him.

Article 11.

(1) Everyone charged with a penal offence has the right to be presumed innocent until proved guilty according to law in a public trial at which he has had all the guarantees necessary for his defence.

(2) No one shall be held guilty of any penal offence on account of any act or omission which did not constitute a penal offence, under national or international law, at the time when it was committed. Nor shall a heavier penalty be imposed than the one that was applicable at the time the penal offence was committed.

Article 12.

No one shall be subjected to arbitrary interference with his privacy, family, home or correspondence, nor to attacks upon his honour and reputation. Everyone has the right to the protection of the law against such interference or attacks.

Article 13.

(1) Everyone has the right to freedom of movement and residence within the borders of each state.

(2) Everyone has the right to leave any country, including his own, and to return to his country.

Article 14.

(1) Everyone has the right to seek and to enjoy in other countries asylum from persecution.

(2) This right may not be invoked in the case of prosecutions genuinely arising from non-political crimes or from acts contrary to the purposes and principles of the United Nations.

Article 15.

(1) Everyone has the right to a nationality.

(2) No one shall be arbitrarily deprived of his nationality nor denied the right to change his nationality.

Article 16.

(1) Men and women of full age, without any limitation due to race, nationality or religion, have the right to marry and to found a family. They are entitled to equal rights as to marriage, during marriage and at its dissolution.

(2) Marriage shall be entered into only with the free and full consent of the intending spouses.

(3) The family is the natural and fundamental group unit of society and is entitled to protection by society and the State.

Article 17.

(1) Everyone has the right to own property alone as well as in association with others.

(2) No one shall be arbitrarily deprived of his property.

Article 18.

Everyone has the right to freedom of thought, conscience and religion; this right includes freedom to change his religion or belief, and freedom, either alone or in community with others and in public or private, to manifest his religion or belief in teaching, practice, worship and observance.

Article 19.

Everyone has the right to freedom of opinion and expression; this right includes freedom to hold opinions without interference and to seek, receive and impart information and ideas through any media and regardless of frontiers.

Article 20.

(1) Everyone has the right to freedom of peaceful assembly and association.

(2) No one may be compelled to belong to an association.

Article 21.

(1) Everyone has the right to take part in the government of his country, directly or through freely chosen representatives.

(2) Everyone has the right of equal access to public service in his country.

(3) The will of the people shall be the basis of the authority of government; this will shall be expressed in periodic and genuine elections which shall be by universal and equal suffrage and shall be held by secret vote or by equivalent free voting procedures.

Article 22.

Everyone, as a member of society, has the right to social security and is entitled to realization, through national effort and international co-operation and in accordance with the organization and resources of each State, of the economic, social and cultural rights indispensable for his dignity and the free development of his personality.

Article 23.

(1) Everyone has the right to work, to free choice of employment, to just and favourable conditions of work and to protection against unemployment.

(2) Everyone, without any discrimination, has the right to equal pay for equal work.

(3) Everyone who works has the right to just and favourable remuneration ensuring for himself and his family an existence worthy of human dignity, and supplemented, if necessary, by other means of social protection.

(4) Everyone has the right to form and to join trade unions for the protection of his interests.

Article 24.

Everyone has the right to rest and leisure, including reasonable limitation of working hours and periodic holidays with pay.

Article 25.

(1) Everyone has the right to a standard of living adequate for the health and well-being of himself and of his family, including food, clothing, housing and medical care and necessary social services, and the right to security in the event of unemployment, sickness, disability, widowhood, old age or other lack of livelihood in circumstances beyond his control.

(2) Motherhood and childhood are entitled to special care and assistance. All children, whether born in or out of wedlock, shall enjoy the same social protection.

Article 26.

(1) Everyone has the right to education. Education shall be free, at least in the elementary and fundamental stages. Elementary education shall be compulsory. Technical and professional education shall be made generally available and higher education shall be equally accessible to all on the basis of merit.

(2) Education shall be directed to the full development of the human personality and to the strengthening of respect for human rights and fundamental freedoms. It shall promote understanding, tolerance and friendship among all nations, racial or religious groups, and shall further the activities of the United Nations for the maintenance of peace.

(3) Parents have a prior right to choose the kind of education that shall be given to their children.

Article 27.

(1) Everyone has the right freely to participate in the cultural life of the community, to enjoy the arts and to share in scientific advancement and its benefits.

(2) Everyone has the right to the protection of the moral and material interests resulting from any scientific, literary or artistic production of which he is the author.

Article 28.

Everyone is entitled to a social and international order in which the rights and freedoms set forth in this Declaration can be fully realized.

Article 29.

(1) Everyone has duties to the community in which alone the free and full development of his personality is possible.

(2) In the exercise of his rights and freedoms, everyone shall be subject only to such limitations as are determined by law solely for the purpose of securing due recognition and respect for the rights and freedoms of others and of meeting the just requirements of morality, public order and the general welfare in a democratic society.

(3) These rights and freedoms may in no case be exercised contrary to the purposes and principles of the United Nations.

Article 30.

Nothing in this Declaration may be interpreted as implying for any State, group or person any right to engage in any activity or to perform any act aimed at the destruction of any of the rights and freedoms set forth herein.

United Nations Millennium Declaration

The General Assembly
Adopts the following Declaration:

United Nations Millennium Declaration

I. Values and principles

1. We, heads of State and Government, have gathered at United Nations Headquarters in New York from 6 to 8 September 2000, at the dawn of a new millennium, to reaffirm our faith in the Organization and its Charter as indispensable foundations of a more peaceful, prosperous and just world.

2. We recognize that, in addition to our separate responsibilities to our individual societies, we have a collective responsibility to uphold the principles of human dignity, equality and equity at the global level. As leaders we have a duty therefore to all the world's people, especially the most vulnerable and, in particular, the children of the world, to whom the future belongs.

3. We reaffirm our commitment to the purposes and principles of the Charter of the United Nations, which have proved timeless and universal. Indeed, their relevance and capacity to inspire have increased, as nations and peoples have become increasingly interconnected and interdependent.

4. We are determined to establish a just and lasting peace all over the world in accordance with the purposes and principles of the Charter. We rededicate ourselves to support all efforts to uphold the sovereign equality of all States, respect for their territorial integrity and political independence, resolution of disputes by peaceful means and in conformity with the principles of justice and international law, the right to self-determination of peoples which remain under colonial domination and foreign occupation, non-interference in the internal affairs of States, respect for human rights and fundamental freedoms, respect for the equal rights of all without distinction as to race, sex, language or religion and international cooperation in solving international problems of an economic, social, cultural or humanitarian character.

5. We believe that the central challenge we face today is to ensure that globalization becomes a positive force for all the world's people. For while globalization offers great opportunities, at present its benefits are very unevenly shared, while its costs are unevenly distributed.

We recognize that developing countries and countries with economies in transition face special difficulties in responding to this central challenge. Thus, only through broad and sustained efforts to create a shared future, based upon our common humanity in all its diversity, can globalization be made fully inclusive and equitable. These efforts must include policies and measures, at the global level, which correspond to the needs of developing countries and economies in transition and are formulated and implemented with their effective participation.

6. We consider certain fundamental values to be essential to international relations in the twenty-first century. These include:

- **Freedom**. Men and women have the right to live their lives and raise their children in dignity, free from hunger and from the fear of violence, oppression or injustice. Democratic and participatory governance based on the will of the people best assures these rights.
- **Equality**. No individual and no nation must be denied the opportunity to benefit from development. The equal rights and opportunities of women and men must be assured.
- **Solidarity**. Global challenges must be managed in a way that distributes the costs and burdens fairly in accordance with basic principles of equity and social justice. Those who suffer or who benefit least deserve help from those who benefit most.
- **Tolerance**. Human beings must respect one other, in all their diversity of belief, culture and language. Differences within and between societies should be neither feared nor repressed, but cherished as a precious asset of humanity. A culture of peace and dialogue among all civilizations should be actively promoted.
- **Respect for nature**. Prudence must be shown in the management of all living species and natural resources, in accordance with the precepts of sustainable development. Only in this way can the immeasurable riches provided to us by nature be preserved and passed on to our descendants. The current unsustainable patterns of production and consumption must be changed in the interest of our future welfare and that of our descendants.
- **Shared responsibility**. Responsibility for managing worldwide economic and social development, as well as threats to international peace and security, must be shared among the nations of the world and should be exercised multilaterally. As the most universal and most representative organization in the world, the United Nations must play the central role.

7. In order to translate these shared values into actions, we have identified key objectives to which we assign special significance.

II. Peace, security and disarmament

8. We will spare no effort to free our peoples from the scourge of war, whether within or between States, which has claimed more than 5 million lives in the past decade. We will also seek to eliminate the dangers posed by weapons of mass destruction.

9. We resolve therefore:

- To strengthen respect for the rule of law in international as in national affairs and, in particular, to ensure compliance by Member States with the decisions of the International Court of Justice, in compliance with the Charter of the United Nations, in cases to which they are parties.
- To make the United Nations more effective in maintaining peace and security by giving it the resources and tools it needs for conflict prevention, peaceful resolution of disputes, peacekeeping, post-conflict peace-building and reconstruction. In this context, we take note of the report of the Panel on United Nations Peace Operations[1] and request the General Assembly to consider its recommendations expeditiously.
- To strengthen cooperation between the United Nations and regional organizations, in accordance with the provisions of Chapter VIII of the Charter.
- To ensure the implementation, by States Parties, of treaties in areas such as arms control and disarmament and of international humanitarian law and human rights law, and call upon all States to consider signing and ratifying the Rome Statute of the International Criminal Court.[2]
- To take concerted action against international terrorism, and to accede as soon as possible to all the relevant international conventions.
- To redouble our efforts to implement our commitment to counter the world drug problem.
- To intensify our efforts to fight transnational crime in all its dimensions, including trafficking as well as smuggling in human beings and money laundering.
- To minimize the adverse effects of United Nations economic sanctions on innocent populations, to subject such sanctions regimes to regular reviews and to eliminate the adverse effects of sanctions on third parties.
- To strive for the elimination of weapons of mass destruction, particularly nuclear weapons, and to keep all options open for achieving

this aim, including the possibility of convening an international conference to identify ways of eliminating nuclear dangers.

- To take concerted action to end illicit traffic in small arms and light weapons, especially by making arms transfers more transparent and supporting regional disarmament measures, taking account of all the recommendations of the forthcoming United Nations Conference on Illicit Trade in Small Arms and Light Weapons.
- To call on all States to consider acceding to the Convention on the Prohibition of the Use, Stockpiling, Production and Transfer of Anti-personnel Mines and on Their Destruction,[3] as well as the amended mines protocol to the Convention on conventional weapons.[4]

10. We urge Member States to observe the Olympic Truce, individually and collectively, now and in the future, and to support the International Olympic Committee in its efforts to promote peace and human understanding through sport and the Olympic Ideal.

III. Development and poverty eradication

11. We will spare no effort to free our fellow men, women and children from the abject and dehumanizing conditions of extreme poverty, to which more than a billion of them are currently subjected. We are committed to making the right to development a reality for everyone and to freeing the entire human race from want.
12. We resolve therefore to create an environment—at the national and global levels alike—which is conducive to development and to the elimination of poverty.
13. Success in meeting these objectives depends, *inter alia*, on good governance within each country. It also depends on good governance at the international level and on transparency in the financial, monetary and trading systems. We are committed to an open, equitable, rule-based, predictable and non–discriminatory multilateral trading and financial system.
14. We are concerned about the obstacles developing countries face in mobilizing the resources needed to finance their sustained development. We will therefore make every effort to ensure the success of the High-level International and Intergovernmental Event on Financing for Development, to be held in 2001.
15. We also undertake to address the special needs of the least developed countries. In this context, we welcome the Third United Nations Conference on the Least Developed Countries to be held in May 2001 and will endeavour to ensure its success. We call on the industrialized countries:

- To adopt, preferably by the time of that Conference, a policy of duty- and quota-free access for essentially all exports from the least developed countries;
- To implement the enhanced programme of debt relief for the heavily indebted poor countries without further delay and to agree to cancel all official bilateral debts of those countries in return for their making demonstrable commitments to poverty reduction; and
- To grant more generous development assistance, especially to countries that are genuinely making an effort to apply their resources to poverty reduction.

16. We are also determined to deal comprehensively and effectively with the debt problems of low- and middle-income developing countries, through various national and international measures designed to make their debt sustainable in the long term.

17. We also resolve to address the special needs of small island developing States, by implementing the Barbados Programme of Action[5] and the outcome of the twenty-second special session of the General Assembly rapidly and in full. We urge the international community to ensure that, in the development of a vulnerability index, the special needs of small island developing States are taken into account.

18. We recognize the special needs and problems of the landlocked developing countries, and urge both bilateral and multilateral donors to increase financial and technical assistance to this group of countries to meet their special development needs and to help them overcome the impediments of geography by improving their transit transport systems.

19. We resolve further:

- To halve, by the year 2015, the proportion of the world's people whose income is less than one dollar a day and the proportion of people who suffer from hunger and, by the same date, to halve the proportion of people who are unable to reach or to afford safe drinking water.
- To ensure that, by the same date, children everywhere, boys and girls alike, will be able to complete a full course of primary schooling and that girls and boys will have equal access to all levels of education.
- By the same date, to have reduced maternal mortality by three quarters, and under-five child mortality by two thirds, of their current rates.
- To have, by then, halted, and begun to reverse, the spread of HIV/AIDS, the scourge of malaria and other major diseases that afflict humanity.

- To provide special assistance to children orphaned by HIV/AIDS.
- By 2020, to have achieved a significant improvement in the lives of at least 100 million slum dwellers as proposed in the "Cities Without Slums" initiative.

20. We also resolve:

- To promote gender equality and the empowerment of women as effective ways to combat poverty, hunger and disease and to stimulate development that is truly sustainable.
- To develop and implement strategies that give young people everywhere a real chance to find decent and productive work.
- To encourage the pharmaceutical industry to make essential drugs more widely available and affordable by all who need them in developing countries.
- To develop strong partnerships with the private sector and with civil society organizations in pursuit of development and poverty eradication.
- To ensure that the benefits of new technologies, especially information and communication technologies, in conformity with recommendations contained in the ECOSOC 2000 Ministerial Declaration,[6] are available to all.

IV. Protecting our common environment

21. We must spare no effort to free all of humanity, and above all our children and grandchildren, from the threat of living on a planet irredeemably spoilt by human activities, and whose resources would no longer be sufficient for their needs.

22. We reaffirm our support for the principles of sustainable development, including those set out in Agenda 21,[7] agreed upon at the United Nations Conference on Environment and Development.

23. We resolve therefore to adopt in all our environmental actions a new ethic of conservation and stewardship and, as first steps, we resolve:

- To make every effort to ensure the entry into force of the Kyoto Protocol, preferably by the tenth anniversary of the United Nations Conference on Environment and Development in 2002, and to embark on the required reduction in emissions of greenhouse gases.
- To intensify our collective efforts for the management, conservation and sustainable development of all types of forests.
- To press for the full implementation of the Convention on Biological Diversity[8] and the Convention to Combat Desertification in those

Countries Experiencing Serious Drought and/or Desertification, particularly in Africa.[9]

- To stop the unsustainable exploitation of water resources by developing water management strategies at the regional, national and local levels, which promote both equitable access and adequate supplies.
- To intensify cooperation to reduce the number and effects of natural and man-made disasters.
- To ensure free access to information on the human genome sequence.

V. Human rights, democracy and good governance

24. We will spare no effort to promote democracy and strengthen the rule of law, as well as respect for all internationally recognized human rights and fundamental freedoms, including the right to development.

25. We resolve therefore:

- To respect fully and uphold the Universal Declaration of Human Rights.[10]
- To strive for the full protection and promotion in all our countries of civil, political, economic, social and cultural rights for all.
- To strengthen the capacity of all our countries to implement the principles and practices of democracy and respect for human rights, including minority rights.
- To combat all forms of violence against women and to implement the Convention on the Elimination of All Forms of Discrimination against Women.[11]
- To take measures to ensure respect for and protection of the human rights of migrants, migrant workers and their families, to eliminate the increasing acts of racism and xenophobia in many societies and to promote greater harmony and tolerance in all societies.
- To work collectively for more inclusive political processes, allowing genuine participation by all citizens in all our countries.
- To ensure the freedom of the media to perform their essential role and the right of the public to have access to information.

VI. Protecting the vulnerable

26. We will spare no effort to ensure that children and all civilian populations that suffer disproportionately the consequences of natural disasters, genocide, armed conflicts and other humanitarian emergencies are given every assistance and protection so that they can resume normal life as soon as possible.

We resolve therefore:

- To expand and strengthen the protection of civilians in complex emergencies, in conformity with international humanitarian law.
- To strengthen international cooperation, including burden sharing in, and the coordination of humanitarian assistance to, countries hosting refugees and to help all refugees and displaced persons to return voluntarily to their homes, in safety and dignity and to be smoothly reintegrated into their societies.
- To encourage the ratification and full implementation of the Convention on the Rights of the Child[12] and its optional protocols on the involvement of children in armed conflict and on the sale of children, child prostitution and child pornography.[13]

VII. Meeting the special needs of Africa

27. We will support the consolidation of democracy in Africa and assist Africans in their struggle for lasting peace, poverty eradication and sustainable development, thereby bringing Africa into the mainstream of the world economy.

28. We resolve therefore:

- To give full support to the political and institutional structures of emerging democracies in Africa.
- To encourage and sustain regional and subregional mechanisms for preventing conflict and promoting political stability, and to ensure a reliable flow of resources for peacekeeping operations on the continent.
- To take special measures to address the challenges of poverty eradication and sustainable development in Africa, including debt cancellation, improved market access, enhanced Official Development Assistance and increased flows of Foreign Direct Investment, as well as transfers of technology.
- To help Africa build up its capacity to tackle the spread of the HIV/AIDS pandemic and other infectious diseases.

VIII. Strengthening the United Nations

29. We will spare no effort to make the United Nations a more effective instrument for pursuing all of these priorities: the fight for development for all the peoples of the world, the fight against poverty, ignorance and disease; the fight against injustice; the fight against violence, terror and crime; and the fight against the degradation and destruction of our common home.

30. We resolve therefore:

- To reaffirm the central position of the General Assembly as the chief deliberative, policy-making and representative organ of the United Nations, and to enable it to play that role effectively.
- To intensify our efforts to achieve a comprehensive reform of the Security Council in all its aspects.
- To strengthen further the Economic and Social Council, building on its recent achievements, to help it fulfil the role ascribed to it in the Charter.
- To strengthen the International Court of Justice, in order to ensure justice and the rule of law in international affairs.
- To encourage regular consultations and coordination among the principal organs of the United Nations in pursuit of their functions.
- To ensure that the Organization is provided on a timely and predictable basis with the resources it needs to carry out its mandates.
- To urge the Secretariat to make the best use of those resources, in accordance with clear rules and procedures agreed by the General Assembly, in the interests of all Member States, by adopting the best management practices and technologies available and by concentrating on those tasks that reflect the agreed priorities of Member States.
- To promote adherence to the Convention on the Safety of United Nations and Associated Personnel.[14]
- To ensure greater policy coherence and better cooperation between the United Nations, its agencies, the Bretton Woods Institutions and the World Trade Organization, as well as other multilateral bodies, with a view to achieving a fully coordinated approach to the problems of peace and development.
- To strengthen further cooperation between the United Nations and national parliaments through their world organization, the Inter-Parliamentary Union, in various fields, including peace and security, economic and social development, international law and human rights and democracy and gender issues.
- To give greater opportunities to the private sector, non-governmental organizations and civil society, in general, to contribute to the realization of the Organization's goals and programmes.

31. We request the General Assembly to review on a regular basis the progress made in implementing the provisions of this Declaration, and ask the Secretary-General to issue periodic reports for consideration by the General Assembly and as a basis for further action.

32. We solemnly reaffirm, on this historic occasion, that the United Nations is the indispensable common house of the entire human family, through which we will seek to realize our universal aspirations for peace, cooperation and development. We therefore pledge our unstinting support for these common objectives and our determination to achieve them.

8th plenary meeting
8 September 2000

Notes

[1] A/55/305-S/2000/809; see *Official Records of the Security Council, Fifty-fifth Year, Supplement for July, August and September 2000*, document S/2000/809.

[2] A/CONF.183/9.

[3] See CD/1478.

[4] Amended protocol on prohibitions or restrictions on the use of mines, booby-traps and other devices (CCW/CONF.I/16 (Part I), annex B).

[5] Programme of Action for the Sustainable Development of Small Island Developing States (*Report of the Global Conference on the Sustainable Development of Small Island Developing States, Bridgetown, Barbados, 25 April-6 May 1994)* (United Nations publication, Sales No. E.94.I.18 and corrigenda), chap. I, resolution 1, annex II).

[6] E/2000/L.9.

[7] *Report of the United Nations Conference on Environment and Development, Rio de Janeiro, 3–14 June 1992* (United Nations publication, Sales No. E.93.I.8 and corrigenda), vol. I: *Resolutions adopted by the Conference,* resolution 1, annex II.

[8] See United Nations Environment Programme, *Convention on Biological Diversity* (Environmental Law and Institution Programme Activity Centre), June 1992.

[9] A/49/84/Add.2, annex, appendix II.

[10] Resolution 217 A (III).

[11] Resolution 34/180, annex.

[12] Resolution 44/25, annex.

[13] Resolution 54/263, annexes I and II.

[14] Resolution 49/59, annex.

Ten Principles of Earth Democracy

Vandana Shiva

1. Ecological Democracy—Democracy of All Life

We are all members of the Earth community. We all have the duty to protect the rights and welfare of all species and all people. No humans have the right to encroach on the ecological space of other species and other people, or treat them with cruelty and violence.

2. Intrinsic Worth of All Species and Peoples

All species, humans and cultures have intrinsic worth. They are subjects, not objects of manipulation or ownership. No humans have the right to own other species, other people or the knowledge of other cultures through patents and other intellectual property rights.

3. Diversity in Nature and Culture

Defending biological and cultural diversity is a duty of all people. Diversity is an end in itself, a value, a source of richness both material and cultural.

4. Natural Rights to Sustenance

All members of the Earth Community including all humans have the right to sustenance—to food and water, to safe and clean habitat, to security of ecological space. These rights are natural rights, they are birthrights given by the fact of existence on earth and are best protected through community rights and commons. They are not given by states or corporations, nor can they be extinguished by state or corporate action. No state or corporation has the right to erode or undermine these natural rights or enclose the commons that sustain all through privatisation or monopoly control.

5. Earth Economy Is Based on Economic Democracy and Living Economy

Earth democracy is based on economic democracy. Economic systems in Earth Democracy protect ecosystems and their integrity, they protect people's livelihoods and provide basic needs to all. In the earth economy there are no disposable or dispensable species or people. The earth economy is a living economy. It is based on sustainable, diverse, pluralistic systems that protect nature and people, are chosen by people, for the benefit of the common good.

6. Living Economies are Built on Local Economies

Conservation of the earth's resources and creation of sustainable and satisfying livelihoods is most caringly, creatively and efficiently and equitably achieved at the local level. Localization of economics is social and ecological imperative. Only goods and services that cannot be produced locally, using local resources, local knowledge should be produced non-locally and traded long distance. Earth democracy is based on vibrant, resilient local economies, which support national and global economies. The global economy does not crush and destroy local economies.

7. Living Democracy

Earth democracy is based on local living democracy with local communities, organised on principles of inclusion and diversity and ecological and social responsibility having the highest authority on decisions related to the environment and natural resources and to the sustenance and livelihoods of people. Authority is delegated to more distant levels of governance on the principle of subsidiarity. Earth democracy is living democracy.

8. Living Knowledge

Earth democracy is based on earth centered and community centered knowledge systems. Living knowledge is knowledge that maintains and renews living processes and contributes to health of the planet and people. It is also living knowledge in that it is embedded in nature and society, is not abstract, reductionist and anti-life. Living knowledge is a commons, it belongs collectively to communities that create it and keep it alive. All humans have a duty to share knowledge. No person or corporation has a right to enclose, monopolize, patent, or exclusively own as intellectual property living knowledge.

9. Balancing Rights with Responsibility

In earth democracy, rights are derived from and balanced with responsibility. Those who bear the consequences of decisions and actions are the decision makers.

10. Globalizing Peace, Care and Compassion

Earth democracy connects people in circles of care, cooperation and compassion instead of dividing them through competition and conflict. Earth democracy globalizes compassion, not greed, and peace, not war.

WE, THE PEOPLE OF COLOR, gathered together at this multinational People of Color Environmental Leadership Summit, to begin to build a national and international movement of all peoples of color to fight the destruction and taking of our lands and communities, do hereby re-establish our spiritual interdependence to the sacredness of our Mother Earth; to respect and celebrate each of our cultures, languages and beliefs about the natural world and our roles in healing ourselves; to ensure environmental justice; to promote economic alternatives which would contribute to the development of environmentally safe livelihoods; and, to secure our political, economic and cultural liberation that has been denied for over 500 years of colonization and oppression, resulting in the poisoning of our communities and land and the genocide of our peoples, do affirm and adopt these Principles of Environmental Justice:

The Principles of Environmental Justice (EJ)

1) **Environmental Justice** affirms the sacredness of Mother Earth, ecological unity and the interdependence of all species, and the right to be free from ecological destruction.

2) **Environmental Justice** demands that public policy be based on mutual respect and justice for all peoples, free from any form of discrimination or bias.

3) **Environmental Justice** mandates the right to ethical, balanced and responsible uses of land and renewable resources in the interest of a sustainable planet for humans and other living things.

4) **Environmental Justice** calls for universal protection from nuclear testing, extraction, production and disposal of toxic/hazardous wastes and poisons and nuclear testing that threaten the fundamental right to clean air, land, water, and food.

5) **Environmental Justice** affirms the fundamental right to political, economic, cultural and environmental self-determination of all peoples.

6) **Environmental Justice** demands the cessation of the production of all toxins, hazardous wastes, and radioactive materials, and that all past and current producers be held strictly accountable to the people for detoxification and the containment at the point of production.

7) **Environmental Justice** demands the right to participate as equal partners at every level of decision-making, including needs assessment, planning, implementation, enforcement and evaluation.

8) **Environmental Justice** affirms the right of all workers to a safe and healthy work environment without being forced to choose between

an unsafe livelihood and unemployment. It also affirms the right of those who work at home to be free from environmental hazards.

9) **Environmental Justice** protects the right of victims of environmental justice to receive full compensation and reparations for damages as well as quality health care.

10) **Environmental Justice** considers governmental acts of environmental injustice a violation of international law, the Universal Declaration On Human Rights, and the United Nations Convention on Genocide.

11) **Environmental Justice** must recognize a special legal and natural relationship of Native Peoples to the U.S. government through treaties, agreements, compacts, and covenants affirming sovereignty and self-determination.

12) **Environmental Justice** affirms the need for urban and rural ecological policies to clean up and rebuild our cities and rural areas in balance with nature, honoring the cultural integrity of all our communities, and provided fair access for all to the full range of resources.

13) **Environmental Justice** calls for the strict enforcement of principles of informed consent, and a halt to the testing of experimental reproductive and medical procedures and vaccinations on people of color.

14) **Environmental Justice** opposes the destructive operations of multinational corporations.

15) **Environmental Justice** opposes military occupation, repression and exploitation of lands, peoples and cultures, and other life forms.

16) **Environmental Justice** calls for the education of present and future generations which emphasizes social and environmental issues, based on our experience and an appreciation of our diverse cultural perspectives.

17) **Environmental Justice** requires that we, as individuals, make personal and consumer choices to consume as little of Mother Earth's resources and to produce as little waste as possible; and make the conscious decision to challenge and reprioritize our lifestyles to ensure the health of the natural world for present and future generations.

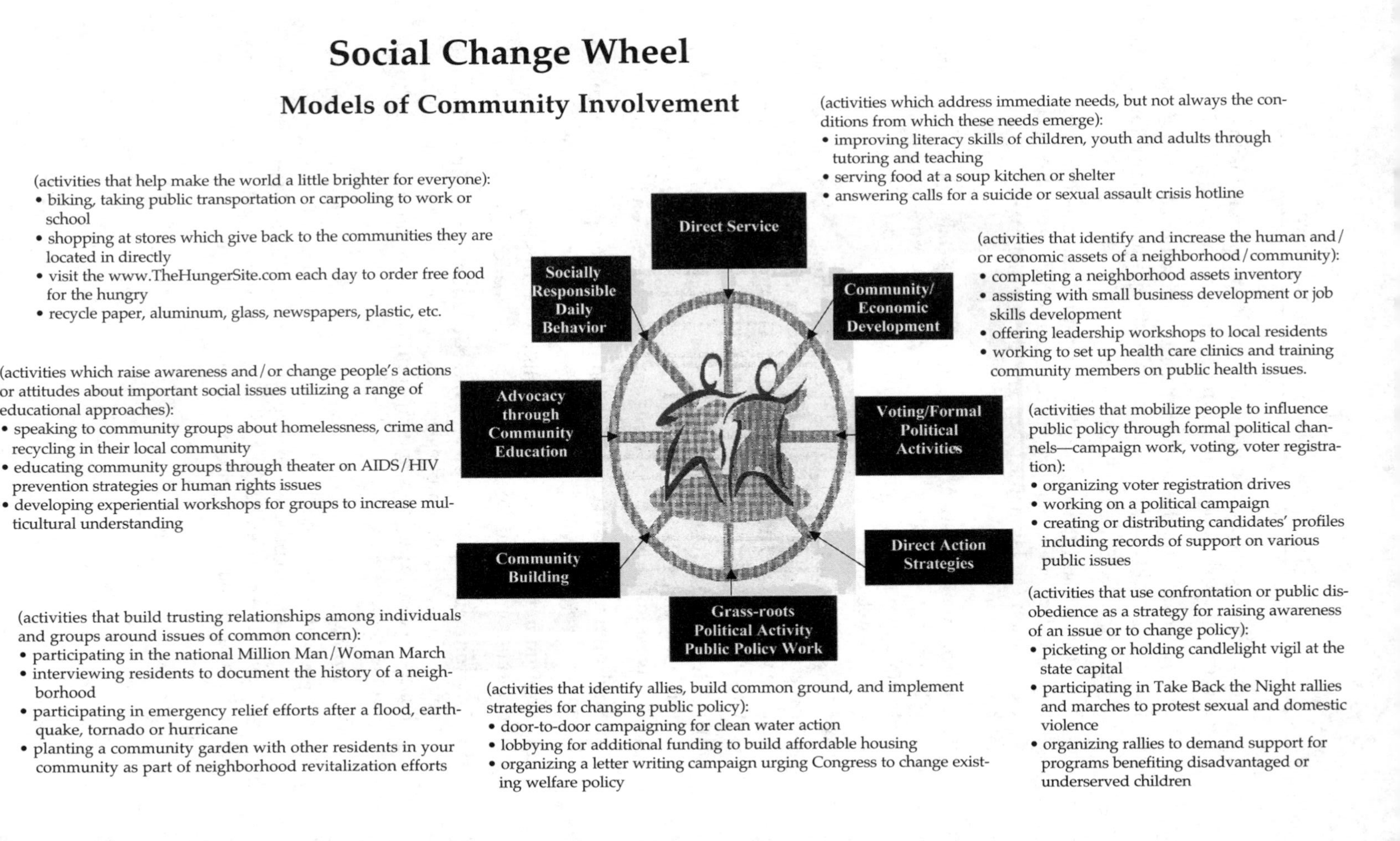
Social Change Wheel
Models of Community Involvement
Direct Service
(activities which address immediate needs, but not always the conditions from which these needs emerge):
• improving literacy skills of children, youth and adults through tutoring and teaching
• serving food at a soup kitchen or shelter
• answering calls for a suicide or sexual assault crisis hotline
Community/ Economic Development
(activities that identify and increase the human and/or economic assets of a neighborhood/community):
• completing a neighborhood assets inventory
• assisting with small business development or job skills development
• offering leadership workshops to local residents
• working to set up health care clinics and training community members on public health issues.
Voting/Formal Political Activities
(activities that mobilize people to influence public policy through formal political channels—campaign work, voting, voter registration):
• organizing voter registration drives
• working on a political campaign
• creating or distributing candidates' profiles including records of support on various public issues
Direct Action Strategies
(activities that use confrontation or public disobedience as a strategy for raising awareness of an issue or to change policy):
• picketing or holding candlelight vigil at the state capital
• participating in Take Back the Night rallies and marches to protest sexual and domestic violence
• organizing rallies to demand support for programs benefiting disadvantaged or underserved children
Grass-roots Political Activity Public Policy Work
(activities that identify allies, build common ground, and implement strategies for changing public policy):
• door-to-door campaigning for clean water action
• lobbying for additional funding to build affordable housing
• organizing a letter writing campaign urging Congress to change existing welfare policy
Community Building
(activities that build trusting relationships among individuals and groups around issues of common concern):
• participating in the national Million Man/Woman March
• interviewing residents to document the history of a neighborhood
• participating in emergency relief efforts after a flood, earthquake, tornado or hurricane
• planting a community garden with other residents in your community as part of neighborhood revitalization efforts
Advocacy through Community Education
(activities which raise awareness and/or change people's actions or attitudes about important social issues utilizing a range of educational approaches):
• speaking to community groups about homelessness, crime and recycling in their local community
• educating community groups through theater on AIDS/HIV prevention strategies or human rights issues
• developing experiential workshops for groups to increase multicultural understanding
Socially Responsible Daily Behavior
(activities that help make the world a little brighter for everyone):
• biking, taking public transportation or carpooling to work or school
• shopping at stores which give back to the communities they are located in directly
• visit the www.TheHungerSite.com each day to order free food for the hungry
• recycle paper, aluminum, glass, newspapers, plastic, etc.

Sources

Sources

pp. 7–14: Presentation for the College of St. Catherine Faculty/Staff Workshop, August 30, 1994, by Joan Mitchell, CSJ.

pp. 15–32: From *Liberating Sanctuary: 100 Years of Women's Education at the College of St. Catherine* edited by Jane Lamm Carroll, Joanne Cavallaro, and Sharon Doherty. Copyright © 2012. Reprinted by permission of Lexington Books.

pp. 33–50: From *More than a Dream: Eighty-five Years at the College of St. Catherine* by Rosalie Ryan, CSJ and Joan Christine Wolkerstorfer. Copyright © 1992 by the College of St. Catherine, St. Paul, Minnesota.

pp. 51–54: From *On Lies, Secrets, and Silence: Selected Prose 1966–1978* by Adrienne Rich. Copyright © 1979 by W. W. Norton and Company. Reprinted by permission of the publisher.

pp. 61–65: From *This Bridge We Call Home: Radical Visions for Transformation* edited by Gloria Anzaldúa and AnaLouise Keating. Copyright © 2002 by Taylor & Francis, Ltd. Reprinted by permission of the publisher via the Copyright Clearance Center.

pp. 66–77: From *Why Are All the Black Kids Sitting Together in the Cafeteria?* by Beverly Daniel Tatum. Copyright © 1997 by Perseus Books Group. Reprinted by permission of the publisher via the Copyright Clearance Center.

pp. 78–82: From *Do You Know Me Now? An Anthology of Minnesota Multicultural Writings* edited by Elisabeth Rosenberg. Copyright © 1997 by Pamela Fletcher. Reprinted by permission.

p. 83: Copyright © 1980 by Lucille Clifton. First appeared in *Two-Headed Woman*, published by The University of Massachusetts Press. Now appears in *Good Woman: Poems and a Memoir 1969–1980*, published by BOA Editions, Ltd.(1987). Reprinted by permission of Curtis Brown, Ltd.

pp. 93–98: Copyright © 1990 by Amy Tan. First appeared in *The Threepenny Review*. Reprinted by permission of the author and the Sandra Dijkstra Literary Agency.

pp. 99–105: From *Leading the Way: Young Women's Activism for Social Change* edited by Mary K. Trigg. Copyright © 2010 by Princeton University Press. Reprinted by permission of the publisher.

pp. 172–182: As appeared in the *Brown Alumni Magazine*, November/December, 1999. Copyright © 1999 by Kenneth R. Miller. Reprinted by permission of the Brown Alumni Magazine.

p. 183: From *The Poems of Emily Dickinson: Reading Edition* edited by Ralph W. Franklin. Published by Harvard University Press.

p. 184: From *Coagulations: New and Selected Poems* by Jayne Cortez. Copyright © 1984 by Jayne Cortez.

pp. 185–196: From *Women and the Word* by Sandra Marie Schneiders. Copyright © 1986 by Saint Mary's College, Notre Dame, Indiana. Reprinted by permission of Paulist Press.

pp. 197–211: From *Black Looks: Race and Representation* by bell hooks. Copyright © 1992. Published by South End Press.

pp. 212–223: From "Working Paper #189 of the Wellesley College Center for Research on Women" by Peggy McIntosh. Copyright © 1988 by Peggy McIntosh. Reprinted by permission of the author.

pp. 224–232: From "White People Facing Race: Uncovering the Myths that Keep Racism in Place" by Peggy McIntosh. Copyright © 2009 by Peggy McIntosh. Reprinted by permission of the author.

pp. 233–247: Reprinted by arrangement with The Heirs to the Estate of Martin Luther King, Jr., c/o Writers House, Inc. as agent for the proprietor. Copyright © 1963 by Martin Luther King, Jr., copyright renewed 1991 by Coretta Scott King.

pp. 279–282: From *The Cancer Journals* by Audre Lorde. Copyright © 1980 by Aunt Lute Books. Reprinted by permission of the publisher.

pp. 283–305: From *Bananas, Beaches and Bases: Making Feminist Sense of International Politics* by Cynthia Enloe. Copyright © 2001 by University of California Press. Reprinted by permission of the publisher via the Copyright Clearance Center.

pp. 290–291: Lyrics to "Are My Hands Clean?" by Bernice Johnson Reagon. Copyright © 1985 by Songtalk Publishing, Inc.

pp. 306–311: First appeared in *The Wind's Twelve Quarters* by Ursula K. LeGuin. Copyright © 1973 by Ursula K. LeGuin. Reprinted by permission of the author and the author's agents, Curtis Brown, Ltd.

pp. 312–313: From *We Are All Magicians* by Ruth Forman. Copyright © 1993 by Ruth Forman. Reprinted by permission of the author.

pp. 314–323: From *Non-Violent Resistance* by Mohandas K. Gandhi. Copyright © 1951 by Navajivan Trust. Reprinted by permission.

pp. 338–348: From *Eyes Open on a World: The Challenges of Change* by the Sisters of St. Joseph of Carondelet. Copyright © 2001 by North Star Press of Saint Cloud, Inc.

pp. 386–409: From *The Life You Can Save* by Peter Singer. Copyright © 2009. Published by Random House, Inc.

pp. 410–420: As appeared in *Cross Currents*, Vol. 58, No. 1, 2008. Copyright © 2008 by John Wiley & Sons, Inc. Reprinted by permission of the publisher via the Copyright Clearance Center.

pp. 421–430: From *Acts of the Christian Martyrs, Texts and Translations* edited and translated by Herbert Musurillo. Copyright © 1972. Reprinted by permission of Oxford University Press, NY via the Copyright Clearance Center.

pp. 431–436: From *Women in Revolutionary Paris, 1789–1795* edited by Darline Gay Levy, translated by Harriet Branson Applewhite and Mary Dunham. Copyright © 1980 by Darline Gay Levy. Published by University of Illinois Press.

pp. 441–447: As appeared in *MFS: Modern Fiction Studies*, Vol. 47, No. 4, Winter, 2001. Copyright © 2001 by Johns Hopkins University Press. Reprinted by permission of the publisher via the Copyright Clearance Center.

pp. 448–450: Copyright © 2002 by Paul Lockhart.

pp. 451–452: As appeared in *Significance: Journal of the Royal Statistical Society*, September, 2011. Copyright © 2011 by John Wiley & Sons, Inc. Reprinted by permission of the publisher via the Copyright Clearance Center.

pp. 455–457: As appeared in *Minnesota Women's Free Press*, Vol. 29, No. 4, April, 2013. Copyright © 2013 by Anne Hamre. Reprinted by permission of the publisher.

pp. 458–468: From *Art Objects: Essays on Ecstasy and Effrontery* by Jeanette Winterson. Copyright © 1995. Published by Random House UK, Ltd.

pp. 469–491: From *Evolution vs Creationism* by Eugenie Scott. Copyright © 2009 by ABC-CLIO, LLC. Reprinted by permission of the publisher via the Copyright Clearance Center.

pp. 492–498: From *The Sociological Imagination* by C. Wright Mills. Copyright © 1959 by Oxford University Press, NY. Reprinted by permission of the publisher via the Copyright Clearance Center.

pp. 499–501: As appeared in *Time*, December 2, 1993. Copyright © 1993 by Time, Inc. Reprinted by permission of the publisher via the Copyright Clearance Center.

pp. 502–512: As appeared in *Feminist Studies*, Vol. 34, No. 1–2, Spring/Summer, 2008. Copyright © 2008 by Feminist Studies, Inc. Reprinted by permission of the publisher via the Copyright Clearance Center.

pp. 539–559: From *Justice and the Politics of Difference* by Iris Marion Young. Copyright © 1990 by Princeton University Press. Reprinted by permission.

pp. 580–589: From *Liberation Theology: An Introductory Reader* by Curt Cadorette. Copyright © 1992 by Orbis Books. Reprinted by permission of the publisher.

pp. 590: From *Time and Materials: Poems 1997–2005* by Robert Hass. Copyright © 2007 by Robert Hass. Reprinted by permission of HarperCollins Publishers.

pp. 602–619: Originally appeared in *Forum on Public Policy*. Copyright © 2010 by Forum on Public Policy. Reprinted by permission of the author.

pp. 634–635: "The Low Road" from *The Moon Is Always Female* by Marge Piercy. Copyright © 1980 by Marge Piercy. Used by permission of Alfred A. Knopf, a division of Random House, Inc.

pp. 636–642: Adapted from *Howard Zinn on History* published by Seven Stories Press, 2000, and *You Can't Be Neutral on a Moving Train* published by Beacon Press, 1994. Copyrights © 2000 and 1994. Reprinted by permission of the publishers.

pp. 660–661: From *Earth Democracy: Justice, Sustainability, and Peace* by Vandana Shiva. Copyright © 2005. Published by South End Press.

p. 664: Adapted in 2010 by College of St. Benedict Campus Ministry from a publication by *Minnesota Campus Compact*, 1996. © copyright 1996 by University of Minnesota.

Author Index

Author Index